Computer Games I

David N.L. Levy

Editor

Computer Games I

With 97 Illustrations

Springer-Verlag

New York Berlin Heidelberg
London Paris Tokyo

Library of Congress Cataloging-in-Publication Data
Computer games.
    Bibliography: p.
    1. Computer games. I. Levy, David N. L.
GV1469.15.C63   1987   794.8′2   87-4754
ISBN 0-387-96496-7 (v. 1)
ISBN 0-387-96609-9 (v. 2)

Typeset by Asco Trade Typesetting Ltd., Hong Kong.
Printed and bound by R. R. Donnelley & Sons, Harrisonburg, Virginia.
Printed in the United States of America.

9 8 7 6 5 4 3 2 1

ISBN 0-387-96496-7 Springer-Verlag New York Berlin Heidelberg
ISBN 3-540-96496-7 Springer-Verlag Berlin Heidelberg New York

Preface

Long before the advent of the electronic computer, man was fascinated by the idea of automating the thought processes employed in playing games of skill. The very first chess "Automaton" captured the imagination of late eighteenth century Vienna, and by the early 1900s there was a genuine machine that could play the chess endgame of king and rook against a lone king.

Soon after the invention of the computer, scientists began to make a serious study of the problems involved in programming a machine to play chess. Within a decade this interest started to spread, first to draughts (checkers) and later to many other strategy games. By the time the home computer was born, there had already been three decades of research into computer games. Many of the results of this research were published, though usually in publications that are extremely difficult (or even impossible for most people) to find. Hence the present volumes.

Interest in computers and programming has now reached into almost every home in the civilized world. Millions of people have regular access to computers, and most of them enjoy playing games. In fact, approximately 80 percent of all software sold for use on personal computers is games software.

Because of this great interest in games, many computer aficionados would like to know how computers play games. In some cases this will be merely out of curiosity; in others, it will be because of the desire to program a computer to play an "intelligent" game. It can be an extremely frustrating, time-consuming, and costly task for the computer enthusiast to locate any specific paper on the subject, and the idea of these books is to provide all of the most important information within one source. This collection of fifty papers, split into two volumes, covers almost the entire spectrum of material on strategy games, and anyone interested in computer games should find here a wealth of interesting and useful material.

Credit for this collection must go to the authors of the various papers which have been included. I have indicated on the first page of each section the original source of the paper, and I have acknowledged, as appropriate, the authors and publishers who have kindly given me permission to reproduce the material.

DAVID N.L. LEVY

Contents (Volume I)

Contents (Volume II)

Introduction

This collection of fifty papers, in two volumes, covers sixteen different games, each of which requires some measure of intelligence to play well. I have divided each volume into chapters, each chapter being devoted to one particular game—apart from the final chapter which is a comprehensive bibliography.

Before discussing the contents of some of the more important chapters, I should first mention two games which I had contemplated including but which, in the end, I decided to omit. The simpler of these is the game of Nim, in which two players alternately remove one or more matches from any of a number of different piles of matches. In the most popular form of the game, the player who removes the last match is the loser. Nim has been solved algorithmically; that is to say, there exists a set of rules which, if followed, guarantee that a player who is in a winning position can find a move which retains the win. This algorithm is described in various mathematics books, including the two excellent (though mathematically advanced) volumes by Berlekamp *et al.* (1982). This algorithm was employed in a machine designed in the 1930s in the United States, and computer games historians can refer to the patent application which can be found on microfilm at most national patent offices (Condon *et al.*, 1940). The reason why I omitted Nim from the collection is that the game does not require genuine intelligence to play perfectly—the existence of an algorithmic solution renders the task "trivial" in the terminology of game theory.

The other game which might have been included is Kalah (also known as Mancala). Kalah is most definitely a game of skill but the literature on Kalah programs does not concentrate sufficiently on the special problems posed by the game itself. Readers who are interested in programming Kalah might have come across references to Russell (1964a, b)—there is very little here of practical use to the Kalah programmer, but Russell's work is possibly the first instance of an iteratively deepening search of the game tree. Another publication which mentions Kalah is Slagle and Dixon (1969), though again the principal interest in that paper lies in other areas.

For reasons of space I decided to omit any papers devoted specifically to tree-searching and/or learning techniques, even though such techniques are very often used in the programming of strategy games.

Backgammon (Chapter 1) is a fine example of the successes achieved by computer scientists in this fascinating field. Hans Berliner, a former World Correspondence Chess Champion, wrote the first program to defeat a human World Champion at a game of skill. Berliner's program won a match against Luigi Villa, played in Monte Carlo during July 1979, and Berliner's two papers describe how he achieved this goal.

Readers will probably know the name Edward O. Thorp from his famous book *Beat the Dealer*, in which the author describes his invention of the card-counting methods which caused the Las Vegas casinos to ban him from playing blackjack, and to change their rules so that the odds did not favor the astute player quite so much. Professor Thorp's analysis of the mathematics of gambling contributes an important section to the chapter on backgammon, since it defines the best play from a number of key end positions. Further mathematical analyses of the game are found in Sections 1.4 and 1.5 which suggest how to handle the doubling cube, the main weapon of the professional backgammon player. The reader who finds some of the mathematics too daunting can nevertheless make use of (and profit from) the results of this research.

Checkers (which is known as draughts in Britain) provided the first example of strong play by a computer program. Although Christopher Strachey was the first to write about programming checkers, it was Samuel's program which became famous when it drew a few games against some of the world's leading human players. There has been relatively little published research on checkers programming since Samuel's second paper (1967), though Arnold Griffith (1974) described a novel (and bizarre!) learning method which he compared with Samuel's ideas. More recently, an even stronger program was written at Duke University, North Carolina, by Eric Jensen and Tom Truscott. The Duke program successfully challenged Samuel's program to a two-game match in 1977, winning both games. Interestingly, Truscott turned to programming checkers only after he had spent many years as one of the more prominent chess programmers. His program DUCHESS competed several times in major computer chess tournaments, usually acquitting itself rather well.

Of all the strategy games to which programmers have devoted their time and effort, none surpasses or equals chess for the sheer magnitude of the work that has been invested during the past 35 years. More has been written about chess programming than about the programming of all other strategy games combined, and it would be an easy matter to fill a whole volume with papers devoted entirely to computer chess. In fact, I have done this (Levy, 1988), leaving Chapter 2 of the present volume to serve as a thorough introduction to the subject.

Computer chess really started with Claude Shannon, whose seminal work dating from the late 1940s is still, in 1988, the foundation of most contemporary chess programs. One of Shannon's articles on the subject forms Section 2.1, while a more detailed description of his ideas can be found in the alternative reference (Shannon, 1950a). In order to provide the reader with a feel for the progress that has been made since Shannon's work, I have included four sections (2.2 to 2.5) that provide a historical survey of the leading programs and some of the more important programming ideas.

I have included Berliner's 1970 paper because it shows how a strong human chess player perceived the deficiencies of chess programs at that time. Berliner is one of the few computer-chess experts who believe that a program should follow human thought processes rather than use the traditional "brute force" approach, and it is interesting that 15 years later the same deficiencies pointed out by Berliner can still be seen in all the strongest chess programs.

The final section in the chapter on chess has been included specifically for the benefit of those who wish to write their own chess programs, as many home-computer owners are now doing. One of the co-authors of this section, Larry Atkin, was part of the famous Slate–Atkin duo whose programs CHESS 3.*n* and CHESS 4.*n*, written at Northwestern University, dominated the world of computer chess for much of the 1970s. A detailed account of their program can be found in Slate and Atkin (1977)—the present paper employs many of the same ideas but has been written with the micro-owner in mind. Peter Frey, the other co-author, is a Professor of Psychology at Northwestern University, and editor of an outstanding collection of articles on computer chess (Frey, 1977a).

The final chapter in this volume is on Scrabble, the proprietary word game which has become the most popular word game in the world. There then follows an extensive bibliography which includes every reference in every paper from both this and the second volume.

CHAPTER 1

Backgammon

1.1. BKG—A Program That Plays Backgammon

Hans J. Berliner

Originally published in July 1977 by the Computer Science Department, Carnegie–Mellon University, Pittsburgh, PA 15213. This work was supported by the Advanced Research Projects Agency of the Office of the Secretary of Defense (Contract F44620-73-C-0074) and is monitored by the Air Force Office of Scientific Research. Reprinted by permission of the author.

Abstract. This paper is both a description of an existing backgammon program and a theoretical discussion of some important issues in evaluation. The program plays a generally competent game at an intermediate level of skill. It correctly solves a high percentage of intermediate level problems in books. Although it only doubles and accepts doubles during the running game, it does several nontrivial things perfectly.

In discussing the structure of evaluation, we consider partitioning all game states into mutually exclusive state-classes. These state-classes are very useful in a knowledge-based system, as they allow relatively easy assimilation of new knowledge. They also permit the building of opponent models based upon what evidence shows the opponent knows in each state-class.

I. Why Yet Another Game?

Backgammon is a game of skill and chance. It is played on a vector of 24 "points." From a predefined starting position, both sides move in opposite directions, with the object of first removing all 15 of one's own men off the end of the vector. There are rules for moving, capturing, re-entering captured men, blocking points so an opponent cannot move there, and finally removing men from the board near the end of the game. The reader not familiar with backgammon would do well to scan the rules of a standard work such as Jacoby and Crawford (Jacoby *et al.*, 1973) before proceeding into this paper in great detail.

The thing that makes backgammon an interesting object of study for AI is that in any given position (of which there are 10^{20} (Levner, 1976)), there are 21 possible combinations that the throw of two dice can produce. Each of these can be played legally in the average board position about 40 different ways. Thus if one were to investigate a backgammon position by tree searching, it would be necessary to deal with a branching factor of more than 800 (!!) at every node. Clearly, this is completely impractical. Therefore backgammon must be approached with evaluation and knowledge in mind. Position P1 will have to preferred over position P2 because it has features that more endear it to the player who can produce it than the features that obtain in P2.

In a game such as chess, it has been customary to search very large trees of 5,000 to 2 million terminal nodes. In such a paradigm, the execution of a terminal evaluation function requires a certain amount of time, which must then be multiplied by the expected number of terminal nodes in the search. Thus designers of chess programs are very circumspect in creating evaluation functions which require lengthy execution times. For this reason certain knowledge that is not trivial to compute is usually left out so that the program may operate faster and search more. Since there can be little or no searching in a practical backgammon program, these contingencies will not apply. On the contrary, it is desirable to apply all possible knowledge to successor positions of the root node, in an attempt to find the best next move. Further, the fact that modern backgammon involves doubling and accepting doubles places an even greater emphasis on the use of knowledge for knowing when to double and when to accept doubles. It is the encoding of knowledge and the subsequent selection effectiveness of the evaluation function that is of interest. This subject is treated in depth in Sections IV and V. However, before going to that part of our research, we describe certain peripheral artifacts that are important for understanding the whole project.

II. The Structure of BKG

BKG is an interactive backgammon program. It is the result of about one man-year of effort since mid-1974. It is written in BLISS (Wulf *et al.*, 1971), a system implementation language, and runs under the TOPS-10 monitor on the PDP-10's at Carnegie–Mellon University. It encompasses more than 80 pages of code, occupies 19K of 36-bit words in core and a further 11K of tables on secondary storage. BKG runs interactively on four different kinds of video terminals (including a graphics terminal which moves the men with a graphic hand, and will upset the board occasionally when BKG loses), and a standard model 33 teletype. These routines were written by Phil Karlton and Steve Rubin at Carnegie–Mellon University.

BKG operates, similarly to many game playing programs, by executing a minor cycle which makes moves within a major one which plays games. When BKG is running interactively, it displays appropriate outputs and prompts at each step of the cycles. The minor cycle (see Figure 1) operates as

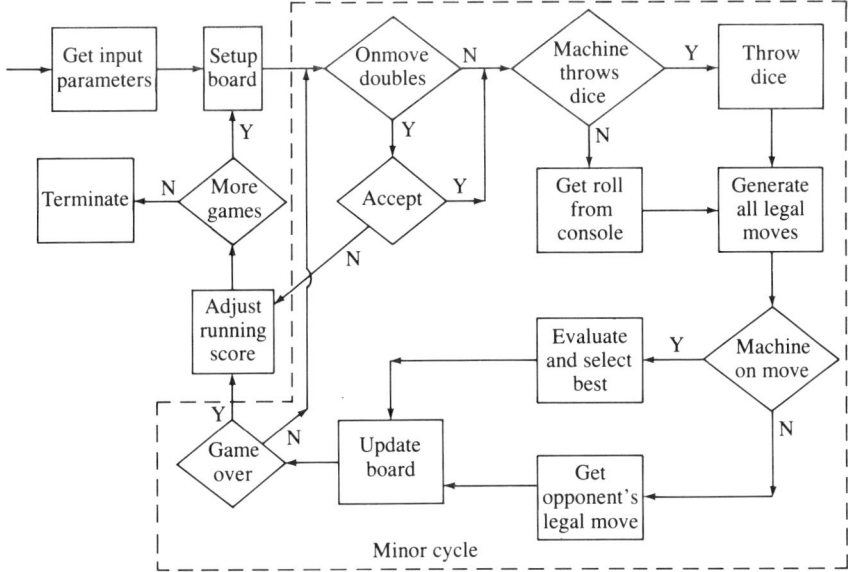

Figure 1

follows: First, BKG checks to see if the side whose turn it now is wishes to double (checking first that it would be legal for that side to do so). If a double is made, BKG asks if the double is accepted. If so, BKG adjusts the position and denomination of the doubling cube and proceeds. If not, the game is over and BKG exits to the major cycle. Next BKG checks to see if it is to throw dice, or receive a roll from the console. BKG uses a random number generator to throw dice. It then generates a list of all possible legal moves for the given roll. If it is the program's turn to play, it serves these potential moves up, one at a time, to the evaluation procedure. It then selects the best. If it is not the machine's turn to play it waits to receive a move from its environment. It then checks the legal move list to see if this move is on the list. If not, it requests a legal move. If the received move is legal, BKG puts it into canonical form. It then executes the legal move by updating the board configuration. If the conditions for one side winning have been met, it exits to the major cycle.

The major cycle is activated whenever a new game is about to begin. If a game is just over, BKG adjusts the overall record of the current competition in favor of the side that just won. It then asks if another game is desired (unless it has been preset for a certain number of games and this number has not been reached as yet). If the answer is negative, the program terminates. Otherwise, it sets the board up, throws dice to see who starts, and yields control to the minor cycle.

BKG can operate in several different modes. Its usual mode is to play a human opponent interactively at a video terminal. However, it can also monitor a game between two opponents while rolling dice for both, and doing the bookkeeping for doubling and accepting decisions. It can also play itself, either while displaying all actions at the terminal, or by only reporting the results of a series of games. For this simulation mode, it is necessary to type in a starting position and the number of iterations desired. For certain types of positions that BKG can play well, this mode can be used to determine within reasonable limits of accuracy what the chances of the respective sides are.

When one or more human opponents are involved, there is the option of letting the humans throw dice for themselves and entering the roll when the program prompts for it. For ordinary purposes this is much too slow a way of playing the program. There is, however, a practical reason for this mode. In tournaments it will be necessary to actually throw dice at the table for both sides, and a method must exist for entering the rolls. It is rather interesting to note as an aside, that while we have seen quite a few illegal moves made in tournaments, this should never happen to BKG, as if a move is not on its legal move list, it would not accept the opponent playing it.

III. Basic Procedures

A. The Move Generator

In discussing move generation, we will refer to the movement of a single man in accordance with the value of a single die face as a move, and the total set of moves associated with a roll of the dice as a play. At first blush it would seem that the design of a move generator for a backgammon program should be a trivial exercise. However, this turns out to be not quite so easy. The reason is that, while it is no problem to attempt to move each man in turn the number of spaces corresponding to the pips on a die face, there are several special conditions that control the way a roll may be played. The basic situation is this: each man may be moved the number of pips on one of the die faces, if the destination space is not off the board and not blockaded by the opponent (he has two or more men on it). Having made one move of one man corresponding to one die face, the same procedure is applied with respect to the other die face. In the case of doubles, the denomination of one die face is applied four times. By simple recursion it is possible to apply each die face to each man in turn, and thus enumerate the whole set of legal moves.

However, there are problems. First, the above procedure will generate many duplicates which we would hope to avoid or eliminate after generation. Second, and more importantly, the procedure outlined will not work for situations in which the moving side has men on the bar (and the only legal moves consist of entering men from the bar), and for those situations where all the men are in the home board (when it is legal to move men to the next point beyond the end of the board and in certain cases even beyond that). Thus on careful examination we determine that there are three distinct states that a board situation can be in:

(1) men on bar;
(2) able to bear off;
(3) all other situations.

Further, it is possible for the state to change during a single play, and the move generator must be able to come to grips with such a situation to generate all legal moves, and only legal moves. A final complication introduced by the rules of backgammon requires that if a full play cannot be made according to the roll, the player must play the largest possible part of the roll. This means that if he can play the full roll, he must do so; and if he can play either die face, he must play the larger.

The move generator understands exactly what moves are legal in each of the three states. As moves are generated which could form a legal play, these are put into a tree form. When move generation has been completed, the tree is scanned and those plays that are legal by our final criterion (use maximum part of roll) are marked as legal plays.

In view of these considerations, we implemented the move generator in the following way. We have a recursive procedure which can call itself a maximum of three times (for doubles) and once for nondoubles. The procedure starts at the location of the man that is furthest away from home for the moving side. It then scans toward home, pausing each time a point is found containing one or more men of the moving side. The die faces are labeled arbitrarily FACE1 and FACE2. The move generator first determines which of the three states the board position is in. It then attempts to apply the current die face to a man on the current point. If it fails in this, it continues the scan until there are no more men or points, whereupon it backtracks. If it succeeds, it updates the board, and if there are still more die faces to apply, it calls itself. In this case, a parameter of this call is the point at which the next scan should commence. For nondoubles this is the same point where the first recursion began. However, for doubles a large saving can be realized by using the current point as argument (since all opportunities to apply the denomination of the die face earlier in the recursion must already have been tried!!). This algorithm will generate all legal moves and only legal moves. For instance, in the case of doubles, if there are more than one man on a point, when the recursive call occurs, the algorithm will attempt to apply the remaining die faces to be played to the remaining men on the point before continuing the scan. Thus, for doubles this algorithm will not generate duplicate plays, while for nondoubles it will. For this reason we use a small modification of the procedure for nondoubles, but this does not concern us here.

B. Special Program Functions

There are several special functions which the program must be able to perform in order to be able to play an interactive game. These include receiving moves, updating the internal representation and that of any display device being used, sending appropriate prompts and messages to the user, being able to double, accept doubles, resign, and accept resignations. We consider all but doubling and resignation to be quite straightforward, so we will only describe the peculiarities of those four functions here.

1. Doubling

According to the rules of modern backgammon, the game is played with a doubling cube which has both a denomination and position. The cube is initialized at value "1," and located in the center (between the two players). The rules specify that either player may before rolling, if the cube is not on his opponent's side, offer to double the stakes by saying "I double," changing the value of the cube to be twice its current value, and offering it to his opponent by placing it on his side. If the opponent accepts the double he gains possession of the cube, so that he is the only player who is next entitled to double, and the game continues for twice the previous stake. If he refuses the game is over, and the appropriate game ending actions must be taken.

It is generally considered by backgammon experts that doubling is what separates the men from the boys (meaning that it is relatively easy to make the right move most of the time but hard to know when a position is good enough to double and bad enough to refuse an opponent's double.) To implement even a mediocre doubling and accepting algorithm is an extremely difficult task. Because of this, BKG at present only permits doubling (in games in which it is playing) in situations where the two sides have disengaged so that captures are no longer possible. This limitation is being remedied in the version we are currently working on. The problem of constructing such decision algorithms are treated in later sections; here we discuss only the requirement for the program to handle doubling in game.

Since it would be rather boring to ask each human player before his roll (if he were legally entitled to double) "Do you want to double?", we have instead created a doubling flag for each human opponent. If a human feels he may want to double on the next roll, he should enable the doubling flag before making his current move. This will result in BKG prompting him with an asterisk before the dice are rolled for him next time (and until the flag is turned off). When the prompt appears, the player may double or just continue. When the doubling flag is not set, BKG will just roll the dice without asking about doubling. This speeds up the game considerably. Of course, for itself BKG does not need such a flag as it can consider its doubling actions in a few microseconds.

When BKG has been doubled, it decides whether or not to accept using the same procedures it uses in deciding whether to double. Whenever a double has been accepted or rejected, the bookkeeping decisions that follow are rather trivial.

2. Resigning

It is, of course, possible to play every game out until someone has actually won. However, it is not infrequent that a situation is reached in which it is no longer possible for one side to win, no matter how fortuitously the fates may treat him. In such a situation it seems appropriate to resign in the interest of time saving and start the next game. BKG will only attempt to resign or allow resignation after the two sides have disengaged. It then calculates after each move the maximum and minimum number of rolls that it could take for each side to get all its men off. Clearly, if the minimum number of rolls of one side is greater than the maximum number of the other side, the first side should resign. This criterion is currently used both for resigning and accepting resignations. However, we do allow the program to try to resign in situations where it may get gammoned (although only when this is somewhat remote) in the hope that the opponent may accept such a resignation. It is also possible to resign a gammon or backgammon, using as criterion the number of rolls needed to get one man off and to get all men out of the opponent's home board. The question of attempting to resign and accept resignations before disengagement will also be taken up in the version we are currently bringing up. This too will involve judgements as to when a position is too good to accept a resignation (the gammoning chances are too high) and when it is so bad that one should be happly to resign (because one could quite easily lose a gammon).

C. Evaluation

The real knowledge and intelligence of BKG are in the procedures that evaluate moves and positions. We describe these in detail in the next two sections.

IV. The Evaluation Procedures

In this section, we describe issues in measuring certain important facets of a board position. In the next section, we describe how the outputs of these measuring functions are used in the overall evaluation. Finally, in Section VI, we describe limitations of various evaluation approaches, and give what we currently feel is the best approach to this problem. In our discussions, we will refer to the two sides as *Onmove* and *Notonmove* (before a move is made) and *Justmoved* and *Nexttomove* after a move is made.

A. Blot Danger Calculation

A blot is a man that is by itself on its point. Such a man is in potential danger of being hit (either right away or at some later time), and being sent back to await its opportunity to re-enter and come around the board again. All other things being equal, it is undesirable to leave blots. However, all other things are seldom equal, and for a variety of reasons (including that it cannot be avoided) blots are left at the end of a play. This procedure calculates the danger to the set of all blots of the moving side, and delivers several values for use by the evaluation procedure.

There are many intricacies to appraising the danger that a set of blots is in. When we first brought the program up, BKG merely noted the existence of blots. It considered all blots equally likely to be hit, and merely delivered a value that represented the total pipcount that would be lost if all blots were to be hit. This was a term that the evaluation procedure attempted to minimize.

However, this measure proved very inadequate; it failed, most importantly, to consider whether any particular blot could be hit by an opposing man. Our next (very small) improvement was to determine that for a blot to be in danger at all, there would have to be an opposing man somewhere in front of it. This produced a small improvement in performance. However, it still failed to get at the degree of endangerment of any blot.

Next we noted that for a blot to be hit it must be a distance of 1, 2, 3, 4, 5, 6, 7, 8, 9, 10, 11, 12, 15, 20, or 24 in front of the hitter,[1] and that for each such distance there is a hit probability corresponding to the number of possible combinations. This new fact produced a very large increment in performance, but it still left untouched several important situations. One of these is that even when a hitter is the right distance away from a hittee, it is at times necessary to have available a set of intermediate points where the hitter is to land. Second, is what is called in backgammon jargon duplication: it is impossible to apply a single die face to more than one move. Thus there is a certain safety for a pair of blots if they can be hit by different men (say) 4 pips away. The point is that if a 4 is rolled only one of the blots can be hit, not both. Third, there was the question of more than one blot being hit with a single roll (something that it is usually wise to avoid), and the question of a single blot being hit simultaneously by two men. This is known as pointing on a blot, and is also something that it is wise to avoid.

As a result of these considerations, we finally implemented a very detailed hit probability procedure which we now describe. We consider any man which is not paired on its point to be a blot, unless it is on the 1 or 2 point in the opponent's home board and the opponent has not yet made more than two points in his home board. We consider any man to be a hitter unless it is part of a pair (and only a pair) in its home board. The reason for the latter is that moving one of such a pair would expose the other to the hittee coming in on the next play, and thus would not really constitute a threat.

We note that there are 40 different ways in which an arbitrary hitter can hit a hittee. To illustrate this consider that there are three different ways in which a hitter three pips away from a hittee can hit it: by a 3, a 2,1, or using 3 parts of a 1,1. This information is encoded in a table of masks which specify which intermediate points must be free, or that only one of a set of two points need be free.

---

[1] [or 16 or 18—EDITOR.]

Our procedure scans the board, starting with the most advanced blot of the moving side, and determines if it is in range of any hitters. If so, then for every hitter it determines all combinations that could be used to hit this blot. It then checks whether the intermediate landing point conditions are satisfied. If so, it enters the location of the hitter in the word corresponding to this combination in the 40-word vector of bit-vectors *Ahit*. At the end of this first pass, the vector *Ahit* contains all the locations of potential hitters, the combination used for the hit, and the location (implicitly) of the hittee.

Next the procedure determines whether the side next-to-move has 0, 1, or more than 1 men on the bar. There is separate section of code for each of these situations. Basically, the procedure examines each word of *Ahit* to see if this combination can be used to hit a man. It starts with the combinations that use only one die face and then goes to the more involved combinations. Each time it finds such a combination it checks to see if the die faces needed for this combination have not been used yet. If so, it marks the faces as used, updates the information on hitting (always assuming that the most advanced blot will be hit if there is a choice), and continues.

If it finds that a combination using only one die face can be used to hit more than one blot, it knows that there exists a combination (the double with that die face) that can be used to hit two blots. If it finds that blots can be hit with more than one single face combination, this means either that a blot can be pointed on or that two blots can be hit with a certain throw. Whenever a blot can be hit by a combination involving two die faces, it checks whether a blot exists on either intermediate point. If so, this combination would hit two blots. In all cases, the values are multiplied by the unused number of ways that this combination can be rolled. At the end of this computation the following values are available:

Piploss = The total number of pips that may be lost due to blots being hit multiplied by the number of rolls that can be used for each hit.
P1 = The number of rolls that hit one or more men.
P2 = The number of ways that more than one blot may be hit, plus the number of ways that a blot may be pointed on.

These data are very adequate to the task at hand. For instance, in situations near the end of the game where one side must break up its safe position and run across "no-man's-land" exposing some blots, BKG does a remarkable job of distributing blots so as to minimize the chance of any being hit. This can be quite difficult even for a master player at times, but this is one of about three or four areas of backgammon play where BKG plays perfectly.

However, there are still some inadequacies to the current approach. The principal one is that the hit probability calculation assumes that it would be desirable to hit any exposed blot. This is usually valid but not always. For instance, the man that would be the hitter might be part of some important blockading or defensive structure and would therefore not want to give that up in order to hit a blot. Also there is the possibility that if the blot were hit it would in turn leave a blot for the opponent. Under certain circumstances (of which we already indicated one earlier) the disadvantages of leaving a blot in the process of hitting a man outweigh the advantages of making such a hit. We have in mind to improve the calculation to report which men are the hitters and name points on which opponent's blots would be left after hitting a blot. However, the program does not seem to be as limited by the lack of this information as by some other things, so this improvement will be postponed until such a time as it seems necessary. We are also aware of the *ad hoc* nature of defining what is a blot and what is a hitter, and will at some future time make these definitions more sensitive to the overall board situation. However, as of this writing the hit probability computation is by far the most sophisticated thing in BKG, encompassing some seven pages of code.

B. Blockading Factor

A blockade consists of a set of points "made" by one side, which prevents an opposing man from having access to those points. Clearly, such points can have a great effect on the opponent's movements, and their location is of great importance. The blockading calculation also has an evolutionary history. It became apparent very early in the development of BKG that it is necessary to distinguish between blockades that have one or more men trapped in front of them, and those that do not. The latter consist only of a potential trap for any man that may be hit.

Initially, we counted the maximum number of contiguous blockading points and squared this number to give greater weight to longer blockades. However, this method overlooks the fact that a blockade of six-in-a-row cannot be spanned, the fact that seven-in-a-row is not better than six-in-a-row, the fact that blockading points do not always have to be contiguous to be effective, and the fact that blockading strength is affected by the distance that a potential blockade runner is away from the blockade. To overcome these objections we developed a table of potential blockades.

We note that since there are only 15 men on a side, it is impossible to have more than seven blockading points. We then computed all combinations of zero to seven blockading points at a distance of 1 to 12 spaces in front of a man. For each configuration we computed the number of rolls that could legally be played by the blockade runner. This is the best measure of the strength of a blockade that we have found. Since a byte of 12 bits uniquely identifies any blocking configuration, and since the number of rolls that can result in getting past the blockade must be between 0 and 36, we constructed a table with bytes of size 6 bits accessed by a 12-bit code describing the blockading configuration. This method results in quick lookup of the essential data. We keep track of:

Escapes = The number of rolls that can be legally played from this point.
Contsq = The point between the location of the furthest back man and own
    9 point where the value of *Escapes* is lowest.

Acontain = 36—*Escapes*(*Contsq*).

Contain = 36—the lowest value of *Escapes* between our 24 point and our 9 point.

It has been found that this information satisfies our needs at the moment.

C. The Running Game

BKG will disengage the forces whenever it has the opportunity to do so, if it is even just slightly ahead in the running game (the race to get all men off). Plays are then evaluated in the following way: Any move that brings a man not already in the home board into the homeboard gets credit for 3 heuristic points (HP). From this is subtracted the number of men already on this point in order to give some encouragement to spreading men out. If the man is brought to the 6 point it gets 10 more HP's, and 10 HP's are subtracted for every space to its destination beyond the 5 point. If all men are in the home board at the end of a play, 200 HP's are added.

At the end of any potential play, BKG evaluates the placement of all men not yet in the home board. For each such man, BKG computes the number of board-crossings the man still has to make to get into the home board, and where the man is placed in its current board. In backgammon terminology a board is a sequence of 6 points (of which there are four, the two home boards and the two outer boards). In general, for the same number of total pips remaining, it is most desirable to have the fewest men left, and have them placed as far back as possible in the board they currently occupy. This allows the most efficient utilization of the most throws. Thus BKG will multiply (3—number of board crossings) by the depth of man in his board. This function seems to produce the desired effect, because it gives the greatest weight to the location of men closest to entering the home board. If the program's side is in danger of gammon, BKG will try to maximize potential rolls of doubles. Thus it will place men so that they can be brought home and one borne off most easily in the event of double 6, 5, 4, 3, or 2.

BKG makes and accepts doubles only during the running game. Until the position is advanced enough so that bearoff tables that give the expected number of rolls to get all men off can be referenced, it uses an algorithm developed by Emmett Keeler (Keeler *et al.*, 1975) of the RAND Corp. This algorithm uses an adjusted pipcount which adds 4/3 pips for every man on the 1 point, 2/3 pips for every man on the 2 point, and 1/3 pip for every man on the 3 point. If one side has borne off fewer men then the other, the (*Account*) of that side is increased by 2 pips for every extra man. Finally, it checks the number of gaps (points unoccupied by own men) in the home board of each side and subtracts the difference from the side having the fewest gaps. This is the adjusted pipcount (*Account*) used in the following computation.

BKG will double if the cube is in the center if its opponent's *Account* is 10% minus 2 pips greater than its own. It will double when it owns the cube if its opponent's *Acount* is 10% minus 1 pip greater than its own. It will accept doubles when it is not more than 10% plus 2 pips behind. This algorithm performs in a basically satisfactory way.

D. Bearing Off

To support decision-making during the bearing-off phase BKG has extensive tables which give the probability for a given position of one side, of bearing off all men in 1, 2, ..., 8 rolls and the expected number of rolls (ENR) to bear all men off. These tables were computed by James J. Gillogly of the RAND Corp. for our use. They are used both in selecting a move and in making doubling and accepting decisions.

The tables cover all situations for up to and including eight men in the home board, and up to and including 25 pips worth of men in the home board. The latter value assures that the tables can handle situations where, for instance, one side has all his men on the 1 and 2 points, but at least five on the 1 point.

The use of the tables in move selection is simple. BKG moves to the position with the lowest ENR. There is one exception to this case; that is, when it is far behind or far enough ahead to have a chance of winning a gammon. In the former case, it moves to the position which has the greatest probability of bearing all men off in the number of rolls that are expected for the opponent to get off. Here the values of probabilities of getting off in N rolls are very useful. When it is far ahead it moves to the position which gives it the greatest chance of bearing all men off in the number of rolls it expects to have before the opponent gets his first man off. It does this by giving additional weight in the computation to the probability of getting off in 1, ..., n rolls, where n is the number of rolls it expects to have before the opponent meets his objective.

For doubling and accepting doubles the situation is more intricate. Whenever, BKG can legally double during this phase, or when it has been doubled, it executes a win probability calculation. If the bear-off position of either side is not in the bear-off probability table, then it uses the Keeler method described above. In that case, the ENR is computed to be the larger of the *Pipcount*/7 and the (number of men left + 1)/2. This will usually overestimate the real ENR somewhat. If the ENR's for both sides are in the table then BKG can calculate the exact probability of the side on move winning by iteratively calculating over N the following equations:

$$W \leftarrow W + (1.0 - W - V) * \text{AWPRB(N)}$$
$$V \leftarrow V + (1.0 - W - V) * \text{AVPRB(N)}$$
$$\text{Until } W + V = 1.0$$

Here, W is probability of *Onmove* winning, and V is probability of *Notonmove* winning. The AWPRB(N) are computed from the bear-off probability tables by the following equation:

$$AWPRB(N) = WPRB(N)/(1.0 - PRBZ)$$
Where: $PRBZ = SUM\ i = 1$ to $N - 1$ of $WPRB(i)$.

If the moving side has a 65% chance of winning, BKG will always double. If the moving side has more than a 79% chance of winning, BKG will always resign if it is the nonmoving side. In between there are many situations in which it makes a great deal of difference how many rolls are left in the game, who has the cube (one should be more cautious in doubling when giving up the cube), and where in between 51% and 65% the win percentage is. We use a set of *ad hoc* tables here, and periodically adjust them when the program appears to be doubling too early or too late.

It should be noted that BKG does a vastly better job of doubling and accepting when using this algorithm than when relying on the Keeler approximation. This can be noticed, for instance, when the position is close but appears to favor one side. When the position changes so that both positions can now be looked up, BKG will frequently double, even though very little appears to have changed from the situation one roll ago for both sides. Upon inspecting the value of the win probability for the moving side, it is not unusual to find it between 60% and 65%; values which were not sufficient to activate Keeler's approximation. For this reason, we are looking at more precise ways of dealing with running game doubling, with the view of being able to obtain an estimate of the win probability of the side on move, rather than the double/don't double decision which Keeler's algorithm estimates. To this end, we are looking at the work of Thorp (Thorp, 1975), and have some ideas of our own for simple approximations which can be tested using our simulation facility.

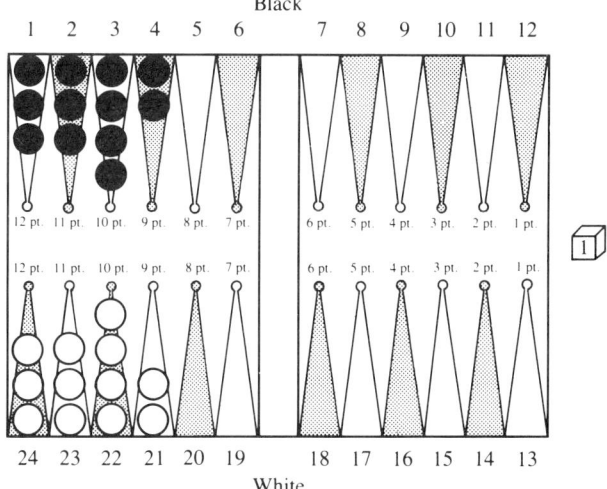

Figure 2

An example of the kind of thing we are talking about is the position in Figure 2. Here the *Acount* for both sides is 36. $36*1.1 - 2 = 38$, so that *Onmove* cannot double. Yet *Onmove* has approximately a 65% chance of winning here, as evidenced by simulations. The power of the bear-off tables is very impressive. Here is another area where the program plays perfectly To illustrate the type of thing BKG does to amaze its author, we show two examples.

In the bottom part of Figure 3, White is to play a 6,2. The 6 must obviously be played from the 21 point. But what is the correct way to play the 2? Almost every human player would say 21–23. However, this is not correct; 22–24 is better. The bear-off tables report the respective ENR's to be 2.748 and 2.739. Upon examination, it turns out that all sequences of future rolls produce the same results in the two positions except when one of the next two rolls is 1,1. If this occurred on the first roll, it would in both positions allow taking three men off. In the preferred position this would leave men on the 21 and 23 points, which allows six additional combinations of getting them both off on the next roll over the other position where the two men would both be on the 22 point. The situation is similar if the 1,1 occurs on the second roll.

The second example in the top part of Figure 3 has similar features. Here Black is to play a 6,1. The 6 must be played from the 4 point, the question is how to play, the 1. Again human players would automatically play 2–1, but this is incorrect. 3–2 is better in all future sequences. Again only those sequences involving a 2,2 make a difference. This would allow getting off in two rolls unless the next roll is 2,1 in the preferred case, but would do no good in the other. The respective ENR's are 2.794 and 2.777.

It may seem that the advantage gained by making the correct play in these

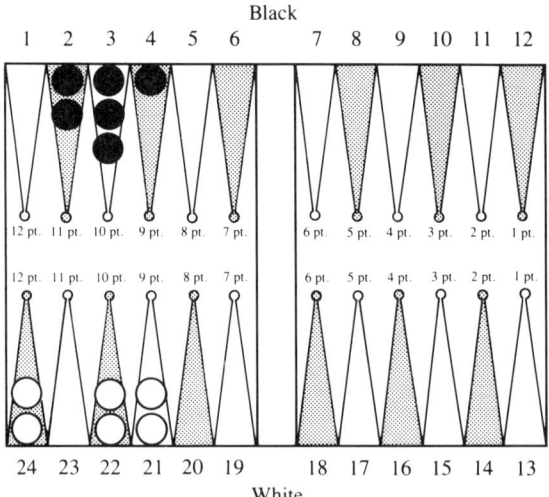

Figure 3

cases is trivial; however, it is certainly worthwhile to improve one's chances in the play when it can be done at no risk. For these two examples it would seem that the rule: "When there are a small odd number of men on the board, play to maximize use of doubles" would seem to be the correct way for humans to capture the knowledge that is contained in the tables.

E. Spacing of Men Around the Board

It is important in backgammon, all other things being equal, not to let groups of men become disconnected from one another. Thus one does not want to advance any men too far, or have any fall too far behind. At the moment we are taking care of this problem by using a second moment of inertia calculation which in general works quite well. We first calculate the center of mass of the moving side after a play. We then calculate *Moment2*—the second moment of inertia of the men located back of the center of mass. In the evaluation process this term will be a debit, and in general BKG will try to minimize this term all other things being equal. It should be noted that this computation also has the desired effect on the men in front of the center of mass (not too far advanced), since advancing men too far, advances the center of mass, thus increasing the number of stragglers and their contribution.

However, as well as this does, it still leaves some things to be desired. Basically, the real issue is whether any man or men is so far behind that it will be very difficult for it to ever join the main force. Or whether any men are so far advanced that they will not play any meaningful role in the game until the bearing-off stage is reached. These two issues are probably best treated separately and we intend to do this in our next revision. It is desirable to maintain stepping stones of safe points for lagging men to join the main force, and it should be relatively simple to devise a measure of the number and nearness to each other of such stepping points as an index of the ease with which lagging men can be brought to safety. Likewise, far advanced men can be debited according to how far advanced they are beyond the last safe man of the opponent. Even with such measures available, we would still plan to retain the second moment term as a useful measure of dispersion of the total force.

F. Other Variables

BKG also computes the values of the following variables which are used in the evaluation process.

1. *Closeboard*—Number of points closed in own home board.—This is a simple counting operation, except at present we subtract 1 for every enemy point in the other's homeboard, and 1 for every two own blots in a homeboard. These approximations are heuristic and will probably be replaced by a more exact calculation at some future time.
2. *Homblots*—The number of blots in own home board.

3. *Builders*—BKG at the end of a play decides which point it would next like to make (based on those already made and a table of values). It then counts the number of men that are extra (single or more than two on a point) that are within 6 points in front of such a point. These men are builders that are available to make this point on a future roll.

4. *Slotted*—When BKG has identified the point it next wants to make, if one of its men is already on this point (either as a result of the present play or a previous one) BKG will assign a value to *Slotted* commensurate will the value of the point (from the point table). Of course, if such a slotted man is in danger of being hit by the opponent on the next roll, this value will be traded off against the risk measured by the hit probability calculation.

5. *Histack*—Accumulates values according to how overloaded this side's points are. It adds 1 point for the third man, 1 for the fourth, 2 more for the fifth, 3 more for the sixth, 4 more for the seventh, etc. This is a quantity to be minimized in the evaluation procedure.

6. In addition to the above variables which require minimal computation, BKG also assign to variables the following quantities:

   Mostback—The point on which the furthest-back man is located (could be the bar).

   Onbar—The number of men on the bar.

   Expallin,Exploff,Expturns,Maxturns,Minturns,Maxloff,Minloff—For these variables the number of half-turns required to meet the stated goal are computed after a situation has been reached in which disengagement is near. Minimum and maximum quantities are self-explanatory. The EXP quantities are based on the sum of the ceilings of the distance that must be covered by each man involved divided by $3\frac{1}{2}$.

   Mobility = Sum of *Escapes* over all men of a side.

   Getbackin(Closeboard,Onbar)—Heuristic table of values for each situation.

   Winfactor = $(Pipcount(Justmoved) + 4 + Acontain(Justmoved)*2)/$
   $(Pipcount(Nexttomove) + Acontain(Nexttomove)*2)$.

   Caploss = Number of pips lost by *Nexttomove* due to captures.

   Edge = $Pipcount(Nexttomove) - Pipcount(Justmoved) - 4$.

   Contfactor = $(Contain(Onmove)^3)/300$.

7. BKG also can compute the following functions on demand (necessary for understanding the next section):

   Ownmen(side,point) = Number of men of "side" on "point."

   Manhome(point) = Returns binary value; true if "point" is in *Onmove's* homeboard.

   Distance(A,B) = Number of pips required to move from "A" to "B."

V. The Evaluation Process

The evaluation process has a long history of experimentation which is still going on. It was apparent, even in the early days of BKG, that a different evaluation procedure had to be used for the running game (forces disengaged) from that used in nonrunning game situations. This is apparent when one considers that *Acontain, Builders*, etc., have no bearing on running-game situations. Similarly, there are certain factors which measure the aggressive worth of a position, the defensive potential of position, and the ease with which men could be brought into the home board, given that the forces are still engaged. Clearly, all these factors are not applicable all the time.

To evaluate any position, we must decide which evaluation computations are applicable. The first step in this process is to decide whether it is a runing-game position or the forces are still engaged. We explained in Section IV how running-game evaluation is done. When the forces are still engaged the evaluation proceeds as follows:

The unit of evaluation is the heuristic point (HP). For all positions where the sides are not yet disengaged the following *GENERAL* evaluation is performed:

$HP \leftarrow HP + Caploss$
     $+ Ownmen(Offboard)*(\text{if } P1 = 0 \text{ then } 22 \text{ else } 3)$
     $+ Mobility/5$
     $+ Getbackin(Closeboard(Justmoved), Onbar(Nexttomove))$
     $- Piploss/Winfactor$
     $- (\text{if not } Manhome(Mostback(Justmoved)) \text{ then } Moment2)$
     $- 2*(Ownmen(Justmoved,1) + Ownmen(Justmoved,2))$
     $- Homblots(Justmoved)^2.$

The evaluation now becomes more sensitive to specific situations. First, we determine whether $Acontain(Justmoved) \leq 6$ in which case *Justmoved* is considered near disengagement and the *NEARDIS* evaluation is performed:

If *Justmoved* appears to be winning; i.e., $Edge \geq 0$ or $Acontain(Nexttomove) \geq 16$ then:

If $P1 \leq 3$ then the following SAFE evaluation is done:

$HP \leftarrow HP + (\text{if } Edge > 0 \text{ then } Edge^2 \text{ else } Acontain(Nexttomove)^3/300)$
     $- Histack(Justmoved)$
     $+ (\text{if } Ownmen(Mostback(Justmoved)) \leq 2 \text{ then } 10)$
          (This makes it easier to break this point and move the men up)
     $+ (\text{if } Manhome(Mostback(Justmoved)) \text{ then}$
          begin   if $Ownmen(Mostback(Justmoved)) \text{ MOD } 2 = 0 \text{ then } 10;$
                    if $(Ownmen(Mostback(Justmoved))$
                         $+ Ownmen(Mostback(Justmoved)+1)) \geq 5 \text{ then } 10;$
     end).

If this is the same state-class we were in previously then
     if $Caploss = 0$ or $P1 > (26 - Edge)/5$ then
          the following GAP evaluation is done:

$$HP \leftarrow HP - (GAP(Justmoved) + P1)$$
$$*(Contfactor + Getbackin(Closeboard(Nexttomove),1)/4)*6$$
$$/Distance(\text{Offboard},Mostback(Justmoved)).$$

Else if this is a new state class then:

$$HP \leftarrow HP + Acontain(Nexttomove)*2 - (1F\ Edge > 0\ \text{then}\ Edge*3).$$

This factor is a measure of how desirable it is to be getting near disengagement, and thus encourages or discourages getting into this state.

Else if *Justmoved* is losing then:

$$HP \leftarrow HP + Acontain(Nexttomove)^3/300.$$
This factor encourages maintaining the best possible actual containment because disengagement is not in the interest of *Justmoved*.

If $Distance(Mostback(Justmoved),Mostback(Nexttomove)) \leq 2$
or $GAP(Justmoved) \leq 1$ then:
$$HP \leftarrow HP + (Expallin(Onmove) - Expallin(Justmoved))/10.$$

This factor encourages *Justmoved* to bring his men efficiently near or into the home board, while being applicable only when *Justmoved*'s position has no holes in it. For this section the important ideas are: If we are ahead and were near disengaged then try to bring men up with minimum danger.

If *Justmoved* is not near disengagement then the following *NOTNEARDIS* computation is performed:

$$HP \leftarrow HP + Slotted(Justmoved)$$
$$+ Builders(Justmoved)$$
$$- Histack(Justmoved)$$
$$+ Acontain(Nexttomove)^3/300$$
$$+ Contain(Nexttomove)^2/50$$
$$+ (\text{If}\ Onbar(Justmoved) = 0\ \text{then}$$
$$\qquad Escapes(Justmoved,Mostback(Justmoved))*2)$$
$$- Escapes(Nexttomove,Mostback(Nexttomove))*2.$$

If *Justmoved* is 10% behind in the *Pipcount* then the *DEFENSE* evaluation function is computed. First, we check to see if there is any danger of gammon or backgammon. In that case:

if $Contain(Nexttomove) \geq 15$ or $Closeboard(Justmoved) \geq 4$ then

we consider if we wish to stay around in the hope of hitting a man. This is because we have some defensive potential in case we do hit the man. In that case the following defensive potential is added in:

$$HP \leftarrow HP + N^3*Distance(Mostback(Justmoved),Mostback(Nexttomove))$$
$$*2 - PRB(1)*100,$$

where N is the number of men that must cross, and PRB(1) is the probability of their crossing in one roll. The latter quantity is found by using the bear-off tables with the input shifted to make it appear that the edge of the board coincides with the location of *Mostback(Justmoved)*.

If $Acontain(Nexttomove) \geq 16$ then:

$$HP \leftarrow HP + 150 + Acontain(Nexttomove)*3.$$

This encourages keeping the opponent blocked in if at all possible.

Unless $Acontain(Nexttomove) = 36$ (*Justmoved* has men trapped in front of a prime), the following *BLOT DANGER* calculation is done:

$$HP \leftarrow HP - (P1*(Getbackin(Closeboard(Nexttomove),1) + Contfactor)) \\ /Winfactor$$

$$- (P2*(Getbackin(Closeboard(Nexttomove),2) + Contfactor)) \\ /Winfactor.$$

If the current play involves changing the location of Mostback then if the new location is further up than *Contsq(Onmove)* then:

$$HP \leftarrow HP + (Acontain(Onmove)^2 - Acontain(Justmoved)^2)/50;$$

It is noteworthy that these evaluation functions produce almost all the recommended ways of playing the opening rolls, thus obviating the need for "opening book knowledge," and also confirming the validity of the evaluation process.

VI. State-Classes and Their Utilization

The above evaluation functions informally partition the state-space into a considerable number of classes. This partitioning is defined purely by the recognition predicates which invoke some evaluation functions and ignore others. The reader will have noted that there are some terms in these functions which are invoked only if this is or is not a new state. This type of recognition produces in effect a different state-class for two identical positions, given that one is reached from a member of the same state-class and the other not. This action is but one unfortunate side-effect of our current method of doing business. Another is that edge-effects exist. An edge-effect is caused by the fact that there are sharp boundaries between state-classes. Thus the program may stay in one state-class because transition to the next normal state-class in the progression toward winning cannot be done favorably—at least not as defined by the evaluation function for the new state-class. This may result in loitering in the current state-class until there is no choice but to make the transition, possibly under much worse circumstances than would have been possible earlier. It is conceivable that if no state-classes existed this type of transition could be done more smoothly.

However, it is almost self-evident that one evaluation function cannot serve to order all positions. To do this, incredible complexities would have to be introduced. Consider the *Slotted* term. Before the opponent has built a strong defensive position, it is worthwhile to expose a man in a slotted context in order to improve one's own position. As the opponent's position gets better, this becomes less and less worthwhile. However, in certain desperate situations, it may again be desirable to take such risks. Finally, in the running game the term has no meaning at all. Clearly, the coefficient of this term must be sensitive to a great deal of context, which in effect makes the coefficient nonlinear and the resulting evaluation function nonlinear. Rather, than evaluate one gigantic nonlinear evaluation function, it seems wiser to evaluate each position in its proper context.

Thus the whole issue of state-classes and their associated evaluation functions is born. The issues associated with state-classes are these: We assume that it is possible to partition all game positions into mutually exclusive state-classes. This is not difficult and can be accomplished by merely having recognizers for a set of state-classes, invoking these recognizers in a canonical order, and putting all not-recognized positions into a grab-bag class. We further assume that within a state-class, a linear polynomial function exists which can order the members of this class according to goodness. It is apparent that this is true in the limit, when there is a state-class for each position; however, the degree to which this is possible when there are a large number of members in a given class is not clear. In practice, it is possible to get very good (if not perfect) orderings, and to split a state-class when the ordering procedure becomes too difficult.

In general, state-classes can be classified into the following categories: (1) essentially won, (2) favorable, (3) about even, (4) unfavorable, and (5) essentially lost. In all cases it is possible to further subdivide the classes into stable and unstable, where in general stability can be thought of as the variability of the end result. Thus the following ordering of these categories represents their general desirability: (1) won stable, (2) won unstable, (3) favorable stable, (4) favorable unstable, (5) even stable, and even unstable, (6) unfavorable unstable, (7) unfavorable stable, (8) lost unstable, and (9) lost stable. Frequently, in order to reach a more favorable class it will be necessary to go first to an unstable class; i.e., take a chance. In general, the side that is closest to winning will want more stable positions and the side that is closest to losing more unstable ones.

However, this is not always the case. The side that has a slightly better position may want to introduce some instability in the hope it will result in an even more favorable position (or even won), while risking losing the advantage or possibly getting slightly the worse of it. This kind of decision is very difficult to program, if all positions are evaluated only on their expectation or game-theoretic value.

Actually, notions such as progress and risk are crutches that are not needed when a universal measure of goodness such as expectation exists, as it does

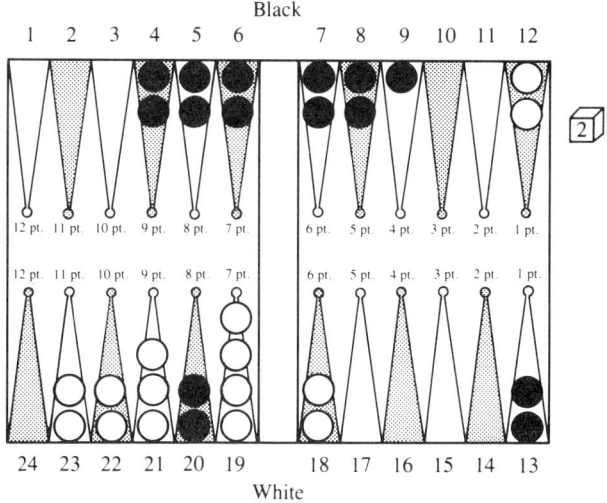

Figure 4

in backgammon. Thus we should always move to the state with the greatest expectation, and state-classes are not needed at all. However, as we pointed out earlier this is only in a system with perfect knowledge. When there is imperfect knowledge, such crutches allow for much smoother performance.

To give an example of move selection across class boundaries, consider the position of Figure 4. In this case *Onmove* is White. The current state-class (1) is characterized by *Onmove* being ahead in the pipcount by 15 pips or more, having to cross exactly two more enemy points with his Mostback, and having $P1 \leq 3$. We can now imagine an evaluation function for this class which would consider the position of the doubling cube, the exact difference in the pipcount, the distance between Mostback and each of the two points that must be crossed, *Contain*(White), the number of stepping stone points of White between the two points of *Nexttomove* that must be crossed, the value of *Closeboard*(White), and the number of pips that are available to be played as slack before any of these values are decreased. Such a function could conceivably deliver an output that would indicate the expectation of White in the particular member of the state-class. Such a function could be derived either by analytic means or by actual simulation of positions in the class to find out how each of the above variables affected the expectation of White. Further, such a function could be tuned as experience is accumulated. Let us assume that such a function exists and predicted that in the situation of Figure 4 White should win 66% of the time, win a gammon 2% of the time, lose 30% of the time and lose a gammon 2% of the time, for a net expectation for White of +0.36.

Now from this position it is possible to move to four state-classes: the present one (class I), an unstable state-class where White has two points to cross, but has a blot in danger of being hit, i.e., $P1 > 3$ (class II), an unstable class where White has only one more point left to cross (class IV), and a stable class where White has only one point left to cross (class III). Further, if a blot is hit in state-classes II or IV, we have another state-class (V) in which White has a man on the bar which must enter in front of Black's blocking position. Each of these state-classes will have their own evaluation functions. Thus when deciding how to play a roll, the play yielding the best expectation will be chosen.

White's win probability, W, in a state where he is to move is the SUM $i = 1$ to n $(T_i * W_i)$ where T_i is the probability of transiting to state i on the play by playing it optimally, and W_i is the probability of winning once state i is reached. If it is Black to play, White's win probability can be computed in a like manner.

This method can be used to decide between plays that result in differing state-classes even though one class may be unstable and the other not. Let us illustrate by an example. Assume that $W = 0.92$ for positions in state-class III. W for positions in state-class II is $PH*W5 + (1 - PH)*W_2$, and W for state class IV is $PH*W_5 + (1 - PH)*W_4$. Here $PH = P1/36$, $W_2 = 0.85$, and $W_4 = 0.92$. To get W_5 we must compute the probability of White escaping over the blockade on his next roll, as otherwise he will be doubled and will have to resign. If he does escape, he has about an even chance in the resulting position. These constants should make clear the computation below. It should be noted that when W for a side that is on roll and can double is ≥ 0.75 (i.e., his expectation ≥ 0.50) he can double and force his opponent's resignation. Thus such terms should be ignored as their value drops to 0. This is true for instance of the term dealing with the situation where White is hit and contained.

We now use this method to decide how to play a difficult roll, 6–1, in Figure 4. There are basically two plays: run one man from the 12 point resulting in a position of class II, or play both men from the 18 point remaining in class I. For the first play:

$$W = 20/36*0.85 + 16/36*2/36*0.5 = 0.48.$$

For the second play, there are five rolls which result in transition to state-class III (2–2, 3–3, 4–4, 5–5, 6–6), 2 rolls that result in a class II position (6–2), eight rolls that result in class IV positions (6–1, 6–3, 6–4, 6–5), and 21 rolls that result in remaining in state-class I. The appropriate computation is:

$$
\begin{aligned}
W = \quad & 5*0.92 && \text{(state-class III)} \\
+ & 8\,(16/36*2/36*0.5 + 20/36*0.85) && \text{(state-class II)} \\
+ & 2\,(23/36*2/36*0.5 + 13/36*0.75) && \text{(state-class IV, 2 blots)} \\
+ & 21*0.55/36 = 20.61/36 = 0.57. && \text{(state-class I, new } W = 0.55)
\end{aligned}
$$

Therefore, it can be seen that it is better to make play two. It should be noted that as the probability of containing a hit man varies with Black's defensive formation, this calculation will also vary accordingly.

The method we have described above can be used for deciding the very important problem of when to move to a state that is in a state-class different from the one we are currently in. However, the whole method assumes that an accurate evaluation function exists for each state-class; i.e., it both orders properly and produces the correct expectation for each member of its class. This is obviously never the case.

Therefore, it is necessary to show how such a system can operate adequately and can be improved in the face of error. For each state-class there are new state-classes that can be reached in one optimal play for each side without a capture being made. We call these classes forward with respect to the original class. Likewise, there are new classes that can be reached from the current class in one optimal play by each side, when there has been at least one capture of a man. We call these classes backward with respect to the original class.

It is possible to start with a class for which we have excellent expectation data, i.e., the class of bearing-off positions that can be looked up in our tables (class B). Next, we consider all classes for which class B is forward, and improve the evaluation function for those classes, tuning the coefficients of existing terms and adding new ones as required. This will improve these evaluation functions. We also note all classes that are backward to this class, and put them on a list together with the name of the current class. We can continue this process indefinitely, but painfully until every class has been encountered. Whenever the evaluation function of a class that is on the backward list is improved, we go back and modify all the evaluation functions of the affected classes. We can then continue our process or go back to one of the classes whose function has just been modified and start anew from there. It is clear that this is a converging procedure. It would probably be necessary to eventually automate this procedure, if for no other reason than that eventually the evaluation functions would become so good that they would do a better job of ordering members of a class than the experimenter would. Such automation, except for the introduction of new terms, has been previously done by Samuel (1959) for checkers. It would appear likely that for a game such as backgammon, it would be possible to get a selection of terms such that no new ones will ever be required. Then it will be merely a matter of tuning old evaluation functions, pulling in a new (but known) term every once in a while to see if it can improve prediction.

As data are collected and the evaluation functions improve, two things become possible. It is possible to keep track of how the prediction works out for the program's own play, which can be used as an indicator of which functions need to be tuned next. It is also possible to keep track of individual opponent's results and come to the conclusion that they do not appraise certain state-classes correctly, and use this information in future games.

VII. Testing of BKG

When testing BKG on typical beginners books, it gets the right answer in excess of 70% of the time. A much better appraisal of the program can be obtained by analyzing its successes and failures on more difficult tasks. For this we chose the problems in a very fine intermediate level book (Holland, 1974). There are 74 doable problems in this book (BKG could not do those which involve doubling decisions before disengagement). We have classified the problems according to the major knowledge required to get the right answer. This is a rather arbitrary way of looking at things, but it is helpful in trying to understand the strengths and lacks in the program. We divided the problems into seven categories:

(1) general positional;
(2) running game: bearoff;
(3) engaged: bearoff;
(4) back game (this a special defensive posture);
(5) timing (this involves advantages that presently exist going away because one side or the other must destroy his position);
(6) defensive plays;
(7) advanced defensive plays (including the return play).

We followed the practice in scoring the results of giving BKG part credit for answers that were not perfectly correct but showed it understood the main point of the problem, although the execution was not perfect. We also deducted part credit when it got the correct answer without understanding what the main problem was. Table 1 shows the results of the tests. In evaluating these results, several things should be noted. The subject matter is relatively advanced, and would for the most part come up in only one of 20 or more games. There are usually on the order of three plausible answers to a problem. BKG is good enough in almost every case to know what these are; thus attaining a score of 33% or less could be regarded more or less as the result of chance. We can see that BKG is extremely good in running game play. Also it has a good understanding of the relative positional advantages. However, its performance in other intermediate level aspects of the game is at best mediocre. It has heuristics to help it do bearing off while still engaged, but these are for run-of-the-mill situations, not for the more sophisticated ones in the test set. It has no specific understanding of the back game. Since

Table 1. Tests of BKG on "Better Backgammon."

Position class	Number	Right	Wrong	Percent correct
Positional	28	$18\frac{3}{4}$	$9\frac{1}{4}$	67
Running bearoff	5	5	0	100
Engaged bearoff	11	2	9	22
Back game	8	$3\frac{1}{4}$	$4\frac{3}{4}$	41
Timing	13	4	9	31
Advanced defense	6	$\frac{1}{2}$	$5\frac{1}{2}$	6
Defense	3	1	2	33

the objectives in the back game are rather different than anything else in backgammon, it will be necessary to implement a specific set of state-classes which recognize back-game potential and how to maintain and destroy it. The problem of timing is one that will be resolved soon. Essentially, this requires having a measure of how many men are presently bound to essential roles in the current evaluation, and how many pips are available to be played by the remaining men before the important men will have to be moved. BKG's only knowledge of defense is that described earlier. It does not understand the concept of coverage, i.e., controlling points on which an opponent's blot may land in the next roll or two. It does not understand that at times it may be beneficial to expose a blot in dire circumstances or to make the "return" play. Thus this series of tests has pinpointed some specific knowledge that BKG lacks and that is not subsumed in its present knowledge base.

VIII. Use of Simulation Facility

It is possible to give BKG a position and ask it to play both sides repeatedly any number of times. In doing these simulations it will play as it ordinarily does; double when allowed and appropriate. There are certain types of positions that BKG plays almost perfectly so that doing such simulations generates useful information for evaluating the position. Included in this class are all running-game positions and those where one side is bearing off with one or fewer points to cross. Thus it is, for instance, possible to determine the expectation of the bearing-off side when there are two opponent's men on the bar, and his home board is closed. Such information is very useful for understanding where certain break even points are. We have, in fact, considered publishing tables of such data for general consumption.

IX. A Game

BKG does not play a brilliant game, as one could for instance say of a chess program when it makes a sacrifice. It plays well and consistently, using its knowledge of probability and positional facets of the game. It makes errors when these facets are misinterpreted due to its evaluation functions or when the appropriate knowledge is not present. The game following on page 28 is representative of the good games it plays.

White: Berliner		Black: BKG	
Roll	Play	Roll	Play
5,4	1–5,12–17	5,6	24–18–13
2,5	5–7–12	3,6	24–18–15
1,3	12–15X,1–2	3,4	25–21,13–10
4,3	12–15,19–23	1,5	6–5,10–5
4,6	15–21X,17–21	6,3	25–22–16
3,1	12–15–16X	2,5	25–23X–18
6,1	0–1,12–18	1,4	25–24–20

(Doubtful play as this blot is too exposed, but Black is lucky).

4,3	17–20X,16–20	3,4	25–22–18X
2,4	0–4,2–4		

(Now would be a good time for Black to double and White should refuse.
However, BKG does not double until disengaged).

		2,6	13–11,18–12X

(BKG does not know about back-game possibilities and thus is happy to hit all
the blots it safely can. Here the back-game is unsound anyway).

5,1	0–1,17–22	1,4	8–7,11–7
3,3	19–22,17–20–23,15–18	3,4	12–9,13–9
3,4	19–23,18–21	6,5	13–7,13–8
2,6	4–10–12	4,5	8–4X,9–4
1,4	0–1,12–16	5,4	13–8,9–5

(Making the 3 point improves Black's gammon chances, but BKG does not want
to leave any shots).

1,2	1–3,16–17	3,6	5–2,8–2
1,3	17–20,21–22	6,1	8–2,8–7
6,2	3–9,22–24	6,3	7–4
2,4	20–24,9–11	6,2	7–5
6,5	11–17–22	5,3	7–2,7–4
1,2	22–24,23–24	3,1	4–3,6–3
5,3	19–24,19–22	1,4	4–0,6–5
6,1	1–7,22–23	3,6	6–0,6–3
6,3	7–13–16	4,6	5–0,5–1X
2,5	No legal move (no luck)	2,2	5–3,5–3–1,2–0 (safe now!)
2,5	0–5–7	4,2	2–0,4–0
5,6	7–12–18	6,4	4–0,3–0
4,5	16–21,18–22	Double	(no chance of gammon remains)
Resign			

1.2. Backgammon Computer Program Beats World Champion

HANS J. BERLINER

Originally published in: *Artificial Intelligence*, vol. 14 (1980), pp. 205–220. Copyright © 1980 by North-Holland Publishing Company. Reprinted by permission of the author and the publisher. This research was sponsored by the Defence Advanced Research Projects Agency (DOD), ARPA Order No. 3597, monitored by the Air Force Avionics Laboratory Under Contract F33615-78-C-1551.

Abstract. On July 15, 1979, a backgammon computer program beat the World Backgammon Champion in a match to 7 points. This is the first time a world champion in a recognized intellectual activity has been defeated by a man-made entity. This paper examines the scientific issues involved in constructing the program, an analysis of its performance, and the scientific significance of the win. We also present our SNAC method of constructing evaluation functions.

1. Introduction

When in the course of cerebral affairs one species succeeds, no matter how slightly, in loosing the shackles of domination placed upon it by its parent species, scientific decorum requires that the facts pertaining to such an event be examined. On July 15, 1979 in Monte Carlo, an event of considerable scientific importance occurred. Luigi Villa, the newly crowned backgammon World Champion, played an exhibition match to 7 points with BKG 9.8, a computer backgammon program developed by me at Carnegie–Mellon University. A winner-take-all purse of $5,000 was at stake. To the surprise of almost everybody, BKG 9.8 won by a score of 7–1. This was the first time that a world champion of a recognized intellectual activity had been defeated by a man-created entity in a head-to-head test of skill. Two questions present themselves: (1) How was this achieved? and (2) What is the significance of the result? We try to answer these questions in this paper.

Why should backgammon be an object of interest to science? Backgammon

(Magriel, 1976) is a game of skill and chance. The chance element is introduced by the throw of dice at each player's turn. The skill comes in selecting the best move associated with the actual dice throw, and in making correct decisions in connection with doubling. Doubling is an action that a player can take that doubles the stakes under which the game is being played. The player being doubled has the choice of giving up the game at the current stake, or continuing the game at doubled stakes with the proviso that only he can make the next double. There is considerable skill involved in making, accepting, or rejecting such doubles.

There is skill involved in selecting the best move too. At a gross level of understanding, the best move is the one that does the most to further one's own objectives and impede the opponent's. Furthering one's own objectives can take the form of actually achieving a known good that is relatively permanent, or creating conditions for the likely achieving of such goods by creating opportunities for favorable dice rolls in the near future. Impeding the opponent involves making it as unlikely as possible for him to roll combinations that will help him in the near future.

The domain of backgammon comprises some 10^{20} positions. Its complexity approximates that of bridge or checkers, both of which can be played as an avocation or very seriously. The playing of excellent backgammon requires the application of considerable amounts of knowledge and intelligence.

Backgammon probably cannot be played by using the chief crutch of most game-playing programs—the look-ahead tree-search. This is because the throw of a pair of dice can produce 21 different results, and each such throw can be played about 20 different ways in the average position. Thus a look-ahead would have to acquiesce to a branching factor of about 400 for each ply of look-ahead; an exponential growth rate that could not be tolerated very long. Thus a computer backgammon program would appear to require evaluation much more than search, very much as humans play the game.

If one uses a linear polynomial evaluation function (one that has a constant coefficient and a single variable per term) in a large domain such as chess, one soon finds out that the function is not sensitive enough. There are features that are important in the opening that are meaningless in the endgame. A linear polynomial will not be sensitive to such problems. The best it can do is to indicate the average value that should be associated with a feature. Experience indicates that this is not sufficient for expert level performance. Samuel's (1959) research first indicated this. Further, Samuel found (1967) that when he used nonlinear terms (where two or more features were related in the same term) his program's performance did not improve. This seemed a puzzling result.

An obvious solution to the deficiencies of the linear polynomial is to break the game up into phases. However, we had previously found (Berliner, 1970) that having game phases for chess also was fraught with difficulties, a condition that was found to exist in backgammon too (Berliner, 1977c). As an outstanding example of such a difficulty, consider the fact that sound advice

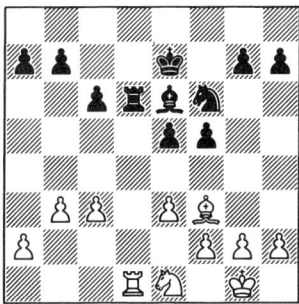

Figure 1. White to play.

in chess is to keep one's King safely in a corner during the middle game, and use it aggressively during the endgame. The fact that the middle game metamorphoses into an endgame creates the difficulty. In such a scheme, there must be a criterion for deciding whether a position is a middle game or an endgame. If a program is faced with an unfavorable endgame situation and a favorable middle game situation, it will go to great extremes to avoid going into an endgame even though the current position is really very close to an endgame, and the endgame is basically unavoidable anyway.

Consider Figure 1. Suppose our evaluation function is designed so that with the material present in the figure it is treated as a middle game, but if one more piece were traded then it would be an endgame. Treated as a middle game, White's King would be considered safe and Black's exposed. In the endgame, White's King would be considered de-centralized, while Black's is centralized. Thus, White would very likely move his Rook in order to avoid the swap and thus consider the position as a middle game with some favorable aspects, rather than an endgame with many unfavorable aspects. Yet this is a very bad action by White as it only increases Black's advantage by making his Rook even stronger, while not avoiding the changing of the character of the position into an endgame.

This behavior is similar to that produced by the horizon effect (Berliner, 1973), which causes a program to believe it has remedied an irremedial problem due to idiosyncracies in the way it conducts its search.

Expert human beings do not have problems such as those above. This convinced me that there was a great deal left to be learned about the structure of evaluation functions. However, investigating evaluation functions in the context of chess creates special problems. In chess, searching interacts with evaluation. Certain positions are considered too volatile to evaluate, so a quiescence search is performed until a set of stable positions is reached. Also, searching for a particular reason (or just brute force searching) will sometimes discover the achievement of some goal that was not at all contemplated when the search was initiated. In such situations move selection is a function not only of knowledge but also of a discovery search. In order to avoid this type of contaminant in investigating evaluation, it was necessary to find a domain that was reasonably complex and where searching had no utility. That is, it should be possible to make decisions based solely on static evaluation, and have evaluation functions to do this. Backgammon appeared to have the desired properties, and in 1974 we began developing a program to play backgammon. The next five sections present the outcome of the research into the structure of evaluation polynomials. They are taken substantively from (Berliner, 1979).

2. Some Preliminaries

In problem solving the analysis takes place in a set of states of the domain, a subset of these that are terminal states (corresponding to the achievement of some goal of the domain), and a set of operators that transform one state into another. In a given domain, it may be possible to apply any of dozens of operators to a given state. Further, the current state may require hundreds of consecutive operator applications in order to arrive at a terminal state. Since such a search grows exponentially with depth, generally no path to a terminal state from a given starting state will be found within a reasonable effort. This is especially true in large domains ($> 10^{14}$ states).

When it is not reasonable to expect the solving process to search toward a terminal state, we must have recourse to knowledge to lead the way to a goal. The knowledge is in the form of "properties" or "features" that can be used to describe any state of the domain. Each such feature can take on a range of values and thus defines a dimension in a hyperspace of features. A polynomial that is the sum of various functions on these features is used to assign values to nodes and thus locate them in the hyperspace. These values are then used to order the nodes with respect to their goodness (closeness to goals of the domain).

The features that are used can represent many facets of the subject domain. Usually, things that are part of the minimal description of a state are also good features. An example from chess might be the location of the King. Other features can be more complex, or patternlike and require the operation upon several primitive features to produce a new feature. This process can be iterated. For instance, to create a feature representing blockading in backgammon it is necessary to first know the location of all (blockading) points on the board that have two or more men of a particular side on it (primitive). Then it is necessary to scan the board to find the location from which it will be hardest for an opposing man to pass through the set of blockading points, and to measure this difficulty. This is definitely not a primitive notion. In fact, it requires a good deal of experimentation in order to determine a function on the set of points that produces a good mapping into the human notion of blockading. The result will be a new feature, and its values will be used in measuring something about the value of a backgammon position.

The selected features are then combined in a polynomial function that is capable of ordering the states of the domain. The chief problem is how to do this so that the ordering is effective. Below, we present the details of our SNAC method (for Smoothness, Nonlinearity, and Application Coefficients) which appears to have remedied all methodological problems in evaluation noted above.

3. Nonlinearity

Linear functions have difficulty in accurately approximating complex behavior over a large range. Consider a simple price relationship between oranges and apples. If we assert that an orange is twice as valuable as an apple, we may be stating something that is correct *on average*. However, this type of advice would not be satisfactory when there is a great orange glut and a shortage of apples. Thus, a linear function seldom is *sensitive* enough over a large range; e.g., it fails to take into account the relative supply of oranges and apples, and will thus prove to be too constricting at times.

However, a linear function is very well behaved. In contrast, multiplying two variables, each of which could have a range of $0:50$, produces a resulting range of $0:2500$. The contribution of such a term to the evaluation could vary widely, causing *stability* problems for the value of the polynomial. Nor would normalizing the result be very satisfactory, since that would essentially suppress any variation at the lower end of the scale.

Another type of problem with nonlinear functions is the *suicide construction*, which we examine below. Say, we have some advice to the system in the form of $S = I * D$, where S is suffering, I is the intensity of pain, and D is the duration of pain. The object is to minimize the value of S (as there will be a minus sign in front of this term in the polynomial). This seems to be a well-formed piece of advice. People, in general, understand that the idea is to reduce both I and D. However, a program that is allowed to manipulate D, when faced with excruciating pain that is difficult to remove, may well recommend suicide, i.e., drive D to 0 at any cost. This usually does not qualify as a solution. However, such advice can be forthcoming even when some other term of the polynomial places a large premium on staying alive. We therefore term a relation, where there exists the potential to manipulate one of the variables in a generally undesirable direction, a *suicide construction*.

Nonlinearity is desirable because of the increased sensitivity it provides, while care must be taken to control volatility and avoid the suicide construction.

4. Smoothness

Any function on the set of features in our evaluation hyperspace will define a surface. Let us consider what can result from a lack of smoothness in the surface. If there is a ridge, a discontinuity, or a sudden step in the surface, then this is a place where the values on one side of such a blemish may be quantitatively very different from those on the other side. Thus, a very small change in the value of some feature could produce a substantial change in the value of the function. When the program has the ability to manipulate such a feature, it will frequently do so to its own detriment. Simply put, the program will act to hurry across such a blemish if it leads to a favorable evaluation, and wait as long as possible to cross it, if it leads to unfavorable consequences. This behavior resembles the horizon effect (Berliner, 1973), although caused by a different set of circumstances. We now name this effect the *blemish effect*. Because of the blemish effect, smoothness is absolutely essential for reliable performance.

Considerations such as the above have been studied in numerical analysis. In fact, the above may seem so obvious that the reader would feel that no one could possibly overlook such a thing. However, this is far from the case. There is very little published on the structure of evaluation polynomials that are used in game playing programs. One exception is the work of Samuel (1959; 1967). Samuel investigates how to achieve nonlinearity without creating an unstable function. His solution, in both cited works is to map a variable with a large range onto a small range. In the earlier work, he creates "binary connective terms" which are a reduction to a binary value of a range that was large to start. Clearly, this will cause the blemish effect in the vicinity where the value of the variable changes from 0 to 1. In the later work, large ranges are reduced to ranges of from 3 to 7 in order to fit more easily into a "signature table" of limited size. Again, the blemish effect will occur near the locations where the value changes occur. We conjecture that the reason that Samuel's program did not perform better after learning nonlinear functions is that the blemish effect caused it to commit serious errors occasionally. Consider the curves in Figure 2, which depict the situation. If the value (along the x-coordinate) of the feature is near the vertical line labeled A, then in the upper curve small variations along the x-coordinate will only produce small variations in the y-coordinate, while in the lower curve they produce no variation at all. However, near the vertical line labeled B, the situation on the lower curve is quite different. Here small variations in the x-coordinate can produce a marked change in the y-coordinate. If the value on either side of the sudden change point can be interpreted as being favorable to the program, it will go to great lengths to select an alternative for which the value will be on that side. We now are able to observe the blemish effect in the performance of older versions of our backgammon program. Thus, one suspects that this difficulty is of very widespread occurrence.

Whenever the coefficient of a nonsmooth term is under the control of the program, the blemish effect can occur. That is what causes the program to make the wrong move in Figure 1. A correct definition of endgame as a smooth function from early middle game to late endgame would appear to avoid this type of problem completely. In this way, the degree of endgameness increases

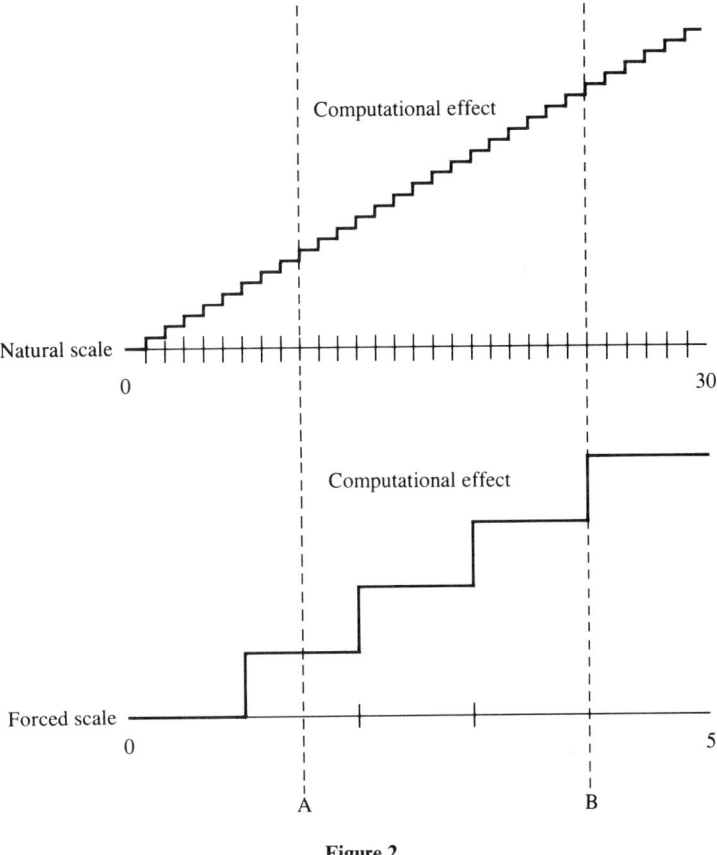

Figure 2

with each swap of material. It is interesting to note that smoothness, thus invoked between known data points creates a transition that is not clearly derivable from the data. Yet, this appears requisite for proficient performance. Further, our studies indicate that the shape of the transition curve does not appear to matter very much.

5. Application Coefficients

We have indicated how sensitivity can be achieved, and how the blemish effect can be avoided by the use of smoothness. However, there is a major problem in avoiding the creation of terms that are very volatile. Otherwise, the program may try to produce some extreme value in the volatile term, because it will outweigh the combined values of all the other terms of the polynomial. This problem arises because it is very difficult to anticipate the range of values that a term may take on over a large domain. This is especially true when functions continue to be changed during program development. Volatility can be avoided by constraining the values that one of the variables can take on. If this were done in a construction such as $S = I * D$, then the volatility of the term would disappear. Yet the constrained variable would provide more sensitivity to context than a constant coefficient. For instance, selecting clothing for a hike could be predicted on the "better safe than sorry" principle, e.g., always wear something warm and take a rain coat (use a constant approach to the problem). However, recognizing that the temperature and barometric pressure usually do not change very much during a few hours allows one to use the readings on these instruments to make more informed choices.

There are two ways of achieving this additional context: (1) by fixing the value of the variable to be that in the original problem situation (frozen variable), i.e., not recomputing it for each new node; and (2) by choosing variables that vary slowly (application coefficients). We have used both methods successfully.

Using the value of a frozen variable gives the problem solving process a global outlook, where all terms using this variable are viewed as they would have been in the original situation. This has the advantage of not letting small variations create too much of an effect, and suppressing volatility for large variations. It has the disadvantage of making the process insensitive to certain kinds of changes. This method is good for functions that require some discrimination to determine the degree to which they apply, but are not required to discriminate minimal changes. This method has been used previously for efficiency reasons, when the cost of recomputing the variable at each new node is high.

The other method is to use *application coefficients.* An application coefficient is a variable that tends to vary slowly with operator applications (moves) due to the nature of the domain. Thus for a set of nodes that are a few operator applications apart, the value of the variable will tend to be relatively constrained. This results in a coefficient that will provide sensitivity without volatility. We give examples of typical application coefficients below.

Our typical evaluation polynomial is of the form $V = A_1 F_1 + A_2 F_2 + \cdots + A_n F_n$, where the A_i's are application coefficients or frozen variables, and the F_i's are functions of features of the domain. We have found that while there are usually many dozens of useful F_i's in a domain, on the order of six or fewer application coefficients appear to emerge. These are strongly related to ideas such as game phase, ease of winning, readiness for attack, etc.

In chess, typical application coefficients are:

(1) What stage the game is in, as denoted by the amount of material on the board, and the degree to which the pieces are still in their original positions.
(2) The degree to which the winning side is winning, indicated by $(W - V)/(W + V)$, where W is the score of the winning side and V that of the losing side.
(3) The ease of being able to win, which is a function of the number of Pawns

left for the winning side and the ease with which they may be exchanged, and the degree to which the position is blockaded.

Similar application coefficients exist in backgammon. Such application coefficients provide a program with context for making decisions. Thus a program that understands the stage of the game in chess, as a function of amount of material on the board, will allow its king to gradually achieve a more central position as the amount of material diminishes. Further, the *suicide construction* can be avoided by using a frozen variable in place of one that can be varied adversely. In the example quoted earlier, the duration of life of the subject becomes frozen, and that value must be used in all functions that could otherwise be subject to the suicide construction.

6. Results

Since October 1978, we have been performing tests on versions of the program named BKG 9.5 through BKG 9.8. The purpose of these tests was to measure the effect of what has been accomplished using SNAC vs. the older method, and to pinpoint remaining areas of weakness. We have three methods of measuring performance of the program:

(1) Performance on a problem set in an intermediate level instruction book (Holland, 1974).
(2) Games against other backgammon programs or earlier versions of our own program.
(3) Performance against human opponents.

The results of these tests are shown in Table 1. The best program we had before using the SNAC method was called BKG 8.0. This program was the result of about 30 man-months of effort. BKG 9.7 was the result of about 8 additional man-months of work, and BKG 9.8 another additional 5 man-months beyond that. In tests on the problem book, BKG 8.0 achieve a score of 45% based on 74 problems that it could attempt. This was a peak performance for this version in the sense that the problems had been used to set certain parameters in the program, thus making it unlikely that small changes in the program would further improve performance on the problem set.

Table 1. Test results of backgammon program performance.

	BKG 8.0 (1977, without SNAC)	BKG 9.5–9.8 (with SNAC)
Problem set from book	45%	66%
Versus best commercial microprocessor	56%	78%
Matches against humans	0–2	3–1
Versus each other	37.9%	62.1%

Without any pretesting, BKG 9.7 achieved 66% on the full set of 77 problems in the same book, and it is highly probable that several additional percentage points of performance could have been gained by small adjustments in the program. However, we have in the last year discontinued the practice of doing this type of tuning as it has been found that many of the problems in books are too contrived (they come up very rarely), and even then answers given by the book are quite often wrong.

Against the best commercially available backgammon microprocessor, BKG 8.0 achieved 56% of the points, while BKG 9.5 (considerably inferior to BKG 9.7) scored 78% of the points in a set of 100 games. BKG 9.7–8 are now much too good to make testing against the microprocessor an interesting task. Our latest tests pitted BKG 8.0 vs. BKG 9.7–8, with BKG 9.7–8 scoring 61.1% of the points.

BKG 8.0 played in the Carnegie–Mellon University backgammon championships in the spring of 1978 and lost its first two matches thus being eliminated. In May 1979, BKG 9.7 played in a tournament of intermediate players in Portola Valley, California and won its first two matches before losing to the ultimate winner of the tourney in the third round. The competition in the California tournament was somewhat better than that in the earlier tourney. Now there is the additional win of the match vs. World Champion Villa. Finally, in October 1979, BKG 9.8 beat Barbara Glazer, the winner of the strong Chicago Invitational tournament, in a single exhibition game. This is the complete performance record of all versions of our program in organized competition.

The reason for all the above accomplishments is the excellent context sensitivity, and the lack of continuity problems that the SNAC method has brought to bear on the backgammon playing ability of the program. Although, versions of BKG beyond 8.0 do have approximately 15–20% more information about backgammon in them, this in no way could account for the difference. In books, problems usually come in pairs where different plays are correct in somewhat similar situations. For a program to solve both problems of such a pair correctly, it must have enough context sensitivity. If this is obtained by having a boundary between the two applicable cases then the boundary must be correct not only for this pair of cases but for all potential pairs of this type. That is frequently asking too much from such a knowledge structure. The smooth phasing over between opposing ideas that is typical of SNAC functions is much more likely to provide both the adequate context due to nonlinearity and the discrimination of those cases that are far enough apart so that they should be handled disparately.

BKG 8.0 has been available on PDP-10 machines for some time and has been regarded as a good game-playing program, and by far the best backgammon program around. Yet, as the above results indicate, the SNAC method has resulted in a rather significant improvement in the program. In evaluating the above, the reader should bear in mind that in backgammon, chance plays a significant role. In the short run, small percentage differences favoring one player are not too significant. However, in the long run a few percentage points are highly indicative of significant skill differences. A 60% edge is quite extreme.

A minimal analysis of the games from the match with Villa has been performed. There were five games in all; BKG 9.8 winning four (doubling accounted for the remainder of its 7 points) and Villa one. The analysis confirms that Villa, as expected, is certainly the better player. Although both sides made some mistakes, BKG 9.8 made two mistakes that could have hurt it very much, but didn't due to a fortunate occurrence at the end of Game 3. Villa did not make any serious errors. BKG 9.8 made several outstanding moves (truly outstanding when one considers they were made by a machine), while Villa had little opportunity to do anything sensational because his style or the opportunities in the games did not permit this.

Villa played 80 nonforced moves during the match. In giving these games to BKG 9.8, and asking it to move in Villa's situation, it 51 times chose the same move as he. Of the 29 times the program would have played differently, there was one occasion where it chose a clearly better move, and seven times when it chose clearly inferior alternatives. The remaining 21 differences would require a cadre of better players than myself to adjudicate their merits. It would have played one game (Game 4) exactly as Villa did.

As to the program's own play, it made at least eight plays ranging from doubtful to obviously bad. However, only one of these bad moves was made in a situation where it could hurt. The other bad moves were bad in a technical sense only; there was a clearly better move, but its betterness would not cause a large difference in the probable outcome of the game. Most of the remaining moves were good, although I do not feel completely qualified to comment on their quality.

BKG 9.8 made a double that ended Game 2, and was considered excellent by watching experts, and was certainly quite remarkable for a machine. The double came in a volatile situation where the game could easily have swung badly against Villa. He declined the double, though the consensus was that he should have accepted. BKG 9.8 made a serious error in accepting a double in Game 3, where expert consensus said it should have declined.

However, the most revealing comments about its play can be summarized as follows: Spectators came to laugh at what was expected to be a mediocre attempt to capture the wisdom of backgammon. Instead they were treated to steady play, wherein mistakes were so few and subtle that only the very best players could discern them. In between, the program showed a great deal of imagination in making correct moves that sometimes even the experts did not anticipate.

7. The Significance of BKG 9.8's Win

This is undoubtedly the most important result achieved to date in contests of machines vs. humans. Yet, I would hesitate to pronounce BKG 9.8 better at backgammon than CHESS 4.7 (the Northwestern University chess program

(Slate *et al.*, 1977) that has dominated computer chess for many years now) is at chess. They are close to equally competent. In order to maintain some perspective, it is probably best to home in on the meaning of BKG 9.8's win from both the positive and negative direction. Let us do the latter first.

This event was not a match for the World Championship. My program did defeat the current World Champion, but it was an exhibition match not involving the title. Further, a match to 7 points is not considered very conclusive in backgammon. A good intermediate player would probably have a 1/3 chance of winning such a match against a world-class player, whereas in a match to 25 points his chances would be considerably diminished. At the time of the match the bookmakers in Monte Carlo were quoting odds of 3 to 2 if you wanted to bet on the machine, and 1 to 2 if you wanted to bet on Villa. Thus the bookmakers apparently thought the program to be very slightly better than a good intermediate player. It would be much more useful in evaluating BKG 9.8's strength to have played a longer series or a number of shorter series, but that will have to wait for some future time.

Further, the conditions of play may have worked somewhat against Villa taking the program seriously at first. It had been arranged that BKG 9.8 should be encased inside a backgammon playing robot was billed as a special feature of the event. Backgammon players in general were aware of the playing capability of microprocessors already on the market, and quite logically assumed that this one would not be much better. Journalists who competed against the program in the week prior to the match found out differently, as they lost approximately 80% of their contests with BKG 9.8. However, this was not general knowledge and would probably have been discounted by the experts anyway. Further, the robot gave a semicomic impression during the event, rolling around controlled by a remote radio link and occasionally speaking and bumping into things. An uninformed person would surely have thought it was there strictly for the entertainment of the participants. However, there was $5,000 at stake, and even a World Champion should be serious for that much money. It should also be pointed out the BKG 9.8 had somewhat the better of the dice rolling. However, its dice were being rolled by a human assistant, not by itself.

On the positive side, the program greatly impressed the spectators, who had thought of the match as largely a publicity stunt, but now came to realize that the program played very well indeed. As related above, the program made a number of outstanding imaginative plays, while never going off the deep end in its use of imagination. This is highly significant, as one of the standard criticisms of programs is that they have no imagination and no understanding of strategic concepts. In Figure 3, which portrays a situation from Game 5, BKG 9.8 shows its excellent grasp of strategy. BKG 9.8 is playing White and has been playing a backgame, predicated on holding the 3 and 5 points against Black's attempts to bring his men home. White now rolled an unfortunate double 2. Many players would be tempted to play 3–5, 19–23, 19–21 to hold their backgame position. However, BKG 9.8 realized, as would professional

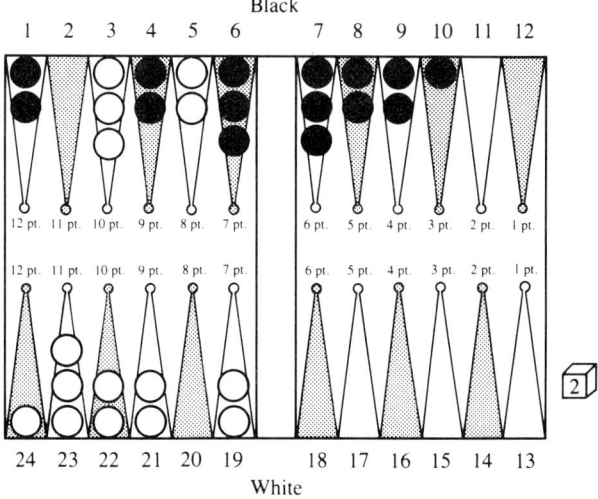

Figure 3

players, that without a good home board the backgame is useless and only risks getting gammoned. Therefore, BKG 9.8 played (3–5)3, 22–24 giving up its backgame and getting ready to run to limit its losses to a single game. Its understanding in this case was widely approved of by the professional players present.

A win in a game of skill and chance is never as convincing as a win in a game of pure skill. However, at the moment one cannot find programs that are capable of competing against top players in activities such as bridge and poker, both games of skill and chance. Measurement of skill in such games is much more difficult than it is in games of pure skill. However, such skill most definitely exists, and in order to compete on near equal terms with a world-class player, one must have a degree of skill that is comparable. This has clearly not been achieved in any of the other games of skill and chance.

8. Present and Future

The program is basically a heuristic program; i.e., it does not use a strong model of backgammon to make its decisions. With the exception of some precomputed tables that are used during bearoff, everything in the program is in the form of finely tuned heuristic functions. This works very well over the vast majority of situations the program is called upon to face. It almost always takes an acceptable action. Yet it is now apparent that many problems in backgammon are amenable to mathematical solution by on the fly solving of closed systems of equations. Several important pieces of such analysis now exist. Our next version will have most of these incorporated in it. Expertise in the areas they cover will then become a matter of whether the equation inputs generated by the program are better than the overall judgment exhibited by its opponent, since it is clear that the opponent would not be able to solve the system of equations in any reasonable amount of time. In the long run, the machine would certainly be favored in such a contest.

Actually, the developmental aspects of the program have had a very interesting effect on my own play. When I began this program, I was little more than a beginner at backgammon. In the process of formulating issues, my own play improved considerably. Since the program can do simulations of an input position by playing it out a large number of times, it has been possible to use it has a scientific tool, both to generate new data for the program itself, and to increase my understanding of backgammon. Although I believe I am still a slightly better player than the program, it is clear that this will not be the case very much longer. The program, as one would expect, is quite inexorable in situations that it understands well. When playing against it, I sometimes ask it to suggest my best move (a playing feature of the program). On such occasions I have a correct response in mind. About 5% or more of the time the program now suggests a better move than the one I had in mind, something that I consider an omen of things to come.

Here the comparison with chess programs is apt. The top chess programs are highly dependent on search speed for their success, while my program moves almost instantaneously. This is because it does essentially no searching, instead doing a lengthy computation in evaluating each alternative in the current situation. Recently, advances in computer chess have been closely related to computing speed, although no doubt some advances would be possible with better evaluation. However, since literally hundreds of thousands of terminal nodes are evaluated in a chess search, efficiency of evaluation is a prime consideration because each additional instruction dedicated to evaluation will be executed those hundreds of thousands of times, creating significant speed decrements in the program. In backgammon, with the program doing no searching the situation is very different. What is required is to bridge the knowledge gap between where the program is now and what is presently known about backgammon. Since functions already in the program are performing excellently, it seems likely that it will be possible to keep adding new knowledge in the same manner as has been done up to now. Each such addition should do something to close the knowledge gap. Further, there is a great deal of disagreement about correct moves between top backgammon players. The advent of computer simulations into backgammon has made it possible to get relatively exact values for situations that could hardly have been appraised analytically. Overall it is clear that backgammon theory is still at an early stage of evolution, compared to games such as chess, checkers, and Go where large bodies of undisputed theory exist. If it is possible to construct strong models of various facets of backgammon play, then it would seem likely that a program would establish new theories and standards of play on its way to becoming a true World Champion.

9. Summary

BKG 9.8 is the result of almost 4 man-years of work. It describes a board position in terms of features. These features, which have been developed over time, form the basis of all program's knowledge, and capture almost all of the "bread and butter" ideas in backgammon. The values of features are combined into a polynomial evaluation function that when applied to a given position assigns a value to it.

The recent improvement of the program is due to the SNAC method that made it possible to:

(1) Organize existing knowledge into functions that are sensitive to local conditions (nonlinearity) without being subject to significant volatility.
(2) Avoid the blemish effect (which used to cause occasional serious errors).
(3) Add new smooth knowledge functions that contribute their part without creating opportunities for new blemish effect situations.

The program at present is probably as capable in its domain as any heuristic program, but not significantly better. However, since its performance is predicated on knowledge rather than search (as is the performance of most chess programs), we expect to continue to produce significant increments in its performance by merely adding new knowledge, a process that under the SNAC method has worked extremely well thus far.

We feel that there are some important lessons to be learned from this work. When chess clouded the evaluation issues that had to be investigated, a domain that did not have these problems was chosen and this allowed substantial progress to be made. Further, the fact that backgammon programs can be tested (as can all game-playing programs) in organized competition allows the reliable detection of quantitative differences in skill. This forces a program developer to face up to the issues of how good his program really is, and what can be done about it. It is this facet that, in my opinion, has been most prominently responsible for the tremendous upsurge in strength of the chess playing programs in the last decade. In the absence of such opportunities for definitive testing, the world must rely on expert testimony to evaluate AI systems. This is clearly less desirable.

Acknowledgments. The author wishes to acknowledge the help of several people who have from time to time helped with the backgammon program by doing all sorts of special purpose programming that I would probably never have got around to. These individuals are Larry Flon, James Gillogly, Phil Karlton, Charles Leiserson, and Roy Levin. Paul Magriel produced some excellent tables to guide BKG's doubling in matches. Discussions with David Slate helped my understanding of the role of smoothness in evaluation. Suggestions by Allen Newell greatly benefitted the formulation of the SNAC concept.

1.3. End Positions in Backgammon

EDWARD O. THORP

Originally published in: *Gambling Times*, October 1978, November 1978, December 1978. Copyright © 1978 Edward Thorp. Reproduction is by permission of the author.

PART I

In "End Positions in Backgammon," you learn useful but simple odds for bearing off with only two men left. Most good players already know this. But, good players, do not go away. Later you will learn facts about backgammon that no one in the world has ever known before. As an introduction to end positions, suppose you are White and it is your turn to roll in the position of Figure 1. The doubling cube is in the middle.

Questions:
1. What is your chance to win?
2. Should you double?
3. How much do you gain or lose by doubling?
4. If you double, should Black accept?
5. How much does Black gain or lose by accepting your double?

White wins only if he bears off on his next roll. So to help us solve end positions of this type, we calculate a table of chances to take off two men in one roll. The exact result is given in Table 1, and the chances to the nearest percent are given by Table 2. To illustrate the use of Table 1, suppose you have a man on the 5 point and a man on the 2 point. Table 1 gives 19 chances in 36 to take both men off on the next roll. This means the exact chance you win in Figure 1 is $19/36 = 0.5277\ldots$. Table 2 gives this to the nearest percent as 53%. This answers Question 1.

To see how Table 1 is calculated, recall that there are 36 *equally likely* outcomes for the roll of two dice. These are listed in Table 3. Think of the two dice as labeled "first" and "second". It might help to use a red die for the "first" die and a white one for the "second" die. Then if the red (first) die shows 5 and

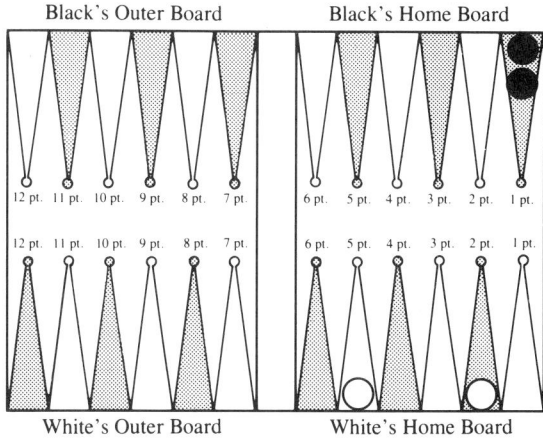

Black's Outer Board   Black's Home Board

12 pt. 11 pt. 10 pt. 9 pt. 8 pt. 7 pt.   6 pt. 5 pt. 4 pt. 3 pt. 2 pt. 1 pt.

White's Outer Board   White's Home Board

Figure 1. You are White, it is your turn to roll, and the doubling cube is in the middle.

Table 1. Chances out of 36 to bear off in one roll with one or two men left.

A man on the	0 pt.	1 pt.	2 pt.	3 pt.	4 pt.	5 pt.	6 pt.
0 pt.	off	36	36	36	34	31	27
1 pt.	36	36	36	34	29	23	15
2 pt.	36	36	26	25	23	19	13
3 pt.	36	34	25	17	17	14	10
4 pt.	34	29	23	17	11	10	8
5 pt.	31	23	19	14	10	6	6
6 pt.	27	15	13	10	8	6	4

Table 2. Percentage chances to bear off in one roll with one or two men left.

A man on the	0 pt.	1 pt.	2 pt.	3 pt.	4 pt.	5 pt.	6 pt.
0 pt.	off	100%	100%	100%	94%	86%	75%
1 pt.	100%	100%	100%	94%	81%	64%	42%
2 pt.	100%	100%	72%	69%	64%	53%	36%
3 pt.	100%	94%	69%	47%	47%	39%	28%
4 pt.	94%	81%	64%	47%	31%	28%	22%
5 pt.	86%	64%	53%	39%	28%	17%	17%
6 pt.	75%	42%	36%	28%	22%	17%	11%

Table 3. The 36 equally likely outcomes of the roll of two dice.

Second die shows→ ↓ First die shows	1	2	3	4	5	6
1	1–1	1–2	1–3	1–4	1–5	1–6
2	2–1	2–2	2–3	2–4	2–5	2–6
3	3–1	3–2	3–3	3–4	3–5	3–6
4	4–1	4–2	4–3	4–4	4–5	4–6
5	5–1	5–2	5–3	5–4	5–5	5–6
6	6–1	6–2	6–3	6–4	6–5	6–6

the white (second) die shows 2, we call the outcome 5–2. If instead the first die shows 2 and the second die shows 5, this is a different one of the 36 rolls and we call it 2–5. Outcomes are named x–y where x is the number the first die shows and y is the number the second die shows.

To see that White has 19 chances in 36 to win, we simply count winning rolls in Table 3. If either die shows at least 2 and the other shows at least 5, White wins. He also wins with 2–2, 3–3, and 4–4. This gives the 19 (shaded) winning outcomes in Table 3. As another example, suppose the two men to bear off are both on the 6 point. Then if the two dice are different, White can not come off in one turn. Of the six doubles, only 3–3 or higher works. This gives 4 ways in 36 or 11%, in agreement with Tables 2 and 3. This simple counting method produces all the numbers in Table 1.

Now we are ready to answer Question 2: Should White double in Figure 1? The answer is Yes, and here's why. We have seen that White wins on average 19 times in 36. If we call the stake 1 unit then, if he does not double, in 36 times he wins 1 unit 19 times and loses 1 unit 17 times for a gain of 2 units/36 times $= 1/18 = 0.055\ldots$. If White does double, Black can either accept or fold. Suppose Black accepts. Then the stakes are 2 units and a calculation like the previous one shows White gains an average of 4 units/ 36 times $= 1/9 = 0.111 \ldots$ unit per time. White gains twice as much as if he did not double. If instead Black folds, then White wins 1 unit at once, which is even better.

This also answers the rest of the questions. Answer to Question 3: White gains an extra 5.55% of a unit, on average, by doubling. Answer to Question 4: Black should accept. He loses 1/9 unit on average by accepting and 1 unit for sure by folding. This answers Question 5: if he makes the error of folding, he loses an extra 8/9 unit or 89%.

The usefulness of Table 2 is generally limited to situations where you have just one or two rolls left before the game ends. But it is surprising how often the table is valuable. Here are some more examples to help alert you to these situations. In Figure 2, Black has the doubling cube. White has just rolled

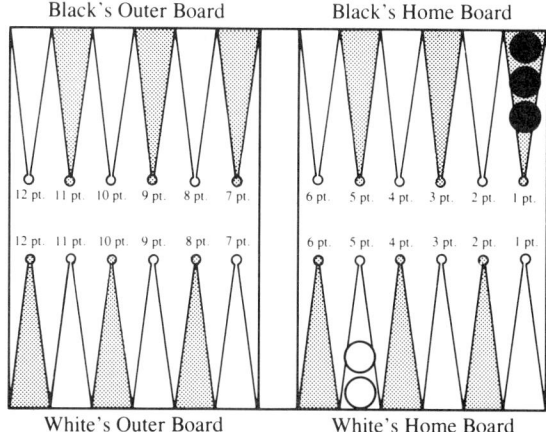

Figure 2. Black has the doubling cube. White has just rolled 2–1. What is the best move?

2–1. How does he play it? If Black rolls doubles on the next turn, he wins at once and it won't matter what White did. So White only needs to consider the case where Black does not roll doubles. Then White will have one more turn and he wants to leave himself with the greatest chance to bear off on that turn. White can move one man from the 5 point to the 4 point and one man from the 5 point to the 3 point. By Table 2, this gives him a 47% chance to win if Black does not roll doubles. Or, White can move one man from the 5 point to the 2 point, leaving the other man on the 5 point. This gives him a 53% chance to win if Black does not roll doubles, so this is the best way to play the 2–1.

In Figure 3, White's problem is to avoid a backgammon: if Black wins before

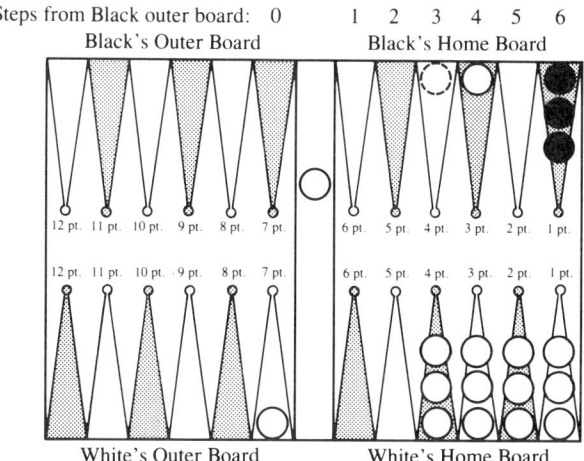

Figure 3. White has just rolled 4–1. What is the best move?

Steps from Black outer board: 0   1   2   3   4   5   6
Black's Outer Board   Black's Home Board

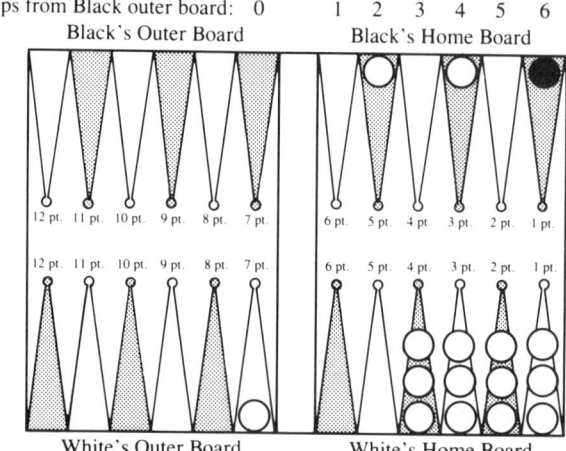

White's Outer Board   White's Home Board

Figure 3(a). After White plays from bar to the black 5 point and Black does not roll doubles.

Steps from Black outer board: 0   1   2   3   4   5   6
Black's Outer Board   Black's Home Board

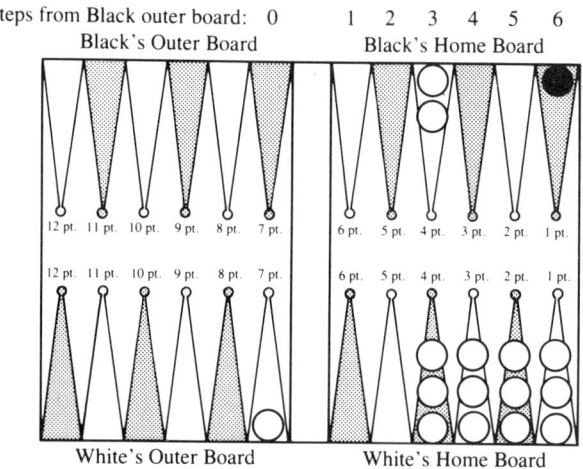

White's Outer Board   White's Home Board

Figure 3(b). After White plays both men to the black 4 point and Black does not roll doubles.

the white men escape from Black's home board, Black will win 3 units. Otherwise he will only gammon White for two units. White must use the 4 to move the man on the bar to the black 4 point (dotted circle). White can move this man on to the black 5 point in which case, if Black does not roll doubles, White's situation on his last turn is shown in Figure 3(a). The chance for White to remove both men from Black's home board on the next roll is the same as the chance to bear off both men when one is on the 4 point and the other is on the 2 point. By Table 2 this is 64%.

Suppose instead White plays both men to the black 4 point. Then Figure 3(b) shows the board if he survives Black's next roll. His chance to save himself from backgammon is the same as bearing off two men from the 3 point in one roll. Table 2 gives 47%. Therefore the play in Figure 3(a) is best. If instead White rolled 4–2 in Figure 3, he could play to leave his two back men on the black 2 and 7 points, giving an 86% chance (Table 2, man on 5 point and man on 0 point) to escape Black's home board on the next roll. Or he could play to leave his two back men no the black 5 and 4 points. This gives only a 69% chance, so is inferior.

An outstanding book on backgammon is Magriel (1977). Most of Table 1 appears there on page 404. A handy reference for practical play is the Doubleday Device (1974). This handy cardboard wheel has most of Table 2 on the back.

Here are some questions to check your understanding of what has been discussed so far. Refer to Figure 2.

1. Should Black double, after White makes the best move?
2. How much would Black gain or lose by so doubling?
3. Should White accept a Black double? If he does, instead of folding, how much does he gain or lose?
4. What is the best way for White to play 3–2 in Figure 2?

PART II

Next we consider the complete exact solution to all backgammon positions when each player has only one or two men left in his own home board. This is the first time this has ever been presented. It was calculated in 1975 by Don Smolen and myself and kept to ourselves until now. However, first I have a comment on Part I of this article.

Readers of Part I realize that it is often not practical or desirable to use the tables during the game. Fortunately, many of these situations are covered by a handy rule that appeared, for instance, in a recent "Sheinwold on Backgammon" column from the *Los Angeles Times*. Sheinwold considers the situation in Figure 4. The problem is whether White should play the 2 so that he leaves his two men on 5 and 2 or on 4 and 3.

We solved this same problem when discussing Figure 2. We saw then from Table 2 that leaving men on 5 and 2 is best because it gives White a 53% chance to get off on the next turn, whereas leaving men on 4 and 3 gives only a 47% chance. Now consider the general question: If you have to leave one or two men after your turn, what is the best "leave"? Assuming that the positions between which you must choose have the *same pip count*, the correct rule, which Sheinwold gives, is:

Rule for leaving one or two men.
(1) If possible, leave one man rather than two.
(2) If you must leave two men, leave them on different points, if possible.
(3) If you still have a choice, move off the 6 point.
(4) If you are already off the 6 point, move the man on the lower point.

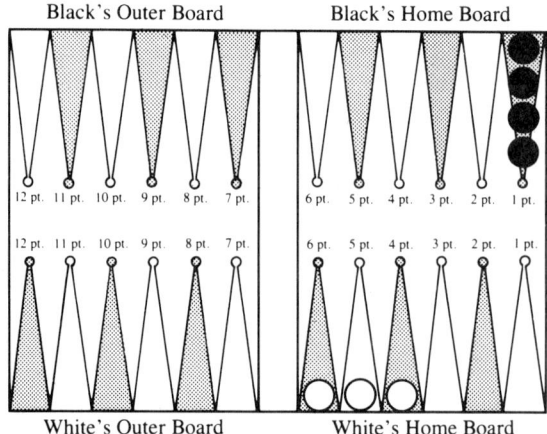

Figure 4. White rolls 6–2 and must bear a man off the 6 point. How should he play the 2?

It is easy to prove this rule is correct by using Table 2. This is shown again here in condensed form as Table 4. To check the rule, we simply check Table 4 for each pip count to see if it always tells us which of two "leaves" to pick. For example, with a pip count of 6, part (1) of the rule says correctly that 0 pt.–6 pt. is best. Then (2) says correctly that among the three remaining

Table 4. Percentage chances to bear off in one roll with one or two men left (from Table 2).

A man on the	1 pt.	2 pt.	3 pt.	4 pt.	5 pt.	6 pt.
0 pt.	100% 1 pip	100% 2 pips	100% 3 pips	94% 4 pips	86% 5 pips	75% 6 pips
1 pt.	100% 2 pips	100% 3 pips	94% 4 pips	81% 5 pips	64% 6 pips	42% 7 pips
2 pt.		72% 4 pips	69% 5 pips	64% 6 pips	53% 7 pips	36% 8 pips
3 pt.			47% 6 pips	47% 7 pips	39% 8 pips	28% 9 pips
4 pt.				31% 8 pips	28% 9 pips	22% 10 pips
5 pt.					17% 10 pips	17% 11 pips
6 pt.						11% 12 pips

two-man positions, 3 pt.–3 pt. is worst. In a similar way, the rule is verified in turn for positions with pip counts of 4, 5, 6, 7, 8, and 10. There is nothing to check for pip counts of 1, 2, 3, and 9 because the choices are equally good for these pip counts. There is nothing to check for counts of 11 and 12 because for these pip counts there is only one choice of position.

More examples illustrating the rule appear in Tzannes and Tzannes (1974). You can use the rule to solve at once test situations 40, 41, 42, and 43. The authors give a rule (page 94) but it is neither as clear nor as simple as ours.

We proved the rule for leaving one or two men just for the case where you will have at most one more turn to play. In that case, the percentages in Table 4 let us compare two positions to see which is better. What if there is a chance that you will have more than one turn? This could happen, for instance, if we change Figure 4 so that Black has five men on the 1 point instead of four. Then Black could roll nondoubles on his next turn, leaving three men on the 1 point; White could roll 1–2 on his next turn, reducing his 5 pt.–2. pt. position to one man on the 4 point; Black could roll nondoubles again, leaving one man on the 1 point; and White then gets a second turn. It turns out that the rule gives the best choice against all possible positions of the opponent, not just those where you will have at most one more turn to play. (Note: There is one possible unimportant exception that might arise, but the error is at most a small fraction of a percent.)

Now we return to the Thorp–Smolen solution of all endgames with just one or two men in each home board. We will label home board positions as follows: $5+3$ where there is a man on the 5 point and a man on the 3 point, with the largest number first. With both men on say the 4 point, we call the position $4+4$. With only one man on say the 5 point we write $5+0$. Think of the 0 as indicating that the second man is on the $0 = $ Off point.

There are six home-board positions with one man, namely $1+0, 2+0, \ldots,$ $6+0$. There are 21 home-board positions with two men. Thus there are 27 one- or two-man positions for each player. (Note: In general, there are exactly $(5 + r)!/5! \, r!$ home-board positions with exactly r men. There are exactly $(6 + r)!/6! \, r! - 1$ home-board positions with from one to r men. Thus since $r = 15$ is possible in the actual game, there are a total of $21!/6! \, 15! - 1 = $ 54,263 different home-board positions for one player. The symbol $r!$, read "r factorial", means $1 \times 2 \times 3 \times \cdots \times r$, Thus $1! = 1, 2! = 2, 3! = 6, 4! = 24,$ etc.)

Table 5 gives the first part of our solution. It tells Player I's "expectation" if I has the move and II owns the cube. By I's expectation we mean the average number of units I can expect to win if the current stake is "one unit," and if both players follow the best strategy. Of course, if a player does not follow the best strategy, his opponent can expect, on average, to do better than Table 5 indicates.

The A above $6+0$ means this column also applies to any count of up to three pips: $1+0, 2+0, 1+1, 3+0,$ or $2+1$. The C above $6+0$ means that this column also applies to $4+0, 3+1, 5+0,$ or $4+1$. The A for Player I means

Table 5. Player I's expected gain or loss, rounded to the nearest percent when Player I is to move and Player II owns the doubling cube. Column labels refer to the II home-board position and row labels refer to the I home-board position. Letters A and C (see text) indicate other Player I or Player II positions that are included with the given headings.

II has→ / I has↓	A, C 6+0	2+2	3+2	4+2 5+1	5+2	3+3 4+3	6+1	5+3	6+2	4+4	6+3	5+4	6+4	5+5	6+5	6+6
2+1 A	100	100	100	100	100	100	100	100	100	100	100	100	100	100	100	100
3+1, 4+0	89	90	90	91	94	95	95	96	96	97	97	97	98	98	98	99
5+0	72	74	75	78	85	87	88	89	90	92	92	92	94	95	95	97
4+1	61	63	65	70	78	82	84	85	86	88	89	89	91	94	94	96
6+0	50	53	56	61	72	76	79	81	82	85	86	86	89	92	92	94
2+2	44	48	51	57	69	74	77	78	80	83	85	85	88	91	91	94
3+2	39	42	46	52	66	71	75	76	78	81	83	83	86	90	90	93
4+2, 5+1	28	32	36	44	60	66	70	72	74	78	80	80	84	88	88	92
5+2	06	11	16	27	48	55	60	63	66	71	73	73	79	84	84	89
3+3	-06	00	06	18	41	50	56	59	62	68	71	71	77	82	82	88
4+3	-06	00	06	18	41	50	56	59	61	67	70	70	76	82	82	88
6+1	-17	-10	-04	09	35	45	51	54	57	64	67	67	74	80	80	87
5+3	-22	-15	-09	05	32	41	48	51	54	61	64	64	71	78	78	85
6+2	-28	-21	-14	01	29	38	45	49	52	59	63	63	70	77	77	84
4+4	-39	-31	-23	-08	22	33	40	44	48	55	59	59	67	74	74	82
6+3	-44	-36	-28	-12	18	28	36	40	44	51	55	55	63	71	71	79
5+4	-44	-37	-30	-14	17	28	35	39	43	51	54	55	62	70	70	78
6+4	-56	-48	-40	-23	06	17	25	29	33	42	46	46	55	63	63	72
5+5	-67	-59	-51	-35	-02	10	19	24	28	37	41	42	51	59	60	70
6+5	-67	-59	-51	-36	-07	03	11	15	19	28	32	33	43	51	53	63
6+6	-78	-71	-64	-50	-25	-17	-09	-05	-01	07	12	12	23	32	36	48

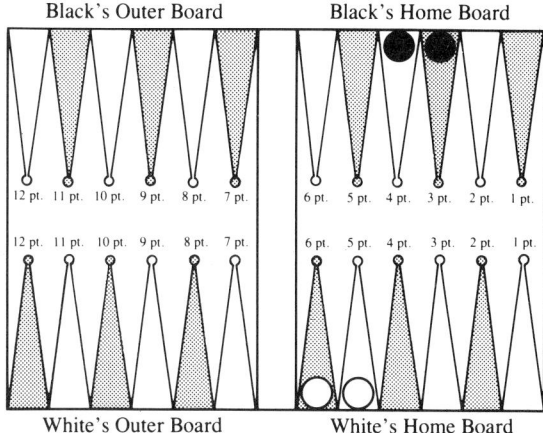

Figure 5. It is White's turn. Black has the cube. Who has the advantage? How much?

the same as for Player II. We illustrate the use of the table with Figure 5. It is White's turn to move so he becomes Player I. We look along the row $6 + 5$ and the column $4 + 3$. Table 5 shows Player I's (White's) expectation as 03 so White has a 3% advantage. He expects to win on average 3% (more exactly 2.54%) of the current stake. If the current stake is $1,000, White should accept a Black offer to "settle" the game if Black offers more than $25.40. If Black offers less, White should refuse.

Table 6 gives the expected gain or loss for Player I when he has the move and the doubling cube is in the middle. Unlike Table 5, in this case I has the option of doubling before he moves. If I does not double, II will be able to double on his next turn. If I doubles, II then has the choice of accepting the double or folding. If II accepts, play continues with doubled stakes and II gets the cube. If II folds, he loses the current (undoubled) stake and the game ends. Table 8 tells whether I should double and whether II should accept.

Table 7 gives the expected gain or loss for Player I when he has the move and the doubling cube is in. In this case, I has the option of doubling before he moves. However, in contrast to Table 6, if I does not double he keeps the cube so II cannot double on his next turn. If I does double, II can accept or fold. If he accepts, the stakes are doubled, play continues, and II gets the cube. If instead II folds, he loses the current (undoubled) stake and the game ends. Table 8 also tells whether I should double and whether II should accept when I has the cube.

In Part III, we will show how to use the tables to play *perfectly* in any of the $27 \times 27 = 729$ end positions covered by the tables. We will run through sample endgames step by step, showing player expectation, doubling strategy, and the best way to play each roll.

Table 6. Player I's expected gain or loss, rounded to the nearest percent, when Player I is to move and the doubling cube is in the middle. The column labels refer to the II home board and the row labels refer to the I home board. Headings are interpreted as in Table 2.

I has↓ \ II has→	A,C 6+0	2+2	3+2	4+2 5+1	5+2	3+3 4+3	6+1	5+3	6+2	4+4	6+3	5+4	6+4	5+5	6+5	6+6
6+0 A,C	100	100	100	100	100	100	100	100	100	100	100	100	100	100	100	100
2+2	89	95	100	100	100	100	100	100	100	100	100	100	100	100	100	100
3+2	78	85	91	100	100	100	100	100	100	100	100	100	100	100	100	100
4+2,5+1	56	64	72	88	100	100	100	100	100	100	100	100	100	100	100	100
5+2	11	22	32	53	95	100	100	100	100	100	100	100	100	100	100	100
3+3,4+3	-06	01	12	36	83	100	100	100	100	100	100	100	100	100	100	100
6+1	-17	-10	-04	19	70	89	100	100	100	100	100	100	100	100	100	100
5+3	-22	-15	-09	10	63	82	95	100	100	100	100	100	100	100	100	100
6+2	-28	-21	-14	01	57	77	91	98	100	100	100	100	100	100	100	100
4+4	-39	-31	-23	-08	44	66	81	88	96	100	100	100	100	100	100	100
6+3	-44	-36	-28	-12	36	57	72	80	88	100	100	100	100	100	100	100
5+4	-44	-37	-30	-14	34	55	71	78	86	100	100	100	100	100	100	100
6+4	-56	-48	-40	-23	13	34	50	58	67	83	91	92	100	100	100	100
5+5	-67	-59	-51	-35	-01	21	39	47	56	74	83	83	100	100	100	100
6+5	-67	-59	-51	-36	-05	08	21	30	38	56	65	66	86	100	100	100
6+6	-78	-71	-64	-50	-22	-10	-02	03	07	16	24	25	46	65	71	96

Table 7. Player I's expected gain or loss, rounded to the nearest percent when Player I is to move and also has the doubling cube. Headings are interpreted as in Table 2. The columns for 6+4, 5+5, 6+5, and 6+6 are the same as for Table 3 so they have been omitted.

II has→ / I has↓	A 2+1	3+1 4+0	5+0	4+1	6+0	2+2	3+2	4+2 5+1	5+2	3+3 4+3	6+1	5+3	6+2	4+4	6+3	5+4
6+0 A, C	100	100	100	100	100	100	100	100	100	100	100	100	100	100	100	100
2+2	89	89	89	89	89	95	100	100	100	100	100	100	100	100	100	100
3+2	78	78	78	78	78	85	91	100	100	100	100	100	100	100	100	100
4+2, 5+1	56	56	56	56	56	64	72	88	95	100	100	100	100	100	100	100
5+2	11	11	19	24	29	32	34	53	83	89	95	98	96	100	100	100
3+3, 4+3	−06	00	09	15	21	24	27	36	70	82	91	88	88	100	100	100
6+1	−17	−10	−00	06	13	16	19	25	63	77	81	80	86	100	100	100
5+3	−22	−15	−05	02	08	12	15	22	57	66	72	78	86	100	100	100
6+2	−28	−21	−10	−03	04	08	11	18	44	57	71	80	88	100	100	100
4+4	−39	−31	−20	−12	−04	−00	04	11	36	55	50	78	86	100	100	100
6+3	−44	−36	−24	−16	−08	−04	00	08	34	34	39	58	67	83	91	92
5+4	−44	−37	−25	−17	−09	−05	−01	07	16	21	22	47	56	74	83	83
6+4	−56	−47	−35	−26	−18	−14	−10	−01	08	14	22	30	38	56	65	66
5+5	−67	−58	−45	−36	−27	−23	−18	−10	05	00	08	13	17	25	30	30
6+5	−67	−58	−45	−37	−29	−24	−20	−12	−08							
6+6	−78	−70	−57	−49	−41	−37	−33	−25								

Table 8. Doubling strategy when Player I has the move. Doubling strategy is the same, whether I has the cube or it is in the middle, except for the shaded region. If Player I has the cube he should not double for positions in the shaded region. If he makes the mistake of doubling, II should accept. When the cube is in the middle, I should double for positions in the shaded region and II should accept.

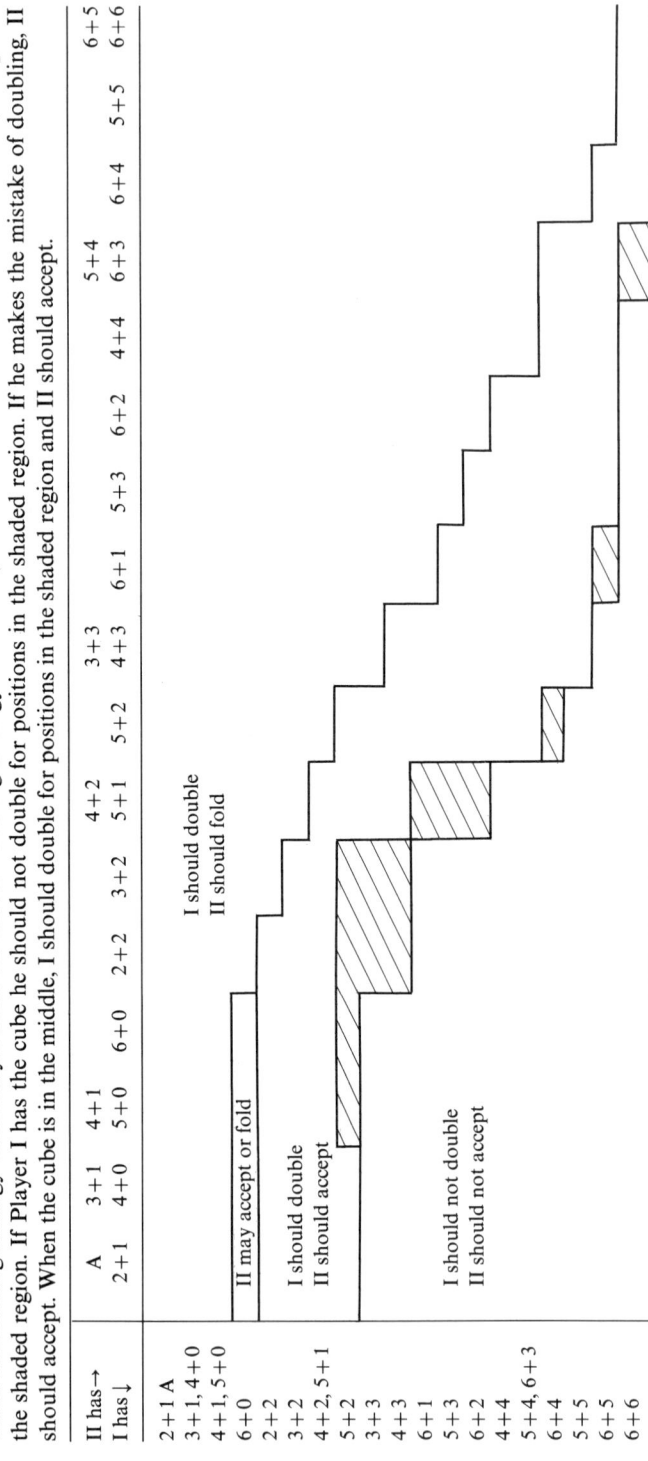

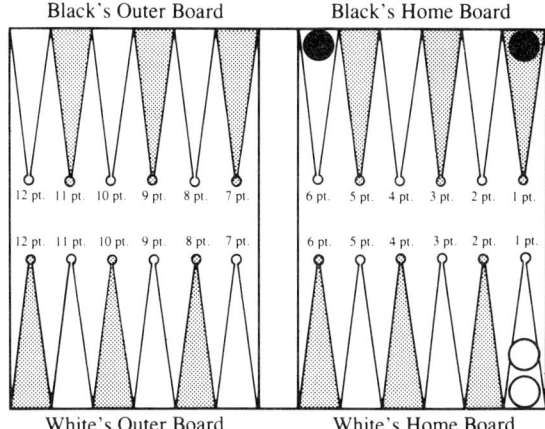

Black's Outer Board   Black's Home Board

White's Outer Board   White's Home Board

Figure 6. (Tzannes and Tzannes) Black is to move. The cube is in the middle. He doubles. Is this correct? Should White accept?

PART III

Here we will illustrate and explain the use of the tables presented in Part II. Consider first Situation 74 from Tzannes and Tzannes (1974). This is shown in Figure 6. It is Black's turn so he is Player I. Black doubles. Should he? If he does, should White accept? If the cube is in the middle, we look in Table 8, row $6+1$, column $1+1$. Black should not double. If he does, White should accept. (This is correctly recommended by Tzannes and Tzannes.) Table 6 shows us that Black's expectation under best play, which means *not* doubling, is -17%. If instead Black has the cube, we use Tables 7 and 8. In this example we get exactly the same answer. This is not always the case, as we will see.

This example is also easy to analyze directly. If Black bears off in his next turn he will win. The chances are $15/36$ (Table 1). If he does not bear off at once, White will win and Black will lose. So if the current stake is 1 unit, and Black does not double, Black's expected gain is $+1$ unit $\times 15/36 - 1$ unit $\times 21/36 = -6/36 = -16\frac{2}{3}\%$. Now suppose Black doubles and White accepts. Then Black's expected gain is $+2$ units $\times 15/36 - 2$ units $\times 21/36 = -12/36 = -33\%$. On average, Black will lose an extra $16\frac{2}{3}\%$ of a unit if he makes the mistake of doubling and White accepts.

It's easy to see from this type of reasoning that if Player I has any two-man position and Player II will bear off on the next turn, then Player I should not double (if he can) when his chance to bear off in one roll is less than 50%. If his chance to bear off is more than 50%, he should double. Referring to the same Table 1 proves this rule which Tzannes and Tzannes cite for these special situations:

> With double three, six–one, six–two
> (or anything worse)

> Keep dumb, hope for the best,
> Anything better, don't delay,
> Double the stakes with zest.

The Tzannes' and Tzannes Situation 73 is similar.

Here is a trickier situation that I do not think you could figure out without help from Tables 4–8. Suppose White has $6+6$, Black has $4+4$, White is on roll and the doubling cube is in the middle. This is shown in Figure 7. How does the game proceed for various rolls?

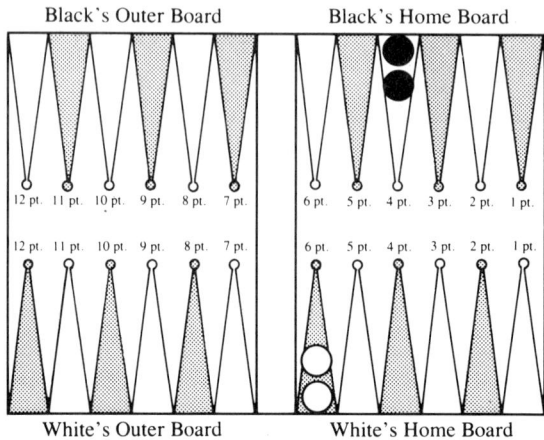

Figure 7. White to roll. The doubling cube is in the middle. Should White double? How does the game proceed for various rolls?

White is Player I. He consults Table 6 and sees his expectation is 16%. But Table 8 tells White not to double. We now show how to use the table to play optimally for a sample series of rolls. Suppose White rolls 3–1. How does he play it? He can end up with $6+2$ or with $5+3$.

The rule from Part I says that $5+3$ looks better because it gives him a greater chance to bear off on the next turn. This is proven by the tables as follows: after White plays, it will be Black's turn. Black will be Player I with $4+4$, White will be Player II with either $5+3$ or $6+2$. The cube will be in the middle. Which is best for White? Consult Table 3. We find Player I (Black) has an expectation of 88% if White has $5+3$, whereas Black has 96% if White has $6+2$. White wants to keep Black's expectation down so he plays to leave $5+3$.

The situation after White makes this move is shown in Figure 8. Black is to roll and the cube is in the middle. Should Black double? Should White accept? Table 8 says Black should double and White should accept. Table 6 says Black's expected gain is 88% of the 1-unit stake. Next Black rolls 2–1. He can leave $4+1$ or $3+2$. The rule from Part I says $4+1$ is better. To confirm this, note that after Black moves, White will be Player I with $5+3$, Black will be Player II with either $4+1$ or $3+2$, and White will have the cube. Therefore

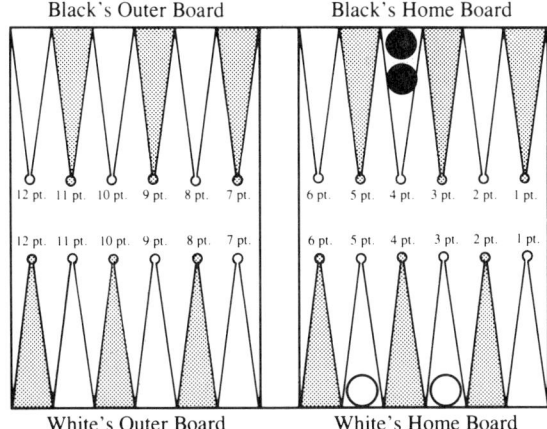

Figure 8. White did not double, then rolled 3–1 in Figure 2 and left 5–3. The cube is in the middle. It is now Black's turn. Black should double, White should accept, and Black's expectation is then 88% of the 1-unit stake.

we consult Table 7, not Table 6. If Black leaves $4+1$, White's expectation is 2% of the current 2-unit stake. If Black leaves $3+2$, White's expectation is 15%. Therefore Black leaves $4+1$.

It is now White's turn. The situation is shown in Figure 9. The stake is 2 units, White's expectation is 2% of 2 units or 0.04 unit and White has the cube. What should he do? Table 8 tells us White should not double. White now rolls 5–2, leaving $1+0$. Black does not have the cube. Table 5 gives his expectation as 61% of 2 units or 1.22 units. He wins or loses on this next roll.

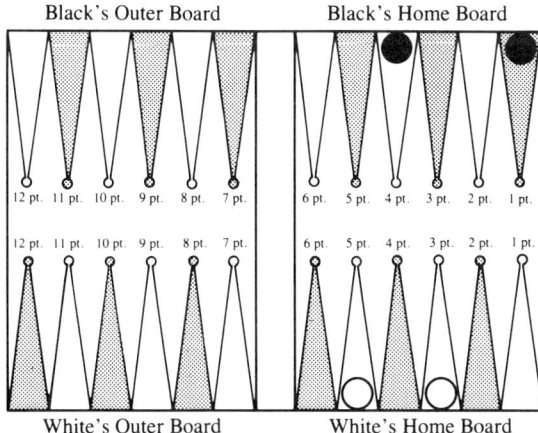

Figure 9. Black doubled, then rolled 2–1 in Figure 3 and left 4–1. The stake is 2 units, it is now White's turn, and he has the cube. White's expectation is 2% of the stake or 0.04 unit. What should White do?

The tables show certain patterns that help you to understand them better. For instance, for a given position it is best for Player I to have the cube. It is next best for Player I if the cube is in the middle and it is worst for Player I for Player II to have the cube. Therefore, for a given position, Player I's expectation is greatest in Table 7, least in Table 5, and in-between in Table 6. For instance, with Player I having $6+6$ and Player II having $4+4$, Player I's expectation is 25% if he has the cube, 16% if it is in the middle, and 7% if Player II has the cube. Sometimes two or even all three of the expectations are the same. For instance, if Player I has $6+6$ and Player II has $6+5$, Player I's expectation is 71% if he has the cube or if it is in the middle. If Player II has the cube, Player I's expectation drops to 36%.

Examination of the doubling strategies in Table 8 shows that the positions where Player I should double and Player II should fold are the same whether Player I has the cube or the cube is in the middle. Although this happens for the two-man end positions we are analyzing here, it is not always true in backgammon. The positions where Player I should double and it does not matter if Player II accepts or folds are also the same in Table 8. But some of the positions where Player I should double and Player II should accept are different. If Player I has the cube Table 8 shows that he should be more conservative. Intuitively, this is because if he has the cube and does not double, he prevents Player II from doubling, whereas if the cube is in the middle Player II cannot be prevented from doubling.

Table 8 leads to an example that will confound the intuition of almost all players. Suppose Player I has $5+2$ and has the cube. Consider two cases (a) Player II has $1+0$ and (b) Player II has $6+0$. In which of these cases should Player I double? Clearly $6+0$ is a worse position that $1+0$. And the worse the position, the more likely we are to double, right? So of the four possible answers (double $1+0$ and $6+0$, double $1+0$ but not $6+0$, double $6+0$ but not $1+0$, do not double $1+0$ or $6+0$) we "know" we can eliminate "double $1+0$, do not double $6+0$", right? WRONG. The only correct answer, from Table 8, is: Double $1+0$ but do not double $6+0$. Try this on your expert friends. They will almost always be wrong. If they do get it right they probably were either "lucky" or read this column. In that case if you ask them to explain why their answer is correct, they probably will not be able to.

You may think that the loss would be slight by doubling $6+0$ erroneously. But you have an expected gain of 29% by not doubling (Table 7), whereas by doubling it can be shown that your expectation drops to only 11%. The exact explanation is complex. The basic idea, though, is that if Player I doubles Player II, Player II accepts, and Player I does not win at once, Player II can use the cube against Player I with great effect at Player II's next turn.

After this was written, Don Smolen pointed out to me that Jacoby and Crawford (1973) discuss what is essentially the same example (they give Player II $4+1$ instead of $6+0$) on pages 116–117 of their excellent *The Backgammon Book*. Table 8 shows that essentially the same situation occurs when Player I has $5+2$ and Player II has $4+1$, $5+0$, $6+0$, $2+2$, or $3+2$ and for no other two-man end positions.

Tables 5, 6, 7, and 8 present, for the first time anywhere, the complete exact solutions to two-man endgames in backgammon. The tables were calculated by a general method I have discovered for getting the complete exact solution to all backgammon positions that are pure races (i.e., the two sides are permanently out of contact). The intricate and difficult computer programs for computing Tables 5 through 8 were written by Don Smolen, so Tables 5 through 8 are our joint work. Don was a computer scientist at Temple University. He is now trading stock options on the floor of the American Stock Exchange. A skilled backgammon player, he won the 1977 American Stock Exchange Tournament.

1.4. Optimal Doubling in Backgammon

EMMETT B. KEELER AND JOEL SPENCER

Originally published in: *Operations Research*, vol. 23, no. 6, November–December 1975, pp. 1063–1071. Reprinted with permission from Operations Research, Operations Research Society of America. No further reproduction permitted without the consent of the copyright owner.

Abstact. This paper shows that the optimal betting strategy for a continuous model of backgammon is to double when you have an 80% chance of winning. We discuss the differences with the published literature on the real game and the problem of infinite expectations. The optimal strategy for a simulation of the endgame is computed by dynamic programming.

Backgammon is a perfect information game, with both players' moves governed by alternating throws of dice. Thus, in theory, there is a best strategy for each player to maximize his chance of winning, and each player can compute his exact probability of winning at any time if the best strategies are followed. Much of the interest of backgammon lies in the betting. Before any of his turns, a player can *double* the stakes, whereupon his opponent can *fold* and pay the doubler 1 unit, or he can play on. If he plays on, only he has the right to *redouble*; that is, the players must alternate doubling. At the nth double, the nondoubler can fold and pay the doubler 2^{n-1} units or he may play on with the stakes at 2^n (and the right to make the next double).

In the first part of this paper, we describe the optimal betting strategy for a continuous model of the game. Later, we discuss how this strategy is modified in the real game. (Although it may upset backgammon aficionados, gammons and backgammons will be considered only as simple wins.)

1. Continuous Games

Consider a two-person game that always ends in some finite time. Let $p(t)$ be the probability at time t that player A will win (given that both players play optimally). If $p(t)$ is a continuous function of time, we call the game continuous. In a noncontinuous game, single moves may cause $p(t)$ to jump (and sometimes drastically, as in Monopoly when Boardwalk with a hotel is hit, and backgammon, especially in the endgame).

With any continuous game, we can associate a game (called the *P-game*) consisting of the unit interval $[0, 1]$ and an indicator. At time t, this indicator is at point $p(t)$. (Call that point the state of the *P*-game.) Player A wins if the indicator reaches 1 before it reaches 0. We now show that the *P*-game indicator for any continuous game moves as a continuous symmetric random walk on $[0, 1]$ although the timescale may be different.

Lemma 1. *Let the P-game be at state x, with $a, b > 0$ such that $0 \leq x - a < x < x + b \leq 1$. Let E be the event that $p(t)$ becomes $x + b$ before it becomes $x - a$. Then the probability of E is $a/(a + b)$.*

Proof. The state $x = \text{prob}[\text{A will win}] = P(E)P[\text{A will win}|E] + P(\sim E)$. $P[\text{A will win}| \sim E]$. Since $p(t)$ is Markovian, however, $p[\text{A will win}|p(t)$ becomes $x + b$ before $x - a] = P[\text{A will win}|p(0) = x + b] = x + b$. Similarly, $P[\text{A will win}| \sim E] = x - a$. (The event $\sim E$ is the event "$p(t)$ becomes $x - a$ before it becomes $x + b$." This is where continuity and a finite end come in.) Thus,

$$x = P(E)(x + b) + [1 - P(E)](x - a), \tag{1}$$

and therefore

$$P(E) = a/(a + b). \tag{2}$$

Example. Basketball is closer to being continuous than most major sports. If we decide *a priori* that UCLA has a 90% chance of beating MIT, how likely is it that at some point in the game, MIT will have a 50% chance of winning? By the lemma, the probability that $P = 50$ before $P = 100$ is $(100 - 90)/[(100 - 90) + (90 - 50)] = \frac{1}{5}$.

2. Backgammon Betting on Continuous Games

Now suppose in a continuous game that only A has the right to double and his probability of winning is $p(t) = \alpha$. For which α should A double? Also, for which β should B fold if A doubles? There may be α at which A has equal expectations whether or not he doubles, and β where B has equal expectations whether he accepts or folds. Assume A doubles at such points α and B folds at such points β. The expected gain to player A is a monotone function of $p(t)$. Thus, by continuity considerations, there will be an α_0 such that A should double if $\alpha \geq \alpha_0$ and should not double if $\alpha < \alpha_0$. We shall call α_0 A's *doubling point*. Similarly, B has a *folding point* β_0, which is the lowest $p(t)$ at which he folds.

Theorem 1. *If both sides play perfectly*, $\alpha_0 = \beta_0$.

Proof. Since B is assumed to play perfectly, A's expectation is less than or equal to the current value of the game. Hence if B would fold, A should double. Therefore A should double at β_0 since B will fold (or do equally poorly if he accepts). So $\alpha_0 \leq \beta_0$. Next, suppose that $\alpha_0 < \gamma < \beta_0$. Let us compare A's strategies of doubling at α_0 with doubling at γ. If A doubles at α_0, either the game will eventually reach state γ or it will not. If it does, A could have waited, since B would have accepted anyway. If the game never reaches state γ, A loses, and loses more by his double at α_0. Therefore to double at $\alpha_0 < \beta_0$ is premature; thus $\alpha_0 \geq \beta_0$ so $\alpha_0 = \beta_0$.

We can use Theorem 1 to solve for α_0. By symmetry, an optimally playing B will double at state $1 - \alpha_0$. When A doubles at α_0, B must have equal expectations whether he folds or accepts. Let K be the current stakes of the game. Then if B folds, he gets $-K$. Assume he accepts. Lemma 1 shows that A will win before B doubles with probability $(2\alpha - 1)/\alpha$. With probability $(1 - \alpha)/\alpha$, B doubles and, since it does not affect the expectations, we can assume A resigns. Thus,

$$-K = 2K[(1 - \alpha)/\alpha - (2\alpha - 1)/\alpha], \tag{3}$$

$$-\alpha = 2[2 - 3\alpha], \tag{4}$$

$$\alpha = 0.8 = 80\%. \tag{5}$$

Now suppose either player has the right to double. When player A doubles, the situation for B is no different from when only A had the right. So B's folding point is still 80%. Again, the argument of Theorem 1 shows that A should not double until $\alpha = 80\%$.

This result completes the strategy. A player doubles if he has at least an 80% chance of winning and accepts a double if he has at least a 20% chance of winning. If both sides play optimally, we can compute $V_A(p)$, the expected gain of player A who is at point p with the right to double. Since A wins when $p = 0.8$ and loses when $p = 0$, by Lemma 1 $V_A(p) = [(p - 0) - (0.8 - p)]/0.8 = (5p/2) - 1$ for $0 \leq p \leq \frac{4}{5}$. Similarly, $V_B(p)$, the value to A of being at probability p when B has the right to double, is $(5p/2) - \frac{3}{2}$ for $\frac{1}{5} \leq p \leq 1$; and $V_C(p)$, the value to A of being at p when both players can double, is $5(2p - 1)/3$ for $\frac{1}{5} \leq p \leq \frac{4}{5}$. Thus, for example, $V_A(\frac{1}{2}) = \frac{1}{4}$ is the value of having the exclusive right to double at the start of the game.

(In our paper (Keeler *et al.*, 1969) we use similar methods to compute optimal betting strategies for a variety of other betting rules, including a fixed number of nonalternating raises and continuous raises.)

The optimal strategy is unique, as it has a positive expectation against any other strategy. (However, see the Appendix for problems that may arise when the expectations do not exist.) Suppose x is the largest probability at which B doubles and y is the smallest probability at which B folds. The most interesting of the four cases to consider is when $x > 0.2$ and $y > 0.8$ (A and B both accept the double). By Lemma 1,

$$V_B(0.8) = (0.8 - x)/(1 - x) + (1 - 0.8)2V_A(x)/(1 - x). \tag{6}$$

The 2 in the second term on the right comes from B's doubling at x and A's accepting. Again by Lemma 1,

$$V_A(x) = 2xV_B(0.8)/0.8 - (0.8 - x)/0.8, \tag{7}$$

and

$$V_C(0.5) = 2[(0.5 - x)V_B(0.8)/(0.8 - x) + 0.3V_A(x)/(0.8 - x)]. \tag{8}$$

Combining (6), (7), and (8), we have $V_C(0.5) = (5x - 1)/4(1 - 2x)$, which is greater than zero for $0.2 < x < 0.5$. The other cases also show positive expectation when $x \neq 0.2$, $y \neq 0.8$.

While "fold at 0.2, double at 0.8" has a positive expectation against any other strategy, it does not take full advantage of the opportunities an inferior opponent provides. Suppose B doubles at $x > 0.2$. A should definitely accept the double. If β_0 is B's folding point, A can double at β_0 if he wants B to fold, or double at $\beta_0 - \varepsilon$ if he wants B to accept. The value of β_0, $\beta_0 = y$, that makes A indifferent has

$$V_B(y) = \tfrac{1}{2}. \tag{9}$$

By Lemma 1,

$$V_B(y) = \{(y - x) + (1 - y)2V_A(x)\}/(1 - x), \tag{10}$$

and

$$V_A(x) = \{x2V_B(y) - (y - x)\}/(y - 0). \tag{11}$$

Combining (9), (10), and (11), we obtain $6y^2 - 9xy - 5y + 8x = 0$. Hence $y = (9x + 5 \pm \{(9x + 5)^2 - 192x\}^{1/2})/12$. When $0.2 \leq x < \tfrac{1}{3}$, there are two roots. If β_0 is greater than the upper root, A doubles at $\beta_0 - \varepsilon$ for an expected gain greater than 1. If β_0 is less than the upper root, A doubles at β_0 and B folds.

For $x > \tfrac{1}{3}$ one must be careful about the "theoretical" problems described in the Appendix. Let us consider A's position if he sets $y = x + \tfrac{1}{3}$ as his doubling point. First assume B accepts this double. Then, by the notation of the Appendix, $M = \tfrac{1}{3}$, $L = x$, $R = \tfrac{2}{3} - x$ so $3LR < M$. Thus the expectations are defined. Solving (10) and (11), we obtain

$$V_A(x) = (x - y)(3x - 1)/\{y(3x - 1) - 2x(3y - 2)\}, \quad \text{(in general),}$$

$$= 1/(3x - 1), \quad \text{(for } y = x + \tfrac{1}{3}\text{),}$$

$$> 0 \quad \text{(as } x > \tfrac{1}{3}\text{).} \tag{12}$$

If, on the other hand, B resigns if doubled at y, the value is

$$V_A(x) = [x - (y - x)]/y = (x - \tfrac{1}{3})/y > 0.$$

In either case, A has positive expectation immediately after B's double. Under such circumstances A can alter his play so as to make his expectation arbitrarily large. Suppose A's expectation after B's double is $\delta > 0$. When B doubles, A should immediately redouble. Then B would redouble right back. Suppose A exchanges $2n$ doubles with B and then—after B's nth double—switches to the doubling point $y = x + \frac{1}{3}$. The stakes have been increased by a factor of 2^{2n}, and A's expectation is now $2^{2n}\delta$. By making the appropriate (large) choice of n A may make his expectation as large as desired. It is a dangerous strategy, for if B suddenly "wises up" (i.e., reads this paper) when the stakes are 2^{1000}, A will be sorry.

Of course, if B's doubling point is $x > \frac{1}{2}$, the analysis is simpler and more intuitively clear. A merely exchanges $2n$ doubles with B and then "throws away" the doubling die.

3. Doubling in Backgammon

If their books can be believed, backgammon experts do not wait for a 0.8 chance of winning to double. For example, Jacoby and Crawford (1973) suggest a redouble at "9 to 5," which is about 0.65, and Goren (1974) gives "2 to 1" or 0.67 as the proper odds. All suggest that there is considerable difference between the first double and later redoubles and recommend accepting doubles only when $p > 0.25$. Is this bad advice, or is our continuous game a poor model for the real game of backgammon?

One possibility is that the advice is practical—if the great mass of players is doubling at around 0.6, a player does better by doubling at 0.7 (rather than 0.8) and keeping such opponents in the game than he does by playing minimax. As we have seen, the optimal strategy is to double just below the novice's folding point, but perhaps because of uncertainty about the novice's evaluation of the game and about his folding point, 0.67 may be safer. (A more cynical view is that experts can make more money by playing their readers than by selling books.)

More important is the fact that backgammon is not really continuous, especially near the end of the game. A player may then know that his next throw is decisive—that after the throw the outcome will be certain. Since the game effectively ends on that throw, a player should double whenever $p > 0.5$. At no time should a player decline a double if $p \geqq 0.25$, since $2[p - (1 - p)] \geqq -1$ at that point. The farther from the end of the game, the less the probability of winning changes with each move, and the closer to each other the doubling point and the folding point become.

To find out exactly how the probability of winning jumps and what effect this has on doubling strategy, we computed the probability of winning and optimal strategies for a simplified version of the later part of a backgammon game. This part of the game is essentially a race to move all one's men to the end of the board. With each turn players throw dice to determine how far they can move. Expert players keep track of the "count," which is the sum of

Table 1. Probability of winning the running game when it is your turn.

		\multicolumn{8}{c}{Your count}							
		30	40	50	60	70	80	90	100
Opponent's count	−10	0.27	0.31	0.33	0.36	0.37	0.38	0.38	0.39
	−5	0.47	0.47	0.47	0.48	0.48	0.48	0.48	0.48
	Even	0.65	0.62	0.61	0.60	0.59	0.59	0.58	0.58
	5	0.79	0.75	0.73	0.70	0.69	0.68	0.67	0.67
	10	0.87	0.84	0.81	0.79	0.78	0.77	0.75	0.74
	15	0.93	0.91	0.88	0.86	0.84	0.83	0.82	0.81
	20	0.97	0.95	0.93	0.91	0.90	0.89	0.87	0.86

the distances remaining for all their men. If it were not for the rule on doublets, we could use the standard statistical results on the distribution of the number of rolls necessary to make $x_i + \cdots + x_n \geq S$, where the x_i are independently drawn from a normal distribution with mean 7 and variance $5\frac{5}{6}$. (A doublet throw of the dice counts four times in backgammon. Thus a pair of fives counts 20 instead of 10.) Instead we "rolled" (on a computer) the dice until they added up to 125, keeping track of when their sum exceeded each number less than 125. We repeated this procedure 1,000 times and used the resulting distribution to compute Table 1. The numbers in Table 1 give the probability that a player will win when it is his turn and his opponent's count is at various distances from his own. Only a large doublet makes a really big shift in the probability of winning. For example, when the counts are 100 and 90, a before-the-throw probability of winning of 0.39 goes to 0.33 with a 5, 0.42 with a 10, and 0.62 with a 20.

We next computed the optimal doubling strategy for a simplified form of the game in which the dice could show either 5 with probability 0.55, 10 with probability 0.36, and 20 with probability 0.09. (The 5 was supposed to replace 3, 4, 5, 6, 7, the 10 to replace 8, 9, 10, 11, 12 and the 20 to replace 16, 20, and 24. The probabilities are set to make the mean $\sim 8\frac{1}{6}$ and the variance $\sim 18\frac{1}{3}$, which are the real backgammon values.) Such a three-valued die is qualitatively very similar to the actual backgammon dice. Indeed, the probabilities of winning shown in Table 2 are close to those in Table 1 in the critical range for doubling. We can compute the optimal actions by dynamic programming, working backwards from the end, and we see that the doubling point approaches 0.8 rather slowly as we move away from the end of the game. Table 3 gives the probabilities for making the first double, for redoubling, and for folding at various points in the game. (Because utility is assumed to be linear, the size of the stake is unimportant, and the redoubling point is the same as the re-redoubling and all further doubling points.) By examining Table 1, we see that a simple formula approximates all these late-game actions. If your count is x, and your opponent's is y:

you double if $y \geq (11/10)x - 1$;   he folds if $y \geq (11/10)x + 2$.

Table 2. A simplified running game.

	Your count							
	30	40	50	60	70	80	90	100
Opponent's count	Probability of winning if it is your turn							
Even	0.64	0.62	0.61	0.60	0.59	0.58	0.58	0.57
+5	0.80	0.76	0.73	0.71	0.70	0.68	0.67	0.66
+10	0.91	0.87	0.84	0.81	0.79	0.78	0.76	0.75
	Optimal Action[a]							
Even								
+5	F	R	R	D	D			
+10	F	F	F	F	F	R	R	R
	Value							
Even	0.48	0.45	0.42	0.40	0.38	0.38	0.38	0.37
+5	1.0	0.92	0.78	0.68	0.65	0.63	0.62	0.60
+10	1.0	1.0	1.0	1.0	1.0	0.97	0.90	0.84

[a] D = You can make first double; opponent should accept.
R = You can also redouble; opponent should accept.
F = You can also redouble; opponent should fold.

Table 3. Cut-off points for optimal strategy.

	Your count				
	30	50	70	90	110
First double	0.65	0.68	0.70	0.72	0.73
Redouble	0.69	0.71	0.72	0.73	0.74
Fold	0.76	0.77	0.78	0.79	0.79

[Another peculiarity in the rules (bearing off) causes a slight wastage of pips on the last few rolls of the dice. This means that the count we have called 50 corresponds to an on-the-board count of 45–50.]

Appendix

Great Expectations

There is a theoretical flaw in our treatment of backgammon doubling points. We have tacitly assumed that the expected value of the game, given doubling strategies for A and B exists. It need not. Suppose A's doubling point is 0.8, which we consider optimal. Now imagine that B sets his doubling point at 0.8. (That is, when A has a 0.8 chance of winning. In this Appendix all doubling

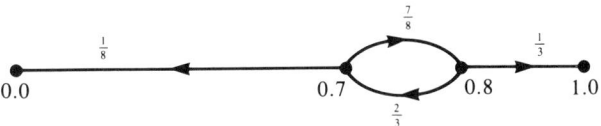

Figure 1

points will be expressed in terms of A's probability of winning.) When the game reaches 0.8, the two players alternate doubles, *ad infinitum*. The game, like life, becomes an absurdity.

The problem of infinite expectations may appear in more subtle guises. Suppose A's doubling point is 0.8 and B's doubling point is 0.7. Let us calculate the expected value to A, beginning at 0.7 with A having the doubling die.

We concern ourselves only with the values 0, 0.7, 0.8, 1, and the transition probabilities as indicated in Figure 1. For $n \geq 0$ with probability $\frac{1}{8}[(\frac{7}{8})(\frac{2}{3})]^n$, the game has $2n$ doubles and then B wins 4^n. With probability $\frac{7}{8}[(\frac{7}{8})(\frac{2}{3})]^n\frac{1}{3}$, the game has $2n + 1$ doubles and then A wins $2 \cdot 4^n$. Thus the expected value to A is

$$\sum_{n=0}^{n=\infty} \frac{7}{8} \cdot \frac{1}{3}[(\frac{7}{8})(\frac{2}{3})]^n 2 \cdot 4^n - \sum_{n=0}^{n=\infty} \frac{1}{8}[(\frac{7}{8})(\frac{2}{3})]^n 4^n.$$

However, both of these sums are *infinite*. A's expectation has both infinite positive and infinite negative components and hence must be regarded as undefined. We easily generalize this case by

Theorem 2. *Let B's doubling point be L and A's doubling point be $L + M$. Set $R = 1 - L - M$. (Assume $0 < L, M, R$.) Suppose both players accept all doubles. Then the game has undefined expectation if and only if*

$$3LR \geqq M. \tag{13}$$

Proof. The situation is exactly as in the example, with terms of the form

$$[LR/(L + M)(R + M)]^n 4^n.$$

Under assumption (13), $4LR/(L + M)(R + M) \geqq 1$; hence the expectation becomes undefined.

As an example, suppose $L = R = 0.35$, $M = 0.3$. Then (13) holds and the expectation is undefined. Intriguingly, this is the doubling strategy advocated by many backgammon experts. It certainly will lead to an exciting game.

What effect does all this have on the practical player? Our answer is: "Essentially none." There are some critical differences between the "pure" game and any real game.

(a) The real game is not continuous.
(b) In a real game, assets are limited to some finite amount.

Suppose that the number of doubles by each player is limited to n. Since this limits the stakes to 4^n, infinite expectations cannot occur. We have shown in our paper (Keeler and Spencer, 1969) that the appropriate first doubling point is then $\alpha(n) = 0.8 + (-1)^n/5.4^n$, which rapidly approaches 0.8.

What are the practical implications of Theorem 2 if, e.g., $L = R = 0.35$? Since the actual game is not continuous, the expectations are finite. In the pure game the expected value of the stake (that is, the amount that changes hands) is infinite. The closer a real game may be mirrored by a continuous game, the larger the expected stake will be. If, e.g., the game consists of watching a random walk on $[0, 1]$ with steps of 10^{-6}, the expected stake will be large indeed. We do not see how to estimate the expected stake in backgammon itself, where—as a very practical problem—it is nearly impossible to calculate the probability of winning with any precision except in the endgame.

In the pure game, if A's doubling point equals $L + M = 0.8$, there will be undefined expectations if B's doubling point equals $L \geq 0.5$. Even more subtle possibilities may occur. If B's nth doubling point is $L_n = 0.5 - \varepsilon_n$ where ε_n rapidly approaches zero, then, with all doubles accepted, there will be undefined expectations. However, there are "reactive" strategies for A that avoid infinite expectations. Essentially, one accepts "absurd" doubles but does not redouble. The following strategy gives finite nonnegative expectation for A against any strategy for B.

Reactive Strategy: Initially, A's doubling point is 0.8. If B doubles at p:

(i) If $p < 0.2$, resign.
(ii) If $0.2 \leq p < 0.49$, accept and make 0.8 the doubling point.
(iii) If $0.49 \leq p < 0.51$, accept and make 0.9 the doubling point.
(iv) If $0.51 \leq p$, accept and throw away the doubling die.

Of course, one may do better against poor players by fine-tuning the doubling point.

Acknowledgment. We would like to thank Thomas Cover for his many helpful suggestions and encouragement.

1.5. On Optimal Doubling in Backgammon

NORMAN ZADEH AND GARY KOBLISKA

Originally published in: *Management Science*, vol. 23, no. 8, April 1977. Copyright ©
1977, The Institute of Management Sciences. Reprinted by permission of The Institute
of Management Sciences.

Abstract. The concept of an effective doubling number for noncontinuous
games is introduced. Computer simulation is employed to determine an extremely accurate strategy for accepting, doubling, and redoubling in running
games.

Introduction

Backgammon is a two-player perfect information game in which a player's
move is governed by a throw of the dice. A player throws the dice and then
moves, after which his opponent throws and moves, etc. If a player rolls, say,
5 and 3, then he may move one man 5 spaces and another man 3 spaces, or
one man 8 spaces. Towards the end of the game, a race usually develops with
the winner being the player who takes his men off first. Race situations may
be accurately approximated by the following contest involving two players,
A and B.

A rolls first and starts out x_A spaces from home, while B begins a distance
x_B from home. (x_A is called player A's *count*). Each player's count is reduced
by the total of his roll. Thus if A's count is 45, and he rolls 5 and 3, his count
becomes 37. Player A wins if and only if his count becomes ≤ 0 before B's
count becomes ≤ 0.

Since gammons and backgammons (these are bonuses) rarely occur in
running games, they will be disregarded.

Players are allowed to double the stakes if they follow betting rules which
will be explained in the next section. We give the optimal doubling and
redoubling strategies for race-type positions. The strategies we present differ
from those given by Keeler and Spencer (1975) because they assumed that the

total of a player's dice could be 5 with probability 11/24, 10 with probability 11/24, and 20 with probability 2/24. In reality, for race purposes, the dice can show any one of 13 numbers.

Continuous Games

Let $p(t)$ denote the probability that player A will win at time t (given both players play optimally). If $p(t)$ is a continuous function of time, we call the game continuous. In backgammon, $p(t)$ is not continuous since it is defined only on nonnegative integers and may jump considerably from one move to the next. We begin by assuming that $p(t)$ is continuous and then make modifications to adjust for its actual discontinuity. The following lemma is from Keeler and Spencer (1975). Observe that A wins if $p(t)$ becomes 1 before it becomes 0.

Lemma 1. *In a continuous game, let the probability of A winning be x, and let $a, b > 0$ be such that $0 \le x - a < x < x + b \le 1$. Let E be the event that $p(t)$ becomes $x + b$ before it becomes $x - a$. Then the probability of E is $a/(a + b)$.*

Proof. We have, by conditioning on whether $p(t)$ first reaches $x + b$ or $x - a$, $x = p(E) \cdot (x + b) + (1 - p(E)) \cdot (x - a)$. This yields

$$p(E) = \frac{x - (x - a)}{(x + b) - (x - a)} = \frac{a}{a + b}.$$

Example 1. Suppose that $x = 0.75$. Then the probability that A wins ($p = 1$ before $p = 0$) is $0.75/1 = 0.75$.

Example 2. Suppose that $x = 0.6$. Then the probability that $x = 0.8$ before $x = 0$ is $0.6/(0.6 + 0.2) = 3/4$.

Lemma 1 may be extended to any linear function of $p(t)$, such as A's expectation. In other words, the probability that A's expectation rises by b before it falls by a is also $a/(a + b)$.

Doubling

In backgammon, the stakes of the game are determined by the doubling cube, which is initially put in the middle of the board with the "1" face up, meaning that the game is initially worth 1 point. During the course of a 1-point game, either player may *double* the stakes before rolling his dice. If A doubles to 2, then B may either concede 1 point to A and start a new game or agree to play the existing game for 2 points. If B elects to play on then only he may redouble.

(All doubles after the first are called redoubles.) Suppose that B decides to play and eventually redoubles to 4. Then A may either give B 2 points and start a new game, or play for 4 with the sole right to redouble, etc. There is no limit to the number of redoubles.

It is shown in Keeler and Spencer (1975) that in a continuous game, A should double or redouble when $p = 0.8$. When A doubles it does not matter whether B accepts or declines, his expectation in both cases is — the current value of the game. To see this, let K denote the value of the game before A doubles. If B accepts, he will own the cube at $2K$. He will win when $p = 0.2$ and lose when $p = 1$. Using Lemma 1, his probability of winning is $0.2/(0.6 + 0.2) = \frac{1}{4}$. Therefore, his expectation is $\frac{1}{4}(2K) - \frac{3}{4}(2K) = -K$, which is what he would lose if he did not accept the double.

Effective Doubling Point in Noncontinuous Games

Because backgammon is not a continuous game, one cannot wait for exactly an 80% chance of winning before doubling. Some doubles will be made at 70%, 74%; others will be made at 84%, 89%, etc. Note that a player's expectation after doubling to $2K$ at 70% is less than K.

In a noncontinuous game, the cube loses some of its value because one might have to reach an 85% position part of the time to win by doubling instead of an 80% position.[1] We may measure this loss of value by approximating our discontinuous game by a continuous one with doubling points D_A for A and D_B for B. Both are functions of the state of the game, i.e., the position of the checkers, whose roll it is, etc. D_A lies between 0.80 and 1. D_B lies between 0.20 and 0. A wins when $p(t) = D_A$, B wins when $p(t) = D_B$.

The loss of cube value to A is measured by the magnitude of $D_A - 0.80$. When $D_A = 0.80$, as is the case in a continuous game, the cube has maximum value since A must travel the minimum distance to win. As D_A moves upward, the cube loses value. When $D_A = 1.0$ the cube has no value to A.

In general, as the race nears the end, D_A will increase since $p(t)$ will become "less continuous." In an even race with 40 spaces to go and the cube in the middle, our results indicate that $D_A \approx 0.88$ and $D_B \approx 0.12$. With 20 pips to go, $D_A \approx 0.90$ and $D_B \approx 0.10$.

Lemma 2. *In a continuous game let $D_A(t)$ and $D_B(t)$ represent the effective doubling points for A and B at time t. Let $p(t)$ represent A's chances of winning at t assuming a cube is not used. Let $p(t, A)$ denote A's chances when holding the cube, and let $p(t, B)$ denote A's chances when B holds the cube. Let $p(t, M)$*

---

[1] Having to reach 70% to double may be shown to be roughly equivalent to having to reach some point >0.80 to double.

denote A's chances when the cube is in the middle. Then we have

$$p(t, A) = p(t)/D_A(t), \tag{1}$$

$$p(t, B) = (p(t) - D_B(t))/(1 - D_B(t)), \tag{2}$$

$$p(t, M) = (p(t) - D_B(t))/(D_A(t) - D_B(t)). \tag{3}$$

Proof. The proof is immediate from Lemma 1. For example, to prove (3), we take $x = p(t)$, $a = p(t) - D_B(t)$, $b = D_A(t) - p(t)$. Then

$$a/(a + b) = (p(t) - D_B(t))/(D_A(t) - D_B(t)).$$

Theorem 1. *In a continuous game with effective doubling points $D_A(t)$, $D_B(t)$ for A and B, respectively, let $M(t)$ denote the greatest value of $p(t)$ for which B can accept A's double. $M(t)$ is called the minimum take point and varies from 75% to 80%. Let $r(t)$ and $d(t)$ denote the minimum values of $p(t)$ for which A can double and redouble, respectively. Then we have*

$$M(t) = 1 - \tfrac{1}{4}(1 - D_B(t)), \tag{4}$$

$$r(t) = \frac{3D_A(t)D_B(t) + D_A(t)}{4D_A(t) - 2(1 - D_B(t))}, \tag{5}$$

$$d(t) = \frac{(D_B(t))^2 + 3D_B(t)(1 - D_A(t)) - D_A(t)}{2D_B(t) - 4D_A(t) + 2}. \tag{6}$$

Proof. We prove (4) first. After A doubles, B's chances of winning given that he owns the cube are $1 - p(t, B)$, which by (2) of Lemma 2 equals

$$1 - \left(\frac{p(t) - D_B(t)}{1 - D_B(t)}\right). \tag{7}$$

B's minimum take point occurs when (7) $= 25\%$, i.e., we have

$$0.25 = 1 - \left(\frac{M(t) - D_B(t)}{1 - D_B(t)}\right).$$

Solving this for $M(t)$ yields (4).

Proof of (5). $r(t)$ is determined by the condition that A's expectation after redoubling be equal to A's expectation before redoubling.

A's expectation before redoubling equals

$$p(t, A)K + (1 - p(t, A))(-K) = K(2p(t, A) - 1).$$

By (1) of Lemma 2, this equals

$$K(2p(t)/D_A(t) - 1). \tag{8}$$

A's expectation after doubling is

$$2K(2p(t, B) - 1), \tag{9}$$

which by (2) of Lemma 2 equals

$$2K\left(\frac{2(p(t) - D_B(t))}{1 - D_B(t)} - 1\right). \tag{10}$$

When $p(t) = r(t)$, we must have (8) = (10), or

$$\frac{2(r(t))}{D_A(t)} - 1 = 2\left(\frac{2(r(t) - D_B(t))}{1 - D_B(t)}\right) - 1. \tag{11}$$

Solving (11) for $r(t)$ yields (5).

The proof of (6) is similar to the proof of (5) and involves equating $2p(t, M) - 1$ to $2(2p(t, B) - 1)$ and solving for $p(t)$.

Optimal Doubling and Redoubling Strategy for Running Games

Recall that a running game may be approximated by a contest between two players A and B with counts x_A and x_B, respectively. We assume that A rolls first. Each player's distance from home is decreased by the total of his roll. Player A wins if his count becomes ≤ 0 before B's count becomes ≤ 0. This approximation is extremely accurate provided that neither player has gaps in his home board or men on the one and two points.

Player A wins if when he takes n rolls to get off, B takes at least n rolls. Let $P(x, n)$ denote the probability that a player with count x gets off in exactly n rolls. Then the probability that A wins is simply $\sum_{j=1}^{\infty} (P(x_A, j) \sum_{k=j}^{\infty} P(x_B, k))$.

This quantity may be calculated exactly using convolutions. Let $f(y)$ denote the probability that a player's total in one roll is y. In backgammon, the minimum roll is 3 and the maximum roll is 24. Thus we have $P(x, 1) = \sum_{y=x}^{24} f(y)$. $P(x, k + 1)$ may be computed using the recursion.

$$P(x, k + 1) = \sum_{y=3}^{24} f(y) \cdot P(x - y, k).$$

Table 1. Probability of winning the running game if it is your turn to roll.

		\multicolumn{11}{c}{Your count}
		10	20	30	40	50	60	70	80	90	100	110
Opponent's count	−20	0	0	5.1	8.3	11.6	14.2	16.5	18.4	20.0	21.4	22.6
	−15	0	7.6	13.2	18.0	21.2	23.7	25.6	27.2	28.5	29.6	30.5
	−10	0	20.3	27.6	31.3	33.6	35.2	36.4	37.3	38.1	38.7	39.3
	−5	32.2	44.4	46.5	47.0	47.4	47.7	47.9	48.0	48.1	48.2	48.3
	Even	78.2	68.7	64.3	62.2	60.8	59.9	59.1	58.5	58.0	57.6	57.3
	+5	90.6	82.9	78.0	74.8	72.4	70.7	69.3	68.2	67.2	66.4	65.7
	+10	94.8	91.1	87.2	84.1	81.6	79.6	77.9	76.5	75.3	74.2	73.2
	+15	99.3	96.0	93.2	90.6	88.4	86.5	84.8	83.3	81.9	80.8	79.7
	+20	99.7	98.3	96.6	94.8	93.0	91.4	89.9	88.5	87.3	86.1	85.0
	+25	99.9	99.4	98.4	97.2	96.0	94.8	93.5	92.4	91.3	90.3	89.3
	+30	100.0	99.8	99.3	98.6	97.8	96.9	96.0	95.1	94.2	93.4	92.5

Table 1 was computed using the above method. It gives the probability (in percent) that a player will win when it is his roll and his opponent's count is at various distances from his own. For example, when A's count is 70 and he is 10 pips ahead, his probability of winning is 77.9%

Keeler and Spencer (1975) computed a similar table by using a method which involved rolling the dice 1,000 times to approximate $P(x, n)$ for all values of x from 1 to 125. It is interesting to note that their results differ from Table 1 by no more than 1%.

Results of the Computer Simulation

To compute the optimal doubling and redoubling strategies and the minimum take points, we began by analyzing racing positions right near the end. One

Table 2. Results of the simulation.

Redouble	Player	Count		
	A	20	0.611	Expectation not doubling
	B	20	0.685	Expectation doubling
Redouble	A	20	0.470	
	B	19	0.435	
Redouble	A	20	0.481	
	B	19	0.472	
Double	A	20	0.330	
	B	18	0.313	
Redouble	A	40	0.744	
	B	44	0.783	
Redouble	A	40	0.693	
	B	43	0.693	
Redouble	A	40	0.689	
	B	43	0.681	
Double	A	40	0.577	
	B	42	0.580	
Redouble	A	70	0.791	
	B	78	0.822	
Redouble	A	70	0.766	
	B	77	0.747	
Redouble	A	70	0.737	
	B	77	0.721	
Double	A	70	0.664	
	B	76	0.652	
Redouble	A	110	0.833	
	B	122	0.866	
Redouble	A	110	0.818	
	B	121	0.796	
Double	A	110	0.757	
	B	120	0.769	
Double	A	110	0.710	
	B	119	0.709	

of us (G. K.) had a piece-moving program which was utilized to compute the optimum doubling and redoubling strategies in actual board positions up to about 12 pips. The computer was instructed to follow these strategies (which are best in actual play) even though they might not coincide exactly with the best strategies for the mathematical race model. In other words, the strategies we obtain are slightly more accurate than those which would be obtained by adhering strictly to the model. From 12 to 20 pips we made intelligent guesses as to the best doubling and redoubling strategies. A CDC 6400 was then asked to compare the expectation after redoubling at 20 vs. 20 versus the expectation by holding on to the cube and rolling. Ten thousand games were played out. The results were used to modify some of the guesses slightly using interpolation and new runs were made with the then accurate strategies. This procedure was repeated at 40 pips, 70 pips, and 110 pips. The program was checked by asking it to print out all information for 50 sample games, both with the cube in the middle and with the cube in A's possession. The results of the runs are given in Table 2. All entries in Table 2 assume that A rolls first. The first entry of each pair gives A's expectation assuming he holds onto the cube for at least one roll. The second entry gives A's expectation assuming he doubles immediately. The term "double" in the leftmost column means that the cube is initially in the middle. Thus the first set of entries in the table indicate that when A's count is 20 and B's count is 20, A's expectation by holding on the cube is 0.611 whereas his expectation by doubling before rolling is 0.685.

Table 3. Optimal doubling strategy in running games.

Minimum	20	40	70	110
Take for opponent	$+2$	$+5\frac{1}{2}$	$+10$	$+14\frac{1}{2}$
Redouble	$-\frac{1}{2}$	$+3$	$+7\frac{1}{2}$	$+11\frac{1}{2}$
Double	$-1\frac{1}{2}$	$+2$	$+6\frac{1}{2}$	$+9\frac{1}{2}$

Table 3 is based on Table 2 and gives the optimal strategy for accepting, doubling, and redoubling. The first column indicates that when your count is 20, you should redouble if your opponent's count is $19\frac{1}{2}$ or more, and double if his count is $18\frac{1}{2}$ or more. Essentially, this means that you should not redouble when his count is 19 unless there is a weakness in his position (a gap or men on the 1 and 2 points, etc.). Your opponent should drop when his count is 23 or higher and take otherwise.

CHAPTER 2

Chess

2.1. A Chess-Playing Machine

CLAUDE E. SHANNON

For centuries philosophers and scientists have speculated about whether or
not the human brain is essentially a machine. Could a machine be designed
that would be capable of "thinking"? During the past decade several large-
scale electronic computing machines have been constructed which are capable
of something very close to the reasoning process. These new computers were
designed primarily to carry out purely numerical calculations. They perform
automatically a long sequence of additions, multiplications, and other arithmetic operations at a rate of thousands per second. The basic design of these
machines is so general and flexible, however, that they can be adapted to
work symbolically with elements representing words, propositions, or other
conceptual entities.

One such possibility, which is already being investigated in several quarters,
is that of translating from one language to another by means of a computer.
The immediate goal is not a finished literary rendition, but only a word-by-word
translation that would convey enough of the meaning to be understandable.
Computing machines could also be employed for many other tasks of a
semirote, semithinking character, such as designing electrical filters and relay
circuits, helping to regulate airplane traffic at busy airports, and routing
long-distance telephone calls most efficiently over a limited number of trunks.

Some of the possibilities in this direction can be illustrated by setting up a
computer in such a way that it will play a fair game of chess. This problem,
of course, is of no importance in itself, but it was undertaken with a serious
purpose in mind. The investigation of the chess-playing problem is intended
to develop techniques that can be used for more practical applications.

The chess machine is an ideal one to start with for several reasons. The
problem is sharply defined, both in the allowed operations (the moves of chess)
and in the ultimate goal (checkmate). It is neither so simple as to be trivial

nor too difficult for satisfactory solution. And such a machine could be pitted against a human opponent, giving a clear measure of the machine's ability in this type of reasoning.

There is already a considerable literature on the subject of chess-playing machines. During the late eighteenth and early nineteenth centuries a Hungarian inventor named Wolfgang von Kempelen astounded Europe with a device known as the Maelzel Chess Automaton, which toured the Continent to large audiences. A number of papers purporting to explain its operation, including an analytical essay by Edgar Allan Poe, soon appeared. Most of the analysts concluded, quite correctly, that the automaton was operated by a human chess master concealed inside. Some years later the exact manner of operation was exposed.

A more honest attempt to design a chess-playing machine was made in 1914 by a Spanish inventor named L. Torres y Quevedo, who constructed a device that played an endgame of King and Rook against King. The machine, playing the side with King and Rook, would force checkmate in a few moves however its human opponent played. Since an explicit set of rules can be given for making satisfactory moves in such an endgame, the problem is relatively simple, but the idea was quite advanced for that period.

An electronic computer can be set up to play a complete game. In order to explain the actual setup of a chess machine, it may be best to start with a general picture of a computer and its operation.

A general-purpose electronic computer is an extremely complicated device containing several thousand vacuum tubes, relays, and other elements. The basic principles involved, however, are quite simple. The machine has four main parts: (1) an "arithmetic organ," (2) a control element, (3) a numerical memory, and (4) a program memory. (In some designs the two memory functions are carried out in the same physical apparatus.) The manner of operation is exactly analogous to a human computer carrying out a series of numerical calculations with an ordinary desk computing machine. The arithmetic organ corresponds to the desk computing machine, the control element to the human operator, the numerical memory to the work sheet on which intermediate and final results are recorded, and the program memory to the computing routine describing the series of operations to be performed.

In an electronic computing machine, the numerical memory consists of a large number of "boxes," each capable of holding a number. To set up a problem on the computer, it is necessary to assign box numbers to all numerical quantities involved, and then to construct a program telling the machine what arithmetical operations must be performed on the numbers and where the results should go. The program consists of a sequence of "orders," each describing an elementary calculation. For example, a typical order may read A 372, 451, 133. This means: add the number stored in box 372 to that in box 451, and put the sum in box 133. Another type of order requires the machine to make a decision. For example, the order C 291, 118, 345 tells the machine to compare the contents of boxes 291 and 118; if the number in box 291 is larger, the machine goes on to the next order in the program; if not, it takes its next order from box 345. This type of order enables the machine to choose from alternative procedures, depending on the results of previous calculations. The "vocabulary" of an electronic computer may include as many as 30 different types of orders.

After the machine is provided with a program, the initial numbers required for the calculation are placed in the numerical memory and the machine then automatically carries out the computation. Of course such a machine is most useful in problems involving an enormous number of individual calculations, which would be too laborious to carry out by hand.

The problem of setting up a computer for playing chess can be divided into three parts: first, a code must be chosen so that chess positions and the chess pieces can be represented as numbers; second, a strategy must be found for choosing the moves to be made; and third, this strategy must be translated into a sequence of elementary computer orders, or a program.

A suitable code for the chessboard and the chess pieces is shown in Figure 1. Each square on the board has a number consisting of two digits, the first digit corresponding to the "rank" or horizontal row, the second to the "file" or vertical row. Each different chess piece also is designated by a number: a pawn is numbered 1, a Knight 2, a Bishop 3, a Rook 4 and so on. White pieces are represented by positive numbers and black pieces by negative ones. The positions of all the pieces on the board can be shown by a sequence of 64 numbers, with zeros to indicate the empty squares. Thus any chess position can be recorded as a series of numbers and stored in the numerical memory of a computing machine.

A chess move is specified by giving the number of the square on which the piece stands and of the one to which it is moved. Ordinarily two numbers

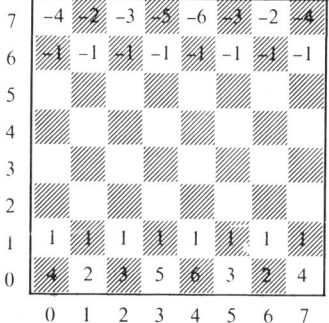

Figure 1. Code for a chess-playing machine is plotted on a chessboard. Each square can be designated by two digits, one representing the horizontal row and the other the vertical. Pieces also are coded in numbers (*see text*).

would be sufficient to describe a move, but to take care of the special case of the promotion of a pawn to a higher piece a third number is necessary. This number indicates the piece to which the pawn is converted. In all other moves the third number is zero. Thus a Knight move from square 01 to 22 is encoded into 01, 22, 0. The move of a pawn from 62 to 72, and its promotion to a Queen, is represented by 62, 72, 5.

The second main problem is that of deciding on a strategy of play. A strightforward process must be found for calculating a reasonably good move for any given chess position. This is the most difficult part of the problem. The program designer can employ here the principles of correct play that have been evolved by expert chess players. These empirical principles are a means of bringing some order to the maze of possible variations of a chess game. Even the high speeds available in electronic computers are hopelessly inadequate to play perfect chess by calculating all possible variations to the end of the game. In a typical chess position there will be about 32 possible moves with 32 possible replies—already this creates 1,024 possibilities. Most chess games last 40 moves or more for each side. So the total number of possible variations in an average game is about 10^{120}. A machine calculating one variation each millionth of a second would require over 10^{95} years to decide on its first move!

Other methods of attempting to play perfect chess seem equally impracticable; we resign ourselves, therefore, to having the machine play a reasonably skillful game, admitting occasional moves that may not be the best. This, of course, is precisely what human players do: no one plays a perfect game.

In setting up a strategy on the machine one must establish a method of numerical evaluation for any given chess position. A chess player looking at a position can form an estimate as to which side, White or Black, has the advantage. Furthermore, his evaluation is roughly quantitative. He may say, "White has a Rook for a Bishop, an advantage of about two pawns"; or "Black has sufficient mobility to compensate for a sacrificed pawn." These judgments are based on long experience and are summarized in the principles of chess expounded in chess literature. For example, it has been found that a Queen is worth nine pawns, a Rook is worth five, and a Bishop or a Knight is worth about three. As a first rough approximation, a position can be evaluated by merely adding up the total forces for each side, measured in terms of the pawn unit. There are, however, numerous other features which must be taken into account: the mobility and placement of pieces, the weakness of King protection, the nature of the pawn formation, and so on. These too can be given numerical weights and combined in the evaluation, and it is here that the knowledge and experience of chess masters must be enlisted.

Assuming that a suitable method of position evaluation has been decided upon, how should a move be selected? The simplest process is to consider all the possible moves in the given position and choose the one that gives the best immediate evaluation. Since, however, chess players generally look more than one move ahead, one must take account of the opponent's various possible responses to each projected move. Assuming that the opponent's reply will be the one giving the best evaluation from his point of view, we would choose the move that would leave us as well off as possible after his best reply. Unfortunately, with the computer speeds at present available, the machine could not explore all the possibilities for more than two moves ahead for each side, so a strategy of this type would play a poor game by human standards. Good chess players frequently play combinations four or five moves deep, and occasionally world champions have seen as many as 20 moves ahead. This is possible only because the variations they consider are highly selected. They do not investigate all lines of play, but only the important ones.

The amount of selection exercised by chess masters in examining possible variations has been studied experimentally by the Dutch chess master and psychologist A. D. De Groot. He showed various typical positions to chess masters and asked them to decide on the best move, describing aloud their analyses of the positions as they thought them through. By this procedure the number and depth of the variations examined could be determined. In one typical case a chess master examined 16 variations, ranging in depth from one Black move to five Black and four White moves. The total number of positions considered was 44.

Clearly, it would be highly desirable to improve the strategy for the machine by including such a selection process in it. Of course one could go too far in this direction. Investigating one particular line of play for 40 moves would be as bad as investigating all lines for just two moves. A suitable compromise would be to examine only the important possible variations—that is, forcing moves, captures and main threats—and carry out the investigation of the possible moves far enough to make the consequences of each fairly clear. It is possible to set up some rough criteria for selecting important variations, not as efficiently as a chess master, but sufficiently well to reduce the number of variations appreciably and thereby permit a deeper investigation of the moves actually considered.

The final problem is that of reducing the strategy to a sequence of orders, translated into the machine's language. This is a relatively straightforward but tedious process, and we shall only indicate some of the general features. The complete program is made up of nine subprograms and a master program that calls the subprograms into operation as needed. Six of the subprograms deal with the movements of the various kinds of pieces. In effect, they tell the machine the allowed moves for these pieces. Another subprogram enables the machine to make a move "mentally" without actually carrying it out: that is, with a given position stored in its memory it can construct the position that would result if the move were made. The seventh subprogram enables the computer to make a list of all possible moves in a given position, and the last subprogram evaluates any given position. The master program correlates and supervises the application of the subprograms. It starts the seventh subprogram making a list of possible moves, which in turn calls in previous subprograms to determine where the various pieces could move. The master program then evaluates the resulting positions by means of the eighth subprogram and compares the results according to the process described above. After comparison of all the investigated variations, the one that gives the best evaluation according to the machine's calculations is selected. This move is translated into standard chess notation and typed out by the machine.

It is believed that an electronic computer programmed in this manner would play a fairly strong game at speeds comparable to human speeds. A machine has several obvious advantages over a human player:

(1) it can make individual calculations with much greater speed;
(2) its play is free of errors other than those due to deficiencies of the program, whereas human players often make very simple and obvious blunders;
(3) it is free from laziness, or the temptation to make an instinctive move without proper analysis of the position;
(4) it is free from "nerves," so it will make no blunders due to overconfidence or defeatism.

Against these advantages, however, must be weighed the flexibility, imagination, and learning capacity of the human mind.

Under some circumstances the machine might well defeat the program designer. In one sense, the designer can surely outplay his machine; knowing the strategy used by the machine, he can apply the same tactics at a deeper level. But he would require several weeks to calculate a move, while the machine uses only a few minutes. On an equal time basis, the speed, patience, and deadly accuracy of the machine would be telling against human fallibility. Sufficiently nettled, however, the designer could easily weaken the playing skill of the machine by changing the program in such a way as to reduce the depth of investigation. This idea was expressed by a cartoon in *The Saturday Evening Post* a while ago.

As described so far, the machine would always make the same move in the same position. If the opponent made the same moves, this would always lead to the same game. Once the opponent won a game, he could win every time thereafter by playing the same strategy, taking advantage of some particular position in which the machine chooses a weak move. One way to vary the machine's play would be to introduce a statistical element. Whenever it was confronted with two or more possible moves that were about equally good according to the machine's calculations, it would choose from them at random. Thus if it arrived at the same position a second time it might choose a different move.

Another place where statistical variation could be introduced is in the opening game. It would be desirable to have a number of standard openings, perhaps a few hundred, stored in the memory of the machine. For the first few moves, until the opponent deviated from the standard responses or the machine reached the end of the stored sequence of moves, the machine would play by memory. This could hardly be considered cheating, since that is the way chess masters play the opening.

We may note that within its limits a machine of this type will play a brilliant game. It will readily make spectacular sacrifices of important pieces in order to gain a later advantage or to give checkmate, provided the completion of the combination occurs within its computing limits. For example, in this position the machine would quickly discover the sacrificial mate in three moves:

White	Black
1 R − K8 ch	R × R
2 Q − Kt4 ch	Q × Q
3 Kt − B6 mate	

Winning combinations of this type are frequently overlooked in amateur play.

The chief weakness of the machine is that it will not learn by its mistakes. The only way to improve its play is by improving the program. Some thought has been given to designing a program that would develop its own improvements in strategy with increasing experience in play. Although it appears to be theoretically possible, the methods thought of so far do not seem to be very practical. One possibility is to devise a program that would change the terms and coefficients involved in the evaluation function on the basis of the results of games the machine had already played. Small variations might be intoduced in these terms, and the values would be selected to give the greatest percentage of wins.

The Gordian question, more easily raised than answered, is: Does a chess-playing machine of this type "think"? The answer depends entirely on how we define thinking. Since there is no general agreement as to the precise connotation of this word, the question has no definite answer. From a behavioristic point of view, the machine acts as though it were thinking. It has always been considered that skillful chess play requires the reasoning faculty. If we regard thinking as a property of external actions rather than internal method the machine is surely thinking.

The thinking process is considered by some psychologists to be essentially characterized by the following steps: various possible solutions of a problem are tried out mentally or symbolically without actually being carried out physically; the best solution is selected by a mental evaluation of the results of these trials; and the solution found in this way is then acted upon. It will be seen that this is almost an exact description of how a chess-playing computer operates, provided we substitute "within the machine" for "mentally."

On the other hand, the machine does only what it has been told to do. It works by trial and error, but the trials are trials that the program designer ordered the machine to make, and the errors are called errors because the evaluation function gives these variations low ratings. The machine makes decisions, but the decisions were envisaged and provided for at the time of design. In short, the machine does not, in any real sense, go beyond what was built into it. The situation was nicely summarized by Torres y Quevedo, who, in connection with his endgame machine, remarked: "The limits within which thought is really necessary need to be better defined ... the automaton can do many things that are popularly classed as thought."

2.2. Chess-Playing Programs and the Problem of Complexity

ALLEN NEWELL, J. C. SHAW, AND H. A. SIMON

Originally published in: *IBM Journal of Research and Development*, vol. 2, 1958, pp. 320–335. Copyright © 1958 IBM Corporation. Reprinted by permission.

Abstract. This paper traces the development of digital computer programs that play chess. The work of Shannon, Turing, the Los Alamos group, Bernstein, and the authors is treated in turn. The efforts to program chess provide an indication of current progress in understanding and constructing complex and intelligent mechanisms.

Man can solve problems without knowing how he solves them. This simple fact sets the conditions for all attempts to rationalize and understand human decision making and problem solving. Let us simply assume that it is good to know how to do mechanically what man can do naturally—both to add to man's knowledge of man, and to add to his kit of tools for controlling and manipulating his environment. We shall try to assess recent progress in understanding and mechanizing man's intellectual attainments by considering a single line of attack—the attempts to construct digital computer programs that play chess.

Chess is the intellectual game *par excellence*. Without a chance device to obscure the contest, it pits two intellects against each other in a situation so complex that neither can hope to understand it completely, but sufficiently amenable to analysis that each can hope to outthink his opponent. The game is sufficiently deep and subtle in its implications to have supported the rise of professional players, and to have allowed a deepening analysis through 200 years of intensive study and play without becoming exhausted or barren. Such characteristics mark chess as a natural arena for attempts at mechanization. If one could devise a successful chess machine, one would seem to have penetrated to the core of human intellectual endeavor.

The history of chess programs is an example of the attempt to conceive and cope with complex mechanisms. Now there might have been a trick—one might have discovered something that was as the wheel to the human leg: a device quite different from humans in its methods, but supremely effective in its way, and perhaps very simple. Such a device might play excellent chess, but would fail to further our understanding of human intellectual processes. Such a prize, of course, would be worthy of discovery in its own right, but there appears to be nothing of this sort in sight.

We return to the original orientation: Humans play chess, and when they do they engage in behavior that seems extremely complex, intricate, and successful. Consider, for example, a scrap of a player's (White's) running comment as he analyzes the position in Figure 1:

Figure 1

"... Are there any other threats? Black also has a threat of Knight to Bishop 5 threatening the Queen, and also putting more pressure on the King's side because his Queen's Bishop can come over after he moves his Knight at Queen 2; however, that is not the immediate threat. Otherwise, his Pawn at King 4 is threatening my Pawn ..."

Notice that his analysis is qualitative and functional. He wanders from one feature to another, accumulating various bits of information that will be available from time to time throughout the rest of the analysis. He makes evaluations in terms of pressures and immediacies of threat, and gradually creates order out of the situation.

How can we construct mechanisms that will show comparable complexity in their behavior? They need not play in exactly the same way; close simulation of the human is not the immediate issue. But we do assert that complexity of behavior is essential to an intelligent performance—that the complexity of a successful chess program will approach the complexity of the thought processes of a successful human chess player. Complexity of response is dictated by the task, not by idiosyncrasies of the human response mechanism.

There is a close and reciprocal relation between complexity and communication. On the one hand, the complexity of the systems we can specify depends on the language in which we must specify them. Being human, we have only limited capacities for processing information. Given a more powerful language, we can specify greater complexity with limited processing powers.

Let us illustrate this side of the relation between complexity and communication. No one considers building chess machines in the literal sense—fashioning pieces of electronic gear into automatons that will play chess. We think instead of chess programs: specifications written in a language, called machine code, that will instruct a digital computer of standard design how to play chess. There is a reason for choosing this latter course—in addition to any aversion we may have to constructing a large piece of special-purpose machinery. Machine code is a more powerful language than the block diagrams of the electronics engineer. Each symbol in machine code specifies a larger unit of processing than a symbol in the block diagram. Even a moderately complicated program becomes hopelessly complex if thought of in terms of gates and pulses.

But there is another side to the relation between communication and complexity. We cannot use any old language we please. We must be understood by the person or machine to whom we are communicating. English will not do to specify chess programs because there are no English-understanding computers. A specification in English is a specification to another human who then has the task of creating the machine. Machine code is an advance precisely because there are machines that understand it—because a chess program in machine code is operationally equivalent to a machine that plays chess.

If the machine could understand even more powerful languages, we could use these to write chess programs—and thus get more complex and intelligent programs from our limited human processing capacity. But communication is limited by the intelligence of the least participant, and at present a computer has only passive capability. The language it understands is one of simple commands—it must be told very much about what to do.

Thus it seems that the rise of effective communication between man and computer will coincide with the rise in the intelligence of the computer—so that the human can say more while thinking less. But at this point in history, the only way we can obtain more intelligent machines is to design them—we cannot yet grow them, or breed them, or train them by the blind procedures that work with humans. We are caught at the wrong equilibrium of a bistable system: we could design more intelligent machines if we could communicate to them better; we could communicate to them better if they were more intelligent. Limited both in our capabilities for design and communication, every advance in either separately requires a momentous effort. Each success, however, allows a corresponding effort on the other side to reach a little further. At some point the reaction will "go," and we will find ourselves at the favorable equilibrium point of the system, possessing mechanisms that are both highly intelligent and communicative.

With this view of the task and its setting, we can turn to the substance of the paper: the development of chess programs. We will proceed historically, since this arrangement of the material will show most clearly what progress is being made in obtaining systems of increasing complexity and intelligence.

Shannon's Proposal

The relevant history begins with a paper by Claude Shannon in 1949 (Shannon, 1950a). He did not present a particular chess program, but discussed many of the basic problems involved. The framework he introduced has guided most of the subsequent analysis of the problem.

As Shannon observed, chess is a finite game. There is only a finite number of positions, each of which admits a finite number of alternative moves. The rules of chess assure that any play will terminate: that eventually a position will be reached that is a win, loss, or draw. Thus chess can be completely described as a branching tree (as in Figure 2), the nodes corresponding to positions and the branches corresponding to the alternative moves from each position. It is intuitively clear, and easily proved, that for a player who can view the entire tree and see all the ultimate consequences of each alternative, chess becomes a simple game. Starting with the terminal positions, which have determinate payoffs, he can work backwards, determining at each node which branch is best for him or his opponent as the case may be, until he arrives at the alternative for his next move.

This inferential procedure—called *minimaxing* in the theory of games—is basic to all the attempts so far to program computers for chess. Let us be sure we understand it. Figure 2 shows a situation where White is to move and has three choices, (1), (2), and (3). White's move will be followed by Black's: (a) or (b) in case move (1) is made; (c) or (d) if move (2) is made; and (e) or (f) if move (3) is made. To keep the example simple, we have assumed that all of Black's moves lead to positions with known payoffs: ($+$) meaning a win for White, (0) meaning a draw, and ($-$) meaning a loss for White. How should White decide what to do—what inference procedure allows him to determine which of the three moves is to be preferred? Clearly, no matter what Black does, move (1) leads to a draw. Similarly, no matter what Black does, move (2) leads

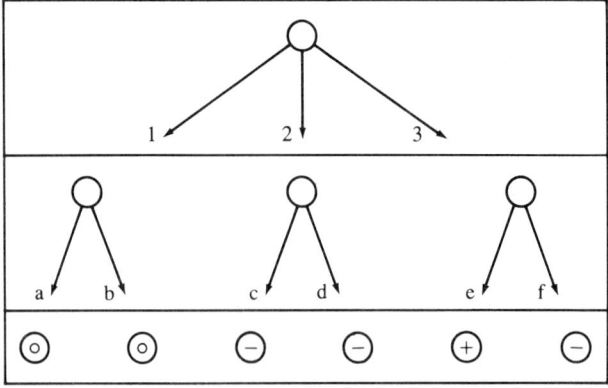

Figure 2. The game tree and minimaxing.

to a loss for White. White should clearly prefer move (1) to move (2). But what about move (3)? It offers the possibility of a win, but also contains the possibility of a loss; and furthermore, the outcome is in Black's control. If White is willing to impute any analytic ability to his opponent, he must conclude that move (3) will end as a loss for White, and hence that move (1) is the preferred move. The win from move (3) is completely insubstantial, since it can never be realized. Thus White can impute a value to a position—in this case draw—by reasoning backwards from known values.

To repeat: If the entire tree can be scanned, the best move can be determined simply by the minimaxing procedure. Now minimaxing might have been the "wheel" of chess—with the adventure ended almost before it had started—if the tree were not so large that even current computers can discover only the minutest fraction of it in years of computing. Shannon's estimate, for instance, is that there are something like 10^{120} continuations to be explored, with less than 10^{16} microseconds available in a century to explore them.

Shannon then suggested the following framework. Playing chess consists of considering the alternative moves, obtaining some effective evaluation of them by means of analysis, and choosing the preferred alternative on the basis of the evaluation. The analysis—which is the hard part—could be factored into three parts. First, one would explore the continuations to a certain depth. Second, since it is clear that the explorations cannot be deep enough to reach terminal positions, one would evaluate the positions reached at the end of each exploration in terms of the pattern of men on the chess board. These static evaluations would then be combined by means of the minimaxing procedure to form the effective value of the alternative. One would then choose the move with the highest effective value. The rationale behind this factorization was the reasonableness that, for a given evaluation function, the greater the depth of analysis, the better the chess that would be played. In the limit, of course, such a process would play perfect chess by finding terminal positions for all continuations. Thus a metric was provided that measured all programs along the single dimension of their depth of analysis.

To complete the scheme, a procedure was needed to evaluate positions statically—that is, without making further moves. Shannon proposed a numerical measure formed by summing, with weights, a number of factors or scores that could be computed for any position. These scores would correspond to the various features that chess experts assert are important. This approach gains plausibility from the existence of a few natural quantities in chess, such as the values of pieces, and the mobility of men. It also gains plausibility, of course, from the general use in science and engineering of linearizing assumptions as first approximations.

To summarize: the basic framework introduced by Shannon for thinking about chess programs consists of a series of questions:

1. Alternatives
   Which alternative moves are to be considered?

2. Analysis
   (a) Which continuations are to be explored and to what depth?
   (b) How are positions to be evaluated statically—in terms of their patterns?
   (c) How are the static evaluations to be integrated into a single value for an alternative?
3. Final choice procedure
   What procedure is to be used to select the final preferred move?

We would hazard that Shannon's paper is chiefly remembered for the specific answers he proposed to these questions: consider all alternatives; search all continuations to fixed depth, n; evaluate with a numerical sum; minimax to get the effective value for an alternative; and then pick the best one. His article goes beyond these specifics, however, and discusses the possibility of selecting only a small number of alternatives and continuations. It also discusses the possibility of analysis in terms of the functions that chess men perform—blocking, attacking, defending. At this stage, however, it was possible to think of chess programs only in terms of extremely systematic procedures. Shannon's specific proposals have gradually been realized in actual programs, whereas the rest of his discussion has been largely ignored. And when proposals for more complex computations enter the research picture again, it is through a different route.

Turing's Program

Shannon did not present a particular program. His specifications still require large amounts of computing for even such modest depths of analysis as two or three moves. It remained for A. M. Turing (Bowden, 1953, Ch. 25) to describe a program along these lines that was sufficiently simple to be simulated by hand, without the aid of a digital computer.

In Table 1 we have characterized Turing's program in terms of the framework just defined. There are some additional categories which will become clear as we proceed. The table also provides similar information for each of the other three programs we will consider.

Turing's program considered all alternatives—that is, all legal moves. In order to limit computation, however, he was very circumspect about the continuations the program considered. Turing introduced the notion of a "dead" position: one that in some sense was stable, hence could be evaluated. For example, there is no sense in counting material on the board in the middle of an exchange of Queens: one should explore the continuations until the exchange has been carried through—to the point where the material is not going to change with the next move. So Turing's program evaluated material at dead positions only. He made the value of material dominant in his static evaluation, so that a decision problem remained only if minimaxing revealed several alternatives that were equal in material. In these cases, he applied a supplementary additive evaluation to the positions reached by making the alternative moves. This evaluation included a large number of factors— mobility, backward pawns, defense of men, and so on—points being assigned for each.

Thus Turing's program is a good instance of a chess-playing system as envisaged by Shannon, although a small-scale one in terms of computational requirements. Only one published game, as far as we know, was played with the program. It proved to be rather weak, for it lost against a weak human player (who did not know the program, by the way), although it was not entirely a pushover. In general its play was rather aimless, and it was capable of gross blunders, one of which cost it the game. As one might have expected, the subtleties of the evaluation function were lost upon it. Most of the numer- ous factors included in the function rarely had any influence on the move chosen. In summary: Turing's program was not a very good chess player, but it reached the bottom rung of the human ladder.

There is no *a priori* objection to hand simulation of a program, although experience has shown that it is almost always inexact for programs of this complexity. For example, there is an error in Turing's play of his program, because he—the human simulator—was unwilling to consider all the alter- natives. He failed to explore the ones he "knew" would be eliminated anyway, and was wrong once. The main objection to hand simulation is the amount of effort required to do it. The computer is really the enabling condition for exploring the behavior of a complex program. One cannot even realize the potentialities of the Shannon scheme without programming it for a computer.

The Los Alamos Program

In 1956 a group at Los Alamos programmed MANIAC I to play chess. (Kister *et al.*, 1957) The Los Alamos program is an almost perfect example of the type of system specified by Shannon. As shown in Table 1, all alternatives were considered; all continuations were explored to a depth of two moves (i.e., two moves for Black and two for White); the static evaluation function consisted of a sum of material and mobility measures; the values were integrated by a minimax procedure,[1] and the best alternative in terms of the effective values was chosen for the move.

In order to carry out the computation within resonable time limits, a major concession was required. Instead of the normal chess board of eight squares by eight squares, they used a reduced board, six squares by six squares. They eliminated the Bishops and all special chess moves: castling, two-square pawn moves in the opening, and *en passant* captures.

---

[1] The minimax procedure was a slight modification of the one described earlier, in that the mobility score for each of the intermediate positions was added in.

The result? Again the program is a weak player, but now one that is capable of beating a weak human player, as the machine demonstrated in one of its three games. It is capable of serious blunders, a common characteristic, also, of weak human play.

Since this is our first example of actual play on a computer, it is worth looking a bit at the programming and machine problems. In a normal 8×8 game of chess there are about 30 legal alternatives at each move, on the average, thus looking two moves ahead brings 30^4 continuations, about 800,000, into consideration. In the reduced 6×6 game, the designers estimate the average number of alternatives at about 20, giving a total of about 160,000 continuations per move. Even with this reduction of five to one, there are still a lot of positions to be looked at. By comparison, the best evidence suggests that a human player considers considerably less than 100 positions in the analysis of a move. (De Groot, 1946) The Los Alamos program was able to make a move in about 12 minutes on the average. To do this the code had to be very simple and straightforward. This can be seen by the size of the program—only 600 words. In a sense, the machine barely glanced at each position it evaluated. The two measures in the evaluation function are obtained directly from the process of looking at continuations: changes in material are noticed if the moves are captures, and the mobility score for a position is equal to the number of new positions to which it leads—hence is computed almost without effort when exploring all continuations.

The Los Alamos program tests the limits of simplification in the direction of minimizing the amount of information required for each position evaluated, just as Turing's program tests the limits in the direction of minimizing the amount of exploration of continuations. These programs, especially the Los Alamos one, provide real anchor points. They show that, with very little in the way of complexity, we have at least entered the arena of human play—we can beat a beginner.

Bernstein's Program

Over the last two years Alex Bernstein, a chess player and programmer at IBM, has constructed a chess-playing program for the IBM 704 (for the full 8×8 board) (Bernstein et al., 1958a; 1958b). This program has been in partial operation for the last 6 months, and has now played one full game plus a number of shorter sequences. It, too, is in the Shannon tradition, but it takes an extremely important step in the direction of greater sophistication: only a fraction of the legal alternatives and continuations are considered. There is a series of subroutines, which we can call plausible move generators, that propose the moves to be considered. Each of these generators is related to some feature of the game: King safety, development, defending own men, attacking opponent's men, and so on. The program considers at most seven alternatives, which are obtained by operating the generators in priority order, the most important first, until the seven are accumulated.

The program explores continuations two moves ahead, just as the Los Alamos program did. However, it uses the plausible move generators at each stage, so that, at most, seven direct continuations are considered from any given position. For its evaluation function it uses the ratio of two sums, one for White and one for Black. Each sum consists of four weighted factors: material, King defense, area control, and mobility. The program minimaxes and chooses the alternative with the greatest effective value.

The program's play is uneven. Blind spots occur that are very striking; on the other hand, it sometimes plays very well for a series of moves. It has never beaten anyone, as far as we know; in the one full game it played it was beaten by a good player (Bernstein et al., 1958b), and it has never been pitted against weak players to establish how good it is.

Bernstein's program gives us our first information about radical selectivity, in move generation and analysis. At seven moves per position, it examines only 2,500 final positions two moves deep, out of about 800,000 legal continuations. That it still plays at all tolerably with a reduction in search by a factor of 300 implies that the selection mechanism is fairly effective. Of course, the selections follow the common and tested lore of the chess world; so that the significance of the reduction lies in showing that this lore is being successfully captured in mechanism. On the other hand, such radical selection should give the program a strong proclivity to overlook moves and consequences. The selective mechanisms in Bernstein's program have none of the checks and balances that exist in human selection on the chess board. And this is what we find. For example, in one situation a Bishop was successively attacked by three pawns, each time retreating one square to a post where the next pawn could attack it. The program remained oblivious to this possibility since the successive pawn pushes that attacked the Bishop were never proposed as plausible moves by the generators. But this is nothing to be unhappy about. Any particular difficulty is removable: in the case of the Bishop, by adding another move generator responsive to another feature of the board. This kind of error correction is precisely how the body of practical knowledge about chess programs and chess play will accumulate, gradually teaching us the right kinds of selectivity.

Every increase in sophistication of performance is paid for by an increase in the complexity of the program. The move generators and the components of the static evaluation require varied and diverse information about each position. This implies both more program and more computing time per position than with the Los Alamos program. From Table 1, we observe that Bernstein's program takes 7,000 words, the Los Alamos program only 600 words: a factor of about 10. As for time per position, both programs take about the same time to produce a move—8 and 12 minutes, respectively. Since the increase in problem size of the 8×8 board over the 6×6 board (about 5 to 1) is approximately canceled by the increase in speed of the IBM 704 over the MANIAC (also about 5 to 1, counting the increased power of the 704 order code), we can say they would both produce moves in the same

8×8 game in the same time. Hence the increase in amount of processing per move in Bernstein's program approximately cancels the gain of 300 to 1 in selectivity that this more complex processing achieves. This is so, even though Bernstein's program is coded to attain maximum speed by the use of fixed tables, direct machine coding, and so on.

We have introduced the comparison in order to focus on computing speed vs. selectivity as sources of improvement in complex programs. It is not possible, unfortunately, to compare the two programs in performance level except very crudely. We should compare an 8×8 version of the Los Alamos program with the Bernstein program, and we also need more games with each to provide reliable estimates of performance. Since the 8×8 version of the Los Alamos program will be better than the 6×6, compared to human play, let us assume for purposes of argument that the Los Alamos and Bernstein programs are roughly comparable in performance. To a rough approximation, then, we have two programs that achieve the same quality of performance with the same total effort by two different routes: the Los Alamos program by using no selectivity and being very fast, and the Bernstein program by using a large amount of selectivity and taking much more effort per position examined in order to make the selection.

The point we wish to make is that this equality is an accident: that selectivity is a very powerful device and speed a very weak device for improving the performance of complex programs. For instance, suppose both the Los Alamos and the Bernstein programs were to explore three moves deep instead of two as they now do. Then the Los Alamos program would take about 1,000 times (30^2) as long as now to make a move, whereas Bernstein's program would take about 50 times as long (7^2), the latter gaining a factor of 20 in the total computing effort required per move. The significant feature of chess is the exponential growth of positions to be considered with depth of analysis. As analysis deepens, greater computing effort per position soon pays for itself, since it slows the growth in number of positions to be considered. The comparison of the two programs at a greater depth is relevant since the natural mode of improvement of the Los Alamos program is to increase the speed enough to allow explorations three moves deep. Furthermore, attempts to introduce selectivity in the Los Alamos program will be extremely costly relative to the cost of additional selectivity in the Bernstein program.

One more calculation might be useful to emphasize the value of heuristics that eliminate branches to be explored. Suppose we had a branching tree in which our program was exploring n moves deep, and let this tree have four branches at each node. If we could double the speed of the program—that is, consider twice as many positions for the same total effort—then this improvement would let us look half a move deeper $(n + \frac{1}{2})$. If, on the other hand, we could double the selectivity—that is, only consider two of the four branches at each node, then we could look twice as deep $(2n)$. It is clear that we could afford to pay an apparently high computing cost per position to achieve this selectivity.

To summarize, Bernstein's program introduces both sophistication and complication to the chess program. Although in some respects—e.g., depth of analysis—it still uses simple uniform rules, in selecting moves to be considered it introduces a set of powerful heuristics which are taken from successful chess practice, and drastically reduce the number of moves considered at each position.

Newell, Shaw, and Simon Program

Although our own work on chess started in 1955 (Newell, 1955), it took a prolonged vacation during a period in which we were developing programs that discover proofs for theorems in symbolic logic. (Newell *et al.*, 1956; 1957) In a fundamental sense, proving theorems and playing chess involve the same problem: reasoning with heuristics that select fruitful paths of exploration in a space of possibilities that grows exponentially. The same dilemmas of speed vs. selection and uniformity vs. sophistication exist in both problem domains. Likewise, the programming costs attendant upon complexity seem similar for both. So we have recently returned to the chess programming problem equipped with ideas derived from the work on logic.

The historical antecedents of our own work are somewhat different from those of the other investigators we have mentioned. We have been primarily concerned with describing and understanding human thinking and decision processes (Newell *et al.*, 1958a). However, both for chess players and for chess programmers, the structure of the task dictates in considerable part the approach taken, and our current program can be described in the same terms we have used for the others. Most of the positive features of the earlier programs are clearly discernible: The basic factorization introduced by Shannon; Turing's concept of a dead position; and the move generators, associated with features of the chess situation, used by Bernstein. Perhaps the only common characteristic of the other programs that is strikingly absent from ours—and from human thinking also, we believe—is the use of numerical additive evaluation functions to compare alternatives.

Basic Organization

Figure 3 shows the two-way classification in terms of which the program is organized. There is a set of goals, each of which corresponds to some feature of the chess situation—King safety, material balance, center control, and so on. Each goal has associated with it a collection of processes, corresponding to the categories outlined by Shannon: a move generator, a static evaluation routine, and a move generator for analysis. The routine for integrating the static evaluations into an effective value for a proposed move, and the final choice procedure are both common routines for the whole program, and therefore are not present in each separate component.

	Goal specification	Move generator	Static evaluation	Analysis generator
King safety				
Material balance				
GOALS — Center control				
Development				
King-side attack				
Promotion				

Figure 3. Basic organization of NSS chess program.

Goals

The goals form a basic set of modules out of which the program is constructed. The goals are independent: any of them can be added to the program or removed without affecting the feasibility of the remaining goals. At the beginning of each move a preliminary analysis establishes that a given chess situation (a "state") obtains, and this chess situation evokes a set of goals appropriate to it. The goal specification routines shown for each goal in Figure 3 provide information that is used in this initial selection of goals. The goals are put on a list with the most crucial ones first. This goal list then controls the remainder of the processing: the selection of alternatives, the continuations to be explored, the static evaluation, and the final choice procedure.

What kind of game the program will play clearly depends on what goals are available to it and chosen by it for any particular move. One purpose of this modular construction is to provide flexibility over the course of the game in the kinds of considerations the program spends its effort upon. For example, the goal of denying stalemate to the opponent is relevant only in certain endgame situations where the opponent is on the defensive and the King is in a constrained position. Another purpose of the modular construction is to give us a flexible tool for investigating chess programs—so that entirely new considerations can be added to an already complex but operational program.

Move Generation

The move generator associated with each goal proposes alternative moves relevant to that goal. These move generators carry the burden of finding positive reasons for doing things. Thus, only the center-control generator will propose $P-Q4$ as a good move in the opening; only the material-balance generator will propose moving out of danger a piece that is *en prise*. These move generators correspond to the move generators in Bernstein's program, except that here they are used exclusively to generate alternative moves and are not used to generate the continuations that are explored in the course of analyzing a move. In Bernstein's program—and *a fortiori* in the Los Alamos program—identical generators are used both to find a set of alternative moves from which the final choice of next move is made, and also to find the continuations that must be explored to assess the consequences of reaching a given position. In our program the latter function is performed by a separate set of analysis generators.

Evaluation

Each move proposed by a move generator is assigned a value by an analysis procedure. We said above that the move generators have the responsibility for finding positive reasons for making moves. Correspondingly, the analysis procedure is concerned only with the acceptability of a move once it has been generated. A generator proposes; the analysis procedure disposes.

The value assigned to a move is obtained from a series of evaluations, one for each goal. The value is a vector, if you like to think of it that way, except that it does not necessarily have the same components throughout the chess game, since the components derive from the basic list of goals that is constructed from the position at the beginning of each move. Each component expresses acceptability or unacceptability of a position from the viewpoint of the goal corresponding to that component. Thus, the material-balance goal would assess only the loss or gain of material; the development goal, the relative gain or loss of *tempi*; the pawn structure goal, the doubling and isolation of pawns; and so on. The value for a component is in some cases a number—e.g., in the material-balance goal where we use conventional piece values: 9 for a Queen, 5 for a Rook, and so on. In other cases the component value is dichotomous, simply designating the presence or absence of some property, like the blocking of a move or the doubling of a pawn.

As in the other chess programs, our analysis procedure consists of three parts: exploring continuations to some depth, forming static evaluations, and integrating these to establish an effective value for the move. By a process that we will describe later, the analysis move generators associated with the goals determine what branches will be explored from each position reached. At the final positon of each continuation, a value is assigned using the static evaluation routines of each goal to provide the component values. The effective value for a proposed move is obtained by minimaxing on these final static values. Minimaxing seems especially appropriate for an analysis procedure that is inherently conservative, such as an acceptance test.

To be able to minimax, it must be possible to compare any two values and decide which is preferable, or whether they are equal in value. For values of the kind we are using, there must be a complete ordering on the vectors that determine them. Further, this ordering must allow variation in the size and composition of the goal list. We use a lexicographic ordering: Each component value is completely ordered within itself; and higher priority values completely dominate lower priority values, as determined by the order of goals on the goal list. To compare two values, then, the first components are compared. If one of these is preferable to the other, this determines the preference for the entire value. If the two components are equal, then the second pair of components is compared. If these are unequal in value, they determine the preference for the entire value, otherwise the next components are compared, and so on.

Final Choice

It is still necessary to select the move to be played from the alternative moves, given the values assigned to them by the analysis procedure. In the other programs the final choice procedure was simply an extension of the minimax: choose the one with highest value. Its obviousness rests on the assumption that the set of alternatives to be considered is a fixed set. If this assumption is relaxed, by generating alternatives sequentially, then other procedures are possible. The simplest, and the one we are currently using, is to set an acceptance level as final criterion and simply take the first acceptable move. The executive routine proceeds down the goal list, activating the move generators of the goals in order of priority, so that important moves are considered first. The executive saves the best move that has been found up to any given moment, and if no moves reach the specified level of acceptability, it makes the best move that was found.

Another possible final choice procedure is to search for an acceptable move that has a double function—that is, a move that is proposed by more than one generator as having a positive effect. With this plan, the executive proceeds down the list of goals in order of priority. After finding an acceptable move, it activates the rest of the generators to see if the move will be proposed a second time. If not, it works from the list of unevaluated moves just obtained to see if any move proposed twice is acceptable. If not, it takes the first acceptable move or the best if none has proved acceptable. This type of executive has considerable plausibility, since the concept of multiple function plays an important role in the chess literature.

Yet a third variation in the final choice procedure is to divide the goals into two lists. The first list contains all the features that should normally be attended to; the second list contains features that are rare in occurrence but either very good or very bad if they do occur. On this second list would be goals that relate to sacrificial combinations, hidden forks or pins that are two moves away, and so on. The executive finds an acceptable move with the first, normal list. Then the rest of the available time is spent looking for various rare consequences derived from the second list.

Analysis

In describing the basic organization of the program we skipped over the detailed mechanism for exploring continuations, simply assuming that certain continuations were explored, the static values computed, and the effective value obtained by minimaxing. But it is clear that the exact mechanisms are very important. The analysis move generators are the main agents of selectivity in the program: They determine for each position arrived at in the analysis just which further branches must be explored, hence the average number of branches in the exploration tree and its average depth. The move generators for the alternatives and the final choice procedure also affect the amount of exploration by determining what moves are considered. But their selection operates only once per move, whereas the selectivity of the analysis generators operates at each step (half-move) of the exploration. Hence the selectivity of the analysis generators varies geometrically with the average depth of analysis.

The exploration of continuations is based on a generalization of Turing's concept of a dead position. Recall that Turing applied this notion to exchanges, arguing that it made no sense to count material on the board until all exchanges that were to take place had been carried out. We apply the same notion to each feature of the board: The static evaluation of a goal is meaningful only if the position being evaluated is "dead" with respect to the feature associated with the goal—that is, only if no moves are likely to be made that could radically alter that component static value. The analysis-move generators for each goal determine for any position they are applied to whether the position is dead with respect to their goal; if not, they generate the moves that are both plausible and might seriously affect the static value of the goal. Thus the selection of continuations to be explored is dictated by the search for a position that is dead with respect to all the goals, so that, finally, a static evaluation can be made. Both the number of branches from each position and the depth of the exploration are controlled in this way. Placid situations will produce search trees containing only a handful of positions; complicated middle game situations will produce much larger ones.

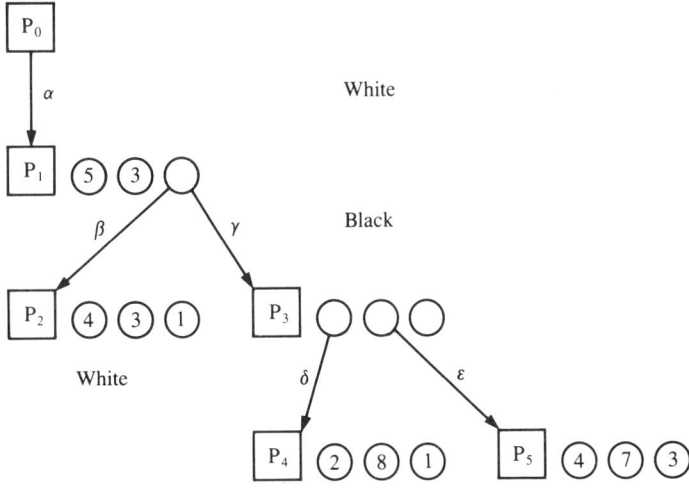

Figure 4. Analysis.

To make the mechanics of the analysis clearer, Figure 4 gives a schematic example of a situation. P_0 is the initial position from which White, the machine, must make a move. The arrow, α, leading to P_1 represents an alternative proposed by some move generator. The move is made internally (i.e., "considered"), yielding position P_1, and the analysis procedure must then obtain the value of P_1, which will become the value imputed to the proposed alternative, α. Taking each goal from the goal list in turn, an attempt is made to produce a static evaluation. For P_1 this attempt is successful for the first and second components, yielding values of 5 and 3, respectively. (Numbers are used for values throughout this example to keep the picture simple; in reality, various sets of ordered symbols are used, their exact structure depending on the nature of the computation.) However, the third component does not find the position dead, and generates two moves, β and γ. The first, β, is considered, leading to P_2, and an attempt is made to produce a static evaluation of it. This proceeds just as with P_1, except that this time all components find the position dead and the static value (4, 3, 1) is obtained. Then the second move, γ, from P_1 is considered, leading to P_3. The attempt to produce a static value for P_3 runs into difficulties with the first component, which generates one move, δ, to resolve the instability of P_3 with respect to its feature. This move leads to P_4 which is evaluable, having the value (2, 8, 1). However, the second component also finds P_3 not dead and generates a single move, ε, leading to P_5. This is also evaluable, having the value (4, 7, 3). The third component finds P_3 dead and therefore contributes no additional moves. Thus the exploration comes to an end with all terminal positions yielding complete static values. Since it is White's move at P_3, White will choose the move with the highest value. This is ε, the move to P_5, with a value of (4, 7, 3) (the first component dominates). The value of this move is the effective value assigned to P_3. Black now has a choice between the move, β, to P_2, yielding (4, 3, 1) and the move, γ, to P_3, yielding (4, 7, 3). Since Black is minimizing, he will choose β. This yields (4, 3, 1) as the effective value of the alternative, α, that leads to P_1, and the end of the analysis.

The minimaxing operation is conducted concurrently with the generation of branches. Thus if P_5, which has a value of (4, 7, 3), had been generated prior to P_4 no further moves would have been generated from P_3, since it is already apparent that Black will prefer P_2 to P_3. The value of P_3 is at least as great as the value of P_5, since it is White's move and he will maximize.

This analysis procedure is not a simple one, either conceptually or technically. There are a number of possible ways to terminate search and reach an effective evaluation. There is no built-in rule that guarantees that the search will converge; the success depends heavily on the ability to evaluate statically. The more numerous the situations that can be recognized as having a certain value without having to generate continuations, the more rapidly the search will terminate. The number of plausible moves that affect the value is also of consequence, as we discussed in connection with Bernstein's program, but there are limits beyond which this cannot be reduced. For example, suppose that a position is not dead with respect to Material Balance and that one of the machine's pieces is attacked. Then it can try to (a) take the attacker, (b) add a defender, (c) move the attacked piece, (d) pin the defender, (e) interpose a man between the attacker and the attacked, or (f) launch a counterattack. Alternatives of each of these types must be sought and tried—they are all plausible and may radically affect the Material Balance.

As an example of the heuristics involved in achieving a static evaluation, imagine that the above situation occurred after several moves of an exploration, and that the machine was already a pawn down from the early part of the continuation. Then, being on the defensive implies a very remote chance of recovering the pawn. Consequently, a negative value of at least a pawn can be assigned to the position statically. This is usually enough in connection with concurrent minimaxing to eliminate the continuation from further consideration.

Summary

Let us summarize our entire program. It is organized in terms of a set of goals: these are conceptual units of chess—King safety, passed pawns, and so on. Each goal has several routines associated with it:

(1) A routine that specifies the goal in terms of the given position;
(2) A move generator that finds moves positively related to carrying out the goal;
(3) A procedure for making a static evaluation of any position with respect to the goal, which essentially measures acceptability;
(4) An analysis move generator that finds the continuations required to resolve a situation into dead positions.

The alternative moves come from the move generators, considered in the order of priority of their respective goals. Each move, when it is generated, is subjected to an analysis. This analysis generates an exploration of the continuations following from the move until dead positions are reached and static evaluations computed for them. The static evaluations are compared, using minimax as an inference procedure, so that an effective value is eventually produced for each alternative. The final choice procedure can rest on any of several criteria: for instance, choosing the first move generated that has an effective value greater than a given norm.

Examples of Goals

In this section we will give two examples of goals and their various components to illustrate the type of program we are constructing. The first example is the center-control goal:

Center Control

Specification
Goal is always operative unless there are no more center pawns to be moved to the fourth rank.

Move generator
(1) Move P − Q4, P − K4 (primary moves).
(2) Prevent the opponent from making his primary moves.
(3) Prepare your own primary moves:
    (a) add a defender to Q4 or K4 square;
    (b) eliminate a block to moving QP or KP.

Static evaluation
Count the number of blocks to making the primary moves.

Analysis move generators
None; static evaluation is always possible.

To interpret this a little: Goals are proposed in terms of the general situation—e.g., for the opening game. The list of goals is made up for a position by applying, in turn, the specification of each of the potential goals. Whether any particular goal is declared relevant or irrelevant to the position depends on whether or not the position meets its specification. For center control, no special information need be gathered, but the goal is declared irrelevant if the center pawns have already been moved to the fourth rank or beyond.

The most important part of the center-control program is its move generator. The generator is concerned with two primary moves: P − Q4 and P − K4. It will propose these moves, if they are legal, and it is the responsibility of the analysis procedures (for all the goals) to reject the moves if there is anything wrong with them—e.g., if the pawns will be taken when moved. So, after 1 P − Q4 P − Q4, the center-control move generator will propose 2 P − K4, but (as we shall see) the evaluation routine of the material balance goal will reject this move because of the loss of material that would result from 2 ... P × P. The center-control generator will have nothing to do with tracing out these consequences.

If the primary moves cannot be made, the center-control move generator has two choices: to prepare them, or to prevent the opponent from making his primary moves. The program's style of play will depend very much on whether prevention has priority over preparation (as it does in our description of the generator above), or *vice versa*. The ordering we have proposed, which puts prevention first, probably produces more aggressive and slightly better opening play than the reverse ordering. Similarly, the style of play depends on whether the Queen's pawn or the King's pawn is considered first.

The move generator approaches the subgoal of preventing the opponent's primary moves (whenever this subgoal is evoked) in the following way. It first determines whether the opponent can make one of these moves by trying the move and then obtaining an evaluation of it from the opponent's viewpoint. If one or both of the primary moves are not rejected, preventive moves will serve some purpose. Under these conditions, the center-control move generator will generate them by finding moves that bring another attacker to bear on the opponent's K4 and Q4 squares or that pin a defender of one of these squares. Among the moves this generator will normally propose are N − B3 and BP − B4.

The move generator approaches the subgoal of preparing its own primary moves by first determining why the moves cannot be made without preparation—that is, whether the pawn is blocked from moving by a friendly piece, or whether the fourth rank square is unsafe for the pawn. In the former case, the generator proposes moves for the blocking piece; in the latter case, it finds moves that will add defenders to the fourth rank square, drive away or pin attackers, and so on.

So much for the center-control move generators, The task of the evaluation routine for the center-control goal is essentially negative—to assure that moves, proposed by some other goal, will not be made that jeopardize control of the center. The possibility is simply ignored that a move generator for some other goal will inadvertently provide a move that contributes to center control. Hence, the static evaluation for center control is only concerned that moves not be made that interfere with P − K4 and P − Q4. A typical example of a move that the center-control evaluation routine is prepared to reject is B − Q3 or B − K3 before the respective center pawns have been moved.

The second example of a goal is material balance. This is a much more extensive and complicated goal than center control, and handles all questions about gain and loss of material in the immediate situation. It does not consider threats like pins and forks, where the actual exchange is still a move away; other goals must take care of these. Both the negative and positive aspects of material must be included in a single goal, since they compensate directly for each other, and material must often be spent to gain material.

Material Balance

Specification
A list of exchanges on squares occupied by own men, and a list of exchanges on squares occupied by opponent's men. For each exchange square there is listed the target man, the list of attackers, and the list of defenders (including, e.g., both Rooks if they are doubled on the appropriate rank or file). For each exchange square a static exchange value is computed by playing out the exchange with all the attackers and defenders assuming no indirect consequences like pins, discovered attacks, etc. Exchange squares are listed in order of static exchange value, largest negative value first. Squares with positive values for the defender are dropped from the list. At the same time a list of all pinned men is generated.

Move generator

Starting with the exchange squares at the top of the list, appropriate moves are generated. If the most important exchange square is occupied by the opponent, captures by attacking pieces are proposed, the least valuable attacker being tried first. If the move is rejected because the attacker is pinned, the next attacker is tried. If the move is rejected for another reason, the possibility of exchange on this square is abandoned, and the next exchange square examined.

If the exchange square under examination is occupied by the program's own piece, a whole series of possible moves is generated:

(a) Try "no move" to see if attack is damaging.
(b) Capture the attacker.
(c) Add a defender not employed in another defense.
(d) Move the attacked piece.
(e) Interpose a man between the attacker and the target; but not a man employed elsewhere, and not if the interposer will be captured.
(f) Pin the attacker with a man not employed elsewhere and not capturable by the attacker.

Static evaluation

For each exchange square, add the values of own men and subtract the values of opponent's men. Use conventional values: $Q-9$, $R-5$, $B-N-3$, $P-1$.

Move generators toward dead positions

A position is dead for this goal only if there are no exchanges, i.e., if the specification list defined above is empty. Then a static evaluation can be made. Otherwise, the various kinds of moves defined under the move generator are made to resolve the exchanges. However, various additional qualifications are introduced to reduce the number of continuations examined. For example, if in a particular exchange material has already been lost and a man is still under attack, the position is treated as dead, since it is unlikely that the loss will be recovered. When a dead position is reached, the static evaluation is used to find a value for the position.

It is impossible to provide here more than a sketchy picture of the heuristics contained in this one goal. It should be obvious from this brief description that there are a lot of them, and that they incorporate a number of implicit assumptions about what is important, and what is not, on the chess board.

Performance of the Program

We cannot say very much about the behavior of the program. It was coded in the spring of 1958 and is not yet fully debugged. Only two goals have been coded: material balance and center control. Development is fully defined as well as a pawn structure goal sufficient for the opening, where its role is primarily to prevent undesirable structures like doubled pawns. These four

Figure 5

goals—material balance, center control, development and pawn structure—
in this order seem an appropriate set for the first phase of the opening game.
Several others—King safety, serious threats, and gambits—need to be added
for full opening play. The serious threats goal could be limited initially to
forks and pins.

We have done considerable hand simulation with the program in typical
positions. Two examples will show how the goals interact. In Figure 5 the
machine is White and the play has been 1 P – K4 P – K4. Assuming the goal
list mentioned above, the material balance move generator will not propose
any moves since there are no exchanges on the board. The center-control
generator will propose P – Q4, which is the circled move in the figure. (In the
illustration, we assume the center-control move generator has the order of
the primary moves reversed from the order described earlier.) This move is
rejected—as it should be—and it is instructive to see why. The move is
proposed for analysis. Material balance does not find the position dead, since
there is an exchange, and generates Black's move, 2 ... P × P. The resulting
position is still not dead, and 3 Q × P, is generated. The position is now dead
for material balance, with no gain or loss in material. The first component
of the static evaluation is "even." There are obviously no blocks to pawn
moves, so that the center-control static value is acceptable. However, the third
component, development, finds the position not dead because there is now
an exposed piece, the Queen. It generates replies that both attack the piece and
develop—i.e., add a tempo. The move 3 ... N – QB3 is generated. This forces
a Queen move, resulting in loss of a tempo for White. Hence development
rejects the move, 2 P – Q4. (The move 3 ... B – B4 would not have sufficed
for rejection by development, since the Bishop could be taken.)

The second example, shown in Figure 6, is from a famous game of Morphy
against Duke Karl of Brunswick and Count Isouard. Play had proceeded
1 P – K4 P – K4; 2 N – KB3 P – Q3; 3 P – Q4. Suppose the machine is Black
in this position. The move 3 ... B – N5 is proposed by material balance to
deal with the exchange that threatens Black with the loss of a pawn. This is
the move made by the Duke and Count. The analysis proceeds by 4 P × P
P × P. This opens up a new exchange possibility with the Queens, which is

Figure 6

tried: 5 Q × Q K × Q; 6 N × P. Thus the pawn is lost in this continuation. Hence, alternative moves are considered at Black's nearest option, which is move 4, since there are no alternative ways of recapturing the Queen at move 5. The capture of White's Knight is possible, so we get: 4′ ... B × N; 5′ P × B P × P; 6′ Q × Q K × Q. This position is rejected by development since the forced King move loses Black his castling privilege, and this loss affects the tempo count. This is a sufficient reason to reject the move 3 ... B − N5, without even examining the stronger continuation, 5″ Q × B, that Morphy as White chose. In our program, 5 P × B is generated before 5 Q × B. Either reply shows that 3 ... B − N5 is unsound.

One purpose of these examples is to illustrate a heuristic for constructing chess programs that we incline to rather strongly. We wish not only to have the program make good moves, but to do so for the right reasons. The chess commentary above is not untypical of human analysis. It also represents rather closely the analysis made by the program. We think this is sound design philosophy in constructing complex programs. To take another example: the four-goal opening program will not make sacrifices, and conversely, will always accept gambits. The existing program is unable to balance material against positional advantage. The way to make the program take account of sacrifices is to introduce an additional goal having to do with them explicitly. The corresponding heuristic for a human chess player is: do not make sacrifices until you understand what a sacrifice is. Stated in still another way, part of the success of human play depends on the emergence of appropriate concepts. One major theme in chess history, for example, is the emergence of the concept of the center and the notion of what it means to control the center. One should not expect the equivalent of such a concept simply to emerge from computation based on quite other features of the position.

Programming

The program we have been describing is extremely complicated. Almost all elements of the original framework put forward by Shannon, which were handled initially by simply uniform rules, have been made variable, and dependent on rather complicated considerations. Many special and highly particular heuristics are used to select moves and decide on evaluations. The program can be expected to be much larger, more intricate, and to require much more processing per position considered than even the Bernstein program.

In the introduction to this paper we remarked on the close connection between complexity and communication. Processes as complex as the Los Alamos program are unthinkable without languages like current machine codes in which to specify them. The Bernstein program is already a very complicated program in machine code; it involved a great deal of coding effort and parts of it required very sophisticated coding techniques. Our own program is already beyond the reach of direct machine coding: It requires a more powerful language.

In connection with the work on theorem-proving programs we have been developing a series of languages, called information processing languages (IPL's). (Newell and Shaw, 1957) The current chess program is coded in one of them, IPL-IV. An information processing language is an interpretive pseudocode—that is, there exists a program in JOHNNIAC machine code that is capable of interpreting a program in IPL and executing it. When operating, JOHNNIAC contains both the machine code and the IPL code.

It is not possible to give in this paper a description of IPL-IV or of the programming techniques involved in constructing the chess program. Basically IPL is designed to manipulate lists, and to allow extremely complicated structures of lists to be built up during the execution of a program without incurring intolerable problems of memory assignment and program planning. It allows unlimited hierarchies of subroutines to be easily defined, and permits recursive definition of routines. As it stands—i.e., prior to coding a particular problem—it is independent of subject matter (although biased towards list manipulation in the same sense that algebraic compilers are biased towards numerical evaluation of algebraic expressions). To code chess, a complete "chess vocabulary" is built up from definitions in IPL. This vocabulary consists of a set of processes for expressing basic concepts in chess: tests of whether a man bears on another man, or whether two men are on the same diagonal; processes for finding the direction between two men, or the first man in a given direction from another; and processes that express iterations over all men of a given type, or over all squares of a given rank. There are about 100 terms in this basic process vocabulary. The final chess program, as we have been describing it in this paper, is largely code in terms of the chess vocabulary. Thus there are four language "levels" in the chess program: JOHNNIAC machine code, general IPL, basic chess vocabulary, and finally the chess program itself.

We can now make a rough assessment of the size and complexity of this program in comparison with the other programs. The table indicates that the program now consists of 6,000 words and will probably increase to 16,000.

Table 1. Comparison of current chess programs.

	Turing	Los Alamos Kister, Stein, Ulam, Walden, Wells	Bernstein Roberts, Arbuckle, Belsky	NSS Newell, Shaw, Simon
Vital statistics				
Date	1951	1956	1957	1958
Board	8 × 8	6 × 6	8 × 8	8 × 8
Computer	Hand simulation	MANIAC-I 11,000 ops/sec	IBM 704 42,000 pos/sec	RAND JOHNNIAC 20,000 ops/sec
Chess program				
Alternatives	All moves	All moves	7 plausible moves Sequence of move generators	Variable Sequence of move generators
Depth of analysis	Until dead (exchanges only)	All moves 2 moves deep	7 plausible moves 2 moves deep	Until dead Each goal generates moves
Static evaluation	Numerical Many factors	Numerical Material, Mobility	Numerical Material, Mobility, Area control, King defense	Nonnumerical Vector of values Acceptance by goals
Integration of values	Minimax	Minimax (modified)	Minimax	Minimax
Final choice	Material dominates Otherwise, best value	Best value	Best value	1. First acceptable 2. Double function

Table 1. (*continued*)

	Turing	Los Alamos Kister, Stein, Ulam, Walden, Wells	Bernstein Roberts, Arbuckle, Belsky	NSS Newell, Shaw, Simon
Programming				
Language		Machine code	Machine code	IPL-IV, interpretive
Data scheme		Single board No records	Single board Centralized tables Recompute	Single board Decentralized List structure Recompute
Time	Minutes	12 min/move	8 min/move	1–10 hrs/move (est.)
Space		600 words	7000 words	Now 6,000 words, est. 16,000
Results				
Experience	1 game	3 games (no longer exists)	2 games	0 games Some hand simulation
Description	Loses to weak player Aimless Subtleties of evaluation lost	Beats weak player Equivalent to human with 20 games experience	Passable amateur Blind spots Positional	Good in spots (opening) No aggressive goals yet

The upper bound is dictated by the size of the JOHNNIAC drum and the fact that JOHNNIAC has no tapes. In terms of the pyramiding structure described above, this program is already much larger than Bernstein's although it is difficult to estimate the "expansion" factor involved in converting IPL to machine code. (For one thing, it is not clear how an "equivalent" machine coded program would be organized.) However, only about 1,000 words of our program are in machine code, and 3,000 words are IPL programs, some of which are as many as ten definitional steps removed from machine code. Further, all 12,000 words on the drum will be IPL program; no additional data or machine code are planned.

The estimated time per move, as shown in Table 1, is from 1 to 10 hours, although moves in very placid situations like the opening will take only a few minutes. Even taking into account the difference in speed between the 704 and JOHNNIAC, our program still appears to be at least ten times slower than Bernstein's. This gap reflects partly the mismatch between current computers and computers constructed to do efficiently the kind of information processing required in chess. (Shaw *et al.*, 1958) To use an interpretive code, such as IPL, is in essence to simulate an "IPL computer" with a current computer. A large price has to be paid in computing effort for this simulation over and above the computing effort for the chess program itself. However, this gap also reflects the difficulty of specifying complex processes; we have not been able to write these programs and attend closely to the efficiency issue at the same time.

On both counts we have felt it important to explore the kind of languages and programming techniques appropriate to the task of specifying complex programs, and to ignore for the time being the costs we were incurring.

Conclusion

We have now completed our survey of attempts to program computers to play chess. There is clearly evident in this succession of efforts a steady development toward the use of more and more complex programs and more and more selective heuristics; and toward the use of principles of play similar to those used by human players. Partly, this trend represents—at least in our case—a deliberate attempt to simulate human thought processes. In even larger part, however, it reflects the constraints that the task itself imposes upon any information processing system that undertakes to perform it. We believe that any information processing system—a human, a computer, or any other—that plays chess successfully will use heuristics generically similar to those used by humans.

We are not unmindful of the radical differences between men and machines at the level of componentry. Rather, we are arguing that for tasks that could not be performed at all without very great selectivity—and chess is certainly one of these—the main goal of the program must be to achieve this selection.

The higher-level programs involved in accomplishing this will look very much the same whatever processes are going on at more microscopic levels. Nor are we saying that programs will not be adapted to the powerful features of the computing systems that are used—e.g., the high speed and precision of current digital computers, which seems to favor exploring substantial numbers of continuations. However, none of the differences known to us—in speed, memory, and so on—affect the essential nature of the task: search in a space of exponentially growing possibilities. Hence the adaptations to the idiosyncrasies of particular computers will all be secondary in importance, although they will certainly exist and may be worth while.

The complexity of heuristic programs requires a more powerful language for communicating with the computer than the language of elementary machine instructions. We have seen that this necessity has already mothered the creation of new information processing languages. But even with these powerful interpretive languages, communication with the machine is difficult and cumbersome. The next step that must be taken is to write programs that will give computers a problem-solving ability in understanding and interpreting instructions that is commensurable with their problem-solving ability in playing chess and proving theorems.

The interpreter that will transform the machine into an adequate student for a human instructor will not be a passive, algorithmic translator—as even the most advanced interpreters and compilers are today—but an active, complex, heuristic problem-solving program. As our explorations of heuristic programs for chess playing and other tasks teach us how to build such an interpreter, they will at last enable us to make the transition from the low-level equilibrium at which man–machine communication now rests to the high-level equilibrium that is certainly attainable.

2.3. Before the Jet Age

DAVID N. L. LEVY

Originally published in: *Chess and Computers*, David N. L. Levy, 1976, pp. 71–112.
© 1976 David N. L. Levy.

The Anderson/Cody Program

In 1959 a Canadian program was demonstrated at the University of Toronto. It was written by Frank Anderson, an International Master, and Bob Cody, and it ran on an IBM 605 computer. The program did not play a complete game but dealt only with simple pawn endings (the most complex was King and two pawns vs. King and pawn). The programmers devised a unique strategy that enabled their program to play these endings perfectly. Their first version could cope with more than 180,000 different positions, a figure that was increased in subsequent versions of the program. When the program was demonstrated at the Canadian Conference of Scientists it played against more than 50 different opponents, each of whom was allowed to choose his own starting position, given the small number of pawns. In each case the program played perfectly.

Unfortunately, the strategy that enabled these endings to be programmed successfully was never documented and the programmers no longer have any written record of it, nor are they able to remember it. In fact, Frank Anderson confessed to me recently that even at the time he could not explain why some of their strategies worked.

The Kotok Program

In 1961 Alan Kotok wrote a chess program for his bachelor's thesis at Massachusets Institute of Technology. His program was written under the guidance of John McCarthy, one of the leading figures in the world of Artificial Intelligence, who was then a professor at MIT.

Kotok's program performed a variable depth search. It looked ahead until a stable position had been reached or until its depth of search reached an arbitary maximum. In order to avoid growing enormous trees the program examined fewer and fewer successor positions as the depth of search increased. Moves were proposed by a plausible move generator whose job it was to find moves that fulfilled various goals. In this respect Kotok's work was similar to that of Newell, Shaw, and Simon. The plausible move generator supplied 4 moves at the root of the tree, 3 at the next level, then 2, 2, 1, 1, 1, 1, 0, 0, ..., etc. In addition to the plausible moves considered at each level the program examined captures and checks.

Kotok's evaluation function used four features: material, pawn structure, center control, and development. Looking at the board from the side of the player about to move, Kotok weighted the 16 center squares in the following way.

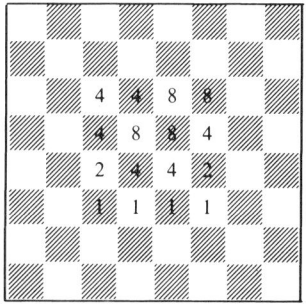

Presumably these weightings were designed to give more credit for attacking squares in the opponent's half of the board, and for attacking squares near his King (the weights 4, 4, 8, 8, for the squares on the sixth rank were adjusted to 8, 8, 4, 4, if the opponent had castled on the left-hand side of the board).

Each center square point was worth one-sixtieth of a pawn at the beginning of the game. After 20 moves center control became less important and after move 30 the feature was discarded.

The program assigned points for each developed piece: 1 for a pawn, rising to 3 or 4 for the other pieces. Each development point was worth one-fifteenth of a pawn at the start of the game but this value too was diminished as the game progressed.

Pawn structure points were each worth one-twentieth of a pawn: For each pawn on an open file the program scored 8 pawn structure points, for each isolated pawn −1, for a backward pawn −5, for a doubled pawn −3 and for a passed pawn 10.

Kotok's work began in the spring of 1961. By the time that he presented his thesis in 1962 his program had played four long game fragments, calculating for between 5 and 20 minutes per move. It played rather poor chess (even for a program) and in one of the four game fragments it made an illegal move, advancing a pawn two squares when the intervening square was occupied.

After graduating from MIT Kotok's interest in computer chess died but his program remained alive. When McCarthy left MIT to take charge of the Artificial Intelligence Laboratory at Stanford University he took Kotok's program with him and improved its tree-searching mechanism.

At the end of 1966 a four-game match began between the Kotok/McCarthy program, running on Stanford University's IBM 7090 computer, and a program developed at the Institute of Theoretical and Experimental Physics in Moscow which used a Soviet M-20 computer. The Soviet program was written by Arlazarov, Adelson-Velsky, Bitman (a Soviet Master), Uskov, and Zhivtovsky.

In two of the games both programs used a basic 3-ply search, in the other two they searched to a depth of 5-ply. The result of the match was an outstanding success for the Soivet program, even though it had been written along the lines of Shannon's primitive type-A strategy and run on a slower machine. The American program, as we have already shown, used Shannon's type-B strategy.

The Soviet program won two games and the other two were agreed drawn when one of them reached move 40. (This agreement, made before the start of the match, was prompted by the abysmal endgame play of both programs.) In the two unfinished games the Soviet program had advantages which would certainly have proved decisive in human master play.

The following article by Arlazarov and Bitman describes the basic elements of their program and analyses the four games of the match. It first appeared in *Shakhmaty vs. SSSR*, number 2, 1968.

Will Machines Ever Outplay Man? (USSR vs. USA)

Even now a lot of chess players are of the opinion that the outcome of a game which has reached a certain position depends not only on the position itself but also on the creative personalities of the players. And this is really so if the chess players are not able to calculate the variations to a sufficient number of moves ahead. In reality, though, the total number of positions which can occur is finite, and in consequence in any given position, including the starting position, the result is uniquely determined.

We have to stress that what we have said above is not just a question of chess or philosophical credo, but it is a fact which can be proved mathematically. Thus, the starting position is drawn or won for White or even won for Black, although we do not yet know which of the three possibilities is the case. If we were able to create a computer which could analyze all possible variations an arbitrary number of moves ahead, then, naturally, we should be able to resolve this question. Unfortunately (or luckily) there is no such machine; moreover, there never can be one. This fact, however, does not exclude the possibility of creating a computer, which with its "iron fist" would be able to defeat any man. People have learned to play chess quite well, and in doing so a human being comes far short of calculating all possible continuations in every position, but rather chooses a small number of them for further analysis. It is only because of this that it is possible to consider main variations quite deeply. This is the strength of a human being, but also his weakness.

A computer can work out the moves and estimate the advantages of the resulting positions much faster than human beings. So, if we can teach a machine to consider only the sensible continuations, then its advantage over a human being will become unquestionable. By the way, a computer plays even more creatively than a man. It does not have stereotypes and it more often finds unexpected and therefore beautiful solutions. The question now is, precisely what does our expression "sensible" mean? The strength of the computer's play depends to a large extent on the answer to this question.

The principles underlying the choice of sensible moves in the American and Soviet programs differ considerably. The completed games allow us to point out the strong and weak sides of these two approaches. The procedure of the American program was closer to that of a human being. On the first move it chose seven continuations by some criteria and for each of these it considered seven possible replies by the opponent. On its second move the program selected only five possibilities for each side. At each succeeding level the number of continuations chosen was reduced and from a certain point only a single-stranded variation was considered.

We, on the other hand, considered all possible continuations for both sides up to a certain level and thereafter only forcing ones: captures and checks. The merit of the first method is that the computer can look quite deeply into the position after the chosen moves; however, the possibility of a bad blunder at the beginning of the variation is not excluded.

Thanks to the fact that the Soviet program does not throw out anything during the first few moves it simply cannot fall into such transparent traps. On the other hand, in choosing among the variations analyzed our computer can err in not considering quiet moves deeply enough, even though forced variations can drag on as far as the fifteenth half-move. We define the depth of the calculations in our programs as the number of half-moves up to the beginning of the forced variations. For example, when we claim that the program plays the game with a depth of calculation of two half-moves it means that the computer considers its own move (really half a move) and the opponent's reply and then examines the consequences of forced variations following on the previous moves.

A forced variation can lead not only to the gain of material, but also to the acquisition of various positional advantages as a result of exchanges. These calculations are done by the chess estimating function [the scoring function—D.N.L.L.]. This takes into account such factors as the mobility of pieces, control of the center, and open lines and the safety of the King, and in respect of the pawn structure considers such factors as the phalanxes, support points, passed pawns, doubled pawns, isolated pawns, isolated pawns on an open file and so on. This estimating function is mainly intended for the opening and middle game, as, indeed, is the whole program.

In the endgame, however, it is more important to devise a plan for a few moves ahead, because the opponent has less opportunity to hinder its realization. Besides, there are considerably fewer plans for the endgame than in the middle game. So, by the end of the game, one can see the final position of very long variations and one can often be sure that a chain of simple moves will lead there.

A program for the endgame will have to be constructed in quite a different way from middle game programs, and the ideas underlying such a program have yet to be worked out properly. The American mathematicians had not yet studied the problem of the endgame either, so it was agreed only to continue the match games up to the fortieth move.

Game 1
White: USSR (Three half-moves)   Black: USA

1 P−K4	P−K4		3 N−B3	B−B4
2 N−QB3	N−QB3		4 B−B4	

In this position, which occurred in the third game as well, the program found the stronger line 4 N × P when playing five half-moves.

4 ...	N−B3		7 B−K3	B−KN5
5 O−O	O−O		8 P−KR3	B−R4
6 P−Q3	P−Q3		9 B−Q5	

The developing moves have finished and the program does not know what to do. Here a human being might have played 9 N − QR4 followed by P − B3, livening the pawns up in the center. It seems though that three half-moves are just not sufficient for seeing the advantages of the resulting position.

   9 ...   B−Q5

It appears that the American program suffers from the same difficulties.

10 P−KN4

In this the program had a "human" idea. It reckons that this move forces an advantageous exchange.

10 ...	B × N		13 R−N1	R−N1
11 QNP × B	B−N3		14 Q−K2	
12 B−N5	R−K1			

In the variation 14 R × P R × R 15 B × N.QB6 the three half-moves have run out and White is still short of material. A computer playing four [five − D.N.L.L.] half-moves would have played 14 R × P.

14 ...   K − R1   15 P − Q4   K − N1

It might appear that in playing 14 ... K − R1 Black was preparing to reply
15 ... P × P against 15 P − Q4, to be followed by 16 P × P B × P 17 B × B
P − Q4, winning a pawn, since White cannot play B × RP +. In fact, however,
neither of the machines saw this line.

16 Q − B4

It is curious that White "thought" five times as long over this bad move as
over most other moves.

16 ...   N − QR4

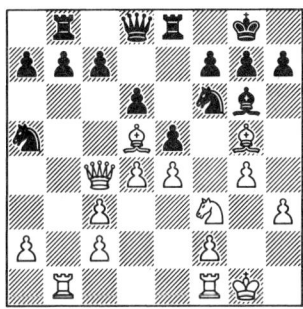

17 B × N

Feeling that something is wrong the program makes an intermediate exchange.
After 17 B × N Q × B 18 Q − Q3 its counting has finished and it thinks all is
well.

17 ...   Q × B   19 P × P   P × P
18 Q − Q3   P − B3

Our program considered the move 19 ... Q − B5 to be best for Black, thinking
that after 20 B − N3 P × P Black wins back the pawn. And if 20 ... B × P,
then it had a pretty variation in reserve: 21 B × KBP + K × B 22 Q × B Q × Q
23 N − N5 + and 24 N × Q.
     This is an example of the complex combinations the computer can carry
out without even noticing the simple intermediate exchange 20 ... N × B,
because after 21 RP × N B × P it thought it was all right.

20 B − N3   R.N1 − Q1   24 R − Q3   R × R
21 Q − K3   P − N3   25 P × R   R − Q1
22 R.B1 − Q1   R − Q3   26 R − R1
23 P − N5   Q − K2

White thinks that Black should play 26 ... N × B and therefore occupies the
open file in advance.

26 ...	Q – Q3		30 R – R4	Q – K3
27 P – Q4	P × P		31 N – K5	Q – K1
28 P × P	N × B		32 P – B4	R – Q3
29 P × N	P – QR4		33 P – B5	

Our program did not see that this move won a pawn, but made the move out of positional considerations.

33 ...	B – R4	34 N – B4	

Now it can see.

34 ...	R – Q1		36 N – B4	B – Q8
35 N × NP	R – N1		37 R – R3	B – B7

Because game two had reached the fortieth move it was decided to call a halt to the match and agree a draw in this game since neither of the opponents had an overwhelming advantage.

Game 2
White: USA   Black: USSR (Three half-moves)

1 P – K4	N – KB3		4 B – N5	P – QR3
2 P – K5	N – Q4		5 B – R4	P – QN4
3 N – KB3	P – K3		6 B – N3	B – N5

This is a typical case of a positional mistake due to an insufficient depth of calculation. Black develops a piece and prevents 7 P – Q4, not noticing that after 6 ... B – N5 7 P – B3 B – B4 (three half-moves have come to an end!) White nevertheless plays 8 P – Q4.

7 N – B3	N – B5	11 B × N	B × B
8 O – O	B – N2	12 B – R3	P – Q3
9 P – Q4	B.N5 × N	13 P × P	
10 P × B	N – Q4		

Our program considered the move 13 P × P to be very weak. Its assessment of the position changed sharply in its own favor.

13 ...	P × P		17 Q – K1	Q – B2
14 R – K1	N – B3		18 B – N4	P – QR4
15 R – K3	O – O		19 B – R3	K – R1
16 Q – K2	B – B5			

However strange it may seem this is not just for "something to do". Black is intending to play 20 ... P – B4, which it cannot do immediately because of the answer R × P.

20 N – N5	P – R3		23 B × R	Q × B
21 N – K4	R.B1 – Q1		24 P – QR3	N – K2
22 N × P	R × N		25 R – K5	N – B3

Now if 26 R — K3 then the game would be drawn by repetition.

| 26 R — QB5 P — K4 | 27 Q — K4 R — R3 |

It is only now that the computer can see that 27 ... R — QB1 can be followed by 28 P — QR4. According to assessments printed out by our computer, its position is worsening very fast. Here we have an example of a position in which the strategy of a deep analysis of a small number of moves does better than a short but comprehensive analysis. White's moves R — QB5, Q — K4 and P — QR4 are essential to any reasonable line of play, while Black cannot interfere with his opponent's plan even by means of the most exotic variations.

| 28 R — Q1 P — N3 | 29 R — Q2 P — N4 |

Defending against the threat of Q — K3, winning a pawn.

30 R — Q1

White can no longer find any move to improve his position.

| 30 ...   P — R5 | 31 R — Q2 P — B3 |

To strengthen such a position is difficult even for a human being. In any case it would need a subtle plan lasting quite a number of moves. This, of course, is beyond the computer's capacity while it has such a shallow depth of calculation. Having no plan Black makes a very weak move. It saw, of course, the reply 32 Q — N6 but considered that after 32 ... Q — B1 it was quite safe. A chess player would never have ended the analysis of a variation in such a position, except perhaps to conclude that it was acceptable.

| 32 Q — K3 P × P | 34 Q — KN3 Q × Q |
| 33 P × P   N — K2 | 35 RP × Q |

Against 35 BP × Q the program was going to play 35 ... R — K3 and the best variation for both sides (following this move) went like this: 36 P — N4 P — B4 37 P × P N × P, getting rid of the weak pawn, since 38 R × N is not possible because of 38 ... R — K8 + 39 K — B2 R — KB8 + and 40 ... R × R.

35 ... N — Q4	38 P × P N × P
36 R — B8 + K — R2	39 P — QB3 N — Q4
37 R — KB8 P — QN5	40 R — QB8 Drawn

From a chess player's point of view, of course, this position is easily won for Black, but both computers showed such a total lack of comprehension of the game that there was no point in examining it further.

Game 3
White: USSR (Five half-moves)   Black: USA

| 1 P — K4   P — K4 | 3 N — B3 B — B4 |
| 2 N — KB3 N — QB3 | 4 N × P! |

This move was quite a surprise for us, since the computer attaches a high value to the right to castle. Nevertheless, the positional advantages secured seem to have pushed the scale in favour of 4 N × P (as against 4 B − B4). Our program gave as the best variation for both sides: 4 ... B × P + 5 K × B N × N 6 P − Q4.

| 4 ... | N × N | 6 P × N | B × P |
| 5 P − Q4 | B − Q3 | 7 P − B4 | |

With this move White "issued" the following optimal sequence: 7 ... B × N + 8 P × B N − B3 9 Q − Q4.

| 7 ... | B × N + | 9 P − K5 | |
| 8 P × B | N − B3 | | |

As in games between human beings plans can change during the play: in its preliminary calculations our program intended to play 9 Q − Q4, but now it can see new possibilities. It is interesting that the line 9 B − B4 was rejected by the program because of 9 ... N × P 10 B × P + K − B1!? and Black wins a pawn because of the threat on ... QB6 and a Queen check on ... KR5.

| 9 ... | N − K5 | 10 Q − Q3 | |

The variation given by the program was this: 10 ... P − Q4 11 P × P ep N × QP 12 B − R3. Note however, that in calculating six half-moves ahead the program did not find the strongest move in the position: 10 Q − Q5!

Why did that happen? Evidently because in the line 10 ... N × P 11 Q − B4 Q − R5 ch 12 P − N3 black is obliged to make a sixth half-move, after which White enters a forcing variation which wins a Knight. Thinking only five half-moves ahead, in the position after 12 P − N3 it appears that Black wins a pawn and so the move 10 Q − Q5 is rejected.

| 10 ... | N − B4 | 12 P − B5 | N − N4 | . |
| 11 Q − Q5 | N − K3 | | | |

In making its twelfth move our program expected 12 ... P − QB3 13 Q − Q3 N − B4 14 Q − Q6.

| 13 P − KR4 | P − KB3 | 14 P × N | P × P |

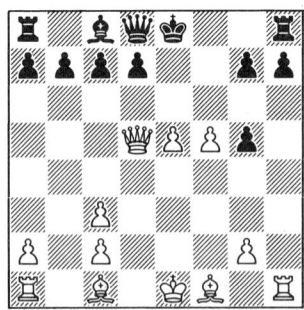

15 R × P!

This simple tactical coup would have been found even with a calculation for one half-move.

15 ...   R − B1   17 Q − Q6
16 R × P   P − B3

After the program made this move it "announced" that Black's only salvation from mate was the variation beginning with the moves 17 ... Q − B3 18 P × Q K − Q1.

17 ...   R × P

Black prefers a faster finish.

18 R − N8 +   R − B1

If 19 ... K − B2 then 20 B − QB4 mate.

19 Q × R mate

Game 4
White: USA   Black: USSR (Five half-moves)

 1 P − K4   N − KB3   3 N − KB3   N − N5
 2 P − K5   N − Q4

This looks senseless. The program is really trying to play 4 ... P − Q4 and the interpolation of 4 P − B3 N.N5 − B3, will not, in the program's opinion, improve White's position.

4 B − N5   P − QB3   6 P − Q4   Q − R4
5 B − R4   P − Q3   7 P − B4

A bad blunder which our program did not expect when it played 6 ... Q − R4.

7 ...   N − B7 + +   9 N − B3   Q − N5
8 K − B1   N × R

The program can see that in quiet continuations White wins the Knight on R1. Now it manages to keep the extra Rook (at least for the present).

10 Q − K2   P × P   17 K − N1   P − QB4
11 P × P   B − K3   18 Q − Q2   P × N
12 Q − Q1   B × P +   19 N × P   P − K3
13 N − K2   P − QN4   20 N − B3   N − B3
14 B − B2   N × B   21 Q − N5   R − Q1
15 Q × N   B × P   22 B − Q2   Q − B8 +
16 N.K2 − Q4   Q − B5 +

The computer is not looking for "beauty": it is simply winning a pawn.

23	B − K1	Q × P	28	P × B	Q × B+
24	Q − B4	B − Q4	29	K − N2	Q × KP
25	Q − N3	Q − K7	30	Q − R4	P − QR4
26	B − B3	P − N5	31	R − QB1	N − Q5
27	B − K1	B × N	32	R − B1	N × P!

The program did not find this move in its earlier analysis. If now 33 K × N, then 33 ... R − Q5! wins the Queen.

33	Q − R3	R − Q6	35	R × N	R × Q+
34	Q − N3	N − K8 +	36	K − B1	Q − QN4 +

The program was intending to play here 36 ... R − N8 + but then found a more lucrative continuation.

37	R − K2	R − QR6	39	K − Q2	
38	K − K1	R − R8 +			

After this the program can see that it is mating.

39	...	Q − Q4 +	41	K − B4	Q − KB4 mate
40	K − K3	R − R6 +			

The problem of creating a chess computer belongs to a young branch of cybernetics—heuristic programming. There is one task facing this discipline the solution of which would have practical applications: to work out methods of orienting in a continuously changing situation depending on a large number of factors which cannot be subjected to a complete mechanical analysis. Chess is an excellent model of such a situation.

In the course of work on chess programs some very valuable heuristic methods have been found which shorten the analysis many times over. Remembering the best moves in deep analyses, the use of forced variations and certain *a priori* evaluations of moves and positions are among these techniques. The heuristic methods discovered in the course of creating chess programs have already found application in the study of networks, finding the minimum of functions of several variables and also in working out the results of some physical experiments.

And as far as the eternal question (which excites all chess players) is concerned of whether the computer will defeat man, the author of this article is bold enough to claim that it will happen in the next 10–15 years.

The Moscow program used an evaluation function with four features:

(1) *Pawn Structure*

Four aspects of pawn structure were considered:

(a) Central Pawns: For each side the central squares are K4, Q4, K5, Q5, K6, and Q6. For each pawn on one of the central squares a bonus of 10 points was given.

(b) The Pawn Phalanx: Two pawns on the same rank and on neighboring files are called a phalanx. N pawns on the same rank and on neighboring files are counted as $N-1$ phalanxes. For each plalanx a bonus of 4 points was scored.

(c) Isolated and Doubled Pawns: Doubled pawns are only penalized if they are also isolated, and isolated pawns that are not doubled are only penalized if they are on a semiopen file. For each such pawn a penalty of 12 points is deducted.

(d) Passed Pawns: For each passed pawn score a bonus of $32-4 \times S$ where S is the number of ranks separating the pawn from the Queening square.

(2) *Mobility*

For each square attacked by a piece, a bonus is scored according to the piece that is doing the attacking. For the King this bonus is 0, for the Queen 1, for a Rook 2, for a Knight or Bishop 5, and for a pawn 0.

This method of scoring encourages minor pieces to be developed before major ones.

(3) *Castling*

When a player castles he scores a bonus of 11 points, but if he forfeits the right to castle he suffers a penalty of 11.

(4) *Material*

The ratios of the values of the pieces are:

pawn $= 1$;
Bishop $=$ Knight $= 3\frac{1}{2}$;
Rook $= 5$;
Queen $= 10$.

The Stanford–Moscow match did much for the development of computer chess by creating the stimulus for further work in the USA. Even as the match was taking place, a new program was being developed at MIT, and the next 8 years saw an explosion of interest in the subject. Computer competitions became more and more frequent and some scientists believed that a master standard chess program was not far away.

The Greenblatt Program

Beginning in mid-November 1966, a chess program was developed on a PDP-6 computer at the Artifical Intelligence Laboratory at MIT. The program was written primarily by Richard Greenblatt, then an undergraduate student, with the assistance of Donald E. Eastlake III. The program was written quickly—by February 1967 it was ready to play in a local tournament where it lost four games and drew one to achieve a rating of 1243 on the United States Chess Federation scale. In March 1967 it played in another tournament, winning one game and losing four. Its performance rating for that event was 1360 and its overall rating went up to 1330. One month later it scored two wins and two losses for a performance rating of 1640. The program was named MAC HACK VI and it was made an honorary member of both the USCF and the Massachusetts Chess Association.

Greenblatt's program contained several powerful interaction aids for locating errors in the program and for improving its performance. These aids included facilities to look, on a cathode ray screen, at the evaluation of any selected node on the game tree, to examine all the factors that caused a move to be considered plausible, to look at the main variation of the program's analysis from each depth-one position analyzed, and to examine statistics on how long the computation took and how many plausible moves were generated at any point. By the use of these facilities and by playing hundreds of games against the program within a few months, Greenblatt was able to produce a program that was efficient, fast, and relatively free of "bugs" (programming errors).

Greenblatt's plausible-move generator had three basic functions. It selected the moves that it considered plausible, put them into their order of merit so as to optimize the advantage of using the alpha–beta algorithm, and calculated certain positional and "developmental" values that would decide the program's move if several moves led to the same static value. The major reason for the quality of the program's play was that considerable chess knowledge was programmed in. In fact there were about 50 chess heuristics used in computing the plausibility of moves, though many of the 50 were only applicable in special cases or at certain stages of the game.

Each square was assigned a value during each plausible-move computation, corresponding roughly to the estimated worth of having another piece bearing on the square or the cost of moving away a piece presently attacking the square. The principal criteria used for assigning these values included the closeness of the square to the center of the board, its proximity to the opponent's King, and its occupation by one of the program's own pieces which is *en prise*. Small values were given for occupation of the square by one of the program's pieces and for its closeness to the opponent's side of the board.

The current developmental value of a piece is the sum of the values for the squares it attacks, plus values accumulated for actual attacks on enemy pieces. When a move is being considered for plausibility the new development value of the piece is calculated assuming the piece to be on its new proposed location. The difference between the new and old developmental values is used as a factor in assessing plausibility, encouraging developing moves and discouraging antipositional ones. Gains or losses in development resulting from blocking or unblocking the opponent's or the program's pieces were also considered in the developmental value. Other factors were added to encourage attacking the opponent's pieces, his weak pawns, his pinned pieces and pieces defending other pieces, etc.

Greenblatt noticed that sometimes his program would give a high plausibility value to an antipositional move because it attacked an enemy piece. If the attack led to material gain, all was well and good; but if the opponent could simply move the attacked piece away then the move was a pointless waste of time. So moves were scored separately on their positional merit and if this proved bad then the move would be rejected if there was a more positional move leading to the same terminal score.

The evaluation function used five features: Material balance, piece ratio, pawn structure, King safety, and center control. The piece ratio term was aimed at promoting exchanges when the program was ahead in material and avoiding them when behind. Greenblatt's pawn structure feature was slightly more reliable than those used in earlier programs because it made allowances for backward pawns as well as for doubled and isolated ones.

The program's tree-search was conducted along the lines of Shannon's type-B strategy, with variable widths of search at different levels of the tree. At the root of the tree the 15 most plausible moves were chosen and ordered.

For each of these the 15 most plausible reply moves were chosen and ordered. Then the nine most plausible replies to these, then nine replies to them and seven moves at depth five. These are the basic settings that were used when the program played tournament games. The only way that the program could fail to consider the indicated number of moves is either that the requisite number of moves simply did not exist or that the alpha–beta algorithm produced a cutoff before all these moves at any node had been examined. Just as efficient tree-searching was sometimes responsible for the basic settings not being reached, so it was often the case that the basic width had to be increased in order to allow for safe checks to be considered, as well as captures (at the first and second level) and at least some of the moves of a reasonable number of pieces. The logic behind this last heuristic is quite sound. If all the moves of a single piece are highly plausible (e.g., those of a Queen because it is *en prise*) then the rest of the board might not be looked at because the number of plausible moves might have reached the basic setting. But by examining the moves of a few other pieces it might be possible to find a clever tactical blow that succeeds even though the Queen is left *en prise*.

The program kept a record of each position considered during its search for a move, together with information concerning the value of that position. If the position arose again during the search, either on part of the same tree (by transposition) or as part of a different tree (e.g., when the program was considering a later move) then the position could be looked up in the table and its value retrieved. This often avoided the necessity of evaluating the same position twice, and it also detected draws by threefold repetition.

If two moves were found by the search to lead to the same static evaluation, the move with the higher plausibility value was preferred. However, in some situations this move was not the most desirable one to make. In order to take such cases into account, two types of modification were made to the values found at the lower levels of the tree. The first modification subtracted a few points if the current move being investigated was marked as being developmentally poor by the plausible-move generator. The second modification subtracted small amounts for moving pieces that had already moved higher up in the tree. This had the effect of avoiding moving pieces twice in the opening, avoiding making moves that result in the moved piece being attacked and forced to retreat, and avoiding making a two-move maneuvre when the maneuvre was possible in one move.

The program's performance was improved by introducing a secondary search whenever the normal tree-search resulted in a new candidate for the best move at the top level. What was done was to move down the principal variation for that move as far as the variation was computed by the plausible-move generator, and then to conduct an additional search, usually limited to two plies although captures and checks could increase this number. The value obtained by the secondary search is then used in place of the value found for the principle variation if it is worse for the side to move. A simple example illustrating the concept of the secondary search is shown in Figure 1.

The program has to move from position P_0. It generates its plausible moves and orders them according to their apparent merit with the best one first. It then examines the apparently best move, M_1 and the resulting position P_1, by looking at the tree below P_1 and backing up the scores in the usual way. Let us say that P_1 is found to have a backed-up score of 20.

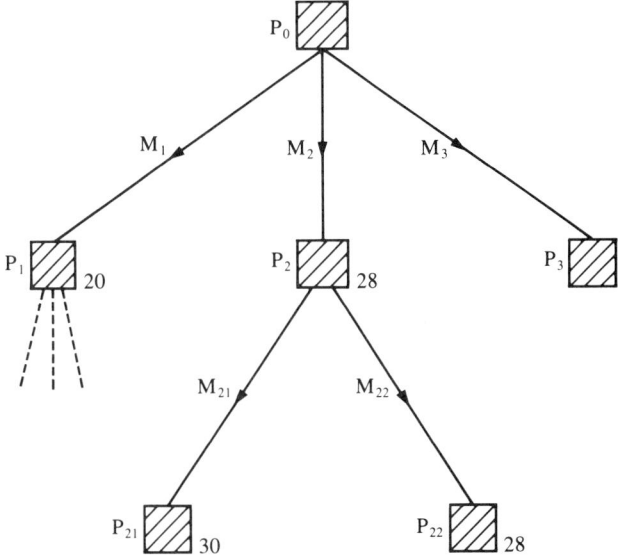

Figure 1. An analysis tree with sample scores illustrating the concept of a secondary search.

The program now looks at M_2 and the resulting position P_2. After examining the tree below P_2 (i.e., P_{21} and P_{22}) the program comes to the conclusion that the score for P_2 is 28 and that the principal variation consists of the moves M_2, M_{22}.

This decision would put M_2 at the top of the list of candidate moves, but before doing so the program checks its analysis by conducting a secondary search from position P_{22}. If this secondary search comes up with a score of less than 28 then this new score is the one assigned to P_2. Otherwise P_2 is assigned a score of 28 and the move M_2 goes to the top of the list of candidates. The search then continues with M_3.

Another feature that was new to chess programs was the use of a small library of opening variations. This "book" was compiled by two MIT students, Larry Kaufmann, who represented the USA in Student Chess Olympiads, and Alan Baisley, an Expert on the USCF scale.

The following game was played by MAC HACK VI when it was only 2 months old. It is the first tournament game played by a computer, and its opponent was rated 2190 on the USCF scale, i.e., almost a Master.

White: Human   Black: MAC HACK VI

1	P−KN3	P−K4	6	P−QB4	P−Q3
2	N−KB3	P−K5	7	N−B3	B−K3
3	N−Q4	B−B4	8	P−Q3	P×P
4	N−N3	B−N3	9	B×P	QN−Q2
5	B−N2	N−KB3	10	P×P	R−QN1

11	B − N2	O − O	34 P − QN4	B − N3
12	O − O	B − N5	35 Q − B2	N − B3
13	Q − B2	R − K1	36 B − K6	N − Q5
14	P − Q4	P − B4	37 R × N	B × R
15	B − K3	P × P	38 Q × P+	K − N2
16	N × P	N − K4	39 Q − N4+	K − R3
17	P − KR3	B − Q2	40 Q × B	Q − K2
18	P − N3	B − QB4	41 Q − R4+	K − N3
19	QR − Q1	Q − B1	42 B − B5+	K − N2
20	K − R2	N − N3	43 Q × RP+	K − B1
21	B − N5	R − K4	44 Q − R8+	K − B2
22	B × N	P × B	45 Q − QR8	Q − B2
23	N − K4	P − B4	46 Q − Q5+	K − N2
24	N − KB6+	K − N2	47 K − N2	Q − K2
25	N × B	Q × N	48 P − KR4	K − R3
26	N − B6	R.1 − K1	49 P − N4	K − N2
27	N × R	R × N	50 P − R5	Q − K7
28	Q − B3	P − B3	51 P − R6+	K − B1
29	R − Q3	R − K7	52 P − R7	Q × KBP+
30	R − Q2	R × R	53 K × Q	K − K2
31	Q × R	N − K4	54 P − R8 = Q	P − R3
32	R − Q1	Q − QB2	55 Q − K6 mate	
33	B − Q5	K − N3		

The next game is the first ever won by a computer program in tournament play. It was played in the second round of the Massachusetts State Championship, March 1967.

White: MAC HACK VI   Black: Human (1510)

1	P − K4	P − QB4	7 B − B4	P − K4
2	P − Q4	P × P	8 B − N3	P − QR3
3	Q × P	N − QB3	9 O − O − O	P − QN4
4	Q − Q3	N − B3	10 P − QR4	B − R3+
5	N − QB3	P − KN3	11 K − N1	P − N5
6	N − B3	P − Q3	12 Q × QP!	B − Q2

If 12 … Q × Q 13 R × Q P × N 14 R × N.KB6 B − Q2 (say) 15 N × P and White is two pawns up. Presumably Human missed the fork of the two Knights by White's Rook.

13	B − R4	B − N2	18 Q − Q5	R − B1
14	N − Q5	N × P	19 N × P	B − K3
15	N − B7+	Q × N	20 Q × N.B6+	R × Q
16	Q × Q	N − B4	21 R − Q8 mate	
17	Q − Q6	B − KB1		

By the time that MAC HACK VI has played in one or two tournaments it had attracted considerable public attention. This became even more the case when it discovered a nice, 9-ply combination that was reputedly missed by some of the US Masters who were shown the same position.

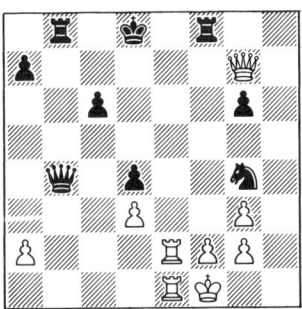

Here MAC HACK found:

1 ...   R × P +!   2 K − N1

If 2 R × R N − R7 + 3 K − K2 (or 3 K − N1 Q × R + 4 K × N Q × R and Black is a Rook ahead) 3 ... Q − N7 + 4 K − Q1 Q − N8 + 5 K − K2 R − N7 mate.

2 ...   R × R   4 Q − B6   R × R +
3 Q − R8 +   K − B2   5 Resigns

MAC HACK VI started a resurgence of interest in computer chess. It was on show in Edinburgh during August 1968 at the triennial congress of the International Federation for Information Processing (IFIP) where it took on all comers and scored about 50%—not a bad result when one realizes that many computer scientists are also stronger than average chess players.

The "Levy Bet"

Immediately after the IFIP'68 congress, the Department of Machine Intelligence and Perception at Edinburgh University held one of its annual "Machine Intelligence Workshops". These meetings brought together many of the most prominent workers in the field of artificial intelligence and the proceedings of the workshops have been published as a well-known series of books by the Edinburgh University Press (*Machine Intelligence 1, ...*, etc).

The Machine Intelligence Workshops were hosted by Donald Michie, Professor of the Edinburgh University department, and during the workshop it was traditional for him to arrange a number of cocktail parties and other social events. It was during one of these parties that my now famous bet was born. I was talking to John McCarthy, Professor of Artificial Intelligence at

Stanford University and one of the world's leading authorities on the subject, and he expressed the opinion that it would only be a matter of time before computer programs could play chess as well as a Grandmaster. I replied that I did not think there would a program that could beat me within 10 years and both he and Michie said that they were sure I was wrong. Intrigued by this challenging opinion I offered to bet each of them £250 that I was right, i.e., that no program would be able to beat me in a match by the end of August 1978. They both accepted the bet with confidence, and my only regret is that I did not make it for a much larger sum, but in those days I was earning less than £1,000 per annum and £500 sounded like a lot of money.

The following year I was asked to present a paper at the Machine Intelligence Workshop and during the course of my presentation I was heckled by Professor Seymour Papert of the Artificial Intelligence Laboratory at MIT. Papert was so sceptical at some of my assertions that I asked him whether he would like to come in on my bet and increase it by £250. He said that he was quite sure that within 5 years, not 10, I would be beaten by a computer program, but I felt that it would have been unfair of me to bet with him on such a short time span. So we agreed that he would become a third member of the consortium. At the time of writing it is already 2 years since Papert's proposed time limit expired. I do not think that his optimism requires any further comment.

In 1970 the Association for Computing Machinery (ACM) held the first chess tournament in which all of the participants were computer programs. The tournament was held in New York as part of the ACM's annual convention and it attracted six entries and widespread publicity. The winner of the tournament was a program called CHESS 3.0 which was written at Northwestern University, Evanston, Illinois. The program will be described in some detail later in this chapter.

The ACM tournament in 1970 was such a success that it was decided to repeat it the following year, and since then it has become a regular event and it usually proves to be the most popular attraction at the ACM convention. I was invited to be the tournament director at the 1971 competition in Chicago where the number of contestants was increased from six to eight. As well as being concerned with the rules of the competition and ensuring fair play, my job was to give a running commentary to the audience so that spectators could understand what was happening in the games. Since 1971 I have performed these duties each year and I must say that I find them far more entertaining than watching most Grandmaster tournaments.

During the 1971 competition I was talking to some of the programmers about my bet. Professor Ed. Kozdrowicki, then of the Bell Telephone Laboratories at Murray Hill, New Jersey, felt sure that I was going to lose and he even offered to increase the bet by $1,000 (about £400). I was still an unprosperous programming assistant and I was afraid to take on such a "big" committment so I said that I would take £250 of his action and Professor Ben Mittman, one of the tournament organizers and the head of the Evanston

installation that had produced the champion program CHESS 3.5 (the son of
CHESS 3.0) took the remainder of the bet. A few hours after Kozdrowicki
came in on the bet his program reached the following position in its game
against GENIE, programmed by Herbert Raymond at the Fleet Computer
Centre in San Diego.

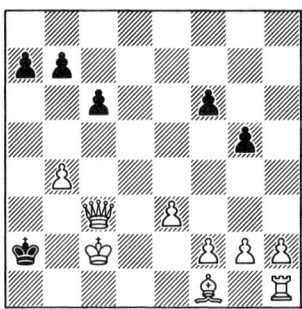

In this position it would appear that White had some advantage. He has
at his disposal two different mates in one (38 B−B4 and 38 Q−N2) as well
as various mates in two, three, four, or indeed almost any number of moves.
But because of a defect that occurs in many chess programs, it was this
plethora of mating continuations that led to COKO's tragedy. Had there been
only one forced mate COKO would have played it, but because there was
more than one mate, and because COKO was unable to distinguish between
the value of a mate in one and the value of a mate in two, three, or four, it
chose between these mating continuations at random.

38 K−B1

This is just as good, from the program's point of view, as giving mate on the
move, since mate still cannot be prevented.

38 ...	P−KB4	39 K−B2

And this just as good as giving mate on the move ...

39 ...	P−B5	42 K−B1	P×P
40 K−B1	P−N5	43 K−B2	P×R=Q
41 K−B2	P−B6		

Now White has one last chance to end the game with a single blow.

44 K−B1???

But this is inexplicable.

44 ...	Q×B+	47 K−B2	Q×RP+
45 K−Q2	Q×P+	48 K−B1	Q−R8+
46 K−B1	Q−N8+	49 K−B2	Q−QN8+

50	K – Q2	P – N6		53	P – K4	K × P
51	Q – B4+	Q – N6		54	P – K5	P – N7
52	Q × Q+	K × Q				

By now COKO's programmers had seen enough and they resigned on behalf of their program. Ed. Kozdrowicki was heard to be muttering something about a bad bet as he left the playing hall.

So by August 1971 my bet had grown to £1,000. By this time I had become an International Master but the standard of the best chess programs had improved little, if at all, since I made the first bet 3 years earlier. As time went on I became more and more confident and I was therefore delighted in the autumn of 1974 when Donald Michie offered to up the stakes. He wanted to increase his stake in the original bet to £500, thereby increasing the total wager to £1,250 (roughly $2,900), and to add a rider that if I did lose this bet then the program that beat me would have been written either by him or under his direction. Since, at that time, the world's strongest chess program was KAISSA, written in Moscow, and since I knew that KAISSA's success in the First World Computer Championships in Stockholm (August 1974) would mean more financial suppport and programming effort for the Moscow group, I felt confident that in the unlikely event that anything did turn sour on me it would be from the East that my victor would come, and not from the West. I therefore accepted both parts of Michie's new wager but I turned down his "offer" to extend the period of the bet from August to December 1978. After all, by August 1978 the value of my winnings will have already been substantially eroded by inflation.

So much for my bet. Let us now look at some of the more recent efforts at producing an electronic Grandmaster.

Soviet Research

Between the time of the Moscow–Stanford match in 1967 and the birth of the KAISSA program in 1971 (see page 149) only one Soviet chess program was heard of. It played very weakly and was annihilated in a game played against the readers of the newspaper *The Ural Worker* (*Uralsky Rabochy*). Each week the program's move would be published in the newspaper and the readers were invited to send in their suggestion for reply moves. The move that received the most votes was played.

The game was published in *Shakhmanty vs. USSR*, number 8, 1968, with notes by Polugayevsky. No details were revealed either concerning the computer or its programmers, perhaps because of the poor play of the program. Here is the game with Polugayevsky's annotations—presumably this is the first mass contest against a computer in history.

White: Readers   Black: Program

1 P – K4   N – QB3

A move suggested by Nimzowitsch. It is not very popular and has almost disappeared from tournaments, but the computer has its own "theoretical taste," which does not coincide with the conclusions of contemporary chess theory.

2 P−Q4 P−Q4   3 N−QB3 P×P

The computer prefers to take the pawn. 3 ... P−K3 is more cautious.

4 P−Q5 N−K4   5 B−KB4

White is quite right in not hurrying to recapture the pawn. By chasing the Knight White tries to make the development of Black's Kingside more difficult.

5 ... N−N3   6 B−N3 P−KB4?

It seems that a computer also has human weaknesses—it can be just as greedy as a human being. The computer does not want to part with the extra pawn, and moreover it threatens 7 ... P−B5.

However, the move ... P−KB4 is obviously antipositional. It weakens the King and opens the KN1−QR7 diagonal. Furthermore, the computer appears to have forgotten one of the most important principles in chess—the principle of development. 6 ... P−QR3 would have been a better solution and if 7 N×P, then 7 ... N−KB3 8 N×N (8 Q−Q4 P−K4! 9 B×KP N×N 10 Q×N Q−K2) 8 ... KP×N. White's position is better but Black will succeed in completing his development. Instead of 7 N×P, 7 Q−Q4 is stronger. After 7 ... N−K3 8 O−O−O, White still has pressure.

7 B−N5+   B−Q2   8 N−R3!

The readers have correctly determined the weak points in their opponent's camp. The White Knight is aiming at K6.

8 ... P−QB3!

A natural move, but since it was made by the computer it deserves an exclamation mark. This move bears witness to the great possibilities of the electronic chess player. Evidently, the computer is able to assess the position correctly. Black's Achilles' Heel is the square K3 and the computer correctly decides not to allow the exchange of his white-squared Bishop, which is the only piece defending that square.

9 B−QB4 Q−N3

White's main threat of 10 N−KN5 followed by 11 P×P and 12 B−B7 mate is noticed by the computer, which prepares to castle Queenside in order to remove the King from the danger zone. However, it does not manage to realize this plan.

Black's position was compromised by his sixth move, but he should have tried as an emergency measure to neutralize his main enemy—the Bishop on QB4. The computer should have "paid attention" to 9 ... P−N4. For example: 10 P×P P×B 11 P×B+ Q×P or 10 B−N3 P−B4 11 P−R4 P−QB5

12 B−R2 P−QR3. And in spite of the strong move 13 P−B3 for White, Black can still put up a fight.

10 Q−Q2   Q−B4

The computer is alert. It avoids the trap prepared by the humans: 10 ... O−O−O 11 N−R4 and the Queen has nowhere to go.

The computer also refuses the "Greek gift"—the pawn on QN7: 10 ... Q × NP 11 R−QN1 Q−R6 12 R × P with an overwhelming advantage for White. Who could say after this move that the computer thinks in a primitive way?

11 P × P

In order to profit from his advantage in development White has to open the game up.

11 ...   B × P

As will transpire later 11 ... P × P 12 O−O−O N−B3 is correct.

12 B−K6!

Well played! Now Black's King's side is frozen and White can calmly prepare for the decisive attack.

12 ...   N−R3

What would a chess player have played in this position? He would have chosen the lesser evil: 12 ... R−Q1 13 B−KB7+ K × B 14 Q × R P−KR3, but the computer cannot part with the exchange. We should note however that the computer's combinative ability is not too bad: it saw the piquant variation: 12 ... P−KR3 13 O−O−O N−B3 14 B−QB7 and then 15 Q−Q8+.

13 O−O−O   N−K4

How else can he defend against 14 B−QB7? If 13 ... Q−R4 then 14 N−KN5 R−Q1 15 Q × R+ Q × Q 16 R × Q+ K × R 17 R−Q1+ K−K1 18 B−QB7 wins.

14 N−KN5   N.R3−N5

Otherwise 15 B × N follows.

15 P−KB3   P−KN3

It has to give up the Knight. The fight is over, but the computer (like some chess players) does not like resigning in time.

16 P × N   B−N2   17 B × N   Q × B

This leads to an attractive finish, the computer "did not like" 17 ... B × B 18 B−B7+ followed by 19 N−K6+ and Black loses his Queen.

Could the computer have seen the final combination? Perhaps, but even a computer is entitled to count on his opponent's mistakes ...

18 Q−Q8+!   R × Q   19 B−B7+

and the computer resigned.

The electronic chess player will undoubtedly try to take revenge on the readers in a fresh match. The future will show whether he can succeed.

Throughout his notes Polugayevsky makes the common mistake of referring to the computer when he really means to say the program. He also calls the computer "he" instead of "it" in his final note, as do many humans when they are playing against a computer program.—D.N.L.L.

The Northwestern Program

The Program written at Northwestern University won the first four ACM tournaments (1970, '71, '72, and '73). It finished second, behind KAISSA, at the First World Computer Championship in Stockholm (1974) and it was second, behind RIBBIT, at the Fifth ACM Tournament (San Diego, 1974). It regained its ACM title at Minneapolis in 1975. The program was written by Larry Atkin, Keith Gorlen, and David Slate while they were students at Northwestern University, and it was improved a little each year, even after its programmers graduated. At the time of writing, Atkin and Slate are working as systems programmers in the same laboratory at Evanston, and Gorlen is with the US Public Health Service at Bethesda, Maryland.

The version of the Northwestern program that first appeared in the ACM tournaments was called CHESS 3.0. As the program has grown in age and strength so its name has been amended and it is currently (1975) called CHESS 4.4. Here is a brief description of how the program decides on its moves.

The program performs a depth-first tree-search using the alpha–beta algorithm. The way in which the program grows the tree is interesting—there is a special routine (segment of the program) whose job it is to choose the next move to be searched or to decide not to search any more moves from some particular node. To choose a move this routine invokes 1 of 15 selector modules, each of which is a different move selection algorithm. A module may select a move and/or it may determine which module is to be used the next time the selection routine is called into operation for the same node. Here is a list of the modules and their functions:

START: this module initializes a node. It calls *GENMOV* to generate and evaluate the legal moves.

LIBRARY: the program has a library of positions that have been "learnt" and this library is searched for a move applicable to the current position. When a position is added to the library a suggested move is also added, this move being either the book move, in the case of a stored opening variation, or the move actually played in that position, in the case of a position already encountered.

ENDPOINT: is evoked to terminate the search of a branch by returning a final evaluation for that branch.

CHPRUNE: tries to find a checking move whose score suggests that it is worth looking at for reasons other than the check.

LMBLAS: looks at the best variation of the previous move tree to see the program's expected response, at that time, if the opponent makes the move predicted by that tree. A human analyses in much the same way—if his opponent makes an expected move a human master will first consider the move that he had planned to make when making his previous move.

ISTBST: chooses the move having the best score from the evaluation function, i.e., the apparently best move.

BSTLAS: chooses the move which turned out best at the last node examined at the same ply level. This is another human approach—if a particular move is strong in reply to one of our opponent's moves, then maybe the same move will be strong in reply to another of his moves.

MORBST: selects up to *L* best-valued moves, where *L* is a preset limit. The limits were usually different for different levels in the tree, though at any one level the limit was the same. It is this limit parameter that determines the width of search and hence, to a great extent, the time taken to make a move.

COMBO: selects a number of the most promising moves as determined by a "combination potential" score.

FLEX: selects moves in almost the same way as *MORBST* but with the difference that it only tries to find moves that defend against a threat not met by previously searched moves.

BANANA SUPER BEYOND: selects moves at ply 1 whose scores are not high enough to justify a full-depth search by previous modules. *SUPER BEYOND* moves are searched to a depth of 3-ply and, if their score looks good, to full depth by the *EXPAND* module. The purpose of *SUPER BEYOND* is to solve such problems as the difficulty of transferring a piece from one square to a better one by passing through a worse one. e.g., a human player would not normally put his Knight on, say, KR3 unless he intended to move it to a good square such as KB4. But since such an operation takes 3-ply it is a good idea to examine a number of moves to that depth.

BEYOND: selects all moves that are not chosen by *SUPER BEYOND* and examines them to a depth of 2-ply. This module is inexpensive in terms of time, but it catches certain kinds of moves that would otherwise not be examined.

EXPAND: re-searches moves that pass the tests set by *BEYOND* and *SUPER BEYOND*. This expansion takes the search to full depth.

QUIESCE: varies the depth of search according to the degree of quiescence of the position.

DONE: terminates the selection of moves from the node currently under consideration.

The program's library of positions can be augmented in two different ways. If the program is in *LEARN* mode then any position added to its library will have a move associated with it. If the program ever reaches this position during the course of a game it will automatically make that move, bypassing the usual tree-search. If the program is set in *ANALYSIS* mode it continually monitors its progress throughout the game. When the evaluation of a current position is significantly different from what was expected during an earlier look-ahead analysis the program assigns credit or blame to its previous four moves and puts these assigned scores into the library. If the same position is encountered in the future, the program uses the credit or blame score to supplement the information gleaned during the normal look-ahead search.

The current version of the Northwestern program, CHESS 4.4, employs an evaluation function with 53 features, and when playing at tournament rates (40 moves in 2 hours) it examines an average of 250,000 positions each time it calculates its move. Of the three members of the programming team only one is a strongish player—David Slate has a USCF Expert's rating. The continued success of their program owes more to the excellence of their programming and to their foresight in building in a number of useful interactive facilities that help them improve their program's play and diagnose its faults.

The following game was played in the third round of the Third ACM Tournament, Boston 1972. At the time of this tournament there was a little thing going on in Iceland between Fischer and Spassky. Possibly prompted by some of the publicity surrounding that match, some of the programs complained during the tournament about spectators in the front row chewing gum and others who were talking too loudly.

White: CHESS 3.6   Black: TECH

1 P−K4	P−K4	4 O−O	B−B4
2 N−KB3	N−QB3	5 N−B3	P−Q3
3 B−N5	N−B3	6 B×N+	

CHESS 3.6 likes to double its opponents' pawns.

| 6 ... | P×B | 8 N×P | O−O |
| 7 P−Q4 | P×P | 9 B−N5 | |

Obviously, CHESS 3.6 could find nothing clear after 9 N×P Q−K1 10 N−Q5 Q×P 11 N×N+ P×N.

| 9 ... | B−KN5 | 10 Q−Q3 | |

It took CHESS 3.6 over 6½ minutes to decide on this move. 10 B×N Q×B 11 Q×B B×N leads nowhere for White.

| 10 ... | B×N | 12 B×N | |
| 11 Q×B | R−N1 | | |

Never missing an opportunity to double its opponent's pawns.

12 ...	Q×B	15 P−KR3	B−K3
13 Q×Q	P×Q	16 P−N4!	
14 P−QN3	R−N5		

Excellent. Fixing Black's KBPs.

| 16 ... | R−Q5 | | |

16 ... P−Q4 looks more logical, but after 17 P−B3 P×P 18 N×P P−KB4 19 N−B6+ K−N2 20 N−R5+ White still has the edge.

| 17 QR−Q1 | R×R | 18 N×R | |

The knight is better placed on K3 than on QB3.

18 ...	K−N2	23 P−B4	R−QR4
19 N−K3	K−N3	24 P−KB5	B−Q2
20 P−KB4	K−N2	25 R−B2	R−K4
21 K−N2	R−QN1	26 R−Q2	P−QR3
22 K−B3	R−N4		

Black can do nothing.

| 27 P−KR4 | P−B4 | | |

A serious positional error, creating a hole for White's knight. Reshevsky annotated this game in the *New York Times* and claimed that after 27 ... P−R3 the position would be even. I. J. Good tried to refute Reshevsky's assessment with the continuation 28 N−N2, threatening 29 N−B4, 30 N−R5+ and

31 N × P, but both Reshevsky and Robert Byrne pointed out that 29 N − B4 could be met by 29 ... K − B1 and 30 N − R5 by 30 ... K − K2, defending the KB3 pawn. There is also the point that 28 N − N2 can be met by 28 ... P − KR4 29 P − N5 P × P 30 P × P P − Q4 equalizing.

The only thing that this analysis proves is that after 27 ... P − R3 White cannot achieve anything with 28 N − N2. However, White's position must surely be superior. He can continue with 28 K − B4 (to prevent the freeing maneuvre ... P − KR4; P − N5 P × P; P × P P − Q4, since now the Rook would be *en prise*) and then play P − N4 preparing for an eventual P − B5.

28 N − Q5	B − B3	31 P × P	P − R4
29 N × QBP	B × P +	32 R × P	B × P
30 K − B4	P − KR4	33 P − R6 + !	

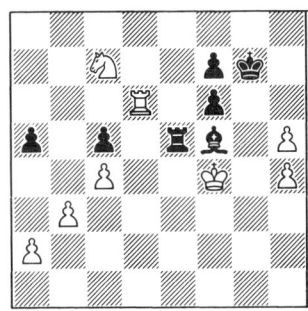

"A stroke of genius"—Reshevsky.

33 ...	K − N3	35 R × P	
34 P − R5 + !	K × P.R4		

White wins a piece. The rest is a matter of technique.

35 ...	R − K7	44 R × P	K − B2
36 K × B	R − KB7 +	45 R − R7 +	K − N3
37 K − K5	R − R7	46 P − R4	R − B4
38 N − Q5	K − N4	47 P − R5	R − B6
39 N − B3	R − R5	48 R − QN7	K − B4
40 R × P	K × P	49 N × P	R − B6
42 N − K4	R − R4 +	50 P − R6	R − R6
42 K − Q6	K − N3	51 P − R7	Black lost on time
43 R − QR7	P − R5		

The Northwestern program has an impressive record against other chess programs. In the first three ACM tournaments it played 10 games and won them all. In the fourth tournament it scored $3\frac{1}{2}$ out of 4 and it was not until the First World Championship Tournament in 1974 that CHESS 4.0 (as it was then called) lost a "serious" game to another program. Later in the same year CHESS 4.0 lost another game to a computer program, this time to RIBBIT from the University of Waterloo. RIBBIT became the first program to stop CHESS 4.0 from winning the ACM tournament.

CHESS 4.0 has not only been successful against other programs. It competed in a tournament with 50 humans at Northwestern University during the winter of 1973/4 and finished in a tie for third place with a score of $4\frac{1}{2}$ out of 6. The average rating of its opponents was 1537 and its performance rating for the tournament was 1736 which places it in the middle of class B on the USCF scale.

TECH

The technology chess program was written by James Gillogly at Carnegie–Mellon University. Its name, TECH, is derived from the basic philosophy that underlines Gillogly's work—he wanted to produce a program that relied almost entirely on technology (i.e., fast computers) and hardly at all on chess heuristics. The aim was to write a program that would simply generate all legal moves to a fixed depth, then evaluate the terminal positions only with respect to material. We have already explained that such an approach can never lead to a program that plays perfect chess, but Gillogly's idea was not to create a Grandmaster program, rather to produce a standard of play against which other programs could be measured. In order to justify the efffort of developing a more complex program it would be necessary that the more complex program could defeat TECH. Since TECH's performance would improve with an increase in computer speeds it could always be used as a "bench-mark" program.

Gillogly's first experiments showed that this ultraprimitive approach did not result in a useful program, since the standard of play was low for any reasonable depth of search. The program often reached a position that was strategically hopeless before it was able to achieve anything by tactics, and it even made tactical blunders through evaluating nonquiescent positions. Gillogly therefore decided to devote a small percentage of the program's computation time to chess heuristics.

His move-generator mechanism consists of two main parts: positional and tactical analysis. The positional analysis routine sorts the moves at the top level of the tree so that the moves with the best superficial positional scores are examined first. This helps to get the most out of the alpha–beta algorithm. No tactical considerations are included in the positional analysis. The tactical analyzer is a "brute-force" tree search which investigates all moves to a fixed depth and evaluates terminal positions provided that they conform to a simple quiescence criteria. The alpha–beta algorithm will select the move at ply-1 that is seen to be materially the best. If there are two or more moves of equal material merit then the first of these is chosen since that is the one whose superficial positional score is the highest. One feature of the technology program that is (in 1975) unique among chess programs is that it uses its opponent's thinking time for its own analysis. While its opponent is thinking it predicts its opponent's move and then begins to compute its reply. If the opponent makes the predicted move then TECH's clock time will be small. In many cases TECH can reply immediately because it predicted its opponent's move long before its opponent had decided on it.

The most important part of the program (in terms of playing ability) is the tactical analysis component (i.e., the brute force search). All moves are searched to a fixed depth, usually 5-ply, and then all captures are examined and all captures in reply to these captures, and so on, until there are no more captures. Even though the alpha–beta algorithm was employed, this search strategy results in as many as 500,000 terminal positions being examined when the program is choosing its move in a tournament game. This is only made possible by the simplicity of the evaluation function (material being the only feature used) and the efficiency of the move generator. Captures are recognized and sorted during move generation with the highest-valued captures being put first on the list. This helps speed up the tree-search since the refutation of a weak move is often a capture.

The positional presorting routine discriminates between moves of equal material value. When used in conjunction with the tactical search routine it can often achieve a satisfactory position from the opening, even though it knows no opening theory. The program distinguishes between five phases of the game and for each phase it employs different heuristics for the positional presort at the top of the tree. Among heuristics that are used throughout the game are one to encourage exchanges when TECH is ahead in material and one to adjust the basic maximum depth for the tactical analysis on the basis of how much time, on average, TECH has for each move before the next time control. If the program has significantly more time available per move than it used (on average) on its previous nine moves, then its depth of search is increased. If it used more time on its previous moves then the depth is decreased.

TECH considers the opening to be the first eight moves. The most important heuristic in the opening evaluation is occupation of the center. Each square on the board is weighted with a desirability value ranging from 0 points for the corners to 8 points for the center. Each move represents a gain or loss of centre control, e.g., the move 1 N − KB3 would yield a gain of 5 points for Center Control. This is multiplied by a priority factor for the piece that moves: pawn = 1, Queen = 1, Rook = 2, Bishop = 3, Knight = 4, and King = − 1. These weightings encourage the development of Knights before Bishops, of minor pieces before major pieces (i.e., bringing out the Queen is discouraged during the opening) and it encourages castling by giving the King a negative priority value so that it scores the greatest number of center control points when it is in a corner.

Each move in the opening is given a final positional score of the center control term plus the value of whichever of the following heuristics apply to the move:

Pawn from K2 to K4: 30 points.
Pawn from K3 to K4: 2 points.
Pawn from Q2 to Q4: 20 points.
Pawn from Q3 to Q4: 2 points.
Kingside castling: 30.
Queenside castling: 10.
N−R3: −15.
Putting a piece on K3 or Q3 where it blocks a pawn: −50.
Moving a Kingside piece: 2.
Playing the Petroff Defense: −50.
Pawn captures towards the center: 5.
Pawn captures away from the center: −5.
Pawn captures leading to doubled isolated pawns: −10.
Advancing a Rook's pawn: −10.
Capturing an undefended center pawn: 50.
Capturing a defended center pawn: −15.

The best way to show the effectiveness of these heuristics is to give some examples of TECH's opening play. Remember that TECH is playing purely from first principles—it has no "book" knowledge whatsoever.

(1) TECH–DAVID, Second ACM Tournament, Chicago 1971. 1 P−K4 P−K3 2 P−Q4 Q−R5 3 N−QB3 N−QB3 4 N−B3 Q−R4 5 B−Q3 Q−N5 6 O−O P−B3 7 B−K3 P−QR3 8 Q−K2 P−KN4.

(2) TECH–CHESS 3.5, Second ACM Tournament, Chicago 1971. 1 P−K4 P−QB4 2 N−KB3 N−QB3 3 P−Q4 P×P 4 N×P N−B3 5 N−QB3 P−Q3 6 B−QB4. Fischer's favorite move! Not bad for a program that knows no theory. 6 ... P−K3 7 O−O P−QR3 8 B−K3 N−K4.

(3) COKO III–TECH, Second ACM Tournament, Chicago 1971. 1 P−K4 P−K4 2 N−KB3 N−QB3 3 B−B4 N−B3 4 P−Q3 P−Q4 5 B×P N×B 6 P×N Q×P 7 N−B3 B−QN5 8 O−O B×N.

(4) SCHACH–TECH, Third ACM Tournament, Boston 1972. 1 P−Q4 P−Q4 2 P−QB4 P×P 3 N−KB3 N−QB3 4 P−K4 P−QN4 5 P−Q5 N−N5 6 B−N5 N−KB3 7 B×N KP×B 8 B−K2 B−QB4.

(5) TECH–USC, Third ACM Tournament, Boston 1972. 1 P−K4 P−QB4 2 N−KB3 N−QB3 3 P−Q4 P×P 4 N×P N−B3 5 N−QB3 P−Q3 6 B−QB4 P−K4 7 N−B5 B−K3 8 Q−Q3 N−QN5.

(6) CHESS 3.6–TECH, Third ACM Tournament, Boston 1972. 1 P−K4 P−K4 2 N−KB3 N−QB3 3 B−N5 N−B3 4 O−O B−B4 5 N−B3 P−Q3 6 B×N+ P×B 7 P−Q4 P×P 8 N×P O−O.

(7) OSTRICH–TECH, Play-off for second place, Third ACM Tournament, Boston 1972. 1 P−QB4 P−K4 2 N−QB3 N−KB3 3 P−K4 N−B3 4 P−Q3 B−B4 5 B−N5 O−O 6 N−B3 P−Q3 7 B−K2 B−K3 8 O−O N−Q5.

(8) TECH–COKO III, Play-off for second place, Third ACM Tournament, Boston 1972. 1 P−K4 P−K4 2 N−KB3 N−KB3 3 P−Q4 B−N5+ 4 B−Q2 B × B+ 5 QN × B P × P 6 N × P O−O 7 B−B4 N × P 8 N × N P−Q4.

These examples should be sufficient to convince the reader that it is quite possible to get reasonable positions in the opening without having any book knowledge.

TECH considers the middle game to begin with move 9 and it continues until one side has less than 1950 points worth of material (in the initial position each side has 4420 on TECH's scale). The center control heuristic is still used in the middle game but the priority factors are slightly altered: pawn = 3, Knight = 4, Bishop = 3, Rook = 2, Queen = 1 and King = 1. Since the pieces have usually found good squares by the middle game, this factor has less influence than in the opening. Each move is credited with a mobility term which is, as usual, the number of potentially legal moves available after the move is made. Movement of a piece into the area near the opponent's King is rewarded in the same way as the center control heuristic, and the net gain is again multiplied by the priority value for that piece. The pawn heuristics are the same as in the opening except that advances of wing pawns score − 5 instead of − 10. If TECH is ahead in material, piece captures score a 10-point bonus. Moving a piece which blocks a KBP or QBP scores 5.

The third, fourth, and fifth phases are devoted to three different types of endgame; endgame with pawns, general endgames, and endgames with only pieces. The most important goals in pawn endgames are advancing one's own passed pawns and blocking those of one's opponent. Each move is credited with the net gain in the realm of passed pawns and this allows TECH to escort its own pawns towards promotion and to block the advance of its opponent's pawns.

Pawn moves are weighted by the rank of their destination and by whether they are opposed.

Rank	Opposed	Unopposed
3	2	3
4	1	5
5	3	10
6	4	13
7	—	23
8	—	80

If TECH has more than one pawn on a file only the first is given this bonus; the other pawns on the same file lose 10 points.

As in the pawn endgame, TECH's main goal in the general endgame is to promote. The pawns are given the same weights for advancing as in the previous paragraph. The material value of a pawn is raised by 20% but if

TECH has two pawns or less then their material value is increased by 90%. This would mean, for example, that if TECH had a Knight and two pawns against a Bishop and one pawn it would not allow its opponent to sacrifice the Bishop in return for the two pawns. A move which places a Rook behind a passed pawn of either color is rewarded with 15 points. The center control term uses priorities of pawn = 0, Knight = 4, Bishop = 3, Rook = 1, Queen = 1 and King = 4. This encourages centralization of the King.

Unlike the other forms of endgame, TECH's goal in the endgame with pieces is to drive its opponent's King to the edge in order to deliver mate. This is achieved by doing a small (2-ply) tree-search and using a special evaluation function that was largely invented by the Northwestern University programming team.

TECH has always been one of the stronger programs of the present generation. At the Second ACM Tournament, Chicago 1971, it finished in a tie for second place from a field of eight programs. It subsequently won the play-off. At the third tournament in Boston, the following year, TECH again tied for second place but this time it was defeated in the play-off by OSTRICH. In 1974, when there were twelve competing programs in the Fourth ACM Tournament at Atlanta, TECH tied for fifth place. The program that finished second in Atlanta was TECH II, written at MIT by Alan Baisley, Stan Kugell, and James Cooper. (Baisley was instrumental in adding the opening library to Greenblatt's program in 1967.) One of the refinements of TECH is its storage of all positions evaluated during the tree-search. If a position occurs again later in the same search (by transposition) or during the search for the next move, it is retrieved from storage and the score associated with it is used instead of being computed for a second time. Since 1973, Gillogly appears to have moved on to other pastures, leaving TECH II to participate in the American and international arenas.

While TECH was active it competed in a number of human tournaments as well as three of the annual ACM events. Between May 1971 and March 1972 it participated in seven human tournaments scoring 12 points from 31 games. Its current (July 1975) USCF rating is 1243 which makes a mockery of some programmers' claims that their programs deserve ratings of 1600–1800.

Let us close this biography of TECH with one of the best games of its career.

White: COKO III   Black: TECH
Second ACM Tournament Chicago 1971

1 P–K4	P–K4	6 P×N	Q×P
2 N–KB3	N–QB3	7 N–B3	B–QN5
3 B–QB4	N–B3	8 O–O	B×N
4 P–Q3	P–Q4	9 P×B	O–O
5 B×P	N×B		

Black has achieved a perfectly satisfactory game from the opening

10 N–N5	B–B4	12 P–QB4
11 R–N1	P–KB3	

A normal computer move, attacking the opponent's Queen, but Black soon takes advantage of the weakness at White's Q4.

12 ...	Q−B4	17 K−R1	N−Q7+
13 N−R3?	B×N	18 P−B3	N×R.B8
14 B−K3	N−Q5	19 Q×N	P−B4
15 P×B	Q−B3	20 R−N5	P−B5
16 P−QB3?	N−B6+		

20 ... P−K5 would open up White's King.

| 21 R−B5 | Q−K3 | 22 B−B1 | P−B3 |

Threatening 23 ... P−QN3.

23 P−Q4   QR−K1?

This move was due to a bug in the program. 23 ... P × P is obvious and correct. Now Black loses a pawn.

24 R×KP	Q−N3	31 Q−B1	Q×BP
25 R×R	Q×R	32 P−Q6	Q−Q5
26 Q−B2	Q−K3	33 Q−K2	Q×QP
27 Q−B1	R−B4	34 Q−K8+	R−B1
28 P−KR4	P−B4!	35 Q−R4	R−B4
29 P−Q5	Q−Q3	36 Q−K8+	R−B1
30 Q−R3	Q−K4	37 Q−R4	Q−K3

TECH knows that it is ahead and so avoids threefold repetition of position.

| 38 Q−N3 | Q−K7! | 39 P−KR3 | R−Q1 |

Forcing the win of the Queen.

40 B×P   R−Q8+

And here COKO's programmers resigned.

KAISSA

Following the success of the Moscow program in the match against Stanford in 1967, little was heard from the Soviet Union about computer chess except for some of Botvinnik's theoretical results. But this did not mean that Soviet scientists had lost interest in the subject. In 1971 a group of programmers at the Institute of Control Science began to rewrite the program that had been used in 1967, and by the following year it was ready, in its new form, to play a match against the readers of the newspaper *Komsomolskaya Pravda*. The two-game match was conducted in the same way as the game played against *The Ural Worker* (see page 136). On most Sundays throughout 1972 the newspaper published KAISSA's moves in each of the two games and the readers sent in their suggested replies. In every case the move suggested by the majority of the readers was chosen and KAISSA's reply was published the following week. KAISSA drew one game and lost the other. The previous year Spassky had played two games against the readers of the same newspaper and scored one win and one draw. Obviously, the combined force of the readership of *Komsomolskaya Pravda* produces rather strong chess and so it is reasonable to assume that KAISSA is also no rabbit.

KAISSA's basic look-ahead was set at 7-ply, with further analysis along variations that involve captures and other forcing moves.

Game 1
White: KAISSA   Black: Readers

  1 P − K4   P − QB4   2 N − QB3

After 40 minutes thought and an examination of over half a million positions.

  2 ...   N − QB3   6 P − Q4   P × P
  3 N − B3   P − Q3   7 B × N   P × N
  4 B − N5   B − Q2   8 B × P   R − N1
  5 O − O   P − KN3   9 B − Q5   B − N2

If 9 ... P × P 10 B × NP R × B 11 Q − Q4, forking the two Rooks.

  10 P − QN3   N − B3   11 B − K3

Before making this move KAISSA examined more than 1,500,000 positions.

  11 ...   Q − B2   16 P × P   P × P
  12 Q − Q4   P − QR4   17 P × B   N − R4
  13 B − QB4   O − O   18 Q − Q3   B − K4
  14 QR − K1   B − B3   19 B − Q4   K − N2
  15 P − K5   B × N   20 R − K3

KAISSA predicted that the continuation would be 20 ... P − B3 21 B × P B × P+ 22 K × B P − Q4+ 23 B − K5.

  20 ...   P − B3   21 R.1 − K1

But now KAISSA changed its mind.

  21 ...   N − B5   26 R − KN1   N − Q4
  22 Q × BP   R.N1 − B1   27 Q × RP   R − QB4
  23 P − QR4   Q − Q2   28 Q − R7+   R − QB2
  24 B × B   BP × B   29 Q − R5   R − QB4
  25 K − R1   Q − R6   30 Q − R7+   R − KB2

Avoiding the draw

  31 Q × R.B5   P × Q   34 B × R   Q × B+
  32 B × N   R − B5   35 R − N2
  33 R × P   R × BP

Declared drawn, since the readers cannot afford to refuse the repetition of moves by 35 ... Q − Q8 + 36 R − N1 Q − B6 + .

Game 2
White: Readers   Black: KAISSA

1 P − QN3

This move was chosen by the newspaper before the readers had been invited to send in their suggestions.

1 ...	P − K4	10	N − K2	R − K1
2 B − N2	N − QB3	11	Q − B2	P − K5
3 P − QB4	P − B3	12	P − Q3	P × P
4 N − QB3	B − N5	13	Q × P	R − B1
5 N − Q5	KN − K2	14	P − B4	B − K2
6 P − QR3	B − Q3	15	P − KR4	P − KR3
7 P − N3	O − O	16	P − R5	N − R1
8 B − N2	N − N3	17	P − K4	P − Q3
9 P − K3	P − B4			

After examining 2,877,000 positions

18 O − O − O	R − B2	25	B − K4	N − B4
19 N × B +	Q × N	26	N − Q5	P − R4
20 N − B3	B − K3	27	P − KN4	N − K2
21 N − Q5	Q − Q2	28	N × N +	R × N
22 N − K3	P × P	29	P − N5	P × P
23 B × KP	N − K2	30	P − KB5	N − B2
24 B × QNP	R − N1			

KAISSA correctly thought that 30 ... B − B2 31 P − R6 P × P 32 Q − QB3 R − K4 33 Q × R would have been even worse.

31 P × B	Q × P	33	Q × Q	R × Q
32 B − Q5	Q − K6 +	34	QR − B1	Resigns

Thus KAISSA made its public debut. When the newspaper games ended the programming team continued to work on the program. Altogether about ten people were involved, including G. Adelson Velsky, Dr. V. Arlazarov, Dr. M. Donskoy, and A. Bitman, a Soviet Master who works at the Institute of Control Science.

KAISSA uses a complex evaluation function involving many features. In fact, it is so complex that when I asked Mikhail Donskoy about it he replied "... I don't even remember what is in it".

The program uses the now familiar method of searching all moves to a specified depth and then considering only captures, checks, other forcing moves and moves that are replies to checks. An upper bound of 30-ply has been put on the depth of these forcing variations but this depth is reached very seldom during the tree-search.

KAISSA uses the alpha–beta algorithm with the slight modification that before the search for a move begins the values of alpha and beta are not set to $-\infty$ and $+\infty$ (as is usually the case) but to rather narrower limits between which the value of the current position is known to lie. In this way the search is reduced still further.

An improvement in the performance of the alpha–beta search is obtained by using what the programmers call the "best move service." They point out that in chess the number of possible moves (less than 10,000) is far smaller than the number of possible positions, and that a classification of moves is therefore much easier than a classification of positions. The underlying principle of the best move service is that a move that was the best in many similar positions would most likely be plausible in the current position.

For each level ten moves are stored. These are the moves that were most frequently the best ones in other position at this level. When ordering the moves from a particular position these "best moves" are put at the head of the list and hence they are considered earlier. The application of the best move service produced a tenfold reduction in the time taken to search trees whose basic depth was 5-ply.

Another innovation was the idea of introducing a dummy move at certain points in the game tree. If it is White's turn to move and Black makes a "blank" move then it is White's turn to move once again. If White can now gain a material advantage then the previous White move must have carried this threat. Under some circumstances a threat can be used to create a cutoff in the search process and this technique can therefore lead to a further reduction in the search time. Another use of the discovery of threats is that they can be included in the list of moves that need to be examined.

KAISSA is able to reduce its search still further by being able to recognize positions that are analogous to positions already examined. If a move is absurd in a particular position then it is likely to be absurd in similar positions and it can therefore be excluded from the search until such time as circumstances appear that change the variation arising after the absurd move. A simple example of this strategy can be shown by considering the following position.

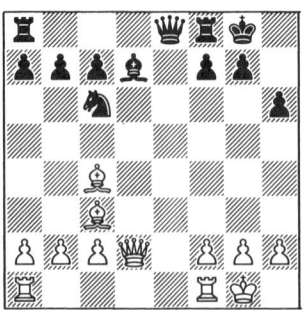

Under normal circumstance a chess program would always consider the moves Q – Q4 and Q – N5 when making a move from this position, and KAISSA's use of the blank move would normally result in these two moves being considered because they are threats. But in the present position both moves are absurd because they put the White Queen *en prise*. Let us assume that White plays 1 P – QR3 and that Black replies 1 ... P – QR4. Now most programs would once again consider Q – Q4 and Q – N5 even though both moves are still absurd *for the same reasons*, but KAISSA has a list of all the squares attacked by each of Black's pieces and it would not consider Q – N5 until Black's KRP had advanced, nor would it examine Q – Q4 until the Black Knight had moved. This is how a human plays chess and KAISSA's programmers point out that the standard of a human's play increases with the accuracy with which he determines when a move rejected earlier as absurd should be reexamined. KAISSA defines absurd moves as those that lead to the immediate loss of material. The only problem in implementing this "method of analogies" is in deciding when the position has changed sufficiently to warrent re-examining a move that was rejected earlier. KAISSA's programmers have made some progress in solving this problem but their research is beyond the scope of this book.

The KAISSA program runs on a British-built ICL 4/70 computer. A version of the program exists that could run on an IBM computer which would be faster and which would therefore allow a greater depth of search and hence stronger play by the program. So far the programmers have been unable to try the IBM version of their program (there are no IBM machines in the Soviet Union) but it is hoped that one will be made available for KAISSA's use at the 1977 World Computer Championship which is due to take place in Toronto. Dr. Arlazarov is of the opinion that if his program can have the use of the biggest and fastest IBM computer then it would be able to play with the strength of a Soviet Candidate-Master. If that proves to be true I might have to work hard to make sure of winning my bet!

KAISSA's first appearance outside the Soviet Union came in August 1974 when it participated in the First World Computer Championships in Stockholm. It won two of its games very convincingly, it was temporarily in trouble in a third and totally lost for much of the game in the vital last round. But in the end KAISSA won all four games and with them the title of World Champion.

2.4. Recent Progress in Computer Chess

MONROE M. NEWBORN

Originally published in: *Advances in Computers*, vol. 18, pp. 59–117. Copyright © 1979 by Academic Press, Inc., reprinted by permission.

1. Introduction

For several hundred years, man has been fascinated by the idea of machines playing chess. When electronic computers arrived in the late 1940s, Wiener (1948), Shannon (1950a, b), and Turing (1953), all prominent names in the world of cybernetics, suggested how man's new creation might so be used. How well they might play could only be guessed. Through the years, many have expressed their opinions, including former world chess champions Mikhail Botvinnik (1970) and Max Euwe (1970).

Based on the ideas of Shannon and Turing, working programs came into existence in the late 1950s and early 1960s (Kister *et al.*, 1957; Bernstein *et al.*, 1958b; Kotok, 1962). They all played rather poorly. To some people the reason was obvious: good players use an entirely different approach. It was argued that until we better understand the approach used by good human players and then write programs to perform in the same way, there would be little progress. Studies of good players suggested they search very small trees (less than 100 nodes) using powerful heuristics to guide the search (de Groot, 1965; Newell and Simon, 1972). The first attempt to program a computer to do the same was reported by Newell *et al.* (1963). Their program played weakly too, mainly because its heuristics were not sufficiently well developed. In fact, the major reason for the lack of success of all early programs was that not nearly enough effort went into any of them.

A little over 10 years ago, two good programs emerged, first the ITEP (Institute of Theoretical and Experimental Physics) program in Moscow, and a year or two later, MAC HACK VI. It was the ITEP program, developed by George M. Adelson-Velskiy, Vladimir L. Arlazarov, A. G. Ushkov, A. Bitman, and A. Zhivatovsky, that in 1966–1967 proved itself superior to an American program developed at MIT by Alan Kotok and John McCarthy in a four-game match in which moves were telegraphed across the Atlantic. The ITEP program won twice and drew twice. In its two victories, the Soviet program carried out exhaustive searches five levels (or plies) deep, continuing deeper along select lines when necessary to arrive at quiescent positions. When searching three levels, instead of five, the program was only able to draw with the Kotok–McCarthy Program (although even in the two drawn games, it had the better position). The latter searched to a depth of four plies in all four games, following capturing sequences somewhat further. Various heuristics were employed to forward prune supposedly bad moves from positions near the root of the tree but as Botvinnik said, the program sometimes "threw the baby out with the bath water" (Botvinnik, 1970).

Two lessons were vividly provided by the match. First, a brute force search of depth D plays significantly stronger chess than one of lesser depths. Second, if one wants to include forward pruning, it is necessary to have very good heuristics. Deeper brute force searches, of course, can be carried out by faster computers. However, some continued to argue that faster computers would never overcome the exponential growth of chess trees, that there may be some improvement in play but not a great deal and that great progress would only come when programs are designed to play as man does. The second lesson was more acceptable and during the next decade, efforts were made to develop good heuristics.

MAC HACK VI programmed by Richard Greenblatt with assistance from Donald Eastlake and Stephen Crocker, emerged in 1967 (Greenblatt *et al.*, 1967). It achieved a good balance between a program based on brute force and one that depended heavily on heuristics for move pruning. MAC HACK VI was the first program to successfully compete in human tournaments, receiving a USCF rating in the 1400s[1] for play in the Massachusetts State Championship in 1967.

In the late 1960s, interest in computer chess started to mushroom. New programs appeared on university campuses across America. In 1970 the Association for Computing Machinery hosted the first major computer chess tournament and has continued to do so every year thereafter at its annual conferences. The first world championship was held in Stockholm in 1974. During the years leading up to Stockholm, CHESS 4.0, the work of David Slate and Larry Atkin (and Keith Gorlen who left the team a few years ago)

---

[1] Most good chess players in America belong to the United States Chess Federation. This organization rates its members. FIDE, the Fédération Internationale des Échecs, is the governing world organization and it too rates its members. FIDE also awards the titles of International Grandmaster and International Master. FIDE ratings for International GMs are about 2500+ and International Masters, 2400+. The USCF ratings are Senior Master, 2400+; Master, 2200+; Expert, 2000+; Class A, 1800+; Class B, 1600+; Class C, 1400+; Class D, 1200+. There are about 150 International Grandmasters (GMs) and 400 International Masters (IMs) in FIDE.

of Northwestern University established itself as the best program in the West (Slate and Atkin, 1977). It went through a series of metamorphoses, starting as CHESS 2.0, becoming CHESS 4.0, at the time of the Stockholm tournament, and finally CHESS 4.7 as of September 1978. On each move, CHESS 4.0 carried out a sequence of exhaustive searches of two plies, three plies, and so on as time permitted, coupled with very thorough extended analysis. KAISSA, the prodigy of Mikhail Donskoy and Arlazarov, dominated efforts in the Soviet Union (see Adelson-Velskiy *et al.*, 1975). KAISSA, too, carried out exhaustive searches, though not a sequence of them, to some fixed depth and forcing sequences still further. Both programs participated at Stockholm with KAISSA capturing the championship (Hayes and Levy, 1976; Mittman, 1974; Newborn, 1975).

An era in computer chess history ended in Stockholm. It was an era in which gradual progress was made. There was progress in software technology making programming, debugging, and testing chess programs much easier. Hardware technology continued to improve as well, MAC HACK VI and CHESS 4.0 had each played thousands of games. Computer centers around the world had copies of them. CHESS 4.0, when running on a CDC 6600, was playing B level chess (although Slate would have said C) and notably better than it played 2 years earlier when running on a CDC 6400. The era was also characterized by unfulfilled expectations and growing pessimism over the future by those who were not sensitive to the progress being made and who felt the programmers were going in the wrong direction.

The year 1975 marked the beginning of, as Berliner calls it, the Jet Age of computer chess (Berliner, 1978). *Computer Chess* (Newborn, 1975) covers events up to and through Stockholm. It is the purpose of Section 2 to survey events following Stockholm including the tail end of the pre-Jet Age era. Over 15 games illustrate the rapid progress made, ending with CHESS 4.7's first victory over a Master. The games show that while CHESS 4.7 is currently the best program, there are several others that are quite strong and improving. Section 3 surveys tree-searching heuristics used in most programs. Chess-specific information in chess programs is considered in Section 4. Three special sections follow: the first discusses endgame play, the next examines speed chess by computers, and the third looks at chess on microcomputers. We conclude in Section 8 with a few comments on the future and discuss briefly what has been learned.

2. After Stockholm

Only 3 months separated the World Championship from the ACM's Fifth United States Computer Chess Championship in San Diego on November 10–12, 1974. Slate and Atkin came prepared to defend their title, a title which they had won for the first time in 1970 and had held ever since. But they were unable to find a CDC 6600 for the tournament (they used a CDC 6600 in Stockholm) and wound up playing on the slower CDC 6400 at Northwestern

University. RIBBIT, the work of Ron Hansen, Russell Crook, and Jim Parry of Waterloo University defeated CHESS 4.0 and won the tournament with a perfect 4–0 record. They used a Honeywell 6050 computer. RIBBIT had won the first Canadian Computer Chess Championship earlier in the year and had finished fourth in Stockholm, and they certainly figured to be contenders. But the concensus was that CHESS 4.0 was not at its best on the CDC 6400. RIBBIT's victory is presented here. Move times are denoted in parentheses. Moves from book are denoted by a "B."

White: RIBBIT   Black: CHESS 4.0

| 1 P–K4(B) | P–QB4(B) | 3 P×P(B) | Q×P(B) |
| 2 P–QB3(B) | P–Q4(B) | 4 P–Q4(B) | P×P(B) |

RIBBIT is now out of book but CHESS 4.0 has two more moves to go.

| 5 P×P(74) | N–QB3(B) | 7 N–B3(67) | Q–Q3(76) |
| 6 N–KB3(84) | B–N5(B) | | |

One move out of book and CHESS 4.0 is on the run!

8 P–Q5(241)	N–N5(174)	12 N–K5+(26)	K–K1(118)
9 B–QN5+(41)	B–Q2(163)	13 P–QR3(234)	Q–Q3(98)
10 B×B+(117)	K×B(86)	14 Q–R4+(41)	...
11 B–K3(317)	Q–QR3(61)		

A low point in CHESS 4.0's career. RIBBIT has established an over-whelming position (see Figure 1) and goes ahead by a Knight and pawn during the next few moves. After the exchange of Queens on move 18, CHESS 4.6 finds itself in a hopeless position.

Figure 1. Position after 14 Q–R4+.

14 ...	N–QB3(119)	19 R–Q1+(92)	K–K3(51)
15 P×N(475)	P×P(60)	20 O–O(231)	N–B3(82)
16 N×P/6(53)	P–K4(44)	21 P–QN4(332)	B–K2(109)
17 N×P/7+(65)	Q–Q2(107)	22 P–R3(69)	P–R4(58)
18 Q×Q+(32)	K×Q(1)	23 R/B–K1(43)	P–R5(85)

24 R − Q3(446)	P − K5(137)	43 N − B6(79)	B − B2(241)
25 B − Q4(49)	R/KR1 − K1(64)	44 R − Q7(258)	B − B5(302)
26 B × N(57)	B × B(75)	45 R × P(214)	B − Q3(158)
27 R × P + (122)	K − B4(77)	46 P − N8 = Q(155)	B × Q(88)
28 R × R(92)	R × R(88)	47 N × B(103)	K − N3(2)
29 P − N4 + (130)	P × Pep(237)	48 R − B5(96)	K − R3(1)
30 P × P(92)	R − K8 + (295)	49 N − Q7(545)	P − N3(3)
31 K − B2(92)	R − QB8(111)	50 R − B6(82)	K − N4(1)
32 P − N4 + (158)	K − N3(78)	51 K − N3(76)	K − R3(1)
33 N − K4(213)	B − K4(187)	52 N − K5(113)	K − N2(2)
34 P − QN5(89)	R − B7 + (88)	53 P − N5(74)	K − N1(4)
35 K − B3(183)	R − KR7(247)	54 N × P(67)	K − R2(1)
36 N − B2(160)	B − B3(140)	55 P − R4(348)	K − N1(1)
37 R − Q6(125)	K − R2(131)	56 P − R5(66)	K − N2(2)
38 R − Q5(161)	B − N7(185)	57 P − R6 + (37)	K − R2(1)
39 K − N3(91)	R × N(87)	58 N − K5(35)	K − R1(1)
40 K × R(57)	B × P(121)	59 P − N6(22)	K − N1(1)
41 P − N6(6)	B − B8(97)	60 K − N4(23)	K − R1(1)
42 P − N7(18)	B − B5(203)	61 R − B8 mate(2)	

2.1. 1975: The Jet Age Arrives

In 1975, Control Data Corporation came out with a new line of super-powerful computers, the CDC CYBER 170 series. David Cahlander of CDC arranged for Slate and Atkin's newest version of their program, CHESS 4.4, to use a CYBER 175 at CDC's corporate headquarters in Minneapolis for the 1975 ACM tournament, the Sixth North American Computer Chess Championship (the tournament's name was changed in deference to the previous year's champion and because usually several Canadian programs compete). The tournament was set for Minneapolis on October 19–21. RIBBIT returned under the new name of TREEFROG. CHAOS, the consistently tough program of Ira Ruben, Fred Swartz, Joe Winograd, William Toikka, and Victor Berman, was back for the third time, having finished second, or in a tie for second, in every tournament that it had previously participated in. DUCHESS, the work of Tom Truscott, Bruce Wright, and Eric Jensen of Duke University, was returning for its secondary try. Eight other programs participated in the four-round event (Levy, 1975).

CHESS 4.4 swept the tournament without facing any trouble along the way. Its fourth round victory over TREEFROG established without a doubt a renewed superiority over the other programs. The strength of the CYBER 175 was the biggest reason for its success. The addition of transposition tables was also a big factor. CHESS 4.4 was searching trees having several hundred thousand nodes.

CHESS 4.4's victory over TREEFROG is presented here. The program started on the CYBER 175, had machine problems, switched to Northwestern's CDC 6400 on move 4, back to the 175 on move 8, back again to the 6400 on move 14, again to the 175 on move 23 where the program really put the pressure on TREEFROG. From move 35 on, CHESS 4.4 coasted to victory on the 6400.

White: CHESS 4.4   Black: TREEFROG

1 P−K4(B)	P−Q4	5 B−K2(116)	P−K3
2 P×P(B)	N−KB3	6 O−O(39)	N−QB3
3 P−Q4(B)	N×P	7 P−B4(118)	N−B3
4 N−KB3(B)	B−N5	8 N−B3(60)	B−N5

CHESS 4.4 changed to a CDC 6400 after move 4 and is now back on the CYBER 175.

9 P−Q5(76)	B×N/QB	12 P×P(36)	R−QN1
10 P×N(83)	Q×Q	13 P−KR3(40)	B−KB4
11 R×Q(40)	B−N5		

Back to the CDC 6400. The position is slightly in CHESS 4.4's favor but at the level the programs are playing, the game is wide open.

14 P−R3(40)	B−B4	19 R−Q2(115)	R×P
15 P−KN4(40)	B−B7	20 P−N5(122)	N−K5
16 R−Q2(32)	B−N6	21 R−Q5(79)	P−KB3
17 N−Q4(97)	B×N	22 B−R5+(89)	K−K2
18 R×B(81)	P−K4		

For the last nine moves CHESS 4.4 has been playing weakly but still has the advantage. White weakened his position in an attempt to push the loss of the advanced pawn over his search horizon. The CDC CYBER 175 takes over for the next dozen moves and clinches the game.

23 B−B3(64)	P−B3	27 B×N(39)	P×B
24 R−R5(52)	B−B7	28 R×P/5+(55)	K−Q3
25 P−N4(25)	R/1−QN1?	29 R/1−K1(40)	...
26 B−K3(28)	N×P/4		

CHESS 4.4 is playing for bigger game than the Black pawns hanging around the board (see Figure 2).

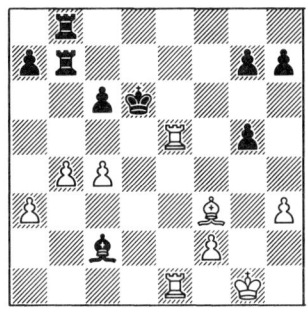

Figure 2. Position after 29 R/1−K1.

29 ...	R − KB2	32 R/6 − K6(86)	R − N3
30 R − K6 + (45)	K − B2	33 R − K8 + (96)	K − Q2
31 R × P + (78)	K − Q1	34 B − Q5(66)	R − B4

The end came on the CDC 6400.

35 R/1 − K7 + (81)	K − Q3	37 B × R(131)	B × B
36 B − K6(88)	R − QB3	38 P − B5 + (67)	Resigns

An error was made entering one of the last few moves into TREEFROG and when the authors realized it, they decided to resign the game.

On October 19, after the third round was completed, Tournament Director David Levy played a simultaneous exhibition against the programs. In 1968, Levy made a $2,000 wager with four leading computer scientists that no computer would defeat him in a match consisting of an even number of games within the next 10 years. Since then, Levy has willingly taken on many chess programs and a few of his games appear in this section. The idea of a simultaneous exhibition originated with Richard Harbeck, who made local arrangements for the Minneapolis affair. One program passed up the exhibiton giving Slate and Atkin the opportunity to enter two versions of CHESS 4.4, one running on a CDC 6400 and the other on a CDC CYBER 175. The programs were set to play at 3 minutes per move. Levy won ten games, drew two, and lost none. His draws, the first by a Master against a computer in any sort of public event, were against CHESS 4.4 running on the CDC CYBER 175, and TREEFROG running on the less awesome Honeywell 6080. The games ended at about 1 A.M. and perhaps Levy was not at his best by then. Levy's game with CHESS 4.4 went as follows.

White: Levy   Black: CHESS 4.4

1 P − Q3   ...

Designed to take CHESS 4.4 out of book.

1 ...	P − K4(173)	5 O − O	B − K2(86)
2 P − KN3	N − QB3(73)	6 P − B3	O − O(50)
3 B − N2	P − Q4(107)	7 P − QN4	P − K5(55)
4 N − KB3	N − B3(51)		

Levy attempts to keep the game quiet, hoping to build up a solid position. CHESS 4.4 has no patience and wants to get into tactical complications. Levy eagerly exchanges Queens when given the opportunity on move 9.

8 P × P	P × P(81)	10 N/3 − Q2	B − KB4(53)
9 Q × Q	R × Q(65)	11 N − B4	B − N5(60)

CHESS 4.4 will now cleverly fox Levy out of a pawn and establish a clear advantage (see Figure 3).

Figure 3. Position after 11 ... B − N5.

12 R − K1	B × P/7(127)	16 N − R3	R − N1(138)
13 N/1 − Q2	B × N(116)	17 R/R − Q1	N − K4(46)
14 N × B	R − Q6(98)	18 R × R	...
15 B − N2	P − QN4(111)		

Again, Levy wants to simplify the position.

18 ...	N × R(34)	20 R × N	P − B4(96)
19 R − K2	N × B(36)	21 P × P	P − QR3(100)

CHESS 4.6 would rather keep its Queenside pawns together and leave Levy's strewn about.

22 N − B2	R − QB1(45)	24 N × P	R − B3(72)
23 N − N4	R × P(74)	25 N − N8?	...

Levy traps his own Knight! He receives some compensation in having two passed Queenside pawns.

25 ...	R − N3(62)	29 B − R3	N − Q4(122)
26 P − QR4	R × N(62)	30 P − N7	N × P(44)
27 P × P	R − QB1(55)	31 B − B8	...
28 P − N6	R − N1(69)		

Although CHESS 4.4 is up a Knight, the position is a bit too difficult for the program to come up with a winning procedure. The remaining 21 moves can be seen to be a standoff although CHESS 4.4 has an extra piece and better chances (Figure 4).

31 ...	K − B1(64)	38 R − B4	K − B2(144)
32 R − B2	B − B3(117)	39 K − B1	P − B4(214)
33 K − N2	K − K2(48)	40 R − B5	K − B3(98)
34 R − Q2	P − N3(69)	41 R − B6+	K − N4(137)
35 R − Q7+	K − B1(67)	42 R − B5	B − Q5(88)
36 R − Q6	B − K4(120)	43 R − B4	B − R1(82)
37 R − QB6	P − B3(63)	44 R − B7	P − R3(272)

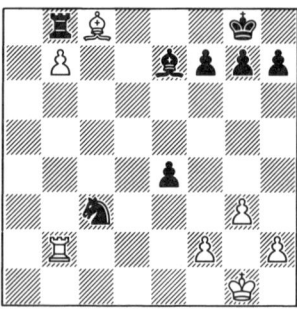

Figure 4. Position after 31 B−B8.

45 R−B6	B−K4(149)	55 R−B4	B−R1(7)
46 R−B5	B−N2(96)	56 R−B5	K−N4(22)
47 R−B7	B−B3(443)	57 P−N4	B−Q5(26)
48 R−B6	B−R1(88)	58 R−B4	B−K4(10)
49 R−B5	K−N5(49)	59 R−B5	K−B3(8)
50 R−B6	K−R4(50)	60 R−B6+	K−N2(35)
51 R−B5	N−R5(9)	61 R−B5	B−Q5(52)
52 R−N5	B−B3(10)	62 R−B7+	K−B3(109)
53 P−R3	N−B6(8)		Drawn by agreement
54 R−B5	B−Q5(11)		

In Levy's game against TREEFROG, he again tried to keep the position closed, was forced into a highly tactical battle and emerged with an advantage and forced mate in four on move 46 (see Figure 5). The mating tree that Levy overlooked, perhaps because he was tired, is shown in Figure 6. Levy was happy to settle for a pawn thinking he was on the road to victory. The game continued:

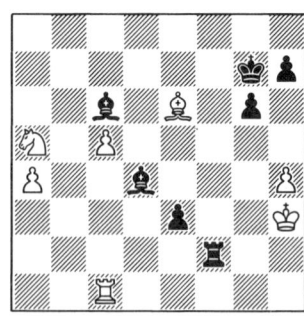

Figure 5. Position in TREEFROG (White) vs. LEVY (Black) after White's 46th move.

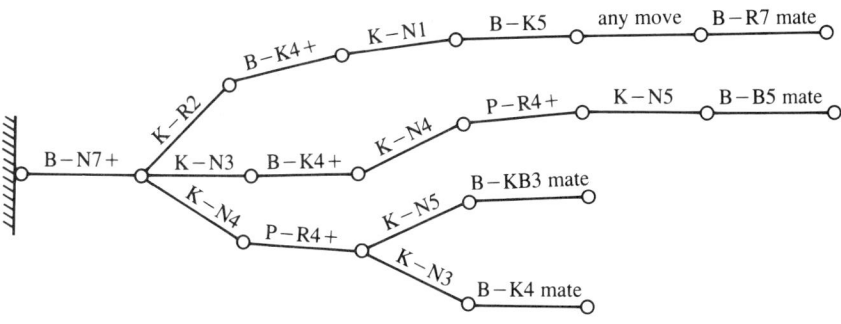

Figure 6. Mating tree: Black to mate in four in the position in Figure 5.

46 ...	B × P/5	49 K − N4	P − R4+
47 P − B6	B − K4	50 K − B3	R − R6?
48 N − B4	R − KR7+		

Levy's second error in five moves. The game ended in a draw on move 71 when it became clear that TREEFROG, with a Rook and Bishop, lacked the technique to defeat Levy, who had a lone Bishop and King.

Two other events took place in 1975 indicating the growing international interest in computer chess. On August 2–3 at the University of Calgary, the Second Canadian Computer Chess Tournament was held. Tony Marsland was the organizer and he implemented his idea of handicapping programs based on the speed of the computers they were running on. Versions of five programs competed: CHESS 3.0, WITA (Marsland's program), COKO 5 (Dennis Cooper and Ed Kozdrowicki), TREEFROG, and X, a program of unknown origin running on a PDP-10 computer [most likely MAC HACK VI or TECH]. X won the tournament with a $2\frac{1}{2}-\frac{1}{2}$ score. Soule and Marsland (1975) conclude that "the results are difficult to assess."

The First German Computer Chess Championship was held at Dortmund on October 8–10. Eight teams participated. The event was part of the Jahrestagung der Gesellschaft fur Informatik. Reinhard Zumkeller was the organizer and David Levy served as Tournament Director. TELL, the work of Johann Joss from Zurich and DAJA, the work of Ludwig Zagler and Sigfried Jahn of the Institut fur Informatik in Munich, finished the three-round Swiss tournament tied for first place with $2\frac{1}{2}$ points apiece. TELL won a playoff game for the championship. The level of play was clearly below the level of the North American tournaments. As Helmut Richter says, "Comparing Dortmond with the First United States Computer Chess Championship, you'll find remarkable parallelisms" (Richter, 1976).

2.2. 1976: The Paul Masson Chess Classic and Other Events

At the initiative of Martin Morrison, currently Executive Director of the United States Chess Federation and at that time the organization's Technical

Director an invitation was extended to CHESS 4.5 to participate in the Paul Masson Chess Classic played on July 23–24. Slate felt that the program was stronger than its rating of 1579 and so he elected to enter it in the B section of the tournament. In the past, the USCF had not been very supportive of activities in computer chess, but in the last two years, articles and information on computer chess have frequently appeared in the USCF's publication, *Chess Life and Review*. In 1977, the USCF established a set of rules under which programs participate in USCF-rated tournaments (Morrison, 1977). In fairness, the earlier lack of interest may have been due to the weak play shown by the programs, although even the first World Computer Chess Championship in Stockholm went unmentioned.

Played in a vineyard on the hillside around Sarasota, California, 756 players gathered for the largest Western tournament ever held. CHESS 4.5, to the astonishment of everybody including Slate and Cahlander (Cahlander was in California, Slate at CDC's new experimental CYBER 176[2] in Minneapolis) won the B section, with a perfect 5–0 record (Morrison, 1976). In an article reporting on CHESS 4.5's performance, Berliner (1976) observes that "to produce a perfect score against that caliber of competition should require a rating in the neighborhood of 1950." CHESS 4.5 was entitled to a prize of $700 but turned it down, an understanding agreed upon before the tournament started.

CHESS 4.6 moved very quickly averaging 55, 54, 59, 25, and 71 seconds in games 1 through 5, respectively. In Round 1, Neil Regan (1693) errored on move 19 in a somewhat complex position and resigned 12 moves later. The program's second-round opponent, Mark Arnold (1704) attempted an unsound sacrifice on move 8 and never recovered. He resigned on move 22. Against Irog Buljan (1751) in Round 3, CHESS 4.5 displayed its endgame talents. After move 48 R × P/2, the position shown in Figure 7 was reached. Berliner doubts whether "any program other than CHESS 4.5 could win this

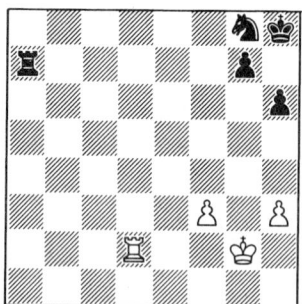

Figure 7. Position after 48 R × P/2 in Buljan. (White vs. CHESS 4.5 (Black)).

---

[2] Cahlander says that the relative speeds of the CDC 6400, CYBER 74, CDC 6600, CYBER 175, and CYBER 176 are 1, 1, 2.75, 6, and 12 respectively.

game against a competent defense. He says "CHESS 4.5 makes it look easy." The win went as follows:

White: Buljan   Black: CHESS 4.5

48 ...	R − R5	64 R − B6 +	R − B3
49 R − Q8	K − R2	65 R − B3	N − B5 +
50 R − Q6	N − B3	66 K − R2	P − R5
51 R − N6	N − R4	67 R − B5	K − R3
52 R − QB6	R − R7 +	68 R − QR5	P − N4
53 K − N1	N − B5	69 R − N5	P − N5
54 P − R4	R − KN7 +	70 R − N8	P − N6 +
55 K − R1	R − N6	71 K − N1	R − B3
56 R − B3	K − N3	72 R − N1	P − R6
57 K − R2	R − R6 +	73 R − R1	R − B3
58 K − N1	R × P/5	74 R − Q1	N − K7 +
59 K − B2	R − R7 +	75 K − R1	R − KN3
60 K − B1	P − R4	76 R − Q6	P − N7 +
61 R − B4	N − Q6	77 K − R2	P − N8 = Q +
62 K − N1	R − R6	78 K × P	Q − KR8 mate
63 K − N2	R × P		

In Round 4, Wesley White (1742) fell prey after only 31 moves. In the final round, Herbert Chu (1784), the program's highest rated opponent, got into a highly tactical battle. Although he had an early advantage, he fell behind on move 19 and resigned on move 30.

The performance was by far the most impressive by a program to date even if one assumes that the California wine may have had an inhibiting influence on the humans. This however was merely the beginning. No one imagined what was just around the corner.

The next major event was ACM's Seventh North American Computer Chess Championship in Houston, October 19–21 (Levy, 1976a). CHESS 4.5 (and the CDC CYBER 176) returned to defend its title. CHAOS was the only other program given any chance, but the authors of CHAOS had done little to improve their program since the previous ACM tournament. TREEFROG's group had lost interest after graduating from Waterloo and did not return. Except for CHESS 4.5, there was perhaps a lull in progress and enthusiasm at Houston. Some of the older programs had retired—TREEFROG, COKO, The Dartmouth Program, TECH and TECH II, for example—and the newer ones such as DUCHESS, BLACK KNIGHT, and BLITZ III were just rounding into form. This latter group would catch up quickly, using the experience of those that came earlier to their advantage. But for the present, CHESS 4.5's edge over the other programs was the largest ever. It was searching trees with 150,000–800,000 nodes per move! CHAOS, running on an Amdahl 470 was searching trees with up to 100,000 nodes per move.

CHESS 4.6 won the tournament defeating WITA in Round 1, DUCHESS in Round 2, and BLACK KNIGHT in Round 3. Its victory over CHAOS in Round 4 was the most lopsided performance played between these two rivals. It is presented here to show the contrast.

Cahlander provided this writer with CHESS 4.6's printout of the game and the data are presented here in digested form. After every White move, there is indicated: (1) the time in seconds; (2) the maximum depth of the iterative exhaustive search; (3) the number of nodes examined × 10^4; and (4) the number of plies that the game followed the continuation expected by the program. If the opponent made the expected reply, that counts for one move.

White: CHESS 4.5   Black: CHAOS

Sicilian Defense

1 P−K4(B)	P−QB4	4 N×P(B)	N−B3
2 N−KB3(B)	N−QB3	5 N−QB3(B)	P−K3
3 P−Q4(B)	P×P	6 N×N(54,6,19,3)	...

This guarantees that CHESS 4.5 will either give CHAOS an isolated Rook's pawn or trade Queens preventing CHAOS from castling. Nothing else looks better.

6 ...	P/N×N	14 B−R3(78,6,24,0)	Q−B6
7 P−K5(85,6,27,4)	N−Q4	15 P−B4(110,6,33,0)	P−B3
8 N×N(255,7,82,1)	P/B×N	16 B−Q6(88,6,28,0)	P−B4
9 B−Q3(77,6,24,0)	P−N3	17 P−R5(93,6,29,0)	K−B2
10 O−O(71,6,23,0)	B−KN2	18 Q−B2(149,6,45,1)	B−KB1
11 Q−K2(66,6,20,1)	B−N2	19 B×B(201,7,67,2)	R/KR×B
12 P−QN3(108,6,33,0)	Q−K2	20 Q−R4(279,7,85,0)	Q−B4+
13 P−QR4(77,6,23,0)	Q−N5	21 K−R1(169,8,58,0)	K−N2

In the position shown in Figure 8, CHESS 4.5 cons CHAOS out of a Bishop for two pawns and a victory two moves later.

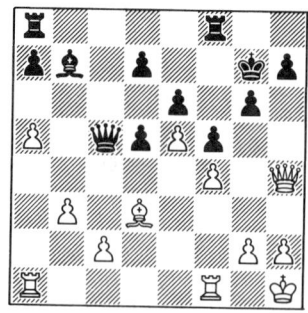

Figure 8. Position after 21 ... K−N2.

22 P – QN4(164,7,57,0)	Q × P/5	24 R × B(64,6,23,0)	Q – R5
23 R/R – N1(113,7,45,2)	Q × P/4	25 B – N5(129,7,51,?)	Time forfeit

CHAOS calculated for over 40 minutes, carrying out deeper and deeper iterations looking for a way to proceed and finally lost on time. CHESS 4.5 saw the continuation 25 ... Q × P/B7 26 R × P/Q R – B2 27 Q – KB6 K – R3 28 R × R.

Once again, Tony Marsland organized a computer chess event in Canada, this time a workshop in Edmonton on June 26–27 (Marsland, 1976). Eight programs participated in a "handicapped" tournament with OSTRICH (Newborn and Arnold) coming out the champion, winning $3\frac{1}{2}$ out of 4 points. In Amsterdam on August 9–11, eight teams participated in the European Computer Chess Championship. The three-round Swiss tournament was won by MASTER with ORWELL and TELL tying for second place (Bakker, 1976).

2.3. 1977: CHESS 4.6 Plays Expert Level Chess

With continuing support from Dave Cahlander and the CDC CYBER 176, Slate and Atkin entered CHESS 4.5 in the 84th Minnesota Open (Minneapolis, Minnesota, February 18–20, 1977), a six-round Swiss tournament open to anyone who wanted to participate. To the great surprise of everyone, the program trounced five players: Warren Stenberg (1969), Charles Fenner (2016), Gerald Ronning (1965), Rick Armagost (1947), and Robert Johnson (1954). Its only defeat was delivered by Walter Morris (2175) (see Cahlander, 1977a). CHESS 4.6 won the tournament and thereby qualified for the Minnesota State Championship that was played the following weekend in Minneapolis. This contest was a "closed tournament," closed to all but the best players in the state, and it was a round robin, that is, everyone played everyone else. The competitors in this event studied games played the previous week by CHESS 4.5, looking for weaknesses. This marks the first time in chess history that computer games were studied seriously by good players concerned with the possibility of losing! Nels Truelson (2079), Peter Thompson (2142), and Lasloe Ficsor (2110) defeated the program in Rounds 1, 2, and 3, respectively. The program defeated Rick Linden (1850) in Round 4 and drew with John Greene (1899) in Round 5. On the basis of the 16 games played in the Paul Masson Chess Classic, the Minnesota Open, and the Minnesota State Championship, CHESS 4.5 received a performance rating of 2099.

We present the endgame of the CHESS 4.5 vs. Stenberg game in Section 6 when specifically discussing endgame play. Berliner (1977a) comments on the CHESS 4.5 vs. Fenner game and the CHESS 4.5 vs. Johnson game. Fenner has the dubious distinction of being the first Expert ever to have lost a tournament game to a computer. The game, with some of Berliner's comments in quotations, follows (see page 166 for an explanation of the information associated with CHESS 4.5's moves).

White: CHESS 4.5   Black: Fenner
                          Sicilian Defense

1 P−K4(B)	P−QB4	7 O−O(110,6,34,0)	B−B4
2 N−KB3(B)	P−K3	8 N−N3(67,6,19,0)	B−R2
3 P−Q4(B)	P×P	9 N−B3(64,4,18,2)	N−B3
4 N×P(B)	P−QR3	10 B−N5(83,6,24,1)	N−K4
5 P−QB4(B)	N−KB3	11 B×N(128,6,36,2)	P×B
6 B−Q3(B)	Q−B2	12 Q−K2(59,6,18,2)	P−Q3

"It appears that Black has gotten the better of the opening having secured the Bishop pair but appearances are deceptive. White has a good game and now finds a way to assert his space advantage."

13 K−R1(47,6,15,4)	B−Q2	15 Q×N(345,7,101,0)	O−O−O
14 P−B4(59,6,19,2)	N×B	16 R/R−Q1(99,6,30,0)	...

"Despite the natural appearance of this move, the immediate P−KB5 is stronger, as it would force Black to move one of the Rooks to KB1 to defend against the threat of P×P." CHESS 4.5 saw 16 ... B−N1 17 P−KR4 P−QN3 18 P−KB5 K−N2 19 P×P B×P. This is a tough position for a program to find a good continuation. CHESS 4.5 feels that White has a $\frac{1}{4}$ pawn advantage.

16 ...   B−B3   17 P−KB5(95,6,28,0) B−N1

"This move attempts to find counterchances, by mate threats along the diagonal. However, the simple 17 ... Q−K2 is in order."

18 P−N3(99,5,25,0) ...

"CHESS 4.5 shows fine judgment in avoiding 18 P×P P×P 19 R×P P−Q4 20 Q−R3 P×P/K5 after which Black's pieces gain new life and his chances improve against the game continuation. Now Q−K2 appears in order for Black after which White can continue with 19 P×P 20 N−Q4 with the better game." The iterative exhaustive search was limited to a depth of five levels the lowest in the game thus far, because, most likely, the alpha−beta window had to be modified on the last iteration (see Section 3.6).

18 ...	P−KR4?!	21 Q×P/3(88,6,27,1)	R/Q1−N1
19 P×P(62,6,21,0)	P−R5	22 P×P(67,6,22,3)	...
20 R×P(71,6,22,3)	P×P/6		

"This is the fly in the ointment. After the incorrect 22 Q−B4, Black would play P−Q4!! with many threats and the better game. Now if 22 ... R×Q 23 P−B8=Q+ R×Q 24 R×R+ K−Q2 25 R−B7+ wins." CHESS 4.5 predicted the game would continue: 22 ... Q×P 23 R×Q R×Q 24 N−R5 B−B2 25 N×B P×N with an evaluation indicating a two-pawn advantage.

22 ...	Q×P	24 N−Q5(197,7,64,0)	...
23 R×Q(161,7,53,2)	R×Q		

"Here Black had the temerity to offer a draw, which was declined" (see Figure 9).

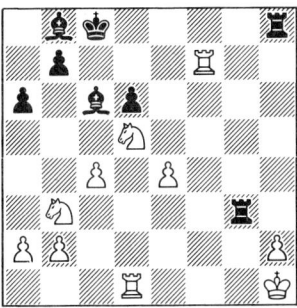

Figure 9. Position after 24 N – Q5.

24 ...   B – K1?!

"Setting a cute trap, which unfortunately for Black is not quite sound."

25 N – N6 + (67,7,26,2)   ...

CHESS 4.5 sees 25 ... K – Q1 R × P/7 26 B – B2 N – B5 27 R – N3 N × P, and feels White is ahead by the equivalent of three pawns.

25 ...   K – Q1   27 R × B + (67,8,24,6)   K – B2
26 R × P/7(266,8,96,0)   B – B3   28 R – QB8 + (1,3,3,3)   ...

"A very clever move, which escaped me when I first saw the game. The point is that on 28 ... K × N, 29 R × P!! and with pieces loose all over the place, Black is lost."

28 ...   R × R   30 K – N1(269,10,112,0)   R – KR1?
29 P × R(102,9,38,2)   B × P +

"30 ... K × N, 31 R × P + was better but hopeless."

31 N – Q5 + (178,8,70,0)   K – B3   32 N – R5 + (204,8,90,?)   Resigns

"On 32 ... K – B4, 33 P – QN4 mate, or 32 ... K – Q2, 33 N – B6 + wins the Bishop. A crisp beautiful game; probably the best ever by a computer, and against a rated Expert." CHESS 4.5 saw winning the Bishop through 32 ... K – Q2 33 N – B6 K – B2 34 N × B R – R4 P – N4. CHESS 4.6 examined just under 400,000 positions per move; each nonbook move averaged 49 seconds.

One month later in New York at the Essex House just off Central Park, CHESS 4.5 gave a simultaneous exhibition itself. Dave Cahlander arranged it as a promotional event at which CDC officially launched the CYBER 176. Taking on ten opponents including Eric Bone (2150), Burt Hochberg (editor of *Chess Life and Review*), Walter Goldwater (an A player and president of the Marshall Chess Club), and one other A player, the program won eight, drew one, and lost one (to Bone). Lasker, who played the Bernstein Program in 1958, said at that time that no program would reach Master status. He observed, after playing CHESS 4.5 that "I am still not ready to admit that a computer will ever attain Master strength, though I will concede that the one made by Control Data Corporation plays better than I had expected anyone would be able to make it do" (Lasker, 1977).

Goldwater (1977) wrote after losing that he was very upset for two days, but after finding out that CHESS 4.5's rating was higher than his, he did not mind quite as much. He said he "phoned various friends—Robert Byrne, Nat Halper, Milton Hanauer—they were upset, too. It was not that they felt I had played worse than usual, but rather that they could see that this was now something to cope with."

As part of the CYBER's coming out party, it also played four games of speed chess with Levy, winning two and losing two. Levy estimated its playing strength at the 2300 level but argued that "it has insufficient positional understanding and strategic planning to enable it to perform at master level under tournament conditions" (Levy, 1977a).

On April 1, Levy went to Carnegie–Mellon University to play a two-game challenge match against CHESS 4.6. He won the first game, and because he could not lose the match, the second game was called off. Donald Michie was a Visiting Professor there and arranged the affair (Michie, 1977). With an audience of 400 watching, Levy steered CHESS 4.5 into a Sicilian opening in which he felt the program had played incorrectly in the past. After Levy's ninth move, the position was as shown in Figure 10. Surely enough, on the first move out the book, CHESS 4.5 continued as Levy had anticipated with 10 N × N (Levy, 1977a). Berliner, who served as commentator for the game, observes that by move 17, CHESS 4.5 had recovered and that in fact Levy was then "probably lost" (Berliner, 1977b), although Levy (1977a) does not agree. On move 26, Berliner says that CHESS 4.5 made the "fatal error." The game went as follows.

Figure 10. Position after 9 ... P – QR3.

White: CHESS 4.5   Black: Levy

1	P – K4(B)	P – QB4	6 P – B3(B)	B – N2
2	N – KB3(B)	P – Q3	7 B – K3(B)	O – O
3	P – Q4(B)	P × P	8 Q – Q2(B)	N – B3
4	N × P(B)	N – KB3	9 B – QB4(B)	P – QR3
5	N – QB3(B)	P – KN3	See Figure 10	

10	N × N(70)?	P × N	13 B – K2(80)	B – K3
11	O – O(209)	N – Q2	14 P – QN3(59)	...
12	P – B4(193)	N – N3		

Levy expected this, pointing out in his analysis that "programs are quite prone to weakening pawn moves because they have little understanding of strong and weak squares."

14 ...	N – B1	15 P – QR3(163)	...

Berliner gives CHESS 4.6 credit for "a fine move which meets the threat of Q – R4." Levy felt that 15 B – Q4 was better.

15 ...	Q – R4	17 P – B5!(121)	...
16 P – QN4(93)	Q – B2		

Opinions differ here. Berliner argues that Levy is probably lost. Levy contends that "White's K5-square is weak and his King's pawn is in danger of becoming isolated."

17 ...	B – Q2	18 B – R6(644)	...

Berliner says that CHESS 4.5 "misjudges the situation and allows the exchange of Queens. With 18 R – B3 this could have been prevented and the attack with B – R6 would be extremely strong." Levy agrees that 18 B – R6 was not best. He suggests that "the correct plan begins with 18 K – R1 followed by R – B3, B – R6, and R – R3."

18 ...	Q – N3 + !	23 R – QN1(107)	N – N3
19 K – R1(115)	Q – Q5	24 R/3 – B1(153)	R/B – QN1
20 Q × Q(25)	B × Q	25 R/N – Q1(46)	P – B3
21 R – B3(118)	B – N2	26 P – QR4?(129)	...
22 B × B(143)	K × B		

Both Berliner and Levy see this as CHESS 4.6's fatal error. Berliner says that "Black's Queenside pawn structure collapses."

26 ...	P – QR4	31 R/1 – B3(118)	P – R5
27 P – N5(68)	P × P/N4	32 P – R4(54)	P – R6
28 P × P/5(134)	R – QB1	33 P × P(391)	P × P
29 R – Q3(143)	R – B4	34 R – K3(249)	B – K3
30 R – N3(243)	R/R – QB1	35 P – R5(245)	P – N4

36 N − Q5(75)	P − R7	40 K − R2(137)	R − B8
37 R − QR3(142)	B × N	41 B − N3(118)	P − R8 = Q
38 P × B(148)	R × P/7	42 R × Q(63)	R × R
39 B − Q1(318)	R − Q7	43 Resigns	

IFIP Congress 77 hosted the Second World Computer Chess Championship in Toronto on August 6–9. Sixteen programs participated in the four-round Swiss style event that was the biggest show yet for the computer chess world. KAISSA, running on an IBM 370/168 returned to defend its title. CHESS 4.6 came as the principal challenger. DUCHESS had been greatly improved as had BELLE, and both figured to be contenders. But at the end of four days, there was no doubt that CHESS 4.6 was best, defeating BCP in Round 1, MASTER in Round 2, DUCHESS in Round 3, and BELLE in Round 4 (and KAISSA in a friendly match following the tournament since the two had not met during regular play). Searching exhaustively to a depth of six plies on most moves and deeper in endgame play was too much for any of its opponents. DUCHESS, improved in the months leading up to the tournament, upset KAISSA in the first round and, although the strongest challenger, was not a threat to the champion.

The game betwen BELLE and CHESS 4.6 to decide the championship went as follows. Slate assisted with the analysis. As can be seen, BELLE played quite strongly but was in contention for no more than the first 24 moves.

White: BELLE   Black: CHESS 4.6

1 P − K4	N − QB3	4 N − B3	B − N5
2 N − KB3	P − K3	5 P − K5	N/N1 − K2
3 P − Q4	P − Q4		

Slate was concerned with the weakness of Black's Kingside. He knows that CHESS 4.6 has no algorithm specifically designed to be aware of the King's vulnerability.

6 P − QR3 ...

BELLE invites CHESS 4.6 to isolate a pawn, something that CHESS 4.6 rarely passes up.

6 ...	B × N+	8 B − N5+	B − Q2
7 P × B	N − R4	9 B − Q3	...

This adds strength to White's Kingside threats.

9 ...	R − QB1	11 N − B3	...
10 N − N5	P − KR3		

Whew! Slate was worried about 11 Q − R5, threatening mate on KB7.

11 ...   P − QB4

Threatening to isolate more pawns!

12	P × P	R × P		15	O − O	R × P/6
13	B − K3	R × P		16	R × R	N × R
14	B × P/7	N − B5		17	B − QB5	...

This is necessary to avoid 17 ... P − QN3.

| 17 | ... | Q − R4 | | 18 | B − Q6 | N − B5 |

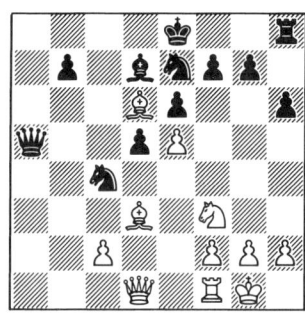

Figure 11. Position after 18 ... N − B5.

(See Figure 11.) Slate was worried about 19 B × N/4. This would strengthen White's Bishop's hold on Q6. White instead rushes to the endgame with

| 19 | Q − R1 | N − B3 | | 21 | R − R1 | B − B1 |
| 20 | Q × Q | N/3 × Q |

This gives Black space to move and eliminate a back row mate.

| 22 | P − B3? | N − B3 | | 23 | R − R4 | ... |

Slate pointed out that 23 B × N is better, solidifying the position of White's remaining Bishop.

| 23 | ... | N × B! |

Slate was concerned that CHESS 4.6 might not play 23 ... N × B because 24 P × N gives White a passed pawn that the program will believe is a serious threat. A search of seven plies is necessary to see how to proceed correctly.

24	P × N	K − Q2		27	R − QR4	P − N4
25	R − KN4	P − KN4		28	R − R1	P − QN5
26	B − B2	K × P

CHESS 4.6 will now have a passed Queen's pawn, which is what it wants.

29	P × P	N × P		33	N − K2	B − N4
30	B − N1	B − Q2		34	N − N1	R − B8
31	K − R1	P − B4		35	R − R5	R × B!
32	N − Q4	R − QB1!

White cannot play 36 R × B because of the mate threat 36 ... N − Q6
37 ... N × P mate!

36	P − B3	B − B8	40	R − R4	B × P +
37	P − R4	R − N7	41	K − N3	B − R4
38	P × P	B × P +	42	K − R3	P − B5
39	K − R2	P × P	43	R − R8	B − N3

CHESS 4.6 threatens mate in one with 44 ... B − B4 mate.

44	K − N4	R − N7 +	49	R − N7	B − B6
45	K − R3	R × N	50	R − KR7	N − Q6
46	K − R2	R − N5	51	R − R3	R − N7 +
47	R − Q8 +	K − K4	52	K − R1	N − B7 mate
48	R − KN8	B − K5			

As exciting as the tournament itself was the presence of Dr. Mikhail
Botvinnik. He was a guest of the tournament and his presence among the
participants added immeasurably to the stature of the event. His own program
PIONEER, is under test in the USSR and nearing the day when it will be
ready to compete. Botvinnik discussed his ideas with the participants, his
pleasure in seeing the progress made so far, and his concern that for programs
to achieve significantly stronger levels of performance, much more selective
search is necessary.

When given the difficult position in Figure 12 (credited to G. Nadareishvili),
PIONEER produced the correct solution after considering only 200 moves.
The computer time required was about 3½ hours! The correct continuation is

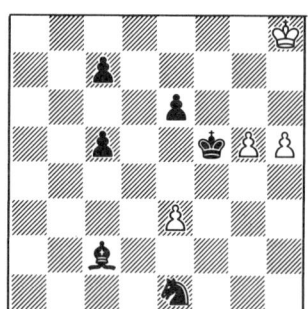

Figure 12. Endgame position with White to move and win (G. Nadareishvili).

1	P − N6	K − B3	3	P − K4!	...
2	P − N7	B − R2			

According to PIONEER, not 3 K × B because 3 ... N − B6 4 P − N8 = Q
N − N5 + 5 Q × N K × Q 6 P − R6 P − B5 7 K − N7 P − B6 8 P − R7 P − B7
9 P − R8 = Q P − B8 = Q 10 Q − R3 + K − N5.

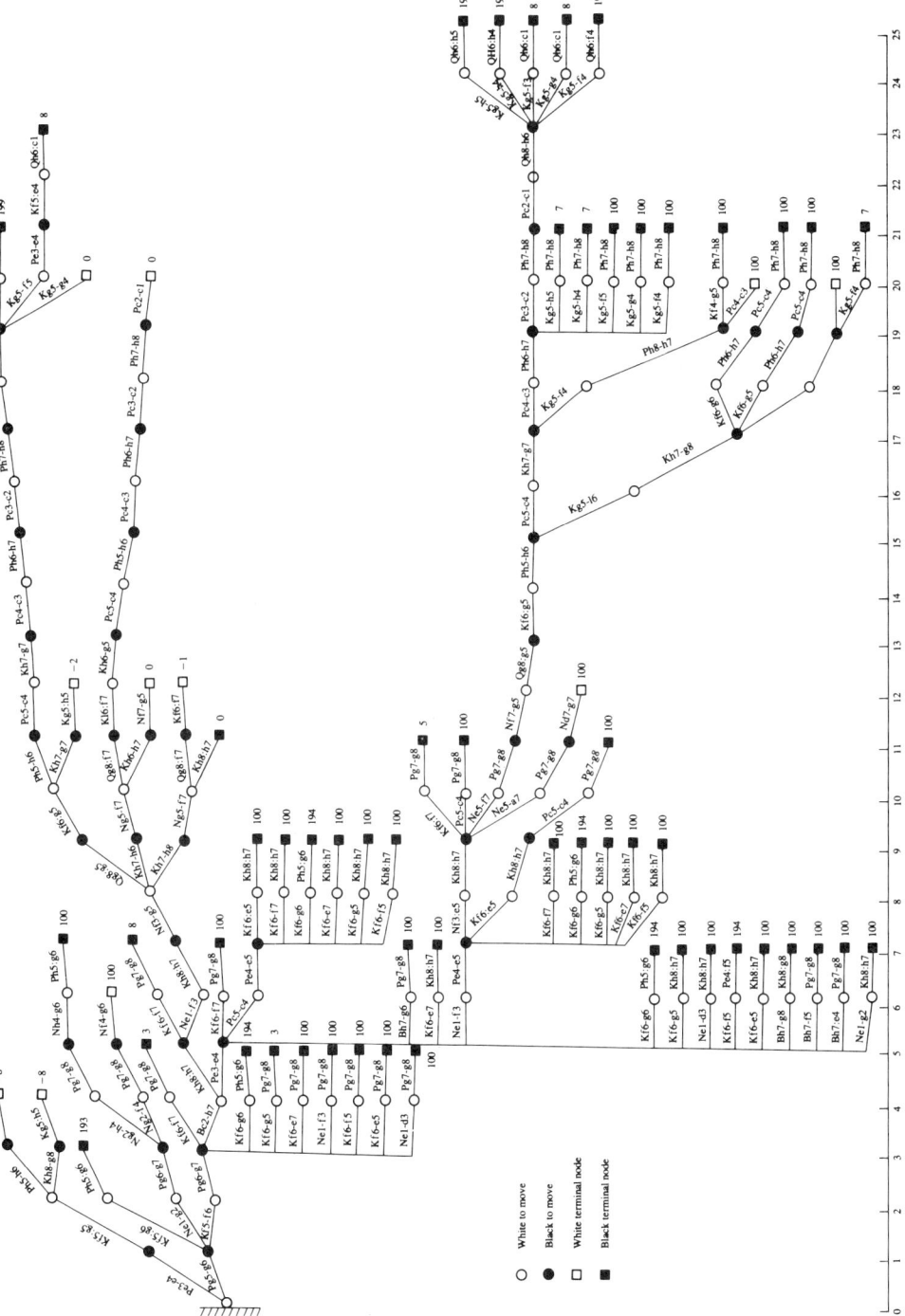

Figure 13. Tree created by PIONEER to solve endgame problem in Figure 12.

3 ...	N — B6	8 P — R6	P — B5
4 P — K5+	N × P	9 K — N7	P — B6
5 K × B	N — B2	10 P — R7	P — B7
6 P — N8 = Q	N — N4+	11 P — R8 = Q	P — B8 = Q
7 Q × N	K × Q	12 Q — R6+!	

PIONEER's tree, redrawn in a readable form from the computer's printout by Botvinnik is shown in Figure 13. The principal continuation was 25 plies long.

On September 16–18, CHESS 4.6 traveled to London via telephone and with Cahlander's help participated in the top section of the Aaronson Chess Tournament. Grandmasters Hort (Czechoslovakia) and Kotov (Soviet Union) were the class of the field. The *Minnesota Chess Journal* (1977) reports that "the electronic monster lost its first game, then won two, and drew the last three for a plus score of $3\frac{1}{2}$–$2\frac{1}{2}$. The three opponents with which it drew in the last three rounds were very strong: Joppen (Switzerland) rated 2200; Seewald (Netherlands), 2160; Flear (Britain), also 2160. The computer's third-round victim was P. Lewin from Britain with a 1680 rating, while its adversaires in the first two rounds were unrated." This is the first time a computer has drawn with a Master in tournament play.

After having had a stunningly successful year, CHESS 4.6 went into the ACM's Eighth North American Computer Chess Tournament in Seattle as a heavy favorite. Twelve programs participated in the four-round event held on October 13–15 (Bailey, 1977); eight of them had participated two months earlier in Toronto. Jack Perkins of NBC-TV covered the tournament and his feature story appeared on the TODAY Show on October 23, 1977. CHESS 4.6 had to be happy with a tie for first place honors with an improved DUCHESS. Undefeated going into the final round, the two met and played each other to a draw. Truscott attributes some of the improvement in DUCHESS to better tree-searching techniques. DUCHESS, as does CHESS 4.6, makes extensive use of transposition tables.

Levy played a simultaneous exhibition against the programs, winning eight, drawing with CHAOS, and losing to CHESS 4.6. The tournament included the participation of the first microcomputer, an Intel 8080, programmed by Arnold Epstein.

DUCHESS's draw with CHESS 4.6 was an exciting game. It seemed for a good part of the game that DUCHESS was going to upset CHESS 4.6, but the champion hung on. We present here the first 32 moves. The remainder of the game appears in Section 5 where endgame play by programs is discussed.

White: DUCHESS   Black: CHESS 4.6

1 P — K4	P — QB4	5 N — B3	P — Q3
2 P — Q4	P × P	6 B — QB4	P — K3
3 P — QB3	P × P	7 O — O	N — B3
4 N × P	N — QB3	8 Q — K2	B — K2

9	R – Q1	P – K4	11	B – Q2	N – Q5
10	B – K3	N – KN5			

CHESS 4.6 does not search deeply enough to see that this loses a pawn.

12	N × N	P × N	16	Q × N	B – N5
13	N – N5	Q – N3	17	Q – R4 +	B – Q2
14	B – B4	N – K4	18	Q – N3	O – O
15	N × P/4	N × B	19	Q × Q	P × Q

We see that CHESS 4.6 would rather castle as it did on move 18 than avoid doubled pawns. DUCHESS has slightly better pawns but CHESS 4.6 has a pair of Bishops.

20	P – QR3	R/B – B1	26	R – Q2	R – QB4
21	R/R – B1	R × R	27	N – K2	R – B3
22	R × R	R – R5	28	P – QR4	B – K3
23	B – K3	B – Q1	29	N – Q4	R – B8 +
24	P – B3	R – R4	30	K – B2	...
25	R – Q1	B – KB3			

CHESS 4.6's check allows White's King to pick up an important tempo in its eventual move to the center to support its pawns.

30	...	B – Q2	32	P × B	R – QN8
31	N – N5	B × N			

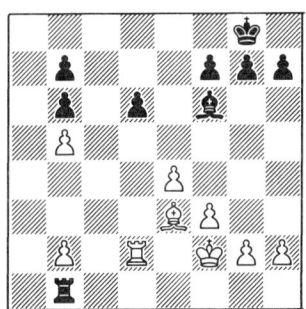

Figure 14. Position after 32 ... R – QN8.

(See Figure 14.) The game is completed on pages 195 and 196 in Section 5.

Bobby Fischer has been closely following developments in computer chess. Some time in the spring of 1977, he played an early version of CHESS CHALLENGER out of curiosity, commenting on its performance in Penrod's *Computer Chess Newsletter* (Penrod, 1977a). He also played three games against MAC HACK VI (Penrod, 1977b). It is not clear what computer or what version of MAC HACK VI was used. The games may be the only published games played by Fischer since winning the World Championship in Iceland.

2.4. 1978: More Accomplishments

The pace of activities continued strongly into 1978. The first tournament exclusively for microcomputers was held on March 3–5 in California (see Section 7).

CHESS 4.6 participated in the Minnesota Twin Cities Open on April 29–30. It entered as the highest rated player and lived up to expectations by winning the tournament with a 5–0 record. Going into the event, the program had a rating of 1936 and Douglas indicates that its performance raised that number by about 35 points. In other recent tournaments, CHESS 4.6 received *performance ratings* over 2100; these performances raised its previously established rating that until the last year or so was somewhere in the 1600s. Chestor, an electronic chessboard controlled by a microprocessor was used for the first time by CHESS 4.6. It sensed moves made on a special chessboard, transmitted them to the CYBER 176, and indicated the CYBER's responses by blinking lights (light-emitting diodes) on a special board.

On May 6, Grandmaster Walter Browne gave a simultaneous exhibition and had the misfortune of losing to CHESS 4.6 on one of the boards. The narration, in *Chess Life and Review* by John Douglas (1978), is delightful. The game lasted 63 moves. CHESS 4.6 predicted 35 of Browne's 58 nonbook moves. In one position CHESS 4.6 searched a tree having 2,158,456 nodes. Douglas indicates that after move 32, Browne had used 22 minutes thinking at the board while CHESS 4.6 had consumed 2 hours 44 minutes, a ratio of almost 1 to 8.

White: W. Browne   Black: CHESS 4.6

1	P–Q4	N–KB3		4	N×P	P–K4
2	P–QB4	P–B4		5	N–N5	B–B4
3	N–KB3	P×P		6	N/1–B3	O–O

Douglas observes that "Browne's Knight move brings CHESS 4.6 out of the opening book. At this point CHESS 4.6 has used 2 minutes and Walter Browne has hardly broken stride as he passed. But now the skid marks in front of the electronic chessboard are added to each time Browne passes by."

7	P–K3	P–Q3		11	O–O	Q–Q2
8	B–K2	P–QR3		12	P–QN3	K–R1
9	N–R3	N–B3		13	B–N2	R–KN1
10	N–B2	B–B4				

Douglas notes that "CHESS 4.6 is having trouble finding something to improve its position. It predicts 14 Q–Q2 P–R3 15 R/R1–Q1 N–K5 16 N×N B×N."

14 N − R4	B − R2		16 R − B1	...
15 B − R3	P − R3			

The editor of *Chess Life and Review* points out that 16 B × P is met with 16 ... B × N!

16 ...	R/R1 − Q1		21 B × B	P × B
17 N − N4	N × N		22 B − K2	B − B4
18 B × N	Q − B2		23 P − B3	P − K5
19 Q − K1	B − B4		24 P − B4	B − Q2
20 B − KB3	B − Q6		25 N − B3	Q − R4

"Now the visiting Master stops, does a double-step, smiles: he's got his thing now. The Queen is out of play. Browne begins a Kingside attack, smiles at the spectators, savors his move."

26 Q − R4 ...

"Thump, smile. It's lucky that the electronic board can only sense the position of the piece and not the force with which it is moved, for Browne's forceful play intimidates the spectators."

26 ...	B − B3		28 P − KN4	P − N5
27 R − QB2	P − QN4		29 N − Q1	R − Q3

CHESS 4.6 expects 30 P − N5 N − R2 31 N − B2 R/1 − Q1 32 B − N4 Q − N3 33 B − B5 but Browne played:

30 N − B2	R/1 − Q1		32 B × R	...
31 R − Q1	R × R+			

"Small thump, walk away, stop, look back, frown."

32 ...	R − Q3		34 R − B1	...
33 Q − N3	Q − Q1			

"Now Browne is defending. Things are not going well at some of the other boards, either, but it is here that Browne spends most of his time" (see Figure 15).

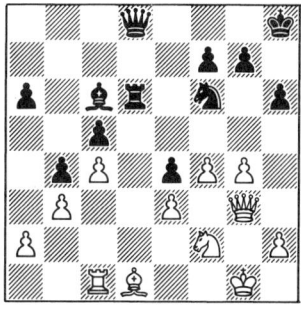

Figure 15. Position after 34 R − B1.

| 34 ... | R − Q7! | 36 P × P | N − R2 |
| 35 P − N5 | P × P | 37 P − N6 | P × P |

CHESS 4.6 is now a whole pawn up!

38 Q × P	Q − R5!	47 R − R1	P − N4
39 Q − B5	B − Q2	48 P × P	R − K4
40 Q − B4	Q × Q	49 P − N4	P − R4
41 P × Q	P − K6	50 N − Q3	R × P +
42 N − K4	P − K7	51 K − B2	P × P
43 B × P	R × B	52 N × P	R − QR4
44 N × P	B − B1	53 K − K3	B − K3
45 R − Q1	R − K1	54 K − Q4	N − N4
46 P − QR3	P × P	55 N − B2	...

Browne offers a draw, but CHESS 4.6 decides to play on.

55 ...	P − R7	58 K − N5	B − Q2 +
56 N − N4	R − R5	59 N − B6	N − B6 +
57 K − B5	N − K5 +		

CHESS 4.6 hammers in "the final nail."

60 K − B5	B × N	63 K − K5	R − Q8
61 K × B	R × P +	64 Resigns	
62 K − Q6	R − Q5 +		

The Jerusalem Conference on Information Technology hosted Israel's first major computer chess event on August 7–9. CHESS 4.6, DUCHESS, CHAOS, OSTRICH, TELL, and BS '66 '76 participated. The programs ran on computers in Israel: CHESS 4.6 on a CDC CYBER 74 at the Hebrew University, DUCHESS on an IBM 370/158, CHAOS and BS '66 '76 sharing an IBM 370/168, OSTRICH on a Nova 3 provided by Data General sales representatives, and TELL on a HP 2000. In general, each program played on a somewhat less powerful system than it was accustomed to. CHESS 4.6, on the CDC CYBER 74, was only able to search trees containing typically 40,000–150,000 nodes, rather than the gigantic trees they are able to handle on the CDC CYBER 176. CHESS 4.6 was unable to use its transpositions table due to a lack of sufficient memory space and was unable to think on its opponent's time for various reasons. While the programs were, perhaps, not at their best, they were still quite strong. Shimon Kagan, the Tournament Director, and an International Master, played speed chess against CHESS 4.6 on Israeli national television. Due to a lack of time, the game was adjudicated a draw after about 20 moves.

DUCHESS won the tournament with a perfect record much to the delight of Truscott. It defeated CHESS 4.6 in Round 2 and CHAOS in Round 3. Kagan commented to the audience halfway through the DUCHESS–CHAOS game that it could have been a game played between two grandmasters.

Against CHESS 4.6, DUCHESS went ahead by a pawn on move 12, an exchange somewhat later, and eventually into an endgame in which it had two passed pawns on the Queenside. After playing very passively for a number of moves, DUCHESS finally got down to the business of pushing its passed pawns forcing CHESS 4.6 to resign on move 60.

Following Seattle, DUCHESS was improved in several ways. Its opening book was improved, searches along checking sequences were improved (DUCHESS follows all checking sequences of up to three moves, rather than just two as it did at Seattle), criteria for trading were made more sophisticated, the King safety algorithm was improved, and the "Knight-on-the-rim-is-dim" algorithm was added. It was also programmed to think on its opponent's time. DUCHESS participated in a three-round B level human tournament at Chapel Hill, North Carolina in the spring of 1978 and received a USCF performance rating of 1783. In that event, DUCHESS won two games and lost one.

The DUCHESS vs. CHESS 4.6 game follows and shows the vincibility of the champion.

White: DUCHESS   Black: CHESS 4.6

1	P−K4	N−QB3		6	O−O	P−QR3
2	P−Q4	P−Q4		7	B−Q3	B−N5
3	P−K5	P−B3		8	P×P	N×P/3
4	N−KB3	B−B4		9	P−B3	P−K4
5	B−QN5	Q−Q2		10	N×P!	B×Q

10 ... N×N is no better. White still is able to hold on to its one-pawn advantage by continuing 11 P−B3.

11	N×Q	N×N		17	P−QN3	P−N4
12	R×B	B−K2		18	P−QR4	P−N5
13	B−B5	R−Q1		19	R−K6	N−R4
14	B−K6	N−B1		20	B−Q1	R−Q3
15	B−N4	N−N3		21	R×R	B×R
16	R−K1	O−O		22	P×P	N−B3

CHESS 4.6 seems to be floundering about using the smaller CYBER 74.

23 B−B3 ...

(See Figure 16.) In this position CHESS 4.6 is willing to play 23 ... R × B feeling that it gains sufficient compensation with 23 ... R × B 24 P × R N × P/Q. This exchanges a Rook for a Bishop and pawn and gives Black a passed pawn and White isolated pawns. The reader might compare this move with move 25 (and in particular the principal continuation found for that move) in the Stenberg vs. CHESS 4.5 endgame on page 194.

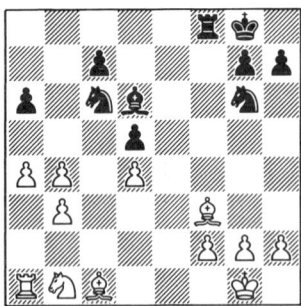

Figure 16. Position after 23 B − B3.

23 ...	R × B		28 K − N2	N − Q7
24 P × R	N × P/Q		29 B − B3	N − K5
25 N − Q2	N − R5		30 B − K1	N − B3
26 B − N2	N/Q × P/B +		31 R − B1	N − R4
27 N × N	N × N +		32 R − B6?	...

DUCHESS plays weakly for the next 20 moves giving CHESS 4.6 every possible chance. White could have played 32 P − N5 leading to a big advantage in a few moves.

32 ...	N − B5 +		45 R − B1	N − K6
33 K − B1	N − Q6		46 R − KR1	P − R7
34 B − Q2	B × P/7		47 B − Q8	N − B2
35 R × P/6	P − R4		48 B × P	N − Q5 +
36 K − K2?	N − B5 +		49 K − N7	B × B
37 K − K3	N − R6		50 K × B	N × P
38 K − Q4?	N × P		51 R × P	K − B4
39 R − R8 +	K − B2		52 K − Q6	P − N4
40 K × P	N − N5		53 K − Q5	P − N5
41 B − N5?	K − N3		54 K − B4	P − N6
42 B − K7	B − N6		55 R − R2	K − K5
43 R − KB8	P − R5		56 K × N	K − Q4
44 K − B6	P − R6		57 R − KN2	K − K4

DUCHESS has finally quenched the fires!

58 R × P	K − Q4		59 P − R5	Resigns

David Levy accepted two more challenges, the first from CHEOPS, the latest effort of Richard Greenblatt, and the second from CHESS 4.7. In the last year or so, Greenblatt added a hardware package to MAC HACK VI. The package was designed to grow trees at nonquiescent terminal positions arrived at by the main PDP computer. Greenblatt told Levy the hardware is capable of evaluating 150,000 positions per second. Feeling that the program was considerably stronger than it had been, Greenblatt extended a challenge to Levy. On August 20, Levy defeated the program in 43 moves. The strength of CHEOPS is difficult to assess based on only one game but I do not believe it is up to the level of the other top programs.

CHESS 4.7's final attempt came in Toronto at the Canadian National Exhibition late in August. A six-game challenge match was played. The first game on August 26 ended in a draw with Levy narrowly escaping defeat. Levy had no difficulties in games two or three. To win his bet he merely had to draw the fourth game. He was quite confident that if he played his own conservative style game, the machine would eventually create its own weaknesses, defeating itself. But he wanted the match to end with him conquering the machine at its own game—in a highly tactical encounter. And thus, he managed to become the first Master to lose a game to a computer in a tournament environment. The fourth game with assistance in annotations by Leon Piasetski and Kevin Spraggett is presented here

White: CHESS 4.7   Black: Levy

Latvian Gambit

1	P−K4(B)	P−K4	6	N×N+(B)	Q×N
2	N−KB3(B)	P−KB4	7	Q−R5+(B)	Q−B2
3	P×P(B)	P−K5	8	Q×Q+(B)	K×Q
4	N−K5(B)	N−KB3	9	N−B3(B)	P−B3
5	N−N4(B)	P−Q4	10	P−Q3(92)	P×P

The game is far from the highly tactical battle that Levy promised. But the blame is not his.

11	B×P(106)	N−Q2	14	P×B(88)	B−B4
12	B−KB4(198)	N−B4	15	O−O(182)	...
13	P−KN4(86)	N×B+			

15 P−B3, and then if 15 ... P−R4, 16 O−O−O P×P 17 P−Q4 gives White a better position. The bias on castling is very high.

15 ...   P−KR4!

Now White's Kingside is in serious trouble. If 16 P−KR3, Black plays 16 ... P×P 17 P×P R−R5! White must play for time:

16	N−R4(125)	B−Q5	17	B−K3(200)	B−K4

Levy preferred to avoid 17 ... B×B 18 P×B giving White strength in the center of the board.

18	P−Q4(153)	B−Q3	21	N−B3(51)	P×P
19	P−KR3(106)	P−QN3	22	P×P(108)	R−R5
20	R/B−K1(236)	B−Q2	23	P−B3(67)	R/1−R1

It looks as though Levy is well on the way to winning his bet (see Figure 17).

Figure 17. Position after 23 ... R/1 − R1.

24 K − B1(120)   B − N6

Levy overlooks 24 ... R − R6 leading shortly to a clearly won position.

25 R − K2(84)	B − B1	28 R/1 − K1(223)	R − N6+
26 K − N2(103)	B − Q3	29 K − B2(74)	R/1 − R6
27 B − N1(67)	R − R6	30 R − K3(135)	B − R3

Zvonko Vranesic, watching in the audience, felt this move is a mistake. Levy may have been concerned with White's pressure on the King's file and may have skipped 30 ... B − B5 for that reason. But if after 30 ... B − B5, White plays 31 R − K7+, then in Piasetski's opinion, 31 ... K − B3 32 R/1 − K3 R − R8 maintains the advantage.

31 N − K2(68)	B × N	33 P − B4!(158)	...
32 R/1 × B(65)	P − B4		

This move, thought out on Levy's time, finally takes pressure off White and turns the game around. Now Black faces great problems to even draw.

33 ...	R × R	35 K − N3(233)	R − R8
34 R × R(334)	R − R5	36 B − B2(109)	R − Q8

According to Piasetski and Spraggett, 36 ... P − B5 is a better line of defense, offering Black better drawing chances.

37 R − R3!(237)   ...

Levy is now in deep trouble.

37 ...	P × P	42 P − N4(126)	B × P
38 R × P+(143)	K − B1	43 R − Q8+(212)	K − B2
39 R − Q7!(188)	R − Q6+	44 R − Q7+(498)	K − B1
40 K − N2(337)	B − B4	45 R × P/4(77)	R − N7
41 R × P/5(172)	R − Q7	46 K − B3!(165)	...

This is necessary to avoid the pin 46 ... B − B4. CHESS 4.7 is on the road to victory. It is searching to a depth of 10 plies on every move!

46 ...	B – B4	52 P – B5(283)	R – R6+
47 R – Q8 + (234)	K – K2	53 K – N4(473)	R – R5+
48 B – R4 + !(90)	K – B2	54 K – R5(247)	R – Q5
49 P – N5(156)	P – N3	55 R – QB7(579)	B – K2
50 R – Q7 + (294)	K – B1	56 P – B6(150)	Resigns
51 P × P(136)	R × P		

However, Levy went on to win the fifth game and the match with a $3\frac{1}{2}$–$1\frac{1}{2}$ score as well as the $2,000 bet.

3. Tree-Searching Techniques (Modifications to the Minimax Algorithm)

The *minimax search algorithm* specifies that, given a position in a two-person game, a tree of all sequences of moves from that position to positions that are won, lost, or drawn be generated and then, assuming each player is attempting to do his best, the algorithm determines the sequence of moves that will optimize each player's chances. The first move on this sequence is the move found best to make in the given position. The entire sequence is called the *principal continuation.*

This strategy, as it stands, is too simple to use in chess programs although it works quite well in programs intended for more elementary games. In most chess positions, such a tree would be astronomical in size containing a completely unmanageable number of move sequences. In chess, it is impossible to follow all move sequences to positions that are won, lost, or drawn. It is possible only to search several moves ahead and assign the resulting position *scores* based on how good they "seem to be." Thus the initial papers on computer chess suggested using a *finite depth minimax search.* All sequences of moves are generated out to some fixed depth, say D, the resulting positions constructed and scored, and then the minimax algorithm used to find the principal continuation. The score of each terminal position is determined by a *scoring function,* a function that examines the material on the board as well as other factors and arrives at a numerical value for the position. Shannon originally suggested a scoring function that considers: (1) material, (2) pawn structure, and (3) mobility. Turing's is only slightly different. More recent programs use more sophisticated functions, but as we see in Section 4, they are still very crude and reflect the chess knowledge of about class C players (if such an analogy is fair to make).

3.1. The Horizon Effect

Both Shannon and Turing were concerned with problems that would be caused by placing a fixed limit on the maximum depth of search. They suggested a variable depth search, one in which all moves are searched out

Figure 18. Position illustrating the horizon effect. From Berliner (1974).

to some fixed depth and certain ones further yet. Turing argued that unless a position is quiescent, that is, void of certain features (Kings in check, pieces *en prise*, certain types of threats, etc.) that make its evaluation unclear, further search is necessary along sequences leading beyond this position. All good programs carry out "extended searching" and some are able to search to depths of 15 to 20 plies along highly forced lines of play.

A search based on the methods described by Shannon and Turing is vulnerable to the *horizon effect*. Berliner's dissertation deals extensively with this subject (Berliner, 1974). Consider, for example, the position in Figure 18 with White to move. Assume a program is carrying out an exhaustive 3-ply search along with extended searching. The program will see in its extended searching that the 3-ply sequence 1 B – N3 P – B5 2 *anything* loses a Bishop for at best a pawn, but will delude itself into believing that 1 P – K5 P × P 2 B – N3 loses only a pawn. The loss of the Bishop through 1 P – K5 P × P 2 B – N3 P – B5 *anything* will not be seen because the first three moves of this sequence lead to a quiescent position and no extended searching will be carried out. The program will continue by playing P – K5, which loses not only the pawn but fails to solve the problem with the Bishop. It will find this out on the next move.

3.2. Forward Pruning

Forward pruning was introduced in the Bernstein chess program in 1956. Rather than searching all moves at each position in a tree, Bernstein's program selected only seven. His program looked four plies deep into a tree with a maximum of $7^4 = 2401$ terminal nodes. The Kotok–McCarthy Program, MAC HACK VI, and early versions of Slate and Atkin's program used forward pruning. However, experience has shown that forward pruning near the root of the tree is very risky and all better current programs do very little of it with, perhaps, the exception of CHAOS.

3.3. The Alpha–Beta Algorithm

The *alpha–beta algorithm,* a modification to the minimax algorithm is a fundamental part of all current chess programs. A program using the alpha–beta algorithm searches a small subtree of the tree searched by a program without it. The subtree always contains the principal continuation found by the minimax algorithm and further, the alpha–beta algorithm always picks the same one. In Knuth and Moore (1975), the history of the algorithm is reviewed. They give McCarthy credit for discovering it, saying that he discussed it with Bernstein as early as 1956. Newell, Shaw, and Simon used a weaker version of the algorithm in their chess program (Newell *et al.,* 1963). Hart and Edwards (1961) published a memorandum describing it but, according to Knuth and Moore, they made no attempt "to indicate why the method worked, much less demonstrate its validity." Brudno (1963) is credited by Knuth and Moore as being first to present a proof of why the algorithm works. The algorithm is described in a number of books and articles, in particular, Nilsson (1971), Knuth and Moore (1975), and Newborn (1975).

The concept of one move *refuting* another is at the heart of the algorithm. The essence is illustrated by the position in Figure 19(a) and the tree in Figure 19(b). Suppose the computer is playing White and White is to move.

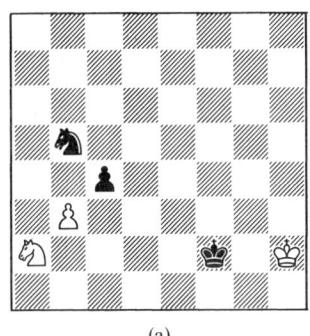

(a)

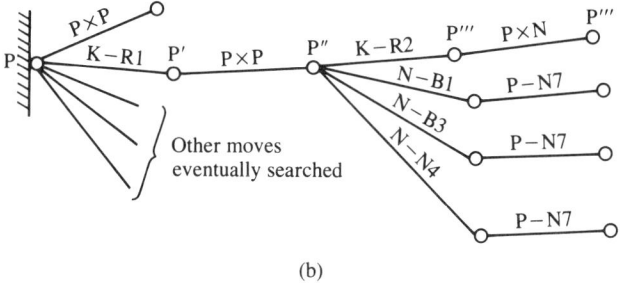

(b)

Figure 19. (a) Position and (b) tree illustrating the alpha–beta algorithm.

Suppose further that a 4-ply search is being carried out. Figure 19(b) shows the following. The first move searched by White is 1 P × P, which the computer finds after looking four levels deep wins a pawn. Later, suppose when searching 1 K − R1 as shown, the first 4-ply continuation considered happens to be 1 K − R1 P × P 2 K − R2 P × N. After scoring position P‴, the computer sees that 2 … P × N refutes 1 K − R1 P × P 2 K − R2. That is 1 P × P looks better than 1 K − R1 P × P 2 K − R2 and searching more moves at P‴ will never change this situation. There is no need to consider any more replies in position P‴ because after finding one refutation there is no need to find another. Further, after checking the three other third-ply moves, the computer will realize that 1 K − R1 is refuted by 1 … P × P and that no other moves in position P′ need be searched. We see that the refutations reduce the number of continuations that are necessary to examine. Slagle and Dixon (1969) showed that the alpha−beta algorithm has the potential of reducing the number of D level terminal positions (the root is level 0) in a tree with fanout N at every node from N^D, required without the alpha−beta algorithm, to as few as:

$$2N^{D/2} − 1 \qquad\qquad D \text{ even,}$$

$$N^{(D+1)/2} + N^{(D−1)/2} − 1 \qquad D \text{ odd.}$$

For example, with $N = 35$ (typical of many chess positions) and $D = 4$, rather than scoring about 1,000,000 terminal positions, a program may get away with scoring no more than about 2000. In practice, several times this number is usually scored.

Being intrigued over the number that is "usually scored," Fuller et al. (1973), Knuth and Moore (1975), Newborn (1977a), and Baudet (1978) carried out theoretical analyses of the *expected number* of terminal nodes scored by an alpha−beta search under various assumptions about the randomness of the terminal node scores. The essence of their results is that even with random terminal node scores, the alpha−beta algorithm cuts down tremendously on the number of terminal nodes scored. The models that were studied led to conservative results. Even better results would have been achieved if terminal node scores were assumed to depend on branch scores and each branch score was a number chosen randomly from the set $\{0, 1, 2, …, k\}$. To model chess, the value of k could be taken as 9. Based on this model, this writer feels that the number of terminal nodes scored would be found to be $O(N^{D/2} \log N)$, where N and D are as previously defined.

Gillogly (1972) and Griffith (1976) carried out empirical studies of the algorithm's efficiency. Their results are difficult to assess. Gillogly's results (1972) in fact led Fuller et al. (1973) to an erroneous functional form for the expected number of terminal nodes scored based on a model in which random numbers from a uniform distribution are assigned to terminal node scores.

The speedup that results by introducing the alpha−beta algorithm into the minimax algorithm depends on the order in which moves are examined at each position in the tree. If the move that turns out to be a refutation is searched first, the speedup that results is greater than if this move is searched after others have been tried. Thus most chess programs have extensive heuristic algorithms that weed out moves that look like they may be refutations; these moves are searched before trying others.

3.4. The Killer Heuristic

The *killer heuristic* was described by Gillogly when detailing TECH (Gillogly, 1972). He observed that if move m_y refutes move m_x, then there is a good chance that m_y might also refute another move, might be a "killer." He suggested that when considering other positions in which m_y can be made, it should be searched first. In Akl and Newborn (1977), it is shown that the benefits from the killer heuristic are closely related to the fanout at each node: For large fanouts, the killer heuristic seems to be more effective in speeding up the search than for small fanouts. Theoretical analyses have not been attempted and await an ambitious mathematician.

3.5. Iterative Deepening

Iterative deepening has been used with surprising success in CHESS 4.6 and DUCHESS. To search $D + 1$ plies requires anywhere from two to ten times as much time as to search D plies. If the best move at ply 1 turns out to be the first one searched, the alpha–beta algorithm generally has more cutoffs and the search goes more quickly than otherwise. The probability that the best move at ply 1 found by a D ply search will turn out to be the best move at ply 1 found by a $D + 1$ ply search is quite high. Statistically then, it is worthwhile to find the principal continuation for a D ply search and use this continuation as the "seed" for a $D + 1$ ply search. CHESS 4.6 carries out iteratively deepening searches to a depth of typically 6 plies, searching to greater depths along certain tactical paths. In the endgame, CHESS 4.6 often carries out iteratively deepening searches to depths of 10–12 plies and much deeper along selective paths.

Programs vary in the amount of the tree saved at each iteration. DUCHESS saves the best move at the first level and the best reply at the second level to each first level move. Good (1968) discussed "progressive deepening" in his "five-year plan," but he did not have exhaustive searches in mind. He argued that good players carry out progressively deepening searches along highly selective lines of play.

3.6. Alpha–Beta Window

An *alpha–beta window* is used in several programs. The alpha–beta search can be speeded up by having a program begin the search assuming that it will not find a win or loss of more than, say, a pawn in the given position. Such a search is said to have a one-pawn window. If at some time during the search a loss of more than a pawn is observed, the search is started anew with a wider window. CHAOS uses an alpha–beta window. Each time the program finishes one iteration of its iteratively deepening search, the window's width is adjusted for the next iteration.

3.7. Transposition Tables

Transposition tables are used by a number of programs including MAC HACK VI, CHESS 4.6, DUCHESS, and CHAOS (Greenblatt *et al.*, 1967; Slate and Atkin, 1977). Positions and their scores are stored as the search progresses. When a new position is reached in the tree, it is checked to see whether it has been searched previously, whether a transposition of moves has lead to the same position. If so, a score can be given to the position by simply assigning it the score stored in the transposition table. However, because of the nature of the alpha–beta search, sometimes this score is, in fact, only a bound on its true score. Sometimes, though, this is enough. Programs that use transposition tables require computers with large memories.

CHESS 4.6 has an input parameter for deciding how large the table should be. Mittman claims CHESS 4.6 speeds up by a factor of about 50% when using maximum table size. Cahlander indicates factors of more than 14 : 1 have been observed. Truscott points out that improvement increases as search depth increases and also as fewer and fewer pieces remain on the board. DUCHESS is programmed to try to make moves that lead to positions that are in the transposition table and thus increase its benefits. Positions are stored in a hash table (Knuth, 1973) and are quickly inserted and retrieved. DUCHESS encodes each position into 22 bytes using a Huffman code (Knuth, 1968).

3.8. The Method of Analogies

Adelson-Velskiy *et al.* (1975) have developed what they call the *method of analogies* to aid KAISSA's search. An attempt is made to see whether a newly reached position is analogous to, that is, has certain of the same characteristics as a position reached earlier. If so, it is not necessary to consider successors of this position; it is assigned the score given to the earlier found analogous position. In some sense this is a generalization of the technique of using transpositions tables.

3.9. Differential Updating of Chess Information

Differential updating of chess information (Scott, 1969) is used to varying degress in all programs. At each terminal node, a program can add up the material value of the pieces on the board to determine the material difference in that position. Alternatively, the program can calculate the material at the root of the tree and differentially update this value as the search progresses. If there is no change in material when going from one position to another, then there is nothing for the program to do. In general, differential updating of chess information results in a significant speedup in a program. Factors other than material can be differentially updated as well. Scott says that each move affects the moves of about three or four other pieces, rather than the 20 or 30 usually on the board. A program can simply update the information related to these few pieces thus saving considerable time.

4. Chess-Specific Information in Chess Programs

Most chess programs understand very little about the game that they are programmed to play! Slate would agree that CHESS 4.6 knows explicitly no more than a class C human player. Good programs know the rules, how much time they have to make their moves, the strength of their opponents, and whether or not to play for a draw in a given position. They also know that mate in one is better than mate in two. Arbitrary values are assigned to the pieces ($K = \infty$, $Q = 9$, $R = 5$, $B = N = 3$, and $P = 1$), although some programs vary these numbers during the course of a game. Many programs incorrectly exchange a Rook and pawn for a Knight and Bishop because they believe they are making an even exchange. They accept sacrifices when they do not find within the search horizon that the opponent can recoup his losses. They refuse to make sacrifices unless the ultimate gains become clear before the search horizon is reached.

They understand when to and when not to trade pieces. When behind, they avoid exchanging non-pawns. The concept of King safety appears in most programs. The King is encouraged to castle and to stay on the side of the board until material drops to some arbitrary level; then the King is encouraged to move to the middle of the board. Pawn structure is also understood. Programs want to create and push passed pawns, sometimes though not hard enough (as DUCHESS vs. CHESS 4.6 shows on page 181) and they avoid isolated and doubled pawns. They understand the concept of mobility (they can count the number of moves in a given position), but tactical concepts such as forks and pins are usually discovered by searching. But this is about all, except for books and some special endgame algorithms.

Opening libraries, usually simply called books, are growing in size. BELLE has the largest, about 100,000 positions, CHESS 4.6, CHAOS, DUCHESS, KAISSA, and several others have books ranging in size from 3,000 to 30,000 positions. Positions, rather than trees of move sequences, are usually stored and thus it is possible for a program to leave its book and return later in the game. Book moves are made in less than a second giving the program more time for middle game moves. Before long programs will use optical scanners to generate their books and then the source will have to be debugged very carefully!

5. Endgame Play

Until recently, endgame play by programs was thought to be their greatest weakness. While the rest of their game was at best class C, their endgame play was atrocious. In the match between the Kotok–McCarthy program and the ITEP program in 1966–1967, both sides agreed games would end at move 40 in order to avoid embarrassing play. In the 1970 ACM Tournament, COKO (White) and J.BIIT (Black) waltzed to a draw in a game in which absolute human novices would have realized how to proceed. After move 81 they reached the position shown in Figure 20. The game ended in a draw with:

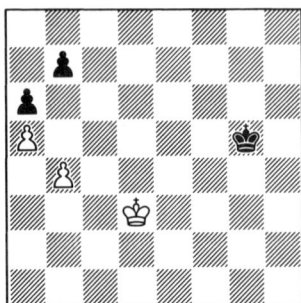

Figure 20. Position reached by COKO (White) vs. J.BIIT (Black) at the 1970 United States Computer Chess Championship.

82 K − K3 K − B4, 83 K − B3 K − K4, 84 K − K3 K − Q4, 85 K − Q3 K − K4, 86 K − K3 K − Q4, 87 K − Q3 K − K4. Drawn by repetition!

A 7-ply search would have shown COKO that its King can capture a pawn if nothing more. COKO, however, was spending barely 2 or 3 seconds on each turn looking for moves with immediate tactical implications and none existed. COKO was simply not programmed to search deeper when time and material on the board permitted. In endgame play with so few pieces on the board, the better programs of today perform exhaustive searches to depths of 10–12 plies, and there is no doubt that they would win this game given COKO's position.

The power of exhaustive search along with some very simple heuristics is enough to permit chess programs to play much more respectable endgames than was believed possible. Heuristics to encourage the King to move toward the center of the board, toward passed pawns, or go into opposition, and heuristics to encourage certain pawn structures go much further than was imagined. In the endgame, transposition tables become much more effective than in the middle game because a higher percentage of positions transpose. This allows CHESS 4.7 and DUCHESS to search considerably deeper than would otherwise be possible.

Two examples of endgame play follow. The first is a victory by CHESS 4.6 over Warren Stenberg (USCF 1969), a professor of mathematics at the Uni-

Figure 21. Stenberg (White) vs. CHESS 4.6 (Black) after Black's move 24.

versity of Minnesota. CHESS 4.6 had a clear advantage entering the endgame, was helped by a blunder on White's 26th move and by White being in serious time trouble. But Stenberg, the first class A player ever to lose to a computer in tournament play, could have recovered if CHESS 4.6 had played as weakly as computers were renowned for. The game was adjourned after move 45 and Stenberg went home and straight to sleep, knowing that he had no real chance. Cahlander provided this writer with CHESS 4.6's printout and what follows is a condensed presentation of the important data. With each Black move by CHESS 4.6, there are indicated the time (in seconds), the search depth of the last iteration, the number of terminal nodes evaluated, and the continuation expected. It is a lot of data, but it is important to record for posterity. Underlined moves in the continuations correspond to moves actually played. Note that 17 out of 32 moves by its opponent were predicted by CHESS 4.6. On move 49, the program predicted its opponent's reply, its own move, and the second reply by the opponent.

The position shown in Figure 21 was reached after Black's move 24. CHESS 4.6 begins the endgame with a slight advantage and has greater freedom for its King and Rook throughout. It keeps White's King on the side of the board and is helped to a premature victory when White errs on move 57. The game, from move 25 on, follows:

White Stenberg	Black CHESS 4.6	Time (sec)	Search depth	Terminal nodes	Continuation expected			
25 P−K4	R−QB1	58	7	183,842	26 P−B4	R−B5	27 N−B2	P−B4
					28 P−QN3	R×P	29 N×R	P×N

CHESS 4.6 seems willing to trade a Rook for a Knight and pawn and the positional advantages of an isolated White Queen's pawn and a passed pawn of its own. But this gives White the edge.

White Stenberg	Black CHESS 4.6	Time (sec)	Search depth	Terminal nodes	Continuation expected
26 N – K3	P – B4	197	8	669,233	27 N × P B × P 28 R – N1 R – B7 29 N – K3 R – K7 30 N – QB4
27 P – QN3	P × P	97	7	342,981	28 N – B4 R – KN1 29 R – Q1 B – B6 30 P – Q6 P – R5 31 P × P K × P
28 N – B4	R – KN1	83	7	267,663	29 R – Q1 B – B6 30 P – Q6 P – K4 31 K – R2 K – K3
29 R – Q1	P – B4	117	7	375,313	30 P – Q6 P – K3 31 R – Q2 K – B3 32 R – R2 K – N4
30 P – Q6	P – K3	167	8	567,651	31 R – Q2 K – B3 32 P – Q7 K – B2 33 R – Q6 P – R4 34 K – B1
31 N – N6 +	K – B3	90	8	307,245	32 N – B4 K – B4 33 R – Q2 B – B3 34 R – R2 R – QR1 35 R – B2
32 N – B4	R – Q1	130	7	415,153	33 R – Q2 K – B4 34 R – R2 R – QR1 35 R – R5 K – Q5
33 N – R5 +	K – Q2	297	9	989,004	34 N – B4 B – B6 35 P – N3 P – K4 36 K – N2 K – K3 37 R – QB1 R – KN1
34 N – B4	B – B6	71	7	232,663	35 P – N3 P – K4 36 K – N2 K – K3 37 R – QB1 R – KN1
35 K – B1	R – KN1	69	7	222,322	36 P – N3 B – B3 37 K – K2 P – R5 38 N – N6 K – B3
36 N – Q2	P – R5	83	7	260,734	37 N – B4 P – B5 38 N – Q2 P – B6 39 N × P/4 P × P 40 K – N1
37 N – B4	P – B5	211	8	746,997	38 N – Q2 B × N 39 R × B P – B6 40 P × P P × P 41 K – K1
38 N – Q2	B × N	96	8	363,181	39 R × B P – R4 40 R – Q4 P – B6 41 P × P P × P 42 K – K1
39 R × B	P – B6	100	8	350,800	40 P × P P × P 41 R – Q3 R – KB1 42 R – Q4 P – R4 43 K – K1
40 P × P	P × P	112	9	448,606	41 R – Q3 R – KB1 42 R – Q4 P – R4 43 R × P/R K × P 44 R – R7 K – Q4 45 P – R4
41 R – Q3	R – KB1	260	10	1,002,080	42 K – K1 R – B4 43 K – Q2 R – Q4 44 R × R P × R 45 K – K3 K × P 46 K × P
42 K – K1	R – B5	96	9	372,796	43 K – Q2 R – B4 44 K – K3 R – Q4 45 R × R P × R 46 K × P K × P
43 K – Q2	R – B4	213	10	753,462	44 K – K3 R – B3 45 K – K4 R – B2 46 R × P R × R 47 K × R K × P 48 K – K4
44 K – B2	R – B4 +	264	8	923,960	45 K – N2 R – K4 46 R × P R – K7 47 K – B1 K × P 48 R – B7 P – K4
45 K – N2	R – KN4	133	9	464,549	46 R × P R – N7 47 K – B2 K × P[a]
46 K – B2	R – KB4	175	9	613,761	47 K – Q2 P – R4 48 K – K3 R – Q4 49 R × R P × R 50 K × P K × P
47 R – Q4	R – B4 +	135	9	520,486	48 K – Q1 R – Q4 49 R × R P × R 50 K – Q2 K × P 51 K – K3 K – K4 52 K × P
48 K – N2	P – R4	175	9	650,408	49 R – Q3 R – B4 50 K – B2 R – B2 51 K – Q2 K – B3 52 K – K3 P – K4
49 R – Q3	R – K4	185	9	656,255	50 R × P R – K7 + 51 K – B1 K × P 52 R – Q3 + K – K4 53 R – Q2 R – K5
50 R × P	R – K7 +	83	9	302,371	51 K – B1 K × P 52 R – B8 K – K4 53 R – B7 R – R7[a]
51 K – B1	K × P	51	8	184,078	52 R – Q3 K – K4 53 R – K3 + R × R 54 P × R K – K5 55 K – Q2 P – K4

White Stenberg	Black CHESS 4.6	Time (sec)	Search depth	Terminal nodes	Continuation expected			
52 K – Q1	R – R7	170	10	647,082	53 R – Q3+	K – K4	54 R – Q2	R × R
					55 K × R	K – Q5	56 P – B3	P – K4
					57 K – K2			
53 R – Q3+	K – B4	(data not available)						
54 K – K1	P – K4	95	9	340,505	55 R – Q2	R – R6	56 R – N2	K – Q5
					57 K – Q2	P – R5	58 K – B2	R – R8
55 P – B4	P × P	99	9	395,263	56 K – Q1	R – KB7	57 K – K1	R – KR7
					58 K – Q1	K – B3	59 R – KB3	K – Q4
					60 R × P	R × P		
56 R – KB3	K – Q5	11	8	48,988	57 R – B2	R × R	58 K × R	K – K5
					59 K – K2	P – B6	60 K – B2	
57 R × P+	K – K6	44	10	197,344	58 K – Q1	K × R	59 K – B1	R – K7
					60 K – N1	R – K6	61 K – R2	R × P/R
					62 K – N2			
58 Resigns								

ᵃ An abbreviated continuation was printed out because the terminal position was found in the transpositions table.

DUCHESS displayed strong endgame play when drawing with CHESS 4.6 at ACM's Seattle tournament. This game gave DUCHESS a first-place tie with CHESS 4.6 and for most of their hard-fought battle, it looked as though DUCHESS would upset the recently crowned world champion. After Black's 32nd move, the game reached the position shown in Figure 14 and repeated in Figure 22. Leo Stefurak (2102 USCF) of the Seattle Chess Club, while observing the game, felt that 33 B – B4 R × P 34 R × R B × R 35 B × P gives DUCHESS (White) a winning advantage. In reply to 33 ... B × P, he felt that 34 B × P gives DUCHESS a larger advantage. The endgame went as follows:

White: DUCHESS   Black: CHESS 4.6

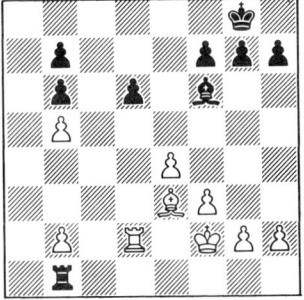

Figure 22. Position after Black's 32nd move in DUCHESS (White) vs. CHESS 4.6 (Black) at Seattle.

33 B × P   R × P   35 K – K3   K – B1
34 R × R   B × R

White has a small advantage at this point. His King is slightly stronger and Black's pawn on Q3 is weak.

| 36 | B – Q4 | B × B + | | 38 | K – Q5 | K – Q2 |
| 37 | K × B | K – K1 | | | | |

White still has a small advantage at this point but probably not enough to win. White might keep his chances alive with 39 P – B4, but instead he makes a move that forces a draw.

39	P – N6	P – N3		46	K – Q4	K – K3
40	P – B4	K – K2		47	K – B4	K – K2
41	P – R3	P – B3		48	P – B5	K – Q1
42	P – R4	K – Q2		49	K – N4	K – Q2
43	P – N4	P – R3		50	K – N5	K – K1
44	P – R5	P × P		51	K – R4	K – K2
45	P × P	K – K2		52	K – N4	K – Q1

53	K – B4	K – K1		56	K – Q4	K – K1
54	K – Q4	K – Q2		57	K – B4	K – B2
55	K – Q5	K – K2			Adjudicated a draw

Both sides were carrying out exhaustive 14–18 plies searches when the game ended.

Three years ago, this writer studied the performance of a simple King and pawns vs. King and pawns endgame program (Newborn, 1977b) on a set of positions from Fine (1941). The program was designed to carry out an exhaustive search to some fixed depth. One of the problems, shown in Figure 23, was far beyond its capabilities. It was estimated that the program would require 25,000 hours of IBM 370/168 time to search deeply enough to find (and understand) the correct solution. Several months ago Cahlander asked CHESS 4.6 to try the problem. CHESS 4.6 carried out an iteratively deepening search to a depth of 26 plies and found the correct principal continuation!

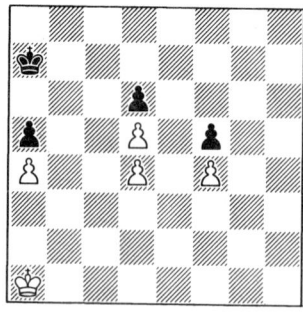

Figure 23. Endgame position from Fine: Problem # 70: White to move and win.

At 25 plies the continuation was wrong. How was CHESS 4.6 able to search so deeply? The answer—transposition tables! In this position a deep search runs across a large number of transpositions. CHESS 4.6 searched to a depth of 26 plies in 632 seconds and examined 3,294,754 terminal positions!

A number of special endgame programs have been developed during the last 10 years. Barbara Huberman, a student of John McCarthy, considered KRK,[3] KBBK, and KBNK endgames (Huberman, 1968). For several types of endgames and based on certain features on the board, positions were divided up into several categories. The categories were then ordered from best to worst (for the winning side). Her strategy involved a breadth first search during which the program tried to find a move that lead to a better position. As soon as one was found, the program was satisfied and search terminated. This resulted in winning, but not necessarily optimal play. Endgames with only pawns on the board were studied by Tan (1972). Piasetski (1976), Michalski and Negri (1976), Clark (1977), and even Bellman (1965).

The most exciting work on special endgames, however, is the (unpublished) work of Ken Thompson. He has developed a large database for the KQKR endgame that plays best chess—wins as quickly and loses as slowly as possible. With each of about 5,000,000 positions, a number n is stored where n is the number of moves for White to move and win. When playing in a game, the program carries out either a 1-ply or a 2-ply search, depending upon which color it is playing (White must be on the move in terminal positions), and searches the database to assign scores to the terminal positions. The database was created by having the program first generate the set of positions with mate on the board. Then, working backward, the computer figured out the number of moves n necessary to reach the nearest of these positions.

The program gave a simultaneous exhibition against six very strong players at the 1977 United States Open Chess Championship in Columbus, Ohio. Playing with the Rook, the program managed to draw four games against, among others, Eugene Meyer (USCF 2350) and John Peters (USCF 2400), while losing to John Meyer, a Life Master in the USCF and to a small horde of players who, having been defeated earlier, banded together on the sixth board. The humans were given about two minutes to make each move.

Thompson has also built large databases for KPKP, KPPK, KRKN, and KRKB. His attempt to use the same approach on KRPKR came to a temporary halt a while ago when he realized that for perfect play, some positions required "Knighting" the pawn when it reached the eight rank. Levy (1976) reports that a program developed by Arlazarov and Futer handles such endgames perfectly. Their work will appear in the next volume of *Machine Intelligence* (Arlazarov and Futer, 1979).

Michie has been interested in endgame programs that select moves by using

---

[3] KRK = King and Rook vs. King, KBBK = King and two Bishops vs. King.

advice stored in an advice table (Michie, 1976). By using 12 pieces of advice and a 4-ply exhaustive search, Michie and Bratko (1978) designed a program to play KRKN endgames that allowed "drawn positions to be indefinitely defended (until terminated by the 50-move rule)." Michie's technique is an excellent one for endgame play but may be very difficult to extend to middle game play.

6. Speed Chess

A pleasant surprise in the last two years has been the strong performances given by the better programs in "speed chess," or "blitz chess" as it is sometimes called. A speed chess game is one in which each side normally is given a total of 5 minutes in which to make all his moves. Most chess games last between 40 and 60 moves and thus it is necessary to set a pace somewhere around 5 seconds per move in order not to lose on time. This is not enough time to play one's best but even at 5 seconds per move, Masters and Grandmasters still play pretty good chess. Masters can compete on equal footing with class A and class B players in speed chess when given only 1 or 2 minutes vs. 5, 6, or even 7 minutes for their opponents. Results from simultaneous exhibitions, where a Master plays 50 A, B, C, and D class players, along with a few beginners, indicate that even a 40–1 time differential still allows the Master to play better.

When Slate and Atkin eliminated forward pruning and incorporated iterative deepening and transposition tables, and when they obtained the services of the CDC CYBER 170 series computers, they found somewhat to their amazement that their program was able to compete in speed chess against Masters. Levy estimated in 1977 that CHESS 4.6 was playing speed chess at around the 2300 USCF level (Levy, 1977a).

When two humans play speed chess, they each waste a few seconds in "overhead" during the course of a game. This is the time required to physically make moves on the board and stop the clock once a move has been decided upon. When a computer plays, it is necessary for an operator to provide assistance. He must observe the opponent's moves, type them into the computer, and make the computer's replies on the board. This "overhead" can amount to 2–4 seconds per move. So the rules when playing Slate and Atkin's program in speed chess are as follows. The human is given 5 minutes to make all his moves as usual. The computer has an internal clock that paces it to play at a rate of 5 seconds per move. If the game lasts 60 moves, CHESS 4.5 loses unless on move 60 it announces that it sees mate in the next few moves.

When playing speed chess, Slate and Atkin's program searches trees having about 10,000–20,000 nodes on the CYBER 176. It carries out exhaustive searches to a depth of 4 or 5 plies in most middle game positions and deeper in the endgame. After making a move, CHESS 4.5 begins calculation of its next move assuming the opponent will respond with the move on the principal continuation. Thus the longer the opponent thinks, the longer the computer thinks in turn! This effect is quite dramatic in speed chess where the human works very hard to find a move and quite often the computer replies instantly.

CHESS 4.5 and later versions of the program have established an impressive list of speed chess victories—against GM Michael Stean and David Levy of England, Hans Berliner, Lawrence Day, and Zvonko Vranesic of Canada, and GM Robert Hübner of West Germany. A game played against Berliner at Carnegie–Mellon in March of 1977 follows. It should be pointed out that Berliner evened his speed chess score against the program by defeating it in a blitz game several months later at the Second World Computer Chess Championship. Berliner has considerable experience playing computers and one wonders to what extent this improves his chances. The game was a highly tactical battle and, although ahead a Bishop to a pawn by the 16th move, Berliner finds himself out-maneuvered and lost by move 20.

White: CHESS 4.6   Black: Berliner

1	P−KB4	P−KN3	5	B−B4	P−K3
2	N−QB3	B−N2	6	O−O	N/1−K2
3	P−K4	P−QB4	7	P−K5	P−Q3
4	N−B3	N−QB3	8	N−K4	...

CHESS 4.6 does not see that this gives up a pawn. It may have seen 8 N−K4 P × P 9 P × P N × P 10 B−N5+ N/K2−B3 11 N × P but not the continuation 11 ... Q−N3 12 B × N+ N × B 13 P−Q4 B × P+ 14 N × B Q × N.

8 ...	P × P	12	N × N	N × N
9 P × P	N × P	13	B−K3	P−QR3
10 B−N5+	N/2−B3	14	B−R4	P−QN4
11 P−Q3	O−O	15	B × P/N?	...

White unnecessarily gives up a Bishop for two pawns and an isolated Black pawn. This evidently satisfies CHESS 4.6. The Bishop can be saved by 15 B−N3 P−B5 16 P × P P × P 17 B−R4.

15 ...	P × B	17	P−Q4	N−B3
16 B × P	R−K1	18	P−B3	P−K4

Berliner wanted to gain space with 18 ... P−K4 and evidently underestimated the strength of CHESS 4.6's next move.

19 N−Q6 ...

(See Figure 24.) From here on Berliner is in trouble; he resigns on move 28.

Figure 24. Position after 19 N − Q6.

19 ... P × P		20 Q − B3! N − K4	

Berliner did not see that this move hangs the Rook. The correct move was simply 20 ... B − Q2.

21 Q × R	P − Q6	25 R − R7	Q − K4
22 N × R	Q × N	26 Q × B +	K − R2
23 P − QR4	P − R4	27 Q − B7	Q − K7
24 P × P	N − N5	28 Q × P	Resigns

After a few games, strong players seem to pick up some of the program's weaknesses and adapt to its style, generally doing much better than at first. But I doubt very much whether a player rated below 2000 USCF can adapt sufficiently to the style of CHESS 4.6 to become the better player. Tom Truscott has indicated that strong chess players adapt to DUCHESS after a number of games. DUCHESS seems to be playing speed chess at around the 1950 USCF level and has defeated several Masters.

It is paradoxical that computers are playing relatively better speed chess than "slow" chess. Church and Church (1977) argue that in speed chess the level of play "deteriorates considerably." Evidently, the play by Masters deteriorates perhaps more than we imagined, the only possible way to explain the rating differential between speed chess and slow chess. In a sense this seems to add support to the work of Simon and Chase (1973). They contend that a Master has stored in his memory some 50,000 chess patterns and has the ability to recognize any of these patterns or combinations of them and make the appropriate response quite quickly. In Newborn (1978b), this writer argues that therefore,

"just as two writers have much the same vocabulary, especially if the two are in close communication, two chess players store a large number of patterns with which they are both familiar. They often anticipate each other's ideas. How many times has a chess player made a bad move, leaving a piece *en prise* for example, only to have his opponent not notice the error. Computers are not programmed to think in terms of patterns on the board in the way people are. Thus when playing computers at speed chess, humans are often thrown off stride by the unusual patterns that arise on the board. The human is forced to revise his thinking between successive moves more frequently than when playing another human. This factor, I believe, accounts for the somewhat weaker play of humans *vis-à-vis* computers in speed chess."

Levy (1977a) argues the difference is because computers play relatively better tactical chess than positional chess, that they do not leave pieces *en prise* and they never miss one-move combinations, etc., and that in speed chess, tactics play a more important role than in slow chess.

7. The Microcomputer Revolution

For well under $1,000, it is now possible to have a computer in your own home, a computer as powerful in many respects as any in existence around 1960. It can be plugged into the wall, it makes no noise, and it weighs about 30 kg. Microcomputers, as they are called, are not as fast or as able to store as many numbers or as easy to work with as are most current minicomputers or full-size computers, but the situation is changing fast. Even with their present capabilities, microcomputers can be programmed to play chess and play respectably indeed. There is a growing number of enthusiasts and programmers busy in their homes, in basements and studies, writing their own programs. Others, who have bought small computers and who are not interested in programming, have obtained one of several commerically available chess programs. Still others have purchased one of the special chess playing machines that are now available for under $500 and which are built around various microprocessors. The more notable of these are CHESS CHALLENGER, BORIS, and COMPU-CHESS.

Several things distinguish microcomputers from larger computers when it comes to their ability to play chess (or to carry out any large numerical computation):

(1) Most microcomputers use an 8-bit word size thus frequently making addressing problems more difficult and making handling large numbers (greater than $\pm 2^7 = \pm 128$) more cumbersome. A gain of perhaps 50% in speed may be achieved by using a 16-bit word size instead of an 8-bit word size as is done by most minicomputers. Still further speedup results by using a 32-bit or larger word size as is the case for IBM 370 series computers and CDC CYBER 170 series computers, respectively.

(2) Memory size is small, typically 4K–8K 8-bit words, as opposed to anywhere from a minimum of 128K 32-bit or 64-bit words in larger computers. Programs running on large computers such as CHESS 4.7, DUCHESS, and CHAOS store several hundred thousand bytes of information as the tree-search progresses and this cannot be done using a small memory. Transposition tables are definitely out until bigger word sizes and bigger memory sizes are available.

(3) Languages and compilers are not as sophisticated as they are on larger systems. Most chess programs for microcomputers are written in either

assembly language or BASIC. Compilers for BASIC often yield code that executes very inefficiently. FORTRAN, the most popular high-level language for chess programs, is becoming available and should improve the situation.

(4) Operating systems are also not in the same league with those available on larger systems. They are slower and much less flexible. Instead of using high-speed disks for program development, small computers use diskettes or inexpensive magnetic tape recording equipment. High-speed line printers are only available for large systems. When developing a chess program, program listings and printouts of parts of the tree are often required. These tasks take considerable time on small systems.

Their major asset is that:

(5) They are cheap to use, essentially free once they have been obtained. Developing chess programs takes vast amounts of computing time and in the past this has slowed the progress of many good programs. The development of CHAOS, for example, has been handicapped because of this.

1978 marked the first year that a microcomputer participated in an ACM tournament. The program, written by Arnold Epstein and called 8080 CHESS, ran on a Processor Technology system. This system uses an Intel 8080 as its central processing unit. The program was in over its head, outclassed by programs on larger computers. In a few years, however, the situation will be very different. With falling memory prices and faster hardware, there will be many good programs running on microprocessors and on all kinds of special purpose contraptions as well, and they will play very strong chess.

About 6 months after Seattle, on March 3–5, 1978, San Jose became the site of the first microcomputer tournament. Eleven microcomputers battled for five rounds during the West Coast Computer Fair. Sargon, the program of Dan and Kathy Spracklen, won with a 5–0 record. Their program ran on a Jupiter II Wave Mate, a 2 MHz Z-80 based system with 8K of memory. Of the special purpose systems, CHESS CHALLENGER and BORIS each finished with a 3–2 record. Unlike the ACM tournaments, all 11 computers appeared in person for the 3-day performance (First Microcomputer Chess Tournament, 1978).

CHESS CHALLENGER was improved in the last few months. Its most current version played OSTRICH at McGill University on July 30, 1978 and an interesting game ensued. OSTRICH's positional play was the major difference; neither side made a serious tactical error. OSTRICH has a provisional Quebec Chess Federation rating of just over 1500 (QCF ratings are slightly less than USCF ratings) and based on its game with CHESS CHALLENGER, the latter deserves a rating around the 1200 level. This is consistent with CHESS CHALLENGER's performance in the C category of the 1978 Quebec Open where it won 7 of 9 points. Its game with OSTRICH went as follows:

White: OSTRICH   Black: CHESS CHALLENGER

1	P – K4(B)	P – QB4(32)	
2	N – KB3(B)	P – Q3(30)	
3	B – N5 +(B)	B – Q2(77)	
4	N – B3(53)	N – KB3(181)	
5	Q – K2(60)	N – B3(182)	
6	O – O(110)	P – K4(657)	
7	P – Q3(140)	N – Q5(199)	
8	B × B +(79)	Q × B(75)	
9	Q – Q1(141)	B – K2(153)	
10	B – N5(106)	P – QR4(640)	
11	P – KR3(160)	R – KN1(547)	
12	P – R3(146)	P – R3(176)	
13	B × N(121)	P × B(152)	

14 K – R1(148)	P – R5(275)
15 N – Q5(223)	B – Q1(261)
16 P – B3(231)	N – N6(167)
17 R – R2(125)	R – QB1(392)
18 N – Q2!(180)	N × N(174)
19 Q × N(92)	R – N3(174)
20 P – Q4(141)	P/B × P(160)
21 P × P(151)	Q – N4(80)
22 R – Q1(342)	Q – B5(238)
23 R/2 – R1(321)	R – B3(333)
24 N – K3(373)	Q × P(273)
25 Q × Q(233)	P × Q(131)
26 R × P(112)	…

Up to this point, CHESS CHALLENGER has been holding ground. The position is shown in Figure 25.

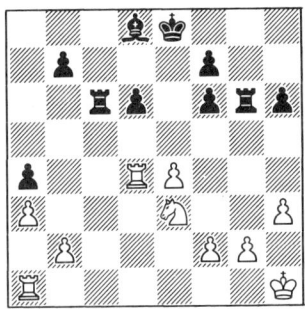

Figure 25. Position after 26 R × P.

26 …	P – N4(123)
27 R/1 – Q1(179)	B – K2(146)
28 N – B5(277)	R – B7(190)
29 R/4 – Q2(151)	R × R(90)
30 R × R(98)	P – R4(107)
31 R – Q5(72)	R – N1(161)
32 R × P/5(100)	R – N3(126)
33 R – N8 +(191)	B – Q1(63)
34 N × P +(146)	K – K2(47)
35 N – B5 +(178)	K – Q2(77)
36 R – N4(153)	B – B2(92)
37 R × P(243)	R – N1(110)

38 P – QN3(328)	B – N3(125)
39 P – B4(134)	B – B2(215)
40 P – N3(125)	R – N1(83)
41 P – QN4(86)	R – K1(84)
42 P – N5(63)	R – QN1(93)
43 R – Q4 +(37)	K – K3(47)
44 N – N7 +(115)	K – K2(73)
45 R – B4(431)	B – Q3(90)
46 N – B5 +(103)	K – K3(246)
47 R – B6(66)	R – Q1(197)
48 P – QR4(54)	P – R5(54)
49 P × P(42)	Resigns

8. Final Observations and the Future

Chess programs have increased remarkably in strength and are presently playing at levels unimagined only a few years ago. In 1970, the best programs played 1400 level chess; by 1974, 1600 level; now in 1978, over 2000. The increased strength can be attributed to a maturing of techniques and faster computers. Before long, the weakest programs participating in the ACM tournaments will be playing at the Expert level.

With advances in both hardware and software continuing at the same rates as they have during the last 10 years, it is highly probable that programs will be playing Master level chess by 1984, Grandmaster level chess by 1988, and better than any human by 1992. (These are conservative estimates!) This speculation is based on the data shown in Figure 26.

Improvement will continue to depend on the process of modifying existing programs, observing how they play, and then making further modifications. Stronger and stronger human players will be required to be involved in this feedback loop as deficiencies become more subtle. Tree-searching techniques and data structures will continue to improve. Rather than giving computers large amounts of chess-specific information, programs will continue to discover this information by searching. Strong programs based on extensive move pruning are still a long way off.

Throughout history, man has regarded himself as a special creature. Once he believed his planet and then his solar system were at the center of the

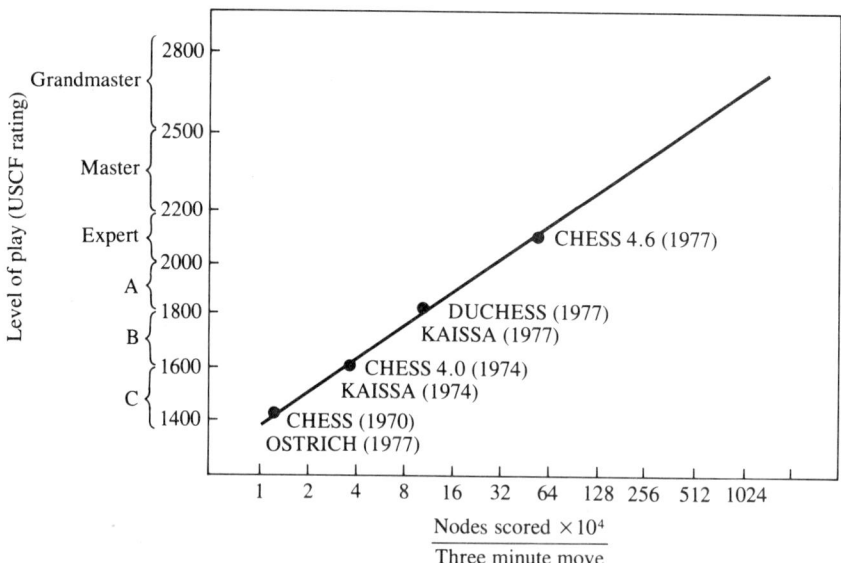

Figure 26. Relationship between playing strength of chess programs and the number of nodes scored per move.

universe, only to discover later that this is not the case. From earliest times, he saw himself as being in a different class than the other inhabitants of the earth. Then 100 years ago, Darwin showed him that he has many relatives. And he always imagined that his intellectual powers are supreme, perhaps uniquely God-given. This belief is being challenged in the twentieth century. With computers competing on an equal footing against all but the best of human players, one more piece of evidence to the contrary has been found.

Man has always been slow in accepting new perspectives of his place in the universe. Old theories have been defended in the light of overwhelming scientific evidence to the contrary. Some will now defend the supremacy of man's intellect by claiming that chess, once thought to be a legitimate test, is, in retrospect, merely a problem of calculation. They will argue that although computers play good chess, they will never write great poetry or compose outstanding music until they are programmed to reason as man does. In time, however, computers may accomplish these feats as well using techniques quite different than man's. What computer chess has taught us is that the effort required will be tremendous.

Acknowledgments. This writer would like to extend a special thanks to Dave Cahlander for the information he provided about the activities of CHESS 4.7. Also to be thanked is Ilan Vardi, formerly a student at McGill and now a graduate student at MIT. Vardi, one of Montreal's top chess players, assisted with the analysis of several games. Finally, the author would like to thank Mrs. Maura Crilly and Mrs. Diane Chan for their gracious help in preparing the manuscript.

2.5. Master Level and Beyond

DAVID N. L. Levy

This section was written specially for the Compendium, to bring up to date (July 1986) the history of computer chess.

The 1980s seem destined to be the era when computer-chess programmers put most of their faith in faster hardware rather than superior programming techniques. The best examples of special purpose hardware being built to generate chess moves and to evaluate chess positions are BELLE (Thompson *et al.*, 1983; Thompson, 1983) and BEBE, written by Tony Scherzer. Their philosophy is simply that brute force is the correct approach and so speed is everything.

BELLE's record of successes in computer tournaments and human events is quite impressive. The program won the World Computer Championship in Linz, Austria, during the summer of 1980, and then took first place at the annual ACM tournaments in 1980, 1981, and 1982. During 1983 it acquitted itself extremely well at the U.S. Open Championship, a tournament in which a number of Grandmasters, International Masters, and National Master players participate, scoring an impressive $8\frac{1}{2}$ out of 12, which corresponds to a performance rating of 2357. As a member of the computer team which took part in the 1983 U.S. Amateur Team Championship, BELLE's performance was equivalent to a rating of 2368. As a result of these events, BELLE's official rating in the U.S. Chess Federation's list rose to 2203, which automatically brought the program the title of U.S. Master (given to players who reach 2200 or higher), and with this title the programmers were presented with a $5,000 cheque from the Fredkin Foundation for programming the first computer that achieved the rank of National Master.

Ever since the late 1970s, some of the best chess programs won occasional speed games against very strong human masters, and occasionally against Grandmasters. In New York, during the 1983 ACM Tournament, I suggested to International Master Bernard Zuckerman that he play a few speed games against BELLE. Zuckerman is without doubt one of the best speed players in the USA, and asked me whether he would own the program's soul if he won every game. Two hours later Zuckerman was reeling from a 5–4 beating!

There is no knowing where special purpose chess hardware may lead. The circuitry that Thompson and Scherzer have built can be integrated into a small number of silicon packages, and it is quite possible that within a few years we will see chess chips that can perform at master level retailing for $10 or less. The doubt in my mind is that the brute force approach will ever lead to play of the calibre of the human World Champion.

Another program which utilizes enormously powerful hardware is CRAY BLITZ, written at the University of Southern Mississippi by Robert Hyatt and Albert Gower. The program runs on the Cray computer which is the world's most powerful commercially available machine. CRAY BLITZ won the 1983 World Computer Championship, and the 1984 ACM Tournament, but in competition games against strong human players it has yet to achieve the high performance ratings of BELLE. Hyatt has announced that in 1986 he will be using a system of parallel CRAYs which is approximately 20 times as powerful as the one currently assigned to his chess program. It remains to be seen whether the combination of a slightly strengthened program with an extra 2-ply of search will be sufficient to take CRAY BLITZ much beyond master level.

The reason why so many chess programmers believe in brute force is that they feel intuitively that an extra few ply of search are all that is needed to produce an electronic Karpov. The stronger chess players amongst the computer chess cognoscenti believe that to be successful a program must think more like a human, utilizing a highly selective search. Most programmers shy away from this approach because they do not possess sufficient knowledge of the game, and in my opinion they are putting their heads in the sand. Chess is a game where planning and concept formation are essential ingredients, and the correct move, particularly in the endgame, often requires an understanding of what is going to happen 20-ply or more into the future. No matter how deep a brute force program searches, I do not believe that this approach will lead to the ultimate goal.

There is, however, one area of chess in which a powerful brute force program can be more impressive than the very strongest human players. I am referring to endgame positions with a very small number of pieces on the board. Ken Thompson has developed a technique for storing every possible configuration with (say) King and Rook vs. King and Queen. By backtracking from all positions where the side with the Queen has actually forced a win (checkmate or win of the Rook), BELLE can play this endgame absolutely perfectly, and it moves instantaneously! This particular endgame configuration is a win for the side with the Queen, but it is far from easy. The first time that International Grandmaster (and former U.S. Champion) Walter Browne tried to win with the Queen against BELLE, he failed!

BELLE has also analyzed other endings, notably King and two Bishops vs. King and Knight. This was thought to be a draw from most positions, but BELLE has shown that it can always be won. Some positions require as many as 67 moves by the winning side, and since the laws of chess normally declare a game to be drawn if 50 successive moves have passed without a pawn move or a capture being made, the International Chess Federation will soon be amending the laws to cater for this exception. (They have already been amended for another exception which has been verified by BELLE.)

Similar results have been achieved by the Soviet program KAISSA for the endings: King, Rook, and pawn vs. King and Rook; and King, Queen, and Knight's pawn vs. King and Queen. That computer programs can outperform the best humans in certain endgame positions is quite impressive, but this work does not advance the more general problem of playing good chess. As hardware becomes faster and faster, endgame configurations with more pieces will be added to the list of positions that can be played perfectly, but such positions are very few. In my opinion, the real breakthrough will come only when someone creates a computer program which can form concepts and sensible plans.

2.6. Experiences Gained in Constructing and Testing a Chess Program

Hans J. Berliner

Originally published in: *Proceedings of IEEE Symposium on System Science and Cybernetics, 1970*, pp. 216–223. Copyright © 1970 IEEE. Reprinted by permission of The Institute of Electrical and Electronic Engineers, Inc., and of the author. This work was begun under the auspices of the International Business Machines Corporation and is currently being sponsored by the Advanced Research Projects Agency of the Office of the Secretary of Defense. (Contract No. F44620-70-C-0107)

Introduction

The state-of-the-art in chess-playing programs, following Greenblatt's (1967) initial successes, has progressed to the point where serious programming is going on at about a half-dozen universities and others are interested. This paper is an attempt to document the structure of one program, and to shed some light on the pitfalls that may be expected and the work involved in developing a competent program. We have endeavored where possible to leave out details given by previous authors.

The author has been one of the top chess players in the United States for 20 years, and is the present World Correspondence Chess Champion. As such we have been interested for some time in the problems of computer chess playing. The work of Shannon (1950) and Turing (1953) seemed to lay a secure foundation upon which such programs could be built. It was therefore rather much of a surprise that the programs produced by early workers in the field turned out to play such weak chess. Having carefully gone over the documents produced by Bernstein *et al.* (1958b), we come to the conclusion that their program evaluated positions at a specified depth, regardless of whether the position was quiescent. Since it is impossible by static means to accurately evaluate a position where each side has threats, it is not too surprising in retrospect to find that their program often made gross blunders. The program of Newell *et al.* (1958b) also did not play very well. Although it was never completely coded, we feel the program design concentrated too much on things of a strategic nature. It is a well-known fact in chess circles, that chess is 90% tactics, and until the tactics are well in hand strategical planning will be of little use. It is the author's contention that, while most of what masters verbalize about chess is on a strategical plane, in reality a master has many levels of "hard wired" tactical analysis routines that process chess situations, and that he is no longer conscious of. Therefore, strategy cannot be effectively introduced until a good representation of the tactical analysis has been implemented.

We interpreted the work of Samuel (1959, 1967) as a demonstration that complex games could be effectively programmed. However, it appeared that his linear polynomial method of evaluation was an outgrowth of his initial goal of demonstrating machine learning. Upon reflection on his results, it seemed that some of his problems could be attributed to the duplication effects that must be present when some 30-odd unrelated factors are applied to produce an evaluation. We consider a small number of well-chosen models of a basic activity (such as pawn structure) to be a better approach. In actuality, no one has tried the factor approach to chess (since there are probably thousands of factors), and Samuel has recently shifted his approach in the direction of models.

It remained for Greenblatt (1967) to avoid the early errors mentioned above and produce a program of notable caliber. His program is a magnificent example of the practical solution of chess programming. Although the program frequently fails to employ ideal solutions (from the chess Masters point of view), these departures seem to be justified by technological expediency and their overall effect is seldom noticed. Greenblatt's program has gone a long way toward solving the tactical problems in chess, and that is its main strength in our opinion. However, significant progress also appears to have been made in incorporating a goal structure and some positional sense into its heuristics.

Our main departure from Greenblatt's approach is as follows: His program works by rapidly paring down the legal alternatives at each node to those that appear to be worth considering. In this process, tactical ideas can be found quickly, but positional moves whose worth is more laborious to discover are frequently left out. We therefore subscribe to the idea of Newell *et al.* (1958b) that almost any amount of processing at a node in a search tree is justified if it helps to avoid false leads in the tree-search. Thus we do not advocate a broad search program that finds the correct move from a set of reasonable alternatives by depth searching. Rather we advocate a program that selects a move as likely to be best after lengthy examination, and only rejects this notion based upon findings in the depth search. This process would then be continued until there no longer appears to be a move that could be better than the best found thus far.

Description of the Program

Most of the above notions had crystallized before work on the program began in May 1968. We had been studying the problems of encoding chess algorithms for several years, and now encouraged by Greenblatt's results, felt it was time to begin developing a program.

It was clear that a chess program should be free from making basic errors that lose material. However, a capable program should also have a feeling for the positional aspects of chess. Positional play involves domination of the board by the pieces. Thus we formulated the following process:

(1) Control of a square by a piece involves the ability of that piece to capture a hypothetical enemy man on that square.
(2) The squares vary in their importance; the central squares being the most important. In order to assign values to the squares in a methodological manner, a superpiece was invented which combined the moves of the Queen and Knight (thus including as subsets the moves of all the pieces). The number of squares that this piece could move to on an open board from any square was calculated to be an indication of the value of the square. From each value was subtracted the number 21, as this is the number of horizontal, vertical, and diagonal squares that could be reached even from the least advantageous location. The result of these manipulations can be seen in Figure 1. This shows excellent agreement with our intuitive notion developed over many years of what the relative values of the squares on the board are.
(3) The effective control of a piece is inversely proportional to its value; thus a weaker piece can exercise more effective control than a stronger one since it is more expendable.
(4) The control for each square is the algebraic sum of the product of the controlling power of each piece and the value of square.
(5) The control of the board is the sum of controls of the individual squares.

This algorithm was discussed with Greenblatt who then incorporated it into his program where it produced a beneficial effect. After 2 years of program development, the board control algorithm still exerts an important effect in giving the program a sense of direction. The importance of board control seems to decrease as pieces disappear from the board, until in the endgame it has little, if any, meaning.

2	3	4	4	4	4	3	2
3	6	8	8	8	8	6	3
4	8	12	12	12	12	8	4
4	8	12	14	14	12	8	4
4	8	12	14	14	12	8	4
4	8	12	12	12	12	8	4
3	6	8	8	8	8	6	3
2	3	4	4	4	4	3	2

Figure 1. Topology of a chessboard.

An initial test of the algorithm, to statically evaluate potential moves in a given position, confirmed expectations but showed another problem. The algorithm had no cares about putting pieces into positions where they could be captured effectively (with a net loss). Thus a method of detecting threats was needed.

The method used was to investigate each occupied square to determine if the nonoccupying side could initiate a favorable capture, and if so, what the optimum gain/loss was from a minimax point of view. This worked very well.

Once threats were identifiable, the algorithm for evaluating positions (which also included a tally of actual material) worked well enough so that a program to play chess was constructed. The program was written in PL/1 and encompassed about 3,500 statements. To date, it has grown only slightly as new code is usually accompanied by a tightening of the old code. The present version of the program has 14 subroutines which do such things as generate the control pattern of a piece, update positions, evaluate positions, control the tree-search, etc.

After some experience in running the program, several important things were noticed:

(1) The program did not know how to handle situations where each side had more than one threat, in fact; several situations (where each side had one threat) were difficult to handle. This arose from the fact that there was no mechanism for detecting the independence of threats and the likelihood of any threat being executed. For instance, if two unprotected Queens were facing each other the program would consider the threat situation equal. What was needed was a threat analyzer which would evaluate the interdependence of threats and also consider whose turn it was to move. Thus in the above example the side whose turn it is to move has an excellent chance of capturing the Queen while the side which just moved has only a small chance of doing so. King checks were included in the threat analysis. In general, the method used was to find the strongest threat for each side. If they were independent, assign each the highest likelihood of being executed. If they were not independent then assign the best threat of the side to move and the second best threat of the side that just moved the highest likelihood; all other threats get a lesser likelihood. The threat coefficients are adjusted so as to be optimistic from the point of view of the moving side. This encourages looking at speculative moves before settling on a safe alternative. This method is now being used, and with a few additional refinements works quite well.

(2) It was very difficult to get the program to do certain kinds of strategic things without having recourse to special heuristics. These were things such as:

(a) Castling Kingside during an early stage of the game.

(b) Not moving pieces twice during an early stage of the game.

(c) Advancing pawns during the endgame when winning, etc.

Special heuristics were put into the program to encourage these things. We would like to emphasize that we consider such heuristics as an admission of defeat. Ideally, we would like behavior of the program to be evoked by a model which deals with such activities. For instance, castling should be evoked as part of a King safety model, rather than by a "do it (all other things being equal) because it is good" heuristic. A collection of such heuristics will eventually become unwieldy and tend to limit further development of the program. The reason such devices were used sparingly here is that no King safety model had been written, and thus there was little option.

Noticing that the program tended to operate in the same manner, regardless of the stage of the game, led to the development of another useful device: the Phase Analyzer. This routine is invoked at the top of the tree, and decides which of the following situations the game is in at present:

(1) one side winning by a large amount;
(2) one of special endgame situations;
(3) early opening;
(4) late opening;
(5) middle game;
(6) endgame.

Before invoking the phase analyzer, the program notes the value of a variable which represents the minimaxed result of the tree-search associated with the last move. This is taken to represent the status of the game—who is winning and by how much. The phase analyzer uses this plus an analysis of the amount of material on the board and the longevity of the game to make the above decisions. The phase analyzer is useful insofar as it can be used to adjust the coefficients in the models in accordance to their importance during that phase of the game. For instance, the value for checking the King diminishes in the endgame. It is also useful for evoking special strategies such as attack the King when you are way ahead. The game status variable is very useful in setting a level of aspiration for the next tree-search.

We have described some interesting features of the program that are used in evaluation, now let us turn to a description of the search procedure, a standard depth-first search is used by the program. Beginning at the starting position, moves are generated by a move generator and each is statically evaluated as generated. The moves are sorted in terms of goodness from the mover's point of view and investigated accordingly. Each move represents a transition to a new position which is in turn investigated until a termination criterion is hit. The structure of the search was at first controlled by a set of parameters input to the program during initialization. These parameters controlled the maximum number of alternatives that the program was allowed to investigate at each level in the tree, and the depth to which it was allowed to search. For instance, the program was usually instructed to investigate at most four moves at the top two levels in the tree, two moves at the next four levels, and one move below that. The program was limited to a depth of search of 14-ply. It testifies to the excellence of the static evaluation function that the program was able to play a reasonable game while considering so few alternatives.

When searching in depth, the program went to the prespecified depth. Then if the threat analysis function indicated there were some unresolved threats for the side next to move, it would keep going, considering only moves related to the threats until there were no more threats or the bottom level was reached. Thus we considered quiescence to be the absence of a threat by the side next to move and the absence of two threats by the moving side. When returning up the tree to a previously visited node with unexplored alternatives, the static evaluation (which is designed to be optimistic) of the next alternative is compared with the backed-up value. If the backed-up value is greater, all alternatives at that level are forward pruned, otherwise the next alternative is investigated. The alpha–beta algorithm (Samuel, 1967) is also used to prevent the program from investigating superseded lines of play.

After some experimentation with the above procedure, which was similar to that of most other programs, and review of results of other workers in the field (Adelson-Velsky et al., 1966; Greenblatt et al., 1967) it became apparent to me that a better method was required. Looking at games being produced by chess automata, it was apparent that the depth of search had little to do with the excellence of the games produced. In fact, Adelson-Velsky et al. include in their paper two games between their program playing at a depth of 4-ply vs. a depth of 3-ply. One contest was won by 3-ply and the other was unfinished.

Similar experiences led us to a detailed study of the trees investigated by the program. It was possible to determine that a large percentage (approximately 75%) of all errors made by the program were due to faulty judgments precipitated by the mechanisms that bring the search to a close once the prespecified boundary is reached. This is at once a startling and revealing discovery. It appears to explain how a 3-ply depth machine can beat a 4-ply machine, since the search termination mechanism is invoked at prespecified levels and thus its effect is random. An example of this effect would be that the search termination mechanism is actuated by the fact that in a terminal position a pawn can be captured. It investigates the capture, but no other moves which happen to include a one-move checkmate.

The overwhelming conclusion of these observations is that search termination introduces an unacceptable level of error into the search. The only reason why such errors do not seem to affect Greenblatt's program too seriously, appears to be that it searches to a minimum of 4-ply and thus errors tend to be further down the tree. However, we have observed the Greenblatt program make bad moves which could not be attributed to anything other than this type of error.

In view of this, we determined to investigate a free form of search which terminated in quiescent positions only and had no special termination procedure; the only bound being the absolute depth limit of 14-ply. We did this with some apprehension since it was difficult to predict the effect on computer time used. Therefore a method was developed for gradually relaxing the search constraints and approaching the free-form search. Surprisingly, this worked very well, and a free-form search is now being used in the program. This depth of search goes to a minimum of 2-ply, except in the endgame where it goes to 4-ply. The width of search is still controlled by an input parameter. Basic quiescence is defined as the complete absence of a threat by either side. All nonquiescent positions at the boundary are investigated until they become quiescent or hit 14-ply. As we progressed toward this state, we discovered several useful tree-search heuristics which helped to keep the search time down. These heuristics deal with the definition of quiescence under a variety of circumstances. For instance, when one side is winning in a portion of the tree by a considerable amount and the losing side has no threats, then it is most likely safe to consider the position quiescent and terminate the search since this is not likely to become the optimum path in the tree. The present search format has increased the average processing time per move vs. the straight 2-ply depth search by approximately sevenfold to an average time of about 65 seconds per move on the IBM 360/67. The actual time per move has ranged between 1 second and 20 minutes, a phenomenon that we find encouraging since it approximates the response time of good tournament players. However, when the program uses much time it is usually because some defect in the static evaluation function leads it to expect something to happen that is not going to happen, and the program spends much time depth-searching without any results. However, this type of phenomenon does not occur often and as the objective function improves, it should be further reduced. On the average, the program examines only 30 nodes in the tree.

These basic improvements in searching had a noticeable effect on the skill of the program, and it began to play at least a half-class better than before. The errors the program now makes are largely attributable to defects in the evaluation function which cause two types of effect: (1) a position is misjudged, or (2) a good move fails to get a high enough evaluation to be considered as an alternative, and thus the variation calculated does not include the best response at all levels. Errors of type (2) predominate; however, when a complete free-form search is instituted (unlimited depth and unlimited width at each node) these errors will disappear also. With a good objective function, such a free-form search should rarely run to large amounts of time.

The analysis of program performance is made possible by four levels of trace facilities which can be turned on and off. In this way it is possible to determine how static evaluations were arrived at, how tree decisions were made, etc. We would encourage anyone writing a chess program to provide similar facilities, as it would be extremely difficult to debug the program and do development work without it.

Another technique that is implemented in this program is worthy of mention. That is the method of incrementally updating positions. When a potential move from a position is explored, most of the new position will be very much like the old. In fact, the only changes are:

(1) The old control field of the moved piece (pieces in the case of castling) must be erased.
(2) The control field of any captured piece must be erased.
(3) The control field of the moved piece(s) must be regenerated at its new position.
(4) There are at most four newly unoccupied or occupied squares (for ordinary moves there are only two). Any piece which moves in a straight line and bears on one of these squares must have its "ray" modified to meet the new conditions.

To do the above required writing some extra code, but resulted in speeding up the program by a factor of four! In computing the new board, it was found that, on average, only 14 squares needed to be recomputed instead of 64 when a new position is generated from scratch.

At the beginning of the game, the program can be set to retrieve its moves from an opening book file. This file contains approximately 200 selected lines of play. It was found that in selecting these lines, careful consideration had to be given to the program's basic ability and style of play. Just because an opening variation is praised in a book on the subject does not make it suitable for the program. When a nonbook move is played, the program may be unable to find why it is inferior (which can be very tricky for even above-average human players). Also the terminating position of the opening variation should be typical of situations that the program handles well, as otherwise it will not know what to do and lose time with vacillation.

Testing the Program

The program was written, tested, and improved over a period of 2 years. Several faults that were found in the program were structural in nature and could not readily be remedied. These are discussed in the section entitled Conclusions and Future Developments.

In retrospect, the testing procedure left much to be desired. Testing usually consisted of the author playing a game or game fragment with the program. This was useful in detecting certain inadequacies of the program, but gave no indication, for instance, of how the program would handle a superior position since it would never achieve one against a much superior player. Other tests consisted on giving the program positions which had special problem features and then noting its response. This would then be repeated after program modifications had been made, until an adequate response was elicited. Probably the most useful tests were those in which the program played a human opponent other than the author. Since the program has little difficulty in beating inexperienced opponents, it was usually rather difficult to find worthy opponents. However, at all levels of skill, interesting things would be found about situations that the program did not handle properly. This usually had to do with coefficients that required adjustment, or special heuristics that the program needed, to better approach a certain problem. One interesting feature was that in superior positions, the program frequently tended to repeat moves—that is, it oscillated from one local optimum to another without having the ability to judge what was necessary for global progress. This problem should be resolved by evoking a planning routine, but since the program has no planning capability, a makeshift solution involving selecting another move (if that was also favorable) was introduced.

In the spring of 1970, we received an invitation to have the program participate in a small open chess tournament at Flint, Michigan. Since the program would be competing in a human tournament, it seemed appropriate to endow it with a name. For this purpose J.BIIT (just because it is there) was chosen. J.BITT duly participated in this event via long distance telephone over the week-end of May 23–24. The overall performance of the program was disappointing as it won only one game and lost four. However, it should have won one of the games it lost and had drawing positions near the end in two other games it lost. Notably, the program did not "blow up" once during the tourney.

Upon returning to Carnegie–Mellon a detailed analysis of the games was undertaken in order to better understand the reasons for the program's performance. Since all five games ended in checkmate, only that portion of the game during which the issue had still not been clearly decided was analyzed. Moves that the program made were classified into four categories as seen through the eyes of a Master:

(1) best possible move;
(2) adequate move;
(3) inferior move;
(4) terrible move (one that goes completely against the requirements of the position).

The results may be seen in Table 1.

It became apparent that in all of its games J.BIIT was doing well (in fact, frequently winning) until it made one or more of its terrible moves. The game

Table 1. Quality of moves.

Category	Best	Adequate	Inferior	Terrible
Game 1	6	9	2	6
Game 2	14	25	10	3
Game 3	15	22	15	3
Game 4	8	6	0	0
Game 5	13	12	4	4
Total	56	74	31	16
Percent	31.7	41.8	17.5	8.0

Table 2. Comparison of Greenblatt program's moves in three games.

Greenblatt moves	Same	Equal	Inferior	Better
Game 1	12	4	5	4
Game 2	14	5	3	8
Game 4	9	3	2	0
Total	35	12	10	12
Percent	50.7	17.4	14.5	17.4

of chess, as played at about the level of the average club player, thus emerges as a sequence of moves distributed about a mean, which will sooner or later contain a decisive error after which the game is too far lost to be recovered. Interestingly, enough excellent moves do not have an opposite effect; that is, they do not create a winning position beyond reach of the opponent. This description is certainly not typical of master level chess, where the game is usually decided by more intricate issues.

On reflection, it became clear that one of the major achievements of Greenblatt had been to develop a program that made relatively few terrible moves. To check this hypothesis we compared the performance of Greenblatt's program in the more important parts of three of the games played. For this purpose we used the version of his program which was discussed in his article, and which is currently running on the PDP-10 at Carnegie–Mellon.

Sixty-nine moves were run for comparison purposes. The responses were classified as follows:

(1) same move as made by J.BIIT;
(2) Different but equally effective move;
(3) inferior move to that made by J.BIIT;
(4) better move than J.BIIT's.

As can be seen from the results in Table 2, this analysis did little to differentiate between the performance of the two programs. Therefore, the seven terrible moves included in the above sample of 69 were analyzed separately. These results are shown in Table 3.

Although the sample is not very large, the results are clear. In fact, the general performance of the Greenblatt program should be better than the results of the table indicate since here it was being asked to take on situations

Table 3. Comparison of Greenblatt program's performance on J.BIIT's terrible moves.

Greenblatt moves	Same	Equal	Inferior	Better
Total	1	2	1	3
Percent	14.3	28.6	14.3	42.8

not of its own making which would thus tend to be alien to its "style" of playing. In conjunction with the previously developed fact that games are lost by the making of very bad moves, this latest datum rounds out the story well: Greenblatt's program makes fewer bad moves (his latest version is surely even better at this) so it tends to perform better. Interesting to note however, when the two programs play against each other, they play on very equal terms (see Appendix). J.BIIT plays more imaginatively and also better positional chess, but the Greenblatt program is steadier.

Further detailed analyses of move printouts showed that six of the 16 terrible moves were caused by: (1) a bug in the program that was not previously identified; and (2) the fact that the program did not "know" that a Rook behind a pawn can effect its ability to advance. These two problems have since been corrected. The other terrible moves were caused by deficiencies in the objective function which will be more difficult to correct, and are best handled by expanding the search space to include more moves at each node.

A sample of games the program has played can be found in the Appendix.

Conclusions and Future Developments

The program described herein will not be developed further by the author as the OS/360/67 under which it operated is no longer being run at Carnegie–Mellon. However, much useful knowledge has been developed from this work, and it is the author's intention to apply this to developing a better program in the future.

Let us first examine some of the more serious shortcomings of today's chess programs.

(A) *They have no coherent planning capability.* A sort of pseudoplanning is achieved by heuristics that point in the right direction, but even simple plans such as transferring a piece to a more important sector are not implemented in any program we know of. This immediately leads to the oscillation phenomenon between local maxima that we spoke of earlier. Since planless programs cannot scan the horizon for plans which would provide a sense of direction, they end up maximizing static features and soon run into oscillating situations.

(B) *They have little sense of what is permanent and what is temporary.* This phenomenon leads them to grab the slightest advantage they can discern, whereas good human players will make judgments as to whether the status quo is favorable and can be maintained and increased. A good example of this is given in Figure 2(a) and (b).

In Figure 2(a) it is safe to say every program will play P − B8/Q which will win the Knight and leave a winning position. However, the maneuver K − Q4 − Q5 forces the Knight away and results in a gain of a whole Queen. In Figure 2(b) the latter maneuver is not possible since the pawn

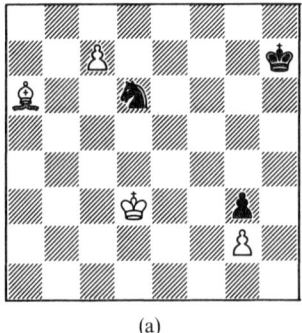   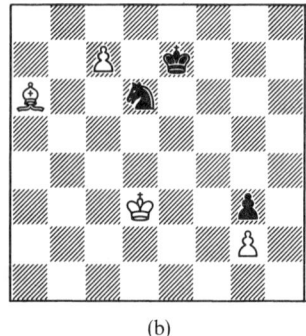

                    (a)   (b)

Figure 2

at QB7 is in imminent danger, so P − B8(Q) is correct, but no program can differentiate the two situations. It is this lack of knowing that certain advantages will not go away that also causes games between computer programs to be rather uninteresting. As soon as a little tension builds up in the position, one program or the other will dissipate it in order to achieve some minimal gain.

(C) *They have no level of aspiration.* This problem is related to the two earlier ones. Programs will work just as hard to avoid losing a pawn when they are a Queen down as when the position is even. When faced with an intricate mate they will give the opponent every benefit of every doubt and instead give up a Rook, little realizing that this spells certain defeat in the future. In fact, the desire to push disagreeable consequences over the search horizon by indulging in temporary distractions is very common feature of the programs we have observed. All this is, of course, due to the fact that the program really does not have any concept of what is going on and instead lives by its objective function which is incapable of evaluating certain outcomes beyond the search horizon.

(D) *They have no ability to benefit from past experience.* One of the most damning aspects of today's chess program is that given the same initial settings, they will play the same game time after time regardless of the game's outcome. Even a weak human player will vary his behavior (perhaps unsuccessfully) after losing a game. However, today's programs have no memory of previous games, and this definitely limits their capability.

The huge number of possible positions makes it difficult to introduce meaningful memory for a chess program. However, it is possible to associate past results in a way similar to Samuel (1959), with the opening book positions. Then for the moves that are computed, the following procedure could be used: All factors used in the objective function at the bottom of the main branch through the search tree are remembered, as well as the value of the objective function. After the program has made four more moves, the latest value of the objective function is examined and if it differs significantly from the earlier value, a slight adjustment of all coefficients involved is done right at that moment. We feel that such changes should be performed in real time and should be permanent, deriving from the program's own experience. The adjustment of each coefficient would, of course, be small, being a function of the total number of data points already sampled.

We see no way that problems such as these can be resolved by programs which depend exclusively on heuristics for guidance. This is because there are basically too many situations to be cataloged. Rather our experience leads us to believe that chess playing is a multilevel activity. Each level collects and synthesizes information into a model of what is going on under the direction of a supervisory level. By appropriate interaction among levels, applying analysis procedures to data models, it should be possible for a program to understand the major aspects of a chess position.

At present, we see at least 11 distinct levels of activity and believe it likely that the final number could be more than twice this. The basic activity levels are:

(1) *Activity of each piece on the board.* This generates the basic control and movement pattern of each piece taking into account the blocking of straight-line pieces by other pieces.
(2) *Interaction of pieces.* This detects the effect of blocking of lines of the straight-line pieces. Effects include pins, discovered attacks, X-rays, control through another piece.
(3) *Activity on a square*
  (a) who control it;
  (b) strategical value;
  (c) capturability of occupying piece.
(4) *Area analysis of related squares*
  (a) color complexes;
  (b) King safety.
(5) *Board analysis*
  (a) sum of board control;
  (b) sum of board threats;
  (c) sum of material;
  (d) sum of strategical values;
  (e) binding of pieces to functions.
(6) *Null move analysis.* Can player not on move do anything meaningful when there are no overt threats?
(7) *Phase analysis.* Determines phase that the game is in and evokes only those lower-level routines appropriate to this phase.
(8) *Goal identification.* When no tactical threats exist to guide the program, a search of goal types appropriate to the particular game phase in question is conducted. These potential goals are listed.
(9) *Strategic planning.* Tests are run to see whether any of the goals listed are

achievable (within the sophistication of the program). Moves that contribute to achieving achievable plans get extra weights in evaluation, and final positions which are *en route* to a planning goal get extra weights.

(10) *Tree-searching.* The tree controls all the above activity and can evoke any of the above routines at any node.

(11) *Learning.* Learning is done in real time at the conclusion of any tree-search and before making a move.

We consider the above structure to be extendable since the lower six levels, being now within the state-of-the-art, would function autonomously, and only the upper levels would require the limited addition of goal types, planning methods, etc. A completely heuristic oriented structure, on the other hand, could grow indefinitely with the addition of new heuristics.

Appendix

Four games and one position played by J.BIIT are presented here. Game 1 was played in the tournament in Flint, Michigan. It is typical insofar as the program gets a good position and then loses it by degrees through not knowing what to do with the advantage. White's peculiar 24th and 28th moves were due to a bug in the program. Game 2 was played against the third board player on the school's city championship chess team. He felt overconfident at the start. The endgame is the best we have ever seen a computer play. Game 3 shows some basic characteristics of the program's play. On move 11 it wants to exchange material because it is ahead, instead of conducting a winning attack. On move 14 it misses the finesse O − O − O after which 15 R × N could be answered by B − B4 ch. When the opponent gets careless it finds a way to regain the piece, and wins the endgame nicely. Game 4 is a typical example of how the version of Greenblatt's program which we have and J.BIIT play. Black could have won a pawn with 11 B − R3 12 P − N3 B − B6. On move 14, White should have played B × N and Black should have retreated the Knight. In the final position neither program wishes to avoid the draw although White stands better. In Position 1, White finds the senseless looking 1 N − K1!! based on a very clever tactical idea.

Game 1. May 23, 1970

White: J.BIIT   Black: Classs B Player

1 P − Q4	P − K3	8 N − QN5	Q − N1
2 P − K4	P − QB4	9 N × B ch	Q × N
3 N − QB3	P × P	10 Q − B5	Q − K2
4 Q × P	N − QB3	11 R − Q1	P − QN3
5 Q − B4	P − KR3	12 Q × Q ch	K × Q
6 N − B3	B − Q3	13 P − B3	P − Q3
7 B − K3	Q − B2	14 B − QN5	B − N2

15	N – Q4	N × N	35	B – N4 ch	K – K1
16	R × N	P – R3	36	B – B3	N – Q2
17	B – Q3	N – B3	37	P – KN4	P – N3
18	O – O	KR – Q1	38	P – R4	K – K2
19	R – N4	P – QN4	39	P – N5	P × P
20	R – QB1	QR – QB1	40	P × P	K – K3
21	P – QR4	B – B3	41	K – N2	K – Q3
22	B – N6	R – Q2	42	K – N3	K – B4
23	P × P	P × P	43	K – B3	K × P
24	R – B2	R – QR1	44	K – K3	P – R6
25	B – K3	R – R5	45	K – Q2	P – R7
26	R × R	P × R	46	P – N4	N – N1
27	P – B3	P – K4	47	B × P	N – B3
28	K – R1	P – Q4	48	B – N2	N × P
29	P × P	R × P	49	B – B6	N – R3
30	R – Q2	N – Q2	50	K – K3	N – B4
31	P – QB4	R – Q3	51	B – K5	N – N6
32	B – K4	R × R	52	B – B6	P – R8/Q
33	B × R	B × B	53	B × Q	N × B
34	P × B	N – B3		and Black won	

Game 2. May 4, 1970

White: J.BIIT   Black: Class B Player

1	P – Q4	P – QB4	22	P – B4	N – B6 ch
2	P – Q5	P – B4	23	R × N ch	N/3 × R
3	N – KB3	P – Q3	24	P – B5 ch	K – Q2
4	N – B3	N – KB3	25	NP × N	R × N
5	Q – Q3	P – K4	26	B – K4	N – B2
6	P – K4	P × P	27	B – K3	P – QN3
7	QN × P	B – B4	28	P – QN4	P × P ch
8	N × P ch	B × N	29	P × P	N – Q3
9	Q × B	N × P	30	B – Q4	R – K1
10	N × P	Q – K2	31	B – Q3	R – K2
11	Q – B8 ch	Q – Q1	32	P – B5	P × P ch
12	Q × Q ch	K × Q	33	P × P	N – N2
13	N – B7 ch	K – K2	34	B – K4	K – B2
14	N × R	N – QB3	35	K – B4	N – R4 ch
15	B – N5 ch	K – K3	36	K – N5	N – N6
16	P – QB4	N/4 – N5	37	B – QB3	P – QR3 ch
17	P – QR3	N – B7 ch	38	K – B4	N – B8
18	K – Q2	N × R	39	B – Q2	N – K7
19	B – Q3	N – N6 ch	40	K – Q3	N – N8
20	K – B3	N/6 – Q5	41	B – N5	R – Q2 ch
21	R – K1 ch	B – K4	42	K – B4	N – K7

43 P – B6	R – Q5 ch	47 B – B4 ch	K – B1
44 K – B5	R – QR5	48 B – K5	N × P/6
45 P – R4	P – R3	49 B × N	R × P
46 B – Q2	N – Q5	50 B – K2	R – R5

The game had to be stopped here, and was adjudicated a win for White. J.BIIT had little difficulty beating the author in the continuation the following day.

Game 3. June 21, 1970

White: Unrated Player   Black: J.BIIT

1 P – K4	P – K4	17 B × B ch	K × B
2 N – KB3	N – QB3	18 P × N	N – Q6
3 B – B4	N – B3	19 R – K2	N × B
4 N – N5	P – Q4	20 K × N	B – B4
5 P × P	P – N4	21 N – R3	P × P
6 B × P	Q × P	22 R × P	KR – K1
7 P – QB4	Q × NP	23 R × R	R × R
8 R – B1	B – Q2	24 N – B3	R – K8 ch
9 N – KB3	P – K3	25 N – Q1	R – R8
10 N – N1	Q × RP	26 P – N4	B – Q5
11 P – Q3	Q – Q3	27 R – N1	R × N
12 P × P	Q × Q ch	28 K – B2	R – R6
13 K × Q	N × P	29 N – N2	R × P
14 R – K1	P – B4	30 K – N3	R × N ch
15 P – B3	P – QR3	31 R × R	B × R
16 B – R4	N – N5	32 K × B	P – KR4
			Resigns

Game 4. January 27, 1970

White: Greenblatt Program (1968 version)   Black: J.BIIT

1 P – K4	P – K4	15 B × N	P × B
2 N – KB3	N – QB3	16 O – O	B – N5
3 P – Q4	P × P	17 P – B3	B – K3
4 N × P	N – B3	18 B – N4	KR – Q1
5 N × N	NP × N	19 QR – K1	P – QR4
6 P – K5	Q – K2	20 B – B3	R – Q6
7 Q – K2	N – Q4	21 P – B4	B – Q4
8 P – QB4	Q – N5 ch	22 P – QR4	P – QB4
9 Q – Q2	N – N3	23 R – K2	B – B3
10 Q × Q	B × Q ch	24 R – R1	B – Q4
11 N – Q2	P – Q4	25 R/1 – K1	B – B3
12 P – QR3	B × N ch	26 R – R1	B – Q4
13 B × B	N × P	27 R/1 – K1	B – B3
14 B – B3	O – O	28 R – R1	
		Drawn by repetition	

Position 1

Probably the best move the program has ever played occurred in the above position. The program playing White played: 1 N − K1. The point is that on replies such as N × N, or N × P/5 the continuation is 2 R × R ch K × R 3 B − N6 ch winning the Queen. Moves such as 1 N − Q4 are tricky, but have no positive effect.

Acknowledgment. The author wishes to express his appreciation to the many people whose ideas have affected the chess program, particularly Drs. Allen Newell and Herbert Simon.

2.7. Creating a Chess Player

Peter W. Frey and Larry R. Atkin

Originally published in: *BYTE*, vol. 3, no. 10 (October 1978), pp. 182–191; no. 11 (November 1978), pp. 162–181; no. 12 (December 1978), pp. 140–157; vol. 4, no. 1 (January 1979), pp. 126–145. Copyright © 1978, 1979 McGraw-Hill, Inc., New York 10020. Used with permission.

PART 1

In a recent *Time* essay (Jastrow, 1978) Robert Jastrow, director of NASA's Goddard Institute for Space Studies, predicted that history is about to witness the birth of a new intelligence, a form superior to humanity's. The pitiful human brain has "a wiring defect" that causes it to "freeze up" when faced with "several streams of information simultaneously." Jastrow suggests that "the human form is not likely to be the standard form for intelligent life" in the cosmos. Even on our own small planet, a new day is near at hand: "In the 1990s, ... the compactness and reasoning power of an intelligence built out of silicon will begin to match that of the human brain."

We have always been fascinated by the idea of a machine that is capable of rational thought. Jastrow is neither the first nor the last person who is betting on rapid improvements in machine intelligence. His expectation that computers will rival humanity within 15 years seems optimistic to anyone who has watched half-a-dozen excited technicians flutter about for several hours trying to bring a crashed system back to life. This prophecy seems even more fanciful to those who have attempted to program machines to cope with pattern recognition, language translation or a complex game such as chess.

The chess environment, in fact, provides a particularly good example of the difficult problems which still need to be solved before silicon intelligence can become a reality. More than 20 years ago, Herbert Simon, a recognized expert in the field of Artificial Intelligence, predicted that within a decade, the world's chess champion would be a computer. This prognostication has not come to pass. Why was an informed scientist like Simon so wrong in his assessment of computer capabilities? A major factor is that computer scientists have often failed to appreciate the level of knowledge which is required to play master-level chess. They have also commonly underestimated the tremendous information-processing capacity of the human brain. Even though chess is a game of logic in which all legal moves can be precisely specified and in which nothing is left to chance, several centuries of intensive analysis have not exhausted the perennial challenge and novelty of the game. Psychologists have been actively studying the human brain for several decades and have discovered a fascinating mystery wrapped within an enigma. The more we learn about the brain, the more we are aware of our lamentable state of ignorance.

The Mind of the Chess Player

At a general level of knowledge, we have several provocative insights on the nature and structure of human chess skill. We know, for example, that the skilled chess player does not examine hundreds of possible continuations before selecting a move. We also know that superior chess players are not formidable "thinking machines" but in fact display a normal range of intelligence scores. Strong chess players, as a group, do not even appear to have special retention abilities such as having "photographic" memories. In most respects, top-flight chess players have the same intellectual capacities as the rest of the population and, in the technical details of move selection, seem to engage in the same type of information processing that is observed in much weaker players.

Our knowledge in these matters is based on the early work of Binet in France and that of de Groot in Holland and on more recent investigations by other scientists in the USSR and the United States. In the late nineteenth century, Binet was surprised to discover that masters did not have a vivid image of the board when playing blindfolded chess. Instead, they seemed to remember positions in abstract terms such as by specific relations among pieces. Interviews with masters clearly indicated that a photographic memory was not a prerequisite for being able to play many simultaneous games of blindfolded chess. In the 1930s and 1940s, de Groot worked with a number of strong chess players (from Grandmasters to strong club players) and had them verbalize their thought processes while selecting a move in a complicated position. His research indicated that Grandmasters' general approach was highly similar to that of weaker players. They analyzed a similar number of moves (about four) from the initial position, a similar number of total moves (about 35), made a similar number of fresh starts (about six), and calculated combinations to the same maximal depth (about seven plies or half-moves, where a move is defined as a play by one side and a response by the other). The only clear measurable difference was that the Grandmasters invariably chose the strongest move while the weaker players did not. Thus de Groot concluded that Grandmasters play better chess because they pick better moves. Unfortunately, this conclusion is not very informative since it is obviously circular. The fact that de Groot's extensive study did not uncover any prominent differences in the move-selection strategies used by strong and average players implies that the analysis procedure itself is not the critical factor which determines chess skill.

An important clue to the difference between skilled and unskilled players was discovered by de Groot when he displayed an unfamiliar chess position to his subjects for a few seconds and then asked them to recall the position from memory. He found that masters recalled almost all the pieces while club players remembered only about half of them. Recent work in this country by Chase and Simon at Carnegie–Mellon University has indicated that novice players recall only about a third of the pieces. Chase and Simon also added an important control procedure. They demonstrated that the differences in recall ability completely disappear if the pieces are positioned randomly. This outcome indicates that the superior memory of the chess master is chess-specific and not a general trait.

Simon and Gilmartin have proposed that skilled chess players learn to recognize a large number of piece combinations as perceptual chunks and perform well in the recall task because they remember four or five chunks rather than four or five pieces like the novice. If the average chunk size is three to four, the skilled player will recall 16 to 18 pieces.

On the basis of this analysis, skill in chess depends on a learned perceptual ability which is highly similar to that acquired by every schoolchild as he or she slowly builds up a large repertoire of words. Initially the child learns to read each word character by character and often does not understand the meaning of the word. The novice chess player perceives the chessboard in a similar way, assessing a position piece by piece and failing to recognize the *meaning* of common piece configurations. The adult reader recognizes words and phrases as basic units (chunks) rather than individual characters and has a recognition vocabulary of approximately 50,000 words. The skilled chess player, in a similar vein, recognizes a very large number of piece configurations (chunks) and understands what they imply both individually and in combination.

The critical aspect of move selection occurs in the first few seconds of the task. Based on his assessment of the position, the skilled player immediately recognizes appropriate long-term and short-term goals and has a good feel for the specific moves which are compatible with these goals. For this reason, only two to four moves on the average are given serious consideration. The difference between the Grandmaster and the Expert lies in the fine distinctions which are made in the first few seconds of their analysis. Skilled chess players can play a remarkably strong game when they are given only 5 seconds for each move. In this short time, it is not possible to make a careful analysis of many different continuations. The player must have an "instinctive" feel for the correct move and be able to recognize key features and to understand both their immediate and long-term implications.

Human chess skill, therefore, is based on two highly refined capacities, pattern recognition and rapid information retrieval. The latter ability depends on the fact that human memory is content-addressable rather than location-addressable like that of a computer. Computer systems often have to search for a specific item of information in memory by conducting an exhaustive, linear search of an entire file. Human memory, however, is organized in an amazingly complex fashion such that most of us can easily recall a specific fact on the basis of a completely novel retrieval cue. For example, name a flower that rhymes with *nose*. In this case, your quick response demonstrates that words are grouped together on the basis of their phonetic similarity (i.e., sound). Your ability to quickly recall words which are similar in meaning to the word *fat* (such as obese, chubby, rotund, flabby, plump, and stout) demonstrates that human memory is also organized by semantic similarity (i.e., meaning). When a person is given a retrieval cue which does not elicit an immediate response, he or she can usually find the correct information after a brief search of related ideas or concepts. This facility contrasts sharply with the extremely limited linear searches which are generally conducted with large computer based storage systems. Even sophisticated computer retrieval strategies which arrange the data base in multilinked lists with elaborate tree structures presently lack the large system efficiency displayed by their biological counterparts.

Pattern recognition and rapid information retrieval are not only key capacities for chess, but are also essential for a wide range of important human problem solving skills. Whether your field is medicine, engineering, plumbing, or computer programming, you would be a complete failure at your job without these essential abilities. Jastrow's claim that machine intelligence will soon equal man's intelligence seems to overlook the important points made in *BYTE* by Ernest Kent. Kent (1978) emphasizes the fact that biological information processors have a vastly different architecture than their silicon imitations. In fact, he suggests that our lack of success in building a thinking machine stems from our attempts "to make a wrench do a screwdriver's job." Our modern high-speed computers were designed to do important tasks which men are not very good at, such as complex mathematical calculations.

The human brain evolved, in contrast, on its ability to identify important environmental events and to quickly recognize their significance. Natural selection has never placed much emphasis on our ability to multiply or our ability to compute the inverse of a matrix. Kent also reminds us that organic evolution worked with a very different kind of hardware than that which is available to the modern computer engineer. Biological information processors have an incredibly slow cycle time, less than 100 operations per second. The basic unit, the neuron, operates in milliseconds rather than in nanoseconds. The brain, however, makes up in quantity and in structural complexity what it lacks in speed. Computers, on the other hand, have many fewer components and a much simpler gating architecture, but are orders of magnitude faster.

It may be that present machine hardware configurations are simply inappropriate for efficient pattern recognition or semantic recall. An analysis of the history of computer chess is instructive. Although there have been numerous advocates for chess programs which imitate human playing methods, only a few have been attempted, and none of these have played reasonable chess. The earliest paper on machine chess, written by Claude Shannon in 1950 (Shannon, 1950a) proposed a mechanical algorithm which was not modeled on human chess play. Shannon suggested a workable procedure for representing the board and piece locations, specified simple mathematical algorithms for generating the legal moves of each piece and gave an example of a straightforward technique for evaluating a position (Frey, 1977, Chapter 3). The key feature of Shannon's proposal was the adoption of the *minimax* technique as described by von Neuman and Morgenstern in 1944. The basic idea of the minimax technique is to assume that the player whose turn it is to play will always choose the move which minimizes his opponent's maximum potential gain. Hence, the name minimax.

The Type B Strategy

One of the difficulties of this approach is that a complete analysis of all possible continuations (type A strategy) very rapidly leads to an overwhelming number of potential positions. The look-ahead tree grows at an exponential rate and with an average, according to de Groot, of 38 legal moves at each position, a search involving three moves (three half-moves for each player) produces over 3 billion (38^6) terminal positions. You may recall that de Groot's research indicated that human players regularly searched a tree to seven plies and sometimes much deeper. Because of this, Shannon concluded that it would not be possible for the machine to consider all possible legal continuations at each *node* of the game tree. Instead, he proposed a type B strategy in which only reasonable (i.e., plausible) moves are pursued at each branching point. If the program considered only five continuations at each node instead of all 38, a 6-ply look-ahead would involve only 15,625 (5^6) terminal positions.

The attractiveness of the type B approach seems overwhelming when the number of terminal positions increases exponentially with depth. The fact that skilled human players explore only a limited number of continuations at each choice point is additional evidence which favors the adoption of this strategy. It is not surprising, therefore, that most programmers have used Shannon's type B strategy in designing a chess program.

Sometimes our understanding of the real world, however, is not always as accurate as we presume. In selecting a type B strategy in preference to a type A strategy, the programmer does not necessarily simplify the problem. This approach was competently implemented in 1967 by Greenblatt at MIT. His program played reasonable, and at that time, fairly impressive chess. The major design problem in a selective search is the possibility that the look-ahead process will exclude a key move at a low level in the game tree. The failure to consider an important move can lead to a very serious miscalculation. A chess game can be lost by a single weak move. For this reason, it is of critical importance that a necessary move not be missed. The type B programs place a critical dependence on the accuracy of their plausible move generator. Chess is an extremely complex game and in many situations a move which at a superficial level seems unlikely, is, in fact, the best one. Grandmasters find these moves while lesser players, including machines, fail to see them. For a decade, several dozen individuals have tried to create a plausible-move generator that is superior to Greenblatt's. The evidence is fairly clear, however, that type B programs have improved very little since 1967.

As strange as it may seem, recent progress in computer chess has come by abandoning the type B strategy. Shannon's logical analysis was made in a "stone-age" hardware environment and without knowledge of several important algorithms. Today, the type A strategy is not as ridiculous as it seemed in 1950. In addition, very few individuals anticipated the immense difficulty involved in constructing a competent plausible-move generator. To become a chess master, a man has to study chess intensively (20 hours or more a week) for at least 5 years. During this time he acquires an immense amount of detailed knowledge about the game of chess. Subtle features of a particular position are recognized immediately and suggest both short-term and long-term goals as well as specific moves. This kind of knowledge is sufficiently abstract that most players find it impossible to verbalize the relevant thought processes. The one factor which stands out clearly, however, is that the chess master has acquired a tremendous library of factual information which can be retrieved quickly and applied in apparently novel situations. No chess program has been able to duplicate this facility and, without it, the creation of a workable plausible-move generator is next to impossible.

When a type A strategy is employed, however, this problem can be bypassed. By making all the moves *plausible*, the program never overlooks a subtle but important one. In fact, by reverting to a brute force search of all possible continuations, the program often finds interesting combinations that are commonly missed even by strong human players. It seems ironic that the brute force approach (full-width searching) produces many more brilliant moves than the smart approach (selective searching). This important discovery was made independently by Slate and Atkin at Northwestern (the authors of the current world champion chess program, CHESS 4.6) and by the Russian KAISSA team.

Minimax and Alpha–Beta Algorithm

Slate and Atkin's work has demonstrated that a full width search can be conducted considerably more efficiently than anyone had previously suspected (including Slate and Atkin, 1977). There are a number of important developments which are responsible for this reassessment. The most important discovery was made in the late 1950s by Newell, Shaw, and Simon as well as by Samuel. Because of the basic logic underlying a minimax search, it is not necessary to search the entire look-ahead tree before selecting the best move. Consider a simple 2-ply search (one move for you and one for your opponent). First you examine one of your possible moves and the 38 or so terminal positions which result from each of your opponent's legal replies. You select the one reply which is best, according to your evaluation function, for your opponent (i.e., the one which minimizes your own maximum potential gain). Next, you consider a second move for yourself and the 38 or so replies that your opponent can make to this move. In considering these moves, you discover that the third reply you examine would give your opponent a better outcome than his best reply to your first candidate. Immediately you realize that it is a complete waste of time for you to analyze any more of his replies to your second candidate. Since you are already guaranteed a worse position after the second move than after the first, it is reasonable to reject the second one and turn to your third candidate. This decision eliminates the need for evaluating 35 of the potential replies to your second candidate. A very tidy saving.

Historically, the score for the best move so far for White has been designated as α and the score for the best move so far for Black has been called β. Thus the name alpha–beta (α–β) algorithm. When the tree is both wide and deep, this algorithm can reduce the number of terminal nodes to a small fraction of the number which would be examined by a complete minimax search. The beauty of this procedure is that it always produces the same result as the full minimax search.

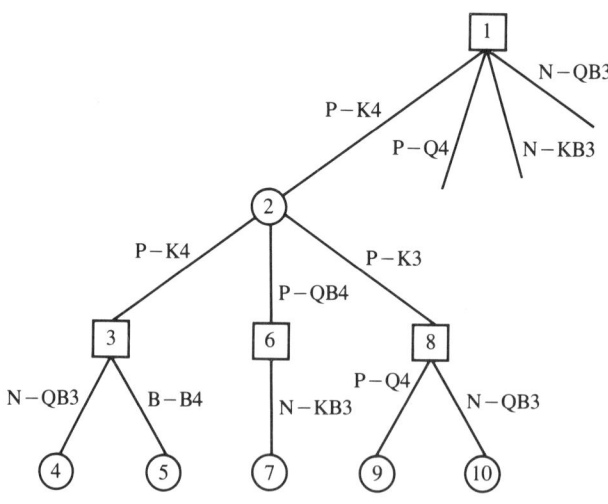

Portion of a game tree for the opening game in chess. Square nodes indicate that White is to play; round nodes that Black is to play. Techniques such as alpha–beta pruning and minimax strategy are used to optimize the use of trees like this.

An important factor in determining the efficiency of the alpha–beta algorithm is the order in which the moves as examined. If White's best moves and Black's best replies are considered first at each choice point, the search of the uniform game tree of height h (number of plies deep) and width d (number of successors at each node) will involve approximately $2 \cdot d^{h/2}$ terminal positions instead of d^h (Knuth and Moore, 1975). The potential magnitude of this saving can be appreciated by considering our previous example with a 6-ply search: 38^6 is more than 3 billion while 2×38^3 is about 110,000. Shannon might have given more consideration to the type A strategy if he had been aware of the alpha–beta algorithm and some of the other technical improvements which were to follow.

General Strategy

To maximize the benefit of the alpha–beta procedure, it is necessary to devise an efficient strategy for generating the moves at each node in an order which is likely to produce a cutoff, such that searching can be terminated at that node. There are several general heuristics which have proven their value time and time again. One is extremely simple and powerful: try capturing moves first. Because a full width search includes many ridiculous moves, a reply which involves a capture will often remove a piece which was "stupidly" placed *en prise* (i.e., attacked and insufficiently defended). Captures also have the beneficial effect of reducing the number of potential offspring. An additional important characteristic of a capturing move is that it will generally have to be examined sooner or later in order to insure the quiescence of the terminal position. Because of this, every capture that is examined early generally reduces the amount of work which will have to be done later. In practice, investigators have reported a speed-up in search time of as much as 2 to 1 by simply putting all the captures at the beginning of the move list.

In addition to captures, there is another class of moves which is also effective for producing cutoffs. These are called *killers* because they are moves which have produced cutoffs in the immediate past and have been specifically remembered for that reason. A short list of killers is maintained by the program and whenever the legal capturing moves fail to produce a cutoff, each of the killers (if legal in the given position) is then examined. This *killer heuristic* is quite effective in producing a move order which enhances the probability of a quick cutoff.

The general features of the alpha–beta algorithm and its important servants, the capture and killer heuristics, were reasonably well known late in the 1960s. In recent years, several important refinements have been added to this list. One of the most important is the staged or iterative alpha–beta search. For example, instead of conducting a 5-ply search all at once the search is done in stages, first a 2-ply search, then a 3-ply search, then a 4-ply search, and finally a 5-ply search. Superficially this might appear to be wasteful since the staged search requires the full 5-ply search eventually anyway. This is not at all the case. As each search is completed, the principal variation (best moves for each side at each depth) is used as the base for the next (1-ply deeper) search. The 3-ply search therefore starts with a move at ply 1 and a reply at ply 2 which has already been proven to be reasonable (from the machine's limited perspective). The 4-ply search starts with reasonable moves at its first three plies. The 5-ply search has the benefit of reasonable moves at its first four plies. Because the efficiency of the alpha–beta algorithm is tremendously sensitive to move ordering, the spill-over in information from one iteration to the next has a surprisingly powerful effect. A single 1-stage 5-ply search might require 120 seconds of processor time. The last segment of the staged 5-ply search might require only half as much time (i.e., 60). Since each iteration requires about five times as much processor time as its predecessor (the exponential character of the look-ahead tree is diminished somewhat by the alpha–beta algorithm), the staged 4-ply search would take about 12 seconds, the staged 3-ply search about 3 seconds, and the 2-ply search about 1 second. The total time for the iterative search would be approximately 76 seconds $(1 + 3 + 12 + 60)$ rather than 120 seconds.

An added benefit of the iterative search, and, incidentally, the reason for its discovery in the first place, is that it provides a useful mechanism for time control. In tournaments, a move must be calculated within a fixed time limit such as 90 to 120 seconds. If one decides to do a 5-ply search in a single stage, it is possible to find onself tied up in calculation after 120 seconds with no idea of how much more time will be needed to complete the search, and without a move to make until the search is completed. In some complex situations the search might take as long as 10 minutes—a disaster for time control. An iterative search allows one to predict the probable duration of the next iteration and to make a decision whether it is cost effective to initiate the next one. If this decision is a go and the search, for some reason, fails to terminate in the anticipated time, the machine can abort and play the move selected by the last iteration. This provides relatively neat and tidy time control. The iterative search was first mentioned by Scott in 1969 and was apparently discovered independently several, years later by Jim Gillogly at Carnegie–Mellon, by Slate and Atkin at Northwestern, and by the Russian KAISSA team.

Refinements to the Type A Strategy

Several other refinements have also made the type A strategy more manageable. One of the time intensive activities involved in tree-searching is move generation. This can be minimized by generating only one move at a time and seeing if it produces a cutoff before generating the next move. If a cutoff occurs and the node is abandoned, one can avoid generating a large number of potential moves. With the *n*-best approach, it is customary to generate all moves at each node and then invest time attempting to decide which ones are worthy of further consideration. Thus the smaller tree, obtained by selective searching, has to be partially paid for by an additional time investment in plausibility analysis.

Another time-intensive activity in the tree-search is the repeated use of the evaluation function. Since many thousands of terminal nodes have to be evaluated in each move selection, any refinement that reduces the work of the evaluation function will pay rich dividends. There are three important techniques which fall in this category. One of these is called *incremental updating*. In order to make an evaluation of a node, it is necessary to have certain key facts available, such as which squares are attacked by each piece, which pieces are present, etc. This information can be newly calculated at each terminal node or can be incrementally maintained by updating the appropriate tables as the tree is generated during the search. This latter procedure is more complex to program but tremendously more efficient in terms of computing time because neighboring terminal positions are highly similar. They usually differ in respect to only a single piece, and therefore the updating procedure requires about 10% of the computations that would be expended if the evaluation data base were recalculated from scratch for each evaluation.

A second refinement in this category is the use of serial organization in the evaluation function. In order to assess the relative merit of a chess position, most programs place heavy emphasis on the material balance (i.e., the relative number of pieces for each side). This tradition is founded on the idea that winning or losing is strongly correlated with being ahead or behind in material. An additional rationale is that this information is readily available and easily updated.

In most programs material factors are so dominant that the other evaluation terms, such as mobility, pawn structure, King safety, area control, etc, taken together almost never account for more than two pawns. Because of this, it makes sense to compute the material balance factor first and then determine if the result is within two pawns of the target value. If not, there is no need to assess the other factors, because the final decision will be independent of their value.

This simple idea encourages one to organize the evaluation function in strict serial order such that influential (heavily weighted) terms are analyzed first and the result examined to see if a decision is possible based on this initial information. If not, the next most influential term(s) are examined and another determination is made. This process is repeated until an escape condition occurs or until all terms have been examined. In most cases, the evaluation will be terminated long before the list of potential terms has been exhausted. This technical refinement can save a significant amount of time.

A third procedure for speeding the evaluation process is to remember past evaluations. For instance, one should avoid reassessing the same position two or more times. In chess, there are many pathways by which one can reach identical positions. In a 3-ply sequence in which the middle move remains constant, for example, the first and third moves can be interchanged and the resulting position will be the same. Transpositions such as this occur frequently in the endgame where the King may have literally hundreds of four-move pathways that end on the same square. Rooks, Bishops, and Queens also have a special facility for reaching a particular destination square in multiple moves rather than in one or two.

A full width search (i.e., type A strategy) greatly accentuates this foolishness. By creating a large table of past positions which have been already evaluated, and using a hashing procedure to check if the present position is in the table, the programmer can completely eliminate a portion of the evaluation effort. In most middle game positions, this technique will produce a 10–50% saving. In certain endgame positions, however, the transposition table can eliminate more than 80% of the evaluation effort. This idea seems to have been implemented first by Greenblatt in 1967.

An extension of this idea is to use the table to store likely moves as well as evaluations. By remembering a move which previously produced a cutoff, the table can facilitate ordering decisions. In addition, the use of the same reply at a familiar position may have the added benefit of increasing the number of transpositions which will be encountered at later nodes. Additional details on the use of a transposition table are discussed in Chapter 4 of Frey (1977).

One of the most difficult challenges for a chess program is the endgame. A machine which calculates a move for each position has difficulty competing with humans who "know" the correct move on the basis of their own or someone else's past experience. There are a huge number of endgame situations in which a specific and highly technical strategy is required. Strong chess players study these intricacies at great length and use this knowledge at the chessboard to avoid unnecessary calculations. For example, a King and a pawn against a lone King is a win in some positions, and a draw otherwise. The same is true for a King and two pawns against a King and a pawn. If a Rook or minor piece is added to each side, the situation changes dramatically. Unfortunately, our present day programs are oblivious to these subtleties. For this reason they can find the correct move only by engaging in prodigious calculations. Their human counterpart, on the other hand, "knows" the correct move after a cursory glance at the position.

Newborn (1977b) has introduced a useful technique for reducing this knowledge gap. The main idea is to categorize familiar endgame positions as wins or draws. Many games end with a King and a pawn fighting a lone King. Skilled players usually terminate the contest before it runs its inevitable course because the outcome is not in doubt. Newborn has shown that it is feasible, taking advantage of the symmetries of the chessboard, to make a bit map that indicates either a win (1) or a draw (0) for each potential square on which the lone King might reside for each of the potential locations of the opposing King and pawn. This knowledge can be encoded in approximately 300-bit boards of 64 bits each (see Frey, 1977, Chapter 5).

Although a tremendous amount of work and chess knowledge is required to complete this task, the end result is well worth the effort. When a position involving two Kings and a pawn is encountered anywhere in the look-ahead tree, it can be immediately scored with 100% accuracy as a win or a draw. This extends the look-ahead horizon of the program by as much as 12–15 plies for these specific situations, and eliminates all the tree-searching effort which would normally be required. Furthermore, it permits accurate evaluations at the end points of a deep search, which allows the program to select a continuation which leads to a favorable endgame. If this approach were extended to a wider range of situations, the machine's present knowledge deficit with respect to the endgame would be greatly reduced.

These programming refinements, together with rapid hardware advances, have made the Shannon type A strategy feasible if not particularly elegant. For this reason it is possible to program a machine to play a game of chess which is free of gross blunders and which sometimes even contains an innovative move or two. Although this approach is clearly not a final solution, it does provide a solid base which can be used as a reliable starting point for future developments.

PART 2: CHESS 0.5

CHESS 0.5 is a program written in Pascal by Larry Atkin, who is coauthor with David Slate of the world championship computer chess program CHESS 4.6. The program is readily adaptable to personal computers having Pascal systems such as the UCSD Pascal project software.

We have attempted to incorporate several features which make the search process more efficient and others which increase the user's options. Both of these enhancements are important. The first set of features (incremental updating, iterative searching, staged-move generation, etc.) were described in general terms in Part 1. These features reduce computation to the point where a move can be selected in a reasonable amount of time even with a full-width search. The second set of features (special control and print commands, accepting chess moves in standard notation) not only add to the pleasure of using the program, but also make the debugging process much easier. The price for these enhancements is a longer, more complicated program. We hope the length of our listing will not discourage the reader from becoming actively involved.

Pascal was developed to provide a logical and systematic higher-level language which could produce reasonably efficient machine code for existing hardware. Computer programs can be conceptualized in terms of two essential parts, descriptions of data and descriptions of actions which are to be performed on the data. Pascal requires that every variable occurring in the program be introduced by a declaration statement which associates an identifier and a data type with that variable. The data type defines the set of values which may be assumed by the variable. Since a chess program involves a large number of variables, our program begins with a long list of declaration statements.

A constant definition introduces an identifier as a synonym for a constant. This is very useful since the value of the constant as stated in the declaration list can be changed at some later date, and this change will then be reflected throughout the program in every place where the constant is used. In the chess program, the values of some of the constants depend on the characteristics of the user's hardware. For example, the values of ZK (maximum search depth) and ZW (move stack limit) will reflect the amount of memory which is available on your system. On personal computers, ZX will generally be set at 7 if you have an 8-bit processor and at 15 if you have a 16-bit processor. Note also that the value of PZX8 depends on the value of ZX. To implement this program on a given computer, it is necessary to insert at the beginning of the program the appropriate values for these constants.

For the sake of clarity, specific data types are declared for a number of different chess concepts and for certain useful indices. The program also takes advantage of the different properties represented in Pascal's data structures: the set, array, and record. It is unlikely that anyone will immediately memorize the names of all the variables. Therefore it is useful to have them listed at the beginning where they can easily be found for later reference.

There is a comment statement accompanying almost every instruction in the program. Although these brief statements may not initially be very meaningful, we expect them to be helpful when the user becomes familiar with the program. Because Pascal requires that all procedures and functions be defined in the serial listing before they are called by another portion of the program, the procedures and functions which are first defined tend to be primitives. The main part of the program is concentrated at the end of the listing.

The portion of the program presented here covers initialization of the program, variable declaration, manipulation of the "bit boards" (used to represent positions on the chessboard), user print routines, and move generation. The second half of the listing will include procedures for evaluation of terminal positions, the look-ahead procedure, and user commands.

```
PROGRAM CHESS(INPUT,OUTPUT);

LABEL

    1,                              (* INITIALIZE FOR A NEW GAME *)
    2,                              (* EXECUTE MACHINES MOVE *)
    9;                              (* END OF PROGRAM *)


CONST

    AA = 1; ZA = 10;                (* CHARACTERS IS A WORD *)
    AC = "A"; ZC = ",";             (* CHARACTER LIMITS *)
    AD = -21; ZD = +21;             (* DIRECTION LIMITS *)
    AJ = 0; ZJ = 73;                (* CHARACTERS IN A STRING *)
    AK = 0; ZK = 16;                (* SEARCH DEPTH LIMITS *)
    AKM2 = -2;                      (* AK-2 *)
```

```
ZKP1 = 17;                          (* ZK+1 *)
AL = 8; ZL = 119;                   (* LARGE BOARD VECTOR LIMITS *)
AZL = -119; ZAL = 119;              (* LARGE BOARD DIFFERENCES
                                       LIMITS *)
AN = 1; ZN = 30;                    (* MESSAGE LIMITS *)
AS = 0; ZS = 63;                    (* BOARD VECTOR LIMITS *)
AT = -1; ZT = 63;                   (* BOARD VECTOR LIMITS AND
                                       ANOTHER VALUE *)
AV = -32767; ZV = +32767;           (* EVALUATION LIMITS *)
AW = 1; ZW = 500;                   (* MOVE STACK LIMITS *)
AX = 0; ZX = 31;                    (* SUBSETS OF SQUARES *)
AY = 0; ZY = 1;                     (* ARRAY OF SUBSETS TO FORM A SET
                                       OF ALL SQUARES ON BOARD *)

LPP = 20;                           (* LINES PER PAGE *)         .
PZX8 = 16777216;                    (* 2^(ZX-7) *)

SYNCF = 1;                          (* FIRST CAPTURE SYNTAX *)
SYNCL = 36;                         (* LAST CAPTURE SYNTAX *)
SYNMF = 37;                         (* FIRST MOVE SYNTAX *)
SYNML = 47;                         (* LAST MOVE SYNTAX *)


TYPE

  (* SIMPLE TYPES *)

TA = AA..ZA;                        (* INDEX TO WORDS OF CHAR *)
TB = BOOLEAN;                       (* TRUE OR FALSE *)
TC = CHAR;                          (* SINGLE CHARACTERS *)
TD = AD..ZD;                        (* DIRECTIONS *)
TE = (B1,B2,B3,B4,S1,S2,S3,S4,N1,N2,N3,N4,N5,N6,N7,N8);
                                    (* NUMBER OF DIRECTIONS *)
TF = (F1,F2,F3,F4,F5,F6,F7,F8);     (* FILES *)
TG = (PQ,PR,PN,PB);                 (* PROMOTION PIECES *)
TH = (H0,H1,H2,H3,H4,H5,H6,H7);
                                    (* TREE SEARCH MODES *)
TI = INTEGER;                       (* NUMBERS *)
TJ = AJ..ZJ;                        (* INDEX TO STRINGS *)
TK = AK..ZK;                        (* PLY INDEX *)
TL = AL..ZL;                        (* LARGE (18X12) BOARD *)
TM = (LITE,DARK,NONE);              (* SIDES *)
TN = AN..ZN;                        (* INDEX TO MESSAGES *)
TP = (LP,LR,LN,LB,LQ,LK,DP,DR,DN,DB,DQ,DK,MT);
                                    (* PIECES:  LIGHT PAWN, LIGHT
                                       ROOK, ... , DARK KING, EMPTY
                                       SQUARE *)
TQ = (LS,LL,DS,DL);                 (* QUADRANTS *)
TR = (R1,R2,R3,R4,R5,R6,R7,R8);     (* RANKS *)
TS = AS..ZS;                        (* SQUARES *)
TT = AT..ZT;                        (* SQUARES, AND ANOTHER VALUE *)
TU = (EP,ER,EN,EB,EQ,EK);           (* TYPES: PAWN, ROOK, ... ,
                                       KING *)
TV = AV..ZV;                        (* EVALUATIONS *)
TW = AW..ZW;                        (* MOVES INDEX *)
TX = AX..ZX;                        (* SOME SQUARES *)
TY = AY..ZY;                        (* NUMBER OF TX'S IN A BOARD *)
TZ = REAL;                          (* FLOATING POINT NUMBERS *)

  (* SETS *)

SC = SET OF AC..ZC;                 (* SET OF CHARACTERS *)
SF = SET OF TF;                     (* SET OF FILES *)
SQ = SET OF TQ;                     (* SET OF CASTLING TYPES *)
SR = SET OF TR;                     (* SET OF RANKS *)
SX = SET OF TX;                     (* SET OF SOME SQUARES *)

  (* RECORDS *)

RB = RECORD                         (* BOARDS *)
  RBTM : TM;                        (* SIDE TO MOVE *)
  RBTS : TT;                        (* ENPASSANT SQUARE *)
  RBTI : TI;                        (* MOVE NUMBER *)
  RBSQ : SQ;                        (* CASTLE FLAGS *)
```

```
CASE INTEGER OF
   0: ( RBIS: ARRAY [TS] OF TP);      (* INDEXED BY SQUARE *)
   1: ( RBIRF: ARRAY [TP,TF] OF TP);(* INDEXED BY RANK AND FILE *)
END;

RA = PACKED ARRAY [TA] OF TC:         (* WORDS OF CHARACTERS *)
RC = ARRAY [TS] OF TP:                (* BOARD VECTORS *)
RN = PACKED ARRAY [TN] OF TC:         (* MESSAGES *)
RJ = PACKED ARRAY [TJ] OF TC:         (* STRINGS *)

RD = PACKED RECORD                    (* SYNTAX DESCRIPTOR FOR
                                         SINGLE SQUARE *)
   RDPC : TB:                         (* PIECE *)
   RDSL : TB:                         (* / *)
   RDKQ : TB:                         (* K OR Q *)
   RDNB : TB:                         (* R, N, OR B *)
   RDRK : TB:                         (* RANK *)
END;

RK = RECORD                           (* KLUDGE TO FIND NEXT BIT *)
   CASE INTEGER OF
      0: (RKTB: SET OF 0..47):        (* BITS *)
      1: (RKTZ: TZ);                  (* FLOATING POINT NUMBER *)
END:

RM = PACKED RECORD                    (* MOVES *)
   RMFR : TS;                         (* FROM SQUARE *)
   RMTO : TS;                         (* TO SQUARE *)
   RMCP : TP;                         (* CAPTURED PIECE *)
   RMCA : TB;                         (* CAPTURE *)
   RMAC : TB;                         (* AFFECTS CASTLE STATUS *)
   RMCH : TB;                         (* CHECK *)
   RMMT : TB;                         (* MATE *)
   RMIL : TB;                         (* ILLEGAL *)
   RMSU : TB;                         (* SEARCHED *)
   CASE RMPR : TB OF                  (* PROMOTION *)
      FALSE: (
         CASE RMOO : TB OF            (* CASTLE *)
            FALSE: (RMEP : TB);       (* EMPASSANT *)
            TRUE : (RMQS : TB);       (* QUEEN SIDE *)
            );
      TRUE : (RMPP : TG);             (* PROMOTION TYPE *)
END;

RS = RECORD                           (* BIT BOARDS *)
   CASE INTEGER OF
      0: (RSSS: ARRAY [TY] OF SX):    (* ARRAY OF SETS *)
      1: (RSTI: ARRAY [TY] OF TI);    (* ARRAY OF INTEGERS *)
END:

RX = ARRAY [TS] OF RS:                (* ATTACK MAPS *)

RY = PACKED RECORD                    (* MOVE SYNTAX DESCRIPTOR *)
   RYLS : RD:                         (* LEFT SIDE DESCRIPTOR *)
   RYCH : TC:                         (* MOVE OR CAPTURE *)
   RYRS : RD:                         (* RIGHT SIDE DESCRIPTOR *)
END;

RE = ARRAY [TM] OF TV:                (* ARRAY OF VALUES *)
RF = ARRAY [TM] OF RM;                (* ARRAY OF MOVES *)


VAR

   (* DATA BASE *)

   BOARD : RB:                        (* THE BOARD *)
   NBORD : ARRAY [TS] OF TP:          (* LOOK-AHEAD BOARD *)
   ATKFR : ARRAY [TS] OF RS;          (* ATTACKS FROM A SQUARE *)
   ATKTO : ARRAY [TS] OF RS:          (* ATTACKS TO A SQUARE *)
   ALATK : ARRAY [TM] OF RS:          (* ATTACKS BY EACH COLOR *)
   TPLOC : ARRAY [TP] OF RS;          (* LOCATIONS OF PIECE BY TYPE *)
   TMLOC : ARRAY [TM] OF RS:          (* LOCATIONS OF PIECE BY COLOR *)
   MOVES : ARRAY [TM] OF RM:          (* MOVES *)
   VALUE : ARRAY [TM] OF TV;          (* VALUES *)
```

```
ALLOC : ARRAY [TK] OF RS;              (* ALL PIECES *)
BSTMV : ARRAY [TK] OF TM;              (* BEST MOVE SO FAR *)
BSTVL : ARRAY [AKM2..ZKP1] OF TV;      (* VALUE OF BEST MOVE *)
CSTAT : ARRAY [TK] OF RS;              (* CASTLING SQUARES *)
ENPAS : ARRAY [TK] OF RS;              (* ENPASSANT SQUARES *)
GENPM : ARRAY [TK] OF RS;              (* PAWN ORIGINATION SQUARES *)
GENTO : ARRAY [TK] OF RS;              (* MOVE DESTINATION SQUARES *)
GENFR : ARRAY [TK] OF RS;              (* MOVE ORIGINATION SQUARES *)
MBVAL : ARRAY [TK] OF TV;              (* MATERIAL BALANCE VALUES *)
MVSEL : ARRAY [TK] OF TI;              (* COUNT MOVES SELECTED BY PLY *)
INDEX : ARRAY [AK..ZKP1] OF TM;        (* CURRENT MOVE FOR PLY *)
KILLR : ARRAY [TK] OF RM;              (* KILLER MOVES BY PLY *)
LINDX : ARRAY [TK] OF TM;              (* LAST MOVE FOR PLY *)
SRCHM : ARRAY [TK] OF TM;              (* SEARCH MODES *)
GOING : TI;                            (* NUMBER OF MOVES TO EXECUTE *)
LSTMV : RM;                            (* PREVIOUS MOVE *)
MAXPS : TV;                            (* MAXIMUM POSITIONAL SCORE *)
MBLTE : TV;                            (* MATERIAL BALANCE LITE EDGE *)
MBPWN : ARRAY [TM] OF TI;              (* NUMBER OF PAWNS BY SIDE *)
MBTOT : TV;                            (* TOTAL MATERIAL ON NBORD *)
NODES : TI;                            (* NUMBER OF NODES SEARCHED *)

JNTK  : TK;                            (* PLY INDEX *)
JNTK  : TK;                            (* ITERATION *)
JNTM  : TM;                            (* SIDE TO MOVE *)
JNTM  : TM;                            (* MOVES STACK POINTER *)

(* LETS *)

FKPSHD : TI;                           (* KING PAWN SHIELD CREDIT *)
FKSANQ : TI;                           (* KING IN SANCTUARY CREDIT *)
FMAXMT : TI;                           (* MAXIMUM MATERIAL SCORE *)
FMODEL : TI;                           (* MODE LIMIT FOR SEARCH *)
FPADCR : ARRAY [TF] OF TI;             (* PAWN ADVANCE CREDIT BY FILE *)
FPBLOK : TI;                           (* PAWN BLOCKED PENALTY *)
FPCONN : TI;                           (* PAWN CONNECTED CREDIT *)
FPFLNX : TI;                           (* PAWN PHALANX CREDIT *)
FROUBL : TI;                           (* DOUBLED ROOK CREDIT *)
FRK7TH : TI;                           (* ROOK ON SEVENTH CREDIT *)
FTRADE : TI;                           (* TRADE-DOWN BONUS FACTOR *)
FTRDSL : TI;                           (* TRADE-DOWN TUNING FACTOR *)
FTRPOK : TI;                           (* PAWN TRADE-DOWN RELAXATION *)
FTRPWN : TI;                           (* PAWN TRADE-DOWN FACTOR *)
FWKING : TI;                           (* KING EVALUATION WEIGHT *)
FWMAJM : TI;                           (* MAJOR PIECE MOBILITY WEIGHT *)
FWMINM : TI;                           (* MINOR PIECE MOBILITY WEIGHT *)
FWPAWN : TI;                           (* PAWN EVALUATION WEIGHT *)
FWROOK : TI;                           (* ROOK EVALUATION WEIGHT *)
WINDOW : TI;                           (* SIZE OF ALPHA-BETA WINDOW *)


(* SWITCHES *)

SWEC : TB;                             (* ECHO INPUT *)
SWPA : TB;                             (* PAGING *)
SWPS : TB;                             (* PRINT PRELIMINARY SCORES *)
SWRE : TB;                             (* REPLY WITH MOVE *)
SWSU : TB;                             (* PRINT STATISTICS SUMMARY *)
SWTR : TB;                             (* TRACE TREE SEARCH *)

(* COMMAND PROCESSING DATA *)

ICARD : RJ;                            (* INPUT CARD IMAGE *)
ILINE : RJ;                            (* CURRENT COMMAND *)
JNTJ  : TJ;                            (* CURRENT INPUT LINE POSITION *)
JNTJ  : TJ;                            (* CURRENT COMMAND POSITION *)

MOVMS : RN;                            (* MOVE MESSAGE *)

(* TRANSLATION TABLES *)

XSPB : ARRAY [TP] OF TB;               (* TRUE FOR SWEEP PIECES *)
XFPE : ARRAY [TP] OF TE;               (* FIRST DIRECTION *)
XLLD : ARRAY [AZL..ZAL] OF TD;         (* DIRECTION FOR LARGE BOARD
                                          SQUARE DIFFERENCES *)
```

```
XLPE : ARRAY [TP] OF TE;          (* LAST DIRECTION *)
XRFS : ARRAY [TF] OF RS;          (* BIT BOARD FOR FILES *)
XRRS : ARRAY [TR] OF RS;          (* BIT BOARD FOR RANKS *)
XNFS : ARRAY [TF] OF RS;          (* COMP BIT BOARD FOR FILES *)
XNRS : ARRAY [TR] OF RS;          (* COMP BIT BOARD FOR RANKS *)
XRSS : ARRAY [TS] OF RS;          (* BIT BOARD FOR 8X8 INDEX *)
XRQM : ARRAY [TQ] OF RM;          (* MOVES FOR CASTLE TYPES *)
XSQS : ARRAY [TQ] OF RS;          (* BIT BOARD FOR CASTLE TYPES *)
XSSX : ARRAY [TS] OF SX;          (* SET ELEMENT FOR 8X8 INDEX *)
XTBC : ARRAY [TB] OF TC;          (* CHARACTERS FOR BOOLEANS *)
XTED : ARRAY [TE] OF TD;          (* DIRECTION NUMBER TO 10X12
                                     SQUARE DIFFERENCE *)
XTGC : ARRAY [TG] OF TC;          (* CHARACTERS FOR PROMOTION *)
XTGMP: ARRAY [TG,TM] OF TP;       (* PIECE FOR PROMOTION TYPE
                                     AND COLOR *)
XTLS : ARRAY [TL] OF TT;          (* 8X8 INDEX FOR 10X12 INDEX *)
XTMA : ARRAY [TM] OF RA;          (* WORDS FOR COLORS *)
XTMQ : ARRAY [TM] OF TQ;          (* CASTLE TYPES FOR SIDE *)
XTMV : ARRAY [TM] OF TV;          (* SCORE FACTOR FOR SIDE *)
XTPC : ARRAY [TP] OF TC;          (* CHARACTERS FOR PIECES *)
XTPM : ARRAY [TP] OF TM;          (* SIDES FOR PIECES *)
XTPU : ARRAY [TP] OF TU;          (* TYPE FOR PIECE *)
XTPV : ARRAY [TP] OF TV;          (* VALUES OF PIECES *)
XTQA : ARRAY [TQ] OF RA;          (* WORDS FOR CASTLES *)
XTQS : ARRAY [TQ] OF TS;          (* TO SQUARES FOR CASTLE TYPES *)
XTRFS: ARRAY [TR,TF] OF TS;       (* 8X8 INDEX FOR RANK AND FILE *)
XTSF : ARRAY [TS] OF TF;          (* FILES FOR SQUARES *)
XTSL : ARRAY [TS] OF TL;          (* 10X12 INDEX FOR 8X8 INDEX *)
XTSR : ARRAY [TS] OF TR;          (* RANKS FOR SQUARES *)
XTSX : ARRAY [TS] OF TX;          (* ELEMENT NUMBER FOR 8X8
                                     INDEX *)
XTSY : ARRAY [TS] OF TY;          (* ARRAY SUBSCRIPT INTO BIT BOARD
                                     FOR 8X8 INDEX *)
XTUC : ARRAY [TU] OF TC;          (* CHARACTER FOR TYPE *)
XTUMP: ARRAY [TU,TM] OF TP;       (* PIECE FOR TYPE AND SIDE *)

XRQSO: ARRAY [TQ] OF RS;          (* UNOCCUPIED SQUARES FOR
                                     CASTLING *)
XRQSA: ARRAY [TQ] OF RS;          (* UNATTACKED SQUARES FOR
                                     CASTLING *)

EDGE : ARRAY [TE] OF RS;          (* EDGES IN VARIOUS DIRECTIONS *)
CORNR: RS;                        (* KING SANCTUARY *)
NULMV: RM;                        (* NULL MOVE *)
OTHER: ARRAY [TM] OF TM;          (* OTHER COLOR *)
SYNTX: ARRAY[SYNCF..SYNML] OF RY; (* MOVE SYNTAX TABLE *)


FUNCTION MAX(A,B:TI):TI;          (* LARGER OF TWO NUMBERS *)

BEGIN
  IF A > B THEN
    MAX := A
  ELSE
    MAX := B;
END; (* MAX *)


FUNCTION MIN(A,B:TI):TI;          (* SMALLER OF TWO NUMBERS *)

BEGIN
  IF A < B THEN
    MIN := A
  ELSE
    MIN := B;
END; (* MIN *)


FUNCTION SIGN(A,B:TI):TI;         (* SIGN OF B APPLIED TO
                                     ABSOLUTE VALUE OF A *)
```

```
BEGIN
  SIGN := TRUNC(B/ABS(B)) * ABS(A);
END;  (* SIGN *)


PROCEDURE SORTIT                          (* SORT PRELIMINARY SCORES *)
  (VAR A:RE;                              (* ARRAY OF SCORES *)
   VAR B:RF;                              (* ARRAY OF MOVES *)
   C:IW);                                 (* NUMBER OF ENTRIES *)

VAR
  INTB : JB;                              (* LOOP EXIT FLAG *)
  INTW : TW;                              (* OUTER LOOP INDEX *)
  INTI : TI;                              (* INNER LOOP INDEX *)
  INTV : TV;                              (* HOLD SCORE *)
  INRM : RM;                              (* HOLD MOVE *)
BEGIN
  FOR INTW := AW+2 TO C DO
  BEGIN
    INTI := INTW - 1;
    INTV := A[INTW];
    INRM := B[INTW];
    INTB := TRUE;
    WHILE (INTI > AW) AND INTB DO
      IF INTV < A[INTI] THEN
      BEGIN
        A[INTI+1] := A[INTI];
        B[INTI+1] := B[INTI];
        INTI := INTI - 1;
      END
      ELSE

        INTB := FALSE;                    (* EXIT *)
    A[INTI+1] := INTV;
    B[INTI+1] := INRM;
  END;
END;  (* SORTIT *)


PROCEDURE ANORS                           (* INTERSECTION OF TWO BIT
                                             BOARDS *)
  (VAR C:RS;                              (* RESULT *)
   A, B:RS);                              (* OPERANDS *)

VAR
  INTY : TY;                              (* BIT BOARD WORD INDEX *)

BEGIN
  FOR INTY := AY TO ZY DO
    C.RSSS[INTY] := A.RSSS[INTY] * B.RSSS[INTY];
END;  (* ANORS *)

PROCEDURE CLRRS                           (* REMOVE SQUARE FROM BIT
                                             BOARD *)
  (VAR C:RS;                              (* BIT BOARD *)
   A:TS);                                 (* SQUARE TO REMOVE *)

BEGIN
  C.RSSS[XTSY[A]] := C.RSSS[XTSY[A]] - XSSX[A];
END;  (* CLRRS *)


PROCEDURE CPYRS                           (* COPY OF A BIT BOARD *)
  (VAR C:RS;                              (* RESULT *)
   A:RS);                                 (* OPERAND *)

VAR
  INTY : TY;                              (* BIT BOARD WORD INDEX *)
```

```
BEGIN
  FOR INTY := AY TO ZY DO
    C.RSSS[INTY] := A.RSSS[INTY];
END;  (* CPYRS *)


PROCEDURE IORRS                          (* UNION OF TWO BIT BOARDS *)
  (VAR C:RS;                             (* RESULT *)
   A, B:RS);                             (* OPERANDS *)

VAR
  INTY : TY;                             (* BIT BOARD WORD INDEX *)

BEGIN
  FOR INTY := AY TO ZY DO
    C.RSSS[INTY] := A.RSSS[INTY] + B.RSSS[INTY];
END;  (* IORRS *)


PROCEDURE NEWRS                          (* CLEAR BIT BOARD *)
  (VAR A:RS);                            (* BIT BOARD TO CLEAR *)

VAR
  INTY : TY;                             (* BIT BOARD WORD INDEX *)

BEGIN
  FOR INTY := AY TO ZY DO
    A.RSSS[INTY] := [];
END;  (* NEWRS *)


PROCEDURE NOTRS                          (* COMPLEMENT OF A BIT BOARD *)
  (VAR C:RS;                             (* RESULT *)
   A:RS);                                (* OPERAND *)

VAR
  INTY : TY;                             (* BIT BOARD WORD INDEX *)

BEGIN
  FOR INTY := AY TO ZY DO
    C.RSSS[INTY] := [AX..ZX]-A.RSSS[INTY];
END;  (* NOTRS *)


FUNCTION NXTTS                           (* NEXT ELEMENT IN BIT BOARD *)
  (VAR A:RS;                             (* BIT BOARD TO LOCATE FIRST
                                            SQUARE, AND THEN REMOVE *)
   VAR B:TS                              (* SQUARE NUMBER OF FIRST SQUARE
                                            IN BIT BOARD *)
  ):TB;                                  (* TRUE IFF ANY SQUARES WERE SET
                                            INITIALLY *)

LABEL
  11;                                    (* RETURN *)

VAR
  INTX : TX;                             (* BIT BOARD BIT INDEX *)
  INTY : TY;                             (* BIT BOARD WORD INDEX *)
  X : RK;                                (* KLUDGE WORD *)

BEGIN
  FOR INTY := ZY DOWNTO AY DO            (* LOOP THRU BIT BOARD WORDS *)
    IF A.RST[INTY] <> 0 THEN
      BEGIN

(*** BEGIN CDC 6000 DEPENDANT CODE *)
(*** FOLLOWING CODE REQUIRES THE 'EXPO' FUNCTION TO RETURN
(*** THE EXPONENT FROM A FLOATING POINT NUMBER.  IT ALSO ASSUMES
(*** THAT FLOATING POINT NUMBERS HAVE 48 BIT COEFFICIENTS RIGHT-
(*** JUSTIFIED IN A WORD, AND THAT SETS ARE RIGHT-JUSTIFIED IN
(*** A WORD. *)
```

```
(*      X.RKTZ := A.RSTI[INTY];          (* FLOAT WORD *)
(*      B := EXPO(X.RKTZ) + INTY * (ZX+1);
(*                                        (* CONVERT TO SQUARE NUMBER *)
(*      X.RKTB := X.RKTB - (47);         (* REMOVE MOST SIGNIFICANT BIT *)
(*      A.RSTI[INTY] := TRUNC(X.RKTZ);   (* INTEGERIZE *)
(*      NXTTS := TRUE;                   (* RETURN A BIT SET *)
(*      GOTO 11;                         (* RETURN *)
(*** END CDC 6000 DEPENDANT CODE *)

(*** BEGIN MACHINE INDEPENDENT CODE *)
    FOR INTX := ZX DOWNTO AX DO          (* LOOP THROUGH BITS IN WORD OF
                                            SET *)

      IF INTX IN A.RSSS[INTY] THEN
      BEGIN
        B := INTX+INTY*(ZX+1);           (* RETURN SQUARE NUMBER *)
        A.RSSS[INTY] := A.RSSS[INTY] - [INTX];
                                         (* REMOVE BIT FROM WORD *)
        NXTTS := TRUE;                   (* RETURN A BIT SET *)
        GOTO 11;                         (* RETURN *)
      END;
(*** END MACHINE INDEPENDENT CODE *)


    END;
  NXTTS := FALSE;                        (* ELSE RETURN NO BITS SET *)
11: (* RETURN *)
END; (* NXTTS *)



FUNCTION CNTRS                           (* COUNT MEMBERS OF A BIT
                                            BOARD *)
  (A:RS):TS;                             (* BIT BOARD TO COUNT *)

VAR
  INTY : TY;                             (* BIT BOARD WORD INDEX *)
  INTS : TS;                             (* TEMPORARY *)
  IMRS : RS;                             (* SCRATCH *)
  INTS : TS;                             (* SCRATCH *)

BEGIN
  INTS := 0;

(*** BEGIN MACHINE INDEPENDENT CODE *)
  CPYRS(IMRS,A);
  WHILE NXTTS(IMRS,INTS) DO
    INTS := INTS+1;                      (* COUNT SQUARES *)
(*** END MACHINE INDEPENDENT CODE *)

(*** BEGIN CDC 6600 DEPENDENT CODE *)
(*** FOLLOWING CODE REQUIRES THE 'CARD' FUNCTION TO
(*** COUNT THE MEMBERS IN A SET. *)
(*FOR INTY := AY TO ZY DO
(*  INTS := INTS + CARD(A.RSSS[INTY]);
(*** END CDC DEPENDENT CODE *)

  CNTRS := INTS;                         (* RETURN SUM *)
END; (* CNTRS *)



PROCEDURE SETRS                          (* INSERT SQUARE INTO BIT
                                            BOARD *)
  (VAR C:RS;                             (* BIT BOARD *)
   A:TS);                                (* SQUARE TO INSERT *)

BEGIN
  C.RSSS[XTSY[A]] := C.RSSS[XTSY[A]] + XSSX[A];
END; (* SETRS *)



PROCEDURE SFTRS                          (* SHIFT BIT BOARD *)
  (VAR A:RS;                             (* RESULT *)
   B:RS;                                 (* SOURCE *)
   C:TE);                                (* DIRECTION *)
```

```
VAR
   INRS : RS;                          (* SCRATCH *)
   INTS : TS:                          (* SCRATCH *)
   INTY : TY;                          (* BIT BOARD WORD INDEX *)

BEGIN

(*** BEGIN MACHINE INDEPENDENT CODE *)
   NEWRS(A):                           (* CLEAR NEW BIT BOARD *)
   WHILE NXTTS(B,INTS) DO
      IF XTLS[XTSL[INTS]+XTED[C]] > 0 THEN
                                       (* SHIFT EACH BIT *)
         SETRS(A,XTLS[XTSL[INTS]+XTED[C]]);
(*** END MACHINE INDEPENDENT CODE *)
(*** BEGIN CDC 6000 DEPENDENT CODE *)
(*** FOLLOWING CODE ASSUMES THAT MULTIPLICATION OR DIVISION
(*** BY A CONSTANT POWER OF 2 IS DONE WITH A SHIFT INSTRUCTION. *)
(*CASE C OF
(*S1:  BEGIN
(*        FOR INTY := AY TO ZY DO          (* SHIFT ONE PLACE *)
(*        BEGIN
(*           B.RSSS[INTY] := B.RSSS[INTY] - EDGE[S1].RSSS[INTY];
(*           A.RSTI[INTY] := B.RSTI[INTY] DIV 2;
(*        END;
(*     END:
(*S2:  BEGIN
(*        FOR INTY := AY TO ZY DO          (* SHIFT WORDS *)
(*        BEGIN
(*           B.RSSS[INTY] := B.RSSS[INTY] - EDGE[S2].RSSS[INTY];
(*           INRS.RSSS[INTY] := B.RSSS[INTY] * [ZX-7..ZX];
(*           A.RSSS[INTY] := B.RSSS[INTY] - [ZX-7..ZX];
(*           A.RSTI[INTY] := A.RSTI[INTY] * 256;
(*        END:
(*        FOR INTY := AY+1 TO ZY DO        (* CARRY BETWEEN WORDS *)
(*           A.RSTI[INTY] := A.RSTI[INTY] + INRS.RSTI[INTY-1] DIV PZX8;
(*     END:
(*S3:  BEGIN
(*        FOR INTY := AY TO ZY DO          (* SHIFT ONE PLACE *)
(*        BEGIN
(*           A.RSSS[INTY] := B.RSSS[INTY] - EDGE[S3].RSSS[INTY];
(*           A.RSTI[INTY] := A.RSTI[INTY] * 2;
(*        END:
(*     END:
(*S4:  BEGIN
(*        FOR INTY := AY TO ZY DO          (* SHIFT WORDS *)
(*        BEGIN
(*           B.RSSS[INTY] := B.RSSS[INTY] - EDGE[S4].RSSS[INTY];
(*           INRS.RSSS[INTY] := B.RSSS[INTY] * [AX..AX+7];
(*           A.RSTI[INTY] := B.RSTI[INTY] DIV 256:
(*        END:
(*        FOR INTY := AY TO ZY-1 DO        (* CARRY BETWEEN WORDS *)
(*           A.RSTI[INTY] := A.RSTI[INTY] + INRS.RSTI[INTY+1] * PZX8;
(*     END:
(*B1:  BEGIN
(*        SFTRS(INRS,B,S1):
(*        SFTRS(A,INRS,S2):
(*     END;
(*B2:  BEGIN
(*        SFTRS(INRS,B,S2):
(*        SFTRS(A,INRS,S3):
(*     END:
(*B3:  BEGIN
(*        SFTRS(INRS,B,S3):
(*        SFTRS(A,INRS,S4):
(*     END:
(*B4:  BEGIN
(*        SFTRS(INRS,B,S4):
(*        SFTRS(A,INRS,S1):
(*     END:
(*N1:  BEGIN
(*        SFTRS(INRS,B,B1):
(*        SFTRS(A,INRS,S2):
(*     END:
(*N2:  BEGIN
(*        SFTRS(INRS,B,B2):
```

```
(*        SFTRS(A,INRS,S2);
(*      END;
(*N3:   BEGIN
(*        SFTRS(INRS,B,B2);
(*        SFTRS(A,INRS,S3);
(*      END;
(*N4:   BEGIN
(*        SFTRS(INRS,B,B3);
(*        SFTRS(A,INRS,S3);
(*      END;
(*N5:   BEGIN
(*        SFTRS(INRS,B,B3);
(*        SFTRS(A,INRS,S4);
(*      END;
(*N6:   BEGIN
(*        SFTRS(INRS,B,B4);
(*        SFTRS(A,INRS,S4);
(*      END:
(*N7:   BEGIN
(*        SFTRS(INRS,B,B4);
(*        SFTRS(A,INRS,S1);
(*      END;
(*N8:   BEGIN
(*        SFTRS(INRS,B,B1);
(*        SFTRS(A,INRS,S1);
(*      END;
(*END;
(*** END CDC 6000 DEPENDENT CODE *)

END;  (* SFTRS *)



FUNCTION INRSTB                        (* SQUARE IN BIT BOARD BOOLEAN *)
  (A:RS;                               (* BIT BOARD *)
   B:TS):TB;                           (* SQUARE IN QUESTION *)

BEGIN
  INRSTB := XSSX[B] <= A.RSSS[XTSY[B]];
END;  (* INRSTB *)



FUNCTION NULRS                         (* NULL BIT BOARD *)
  (A:RS)                               (* BIT BOARD TO CHECK *)
   :TB;                                (* TRUE IF BIT BOARD EMPTY *)

VAR
  INTY : TY;                           (* BIT BOARD WORD INDEX *)
  INTB : TB;                           (* TEMPORARY VALUE *)

BEGIN
  INTB := TRUE;
  FOR INTY := AY TO ZY DO
    INTB := INTB AND (A.RSTI[INTY] = 0);
  NULRS := INTB;
END;  (* NULRS *)



FUNCTION NULMVB                        (* NULL MOVE BOOLEAN *)
  (A:RM)                               (* MOVE TO TEST *)
   :TB;                                (* TRUE IF NULL MOVE *)
BEGIN
  WITH A DO
    NULMVB := RMAC AND RMPR AND (NOT RMCA);
END;  (* NULMVB *)



PROCEDURE INICON;                      (* INITIALIZE GLOBAL CONSTANTS *)

VAR
  INTD : TD;                           (* DIRECTION INDEX *)
  INTE : TE;                           (* DIRECTION *)
```

```
INTF : TF;                          (* FILE INDEX *)
INTI : TI;                          (* SCRATCH *)
INTL : TL;                          (* LARGE BOARD INDEX *)
INTQ : TQ;                          (* CASTLE TYPE INDEX *)
INTR : TR;                          (* RANK INDEX *)
INTT : TT;                          (* SQUARE INDEX *)
INTX : TX;                          (* SET ELEMENT INDEX *)
INTY : TY;                          (* BIT BOARD WORD INDEX *)
INTI : TI;                          (* SCRATCH *)
INRS : RS;                          (* SCRATCH *)

PROCEDURE INISYN                    (* INITIALIZE MOVE SYNTAX
                                       TABLE ENTRY *)
  (A:RA);                           (* MOVE SYNTAX *)

BEGIN
  WITH SYNTX[INTI] DO
  BEGIN
    WITH RYLS DO
    BEGIN
      ROPC := TRUE;
      ROSL := A(AA+0) <> " ";
      ROKQ := A(AA+1) <> " ";
      RONB := A(AA+2) <> " ";
      RORK := A(AA+3) <> " ";
    END;
    RYCH := A(AA+4);
    WITH RYRS DO
    BEGIN
      ROPC := A(AA+5) <> " ";
      ROSL := A(AA+6) <> " ";
      ROKQ := A(AA+7) <> " ";
      RONB := A(AA+8) <> " ";
      RORK := A(AA+9) <> " ";
    END;
  END;
  INTI := INTI+1;
END;  (* INISYN *)


PROCEDURE INIXTP                    (* INITIALIZE PIECE TRANSLATION
                                       TABLES *)
  (A : TP;                          (* PIECE TO BE TRANSLATED *)
   B : TC;                          (* DISPLAY EQUIVALENT *)
   C : TM;                          (* COLOR OF PIECE *)
   D : TU;                          (* TYPE OF PIECE *)
   E : TB;                          (* TRUE IF SWEEP PIECE *)
   F : TE;                          (* FIRST DIRECTION OF MOVEMENT *)
   G : TE;                          (* LAST DIRECTION OF MOVEMENT *)
   H : TV);                         (* VALUE OF PIECE *)

BEGIN
  XTPC[A] := B;
  XTPM[A] := C;
  XSPB[A] := E;
  XFPE[A] := F;
  XLPE[A] := G;
  XTPU[A] := D;
  XTPV[A] := H;
  IF A <> NT THEN
    XTUMP[D,C] := A;
END;  (* INIXTP *)


BEGIN  (* INICON *)

  (** INITIALIZE PIECE CHARACTERISTICS *)

  INIXTP(LP,"A",LITE,EP,FALSE,B1,B2,1*64);
  INIXTP(LR,"B",LITE,ER,TRUE ,S1,S4,5*64);
  INIXTP(LN,"C",LITE,EN,FALSE,N1,N8,3*64);
  INIXTP(LB,"D",LITE,EB,TRUE ,B1,B4,3*64);
  INIXTP(LQ,"E",LITE,EQ,TRUE ,B1,S4,9*64);
  INIXTP(LK,"F",LITE,EK,FALSE,B1,S4,8);
```

```
INIXTP(DP,"1",DARK,EP,FALSE,B3,B4,-1*64);
INIXTP(DR,"2",DARK,ER,TRUE ,S1,S4,-5*64);
INIXTP(DN,"3",DARK,EN,FALSE,N1,N6,-3*64);
INIXTP(DB,"4",DARK,EB,TRUE ,B1,B4,-3*64);
INIXTP(DQ,"5",DARK,EQ,TRUE ,B1,S4,-9*64);
INIXTP(DK,"6",DARK,EK,FALSE,B1,S4,0);
INIXTP(MT,"-",NONE,EP,FALSE,B2,B1,0);

XTGMP(PQ,LITE) := LQ;   XTGMP(PQ,DARK) := DQ;   XTGC(PQ) := "Q";
XTGMP(PR,LITE) := LR;   XTGMP(PR,DARK) := DR;   XTGC(PR) := "R";
XTGMP(PN,LITE) := LN;   XTGMP(PN,DARK) := DN;   XTGC(PN) := "N";
XTGMP(PB,LITE) := LB;   XTGMP(PB,DARK) := DB;   XTGC(PB) := "B";

XTUC(EK) := "K";
XTUC(EQ) := "Q";
XTUC(ER) := "R";
XTUC(EN) := "N";
XTUC(EB) := "B";
XTUC(EP) := "P";

(** INITIALIZE OTHER CONSTANTS *)

XTBC(FALSE) := "-";
XTBC(TRUE ) := "*";

OTHER(LITE) := DARK;   XTMV(LITE) :=  1;
OTHER(DARK) := LITE;   XTMV(DARK) := -1;
OTHER(NONE) := NONE;

XTMA(LITE) := "   WHITE ";
XTMA(DARK) := "   BLACK ";
XTMA(NONE) := "   NO ONE ";

XTQA(LS) := "WHITE KING";
XTQA(LL) := "WHITE LONG";
XTQA(DS) := "BLACK KING";
XTQA(DL) := "BLACK LONG";

(** INITIALIZE 18X12 TO 8X8 AND 8X8 TO 18X12 TRANSLATION TABLES *)

FOR INTL := AL TO ZL DO            (* LOOP THROUGH LARGE BOARD *)
  XTLS(INTL) := -1;               (* PRESET ARRAY TO OFF BOARD *)

INTL := 21;                       (* INDEX OF FIRST SQUARE ON LARGE
                                     BOARD *)
INTT := -1;                       (* INDEX OF FIRST SQUARE ON SMALL
                                     BOARD *)
FOR INTR := R1 TO R8 DO            (* LOOP THROUGH RANKS *)
BEGIN
  FOR INTF := F1 TO F8 DO          (* LOOP THROUGH FILES *)
  BEGIN
    INTT := INTT+1;               (* ADVANCE SMALL BOARD INDEX *)
    XTRFS(INTR,INTF) := INTT;      (* SET MATRIX TO VECTOR
                                     TRANSLATION *)
    XTLS(INTL) := INTT;           (* SET LARGE BOARD TRANSLATION
                                     TABLE WITH SMALL BOARD
                                     INDEX *)
    XTSL(INTT) := INTL;           (* SET SMALL BOARD TRANSLATION
                                     TABLE WITH LARGE BOARD
                                     INDEX *)
    XTSR(INTT) := INTR;           (* SET RANK OF SQUARE *)
    XTSF(INTT) := INTF;           (* SET FILE OF SQUARE *)
    INTL := INTL+1;               (* ADVANCE LARGE BOARD INDEX *)
  END;
  INTL := INTL+2;                 (* ADVANCE LARGE BOARD INDEX TO
                                     SKIP BORDER *)
END;

(** INITIALIZE 8X8 TO BIT BOARD TABLES *)

INTT := -1;
FOR INTY := AY TO ZY DO
BEGIN
  FOR INTX := AX TO ZX DO
```

```
    BEGIN
      INTT := INTT+1;
      XTSX[INTT] := INTX;
      XTSY[INTT] := INTY;
      XSSX[INTT] := [INTX];
      NEWRS(XRSS[INTT]);
      XRSS[INTT].RSSS[INTY] := [INTX];
    ENO;
ENO;

(** INITIALIZE CONSTANT BIT BOARDS *)

FOR INTR := R1 TO R8 OO
  NEWRS(XRRS[INTR]);

FOR INTF := F1 TO F8 OO
  NEWRS(XRFS[INTF]);

FOR INTR := R1 TO R8 OO
  FOR INTF := F1 TO F8 OO
  BEGIN
    SETRS(XRRS[INTR],XTRFS[INTR,INTF]);
    SETRS(XRFS[INTF],XTRFS[INTR,INTF]);
  ENO;

FOR INTF := F1 TO F8 OO
  NOTRS(XNFS[INTF],XRFS[INTF]);

FOR INTR := R1 TO R8 OO
  NOTRS(XNRS[INTR],XRRS[INTR]);

(** INITIALIZE EDGES *)

CPYRS(EDGE[S1],XRFS[F1]);
CPYRS(EDGE[S2],XRRS[R8]);
CPYRS(EDGE[S3],XRFS[F8]);
CPYRS(EDGE[S4],XRRS[R1]);
IORRS(EDGE[B1],EDGE[S1],EDGE[S2]);
IORRS(EDGE[B2],EDGE[S2],EDGE[S3]);
IORRS(EDGE[B3],EDGE[S3],EDGE[S4]);
IORRS(EDGE[B4],EDGE[S4],EDGE[S1]);
IORRS(EDGE[N1],EDGE[B1],XRRS[R7]);
IORRS(EDGE[N2],EDGE[B2],XRRS[R7]);
IORRS(EDGE[N3],EDGE[B2],XRFS[F7]);
IORRS(EDGE[N4],EDGE[B3],XRFS[F7]);
IORRS(EDGE[N5],EDGE[B3],XRRS[R2]);
IORRS(EDGE[N6],EDGE[B4],XRRS[R2]);
IORRS(EDGE[N7],EDGE[B4],XRFS[F2]);
IORRS(EDGE[N8],EDGE[B1],XRFS[F2]);

(** INITIALIZE CORNER MASK *)

IORRS(INRS,XRRS[R1],XRRS[R2]);
IORRS(INRS,INRS,XRRS[R7]);
IORRS(INRS,INRS,XRRS[R8]);
IORRS(CORNR,XRFS[F1],XRFS[F2]);
IORRS(CORNR,CORNR,XRFS[F7]);
IORRS(CORNR,CORNR,XRFS[F8]);
ANORS(CORNR,CORNR,INRS);

(** INITIALIZE DIRECTION TABLE *)

              XTED[N1]:= 19;                    XTED[N2]:= 21;
XTED[N8]:=  8;XTED[B1]:=  9;XTED[S2]:= 10;XTED[B2]:= 11;XTED[N3]:= 12;
              XTED[S1]:= -1;                    XTED[S3]:=  1;
XTED[N7]:=-12;XTED[B4]:=-11;XTED[S4]:=-10;XTED[B3]:= -9;XTED[N4]:= -8;
              XTED[N6]:=-21;                    XTED[N5]:=-19;

(** INITIALIZE SQUARE DIFFERENCE TO DIRECTION TABLE *)

FOR INTI := AZL TO ZAL OO
  XLLD[INTI] := 0;
FOR INTE := B1 TO S4 OO
BEGIN
  INTD := XTED[INTE];
```

```
    FOR IMTI I= 1 TO 7 DO
      XLLD(IMTI*INTO) I= INTO;
  ENO;
  FOR INTE I= N1 TO N8 DO
    XLLD(XTEO(INTE)) I= XTEO(INTE);

  (** INITIALIZE CASTLING TRANSLATION TABLES *)

  IORRS(XSQS(LS),XRSS(XTRFS(R1,F8)),XRSS(XTRFS,R1,F5)));
  IORRS(XSQS(LL),XRSS(XTRFS(R1,F1)),XRSS(XTRFS(R1,F5)));
  IORRS(XSQS(OS),XRSS(XTRFS(R8,F8)),XRSS(XTRFS(R8,F5)));
  IORRS(XSQS(OL),XRSS(XTRFS(R8,F1)),XRSS(XTRFS(R8,F5)));

  IORRS(XRQSO(LS),XRSS(XTRFS(R1,F6)),XRSS(XTRFS(R1,F7)));
  IORRS(XRQSO(LL),XRSS(XTRFS(R1,F4)),XRSS(XTRFS(R1,F3)));
  IORRS(XRQSA(LS),XRSS(XTRFS(R1,F5)),XRQSO(LS)));
  IORRS(XRQSA(LL),XRSS(XTRFS(R1,F5)),XRQSO(LL)));
  IORRS(XRQSO(LL),XRSS(XTRFS(R1,F2)),XRQSO(LL)));

  IORRS(XRQSO(OS),XRSS(XTRFS(R8,F6)),XRSS(XTRFS(R8,F7)));
  IORRS(XRQSO(OL),XRSS(XTRFS(R8,F4)),XRSS(XTRFS(R8,F3)));

  IORRS(XRQSA(OS),XRSS(XTRFS(R8,F5)),XRQSO(OS)));
  IORRS(XRQSA(OL),XRSS(XTRFS(R8,F5)),XRQSO(OL)));
  IORRS(XRQSO(OL),XRSS(XTRFS(R8,F2)),XRQSO(OL)));

  FOR INTQ I= LS TO OL DO
    WITH XRQM(INTQ) DO
    BEGIN
      RMCP I= MT;
      RMCA I= FALSE;
      RMAC I= TRUE;
      RMCH I= FALSE;
      RMMT I= FALSE;
      RMIL I= FALSE;
      RMSU I= FALSE;
      RMPR I= FALSE;
      RMOO I= TRUE;
    ENO;

  XRQM(LS).RMFR I= XTRFS(R1,F5); XRQM(LS).RMTO I= XTRFS(R1,F7);
  XRQM(LL).RMFR I= XTRFS(R1,F5); XRQM(LL).RMTO I= XTRFS(R1,F3);
  XRQM(OS).RMFR I= XTRFS(R8,F5); XRQM(OS).RMTO I= XTRFS(R8,F7);
  XRQM(OL).RMFR I= XTRFS(R8,F5); XRQM(OL).RMTO I= XTRFS(R8,F3);

  XRQM(LS).RMQS I= FALSE;
  XRQM(LL).RMQS I= TRUE;
  XRQM(OS).RMQS I= FALSE;
  XRQM(OL).RMQS I= TRUE;

  XTMQ(LITE) I= LS;
  XTMQ(DARK) I= OS;

  XTQS(LS) I= XTRFS(R1,F8);
  XTQS(LL) I= XTRFS(R1,F1);
  XTQS(OS) I= XTRFS(R8,F8);
  XTQS(OL) I= XTRFS(R8,F1);

  (** INITIALIZE NULL MOVE *)

  WITH NULMV DO
  BEGIN
    RMFR I= AS;
    RMTO I= AS;
    RMCP I= MT;
    RMCA I= FALSE;
    RMAC I= TRUE;
    RMCH I= FALSE;
    RMMT I= FALSE;
    RMIL I= FALSE;
    RMSU I= FALSE;
    RMPR I= TRUE;
    RMPP I= PB;
  ENO;
```

```
(** INITIALIZE COMMAND PROCESSING VARIABLES *)

JMTJ := ZJ;
ICARD(ZJ) := ";";
ILINE(ZJ) := ";";

(** INITIALIZE MOVES SYNTAX TABLE *)

INTI := SYNCF;
INISYN("     *P        ");
INISYN("     *P/   1");
INISYN("/   1*P        ");
INISYN("     *P/  R ");
INISYN("/ R *P        ");
INISYN("     *P/ R1");
INISYN("/ R1*P        ");
INISYN("     *P/KR ");
INISYN("/KR *P        ");
INISYN("     *P/KR1");
INISYN("/KR1*P        ");
INISYN("/   1*P/  1");
INISYN("/ R *P/ R ");
INISYN("/   1*P/ R ");
INISYN("/ R *P/  1");
INISYN("/ R1*P/  1");
INISYN("/   1*P/ R1");
INISYN("/ R1*P/ R ");
INISYN("/ R *P/ R1");
INISYN("/KR *P/  1");
INISYN("/   1*P/KR ");
INISYN("/KR *P/ R ");
INISYN("/ R *P/KR ");
INISYN("/   1*P/KR1");
INISYN("/KR1*P/  1");
INISYN("  R *P/KR1");
INISYN("/KR1*P/ R ");
INISYN("/ R1*P/ R1");
INISYN("/KR *P/ R1");
INISYN("/ R1*P/KR ");
INISYN("/KR *P/KR ");
INISYN("/KR1*P/ R1");
INISYN("/ R1*P/KR1");
INISYN("/KR1*P/KR ");
INISYN("/KR *P/KR1");
INISYN("/KR1*P/KR1");

INISYN("     -     R1");
INISYN("     -    KR1");
INISYN("/   1-     R1");
INISYN("/ R -     R1");
INISYN("/   1-    KR1");
INISYN("/ R -    KR1");
INISYN("/ R1-     R1");
INISYN("/KR -     R1");
INISYN("/ R1-    KR1");
INISYN("/KR -    KR1");
INISYN("/KR1-    KR1");

(** INITIALIZE LETS *)

FKPSMO := 10;
FKSAMQ := 150;
FMAXMT := 256;
FMODEL := 10;
FPAOCR(F1) := 0;
FPAOCR(F2) := 0;
FPAOCR(F3) := 5;
FPAOCR(F4) := 10;
FPAOCR(F5) := 15;
FPAOCR(F6) := 5;
FPAOCR(F7) := 0;
FPAOCR(F8) := 0;
FPBLOK := 20;
FPCOMM := 5;
```

```
FPFLNX := 12:
FRDUBL := 60:
FRK7TM := 120:
FTRADE := 36:
FTROSL := 5156:
FTRPOK := 2:
FTRPWN := 8:
FWKING := 50:
FWMAJM := 1:
FWMINM := 200:
FWPAWM := 108:
FWROOK := 2:
WINDOW := 30:

(** INITIALIZE SWITCHES *)

SWEC := TRUE:
SWPA := TRUE:
SWPS := FALSE:
SWRE := TRUE:
SWSU := FALSE:
SWTR := FALSE:

(** INITIALIZE MAIN LOOP CONTROL VARIABLES *)

GOING := 0;

END;  (* INICON *)


PROCEDURE INITAL(VAR A:RB):          (* INITIALIZE FOR A NEW GAME *)

VAR
  INTF : TF;                         (* FILE INDEX *)
  INTR : TR;                         (* RANK INDEX *)

BEGIN
  WITH A DO
  BEGIN
    RBTM := LITE;                    (* SIDE TO MOVE *)
    RBTS := -1;                      (* NO ENPASSANT SQUARE *)
    RBTI := 0;                       (* GAME HAS NOT STARTED *)
    RBSQ := (LS,LL,DS,DL);           (* ALL CASTLING MOVES LEGAL *)
    FOR INTF := F1 TO F8 DO          (* LOOP THROUGH ALL FILES *)
    BEGIN
      RBIRF[R2,INTF] := LP;          (* SET LIGHT PAWNS ON BOARD *)
      FOR INTR := R3 TO R6 DO        (* LOOP THRU MIDDLE OF BOARD *)
        RBIRF[INTR,INTF] := MT;      (* SET MIDDLE OF BOARD EMPTY *)
      RBIRF[R7,INTF] := DP;          (* SET DARK PAWNS ON BOARD *)
    END;
    RBIRF[R1,F1] := LR;              (* SET REMAINDER OF PIECES ON
                                        BOARD *)

    RBIRF[R1,F2] := LN;
    RBIRF[R1,F3] := LB;
    RBIRF[R1,F4] := LQ;
    RBIRF[R1,F5] := LK;
    RBIRF[R1,F6] := LB;
    RBIRF[R1,F7] := LN;
    RBIRF[R1,F8] := LR;
    RBIRF[R8,F1] := DR;
    RBIRF[R8,F2] := DN;
    RBIRF[R8,F3] := DB;
    RBIRF[R8,F4] := DQ;
    RBIRF[R8,F5] := DK;
    RBIRF[R8,F6] := DB;
    RBIRF[R8,F7] := DN;
    RBIRF[R8,F8] := DR;

    MOVMS := " ENTER MOVE OR TYPE GO.        ";
    WRITELN(MOVMS);
    LSTMV := NULMV;                  (* INITIALIZE PREVIOUS MOVE *)
  END;
END;  (* INITAL *)
```

```
PROCEDURE PAUSER;                           (* PAUSE FOR CARRIAGE RETURN *)

BEGIN
  IF SWPA THEN
  BEGIN
    WRITELN(" PAUSING ");
    READLN;
  END;
END;  (* PAUSER *)



PROCEDURE PRIMOV(A:FM);                      (* PRINT A MOVE *)

BEGIN
  WITH A DO
  BEGIN
    WRITE(" FROM ",FMFR:2," TO ",RMTO:2);
    IF NULMVB(A) THEN
      WRITE(", NULL MOVE")
    ELSE
    BEGIN
      IF RMCA THEN
        WRITE(", CAPTURE ",XFPC(RMCP),",")
      ELSE
        WRITE(", SIMPLE,");
      IF NOT RMAC THEN
        WRITE(" NO");
      WRITE(" ACS");
      IF RMCH THEN
        WRITE(", CHECK");
      IF RMMT THEN
        WRITE(", MATE");
      IF RMIL THEN
        WRITE(", ILLEGAL");
      IF RMSU THEN
        WRITE(", SEARCHED");
      CASE RMPR OF
      FALSE:  (* NOT PROMOTION *)
        CASE RMOO OF
        FALSE:  (* NOT CASTLE *)
          IF RMEP THEN
            WRITE(", ENPASSANT");
        TRUE:  (* CASTLE *)
          BEGIN
            WRITE(", CASTLE ");
            IF RMQS THEN
              WRITE("LONG")
            ELSE
              WRITE("SHORT");
          END;
        END;
      TRUE:   (* PROMOTION *)
        BEGIN
          WRITE(", PROMOTE TO ");
          CASE RMPP OF
          PQ:  WRITE("QUEEN");
          PR:  WRITE("ROOK");
          PB:  WRITE("BISHOP");
          PN:  WRITE("KNIGHT");
          END;
        END;
      END;
    END;
  END;
  WRITELN(".");
END;  (* PRIMOV *)



PROCEDURE PRINTB(A:RC);                      (* PRINT A BOARD *)

VAR
  INTR : TR;                                 (* RANK INDEX *)
  INTF : TF;                                 (* FILE INDEX *)
```

```
BEGIN
  WRITELN;                            (* WRITE A BLANK LINE *)
  FOR INTR := R8 DOWNTO R1 DO         (* LOOP DOWN THROUGH RANKS *)
  BEGIN
    WRITE (" ",ORD(INTR)+1:1," ");    (* OUTPUT RANK LABEL *)
    FOR INTF := F1 TO F8 DO           (* LOOP ACROSS THROUGH FILES *)
      WRITE (XTPC[A[XTRFS[INTR,INTF]]]);
                                      (* OUTPUT CONTENTS OF SQUARE *)
    WRITELN;                          (* WRITE OUT A RANK *)
  END;
  WRITELN ("  W RNBQKBNR");           (* WRITE OUT BOTTOM LABEL *)
END;  (* PRINTB *)



PROCEDURE PRINBB(A:FS);               (* PRINT A BIT BOARD *)

VAR
  INTR : TR;                          (* RANK INDEX *)
  INTF : TF;                          (* FILE INDEX *)

BEGIN
  WRITELN;                            (* WRITE OUT A BLANK LINE *)
  FOR INTR := R8 DOWNTO R1 DO         (* LOOP DOWN THROUGH RANKS *)
  BEGIN
    WRITE (" ",ORD(INTR)+1:1," ");    (* OUTPUT RANK LABEL *)
    FOR INTF := F1 TO F8 DO           (* LOOP ACROSS THROUGH FILES *)
      WRITE (XTBC[INRSTB(A,XTRFS[INTR,INTF])]);
                                      (* OUTPUT CONTENTS OF SQUARE *)
    WRITELN;                          (* WRITE OUT A RANK *)
  END;
  WRITELN ("  W RNBQKBNR");           (* WRITE OUT BOTTOM LABEL *)
END;  (* PRINBB *)



PROCEDURE PRINAM(A:FX);               (* PRINT ATTACK MAP *)

VAR
  INTR, JNTR : TR;                    (* RANK INDICES *)
  INTF, JNTF : TF;                    (* FILE INDICES *)

BEGIN
  WRITELN;
  FOR INTR := R8 DOWNTO R1 DO
  BEGIN
    ,FOR JNTR := R8 DOWNTO R1 DO
    BEGIN
      FOR INTF := F1 TO F8 DO
      BEGIN
        WRITE(" ");
        FOR JNTF := F1 TO F8 DO
        BEGIN
          WRITE(XTBC[INRSTB(A[XTRFS[INTR,INTF]],XTRFS[JNTR,JNTF])]);
        END;
        WRITE(" ");
      END;
      WRITELN;
    END;
    WRITELN;
    IF INTR IN [R1,R3,R5,R7] THEN PAUSER;
  END;
END;  (* PRINAM *)



PROCEDURE PRISWI(A:FA;B:TB);          (* PRINT A SWITCH *)

BEGIN
  WRITE(" ",A[AA],A[AA+1]);
  IF B THEN
    WRITELN(" ON")
  ELSE
    WRITELN(" OFF");
END;  (* PRISWI *)
```

```
PROCEDURE MBEVAL;                        (* EVALUATE MATERIAL BALANCE *)

VAR
  INTI , TI;                             (* COUNT PAWNS OF WINNING SIDE *)

BEGIN
  IF MBLTE <> 0 THEN
    IF MBLTE > 0 THEN
      INTI := MBPWN(LITE)
    ELSE
      INTI := MBPWN(DARK)
  ELSE
    INTI := 0;

  MBEVAL(JNTK) := SIGN(MIN(MIN(FMAXMT,ABS(MBLTE))
    +FTRADE*ABS(MBLTE)*(FTRDSL-MBTOT)*(4*INTI+FTRPOK)
    DIV (4*INTI+FTRPWN) DIV 262144,16320),MBLTE);

END;  (* MBEVAL *)



PROCEDURE MBCAPT                         (* EVALUATE MATERIAL AFTER
                                            CAPTURE *)

  (A:TP);                                (* PIECE CAPTURED *)

BEGIN
  MBTOT := MBTOT - ABS(XTPV(A));         (* TOTAL MATERIAL ON BOARD *)
  IF XTPU(A) = EP THEN
    MBPWN(XTPM(A)) := MBPWN(XTPM(A)) - 1;
                                         (* REMOVE PAWN IF NECESSARY *)
  MBLTE := MBLTE - XTPV(A);              (* LITE ADVANTAGE *)
  MBEVAL;                                (* EVALUATE MATERIAL *)
END;  (* MBCAPT *)



PROCEDURE MBTPAC                         (* REMOVE CAPTURE FROM
                                            MATERIAL BALANCE DATA.  THIS
                                            IS THE INVERSE OF MBCAPT *)

  (A:TP);                                (* PIECE UNCAPTURED *)

BEGIN
  MBTOT := MBTOT + ABS(XTPV(A));
  IF XTPU(A) = EP THEN
    MBPWN(XTPM(A)) := MBPWN(XTPM(A)) + 1;
  MBLTE := MBLTE + XTPV(A);
END;  (* MBTPAC *)



PROCEDURE MBPROM                         (* EVALUATE MATERIAL BALANCE
                                            CHANGE DUE TO PAWN
                                            PROMOTION *)

  (A:TP);                                (* PIECE TO PROMOTE TO *)

BEGIN
  MBTOT := MBTOT + ABS(XTPV(A)-XTPV(XTUMP(EP,XTPM(A))));
                                         (* TOTAL MATERIAL ON BOARD *)
  MBPWN(XTPM(A)) := MBPWN(XTPM(A)) - 1;(* COUNT PAWNS *)
  MBLTE := MBLTE + XTPV(A)-XTPV(XTUMP(EP,XTPM(A)));
  MBEVAL;                                (* EVALUATE RESULT *)
END;  (* MBPROM *)



PROCEDURE MBMORP                         (* REMOVE PAWN PROMOTION
                                            FROM MATERIAL BALANCE DATA.
                                            THIS IS THE INVERSE
                                            OF MBPROM *)

  (A:TP);                                (* PIECE PROMOTED TO *)

BEGIN
  MBTOT := MBTOT - ABS(XTPV(A)-XTPV(XTUMP(EP,XTPM(A))));
```

```
   MBPWN(XTPM(A)) := MBPWN(XTPM(A)) + 1;
   MBLTE := MBLTE - (XTPV(A)-XTPV(XTUMP(EP,XTPM(A))));
ENO;  (* MBMORP *)



PROCEOURE AOOATK                      (* ADD ATTACKS OF PIECE TO DATA
                                         BASE *)
   (A:TS);                            (* SQUARE OF PIECE TO ADD
                                         ATTACK *)

VAR
   INTB : TB;                         (* LOOP CONTROL BOOLEAN *)
   INTO : TO;                         (* CURRENT DIRECTION OFFSET *)
   INTE : TE;                         (* CURRENT DIRECTION INDEX *)
   INTM : TM;                         (* COLOR OF CURRENT PIECE *)
   INTP : TP;                         (* CURRENT PIECE *)
   INTT : TT;                         (* RUNNING SQUARE *)

BEGIN
   INTP := NBORD(A);                  (* PIECE OF INTEREST *)
   INTM := XTPM(INTP);                (* COLOR *)
   FOR INTE := XFPE(INTP) TO XLPE(INTP) DO
   BEGIN
      INTT := A;                      (* INITIALIZE RUNNING SQUARE *)
      INTB := XSPB(INTP);             (* TRUE IF SWEEP PIECE *)
      INTO := XTEO(INTE);             (* OFFSET *)
      REPEAT
         INTT := XTLS(XTSL(INTT) + INTO);  (* STEP IN PROPER DIRECTION *)
         IF INTT >= 0 THEN
         BEGIN
            SETRS(ATKFR(A),INTT);
            SETRS(ATKTO(INTT),A);
            SETRS(ALATK(INTM),INTT);
            IF NBORD(INTT) <> MT THEN
               INTB := FALSE;
         ENO
         ELSE
            INTB := FALSE;
      UNTIL NOT INTB;
   ENO;
ENO;  (* AODATK *)



PROCEOURE AODLOC                      (* ADD PIECE TO DATA BASE *)
   (A:TS;                             (* SQUARE WITH NEW PIECE ON IT *)
    B:TP);                            (* NEW PIECE TO ADD *)


BEGIN
   CLRRS(TPLOC(MT),A);                (* BIT BOARD OF EMPTY SQUARES *)
   SETRS(TPLOC(B),A);                 (* BIT BOARD OF ALL SAME PIECE *)
   SETRS(TMLOC(XTPM(B)),A);           (* BIT BOARD OF ALL SAME COLOR *)
   SETRS(ALLOC(JMTK),A);              (* BIT BOARD OF ALL PIECES *)
   NBORD(A) := B;                     (* SET NEW PIECE ON BOARD *)
ENO;  (* AODLOC *)



PROCEOURE CLSTAT;                     (* CLEAR POSITION STATUS *)

BEGIN
   WITH BOARD DO
   BEGIN
      RBTM := LITE;                   (* WHITE TO MOVE *)
      RBTS := -1;                     (* NO ENPASSANT *)
      RBSQ := ();                     (* NO CASTLING LEGAL *)
   ENO;
ENO;  (* CLSTAT *)



PROCEOURE CUTATK                      (* CUT ATTACKS THROUGH SQUARE *)
   (A:TS);                            (* SQUARE *)
```

```
VAR
  IMRS : RS;                          (* ATTACKING PIECES *)
  IMTS : TS;                          (* ATTACKING PIECE SQUARE *)
  IMRS : RS;                          (* SCRATCH *)
  INTO : TO;                          (* STEP SIZE *)
  INTM : TM;                          (* ATTACKING PIECE SIDE *)
  INTL : TL;                          (* NO LONGER ATTACKED SQUARE *)
  INTT : TT;                          (* NO LONGER ATTACKED SQUARE *)

BEGIN
  CPYRS(IMRS,ATKTO(A));               (* ALL PIECES ATTACKING SQUARE *)
  WHILE NXTTS(IMRS,INTS)) DO
    IF XSPB(NBORD(INTS)) THEN         (* IF SWEEP PIECE *)
    BEGIN
      INTO := XLLD(XTSL(A)-XTSL(INTS));
                                      (* STEP SIZE ON 10 X 12 BOARD *)
      INTM := XTPM(NBORD(INTS));      (* SIDE OF ATTACKING PIECE *)
      INTL := XTSL(A)+INTO;           (* FIRST SQUARE BEYOND PIECE *)
      INTT := XTLS(INTL);             (* FIRST SQUARE BEYOND PIECE ON
                                         8X8 BOARD *)
      WHILE INTT > AT DO              (* WHILE ON BOARD *)
      BEGIN
        CLRRS(ATKFR(INTS),INTT);      (* CLEAR ATTACK MAP *)
        CLRRS(ATKTO(INTT),INTS);
        ANDRS(IMRS,ATKTO(INTT),TMLOC(INTM));
                                      (* OTHER ATTACKS ON SQUARE BY
                                         SAME SIDE *)
        IF NULRS(IMRS) THEN           (* IF NO ATTACKS BY THAT SIDE *)
          CLRRS(ALATK(INTM),INTT);    (* CLEAR ATTACKS BY SIDE *)
        IF NBORD(INTT) = MT THEN
        BEGIN
          INTL := INTL+INTO;          (* STEP BEYOND SQUARE *)
          INTT := XTLS(INTL);
        END
        ELSE
          INTT := AT;                 (* STOP SCAN *)
      END;
    END;
END;  (* CUTATK *)


PROCEDURE DELATK                      (* DELETE ATTACKS FROM SQUARE *)
  (A:TS);                             (* SQUARE TO REMOVE PIECE *)

VAR
  IMRS : RS;                          (* SQUARES ATTACKED BY PIECE ON
                                         SQUARE *)
  IMRS : RS;                          (* SCRATCH *)
  INTS : TS;                          (* SQUARE ATTACKED BY PIECE ON
                                         SQUARE *)
  INTM : TM;                          (* SIDE OF PIECE ON SQUARE *)

BEGIN
  CPYRS(IMRS,ATKFR(A));               (* SQUARES ATTACKED BY PIECE
                                         ON SQUARE *)
  NEWRS(ATKFR(A));                    (* CLEAR ATTACKS FROM SQUARE *)
  INTM := XTPM(NBORD(A));             (* SIDE OF PIECE ON SQUARE *)
  WHILE NXTTS(IMRS,INTS) DO           (* LOOP THROUGH ALL ATTACKS BY
                                         PIECE *)
  BEGIN
    CLRRS(ATKTO(INTS),A);             (* CLEAR ATTACK TO OTHER
                                         SQUARE *)
    ANDRS(IMRS,ATKTO(INTS),TMLOC(INTM));
                                      (* OTHER ATTACKS BY SAME SIDE *)
    IF NULRS(IMRS) THEN
      CLRRS(ALATK(INTM),INTS);        (* CLEAR ATTACKS BY SIDE *)
    CLRRS(TPLOC(NBORD(A)),A);         (* CLEAR PIECE *)
    CLRRS(TMLOC(INTM),A);             (* CLEAR PIECE FROM SIDE *)
    CLRRS(ALLOC(JNTK),A);             (* CLEAR PIECE FROM ALL PIECES *)
    SETRS(TPLOC(MT),A);               (* SET EMPTY *)
    NBORD(A) := MT;
  END;
END;  (* DELATK *)
```

```
PROCEDURE PRPATK                          (* PROPAGATE ATTACKS THROUGH
                                             SQUARE *)
   (A:TS);                                 (* SQUARE *)

VAR
   INRS : RS;                              (* ATTACKING PIECES *)
   INTS : TS;                              (* ATTACKING PIECE SQUARE *)
   INTD : TD;                              (* STEP SIZE *)
   INTM : TM;                              (* ATTACKING PIECE SIDE *)
   INTL : TL;                              (* NEW ATTACKED SQUARE *)
   INTT : TT;                              (* NEW ATTACKED SQUARE *)

BEGIN
   CPYRS(INRS,ATKTO(A));                   (* ALL PIECES ATTACKING SQUARE *)
   WHILE NXTTS(INRS,INTS) DO
      IF XSPB(NBORD(INTS)) THEN            (* IF SWEEP PIECE *)
      BEGIN
         INTD := XLLD(XTSL(A)-XTSL(INTS));
                                           (* STEP SIZE ON 10 X 12 BOARD *)
         INTM := XTPM(NBORD(INTS));        (* SIDE OF ATTACKING PIECE *)
         INTL := XTSL(A)+INTD;             (* FIRST SQUARE BEYOND PIECE *)
         INTT := XTLS(INTL);               (* FIRST SQUARE BEYOND PIECE ON
                                             8X8 BOARD *)

         WHILE INTT >= 0 DO                (* WHILE ON BOARD *)
         BEGIN
            SETRS(ATKFR(INTS),INTT);       (* SET ATTACK MAP *)
            SETRS(ATKTO(INTT),INTS);
            SETRS(ALATK(INTM),INTT);       (* SET ATTACKS BY SIDE *)
            IF NBORD(INTT) = MT THEN
            BEGIN
               INTL := INTL+INTD;          (* STEP BEYOND SQUARE *)
               INTT := XTLS(INTL);
            END
            ELSE
               INTT := -1;                 (* STOP SCAN *)
         END;
      END;
END;  (* PRPATK *)



PROCEDURE GAINIT                           (* UNPROCESS CAPTURE MOVE *)
   (A:RM);                                 (* CAPTURE MOVE *)

BEGIN
   WITH A DO
   BEGIN
      ADDLOC(RMFR,NBORD(RMTO));            (* PUT PIECE ON ORIGINAL
                                             SQUARE *)

      ADDATK(RMFR);                        (* STOP ATTACKS AT THIS SQUARE *)
      CUTATK(RMFR);                        (* REMOVE THEM FROM
      DELATK(RMTO);                           DESTINATION SQUARE *)

      ADDLOC(RMTO,RMCP);                   (* REPLACE CAPTURED PIECE *)
      ADDATK(RMTO);
      MBTPAC(NBORD(RMTO));                 (* UPDATE SCORE *)
   END;
END;  (* GAINIT *)



PROCEDURE LOSEIT                           (* PROCESS CAPTURE MOVE *)
   (A:RM);                                 (* CAPTURE MOVE *)

BEGIN
   WITH A DO
   BEGIN
      MBCAPT(NBORD(RMTO));                 (* UPDATE SCORE *)
      DELATK(RMTO);                        (* DELETE ATTACKS OF CAPTURED
                                             PIECE *)

      ADDLOC(RMTO,NBORD(RMFR));            (* ADD PIECE TO DESTINATION
                                             SQUARE *)

      DELATK(RMFR);                        (* DELETE ATTACKS OF MOVING
                                             PIECE *)
```

```
      PRPATK(RMFR);                 (* PROPAGATE ATTACKS THROUGH
                                       FROM SQUARE *)
      ADDATK(RMTO);                 (* ADD ATTACKS OF MOVING PIECE *)
    END;
END;  (* LOSEIT *)



PROCEDURE MOVEIT                    (* PROCESS ORDINARY MOVE *)
  (A:RM);                           (* ORDINARY MOVE *)

BEGIN
  WITH A DO
    BEGIN
      ADDLOC(RMTO,NBORD(RMFR));     (* ADD PIECE TO NEW SQUARE *)
      CUTATK(RMTO);                 (* CUT ATTACKS THROUGH NEW
                                       SQUARE *)
      DELATK(RMFR);                 (* DELETE ATTACKS FROM OLD
                                       SQUARE *)
      PRPATK(RMFR);                 (* PROPAGATE ATTACKS THROUGH OLD
                                       SQUARE *)
      ADDATK(RMTO);                 (* ADD ATTACKS FROM NEW SQUARE *)
    END;
END;  (* MOVEIT *)



PROCEDURE RTRKIT                    (* UNPROCESS ORDINARY MOVE *)
  (A:RM);                           (* THE MOVE TO RETRACT *)

BEGIN
  WITH A DO
    BEGIN
      ADDLOC(RMFR,NBORD(RMTO));     (* PUT PIECE ON ORIGINAL
                                       SQUARE *)
      CUTATK(RMFR);                 (* CUT ATTACKS THROUGH ORIGINAL
                                       SQUARE *)
      DELATK(RMTO);                 (* DELETE ATTACKS FROM
                                       DESTINATION SQUARE *)
      PRPATK(RMTO);                 (* PROPAGATE ATTACKS THROUGH
                                       DESTINATION SQUARE *)
      ADDATK(RMFR);                 (* ADD ATTACKS FROM ORIGINAL
                                       SQUARE *)
    END;
END;  (* RTRKIT *)



PROCEDURE PAWNIT                    (* UNPROMOTE A PAWN *)
  (A:RM);                           (* PROMOTION MOVE *)

BEGIN
  WITH A DO
    BEGIN
      MBMORP(NBORD(RMTO));                (* UPDATE SCORE *)
      NBORD(RMTO) := XTUMP(EP,XTPM(NBORD(RMTO)));
    END;
END;  (* PAWNIT *)



PROCEDURE PROACA                    (* PROCESS CASTLE STATUS
                                       CHANGES *)
  (A:TS);                           (* SQUARE *)

VAR
  INRS : RS;                        (* SCRATCH *)
  INRS : RS;                        (* SCRATCH *)

BEGIN
  CLRRS(CSTAT[JNTK],A);             (* CLEAR THIS SQUARE *)
  ANDRS(INRS,CSTAT[JNTK],XRRS(XTSR(A)));
                                    (* CASTLE BITS FOR THIS SIDE *)
  IF NOT INRSTB(INRS,XTRFS(XTSR(A),FS)) THEN
                                    (* IF KING MOVE *)
```

```
       ANDRS(CSTAT[JNTK],CSTAT[JNTK],XNRS[XTSR[A]]);
                                         (* CLEAR ALL CASTLE MOVES FOR
                                            SIDE *)
       ANDRS(INRS,INRS,XRFS[F8]);        (* KING ROOK SQUARE *)
       ANDRS(INRS,INRS,XRFS[F1]);        (* QUEEN ROOK SQUARE *)
       IORRS(INRS,INRS,INRS);            (* BOTH ROOK SQUARES *)
       IF NULRS(INRS) THEN               (* IF BOTH ROOKS GONE *)
         ANDRS(CSTAT[JNTK],CSTAT[JNTK],XNRS[XTSR[A]]);
END;  (* PROACA *)



PROCEDURE PROACS                         (* PROCESS MOVES AFFECTING CASTLE
                                            STATUS *)
   (A:RM);                               (* MOVE WITH RMAC *)

BEGIN
   WITH A DO
   BEGIN
      IF INRSTB(CSTAT[JNTK],RMFR) THEN   (* FROM SQUARE *)
        PROACA(RMFR);
      IF INRSTB(CSTAT[JNTK],RMTO) THEN   (* TO SQUARE *)
        PROACA(RMTO);
   END;
END;  (* PROACS *)



PROCEDURE PROMOT                         (* PROCESS PROMOTION *)
   (A:RM);                               (* PROMOTION MOVE *)

BEGIN
   WITH A DO
   BEGIN
      MBPROM(XTGMP[RMPP,JNTM]);          (* UPDATE SCORE *)
      NBORD(RMFR) := XTGMP[RMPP,JNTM];
   END;
END;  (* PROMOT *)



PROCEDURE CREATE;                        (* CREATE GLOBAL DATA BASE *)

VAR
   INRS : RS;                            (* SCRATCH BIT BOAPD *)
   INTM : TM;                            (* COLOR INDEX *)
   INTP : TP;                            (* PIECE INDEX *)
   INTQ : TQ;                            (* CASTLE TYPE INDEX *)
   INTS : TS;                            (* SQUARE INDEX *)

BEGIN
   WITH BOARD DO
   BEGIN

      JNTM := AM+1;                      (* INITIALIZE MOVES STACK
                                            POINTER *)
      JNTK := AK;                        (* PLY INDEX *)
      JNTM := RBTM;                      (* SIDE TO MOVE *)

      NODES := 0;                        (* INITIALIZE TOTAL NODES *)

      LINDX[JNTK] := JNTM;               (* MOVES ARRAY LIMIT *)
      SRCHM[JNTK] := MQ;                 (* SEARCH MODE *)

      FOR INTS := AS TO ZS DO
      BEGIN
         NEWRS(ATKFR[INTS]);             (* CLEAR ATTACKS FROM *)
         NEWRS(ATKTO[INTS]);             (* CLEAR ATTACKS TO *)
         NBORD[INTS] := MT;              (* CLEAR LOOKAHEAD BOARD *)
      END;

      NEWRS(ALLOC[JNTK]);                (* CLEAR ALL PIECE LOCATIONS *)

      FOR INTP := LP TO MT DO
        NEWRS(TPLOC[INTP]);              (* CLEAR PIECE LOCATIONS *)
```

```
FOR INTM := LITE TO NONE DO
BEGIN
   NEWRS(TMLOC[INTM]);            (* CLEAR COLOR LOCATIONS *)
   NEWRS(ALATK[INTM]);            (* CLEAR COLOR ATTACKS *)
END;

MBTOT := 0;
MBPWN[LITE] := C;
MBPWN[DARK] := 0;
MBLTE := 0;

FOR INTS := AS TO ZS DO
   IF RBIS[INTS] <> MT THEN
   BEGIN
      ADDLOC(INTS,RBIS[INTS]);
      MBTPAC(RBIS[INTS]);
   END
   ELSE
      SETRS(TPLOC[MT],INTS);

MBEVAL;                           (* EVALUATE MATERIAL *)

CPYRS(INRS,ALLOC[JNTK]);          (* COPY BIT BOARD OF ALL
                                     PIECES *)

WHILE NXTTS(INRS,INTS) DO
   ADDATK(INTS);                  (* ADD ATTACKS OF ALL PIECES *)

NEWRS(CSTAT[JNTK]);               (* INITIALIZE CASTLING SQUARES *)
FOR INTQ := LS TO DL DO
   IF INTQ IN RBSQ THEN
      IORRS(CSTAT[JNTK],CSTAT[JNTK],XSQS[INTQ]);

NEWRS(ENPAS[JNTK]);               (* INITIALIZE ENPASSANT SQUARE *)
IF RBTS >= 0 THEN
   SETRS(ENPAS[JNTK],RBTS);

CPYRS(GENPN[JNTK],TPLOC[XTJMP[EP,JNTM]]);
NOTRS(GENTO[JNTK],TMLOC[JNTM]);
NOTRS(INRS,GENPN[JNTK]);
ANORS(GENFR[JNTK],TMLOC[JNTM],INRS);
END;
END;  (* CREATE *)


PROCEDURE ONDATE                  (* DOWNDATE DATA BASE TO BACK
                                     OUT A MOVE *)
   (A:RM);                        (* THE MOVE TO RETRACT *)

VAR
   INTS : TS;                     (* SCRATCH *)
   INTR : TR;                     (* ROOK RANK FOR CASTLING *)
   INTF : TF;                     (* ROOK FILE FOR CASTLING *)

   RKFR : TS;                     (* ROOK FROM SQUARE *)
   RKTO : TS;                     (* ROOK TO SQUARE *)

BEGIN
   WITH A DO
   BEGIN
      CASE ORD(RMCA)*4 + ORD(RMAC)*2 + ORD(RMPR) OF
         0: (* ORDINARY MOVE *)
            RTRKIT(A);
         1: (* PAWN MOVE AND PROMOTE *)
            BEGIN
               PAWNIT(A);
               RTRKIT(A);
            END;
         2: (* MISCELLANEOUS ACS *)
            IF RMOO THEN
            BEGIN  (* CASTLE *)
               IF RMQS THEN
                  INTF := F1          (* ROOK ON QUEEN ROOK FILE *)
               ELSE
                  INTF := F8;         (* ROOK ON KING ROOK FILE *)
               INTR := XTSR[RMFR];    (* ROOK FILE *)
```

```
            RKFR := XTRFS(INTR,INTF);    (* ROOK FROM SQUARE *)
            RKTO := (RMFR+RMTO) DIV 2;   (* ROOK TO SQUARE *)
            ADDLOC(RKFR,NBORD(RKTO));    (* REPLACE ROOK *)
            DELATK(RKTO);
            PRPATK(RKTO);
            ADDATK(RKFR);
            RTRKIT(A);                   (* RETRACT KING MOVE *)
          END
          ELSE  (* NOT CASTLE *)
            RTRKIT(A);
      3:  (* NULL MOVE *)
      4:  (* CAPTURE *)
          IF RMEP THEN
          BEGIN  (* CAPTURE ENPASSANT *)
            INTS := XTRFS(XTSR(RMFR),XTSF(RMTO));
            ADDLOC(INTS,RMCP);
            CUTATK(INTS);
            ADDATK(INTS);
            RTRKIT(A);                   (* RETRACT PAWN MOVE *)
            MBTPAC(NBORD(INTS));         (* ADD PIECE TO SCORE *)
          END
          ELSE  (* CAPTURE NOT ENPASSANT *)
            GAINIT(A);
      5:  (* CAPTURE AND PROMOTE *)
          BEGIN
            PAWNIT(A);                   (* UNPROMOTE *)
            GAINIT(A);                   (* UNCAPTURE *)
          END;                                        •
      6:  (* CAPTURE ACS *)
          GAINIT(A);                     (* UNCAPTURE *)
      7:  (* CAPTURE ROOK ACS, PROMOTE *)
          BEGIN
            PAWNIT(A);
            GAINIT(A);
          END;
    END;
    JNTM := LINDX(JNTK);                 (* RESET MOVE GENERATION
                                            POINTER *)
    JNTK := JNTK-1;                      (* BACK UP PLY INDEX *)
    JNTM := OTHER(JNTM);                 (* SWITCH SIDE TO MOVE *)
  END;
END;  (* UNDATE *)


FUNCTION UPDATE                          (* UPDATE DATA BASE FOR A MOVE *)
  (VAR A:RM)                             (* THE MOVE *)
  :TB;                                   (* RETURNS TRUE IF MOVE IS
                                            LEGAL *)


VAR
  INRS : RS;                             (* SCRATCH *)
  IMRS : RS;                             (* SCRATCH *)
  INTS : TS;                             (* SCRATCH *)
  INTF : TF;                             (* ROOK FILE FOR CASTLING *)
  INTR : TR;                             (* ROOK RANK FOR CASTLING *)
  RKTO : TS;                             (* ROOK DESTINATION SQUARE *)
  RKFR : TS;                             (* ROOK ORIGIN SQUARE *)

BEGIN
  WITH A DO
    BEGIN
      JNTK := JNTK+1;                    (* ADVANCE PLY INDEX *)
      NEWRS(ENPAS(JNTK));                (* CLEAR ENPASSANT BIT BOARD *)
      CPYRS(CSTAT(JNTK),CSTAT(JNTK-1));  (* INITIALIZE CASTLE STATUS *)
      CPYRS(ALLOC(JNTK),ALLOC(JNTK-1));  (* INITIALIZE ALL LOCATIONS *)
      MBVAL(JNTK) := MBVAL(JNTK-1);      (* INITIALIZE MATERIAL SCORE *)
      LINDX(JNTK) := JNTM;               (* MOVES ARRAY LIMIT *)
      CASE ORD(RMCA)*4 + ORD(RMAC)*2 + ORD(RMPR) OF
        0:  (* ORDINARY MOVE *)
          IF RMEP THEN
          BEGIN                          (* PAWN MOVE 2 SPACES *)
            SFTRS(INRS,XRSS(RMTO),S1);
            SFTRS(IMRS,XRSS(RMTO),S3);
```

```
                IORRS(INRS,INRS,INRS);            (* SQUARES NEXT TO DESTINATION *)
                ANDRS(INRS,INRS,TPLOC(XTJMP(EP,OTHER(JNTM))));
                                                  (* INTERSECT WITH ENEMY PAWNS *)
             IF NOT NULRS(INRS) THEN
                SETRS(ENPAS(JNTK),(RMTO+RMFR) DIV 2);
                                                  (* SET ENPASSANT SQUARE *)
                MOVEIT(A);                        (* MOVE PAWN *)
            END
            ELSE
                MOVEIT(A);                        (* MOVE PIECE *)
   1:   (* MOVE AND PROMOTE *)
        BEGIN
            PROMOT(A);                            (* PROMOTE PAWN *)
            MOVEIT(A);                            (* MOVE PROMOTED PIECE *)
        END;
   2:   (* MISCELLANEOUS ACS *)
        BEGIN
           IF RMOO THEN
            BEGIN   (* CASTLE *)
                IF RMQS THEN
                    INTF := F1               (* ROOK ON QUEEN ROOK FILE *)
                ELSE
                    INTF := F8;              (* ROOK ON KING ROOK FILE *)
                INTR := XTSR(RMFR);          (* ROOK ON KINGS RANK *)
                RKFR := XTRFS(INTR,INTF);    (* ROOK ORIGIN SQUARE *)
                RKTO := (RMFR+RMTO) DIV 2;(* ROOK DESTINATION SQUARE *)
                ANDRS(CSTAT(JNTK),CSTAT(JNTK),XNRS(INTR));
                                             (* DISALLOW FURTHER CASTLING
                                                BY THIS SIDE *)
                ADDLOC(RKTO,NBORD(RKFR)); (* PUT ROOK ON NEW SQUARE *)
                ADDATK(RKTO);             (* ADD ITS ATTACKS *)
                DELATK(RKFR);             (* DELETE FROM ORIGINAL SQUARE *)
                MOVEIT(A);                (* MOVE KING *)
            END
            ELSE  (* NOT CASTLE *)
            BEGIN
                PROACS(A);                   (* PROCESS CASTLE STATUS MODS *)
                MOVEIT(A);                   (* MOVE TO OR FROM KING OR ROOK
                                                SQUARE *)
            END;
        END;
   3:;  (* NULL MOVE *)
   4:   (* CAPTURE *)
        IF RMEP THEN
        BEGIN   (* CAPTURE ENPASSANT *)
            INTS := XTRFS(XTSR(RMFR),XTSF(RMTO));
                                             (* CAPTURED PAWN SQUARE *)
            MBCAPT(NBORD(INTS));             (* UPDATE SCORE *)
            DELATK(INTS);                    (* DELETE CAPTURED PAWN
                                                ATTACKS *)
            PRPATK(INTS);                    (* PROPAGATE ATTACKS THROUGH
                                                PAWN *)
            MOVEIT(A);                       (* MOVE CAPTURING PAWN *)
        END
        ELSE   (* CAPTURE NOT ENPASSANT *)
            LOSEIT(A);                       (* PROCESS CAPTURE *)
   5:   (* CAPTURE AND PROMOTE *)
        BEGIN
            PROMOT(A);                       (* PROMOTE PAWN *)
            LOSEIT(A);                       (* PROCESS CAPTURE WITH PROMOTED
                                                PIECE *)
        END;
   6:   (* CAPTURE ACS *)
        BEGIN
            PROACS(A);                       (* PROCESS CASTLE STATUS MODS *)
            LOSEIT(A);                       (* PROCESS ROOK CAPTURE *)
        END;
   7:   (* CAPTURE ROOK ACS, PROMOTE *)
        BEGIN
            PROMOT(A);                       (* PROMOTE PAWN *)
            PROACS(A);                       (* CHANGE CASTLE STATUS *)
            LOSEIT(A);                       (* PROCESS ROOK CAPTURE *)
        END;
END;
```

```
    (* INITIALIZE MOVE GENERATION *)

    JNTM := OTHER(JNTM);                    (* SWITCH SIDE TO MOVE *)
    CPYRS(GENPN(JNTK),TPLOC(XTJMP(EP,JNTM)));
    NOTRS(GENTO(JNTK),TMLOC(JNTM));
    NOTRS(INRS,GENPN(JNTK));
    ANORS(GENFR(JNTK),TMLOC(JNTM),INRS);

    (* DETERMINE IF MOVE LEAVES KING IN CHECK, OR MOVES
       KING INTO CHECK *)

    ANORS(INRS,TPLOC(XTJMP(EK,JNTM)),ALATK(OTHER(JNTM)));
    RMCH := NOT NULRS(INRS);
    ANORS(INRS,TPLOC(XTJMP(EK,OTHER(JNTM))),ALATK(JNTM));
    RMIL := NOT NULRS(INRS);
    UPDATE := NOT RMIL;
    IF NOT RMIL THEN                        (* COUNT LEGAL MOVES *)
      MVSEL(JNTK-1) := MVSEL(JNTK-1) + 1;

    (* INITIALIZE MOVE SEARCHING *)

    SRCHM(JNTK) := M1;
    NODES := NODES+1;                       (* COUNT NODES SEARCHED *)
  END;
END;  (* UPDATE *)



PROCEDURE GENONE                           (* STACK ONE GENERATED MOVE *)
  (A:TT;                                    (* FROM SQUARE *)
   B:TS);                                   (* TO SQUARE *)

VAR
  INRS : RS;                                (* SCRATCH *)

BEGIN
  WITH MOVES(JNTW) DO
  BEGIN
    RMFR := A;                              (* FROM SQUARE *)
    RMTO := B;                              (* TO SQUARE *)
    RMCP := NBORD(B);                       (* CAPTURED PIECE *)
    RMCA := (NBORD(B) <> MT);               (* CAPTURE *)
    IORRS(INRS,XRSS(A),XRSS(B));
    ANORS(INRS,INRS,CSTAT(JNTK));
    RMAC := NOT NULRS(INRS);                (* AFFECTS CASTLE STATUS *)
    RMCH := FALSE;                          (* CHECK *)
    RMMT := FALSE;                          (* MATE *)
    RMIL := FALSE;                          (* ILLEGAL *)
    RMSU := FALSE;                          (* SEARCHED *)
    RMPR := FALSE;                          (* PROMOTION *)
    RMOO := FALSE;                          (* CASTLE *)
    RMEP := FALSE;                          (* ENPASSANT *)
  END;
  VALUE(JNTW) := 0;                         (* CLEAR VALUE *)
  IF JNTW < ZW THEN
    JNTW := JNTW+1;                         (* ADVANCE MOVES STACK POINTER *)
END;  (* GENONE *)



PROCEDURE PWNPRO;                          (* GENERATE ALL PROMOTION
                                              MOVES *)

VAR
  INTG : TG;                                (* PROMOTION TYPE *)

BEGIN
  MOVES(JNTW-1).RMPR := TRUE;               (* SET PROMOTION *)
  MOVES(JNTW-1).RMPP := PQ;                 (* PROMOTE TO QUEEN FIRST *)
  FOR INTG := PR TO PB DO                   (* GENERATE OTHER PROMOTIONS *)
  BEGIN
    MOVES(JNTW) := MOVES(JNTW-1);           (* COPY LAST MOVE *)
    MOVES(JNTW).RMPP := INTG;               (* CHANGE PROMOTE TO PIECE *)
    JNTW := JNTW+1;                         (* ADVANCE MOVE INDEX *)
  END;
END;  (* PWNPRO *)
```

```
PROCEDURE GENPWN                        (* GENERATE PAWN MOVES *)
   (A:RS;                               (* PAWNS TO MOVE *)
    B:RS);                              (* VALID DESTINATION SQUARES *)


VAR
   IMRS, IMRS : RS;                     (* SCRATCH *)
   INTS : TS;                           (* DESTINATION SQUARE *)

BEGIN
   IF JNTM = LITE THEN
   BEGIN                                (* WHITE PAWNS *)
     SFTRS(IMRS,A,S2);                  (* ADVANCE ONE RANK *)
     ANORS(IMRS,TPLOC[MT],IMRS);        (* ONLY TO EMPTY SQUARES *)
     CPYRS(IMRS,IMRS);                  (* SAVE FOR 2 SQUARE MOVES *)
     ANORS(IMRS,B,IMRS);                (* ONLY VALID DESTINATION
                                           SQUARES *)

     WHILE NXTTS(IMRS,INTS) DO
     BEGIN
       GENONE(XTLS[XTSL[INTS]-XTED[S2]],INTS);
                                        (* GENERATE SIMPLE PAWN MOVES *)
       IF INTS >= XTRFS[R8,F1] THEN
         PWNPRO;                        (* PROCESS PROMOTION *)
     END;
     ANORS(IMRS,IMRS,XRRS[R3]);         (* TAKE ONLY PAWNS ON THIRD *.
     SFTRS(IMRS,IMRS,S2);               (* ADVANCE ONE MORE RANK *)
     ANORS(IMRS,IMRS,TPLOC[MT]);        (* ONLY TO EMPTY SQUARES *)
     ANORS(IMRS,IMRS,B);                (* ONLY VALID DESTINATION
                                           SQUARES *)

     WHILE NXTTS(IMRS,INTS) DO
     BEGIN
       GENONE(XTLS[XTSL[INTS]-2*XTED[S2]],INTS);
                                        (* GENERATE DOUBLE PAWN MOVES *)
       MOVES[JNTW-1].RMEP := TRUE;      (* FLAG AS TWO SQUARES *)
     END;

     SFTRS(IMRS,A,B1);                  (* TRY CAPTURES TO THE LEFT *)
     IORRS(IMRS,TMLOC[OTHER[JNTM]],ENPAS[JNTK]);
                                        (* OPPONENT PIECES + EP SQUARE *)
     ANORS(IMRS,IMRS,B);                (* VALID DESTINATION SQUARES *)
     ANORS(IMRS,IMRS,IMRS);             (* CAPTURE MOVES TO LEFT *)
     WHILE NXTTS(IMRS,INTS) DO
     BEGIN
       GENONE(XTLS[XTSL[INTS]-XTED[B1]],INTS);
                                        (* GENERATE CAPTURE MOVE *)
       MOVES[JNTW-1].RMCA := TRUE;      (* FLAG CAPTURE *)
       MOVES[JNTW-1].RMEP := IMRSTB(ENPAS[JNTK],INTS);
                                        (* FLAG ENPASSANT CAPTURE *)
       IF MOVES[JNTW-1].RMEP THEN
         MOVES[JNTW-1].RMCP := OP;      (* SET CAPTURED PIECE TYPE *)
       IF INTS >= XTRFS[R8,F1] THEN
         PWNPRO;                        (* PROCESS PROMOTION *)
     END;

     SFTRS(IMRS,A,B2);                  (* TRY CAPTURES TO THE RIGHT *)
     IORRS(IMRS,TMLOC[OTHER[JNTM]],ENPAS[JNTK]);
                                        (* OPPONENT PIECES + EP SQUARE *)
     ANORS(IMRS,IMRS,B);                (* VALID DESTINATION SQUARES *)
     ANORS(IMRS,IMRS,IMRS);             (* CAPTURE MOVES TO LEFT *)
     WHILE NXTTS(IMRS,INTS) DO
     BEGIN
       GENONE(XTLS[XTSL[INTS]-XTED[B2]],INTS);
                                        (* GENERATE CAPTURE MOVE *)
       MOVES[JNTW-1].RMCA := TRUE;      (* FLAG CAPTURE *)
       MOVES[JNTW-1].RMEP := IMRSTB(ENPAS[JNTK],INTS);
                                        (* FLAG ENPASSANT CAPTURE *)
       IF MOVES[JNTW-1].RMEP THEN
         MOVES[JNTW-1].RMCP := OP;      (* SET CAPTURED PIECE TYPE *)
       IF INTS >= XTRFS[R8,F1] THEN
         PWNPRO;                        (* PROCESS PROMOTION *)
     END;
   END
   ELSE
   BEGIN                                (* BLACK PAWNS *)
     SFTRS(IMRS,A,S4);                  (* ADVANCE ONE RANK *)
     ANORS(IMRS,TPLOC[MT],IMRS);        (* ONLY TO EMPTY SQUARES *)
```

```
   CPYRS(INRS,INRS);                    (* SAVE FOR 2 SQUARE MOVES *)
   ANORS(INRS,8,INRS);                  (* ONLY VALID DESTINATION
                                           SQUARES *)

   WHILE NXTTS(INRS,INTS) DO
   BEGIN
     GENONE(XTLS(XTSL(INTS)-XTED(S4)),INTS);
                                        (* GENERATE SIMPLE PAWN MOVES *)

     IF INTS <= XTRFS(R1,F8) THEN
       PWNPRO;                          (* PROCESS PROMOTION *)
   END;
   ANORS(INRS,INRS,XRRS(R6));           (* TAKE ONLY PAWNS ON THIRD *)
   SFTRS(INRS,INRS,S4);                 (* ADVANCE ONE MORE RANK *)
   ANORS(INRS,INRS,TPLOC(MT));          (* ONLY TO EMPTY SQUARES *)
   ANORS(INRS,INRS,8);                  (* ONLY VALID DESTINATION
                                           SQUARES *)

   WHILE NXTTS(INRS,INTS) DO
   BEGIN
     GENONE(XTLS(XTSL(INTS)-2*XTED(S4)),INTS);
                                        (* GENERATE DOUBLE PAWN MOVES *)
     MOVES(JNTW-1).RMEP := TRUE;        (* FLAG AS TWO SQUARES *)
   END;

   SFTRS(INRS,A,83);                    (* TRY CAPTURES TO THE LEFT *)
   IORRS(INRS,TMLOC(OTHER(JNTM)),ENPAS(JNTK));
                                        (* OPPONENT PIECES + EP SQUARE *)
   ANORS(INRS,INRS,8);                  (* VALID DESTINATION SQUARES *)
   ANORS(INRS,INRS,INRS);               (* CAPTURE MOVES TO LEFT *)
   WHILE NXTTS(INRS,INTS) DO
   BEGIN
     GENONE(XTLS(XTSL(INTS)-XTED(83)),INTS);
                                        (* GENERATE PAWN CAPTURE MOVE *)
     MOVES(JNTW-1).RMCA := TRUE;        (* FLAG CAPTURE *)
     MOVES(JNTW-1).RMEP := INRSTB(ENPAS(JNTK),INTS);
                                        (* FLAG ENPASSANT CAPTURE *)

     IF MOVES(JNTW-1).RMEP THEN
       MOVES(JNTW-1).RMCP := LP;        (* SET CAPTURED PIECE TYPE *)
     IF INTS <= XTRFS(R1,F8) THEN
       PWNPRO;                          (* PROCESS PROMOTION *)
   END;

   SFTRS(INRS,A,84);                    (* TRY CAPTURES TO THE RIGHT *)
   IORRS(INRS,TMLOC(OTHER(JNTM)),ENPAS(JNTK));
                                        (* OPPONENT PIECES + EP SQUARE *)
   ANORS(INRS,INRS,8);                  (* VALID DESTINATION SQUARES *)
   ANORS(INRS,INRS,INRS);               (* CAPTURE MOVES TO LEFT *)
   WHILE NXTTS(INRS,INTS) DO
   BEGIN
     GENONE(XTLS(XTSL(INTS)-XTED(84)),INTS);
                                        (* GENERATE PAWN CAPTURE MOVE *)
     MOVES(JNTW-1).RMCA := TRUE;        (* FLAG CAPTURE *)
     MOVES(JNTW-1).RMEP := INRSTB(ENPAS(JNTK),INTS);
                                        (* FLAG ENPASSANT CAPTURE *)
     IF MOVES(JNTW-1).RMEP THEN
       MOVES(JNTW-1).RMCP := LP;        (* SET CAPTURED PIECE TYPE *)
     IF INTS <= XTRFS(R1,F8) THEN
       PWNPRO;                          (* PROCESS PROMOTION *)
   END;
 END;
END; (* GENPWN *)


PROCEDURE GENFSL                        (* GENERATE ALL MOVES FROM
                                           A SET OF SQUARES *)

  (A:RS);                               (* ORIGIN SET OF SQUARES *)

VAR
  INRS : RS;                            (* OUTER LOOP BIT BOARD *)
  INRS : RS;                            (* INNER LOOP BIT BOARD *)
  IPRS : RS;                            (* PAWN ORIGIN BIT BOARD *)
  INTS : TS;                            (* OUTER LOOP SQUARE NUMBER *)
  INTS : TS;                            (* INNER LOOP SQUARE NUMBER *)

BEGIN
  ANORS(INRS,A,GENFR(JNTK));            (* ONLY VALID FROM SQUARES *)
```

```
      NOTRS(IMRS,A):
      ANDRS(GENFR[JNTK],GENFR[JNTK],IMRS):  (* REMOVE ORIGIN SQUARES *)
      ANDRS(IPRS,A,GENPM[JNTK]):            (* VALID PAWN FROM SQUARES *)
      ANDRS(GENPM[JNTK],GENPM[JNTK],IMRS):  (* REMOVE PAWNS *)

      WHILE NXTTS(IMRS,IMTS) DO             (* LOOP THROUGH ORIGINS *)
      BEGIN
         ANDRS(IMRS,ATKFR[INTS],GENTO[JNTK]):
                                            (* GET UNPROCESSED DESTINATION
                                               SQUARES *)
         WHILE NXTTS(IMRS,IMTS) DO          (* LOOP THROUGH DESTINATIONS *)
            GENONE(INTS,IMTS):              (* GENERATE MOVE *)
      END:
      GENPWN(IPRS,GENTO[JNTK]):             (* GENERATE PAWN MOVES *)
END:  (* GETFSL *)


PROCEDURE GENTSL                            (* GENERATE ALL MOVES TO A
                                               SET OF SQUARES *)
   (A:RS):                                  (* TARGET SET OF SQUARES *)

VAR
   IMRS : RS;                               (* OUTER LOOP BIT BOARD *)
   IMRS : RS;                               (* INNER LOOP BIT BOARD *)
   IPRS : RS;                               (* PAWN BIT BOARD *)
   IMTS : TS;                               (* OUTER LOOP SQUARE NUMBER *)
   IMTS : TS;                               (* INNER LOOP SQUARE NUMBER *)

BEGIN
   ANDRS(IMRS,A,GENTO[JNTK]):               (* ONLY VALID TO SQUARES *)
   NOTRS(IMRS,A):
   ANDRS(GENTO[JNTK],GENTO[JNTK],IMRS):     (* REMOVE DESTINATION SQUARES *)
   CPYRS(IPRS,IMRS):                        (* SAVE FOR PAWN MOVES *)

   WHILE NXTTS(IMRS,IMTS) DO                (* LOOP THROUGH DESTINATIONS *)
   BEGIN
      ANDRS(IMRS,ATKTO[INTS],GENFR[JNTK]):
                                            (* GET PIECES OF SIDE TO MOVE *)
      WHILE NXTTS(IMRS,IMTS) DO             (* LOOP THROUGH ORIGINS *)
         GENONE(IMTS,INTS):                 (* GENERATE MOVE *)
   END:
   GENPWN(GENPM[JNTK],IPRS):                (* GENERATE PAWN MOVES *)
END:  (* GENTSL *)


PROCEDURE GENCAP;                           (* GENERATE CAPTURE MOVES *)

VAR
   IMRS : RS;                               (* DESTINATION SQUARES *)

BEGIN
   IORRS(IMRS,ENPAS[JNTK],TMLOC[OTHER[JNTM]]):
   GENTSL(IMRS):                            (* GENERATE MOVES TO
                                               ENEMY SQUARES *)
END:  (* GENCAP *)


PROCEDURE GENCAS:                           (* GENERATE CASTLE MOVES *)

VAR
   INTQ : TQ:                               (* CASTLE TYPE INDEX *)
   IMRS : RS:                               (* OCCUPIED SQUARES TEST *)
   IMRS : RS:                               (* ATTACKED SQUARES TEST *)

BEGIN
   FOR INTQ := XTMQ[JNTM] TO SUCC(XTMQ[JNTM]) DO
   IF INRSTB(CSTAT[JNTK],XTQS[INTQ]) THEN
                                            (* IF CASTLING IS LEGAL *)
   BEGIN
      ANDRS(IMRS,XRQSO[INTQ],ALLOC[JNTK]):
                                            (* CHECK OCCUPIED SQUARES *)
```

```
    ANORS(INRS,XPOSA(INTQ),ALATK(OTHER(JNTM)));
                                      (* CHECK ATTACKED SQUARES *)
    IF NULRS(INRS) AND NULRST(NRS) THEN
                                      (* IF CASTLING IS LEGAL AND
                                         POSSIBLE *)
    BEGIN
      MOVES(JNTW) := XRQM(INTQ);      (* GENERATE CASTLING MOVE *)
      VALUE(JNTW) := 0;
      JNTW := JNTW+1;
    END;
  END;
END; (* GENCAS *)



PROCEDURE GENALL;                     (* GENERATE ALL LEGAL MOVES *)

BEGIN
  GENFSL(ALLOC(JNTK));                (* GENERATE SIMPLE MOVES *)
  GENCAS;                             (* GENERATE CASTLE MOVES *)
END; (* GENALL *)



PROCEDURE LSTMOV;                     (* LIST LEGAL PLAYERS MOVES *)

VAR
  INTW : TW;                          (* MOVES INDEX *)

BEGIN
  CREATE;                             (* CREATE DATA BASE *)
  GENALL;                             (* GENERATE ALL MOVES *)
  FOR INTW := AW+1 TO JNTW-1 DO
  BEGIN
    IF UPDATE(MOVES(INTW)) THEN;      (* SET ILLEGAL FLAG *)
    DNDATE(MOVES(INTW));
  END;
END; (* LSTMOV *)
      .

PROCEDURE THEMOV                      (* MAKE THE MOVE FOR REAL *)
    (A:RM);                           (* THE MOVE TO MAKE *)

VAR
  INT8 : T8;                          (* SCRATCH *)
  INRS : RS;                          (* SCRATCH *)
  INTQ : TQ;                          (* CASTLE TYPE INDEX *)
  INTS : TS;                          (* SCRATCH *)

BEGIN
  LSTMV := A;                         (* SAVE AS PREVIOUS MOVE *)
  INT8 := JPDATE(A);                  (* UPDATE THE DATA BASE *)
  WITH BOARD DO                       (* AND COPY ALL THE RELEVANT DATA
                                         BACK DOWN *)
  BEGIN
    RBTM := JNTM;                     (* SIDE TO MOVE *)
    CPYRS(INRS,ENPAS(JNTK));
    IF NXTTS(INRS,INTS) THEN          (* FIND ENPASSANT SQUARE *)
      RBTS := INTS
    ELSE
      RBTS := AT;
    IF JNTM = DARK THEN
      RBTI := RBTI+1;                 (* ADVANCE MOVE NUMBER *)
    FOR INTQ := LS TO DL DO
      IF INRSTB(CSTAT(JNTK),XTQS(INTQ)) THEN
        RBSQ := RBSQ+(INTQ)           (* CASTLE LEGAL *)
      ELSE
        RBSQ := RBSQ-(INTQ);          (* CASTLE NOT LEGAL *)
      FOR INTS := AS TO ZS DO
        RBIS(INTS) := NBORD(INTS);    (* COPY POSITION *)
  END;
END; (* THEMOV *)
```

The most important part of the variable declaration list in terms of under-standing the program is the portion which specifies the global database. This includes the current board (BOARD, a record) and a number of important arrays. The look-ahead board (NBORD) is an array listing the piece occupying each square. The attacks emanating from each square are represented by ATKFR, an array which lists an 8×8 bit board for each of the 64 squares. The attacks to each square are represented by a similar array, ATKTO. The combined attacks for each side are represented by a two-item array of 8×8 bit boards called ALATK.

The location of all pieces by type is represented by an array of twelve 8×8 bit boards, TPLOC. The location of all pieces by color is represented by an array of two 8×8 bit boards, TMLOC. The moves are stored in an array (MOVES) of records. Each record (RM) contains information about the from square, to square; whether a capture is involved and the type of piece captured, whether the move affects castle status, involves check or mate, involves a piece promotion, and whether the move has been searched yet. Additional arrays provide information on castling squares, *en passant* squares, the location of all pieces, the location of pawns, etc. To be successful, a chess program must organize the database in a logical manner and be able to manipulate it efficiently.

For reasons of efficiency, the program often stores the same information in two or more different ways. Because of this, it is necessary to be able to translate from one form to the other. These activities are handled by special arrays. For example, the XTPC array allows one to use a piece designator (LP, LQ, LK, DQ, etc) as in index and returns the corresponding character (1–6 for Black pieces and A–F for White pieces) which is used when a board representation is printed on the terminal.

There are several general purpose routines which are needed by the pro-gram. Two functions, MIN and MAX, provide the smaller or larger of two numbers upon request. A third function, SIGN, applies the sign of one number to the absolute value of another number. A general purpose sort routine, SORTIT, is also provided.

Manipulating the Bit Boards

There are a number of primitive operations which involve the manipulation of information represented in bit board form. A bit board is one or more computer words which have a bit set in specific locations to represent the occurrence or nonoccurrence of a particular event. For example, eight 8-bit words can be used to represent the eight rows of a chessboard. Each bit cor-responds to one square. To represent the location of all White pawns, a bit is set (i.e., 1) in the proper locations and all other locations remain clear (i.e., 0). This method for representing and manipulating information is very useful in chess programming. For this reason, the first actions defined by our chess program are a set of procedures and functions for manipulating bit boards.

The actions represented are:

 (1) the intersection of two bit boards (ANDRS);
 (2) the union of two bit boards (IORRS);
 (3) the complement of a bit board (NOTRS);
 (4) setting a bit in a bit board (SETRS);
 (5) removing a bit from a bit board (CLRRS);
 (6) counting the number of bits that are set on a bit board (CNTRS);
 (7) making a copy of a bit board (CPYRS);
 (8) setting all bits to 0 (NEWRS);
 (9) shifting all bits in a particular direction (SFTRS);
(10) determining whether a particular bit is set (INRSTB);
(11) determining whether a bit board is empty, i.e., has no bit set (NULRS); and
(12) finding and reporting integer value for a location where a bit is set (NXTTS).

Since these routines are used repeatedly by the program, you can decrease the move calculation time quite a bit by implementing these primitives in assembly language. You will note that the function NXTTS is written in two ways: machine independent code, and code which is compatible only with the Control Data 6000 series machines. There are a number of places in the program where execution time can be enhanced by substituting machine dependent code which takes advantage of one or more special features of the hardware you are using. It would be helpful, also, if functions in Pascal could return an array or record instead of just a single value. There are many places in the program where this type of function would be more logical and more efficient than using a procedure (i.e., subroutine). If one were to consider the best of all possible worlds, it would be especially nice if the bit map manipulations could be compiled in line. With the Pascal arrangement, many of the procedure calls take as much time as the execution of the procedure.

Initial Steps

It is also necessary at the beginning of the program to provide values for the variables which define the chess environment, such as piece characteristics. For example, a White pawn is represented as LP for some purposes and as the letter A for other purposes. It has the color LITE, is not a sweep piece, and moves only in certain directions. It is necessary to initialize the translation tables, the constant, and variable 8×8 bit boards, and a number of other tables. The three routines which are called to do this when the program is first activated are INISYN, INIXTP, and INICON. A fourth procedure

(INITAL) is called by the main program to get ready for a new game. It will be called more than once if the user wishes to play more than one game.

During the development of the program, it is necessary to determine whether the individual procedures are functioning properly. To do this, it is helpful to have a few primitive print routines which can provide information about the internal workings in a form which is understandable to the programmer. These same routines are also called by the main input/output (IO) routine (READER) which appears later in the program.

One of these routines (PRIMOV) prints an internal representation of the machine's move. Another prints an 8×8 array representing the board (PRINTB). This consists of numbers for Black's pieces (Black pawn = 1; Black King = 6) and letters for White's pieces (White pawn = A; White King = F) with empty squares represented by a $-$. The PRINBB routine prints an 8×8 array representing a bit board. In this case an asterisk (*) stands for a square where a bit is set and a minus sign ($-$) stands for a square where a bit has not been set. An attack map is printed by PRINAM and this consists of 64 (one for each square) 8×8 bit maps in which an * stands for a bit which is set and a $-$ stands for a clear bit.

Other useful print routines include one which permits a user controlled pause during printing (PAUSER) and one which informs the programmer of the status of particular control switches (PRISWI). Because of Pascal's serial requirement (i.e., every procedure must be defined before it can be called by another procedure), these routines appear early in the program so that they can be used to test the procedures and functions which follow.

In Part 1 we mentioned incremental updating as an important feature of an efficient chess program. It is necessary to apply an evaluation function to the terminal nodes of the look-ahead tree. These evaluations, if they are at all sophisticated, require a substantial amount of detailed information about the position. Although it is possible to calculate this information separately for each evaluation, this is not a very efficient procedure, because adjacent nodes are almost identical. Most of the information which would be calculated each time would be redundant. A more efficient alternative is to "update" and "downdate" the relevant database incrementally as the program moves about in the look-ahead tree. This capability requires quite a bit of special programming.

Several primitive routines are very useful for this. If the move involves a capture, it is necessary to change the material balance function. The actual scoring itself is handled by MBEVAL. This routine is called either by MBCAPT or MBTPAC when a piece is lost (update) or gained (downdate); or by MBPROM or MBMORP when a pawn is promoted (update); or when a newly promoted pawn is demoted (downdate). There are other changes which are required in the database for both capture and noncapture moves. The new squares which are attacked by the piece need to be added to the attack maps (ATKFR, ATKTO, ALATK). This is done by ADDATK. The new square for the piece is added to the database by ADDLOC. The attacks of sliding pieces which are blocked by the newly moved piece are recomputed by CUTATK. The attacks of sliding pieces which are unblocked by vacating the former square are recomputed by PRPATK. The attacks which emanated from the piece on its former square are deleted by DELATK. These primitive routines are called by LOSEIT when a capture is involved or by MOVEIT otherwise. If the move affects castling status, the necessary database changes are made by PROACA and PROACS. If a pawn promotion is involved, PROMOT makes the necessary adjustments.

Move Generation

A major part of any chess program is the move-generation module. Because of the complexity of the game, many programs simply ignore some of the more unusual moves, such as Queenside castling, *en passant* pawn captures, or promotion of a pawn to a piece other than a Queen (i.e., underpromotion). This arrangement will suffice to play legal chess, but it may be costly if one of the omitted move types is highly desirable in a specific game situaton. In addition, an incomplete move generation facility prevents the machine from checking the legality of its opponent's moves.

Rather than being satisfied with an approximate solution, we have heeded the old maxim, "If a job is worth doing, it is worth doing well," and have implemented a move generator which permits the program to play a complete game of legal chess. As you can see from the listing, this requires extensive programming.

The first step in move generation is to create the database for the important features of the existing board configuration. This is done by CREATE. Once a move has been selected, it is necessary to change the database. This is done by UPDATE which makes use of the routines which were just described (e.g., ADDATK, CUTATK, ADDLOC, CLSTAT, PRPATK, DELATK, MOVEIT, LOSEIT). The move is placed on the move stack by GENONE. Special routines exist for generating moves which involve the promotion of a pawn (PWNPRO) and for generating the standard pawn moves (GENPWN). When a move is tried and produces an α–β cutoff, the program backs down the look-ahead tree and begins to explore moves at a different node. Several procedures are employed to downdate the database. These include the main routines RTRKIT and DNDATE, which are essentially the complement of MOVEIT and UPDATE. Two other procedures are also needed, one to unpromote a pawn (PAWNIT) and one to resurrect a captured piece (GAINIT). This set of routines permits the program to move about the look-ahead tree and incrementally update or downdate the database.

The executive routines which are responsible for move generation are GENFSL, which generates all legal moves from a set of squares, and GENTSL, which generates all legal moves to a set of squares. The rationale for having two routines is that we wish to generate the moves in stages. For example, captures should be searched first at each node (i.e., the capture heuristic). To do this, we identify the square locations of the opponent's pieces, and then call GENTSL to generate all capturing moves. These moves are searched before any other moves are generated. If one of these produces a cutoff the rest of the moves need not be generated at all. A third executive routine (GENCAS) generates all castling moves. These moves are generated after the captures if castling is still legal.

A fourth executive routine for move generation is GENALL. This procedure generates all legal moves and is used by the program to check the legality of the opponent's move. It is called by LSTMOV which makes a list of all the legal moves and each of these are compared with the opponent's move by YRMOVE (presented later). If the opponent's move is not on the list, the machine prints "illegal move." If the opponent's move is compatible with more than one of the moves on the list (e.g., P — R3 could be either P — QR3 or P — KR3), the machine prints the message, "ambiguous move." When the machine has completed its own move selection or has determined that the opponent's move is legal and not ambiguous, the move is actually made by THEMOV.

PART 3: CHESS 0.5 (continued)

Evaluating Terminal Positions

Another important aspect of any chess program is the function which provides a static evaluation of terminal positions in the look-ahead tree. In the present program, this routine also doubles as a preliminary scoring function for sorting moves at the first ply, at the beginning of the look-ahead search. Since the evaluation function is used repetitively in the search, efficiency demands that it be carefully engineered. We have left this task as an exercise for the reader. Our function presently includes only a few basic essentials.

The most important feature is material. We employ essentially the same function for this that is used by CHESS 4.5. A trade-down bonus is also incorporated, i.e., trade pieces but not pawns when ahead in material. A second feature which is considered is piece mobility. The mobility of Knights and Bishops is weighted more heavily than that for Rooks and Queens. Special credit is given to a King which is located in one of the four corner squares in each corner of the board, i.e., 16 squares total. This encourages early castling. Pawn structure is considered by providing a bonus for advancing the pawns in the four center files, for having a pawn near the King, and for having a pawn adjacent to or defended by another pawn. This indirectly penalizes isolated or backward pawns. There is a direct penalty if the square in front of a pawn is occupied. The position of the Rooks is considered by providing a bonus for placing a Rook on the seventh rank and for attacking another Rook of the same color (i.e., doubled Rooks). The executive routine for these assessments is EVALU8.

The Look-Ahead Procedure

The look-ahead procedure is controlled by an executive routine called SEARCH. Several subprocedures are also defined which handle specific tasks. NEWBST keeps track of the move which is currently thought to be best, and dynamically reorders the moves at the first ply level each time a new best-move is selected. MINMAX determines whether the move under consideration will produce an $\alpha-\beta$ cutoff. SCOREM is called into action when the program can find no legal moves at a node. It determines whether the position should be scored as a checkmate or as a stalemate. SELECT is responsible for move ordering at each node. It determines whether there are any more moves to be searched and if so, makes sure that they are generated in the correct order (i.e., captures, killers, castling moves, and then the remaining moves).

SEARCH incorporates a number of important features which make the look-ahead search more efficient. These include staged move generation, preliminary ordering scores, setting a narrow $\alpha-\beta$ window at the beginning of the search, conducting the search in an iterative fashion, and dynamically recording moves at the first ply as the search proceeds. Because of these features, the full-width search takes a long time instead of taking forever.

User Commands

For the user's convenience, the program should be able to respond to a few simple commands. Inputs to the program are processed by a lengthy routine, READER, which has many component subprocedures. The translation of the input string is handled by a group of routines: RDRERR, RDRGNT, RDRSFT, RDRCMP, RDLINE, RDRMOV, and RDRNUM. Each of the commands is executed by a separate routine.

When the human player wishes to terminate the game before it has reached its conclusion (e.g., when he is hopelessly lost and does not want to stay around to be crushed), he can simply type an END command and the ENDCMD routine will terminate the program. If the user simply wishes to start a new game, he can type INIT and the INICMD routine will set up for a new game. If the user would like to set up a specific position from the previous game or some other game, he can call the BOACMD routine, which will set up any position he desires. To use this instruction, the pieces are designated in the standard way (e.g., K, Q, R, B, N, and P) and the colors are designated by L for light and D for dark. The board is described by starting at the lower left-hand corner and listing, row by row, the 64 squares. Numbers are used to represent consecutive empty squares. The command to set up the position after 1 P−K4 P−K4 2 N−KB3 N−QB3 is: BOARD, LRNBQKB1 RPPPP1PPP5N24P34DP32N4PPPP1PPPR1BQKBNR.

If the human player is lazy or simply wishes to test the program, he or she can type GO and the machine will select a move. By repeatedly typing GO the user can sit back and watch the machine play against itself. The routine that handles this is GONCMD. To specify a value for selected program parameter variables, the player can use LETCMD. For example, the amount of time the machine spends calculating a move can be controlled by specifying a limit for the number of nodes to be searched. The command LET FNODEL = 1,000 will cause the machine to set a target value of 1,000 for the number of nodes to be searched. In this case it will not start another iteration if it has already searched 1,000 nodes. If the user is confused about the current board configuration, the command PRINT will activate PRICMD which calls PRINTB for a representation (8 × 8 array) of the board. For diagnostic purposes the user can also ask for other information. The routine PAMCMD is activated by PB and provides an 8 × 8 attack map for each of the 64 squares. The routine POPCMD is activated by PO and gives information concerning the side to move (White or Black), the *en passant* status after the last move, the present castle status, and the move number. If the user types PM, the routine PMVCMD will provide a list of all moves which are legal for the side to move in the current position. The command PL activates PLECMD which prints the value of a designated variable; for example, the user can determine the present limit for the number of nodes to be searched by typing PL FNODEL.

The user also has control over several switches. He can ask the machine to repeat (echo) each entry, to pause after 20 lines of output, and to reply automatically each time the opponent enters a move. These switches are set by the switch commands (e.g., SW EC OFF), and are processed by SWICMD. If the user wishes to manually alter one or more of the status conditions (e.g., side to move, move number, *en passant*, castling), this can be done by activating STACMD.

Notes on Notation

The program also processes standard chess notation. This is not strictly necessary. Many programs use their own convention for entering and reporting moves. A common procedure is to denote the squares using a number (1–8) for each row and a letter (a–h) for each column. A move is defined by listing the present square of the piece and then the destination square. For example, the common opening move, P − K4, would be e2e4. Moving the White Knight on the Kingside from its original square to KB3 would be g1f3. This convention works nicely but it forces an experienced chess player to learn a new system. Most would prefer standard chess notation.

Because there are multiple ways to express the same move in standard notation, the translation routine needs to be fairly sophisticated. Consider a position in which the White Queen's Rook is on its original square and the neighboring Knight and Bishop have been moved. A more which places the Rook on the Queen Bishop file can be designated as R − B1, R − QB1, R/1 − B1, R/1 − QB1, R/R1 − B1, or R/R1 − QB1. It is important that the program recognize that each of these character strings represents the same move. How is this done?

One way is to have the machine generate a list of all legal moves and then compare each of these with the move entered by the player. If this move matches one on the list, that move is noted. The rest of the list is then checked and if no more matches are found, the noted move is assumed to be the correct one. If no match is found, the machine prints "illegal move." If a second match is found (e.g., P − B3 matches both P − KB3 and P − QB3), the machine prints "ambiguous move." The process of translating the opponent's move into machine compatible form and checking its legality or ambiguity is done by YRMOVE. The process of translating the machine's move into standard notation is handled by MYMOVE. Both of these procedures call MINENG, which is responsible for constructing the appropriating character strings.

Final Thoughts

This completes our listing of our demonstration chess program. Despite the program's length, there are many desirable features which have been omitted. The reader with an interest in chess and programming should use this listing as a starting point for developing a program. The time required for move calculation can be reduced by writing machine-dependent code for some of the frequently used routines. There are also features which can be added to improve the level of play.

One useful addition would be an opening library. An effective technique for this is described by Slate and Atkin in their chapter in *Chess Skill in Man and Machine* (Frey, 1977a). An opening library provides the user with a challenging set of opening moves and directs the game into situations which are familiar to the experienced chess player. By including various options at the early choice points and using a random selection procedure, the programmer can insure that the machine will not always select the same move squence. The programmer can also give the user the option of specifying a particular opening against which he would like to practice. For important matches, the programmer can prepare surprise openings for the machine in order to gain a psychological edge on the opponent.

The second half of CHESS 0.5, written in Pascal. This portion of the program covers evaluation of terminal nodes, the look-ahead procedure, and user commands.

```
PROCEDURE EVALU8;                         (* EVALUATE CURRENT POSITION *)

VAR
  INTV : TV;                              (* SCORE *)


  FUNCTION EVKING                         (* EVALUATE KING *)
    (A:RS;                                (* KING BIT BOARD *)
     B:RS):TV;                            (* FRIENDLY PAWN BIT BOARD *)

  VAR
    INTS : TS;                            (* SCRATCH *)
    INRS : RS;                            (* SCRATCH *)
    INTV : TV;                            (* SCRATCH *)
  BEGIN
    ANDRS(INRS,A,CORNR);
    IF NULRS(INRS) THEN                   (* KING NOT IN CORNER *)
      INTV := 0
    ELSE
      INTV := FKSANQ;                     (* KING SAFELY IN CORNER *)

    INRS := A;
    IF NXTTS(INRS,INTS) THEN
    BEGIN
      ANDRS(INRS,ATKFR[INTS],B);          (* FIND PAWNS NEXT TO KING *)
      INTV := INTV + CNTRS(INRS)*FKPSHO;
                                          (* CREDIT EACH CLOSE PAWN *)
    END;

    EVKING := INTV;                       (* RETURN KING SCORE *)
  END; (* EVKING *)



  FUNCTION EVMOBL                         (* EVALUATE MOBILITY *)
    (A,B:TP):TV;                          (* PIECE TYPES TO EVALUATE *)

  VAR
    INRS : RS;                            (* SCRATCH *)
    INTS : TS;                            (* SCRATCH *)
    INTV : TV;                            (* SCRATCH *)

  BEGIN
    IORRS(INRS,TPLOC[A],TPLOC[B]);        (* MERGE PIECE TYPES *)
    INTV := 0;                            (* INITIALIZE COUNT *)
    WHILE NXTTS(INRS,INTS) DO             (* COUNT ATTACKS *)
      INTV := INTV + CNTRS(ATKFR[INTS]);
    EVMOBL := INTV;                       (* RETURN TOTAL ATTACKS *)
  END; (* EVMOBL *)



  FUNCTION EVPAWN                         (* EVALUATE PAWNS *)
    (A:RS;                                (* LOCATION OF PAWNS *)
     B:TE;                                (* PAWN FORWARD DIRECTION *)
     C:TR):TV;                            (* PAWN HOME RANK *)

  VAR
    INRS : RS;                            (* SCRATCH *)
    IHRS : RS;                            (* SCRATCH *)
    INTS : TS;                            (* SCRATCH *)
    INTV : TV;                            (* SCRATCH *)
  BEGIN
    SFTRS(INRS,A,S1);
    ANDRS(INRS,INRS,A);                   (* BIT SET FOR SIDE BY SIDE *)
    INTV := CNTRS(INRS)*FPFLNX;           (* SCORE PHALANX *)

    SFTRS(INRS,A,B1);
    ANDRS(INRS,INRS,A);                   (* BIT SET FOR PAWN DEFENSE *)
    INTV := INTV + CNTRS(INRS)*FPCONN;    (* CREDIT CONNECTED PAWNS *)

    SFTRS(INRS,A,B2);
```

```
ANDRS(INRS,INRS,A);
INTV := INTV + CNTRS(INRS)*FPCONN;   (* AND OTHER CONNECTED PAWNS *)

SFTRS(INRS,A,B);                     (* MOVE FORWARD *)
NOTRS(INRS,TPLOC[MT]);               (* OCCUPIED SQUARES *)
ANDRS(INRS,INRS,INRS);               (* BLOCKED PAWNS *)
INTV := INTV - CNTRS(INRS)*FPBLOK;   (* PENALIZE BLOCKED PAWNS *)

CPYRS(INRS,A);
WHILE NXTTS(INRS,INTS) DO            (* FOR EACH PAWN *)
  INTV := INTV +(ABS(ORD(C)-ORD(XTSR[INTS])))*FPADCR[XTSF[INTS]];
                                     (* CREDIT PAWN ADVANCEMENT *)

EVPAWN := INTV;                      (* RETURN PAWN SCORE *)
END;  (* EVPAWN *)



FUNCTION EVROOK                      (* EVALUATE ROOKS *)
  (A:RS;                             (* ROOK LOCATIONS *)
   B:RS):TV;                         (* SEVENTH RANK *)

VAR
  INTV : TV;                         (* SCRATCH *)
  INTI : TI;                         (* SCRATCH *)
  INTS : TS;                         (* SCRATCH *)
  INRS : RS;                         (* SCRATCH *)

BEGIN
  INTV := 0;                         (* INITIALIZE *)
  INRS := A;
  IF NXTTS(INRS,INTS) THEN           (* LOCATE FIRST ROOK *)
  BEGIN
    ANDRS(INRS,A,ATKFR[INTS]);
    IF NOT NULRS(INRS) THEN          (* ROOK ATTACKS FRIENDLY ROOK *)
      INTV := INTV + FRDUBL;         (* GIVE DOUBLED ROOK CREDIT *)
  END;

  ANDRS(INRS,A,B);                   (* ROOKS ON SEVENTH *)
  INTI := CNTRS(INRS);
  EVROOK := INTV + INTI*INTI*FRK7TH; (* CREDIT ROOKS ON SEVENTH *)
END;  (* EVROOK *)



BEGIN
  IF XTMV[JNTM]*MBVAL[JNTK] + MAXPS <= BSTVL[JNTK-2] THEN
                                 (* MOVE WILL PRUNE ANYWAY *)
    INTV := XTMV[JNTM] * MBVAL[JNTK]
  ELSE
  BEGIN
    INTV :=(  FWPAWN*(EVPAWN(TPLOC[LP],S2,R2)-EVPAWN(TPLOC[DP],S4,R7))
            + FWMINM*(EVNOBL(LB,LN)            -EVNOBL(DB,DN)         )
            + FWMAJM*(EVNOBL(LR,LQ)            -EVNOBL(DR,DQ)         )
            + FWROOK*(EVROOK(TPLOC[LR],XRRS[R7])
                                   -EVROOK(TPLOC[DR],XRRS[R2])        )
            + FWKING*(EVKING(TPLOC[LK],TPLOC[LP])
                                   -EVKING(TPLOC[DK],TPLOC[DP])       )
           ) DIV 64;
    MAXPS := MAX(MAXPS,ABS(INTV));
    INTV := XTMV[JNTM]*(MBVAL[JNTK]+INTV);
  END;
  IF SWTR THEN
  BEGIN
    WRITE(" EVALU8",JNTK,JNTM,INDEX[JNTK],INTV);
    PRIMOV(MOVES[INDEX[JNTK]]);
  END;
  VALUE[INDEX[JNTK]] := INTV;        (* RETURN SCORE *)
END;  (* EVALU8 *)



FUNCTION SEARCH                      (* SEARCH LOOK-AHEAD TREE *)
  :TM;                               (* RETURNS THE BEST MOVE *)
```

```
LABEL
  11,                                 (* START NEW PLY *)
  12,                                 (* TRY DIFFERENT FIRST MOVE *)
  13,                                 (* FLOAT VALUE BACK UP *)
  14,                                 (* FIND ANOTHER MOVE *)
  15,                                 (* BACK UP A PLY *)
  16;                                 (* EXIT SEARCH *)


  PROCEDURE NEWBST                    (* SAVE BEST MOVE INFORMATION *)
    (A:TK);                           (* PLY OF BEST MOVE *)

  VAR
    INTW : TW;                        (* MOVES INDEX *)
    INRM : RM;                        (* SCRATCH *)

  BEGIN
    BSTMV[A] := INDEX[A+1];           (* SAVE BEST MOVE *)
    IF A = AK THEN                    (* AT FIRST PLY *)
    BEGIN
      INRM := MOVES[BSTMV[A]];        (* SAVE BEST MOVE *)
      FOR INTW := BSTMV[A]-1 DOWNTO AW+1 DO
        MOVES[INTW+1] := MOVES[INTW]; (* MOVE OTHER MOVES DOWN *)
      MOVES[AW+1] := INRM;            (* PUT BEST AT BEGINNING *)
      BSTMV[AK] := AW+1;              (* POINTS TO BEST MOVE *)
    END
    ELSE
      IF NOT MOVES[BSTMV[A]].RMCA THEN
        KILLR[JNTK] := MOVES[BSTMV[A]];(* SAVE KILLER MOVE *)
  END;  (* NEWBST *)




  FUNCTION MINMAX                     (* PERFORM MINIMAX OPERATION *)
    (A:TK)                            (* PLY TO MINIMAX AT *)
     :TB;                             (* TRUE IF REFUTATION *)

  BEGIN
    MINMAX := FALSE;                  (* DEFAULT IS NO PRUNING *)
    IF SWTR THEN
      WRITE(" MINMAX",A,-BSTVL[A-1],BSTVL[A],-BSTVL[A+1]);
    IF -BSTVL[A+1] > BSTVL[A] THEN
    BEGIN
      BSTVL[A] := -BSTVL[A+1];
      NEWBST(A);                      (* SAVE BEST MOVE *)
      MINMAX := BSTVL[A+1] <= BSTVL[A-1];
                                      (* RETURN TRUE IF REFUTATION *)
      IF SWTR THEN
        WRITE(" NEW BEST. PRUNE: ",BSTVL[A+1] <= BSTVL[A-1]);
    END;
    IF SWTR THEN
      WRITELN;                        (* PRINT TRACE LINE *)
  END;  (* MINMAX *)




  PROCEDURE SCOREM;                   (* SCORE MATE *)

  BEGIN
    MOVES[INDEX[JNTK]].RMM := TRUE;   (* INDICATE MATE *)
    IF MOVES[INDEX[JNTK]].RMCM THEN   (* CHECKMATE *)
      VALUE[INDEX[JNTK]] := 64*JNTK - ZV
    ELSE                              (* STALEMATE *)
      VALUE[INDEX[JNTK]] := 0;
    IF SWTR THEN
      WRITELN(" SCOREM",JNTK,JNTW,INDEX[JNTK],VALUE[INDEX[JNTK]]);
  END;  (* SCOREM *)




  FUNCTION SELECT                     (* SELECT NEXT MOVE TO SEARCH *)
     :TB;                             (* TRUE IF MOVE RETURNED *)
```

```
LABEL
  21,                             (* NEW SEARCH MODE *)
  22;                             (* EXIT SELECT *)

VAR
  INTB : TB;                      (* RETURN VALUE *)
  INTK : TK;                      (* SCRATCH *)
  INTW : TW;                      (* MOVE INDEX *)
  INTW : TW;                      (* SCRATCH *)
  INTV : TV;                      (* SCRATCH *)


  PROCEDURE SELDON;               (* SELECT EXIT - DONE.
                                     CALLED WHEN NO FURTHER
                                     MOVES ARE TO BE SEARCHED
                                     FROM THIS POSITION.
                                     THE CURRENT POSITION MUST
                                     HAVE BEEN EVALUATED. *)

  BEGIN
    INTB := FALSE;                (* RETURN NO MOVE SELECTED *)
    IF SWTR THEN
      WRITELN(" SELECT",JNTK," END.");
    GOTO 22;                      (* EXIT SELECT *)
  END; (* SELDON *)


  PROCEDURE SELMOV                (* SELECT EXIT - SEARCH.
                                     CALLED WHEN A MOVE TO
                                     BE SEARCHED HAS BEEN
                                     FOUND. *)
    (A:TW);                       (* INDEX TO SELECTED MOVE *)

  BEGIN
    INTB := TRUE;                 (* RETURN MOVE SELECTED *)
    INDEX[JNTK+1] := A;           (* POINT TO SELECTED MOVE *)
    MOVES[A].RMSU := TRUE;        (* FLAG MOVE AS SEARCHED *)
    IF SWTR THEN
    BEGIN
      WRITE(" SELECT",JNTK,ORD(SRCHM[JNTK]),A);
      PRIMOV(MOVES[A]);
    END;
    GOTO 22;                      (* EXIT SELECT *)
  END; (* SELMOV *)


  PROCEDURE SELNXT                (* SELECT EXIT - NEW MODE.
                                     CALLED WHEN A NEW SEARCH
                                     MODE IS TO BE SELECTED *)
    (A:TH);                       (* NEW SEARCH MODE *)

  BEGIN
    INDEX[JNTK+1] := LINDX[JNTK]-1; (* RESET MOVES POINTER *)
    SRCHM[JNTK] := A;             (* CHANGE SEARCH MODE *)
    GOTO 21;                      (* EXECUTE NEXT MODE *)
  END; (* SELNXT *)


  PROCEDURE SELANY;               (* SEARCH ALREADY GENERATED
                                     AND NOT ALREADY SEARCHED *)

  VAR
    INTW : TW;                    (* MOVES INDEX *)

  BEGIN
    FOR INTW := INDEX[JNTK+1]+1 TO JNTW-1 DO
      IF NOT MOVES[INTW].RMSU THEN
        SELMOV(INTW);
  END; (* SELANY *)
```

```
BEGIN
21:   (* NEW SEARCH MODE *)
  CASE SRCHM[JNTK] OF

    M0:  (* INITIALIZE FOR NEW MOVE *)
         BEGIN
           MVSEL[JNTK] := 0;           (* CLEAR MOVES SEARCHED *)
           INTV := BSTVL[JNTK-2];      (* SAVE ALPHA *)
           BSTVL[JNTK-2] := -ZV;       (* INHIBIT PRUNING IN EVALU0 *)
           MAXPS := 0;                 (* INITIALIZE MAXIMUM POSITIONAL
                                          SCORE *)
           GENALL;                     (* GENERATE ALL MOVES *)
           FOR INTW := AW+1 TO JNTW-1 DO
           BEGIN
             IF UPDATE(MOVES[INTW]) THEN
             BEGIN
               INDEX[JNTK] := INTW;    (* POINT TO CURRENT MOVE *)
               EVALU0;                 (* SCORE POSITION *)
             END;
             ONDATE(MOVES[INTW]);
           END;
           BSTVL[JNTK-2] := INTV;      (* RESTORE ALPHA *)
           SORTIT(VALUE,MOVES,JNTW-1);
                                       (* SORT PRELIMINARY SCORES *)
           FOR INTK := AK TO ZK DO
             KILLR[INTK] := NULMV;     (* CLEAR KILLER TABLE *)
           IF SWTR OR SWPS THEN
             FOR INTW := AW+1 TO JNTW-1 DO
             BEGIN
               WRITE(" PRELIM",INTW,VALUE[INTW]);
               PRIMOV(MOVES[INTW]);    (* PRINT PRELIMINARY SCORES *)
               IF INTW/LPP = INTW DIV LPP THEN
                 PAUSER;
             END;
           SELNXT(M6);                 (* SEARCH ALL MOVES *)
         END;

    M1:  (* INITIALIZE AT NEW DEPTH *)
         BEGIN
           MVSEL[JNTK] := 0;           (* CLEAR MOVES SEARCHED *)
           IF JNTK > JNTK THEN
           BEGIN
             EVALU0;                   (* EVALUATE CURRENT POSITION *)
             INDEX[JNTK+1] := AW;
             BSTVL[JNTK+1] := -VALUE[INDEX[JNTK]];
             IF MINMAX(JNTK) OR (JNTK = ZK) THEN
               SELDON;                 (* THIS MOVE PRUNES *)
             SRCHM[JNTK] := M2;        (* CAPTURE SEARCH *)
           END
           ELSE
             SRCHM[JNTK] := M3;        (* CAPTURES IN FULL SEARCH *)
           GENCAP;                     (* GENERATE CAPTURES *)
           SELNXT(SRCHM[JNTK]);        (* CHANGE SEARCH MODE *)
         END;

    M2:  (* CAPTURE SEARCH *)
         BEGIN
           INTW := AW;                 (* BEST MOVE POINTER *)
           INTV := AV;                 (* BEST VALUE *)
           FOR INTW := LINDX[JNTK] TO JNTW-1 DO
             WITH MOVES[INTW] DO
               IF NOT RMSU THEN
                 IF ABS(XTPV[RMCP]) > INTV THEN
                 BEGIN
                   INTV := ABS(XTPV[RMCP]);

                   INTW := INTW;
                 END;
           IF INTW <> AW THEN          (* MOVE FOUND *)
             SELMOV(INTW)              (* SELECT BIGGEST CAPTURE *)
           ELSE
             SELDON;                   (* QUIT *)
         END;
```

```
M3:   (* FULL WIDTH SEARCH - CAPTURES *)
      BEGIN
        INTW := AW;                    (* BEST MOVE POINTER *)
        INTV := AV;                    (* BEST VALUE *)
        FOR INTW := LINDX[JNTK] TO JNTW-1 DO
          WITH MOVES[INTW] DO
            IF NOT RMSU THEN
              IF ABS(XTPV[RMCP]) > INTV THEN
                BEGIN
                  INTV := ABS(XTPV[RMCP]);

                  INTW := INTW;
                END;
        IF INTW <> AW THEN             (* MOVE FOUND *)
          SELMOV(INTW)                 (* SELECT BIGGEST CAPTURE *)
        ELSE
          IF NOT NULMVB(KILLR[JNTK]) THEN
          BEGIN
            INTW := JNTW;              (* SAVE CURRENT MOVES INDEX *)
            GENFSL(XRSS[KILLR[JNTK].RMFR]);
                                       (* GENERATE MOVE BY KILLER *)
            SRCHM[JNTK] := M4;         (* SET NEXT SEARCH MODE *)
            FOR INTW := INTW TO JNTW-1 DO
                                       (* LOOK AT MOVES BY KILLER *)
              IF KILLR[JNTK].RMTO = MOVES[INTW].RMTO THEN
                SELMOV(INTW);          (* SELECT KILLER MOVE *)
          END;
        SELNXT(M4);                    (* GO TO NEXT STATE *)
      END;

M4:   (* INITIALIZE SCAN OF CASTLE MOVES AND OTHER MOVES
          BY KILLER PIECE *)
      BEGIN
        GENCAS;                        (* GENERATE CASTLE MOVES *)
        SELNXT(M5);                    (* GO TO NEXT STATE *)
      END;

M5:   (* FULL WIDTH SEARCH - CASTLES AND OTHER MOVES BY KILLER
          PIECE *)
      BEGIN
        SELANY;                        (* SELECT ANY MOVE *)
        GENFSL(ALLOC[JNTK]);           (* GENERATE REMAINING MOVES *)
        SELNXT(M6);                    (* NEXT SEARCH MODE *)
      END;

M6:   (* FULL WIDTH SEARCH - REMAINING MOVES *)
      BEGIN
        SELANY;                        (* SELECT ANYTHING ON LIST *)
        IF MVSEL[JNTK] = 0 THEN
          SCOREM;                      (* SCORE MATE *)
        SELDON;                        (* EXIT SELECT *)
      END;

M7:   (* RESEARCH FIRST PLY *)
      BEGIN
        JNTW := LINDX[AK+1];           (* POINT TO ALREADY GENERATED
                                          MOVES *)
        MVSEL[AK] := 0;                (* RESET MOVES SEARCHED *)
        FOR INTW := AW+1 TO JNTW-1 DO
          MOVES[INTW].RMSU := FALSE;
                                       (* CLEAR SEARCHED BIT *)
        IF SWTR THEN
          WRITELN(" REDO ",JNTK,BSTVL[AK-2],BSTVL[AK-1]);
        SELNXT(M6);                    (* SEARCH ALL MOVES *)
      END;
  END;

22:   (* SELECT EXIT *)
  SELECT := INTB;                      (* RETURN VALUE *)
END;  (* SELECT *)

BEGIN  (* SEARCH *)
  BSTMV[AK] := AW;                     (* INITIALIZE MOVE *)
  INDEX[JNTK] := AW;                   (* INITIALIZE TREE *)
  MOVES[AW] := LSTMV;                  (* INITIALIZE MOVE *)
```

```
EVALU8;                              (* INITIAL GUESS AT SCORE *)
BSTVL[AK-2] := VALUE[AW] - WINDOW;   (* INITIALIZE ALPHA-BETA
                                        WINDOW *)
BSTVL[AK-1] := - VALUE[AW] - WINDOW;
JNTK := AK+1;                        (* INITIALIZE ITERATION NUMBER *)
WHILE (NODES < FNODE) AND (JNTK < MAX(ZK DIV 2, ZK-8)) DO
BEGIN

11:  (* START NEW PLY *)
     BSTVL[JNTK] := BSTVL[JNTK-2];       (* INITIALIZE ALPHA *)

12:  (* DIFFERENT FIRST MOVE *)
     IF NOT SELECT THEN
     BEGIN
       BSTVL[JNTK] := VALUE[INDEX[JNTK]];
       NEWBST(JNTK);
     END
     ELSE
     BEGIN
       IF UPDATE(MOVES[INDEX[JNTK+1]]) THEN
         GOTO 11                         (* START NEW PLY *)
       ELSE
       BEGIN
         DNDATE(MOVES[INDEX[JNTK]]);
         GOTO 12;                        (* FIND ANOTHER MOVE *)
       END;

13:  (* FLOAT VALUE BACK *)
     IF MINMAX(JNTK) THEN
       GOTO 15;                          (* PRUNE *)

14:  (* FIND ANOTHER MOVE AT THIS PLY *)
     IF SELECT THEN
       IF UPDATE(MOVES[INDEX[JNTK+1]]) THEN
         GOTO 11                         (* START NEW PLY *)
       ELSE
       BEGIN
         DNDATE(MOVES[INDEX[JNTK]]);
         GOTO 14;                        (* FIND ANOTHER MOVE *)
       END;
     END;

15:  (* BACK UP A PLY *)
     IF JNTK > AK THEN
     BEGIN (* NOT DONE WITH ITERATION *)
       DNDATE(MOVES[INDEX[JNTK]]);       (* RETRACT MOVE *)
       GOTO 13;
     END;

       (* DONE WITH ITERATION *)
     IF (BSTVL[AK] <= BSTVL[AK-2]) OR (BSTVL[AK] >= -BSTVL[AK-1]) THEN
     BEGIN  (* NO MOVE FOUND *)
       IF MVSEL[AK] = 8 THEN
       BEGIN (* NO LEGAL MOVES *)
         GOTO 16;                        (* GIVE UP *)
       END;
       BSTVL[AK-2] := -ZV;               (* SET ALPHA-BETA WINDOW LARGE *)
       BSTVL[AK-1] := -ZV;
       SRCHM[AK] := H7;
       JNTW := AK+1;
       GOTO 11;                          (* TRY AGAIN *)
     END;
     BSTVL[AK-2] := BSTVL[AK] - WINDOW;  (* SET ALPHA BETA WINDOW *)
     BSTVL[AK-1] := - BSTVL[AK] - WINDOW;
     JNTK := JNTK+1;                     (* ADVANCE ITERATION NUMBER *)
     SRCHM[AK] := H7;
   END;

16:  (* EXIT SEARCH *)
     SEARCH := BSTMV[AK];                (* RETURN BEST MOVE *)
END; (* SEARCH *)



PROCEDURE READER;                        (* READ INPUT FROM USER *)
```

```
LABEL
  11;                                     (* COMMAND FINISHED EXIT *)

VAR
  INRA : RA;                              (* SCRATCH TOKEN *)
  INTJ : TJ;                              (* ECHO COMMAND INDEX *)


  PROCEDURE RDRERR(A:RN);                 (* PRINT DIAGNOSTIC AND EXIT *)

  VAR
    INTJ : TJ;                            (* STRING INDEX *)
    INTN : TN;                            (* MESSAGE INDEX *)

  BEGIN
    IF NOT SWEC THEN                      (* ECHO LINE IF NOT ALREADY
                                             DONE *)
    BEGIN
      WRITE(" ");
      FOR INTJ := AJ TO ZJ-1 DO
        WRITE(ILINE[INTJ]);               (* WRITE INPUT LINE *)
      WRITELN;
    END;
    FOR INTJ := AJ TO JNTJ DO
      WRITE(" ");                         (* LEADING BLANKS BEFORE ARROW *)
    WRITELN("---");                       (* POINTER TO ERROR *)
    FOR INTN := AN TO ZN DO
      WRITE(A[INTN]);                     (* WRITE DIAGNOSTIC *)
    WRITELN;
    GOTO 11;                              (* COMMAND EXIT *)
  END;  (* RDRERR *)



  FUNCTION RDRGNT(VAR A:RA):TB;           (* GET NEXT TOKEN FROM COMMAND
                                             RETURNS TOKEN IN A.
                                             RETURNS TRUE IF NON-EMPTY
                                             TOKEN.
                                             A TOKEN IS ANY CONSECUTIVE
                                             COLLECTION OF ALPHANUMERIC
                                             CHARACTERS.
                                             LEADING SPECIAL CHARACTERS
                                             IGNORED. *)


  VAR
    INTJ : TJ;                            (* STRING INDEX *)

  BEGIN
    WHILE (JNTJ < ZJ) AND (ORD(ILINE[JNTJ]) >= ORD("+")) DO
      JNTJ := JNTJ+1;
    A := "          ";
    INTJ := AA;
    WHILE (JNTJ < ZJ) AND (INTJ < ZA) AND (ILINE[JNTJ] IN ["A".."9"]) DO
    BEGIN
      A[INTJ] := ILINE[JNTJ];             (* COPY CHARACTER TO TOKEN *)
      INTJ := INTJ+1;                     (* ADVANCE POINTERS *)
      JNTJ := JNTJ+1;
    END;
    RDRGNT := INTJ <> AA;                 (* RETURN TRUE IF ANYTHING
                                             MOVED *)
    WHILE (INTJ < ZJ) AND (ILINE[JNTJ] IN ["A".."9"]) DO
      JNTJ := JNTJ+1;                     (* SKIP REST OF TOKEN *).
  END;  (* RDRGNT *)



  PROCEDURE RDRSFT;                       (* SKIP FIRST TOKEN IN COMMAND
                                             LINE *)

  VAR
    INRA : RA;                            (* SCRATCH *)
    INTB : TB;                            (* SCRATCH *)
```

```
BEGIN
  JNTJ := AJ;                           (* INITIALIZE SCAN *)
  INTB := RDRGNT(INRA);                 (* THROW AWAY FIRST TOKEN *)
END;  (* RDRSFT *)




PROCEDURE RDRCMD                        (* TEST FOR AND EXECUTE COMMAND
                                           EXITS TO COMMAND EXIT IF
                                           COMMAND IS PROCESSED. *)

  (A:RA;                                (* POTENTIAL COMMAND KEYWORD *)
   PROCEDURE XXXCMD);                   (* PROCEDURE TO EXECUTE
                                           COMMAND *)

BEGIN
  IF INRA = A THEN
    BEGIN
      XXXCMD;                           (* EXECUTE COMMAND *)
      GOTO 11;                          (* EXIT *)
    END;
END;  (* RDRCMD *)




PROCEDURE RDLINE;                       (* GET NEXT INPUT LINE FROM
                                           USER *)

VAR
  INTC : TC;                            (* SCRATCH *)
  INTJ : TJ;                            (* STRING INDEX *)

BEGIN
  READLN;                               (* ADVANCE TO NEXT LINE *)
  INTJ := AJ;
  WHILE NOT EOLN AND (INTJ < ZJ) DO
    BEGIN
      READ(ICARD[INTJ]);                (* COPY INPUT LINE *)
      INTJ := INTJ+1;
    END;
  WHILE NOT EOLN DO
    READ(INTC);                         (* SKIP REST OF INPUT LINE *)
  WHILE INTJ < ZJ DO
    BEGIN
      ICARD[INTJ] := " ";               (* BLANK REST OF LINE *)
      INTJ := INTJ+1;
    END;
  ICARD[ZJ] := ":";                     (* SET END OF COMMAND *)
  JNTJ := AJ;                           (* RESET INPUT LINE POINTER *)
END;  (* RDLINE *)




FUNCTION RDRMOV:TB;                     (* EXTRACT NEXT COMMAND
                                           FROM INPUT LINE.
                                           RETURNS TRUE IF NON-EMPTY
                                           COMMAND. *)

VAR
  INTJ : TJ;                            (* STORING POINTER *)

BEGIN
  WHILE (JNTJ < ZJ) AND (ICARD[JNTJ] = " ") DO
    JNTJ := JNTJ+1;                     (* SKIP LEADING BLANKS *)
  INTJ := AJ;
  WHILE (JNTJ < ZJ) AND (ICARD[JNTJ] <> ":") DO
    BEGIN
      ILINE[INTJ] := ICARD[JNTJ];
      INTJ := INTJ+1;
      JNTJ := JNTJ+1;
    END;
  IF (ICARD[JNTJ] = ":") AND (JNTJ < ZJ) THEN
    JNTJ := JNTJ+1;                     (* SKIP SEMI-COLON *)
  RDRMOV := INTJ <> AJ;                 (* RETURN TRUE IF NON-EMPTY *)
  WHILE INTJ < ZJ DO
```

```
        BEGIN
          ILINE[INTJ] := " ";                 (* BLANK FILL LINE *)
          INTJ := INTJ+1;
        END;
        ILINE[ZJ] := ";";                      (* STORE COMMAND TERMINATOR *)
        JNTJ := AJ;                            (* PRESET COMMAND SCAN *)
    END;  (* RDRMOV *)


    FUNCTION RDRNUM:TI;                        (* CRACK NUMBER FROM COMMAND
                                                  LINE.  RETURNS NUMBER IF NO
                                                  ERROR.  EXITS TO COMMAND EXIT
                                                  IF ERROR. *)

    VAR
      INTB : TB;                               (* SIGN *)
      INTI : TI;                               (* VALUE *)

    BEGIN
      WHILE (JNTJ < ZJ) AND (ILINE[JNTJ] = " ") DO
        JNTJ := JNTJ+1;                        (* SKIP LEADING BLANKS *)
      IF ILINE[JNTJ] = "-" THEN
      BEGIN
        INTB := TRUE;                          (* NUMBER IS NEGATIVE *)
        JNTJ := JNTJ+1;                        (* ADVANCE CHARACTER POINTER *)
      END
      ELSE
      BEGIN
        INTB := FALSE;                         (* NUMBER IS POSITIVE *)
        IF ILINE[JNTJ] = "+" THEN
          JNTJ := JNTJ+1;                      (* SKIP LEADING + *)
      END;
      INTI := 0;
      WHILE ILINE[JNTJ] IN ["0".."9"] DO
      BEGIN
        IF INTI < MAXINT/10 THEN
          INTI := 10*INTI+ORD(ILINE[JNTJ])-ORD("0")
        ELSE
          RDRERR(" NUMBER TOO LARGE             ");
        JNTJ := JNTJ+1;                        (* ADVANCE *)
      END;
      IF ILINE[JNTJ] IN ["A".."Z"] THEN
        RDRERR(" DIGIT EXPECTED                 ");
      IF INTB THEN
        INTI := -INTI;                         (* COMPLEMENT IF NEGATIVE *)
      RDRNUM := INTI;                           (* RETURN NUMBER *)
    END;  (* RDRNUM *)


    PROCEDURE BOACMD;                          (* COMMAND - SET UP POSITION *)

    VAR
      INTM : TM;                               (* COLOR *)
      INTS : TS;                               (* POSITION ON BOARD *)


      PROCEDURE BOAADV(A:TI);                  (* ADVANCE N FILES *)

      BEGIN
        IF INTS+A < ZS THEN
          INTS := INTS+A
        ELSE
          INTS := ZS;
      END;  (* BOAADV *)


      PROCEDURE BOASTO(A:TP);                  (* STORE PIECE ON BOARD *)

      BEGIN
        BOARD.RBIS[INTS] := A;
        IF INTS < ZS THEN
          INTS := INTS+1;
      END;  (* BOASTO *)
```

```
BEGIN  (* BOACMD *)
  CLSTAT;                              (* CLEAR STATUS FLAGS *)
  LSTMV := NULMV;                      (* CLEAR PREVIOUS MOVE *)
  FOR INTS := AS TO ZS DO
    BOARD.RBIS[INTS] := MT;            (* CLEAR BOARD *)
  INTM := LITE;
  INTS := 0;
  REPEAT
    IF ILINE[JNTJ] IN ("P","R","N","B","Q","K","L","D","1".."8"] THEN
    CASE ILINE[JNTJ] OF
      "P": BOASTO(XTUMP(EP,INTM));
      "R": BOASTO(XTUMP(ER,INTM));
      "N": BOASTO(XTUMP(EN,INTM));
      "B": BOASTO(XTUMP(EB,INTM));
      "Q": BOASTO(XTUMP(EQ,INTM));
      "K": BOASTO(XTUMP(EK,INTM));
      "L": INTM := LITE;
      "D": INTM := DARK;
      "1","2","3","4","5","6","7","8":
          BOAADV(ORD(ILINE[JNTJ])-ORD("0"));
    END
    ELSE
      IF ILINE[JNTJ] IN ("A".."9"] THEN
      BEGIN
        FOR INTS := AS TO ZS DO
          BOARD.RBIS[INTS] := MT;
          CLSTAT;                      (* CLEAR STATUS *)
          RORERR(" ILLEGAL BOARD OPTION        ");
      END;
    JNTJ := JNTJ+1;
  UNTIL JNTJ = ZJ;
END;  (* BOACMD *)


PROCEDURE ENDCMD;                      (* COMMAND - END PROGRAM *)

BEGIN
  GOTO 9;                              (* END PROGRAM *)
END;  (* ENDCMD *)


PROCEDURE GOMCMD;                      (* COMMAND - GO M MOVES *)

BEGIN
  GOING := RORNUM;                     (* CRACK NUMBER *)
  IF GOING <= 0 THEN
    GOING := 1;
  GOTO 2;                              (* EXECUTE MACHINES MOVE *)
END;  (* GOMCMD *)


PROCEDURE INICMD;                      (* COMMAND - INITIALIZE FOR A NEW
                                          GAME *)

BEGIN
  GOTO 1;                              (* INITIALIZE FOR A NEW GAME *)
END;  (* INICMD *)


PROCEDURE LETCMD;                      (* COMMAND - CHANGE VARIABLE *)

LABEL
  21;                                  (* LET COMMAND EXIT *)

PROCEDURE LETONE                       (* TEST FOR AND SET ONE
                                          VARIABLE *)
  (A:RA;                               (* VARIABLE NAME *)
   VAR B:TI);                          (* VARIABLE *)

BEGIN
  IF A = INRA THEN
  BEGIN
```

```
    B := RDRNUM;                          (* GET VALUE *)
      GOTO 21;                            (* EXIT *)
    END;
END;  (* LETONE *)


BEGIN
  IF RDRGNT(INRA) THEN
  BEGIN
    LETONE("FKPSHO      ",FKPSHO);
    LETONE("FKSANQ      ",FKSANQ);
    LETONE("FMAXMT      ",FMAXMT);
    LETONE("FNODEL      ",FNODEL);
    LETONE("FPADQR      ",FPADCR(F1));
    LETONE("FPADQN      ",FPADCR(F2));
    LETONE("FPADQB      ",FPADCR(F3));
    LETONE("FPADQF      ",FPADCR(F4));
    LETONE("FPADKF      ",FPADCR(F5));
    LETONE("FPADKB      ",FPADCR(F6));
    LETONE("FPADKN      ",FPADCR(F7));
    LETONE("FPADKR      ",FPADCR(F8));
    LETONE("FPBLOK      ",FPBLOK);
    LETONE("FPCOMM      ",FPCOMM);
    LETONE("FPFLNX      ",FPFLNX);
    LETONE("FRDUBL      ",FRDUBL);
    LETONE("FRK7TH      ",FRK7TH);
    LETONE("FTRADE      ",FTRADE);
    LETONE("FTRDSL      ",FTRDSL);
    LETONE("FTRPOK      ",FTRPOK);
    LETONE("FTRPWN      ",FTRPWN);
    LETONE("FWKING      ",FWKING);
    LETONE("FWMAJM      ",FWMAJM);
    LETONE("FWMINM      ",FWMINM);
    LETONE("FWPAWN      ",FWPAWN);
    LETONE("FWROOK      ",FWROOK);
    LETONE("WINDOW      ",WINDOW);
    RORERR(" ILLEGAL LET VARIABLE NAME      ");
  END;
21:  (* LET COMMAND EXIT *)
END;  (* LETCMD *)


PROCEDURE PLECMD;                         (* COMMAND - PRINT VARIABLE *)

LABEL
  21;                                     (* PRINT LET COMMAND EXIT *)

PROCEDURE PRIONE                          (* TEST FOR AND PRINT VARIABLE *)
  (A:RA;                                  (* TEST VARIABLE NAME *)
   B:TI);                                 (* VARIABLE *)

BEGIN
  IF INRA = A THEN
  BEGIN
    WRITELN(A,B);
    GOTO 21;                              (* EXIT *)
  END;
END;  (* PRIONE *)


  BEGIN  (* PLECMD *)
    WHILE RDRGNT(INRA) DO
    BEGIN
      PRIONE("FKPSHO      ",FKPSHO);
      PRIONE("FKSANQ      ",FKSANQ);
      PRIONE("FMAXMT      ",FMAXMT);
      PRIONE("FNODEL      ",FNODEL);
      PRIONE("FPADQR      ",FPADCR(F1));
      PRIONE("FPADQN      ",FPADCR(F2));
      PRIONE("FPADQB      ",FPADCR(F3));
      PRIONE("FPADQF      ",FPADCR(F4));
      PRIONE("FPADKF      ",FPADCR(F5));
```

```
        PRIONE("FPADKB      ",FPADCR[F6]);
        PRIONE("FPADKN      ",FPADCR[F7]);
        PRIONE("FPADKR      ",FPADCR[F8]);
        PRIONE("FPBLOK      ",FPBLOK);
        PRIONE("FPCOMN      ",FPCOMN);
        PRIONE("FPFLNX      ",FPFLNX);
        PRIONE("FRDUBL      ",FRDUBL);
        PRIONE("FRK7TH      ",FRK7TH);
        PRIONE("FTRADE      ",FTRADE);
        PRIONE("FTRDSL      ",FTRDSL);
        PRIONE("FTRPOK      ",FTRPOK);
        PRIONE("FTRPWN      ",FTRPWN);
        PRIONE("FWKING      ",FWKING);
        PRIONE("FWMAJM      ",FWMAJM);
        PRIONE("FWMINM      ",FWMINM);
        PRIONE("FWPAWN      ",FWPAWN);
        PRIONE("FWROOK      ",FWROOK);
        PRIONE("WINDOW      ",WINDOW);
        RORERR(" ILLEGAL VARIABLE NAME        ");

21;   (* PRINT LET CCMMAND EXIT *)
  END;
END;   (* PLECMO *)



PROCEDURE PRICMO;                       (* COMMAND - PRINT BOARD *)

BEGIN
  IF RORGNT(INRA) THEN
    PRINTB(NBORD)
    ELSE
    PRINTB(BOARD.RBIS);
END;   (* PRICMO *)



PROCEDURE PAMCMO;                       (* COMMAND - PRINT ATTACK MAP *)

BEGIN
  WHILE RORGNT(INRA) DO
    IF INRA[AA] = "T" THEN
      PRINAM(ATKTO)
      ELSE
      IF INRA[AA] = "F" THEN
        PRINAM(ATKFR)
        ELSE
        RORERR(" ATTACK MAP NOT 'TO' OR 'FROM'");
END;   (* PAMCMO *)



PROCEDURE POPCMO;                       (* COMMAND - PRINT OTHER STUFF *)

VAR
  INTQ : TQ;                            (* CASTLE TYPE INDEX *)

BEGIN
  WITH BOARD DO
  BEGIN
    WRITELN(XTMA[RBTM]," TO MOVE.");
    WRITELN(RBTS," ENPASSANT.");
    WRITELN("MOVE NUMBER",RBTI);
    FOR INTQ := LS TO DL DO
      IF INTQ IN RBSQ THEN
        WRITELN(XTQA[INTQ]," SIDE CASTLE LEGAL.");
  END;
END;   (* POPCMO *)



PROCEDURE PMVCMO;                       (* COMMAND - PRINT MOVE LIST *)

VAR
  INTW : TW;                            (* MOVES LIST INDEX *)
```

```
BEGIN
  LSTMOV;                              (* LIST LEGAL MOVES *)
  FOR INTW := AW TO JNTW-1 DO
  BEGIN
    WRITE(INTW:4," ");
    PRIMOV(MOVES(INTW));
    IF INTW/LPP = INTW DIV LPP THEN
      PAUSER;
  END;
END;  (* PMVCMD *)



PROCEDURE SWICMD;                      (* COMMAND - FLIP SWITCH *)

LABEL
  21;                                  (* SWITCH OPTION EXIT *)


  PROCEDURE SWIONE                     (* PROCESS ONE SWITCH *)
    (A:RA;                             (* SWITCH NAME *)
     VAR B:TB);                        (* SWITCH *)

  VAR
    INTJ : TJ;                         (* SAVE COMMAND INDEX *)

  BEGIN
    IF INRA = A THEN
    BEGIN
      INTJ := JNTJ;                    (* SAVE CURRENT POSITION *)
      IF RDRGNT(INRA) THEN
      BEGIN
        IF INRA = "ON       " THEN
          B := TRUE                    (* TURN SWITCH ON *)
        ELSE
          IF INRA = "OFF      " THEN
            B := FALSE                 (* TURN SWITCH OFF *)
          ELSE
            JNTJ := INTJ;              (* RESTORE CURRENT POSITION *)
        PRISWI(A,B);                   (* PRINT SWITCH VALUE *)
      END
      ELSE
        PRISWI(A,B);
      GOTO 21;                         (* SWITCH OPTION EXIT *)
    END;
  END;  (* SWIONE *)


BEGIN  (* SWICMD *)
21:  (* SWITCH OPTION EXIT *)
  WHILE RDRGNT(INFA) DO
  BEGIN
    SWIONE("EC        ",SWEC);
    SWIONE("PA        ",SWPA);
    SWIONE("PS        ",SWPS);
    SWIONE("RE        ",SWRE);
    SWIONE("SU        ",SWSU);
    SWIONE("TR        ",SWTR);
    RDRERR(" INVALID SWITCH OPTION        ");
  END;
END;  (* SWICMD *)



PROCEDURE STACMD;                      (* COMMAND - STATUS CHANGES *)

LABEL
  21;                                  (* STATUS COMMAND OPTION EXIT *)
VAR
  INRA : RA;                           (* CURRENT TOKEN *)
  INTW : TW;                           (* SIDE BEING PROCESSED *)
```

```
PROCEDURE STAEPF                        (* PROCESS EP FILE *)
  (A:RA:                                (* TEST TOKEN *)
   B:TF);                               (* EQUIVALENT FILE *)

BEGIN
  IF A = INRA THEN
  BEGIN
    IF INTM = LITE THEN
      BOARD.RBTS := XTRFS[R6,B]
    ELSE
      BOARD.RBTS := XTRFS[R3,B];
    GOTO 21;                            (* EXIT STATUS OPTION *)
  END;
END; (* STAEPF *)



PROCEDURE STACAK;                       (* ALLOW CASTLE KING SIDE *)

BEGIN
  IF INTM = LITE THEN
    BOARD.RBSQ := BOARD.RBSQ + [LS]
  ELSE
    BOARD.RBSQ := BOARD.RBSQ + [DS];
END; (* STACAK *)



PROCEDURE STACAQ;                       (* ALLOW CASTLE QUEEN SIDE *)

BEGIN
  IF INTM = LITE THEN
    BOARD.RBSQ := BOARD.RBSQ + [LL]
  ELSE
    BOARD.RBSQ := BOARD.RBSQ + [DL];
END; (* STACAQ *)



PROCEDURE STADRK;                       (* SET BLACK OPTIONS *)

BEGIN
  INTM := DARK;
END; (* STADRK *)



PROCEDURE STAENP;                       (* SET ENPASSANT FILE *)

BEGIN
  IF NOT RDRGNT(INRA) THEN
  BEGIN
    CLSTAT;                             (* CLEAR STATUS *)
    RORERR(" ENPASSANT FILE OMITTED        ");
  END;

  STAEPF("QR          ",F1);
  STAEPF("QN          ",F2);
  STAEPF("QB          ",F3);
  STAEPF("Q           ",F4);
  STAEPF("K           ",F5);
  STAEPF("KB          ",F6);
  STAEPF("KN          ",F7);
  STAEPF("KR          ",F8);
  CLSTAT;                               (* CLEAR STATUS *)
  RORERR(" ILLEGAL ENPASSANT FILE       ");
END; (* STAENP *)



PROCEDURE STAGOS;                       (* SET SIDE TO MOVE *)

BEGIN
  BOARD.RBTM := INTM;
  JNTM := INTM;
END; (* STAGOS *)
```

```
PROCEDURE STALIT;                      (* SET WHITE OPTIONS *)

BEGIN
  INTM := LITE;
END;  (* STALIT *)



PROCEDURE STANUM;                      (* SET MOVE NUMBER *)

BEGIN
  BOARD.RBTI := RDRNUM;
END;  (* STANUM *)



PROCEDURE STAOPT                       (* TEST STATUS OPTION *)
  (A:RA;                               (* TEST OPTION *)
   PROCEDURE STAXXX);                  (* PROCEDURE TO EXECUTE IF
                                          EQUAL *)

BEGIN
  IF INRA = A THEN
  BEGIN
    STAXXX;                            (* EXECUTE PROCEDURE *)
    GOTO 21;                           (* EXIT STATUS OPTION *)
  END;
END;  (* STAOPT *)



BEGIN  (* STACMD *)
  CLSTAT;                              (* CLEAR STATUS *)
  INTM := LITE;                        (* DEFAULT SIDE WHITE *)
21:  (* STATUS OPTION EXIT *)
  WHILE RDRGNT(INRA) DO
  BEGIN
    STAOPT("D          ",STADRK);
    STAOPT("EP         ",STAENP);
    STAOPT("G          ",STAGOS);
    STAOPT("L          ",STALIT);
    STAOPT("M          ",STANUM);
    STAOPT("OO         ",STACAK);
    STAOPT("OOO        ",STACAQ);
    CLSTAT;
    RORERR(" INVALID STATUS OPTION        ");
  END;
END;  (* STACMD *)



PROCEDURE WHACMD;                      (* COMMAND - WHAT? *)

BEGIN
  WRITELN(MOVMS);                      (* PRINT LAST MESSAGE *)
END;  (* WHACMD *)



BEGIN  (* READER *)
11:  (* COMMAND EXIT *)
  WHILE NOT RDRMOV DO
    ROLINE;
    IF SWEC THEN                       (* ECHO LINE *)
    BEGIN
      WRITE("  ");
      FOR INTJ := AJ TO ZJ-1 DO
        WRITE(ILINE[INTJ]);
      WRITELN;
    END;
    IF ILINE[AJ+1] IN ["A".."W","Y","Z"] THEN
    BEGIN
      INRA := "          ";           (* EXTRACT KEYWORD *)
      INRA[AA] := ILINE[AJ];
      INRA[AA+1] := ILINE[AJ+1];
      RDRSFT;                          (* SKIP FIRST TOKEN *)
      RORCMD("BO         ",BOACMD);
```

```
            RORCMO("EN           ",ENDCMO);
            RORCMO("GO           ",GONCMO);
            RORCMO("IN           ",INICMO);
            RORCMO("LE           ",LETCMO);
            RORCMO("PB           ",PAMCMO);
            RORCMO("PO           ",POPCMO);
            RORCMO("PL           ",PLECMO);
            RORCMO("PM           ",PMVCMO);
            RORCMO("PR           ",PRICMO);
            RORCMO("ST           ",STACMO);
            RORCMO("SW           ",SWICMO);
            RORCMO("WH           ",WHACMO);
            RORERR(" INVALID COMMAND              ");
        END;
    END;  (* READER *)


    PROCEDURE MINENG                    (* GENERATE MINIMUM
                                           ENGLISH NOTATION *)
        (A:RM;                          (* MOVE TO NOTATE *)
         B:RA);                         (* LEADING COMMENT *)

    VAR
        INTN : TN;                      (* MESSAGE INDEX *)

        PROCEDURE ADDCHR                (* ADD CHARACTER TO MESSAGE *)
            (A:TC);                     (* CHARACTER *)

        BEGIN
            MOVMS[INTN] := A;           (* ADD CHARACTER *)
            IF INTN < ZM THEN
                INTN := INTN+1;         (* ADVANCE POINTER *)
        END;  (* ADDCHR *)


        PROCEDURE ADDSQR                (* ADD SQUARE TO MESSAGE *)
            (A:TS;                      (* SQUARE TO ADD *)
             B:RO);                     (* SQUARE SYNTAX *)

        BEGIN
            WITH B DO
            BEGIN
                IF RDPC THEN
                    ADDCHR(XTUC[XTPU[NBORD[A]]]);
                IF RDSL THEN
                    ADDCHR("/");
                IF ROKQ THEN
                    IF XTSF[A] IN [F1..F4] THEN
                        ADDCHR("Q")
                    ELSE
                        ADDCHR("K");
                IF RDNB THEN
                    CASE XTSF[A] OF
                        F1,F8: ADDCHR("R");
                        F2,F7: ADDCHR("N");
                        F3,F6: ADDCHR("B");
                        F4   : ADDCHR("Q");
                        F5   : ADDCHR("K");
                    END;
                IF RDRK THEN
                    IF JNTM = LITE THEN
                        CASE XTSR[A] OF
                            R1: ADDCHR("1");
                            R2: ADDCHR("2");
                            R3: ADDCHR("3");
                            R4: ADDCHR("4");
                            R5: ADDCHR("5");
                            R6: ADDCHR("6");
                            R7: ADDCHR("7");
                            R8: ADDCHR("8");
                        END
                    ELSE
                        CASE XTSR[A] OF
                            R1: ADDCHR("8");
```

```
            R2: AODCHR("7");
            R3: AODCHR("6");
            R4: AODCHR("5");
            R5: AODCHR("4");
            R6: AODCHR("3");
            R7: AODCHR("2");
            R8: AODCHR("1");
        END;
  END;
END;  (* ADDSQR *)



PROCEDURE ADDWRD                  (* ADD WORD TO MESSAGE *)
  (A:RA:                          (* TEXT OF WORD *)
   B:TA);                         (* LENGTH OF WORD *)

VAR
  INTA : TA;                      (* CHARACTER INDEX *)

BEGIN
  FOR INTA := AA TO B DO
    ADDCHR(A[INTA]);
END;  (* ADDWRD *)



FUNCTION DIFFER                   (* COMPARE MOVES *)
  (A,B:RM)                        (* MOVES TO COMPARE *)
   :TB;                           (* TRUE IF MOVES ARE DIFFERENT *)

VAR
  INTB : TB;                      (* SCRATCH *)

BEGIN
  INTB := (A.RMFR <> B.RMFR) OR
          (A.RMTO <> B.RMTO) OR
          (A.RMCP <> B.RMCP);
  IF A.RMPR = B.RMPR THEN
    IF A.RMPR THEN
      DIFFER := INTB OR (A.RMPP <> B.RMPP)
    ELSE
      IF A.RMOQ = B.RMOQ THEN
        IF A.RMOO THEN
          DIFFER := INTB OR (A.RMQS <> B.RMQS)
        ELSE
          DIFFER := INTB
      ELSE
        DIFFER := TRUE
  ELSE
    DIFFER := TRUE;
END;  (* DIFFER *)



PROCEDURE SETSQD                  (* DEFINE SPECIFIC SQUARE
                                     DESCRIPTOR *)
  (A:TS;                          (* SQUARE TO DESCRIBE *)
   B:RD;                          (* SYNTAX TO USE *)
   VAR C:SR;                      (* SET OF POSSIBLE RANKS *)
   VAR D:SF);                     (* SET OF POSSIBLE FILES *)

BEGIN
  C := (R1..R8);                  (* INITIALIZE TO DEFAULTS *)
  D := (F1..F8);
  WITH B DO
  BEGIN
    IF RDKQ AND RDN8 THEN
      D := (XTSF(A));
    IF (NOT RDKQ) AND RDN8 THEN
      CASE XTSF(A) OF
        F1,F8: D := (F1,F8);
        F2,F7: D := (F2,F7);
        F3,F6: D := (F3,F6);
        F4   : D := (F4);
        F5   : D := (F5);
      END;
```

```
        IF RORK THEN
          C := [XTSR[A]];
      END;
END;  (* SETSQO *)



    PROCEDURE MINGEN                    (* PRODUCE MINIMUM
                                           ENGLISH NOTATION FOR
                                           MOVES AND CAPTURES *)

      (A:RM;                            (* MOVE OR CAPTURE *)
       B:TI;                            (* FIRST SYNTAX TABLE ENTRY *)
       C:TI);                           (* LAST SYNTAX TABLE ENTRY *)

    LABEL
      21,                               (* EXIT AMBIGUOUS MOVE SCAN *)
      22;                               (* EXIT MINGEN *)

    VAR
      INTG : TG;                        (* PROMOTION PIECE *)
      INTI : TI;                        (* SYNTAX TABLE INDEX *)
      INTM : TM;                        (* MOVES INDEX *)
      INLR : SR;                        (* RANKS DEFINED ON LEFT *)
      INRR : SR;                        (* RANKS DEFINED ON RIGHT *)
      INLF : SF;                        (* FILES DEFINED ON LEFT *)
      INRF : SF;                        (* FILES DEFINED ON RIGHT *)

    BEGIN
      FOR INTI := B TO C DO             (* FOR EACH SYNTAX ENTRY *)
        WITH SYNTX[INTI] DO
        BEGIN
          IF A.RMPR THEN
            INTG := A.RMPP
          ELSE
            INTG := PB;
          SETSQO(A.RMFR,RYLS,INLR,INLF); (* SET SQUARE SETS *)
          SETSQO(A.RMTO,RYRS,INRR,INRF);
          FOR INTM := AW+1 TO JNTW-1 DO
            IF DIFFER(MOVES[INTM],A) THEN
              IF (NBORD(A.RMFR) = NBORD(MOVES[INTM].RMFR)) AND
                 (A.RMCP = MOVES[INTM].RMCP) THEN
                WITH MOVES[INTM] DO
                  IF (XTSR[RMFR] IN INLR) AND
                     (XTSR[RMTO] IN INRR) AND
                     (XTSF[RMFR] IN INLF) AND
                     (XTSF[RMTO] IN INRF) AND
                     ((RMPR AND (INTG = RMPP)) OR (NOT RMPR)) THEN
                    GOTO 21;            (* ANOTHER MOVE LOOKS THE SAME *)

          (* NO OTHER MOVE LOOKS THE SAME *)
          ADDSQR(A.RMFR,RYLS);          (* ADD FROM SQUARE *)
          ADDCHR(RYCH);                 (* ADD MOVE OR CAPTURE *)
          ADDSQR(A.RMTO,RYRS);          (* ADD TO SQUARE *)
          GOTO 22;                      (* EXIT MINGEN *)
      21: (* TRY NEXT SYNTAX *)
        END;
      22: (* EXIT MINGEN *)
    END;  (* MINGEN *)


BEGIN  (* MINENG *)
  MOVMS := "                          ";
                                        (* CLEAR MESSAGE *)
  INTM := AW+1;                         (* INITIALIZE MESSAGE INDEX *)
  ADDWRD(B,ZA);                         (* ADD INITIAL COMMENT *)
  ADDWRD("-       ",2);
  WITH A DO
  BEGIN
  IF RMOO THEN                          (* CASTLE *)
  BEGIN
    ADDWRD("O-O     ",3);
    IF RMQS THEN
      ADDWRD("-O      ",2);
  END
  ELSE                                  (* NOT CASTLE *)
    IF RMCA THEN                        (* CAPTURE *)
      MINGEN(A,SYNCF,SYNCL)
```

```
      ELSE                          (* SIMPLE MOVE *)
        MINGEN(A,SYNMF,SYNML);
    IF RMPR THEN                    (* PROMOTION *)
    BEGIN
      ADDCHR("=");
      ADDCHR(XTGC(RMPP));
    END;
    ADDWRD(".        ",3);
    IF RMCH THEN                    (* CHECK *)
    BEGIN
      ADDWRD("CHECK   ";5);
      IF RMMT THEN                  (* CHECKMATE *)
        ADDWRD("MATE    ",4);
      ADDCHR(".");
    END
    ELSE
      IF RMMT THEN                  (* STALEMATE *)
        ADDWRD("STALEMATE.",10);
  END;
END; (* MINENG *)



PROCEDURE MYMOVE;                   (* MAKE MACHINES MOVE *)

VAR
  INRM : RM;                        (* THE MOVE *)

BEGIN
  CREATE;                           (* INITIALIZE DATA BASE *)
  INRM := MOVES[SEARCH];            (* FIND THE BEST MOVE *)
  IF INRM.RMIL THEN
  BEGIN                             (* NO MOVE FOUND *)
    GOING := 0;
    IF LSTMV.RMCH THEN              (* CHECKMATE *)
      WRITELN(" CONGRATULATIONS.")
    ELSE                            (* STALEMATE *)
      WRITELN(" DRAWN. ")
  END
  ELSE
  BEGIN
    MINENG(INRM," MY MOVE ");       (* TRANSLATE MOVE TO ENGLISH *)
    WRITELN(MOVMS);                 (* TELL THE PLAYER *)
    THEMOV(INRM);                   (* MAKE THE MOVE *)
    IF SWSU THEN
      WRITELN(BOARD.RBTI,".",NODES," NODES.",BSTVL[AK]);
  END;
END; (* MYMOVE *)



PROCEDURE YRMOVE;                   (* MAKE PLAYERS MOVE *)

LABEL
  11, 12, 13, 14, 15,               (* SYNTAX NODES *)
  16,                               (* SYNTAX ERROR *)
  17,                               (* AMBIGUOUS MOVE *)
  18;                               (* NORMAL EXIT *)

VAR
  INTB : TB;                        (* VALID MOVE FOUND *)
  INTC : TC;                        (* CURRENT CHARACTER *)
  INTM : TJ;                        (* MOVES INDEX *)

  INTP : TP;                        (* MOVING PIECE *)
  INCP : TP;                        (* CAPTURED PIECE *)
  IFCA : TB;                        (* CAPTURE *)
  IFPR : TB;                        (* PROMOTION *)
  IFOO : TB;                        (* CASTLE *)
  IFQS : TB;                        (* QUEEN SIDE CASTLE *)
  INTG : TG;                        (* PROMOTION TYPE *)
  IFMV : TB;                        (* MOVE FOUND *)

  IFLD : TB;                        (* R, N, OR B ON LEFT *)
  IFLF : TB;                        (* K OR Q ON LEFT *)
  IFRD : TB;                        (* R, N, OR B ON RIGHT *)
  IFRF : TB;                        (* K OR Q ON RIGHT *)
```

```
INLF : SF;                                 (* FILES ON LEFT *)
INLR : SR;                                 (* RANKS ON LEFT *)
INRF : SF;                                 (* FILES ON RIGHT *)
INRR : SR;                                 (* RANKS ON RIGHT *)

INRM : RM;                                 (* THE MOVE *)

FUNCTION NCHIN                             (* DETERMINE IF NEXT INPUT
                                              CHARACTER IS NOT IN A GIVEN
                                              SET *)
  (A:SC;                                   (* SET OF CHARACTERS TO CHECK *)
   PROCEDURE YRMXXX)                       (* SEMANTICS ROUTINE TO CALL
                                              IF NEXT CHARACTER IS IN SET *)
   :TB;                                    (* TRUE IF CHARACTER IS NOT IN
                                              SET *)

VAR
  INTB : TB;                               (* SCRATCH *)

BEGIN
  INTB := NOT (INTC IN A);
  IF NOT INTB THEN
    BEGIN
      YRMXXX;                              (* EXECUTE SEMANTICS ROUTINE *)
      JNTJ := JNTJ+1;                      (* ADVANCE PAST CHARACTER *)
      WHILE (JNTJ < ZJ)
        AND ((ILINE[JNTJ] = " ") OR (ORD(ILINE[JNTJ]) > ORD(ZC))) DO
        JNTJ := JNTJ+1;                    (* SKIP BLANKS *)
      INTC := ILINE[JNTJ];                 (* NEXT CHARACTER *)
      IF (INTC = ".") OR (INTC = ";") THEN
        GOTO 15;                           (* EXIT SCAN *)
    END;
    NCHIN := INTB;                         (* RETURN TRUE IF CHARACTER IS
                                              NOT IN STRING *)
END;  (* NCHIN *)



PROCEDURE YRMMIT;                          (* FOUND A MOVE.  EXITS
                                              TO AMBIGUOUS MOVE IF THIS
                                              IS THE SECOND POSSIBLE MOVE.
                                              SAVES THE MOVE IN INRM
                                              OTHERWISE.  *)

BEGIN
  IF IFMV THEN GOTO 17;                    (* SECOND POSSIBLE MOVE *)
  IFMV := TRUE;                            (* FIRT POSSIBLE MOVE *)
  INRM := MOVES[INTW];                     (* SAVE MOVE *)
END;  (* YRMMIT *)



PROCEDURE YRMCOM;                          (* COMPARE SQUARES.  CALLS YRMMIT
                                              IF MOVES[INTW] MOVES THE
                                              RIGHT TYPE OF PIECE, CAPTURES
                                              THE RIGHT TYPE OF PIECE, AND
                                              MOVES TO AND FROM POSSIBLE
                                              SQUARES *)

BEGIN
  WITH MOVES[INTW] DO
    IF (XTSR(RMFR) IN INLR) AND
       (XTSF(RMFR) IN INLF) AND
       (XTSR(RMTO) IN INRR) AND
       (XTSF(RMTO) IN INRF) AND
       (NOT RMIL) AND
       (BOARD.RBIS[RMFR] = INTP) THEN
      IF RMCA = IFCA THEN
        IF RMCA THEN
          IF RMCP = INCP THEN
            YRMMIT
          ELSE
        ELSE
          YRMMIT;
END;  (* YRMCOM *)
```

```
PROCEDURE YRMCAP;                    (* SEMANTICS - CAPTURE *)

BEGIN
  IFCA := TRUE;
END;  (* YRMCAP *)



PROCEDURE YRMCAS;                    (* SEMANTICS - CASTLE *)

BEGIN
  IFOO := TRUE;
END;  (* YRMCAS *)



PROCEDURE YRMCPC;                    (* SEMANTICS - CAPTURED PIECE *)

BEGIN
  CASE INTC OF
    "P": INCP := XTUMP[EP,OTHER[JNTM]];
    "R": INCP := XTUMP[ER,OTHER[JNTM]];
    "N": INCP := XTUMP[EN,OTHER[JNTM]];
    "B": INCP := XTUMP[EB,OTHER[JNTM]];
    "Q": INCP := XTUMP[EQ,OTHER[JNTM]];
  END;
END;  (* YRMCPC *)



PROCEDURE YRMCQS;                    (* SEMANTICS - CASTLE LONG *)

BEGIN
  IFQS := TRUE;
END;  (* YRMCQS *)



PROCEDURE YRMLKQ;                    (* SEMANTICS - K OR Q ON LEFT *)

BEGIN
  CASE INTC OF
    "K": INLF := [F5..F8] * INLF;    (* KING SIDE *)
    "Q": INLF := [F1..F4] * INLF;    (* QUEEN SIDE *)
  END;
  IFLF := TRUE;
END;  (* YRMLKQ *)



PROCEDURE YRMLRB;                    (* SEMANTICS - R, N, OR B ON
                                        LEFT *)

BEGIN
  CASE INTC OF
    "R":  INLF := [F1,F8] * INLF;    (* ROOK FILE *)
    "N":  INLF := [F2,F7] * INLF;    (* KNIGHT FILE *)
    "B":  INLF := [F3,F6] * INLF;    (* BISHOP FILE *)
  END;
  IFLD := TRUE;
END;  (* YRMLRB *)



PROCEDURE YRMLRK;                    (* SEMANTICS - RANK ON LEFT *)

BEGIN
  IF JNTM = LITE THEN
  CASE INTC OF
    "1": INLR := [R1];
    "2": INLR := [R2];
    "3": INLR := [R3];
    "4": INLR := [R4];
    "5": INLR := [R5];
    "6": INLR := [R6];
```

```
        "7": INLR := [R7];
        "8": INLR := [R8];
      END
    ELSE
      CASE INTC OF
        "1": INLR := [R8];
        "2": INLR := [R7];
        "3": INLR := [R6];
        "4": INLR := [R5];
        "5": INLR := [R4];
        "6": INLR := [R3];
        "7": INLR := [R2];
        "8": INLR := [R1];
      END;
END;  (* YRMLRK *)



PROCEDURE YRMNUL;                       (* SEMANTICS - NULL *)

BEGIN
END;  (* YRMNUL *)



PROCEDURE YRMPCM;                       (* SEMANTICS - PIECE MOVED *)

BEGIN
  CASE INTC OF
    "P": INTP := XTUMP[EP,JNTM];        (* PAWN *)
    "R": INTP := XTUMP[ER,JNTM];        (* ROOK *)
    "N": INTP := XTUMP[EN,JNTM];        (* KNIGHT *)
    "B": INTP := XTUMP[EB,JNTM];        (* BISHOP *)
    "Q": INTP := XTUMP[EQ,JNTM];        (* QUEEN *)
    "K": INTP := XTUMP[EK,JNTM];        (* KING *)
  END;
END;  (* YRMPCM *)



PROCEDURE YRMPRO;                       (* SEMANTICS - PROMOTION *)

BEGIN
  CASE INTC OF
    "R": INTG := PR;                    (* ROOK *)
    "N": INTG := PN;                    (* KNIGHT *)
    "B": INTG := PB;                    (* BISHOP *)
    "Q": INTG := PQ;                    (* QUEEN *)
  END;
  IFPR := TRUE;
END;  (* YRMPRO *)



PROCEDURE YRMRKQ;                       (* SEMANTICS - K OR Q ON RIGHT *)

BEGIN
  CASE INTC OF
    "K": INRF := [F5..F8] * INRF;       (* KING SIDE *)
    "Q": INRF := [F1..F4] * INRF;       (* QUEEN SIDE *)
  END;
  IFRF := TRUE;
END;  (* YRMLKQ *)



PROCEDURE YRMRRB;                       (* SEMANTICS - R, N, OR B ON
                                           RIGHT *)

BEGIN
  CASE INTC OF
    "R": INRF := [F1,F8] * INRF;        (* ROOK FILE *)
    "N": INRF := [F2,F7] * INRF;        (* KNIGHT FILE *)
    "B": INRF := [F3,F6] * INRF;        (* BISHOP FILE *)
  END;
```

```
   IFRO := TRUE;
END;  (* YRMLRB *)


PROCEDURE YRMRRK;                         (* SEMANTICS - RANK ON RIGHT *)

BEGIN
   IF JNTM = LITE THEN
     CASE INTC OF
       "1": INRR := [R1];
       "2": INRR := [R2];
       "3": INRR := [R3];
       "4": INRR := [R4];
       "5": INRR := [R5];
       "6": INRR := [R6];
       "7": INRR := [R7];
       "8": INRR := [R8];
     END
   ELSE
     CASE INTC OF
       "1": INRR := [R8];
       "2": INRR := [R7];
       "3": INRR := [R6];
       "4": INRR := [R5];
       "5": INRR := [R4];
       "6": INRR := [R3];
       "7": INRR := [R2];
       "8": INRR := [R1];
     END;
END;  (* YRMLRK *)



BEGIN  (* YRMOVE *)
   INTB := FALSE;
   WHILE NOT INTB DO
   BEGIN
     READER;                              (* READ NEXT MOVE *)
     LSTMOV;                              (* LIST LEGAL MOVES *)
     IFCA := FALSE;
     IFPR := FALSE;
     IFOO := FALSE;
     IFQS := FALSE;
     IFLD := FALSE;
     IFLF := FALSE;
     IFRD := FALSE;
     IFRF := FALSE;
     INTP := MT;
     INCP := MT;
     INLF := [F1..F8];
     INRF := [F1..F8];
     INLR := [R1..R8];
     INRR := [R1..R8];

     INTC := ILINE[JNTJ];

     IF    NCHIN(["P","R","N","B","Q","K"],YRMPCM) THEN GOTO 14;
     IF    NCHIN(["/"]                   ,YRMNUL) THEN GOTO 11;
     IF    NCHIN(["K","Q"]               ,YRMLKQ) THEN;
     IF    NCHIN(["R","N","B"]           ,YRMLRB) THEN;
     IF    NCHIN(["1".."8"]              ,YRMLRK) THEN;
11:  (* LEFT SIDE DONE *)
     IF NOT NCHIN(["-"]                  ,YRMMUL) THEN GOTO 12;
     IF    NCHIN(["*","X"]               ,YRMCAP) THEN GOTO 16;
     IF    NCHIN(["P","R","N","B","Q"]   ,YRMCPC) THEN GOTO 16;
     IF    NCHIN(["/"]                   ,YRMNUL) THEN GOTO 13;
12:  (* RIGHT SIDE SQUARE *)
     IF    NCHIN(["K","Q"]               ,YRMRKQ) THEN;
     IF    NCHIN(["R","N","B"]           ,YRMRRB) THEN;
     IF    NCHIN(["1".."8"]              ,YRMRRK) THEN;
13:  (* PROMOTION *)
     IF    NCHIN(["="]                   ,YRMNUL) THEN GOTO 15;
     IF    NCHIN(["R","N","B","Q"]       ,YRMPRO) THEN GOTO 16;
     GOTO 15;
```

```
14:   (* CASTLING *)
      IF      NCHIN(("O","O")                    ,YRMNUL) THEN GOTO 16;
      IF      NCHIN(("-")                        ,YRMNUL) THEN GOTO 16;
      IF      NCHIN(("O","O")                    ,YRMCAS) THEN GOTO 16;
      IF      NCHIN(("-")                        ,YRMCQS) THEN GOTO 15;
      IF      NCHIN(("O","O")                    ,YRMNUL) THEN GOTO 16;
15:   (* SYNTAX CORRECT *)

      IF IFRF AND NOT IFRO THEN
        INRF := INRF * (F4,F5);                  (* SELECT K OR Q FILE *)
      IF IFLF AND NOT IFLO THEN
        INLF := INLF * (F4,F5);                  (* SELECT K OR Q FILE *)
      IFMV := FALSE;                             (* NO MOVE FOUND YET *)
      INTW := AW;                                (* INITIALIZE INDEX *)
      WHILE INTW < JNTW DO
        WITH MOVES(INTW) DO
        BEGIN
          IF RMPR = IFPR THEN
            IF RMPR THEN
              IF RMPP = INTG THEN                (* CORRECT PROMOTION TYPE *)
                YRMCOM                           (* COMPARE SQUARES AND PIECES *)
              ELSE
            ELSE                                 (* NOT PROMOTION *)
              IF RMOO = IFOO THEN
                IF RMOO THEN                     (* CASTLING *)
                  IF RMQS = IFQS THEN            (* CASTLING SAME WAY *)
                    YRMMIT
                  ELSE
                ELSE                             (* NOT CASTLING *)
                  YRMCOM;                        (* COMPARE SQUARES AND PIECES *)
          INTW := INTW+1;                        (* ADVANCE MOVES INDEX *)
        END;
      IF IFMV THEN                               (* ONE MOVE FOUND *)
      BEGIN
        MINENG(INRM,"YOUR MOVE ");               (* CONVERT TO OUR STYLE *)
        WRITELN(MOVMS);                          (* PRINT MOVE *)
        THEMOV(INRM);                            (* MAKE THE MOVE *)
        INTB := TRUE;                            (* EXIT YRMOVE *)
      END
      ELSE                                       (* NO MOVES FOUND *)
        WRITELN(" ILLEGAL MOVE.");
      GOTO 18;                                   (* EXIT *)

16:   (* SYNTAX ERROR *)
      WRITELN(" SYNTAX ERROR.");
      GOTO 18;                                   (* EXIT *)

17:   (* AMBIGUOUS MOVE *)
      WRITELN(" AMBIGUOUS MOVE.");
18:   (* EXIT *)
  END;
END;   (* YRMOVE *)



BEGIN   (* THE PROGRAM *)
  WRITELN(" HI.  THIS IS CHESS .5");
  INICON;                                        (* INITIALIZE CONSTANTS *)

1:   (* INITIALIZE FOR A NEW GAME *)
  INITAL (BOARD);                                (* INITIALIZE FOR A NEW GAME *)
  REPEAT
    REPEAT
      YRMOVE;                                    (* EXECUTE PLAYERS MOVE *)
    UNTIL SWRE;

2:   (* EXECUTE MACHINES MOVE *)
    REPEAT
      MYMOVE;
      IF GOING > 0 THEN
        GOING := GOING-1;
    UNTIL GOING = 0;
  UNTIL FALSE;

9:   (* END OF PROGRAM *)
END.
```

A second and somewhat more challenging project would be to develop a transposition table for the program. This requires the availability of unused memory (at least 8K bytes and preferably 16K or 32K bytes), an efficient hashing scheme, and a set of decision rules to select among positions when a collision occurs (i.e., two positions hash to the same address in the table). Another problem is that the use of a staged evaluation process and the $\alpha-\beta$ algorithm often provides an imprecise evaluation score (i.e., the machine has determined that a position was not optimal but has not invested the time to find out exactly how bad it was). If the programmer succeeds with the transposition table, however, move calculation will take 30–50% less time in most middle game positions and 60–90% less time in many endgame positions.

A third area for improvement is the evaluation function. Our program presently has only a rudimentary function. The reader should compare it with the one used by CHESS 4.5 which is described in detail by Slate and Atkin. Their evaluation function provides an excellent starting point for revising our present function. In Part 4 we will discuss the advantages of using a conditional evaluation function, i.e., one that changes depending on the stage of the game and on the presence of special features. One implementation of this strategy is the special endgame program described by Monroe Newborn in *Chess Skill in Man and Machine* (Frey, 1977a).

It is appropriate for us to add two important disclaimers at this juncture. Although we have carefully tested each of the routines in the program and played several chess games, it is still possible that there are a few minor bugs in the program. If you find one, a letter to one of us or to *BYTE* would be appreciated. Second, our chess program was written primarily for pedagogical purposes. For this reason it is not a production program and does not run very efficiently. If you are the competitive type, our program should provide many useful ideas, but you should not expect it to compete successfully in tournament play unless you make extensive modifications and additions.

A chess program has a tendency to grow and change its personality as the programmer becomes more familiar with each of its many limitations. It provides a constant challenge for those of us who are too compulsive to tolerate obvious weaknesses. In fact one must be careful not to become totally obsessed with this project. We do not wish any of you to lose your job or your spouse because of a chess program.

PART 4: STRATEGY IN COMPUTER CHESS

The chess program that we have presented in Parts 2 and 3 represents a modern implementation of the basic type A strategy described by Shannon (1950a). If run on a powerful computer, this type of program can play a reasonably good game of chess. Its major weakness lies in its inability to engage in long-range planning. In many middle and endgame positions, it will make seemingly aimless moves. Once it attains a position which optimizes the general heuristic goals of its evaluation function, it is faced with the prospect of finding a move which alters the position as little as possible. If the opponent is skillful in developing a long-range attack while not providing any immediate targets, the machine may simply shuffle its pieces back and forth until its position becomes hopeless. The absence of reasonable goal directed behavior is a common limitation of problem solving techniques which are based solely on forward search. The solution of this problem would have important implications for a wide variety of Artificial Intelligence tasks.

To play a strong game of chess, it is necessary to have a plan. To have a plan, however, the program must recognize specific patterns and relate them to appropriate goals. This, in turn, requires that the program have access to the detailed kind of chess knowledge which is characteristic of the skilled human player. Thus, we seem to have come round in a circle. In order to avoid selective searching, we have adopted a strategy which does not require very much chess knowledge. In examining the weaknesses of this approach, we discover that the forward search can only be truly successful if we have a clear idea of what we are looking for. To know what we are looking for, however, we must have more knowledge about chess.

So where do we go from here? The highly skilled players who are familiar with the chess programming literature (notably, Berliner, Botvinnik, and Levy) are unanimous in their enthusiasm for a selective search strategy. Berliner (1974), for example, advocates a procedure in which very small (for a computer) look-ahead trees are generated, e.g., 200–500 nodes. His idea is that the program should make an intensive analysis at each node "in order to ascertain the truth about each issue dealt with." Chess knowledge should play a primary role in directing the tree-search. The search itself would discover additional relevant information and this would provide an even more knowledgeable focus for the search. This procedure is analogous to the progressive deepening technique which de Groot discovered in the human Grandmaster and is the exact antithesis of the brute force (type A) strategy (see Part 1).

The efforts of the last decade have demonstrated that the selective search strategy is harder to implement than the full-width approach. In addition, full-width searching has consistently produced superior chess. Despite this, there is hardly anyone familiar with chess programming who does not believe that further progress depends on increasing the amount of chess knowledge in the program. The key question is not whether this should be done but how to do it. Since the selective search approach has not led to notable progress, perhaps it is time to consider a different approach.

We believe that a viable alternative exists which combines the proven virtues of the full-width procedure with the potential advantage of a goal-directed search. The central idea is the development of a unique evaluation function for each position. In addition to the general heuristics which are presently employed, evaluations should consider features which are germane to appropriate goals.

According to this plan, move selection would involve two separate stages. In the first phase, a static analysis of the position would be made in an attempt to discover key patterns. This process would involve a hierarchical analysis in which the features of the position would be compared with a general set of library patterns. Highly specific features would be identified and relevant chess-specific knowledge would be accessed. This information, including appropriate short-term and long-term goals, would be used to construct a conditional evaluation function which would assess the usual general features (e.g., Material, Mobility, King Safety, etc.) and also other features which are meaningful only in specific situations. Once the conditional evaluation function has been constructed, the second phase of analysis would begin, a conventional full-width tree-search employing the special evaluation function.

The first phase of this process would rely heavily on domain specific knowledge (i.e., information about chess). It would require a pattern recognition facility and an organizational plan for storing a vast amount of chess knowledge in a manner conducive to rapid retrieval. When this first phase was successful in identifying appropriate goals and producing relevant modifications in the evaluation function, the full-width search which followed would select a move which was thematic with the appropriate goal. If the first phase were unable to identify a key feature, the evaluation function would employ the same general heuristics which it presently uses. For this reason, the pattern recognition and information retrieval modules can be gradually implemented without a lengthy period in which serious blunders are frequent occurrences. This is a major advantage that the conditional evaluation function has in comparison to a selective search strategy.

Chess Structure

To implement a conditional evaluation function, it is necessary to develop a hierarchical descriptive structure for chess. At the top level, one can make the conventional distinctions between the opening, the middle game, and the endgame. Within each of these three major divisions, there would be many specific subdivisions. Within each subdivision, there would be many specific variations.

The opening has three major themes: to develop a pawn structure which is favorable for you but unfavorable for your opponent; to increase the mobility of your minor pieces and limit the mobility of your opponent's minor pieces; and to castle as soon as possible and delay your opponent's opportunity to castle. These general goals provide a framework for evaluating specific variations. They do not provide a specific prescription for selecting a move because a sequence of moves which is thematic with these goals may have a tactical refutation. An apparently good move may not work because it loses material. For this reason, general principles are best applied at the terminal points of a look-ahead search rather than being used as a checklist for selecting the most thematic move as advocated by Church and Church in Frey (1977a).

The tournament player who knows opening theory as well as many specific move variations will have a clear advantage over an opponent who knows the general principles but is not familiar with the specific variations. For this reason, tournament players and good chess programs rely on a library of memorized opening variations. The contestant who has carefully planned his opening variations can often gain an important advantage early in the game. To maximize the benefit of a well-prepared opening library, it is also necessary to continue the general theme of the opening once the predigested move sequences have been exhausted. At this stage it is necessary to have a conditional evaluation function. When the machine leaves the library and starts to use a look-ahead procedure to calculate its move, it should use an evaluation function that augments general opening principles with special goals which are thematic with that type of opening.

A portion of the work required to implement this proposal has already been started. Chess specialists have prepared highly detailed analyses of specific opening variations and have developed well-defined rules for categorizing different move sequences into specific subdivisions. For example, a game which starts: 1 P−K4 P−K3 is labeled as the French defense. If the game continues 2 P−Q4 P−Q4 3 N−QB3 B−N5, it is called the Nimzovich (or Winawer) variation of the French defense. If it continues 2 P−Q4 P−Q4 3 N−QB3 N−KB3, the game is labeled as the classical variation. A continuation of 2 P−Q4 P−Q4 3 N−QB3 P × P is called either the Rubinstein variation or the Burn variation depending upon subsequent moves. A different approach develops from 2 P−Q4 P−Q4 3 N−Q2, which is labeled as the Tarrasch variation. And there are many more. The important point, however, is that each of these variations can be objectively identified, and that for each there are well-developed strategical ideas and specific immediate goals. These ideas can be stored in the opening library and can be retrieved when the machine leaves the library. In addition to general opening heuristics, the evaluation function would reflect the specific theoretical ideas which are appropriate to the particular opening at hand. In principle, this idea can be implemented without difficulty. In practice, however, a tremendous amount of chess knowledge is needed and hours and hours of effort are required. To our knowledge no serious attempt has yet been made to implement this strategy. The information on opening theory is needed only once during a game and thus could be stored on disk, since rapid access is not critical.

Pattern Recognition and the Middle Game

From a conceptual point of view, the application of chess knowledge to the evaluation function in the middle game is much more challenging. In this case, pattern recognition becomes an important ingredient. In implementing a goal oriented move selection strategy, Church and Church (1977) limited their middle game strategy to either a Kingside attack, a Queenside attack, or concentration on a weak point (i.e., a target). The Kingside or Queenside attack is triggered when the machine determines that it has superior forces on one side or the other. This determination can be based on who controls key squares. In calculating the power relationship of different pieces over given squares, it is important to note that less valuable pieces exert more control than valuable pieces. A pawn has greater control over territory than a Queen because it is harder to dislodge. If an attack on one side or the other is deemed appropriate, the evaluation function can be modified to give an extra bonus for moves which augment the attack on that side and for moves which increase the pressure on critical squares.

Pattern analysis is also important in detecting an appropriate target. There are several well-known chess relations which provide obvious targets for attack. One is the *backward pawn* which is prevented from advancing by a pawn or a minor piece. Another natural target is the minor piece which is pinned to the King or Queen. The third is the overworked piece, a key element in the defense against two or more different attacks. If the latter is removed in an exchange, the pieces it is defending will be open for attack. A fourth natural target is a square which would permit a Knight to fork two major pieces (i.e., Rook, Queen, King) or a Bishop to skewer two major pieces. If the machine threatens to control that square and to locate an appropriate piece there, the opponent will be forced to devise a defense. Once one of these targets has been detected, the evaluation function can be modified to give a bonus for moves directed at the target. In addition, a plan might be devised to encourage the use of a decoy (a pawn or minor piece which is sacrificed to bring an important piece to a particular square) or to capture a piece which is serving an important defensive function.

A Chess "Snapshot"

In the past, programmers have attempted to implement such plans by using a selective search (e.g., Berliner, Zobrist, and Carlson) or by using no search at all (e.g., Church and Church). Zobrist and Carlson (1973) have developed an innovative technique in which "computer snapshots" are devised which summarize important piece relationships such as attacks, pins, skewers, forks, etc., which presently exist in the given position, or which could occur after one or two moves. Each snapshot is given a weight based on the relative values of the pieces involved and the location of the pieces in respect to the opposing King and the center of the board. The weighted snapshots are then used to select moves for inclusion in a Shannon type B tree-search. This procedure provides considerable goal direction to the move selection process.

Although the Zobrist-Carlson snapshot procedure has much to offer (including a highly efficient bit map implementation strategy), it incorporates a common problem shared by all selective search techniques. Occasionally an important continuation is overlooked and this results in the selection of an inappropriate move which may be a gross blunder. By implementing the plans derived from the computer snapshots in the form of a conditional evaluation function, instead, the program can benefit from goal directedness without risking the oversights which are characteristic of selective searching. In this way, the machine can retain the benefits of the full-width search and at the same time engage in strategic planning.

There is a special class of positions for which this approach is especially appropriate. In his thesis at Carnegie–Mellon University Berliner described a special problem, the horizon effect, which plagues the conventional look-ahead approach (see Frey, 1977a, pages 73–77). One version of this problem involves a piece which is trapped and cannot be saved. Forward searching programs often engage in a bit of foolishness by making forcing but poor moves (such as attacking pieces with pawns or sacrificing pawns for no advantage) which delay the capture of the trapped piece and push its eventual loss beyond the horizon of the tree search. By doing this, the program erroneously concludes that the piece is safe, when in reality the planned move sequence weakens a reasonable position and is still insufficient to save the piece. In this type of situation, the trapped piece should be given up for lost and the program should do its best to take advantage of the tempo required by the opponent to capture the piece. A piece whose time has come is sometimes referred to as a desperado. The only option available is to make the opponent pay as dearly as possible for the capture. If the desperado can be traded for a pawn or a piece of lesser value, this is preferable to being given up for nothing.

This strategy can be implemented with a conditional evaluation function by simply assuming that the trapped piece has a material value of zero. This change would cause the search process to trade the piece for the highest valued candidate that can be found. This is obviously better than having the program engage in useless sacrifices of position and material in a hopeless attempt to resurrect a lost piece. The key element to this implementation is the ability to determine when a piece is truly lost and can be labeled as a desperado. This is a very difficult problem even for a very sophisticated pattern analysis facility.

Endgame Considerations

The most interesting application of the conditional evaluation function is in the endgame. Because endgame strategy is highly dependent on the specific characteristics of the position, a general purpose evaluation function is not very effective. It is necessary to understand what is required in a given position and then select moves which are clearly directed at an appropriate goal. Church and Church list three common goals in the endgame: to mate the opponent's King, capture a weak pawn, or promote a pawn. In this case, pattern analysis is important. First the machine must be able to identify the position as one belonging to the endgame. Then it has to determine whether a mate attempt is reasonable or whether a pawn can be captured or promoted. Church and Church (see Frey, 1977a) describe a general strategy for identifying and capturing a weak pawn. Although their approach does not involve a forward tree-search, the specific techniques which they describe can be adapted to the full-width search strategy. Let us consider several specific endgame positions involving either a mate, a pawn capture, or a pawn promotion.

For a number of mating situations, a specific algorithm (step-by-step instructions) or a complete lookup table can be developed to produce mate in a minimum number of moves. Typical applications would be King and Queen vs. King; King and Rook vs. King; and King, Bishop, and Knight vs. King. The mating algorithm for each case would include rules for assigning the potential piece relationships into a few general categories, and a prescription for an appropriate type of move for each category. This approach requires no search. A second approach involving a lookup table is even more explicit. An appropriate move is stored in a table for every possible piece configuration. To play the mate perfectly, the machine uses the position to determine an address in the table and then simply reads the correct move.

Both of these procedures are perfectly feasible and avoid many problems which can be encountered in the endgame. The limitation of this approach is that there are a very large number of mating situations and a tremendous amount of work would be required to make a detailed analysis of each one. In addition, this strategy requires the storage of a great deal of information which would be used only infrequently.

A third approach, and one which is thematic with the idea of conditional evaluations, is to make a small modification in the evaluation function for each specific mating situation. The notion is that a shallow search combined with a few key ideas should suffice to produce a mate in a reasonable number of moves. With King and Queen or King and Rook vs. King, it is sufficient for the program to "know" that the defending King must be forced to the edge. To do this, the program simply needs to add bonus points to the evaluation function when the defending King is near the edge. The size of the bonus should be a linear function of closeness to the edge. This modification of the evaluation function causes the minimax search to select a pathway in the look-ahead tree which forces the defending King to the edge.

With King, Bishop, and Knight against King, the job is slightly more complicated. In this case it is important to know that the defending King must be forced to one of the two corners having the same color as the Bishop's squares. The trick is to add a large bonus when the defending King is on the appropriate corner squares and a smaller credit when it is near these corners. This modification will cause the minimax procedure to find a sequence of moves which forces the defending King into one of the appropriate corners. The general theme is that the full-width search is a powerful device by itself and that the addition of a small amount of chess knowledge is sufficient to produce the desired outcome.

Kings and Pawns in the Endgame

Some of the most challenging positions in the endgame involve only Kings and pawns. Many of these require an approach which is more sophisticated than those described previously. Consider, for example, the position diagrammed in Figure 1. This is a modification of a position presented in Berliner's thesis which demonstrates one of the major weaknesses of a full-width forward search. White has a pawn on f6 which could advance and be promoted if the Black King were out of the way. [*Algebraic notation is used throughout this article to designate chessboard squares. The horizontal rows (ranks) are numbered from 1–8, starting at the bottom (White). The files are labeled a–h from left to right.*] To win, White must do an end run with his King and bring it to the aid of the pawn. Since Black cannot attack White's pawns on c3 or g5 without leaving the passed pawn, he is helpless to stop White's maneuver. Although this analysis is obvious at a glance to an experienced player, a program that discovers truth by doing a full-width search is faced with a difficult problem. In order to determine that the King can force promotion of the pawn, White must complete a look-ahead search of approximately 35 plies. This is beyond the scope of even the most powerful computer. If the machine employs a general purpose algorithm which encourages the King to centralize its position during the endgame, it will search for a pathway which eventually places it on its present square (f4) or one of the neighboring squares (e3 or f3). Because of this, the correct sequence of moves would never be discovered.

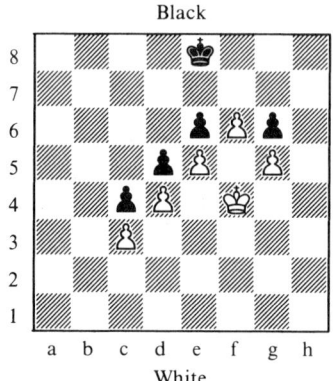

Black

White

Figure 1. Chess position which demonstrates a weakness of the *full-width forward search*. In this example, White has a pawn on square f6 which could advance and be promoted if the Black King were out of the way. To win, the White King must come to the aid of the pawn. Since Black cannot attack White's pawns on c3 or g5 without leaving the passed pawn, he is helpless to stop White's maneuver. Although this analysis is obvious to an experienced player, a program using a full-width search would have to search its decision tree to a depth of 35 plies (i.e., 35 half-moves; a ply is defined as a move by one side) in order to come to same conclusion.

In order for a full-width search to make progress in this type of position, the evaluation function must produce goal direction. One way to do this is to provide a bonus for moves which reduce the distance between the White King and the passed pawn. A secondary goal is to reduce the distance between the White King and any Black pawns which are not defended by another pawn. A tertiary goal is to centralize the White King. The first step in developing a specific implementation of this plan is to identify the territory which is denied to the White King. For this purpose, we wish to determine which squares are controlled by the pawns. The White King cannot move to a square occupied by one of is own pawns, nor can it move to a square attacked by an opposing pawn. Figure 2 presents a map of the position with each of the forbidden squares darkened. The location of these "taboo" squares provides the defining boundaries for potential access routes to the desired goals. The second step in implementing this plan is to use a technique described by Church and Church. Starting at each goal object, work backward toward the attacking piece(s). In our case, we are interested in creating a reward gradient which encourages the White King to approach its own passed pawn and the target pawns. To do this, we consider one goal object at a time. All passed pawns are identified. In our example, only the White pawn at f6 qualifies. The two squares diagonally in front of it (e7 and g7) are each credited with 8 "points" each. All squares immediately adjacent to these squares (but not including squares inaccessible to the White King) are credited with 7 points. Next all squares adjacent to these squares (excluding inaccessible squares) are credited with 6 points. This process is continued until we run out of squares or until we have assigned all credits down to and including 1.

The next step in the process is to identify Black pawns which are not

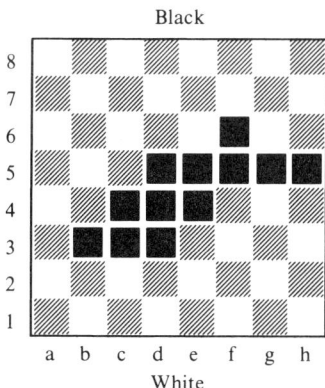

Black

White

Figure 2. Forbidden squares in the Figure 1 position used to help White (the computer) evaluate the position more efficiently. The White King cannot move to a square occupied by one of its own pawns, nor can it move to a square attacked by an opposing pawn. All of these squares are darkened in the figure. This diagram is used in implementing the goal directed technique described by Church and Church (see Figure 3).

defended by other pawns (i.e., targets). In this case, the pawns at e6 and g6 qualify. Credit these two squares and the adjacent ones with 5 points each, excluding darkened squares. Next, credit squares adjacent to these with 4 points. Continue this process until all available squares have been exhausted or until the value of 1 has been assigned. This process is executed independently for each target pawn. The last step involves credit for centralization. The four most central squares (d4, d5, e4, e5) are credited with 3 points. The squares which surround these squares are credited with 2 points. The squares which surround those squares are credited with 1 point. Points are then removed from any square which is inaccessible to the White King. When this process has been completed, the credits are totaled for each square to provide a bonus map for the White King. This map is presented in Figure 3. By applying this bonus map to the terminal positions of the look-ahead search, the evaluation process will select a move sequence which causes the White King to gravitate in the proper direction. In fact, the correct sequence of moves will be selected even if White is restricted to a 5-ply search each time a move is selected. The bonus map, though simple in concept, has a tremendously beneficial effect.

There is an additional point which needs consideration. In our exposition, we have assumed that the pawns remained stationary. If a pawn were to move, the bonus map would have to be changed. This is not a major problem,

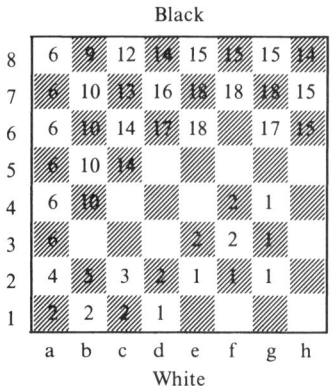

Black

	a	b	c	d	e	f	g	h
8	6		12		15		15	
7		10		16		18		15
6	6		14		18		17	
5		10						
4	6						1	
3						2		
2	4		3		1		1	
1		2		1				

White

Figure 3. Bonus map for the White King in the position of Figure 1, based on a technique described by Church and Church (1977). A goal is established for a particular attacking piece, in this case the White King, and an iterative numerical technique is used to implement it. The goal is to encourage the White King to approach its own passed pawn and the target pawns. (A target pawn is an enemy pawn not defended by other pawns.) Numerical figures of merit are assigned to strategic squares close to White's passed pawn and Black's undefended pawns. Points are also awarded or subtracted for positional characteristics such as centralization of squares, etc. A type of flow algorithm assigns lower and lower values to squares in direct proportion to their distances from the strategic squares, avoiding any forbidden squares. The resulting map of numbered squares enables the King to find the right pathway by constantly searching for ascending values of squares whenever possible.

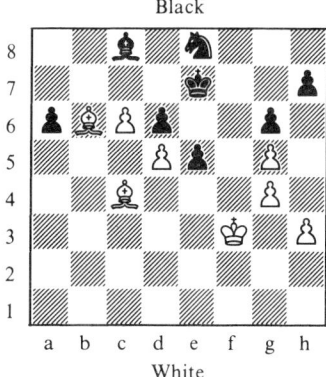

Figure 4. Another endgame position, analyzed by the method of Church and Church in Figures 5 and 6.

however, since there are only a small number of positions than can result from pawn moves, and once the bonus map has been computed for a given configuration, it can be stored and used each time that configuration is encountered in the look-ahead tree. For this reason, the calculations which are required will not be particularly time consuming.

Another example of this strategy is based on the position presented in Figure 4. This is a slight modification of Figure 6.7 from the chapter of *Chess Skill in Man and Machine* by Church and Church (Frey, 1977a). To apply our technique with respect to the bonus map for the White King it is necessary to determine which squares are not accessible to the White King by virtue of pawn control. As before, these include squares occupied by White pawns and squares attacked by Black pawns. The relevant squares are darkened in Figure 5.

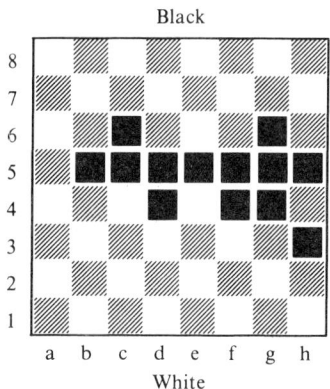

Figure 5. Forbidden squares for the position in Figure 4.

The next step is to locate passed pawns for White. There is only one and it is located at c6. The two squares diagonally in front of this pawn (b7 and d7) are credited with 8 points. Squares adjacent to these squares which are not among the darkened squares in Figure 5 are credited with 7 points. Squares adjacent to these receive 6 points. This process is continued until there are no more available squares or until the credit value of 1 has been assigned. The next step is to determine whether any Black pawns are potential targets. As before, a target pawn is defined as one which is not defended by a friendly pawn. In the present example, there are three candidates: the pawns at a6, d6, and h7. For each pawn, the value of 5 is credited to the pawn's square and the adjacent squares. Then the value of 4 is credited to each adjacent square. This process of establishing a gradient of decreasing values from 5 down to 1 as distance increases from the target is continued until the last values have been assigned. This is done for each target pawn and in each case, squares darkened in Figure 5 are always excluded from the process. The last assignment process is conducted for centralization, with center squares (d4, d5, e4, and e5) receiving 3 credits each and neighboring squares receiving 2 credits. The squares one move in from the edge are assigned the value of 1 and then credits are removed from any square which has been darkened. The final step in developing a bonus map for the White King is to total the credits for each square.

The composite map is presented in Figure 6. This set of bonus points will encourage the White King to move in the appropriate direction. Without this strategy an 11-ply search would be required for White to discover that the pawn at a6 can be captured. With the implementation of these attack gradients for the White King, however, the correct move can be selected with only a 3-ply search. As was the case in the previous example, the establishment of a plan within the evaluation function produces a goal-directed search without

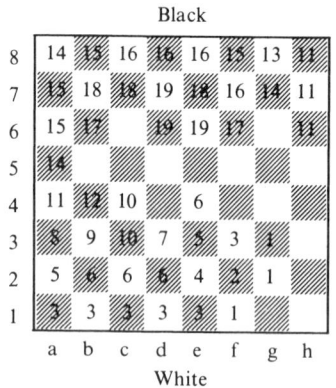

Figure 6. Bonus map for the position of Figure 4. Without this map, an 11-ply search would be required for the computer (White) to discover that the pawn at a6 can be captured. Using the map, only a 3-ply search is required.

requiring an enormous look-ahead tree. This increase in efficiency is highly desirable.

Because the process is directed by the location of the pawns, changes in the map will occur infrequently and therefore only a relatively small number of bonus maps will be required for any one search. Once a map has been calculated for a particular pawn configuration, it can be stored and used later whenever it is needed. Although this strategy seems to work well in the examples we have presented, it is reasonable to ask whether this procedure will work in all endgame situations. Unfortunately, the answer is no.

Consider the position presented in Figure 7. This is a famous endgame problem which appears as diagram 70 in Reuben Fine's classic chess book, *Basic Chess Endings* (Fine, 1941). It was analyzed in 1975 by Monroe Newborn to determine if his special endgame program, PEASANT, could solve it. After several unsuccessful efforts, Newborn concluded that the problem would require about 25,000 hours of processor time before a solution could be found (Frey, 1977a). The problem is difficult, but not as impossible as Newborn suggests. Because PEASANT does not have a transposition table, the program did not take advantage of the tremendous number of identical terminal positions which are encountered when an exhaustive search is made of this position. Because the pawns are locked, the only moves which are possible are King moves, and this greatly increases the potential number of transpositions.

The position was submitted to Northwestern's chess program CHESS 4.5 running on the CYBER 176 system at Control Data headquarters in Minneapolis. David Cahlander discovered that CHESS 4.5 could solve the problem after a 26-ply search! This required 10 minutes of processor time on the powerful CYBER 176. Although it is interesting to know that the problem can be

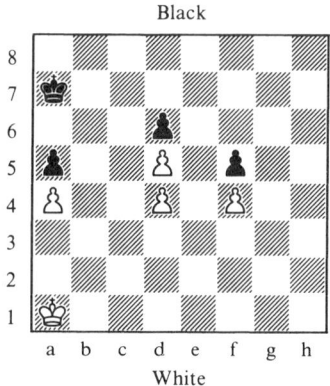

Figure 7. A chess position which can be analyzed efficiently by means of the *coordinate square* concept proposed by Ken Church. In this approach, the Black King must *coordinate* precisely with the White King in order to successfully defend its pawns. The technique is illustrated in Table 1.

solved by a brute-force search, this type of solution is not particularly elegant and it requires a level of hardwave sophistication that is not likely to be available in the small system for a few years yet.

The Coordinate Squares Approach

What can be done to make this problem more manageable? Interestingly enough, there is a rather neat approach to problems of this type which has been examined in some detail by Ken Church in his undergraduate thesis at MIT. Working with Richard Greenblatt as his advisor, Church applied the chess concept of coordinate squares to this position. The basic notion is that the Black King must coordinate precisely with the moves of the White King in order to successfully defend its pawns. For any particular square which the White King occupies, there are only a limited number of squares which the Black King can occupy and still hold his act together.

In his thesis, Ken Church presents a fairly extensive analysis of King and pawn endgames. For our present purpose, we will limit our analysis to King and pawn endgames in which the pawns are locked and we will modify Church's approach to suit our conditional evaluation strategy. The major difference is that Church attempts to discover a complete solution to the problem using the coordinate squares idea. We propose, instead, to use the coordinate squares approach to provide the evaluation function with additional chess knowledge. With this modification, a full-width search of reasonable depth can find the correct move.

Using Figure 7 as an example, the first step in this process is to determine which squares are denied to each of the Kings by the existing pawn configuration: By noting that each King cannot move to a square that is occupied by its own pawn or that is attacked by an opponent's pawn, one can easily determine that squares a4, b4, c5, d4, d5, e4, e5, f4, and g4 are denied to the White King. Likewise, squares a5, b5, c5, c6, d6, e5, e6, f6, and g6 are denied to the Black King. Neither side has a passed pawn, but there are multiple targets, since none of the pawns are defended by friendly pawns.

By applying the strategy described earlier, it is possible to calculate a composite attack map for the White King on the basis of the target pawns at a5, d6, and f5 and taking into account the centralization subgoal. The resulting map for Fine's position is presented in Figure 8. The squares without a number are the squares which are denied to the White King because of the pawn structure. Given the position of the White King (a1), a shallow search using this attack map as part of the evaluation function would encourage the White King to approach the target pawn at a5 (e.g., b2, c3, c4, b5, a5). If the Black King were more than five moves from a5, this sequence of moves would lead to success. Given that the Black King is at a7, however, this plan is doomed to failure. In fact, the first move in the sequence, b2, is fatal and transforms a winning position into a draw. There are two important conclusions that follow

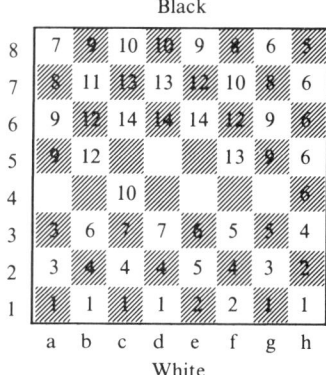

Figure 8. Bonus map for the position of Figure 7, a composite attack map for White based on the target pawns at a5, d6 and f5, and taking into account the centralization subgoal.

from this discovery. The first is that our simple goal-gradient approach does not always work. The second is that chess endgames are much more difficult than a novice player might suppose.

Let us extend Ken Church's ideas and apply the concept of coordinate squares to this position. First, we wish to assign each of the squares to one of three categories: under the influence of the Black King, under the influence of the White King, or contested. To do this we compute the distance from each King to each square, given the constraints imposed by the existing pawn structure. This creates two distance maps, one for the White King and one for the Black King. For squares which are not accessible to one or both of the Kings, we assign a distance score based on the number of King moves required to reach that square by traveling across accessible squares. Next, each square which is closer in moves to the Black King than to the White King and is not denied to the Black King is assigned to Black. Each square which is closer to the White King than to the Black King and is not denied to the White King is assigned to White. The remaining squares are assigned to the contested category. The results of this procedure are summarized in Figure 9. The squares assigned to Black are indicated by the letter B and the squares assigned to White are indicated by a W. The blank squares belong in the contested category.

If the territory under the influence of either King is adjacent to an opponent's pawn, the contest is essentially settled since that pawn would be open for capture. Since this is not the case for the present position, we wish to define a special category of squares called *frontier squares*. A frontier square is any square under your influence that is adjacent to an accessible contested square or is adjacent to an accessible square under the influence of the opponent.

For the position diagrammed in Figure 7, the frontier squares for White are c4 and h4. The next step is determine, for each of these frontier squares, the set of squares under Black's influence which, if the Black King were located

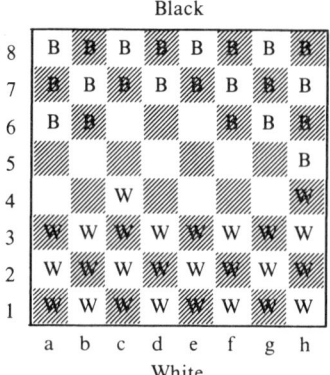

Black

White

Figure 9. The square control concept applied to the position of Figure 7. Each of the squares is assigned to one of three categories: under the influence of the Black King, under the influence of the White King, or contested. To do this, the distance from each King to each square is computed, given the constraints imposed by the existing pawn structure. Each square closer in moves to the Black King and not denied to the Black King is assigned to Black, and vice versa. The remaining squares are labeled as contested. Through a complex series of manipulations and the use of so-called frontier squares (see text), White is actively directed to attack Black's pawns using the strategy of trying to prevent Black from moving onto strategic coordinate squares which are vital to Black's defense.

on that square, would prevent the White King from moving from the frontier square to any of the contested squares or to any of Black's squares. For the frontier square at c4, the Black King would have to be at either a6 or b6 to prevent the White King from penetrating to b5. For the frontier square at h4, the Black King would have to be at g6 or h6 to prevent penetration by the White King. (Note that the Black King could not legally be at h5 if the White King were at h4.) These defense squares for Black can be determined by the machine by placing the White King on the frontier square and conducting a shallow tree-search with White to move first and determining empirically which locations for the Black King successfully repel the invader.

The next step in this process is to determine the shortest distance betwen each pair of frontier squares. For the present position, there are only two frontier squares and thus one minimal distance. Five King moves are required to travel between the two frontier squares. If Black is to be successful in defending, the Black King must be able to move from a defense square for h4 to a defense square for c4 in the same number or in fewer moves than it takes the White King to travel between the two frontier squares.

For this reason, each square in Black's defense set for c4 must be five or fewer moves from one of the defense squares for h4. Also, each square in the defense set for h4 must be five or fewer moves from one of the defense squares for c4. This requirement places a further restriction on those squares which satisfy the necessary defense conditions. One will note that a6 is six moves from the nearest square in the defense set for h4. Also, h6 is six moves from the nearest square in the defense set for c4. Therefore, the true defense set for c4 contains only b6 (a6 will not suffice). The true defense set for h4 contains only g6 (h6 will not suffice). Thus, we have determined that when the White King is on c4 and has the move, there is one, and only one, coordinate square for the Black King (b6). If the White King is on h4 and has the move, there is one, and only one, coordinate square for the Black King (g6).

The next step is to generalize this analysis to squares in White's territory which are immediately adjacent to the frontier squares. In this case, squares b3, c3, d3, g3, and h3. The square at b3 is one King move from the frontier squares at c4 and six moves from the frontier square at h4. If the White King is at b3, therefore, the Black King must be on a square which is simultaneously one move from b6 and six or fewer moves from g6. The squares which satisfy this condition (i.e., the coordinate squares for b3) are a6, a7, b7, and c7. The same set of calculations can be made for the other adjacent squares. The coordinate squares for c3 are b7 and c7. For d3, there is only one coordinate square, namely c7. Since the White King can move directly from c3 to d3 and Black must move to c7, and only c7, to maintain his defense, it is not possible for him to be on c7 when the White King is on c3. If he were, he would not be able to move when White moved from c3 to d3 and still satisfy the defense requirements. For this reason, only square b7 is sufficient for Black when White is on c3. In addition, since b3 is adjacent to c3, the coordinate square for c3 is not available for b3. Thus the set for b3 is further restricted to a6, a7, and c7.

If we examine g3, we will discover that it is one move from the frontier square at h4 and four moves from the frontier square at c4. This implies that the Black King must be on a square which is one move from b6 and four or fewer moves from g6. There are only two squares which satisfy this requirement, namely, f6 and f7. Therefore we can conclude that no square other than f6 or f7 will serve as a coordinate for g3. When we examine h3, we will find that there are three potential coordinate squares: f6, f7, and g7. Since this set shares f6 and f7 with the defense squares for g3, further restrictions are implied. It is not possible for the same square to serve as a coordinate square for two adjacent squares since it is not possible for Black to pass when it is his turn to move. Therefore if f6 is assigned to h3, then f7 *must* be assigned to g3. If f7 is assigned to h3, then f6 *must* be assigned to g3.

The next step in this process is to determine the set of coordinate squares for each square on the minimum pathway(s) between the two frontier squares for which the coordinate squares have not yet been determined. The new squares are e2, e3, f2, and f3. By following the same analysis as before, we can determine that the coordinate squares for e2 and e3 are d7 and d8. The coordinate squares for f2 and f3 are e7 and e8. Because of adjacency restrictions, the assignment of one of these values automatically restricts the other square to the remaining value.

The results of our coordinate square analysis are summarized in Table 1. When it is Black's turn to move and White has moved to one of the squares

Table 1. Results of the coordinate square analysis for the position of Figure 7. Shown are the potential squares for the Black King which defend against the White King's threats when it is White's turn to move.

Square of the White King	Coordinate squares for the Black King
b3	a6, a7, c7
c3	b7
c4	b6
d3	c7
e2	d7, d8
e3	d7, d8
f2	e7, e8
f3	e7, e8
g3	f6, f7
h3	f6, f7, g7
h4	g6

listed in the table, Black must be able to move to a coordinate square. For this reason, the evaluation function for the machine can be modified to give a bonus of 20 points to White for any terminal position in the look-ahead tree where it is Black's turn to move and the Black King is more than one move from a necessary coordinate square. If it is White's turn to move, a 20-point bonus will be awarded to any terminal position in the look-ahead tree where Black is not located on a necessary coordinae square.

Let us consider how this in combination with the White King attack map (Figure 8) will affect the outcome of the look-ahead search. The machine will try to find a pathway to squares c3 or d3 because their attack value of 7 is higher than any of the surrounding squares. Even better would be a pathway to c4, since its attack value of 10 is larger than 7. In each of these cases, the machine will also try to satisfy the condition that Black cannot be on a proper coordinate square when the White King reaches c3, d3, or c4 so that the additional 20-point bonus is also earned. In attempting to do this, it will find that if the White King moves from a1 to either a2 or b2 on his first move, the 20 point bonus will be lost forever. The reason is that either of these moves allows the Black King to coordinate and, because of the minimax strategy, the tree-search will always assume replies for Black which maintain this coordination. If the White King's first move is to square b1, the Black King cannot coordinate and the 20-point bonus will still be available at some of the terminal positions in the tree. It is not surprising, therefore, to find Reuben Fine advising that K − N1 is the only move for White which preserves the win.

In order for the machine to find this move, assuming that both the attack map and the coordinate squares information are incorporated in the evaluation function, a search of nine plies is required. This is a tremendous improvement over the 26-ply search required by the unmodified program. In order to actually win a Black pawn, the White King must move to c3 or c4 with Black not in coordination and make a 13-ply look-ahead search. If the White King moves to d3 with Black not in coordination, an 11-ply search will suffice. In order to prevent a draw, White will avoid repeating identical positions and thus will eventually travel to e3. From this vantage point, the win of a pawn can be visualized with a 9-ply search. Therefore, the problem could be solved by the machine if it searched to a depth of nine plies for each move calculation. With a program such as CHESS 4.5, a 9-ply search for this position can be conducted in less than 2 minutes on even a medium power computer.

The procedures which we have described are applicable to a wide range of endgame positions. The coordinate squares analysis demonstrates that even highly complex endgame positions are manageable when the full-width search employs a sufficiently knowledgeable evaluation function. Although the examples we have discussed encompass only a few types of chess positions, we hope that the reader will envision the power which is potentially available when the evaluation function is modified to incorporate relevant chess knowledge. The implementation of this approach on a broad scale should eventually produce chess programs which can be run on medium power machines and still compete on equal terms with strong human players.

Quiescence

Another important area for the application of chess knowledge is the problem of *quiescence*. It is essential that the static evaluation function not be applied to a turbulent position. If the next move has the potential to produce a major perturbation of the situation, the evaluation which is rendered will not be accurate. For example, it makes little sense to apply a static evaluation function in the middle of a piece exchange or when one of the Kings is in check. In each case, the judgment which is rendered will not be reliable. For this reason CHESS 4.5 presently goes beyond the predetermined search depth at "terminal" positions where a capture might be profitable for the side whose turn it is to move, where certain types of checking moves are possible, or where a pawn is on the seventh rank. This extended search facility is called the quiescence search, and its major objective is to produce reasonably static positions for which the evaluation function can provide accurate assessments.

A weakness of this present implementation is that the definition of a turbulent position is much too narrow. There are many situations in addition to capture threats, checks on the King, and pawn promotion threats which are clearly turbulent. Larry Harris has characterized some of these in Chapter 7 of *Chess Skill in Man and Machine*. Harris includes in this category positions which involve a pawn lever, a back rank mate threat, or sacrifice potential. The interested reader can consult Harris' chapter for operational definitions of these patterns. It is essential to note that these and other important patterns are not easily detected. In each case, a fairly sophisticated pattern analysis capability is required. A reasonable goal for improving the present forward search chess programs would be the development of an efficient procedure for detecting potential sources of turbulence. The central objective would be to use this information as one of the decision criteria for terminating search at a node. If the position is not quiescence in respect to a potential perturbation which has been detected, the look-ahead process should be continued.

For example, during the opening when the machine leaves its library with information that the control of a particular square is an important objective, the decisions about search termination can consider whether the position is quiescent in respect to perturbations which might influence control of the key square. Another example of this idea involves the endgame. If the preliminary analysis indicates that a particular pawn should be an attack target, the decision for search termination should consider whether each position is quiescent with respect to this goal. Positions at the predetermined depth level will be evaluated only if all potential attacks are more than two moves away from the target. When one or more attackers are close to the goal, the search process will be continued to determine if capture is feasible. This modification of the search process introduces a goal directed selective search at the terminal positions of the full-width tree. The addition of several extra plies of search at relevant nodes in the tree can mean the difference between finding and just missing an important continuation. This type of facility is difficult to implement and difficult to control properly, but the potential gains are such that the effort is worthwhile.

Establishing Appropriate Goals

In order to implement this goal direction feature in the evaluation function and quiescence search, it is necessary to recognize that a goal which may be of paramount importance at the base node of the look-ahead tree may no longer be relevant at some of the terminal nodes. Intervening moves may accomplish the necessary goal or may alter the situation such that it is no longer possible. In these cases, the conditional evaluation function would be directed at an inappropriate goal. One way to deal with this problem would be to select goals which were both general and long range. In this case, they should continue to be relevant at the terminal nodes of the look-ahead tree. Unfortunately, this is a fairly severe limitation on the goal-directed search and is therefore not desirable. A second approach would be to apply pattern analysis at each terminal node instead of at the base node only. In this case, the goals which were selected would always be relevant to the position. This procedure would be very time-consuming, since feature analysis is a complex process. The essential aspect of the problem is a time relevance tradeoff in which a guarantee that relevant goals are being pursued requires a heavy investment in additional computing time. The third and most reasonable approach would be to designate which features of the position are crucial to each particular goal and to incrementally update our goals (and thus the evaluation function and the decision rules for the quiescence search) whenever these features change. This is a highly sophisticated approach which would be difficult to implement.

Conclusion

Let us summarize our conclusions and relate them to the world of personal computing. We have attempted to argue that a full-width search strategy is feasible with a small computer, and that ultimately this approach will produce better chess than a selective search strategy. For this plan to be successful, it is necessary to employ software and hardware suited to the task. The software must incorporate recent improvements in tree-searching strategy (i.e., $\alpha-\beta$ pruning, the capture and killer heuristics, iterative searching, staged move generation, incremental updating, serial evaluation, and transposition analysis) as well as other refinements such as conditional evaluations which provide goal direction to the search process.

On the hardware side, it is necessary to have a reasonably powerful system. Although there have been a number of recent efforts to program micro-processor systems to play chess, the games which have resulted have not been comparable to those played by established large system programs. Although it is quite an accomplishment to produce even rudimentary chess from a microprocessor system, the level of play to date is not very encouraging. An example of this type of game appeared in March 1978 *BYTE*, "Microchess 1.5 versus Dark Horse," page 166.

The type of chess program described in this article requires reasonably powerful hardware in order to provide an interesting game. Because of the many operations requiring bit map manipulation, a 16-bit processor is much more desirable than an 8-bit processor. It is more efficient to represent a set of 64 squares with four 16-bit words than with eight 8-bit words. With a need for computing power in mind, one might select a microprocessor system based on one of the new high-speed 16-bit processors such as the Zilog Z-8000 or the Intel 8086. In addition, this type of program will require quite a bit of memory. The program itself will require aboout 20K bytes and the trans-position table, if implemented, will need at least another 20K bytes. If the programmer plans to add chess knowledge for conditional evaluations, a total of 64K bytes is desirable. An opening library which is sufficient to keep a skilled opponent on his toes requires disk storage.

These considerations may dampen the enthusiasm of many would-be chess programmers. On the other hand, a realistic orientation at the start could save a great deal of grief along the way. When implemented on fairly sophisticated hardware, our demonstration chess program will usually provide a reasonable chess move after 2 or 3 minutes of computation. If more time is available (e.g., selecting a move for a postal chess game by letting the machine "think" for several hours), a fairly respectable level of play can be anticipated. With future hardware improvements, this type of program may soon become reasonably competitive at tournament time limits, even on a personal computing system.

[Editor's note: Throughout this paper the authors refer frequently to the book "*Chess Skill in Man and Machine*" (Frey, 1977a). Frey's book is a collection of papers on Computer Chess, presented at a symposium held at Northwestern University. In my opinion it is an outstanding contribution to the field, and I would most strongly recommend it to anyone interested in the subject.— D.N.L.L.]

CHAPTER 3

Checkers (Draughts)

3.1. Logical or Nonmathematical Programs

CHRISTOPHER S. STRACHEY

Originally published in: *Proceedings of the Association for Computing Machinery Conference, Toronto*, 1952, pp. 46–49. Copyright © 1952 Association for Computing Machinery, Inc., reprinted by permission.

A large part of any mathematical program is concerned with operations which are not strictly mathematical at all. Examples of this are the input and output routines, the arrangements for calling in various subroutines when required and, above all, the general organization of the problem as a whole. It is an interesting fact that these nonmathematical parts of the program often take many more instructions than the mathematics proper. As an example, in a problem which involved the step by step integration of a simple nonlinear differential equation, the actual integration cycle used 70 instructions, the arrangements to print out the results and to stop the integration at the required point used a further 48 instructions and a printing subroutine of 64 instructions—a total of 112 instructions. The problem required this integration to be performed a large number of times with different parameters; the organization involved in doing this, and in arranging that the parameters should be fed into the machine in the simplest possible form, used to fewer than 250 instructions and subroutines totalling about 150 instructions. This may be a rather extreme case, but it is generally true to say, I think, that the nonmathematical parts of the program use far more instructions than one would at first sight expect, and that a relatively large part of effort in preparing the program is spent dealing with these nonmathematical operations.

The reason for this is twofold. First, these operations, being essentially logical in nature and not mathematical, are exceedingly diverse. There is, so far as I know, no really satisfactory notation in use for dealing with them and they are therefore correspondingly difficult to think about. The second reason, is that the machines have been designed principally to perform mathematical operations. This means that while it is perfectly possible to make them do logic, it is necessarily a rather cumbersome process. The difficulty, of course, is to decide what further functions would be of assistance with the logic. The B-line facility of the Ferranti machines is certainly a big step in the right direction, but there is still a long way to go. I do not propose to go any further into this question here, except to say that I think it is a point worth a good deal of consideration in the design of any further machines.

Instead, I want to discuss a slightly different group of programs: those which are wholly or almost wholly nonmathematical in nature. These programs are extremely varied and I shall therefore confine myself to describing a few typical ones very briefly.

The first and most generally known type I want to mention is the floating-point routine. It is often of great assistance to be able to use a floating binary or decimal point, and for machines which have not got this facility built into the hardware, the simplest way to do this is to use an interpretive floating-point routine. A routine of this type takes a single "instruction" (sometimes called a coded instruction) which is usually of the same general form as the normal instructions and interprets it as the sequence of ordinary instructions needed to carry out the floating-point operation called for. A routine of this type makes it as simple to code a program for floating-point arithmetic as for fixed-point arithmetic, but it has the disadvantage of being rather slow. A single floating-point operation usually takes about 60 single operation times. This means that if speed is important, and it usually is, it is best to arrange that as much as possible shall be carried out by normal uncoded instructions. It is remarkable how far this can be carried—a very large part of the program consists of counting cycles, performing discriminations, and transferring numbers to and from the accumulator and multiplier register. If the floating-point program is arranged so that these can all be done by normal instructions, remarkably few coded instructions will be necessary. This means arranging for the stores used as the floating-point accumulator and multiplier registers to be always in the standard form so that direct transfers are possible, and choosing the standard form so that the numerical part of the number is in the most significant, and the exponent in the least significant, part of the combined number so that normal discriminations or sign can be performed. With these precautions, an interpretive floating-point program need only take about ten times as long as the corresponding program using a fixed point.

Another interesting group of logical programs are those intended to assist the programmer. There is one just coming into use at Manchester which will perform the entire coding of a problem from a sequence of quasi-algebraic symbols. In order to use this program properly, it is still necessary to have a good working knowledge of the machine, and the symbolism it uses is not exactly that of normal mathematics, but it certainly makes the preparation of simple programs an extremely easy and painless affair. This program is a first and very important step, I think, towards the ideal stage of getting a machine to accept ordinary mathematical equations in the normal symbolism, and from them to prepare its own program. Programs of this type whose function is to take over some of the work now done by the programmer will, I hope, become increasingly common.

Finally, I should like to describe in slightly more detail a program I have just completed which makes the machine play a game of draughts.

The same of draughts occupies an intermediate position between the extremely complex games such as chess, and the relatively simple games such as Nim or noughts-and-crosses for which a complete mathematical theory exists. There are several programs in existence which will play the simple games but most of them use the complete mathematical theory so that the outcome of the game is no longer uncertain. In spite of a good deal of newspaper comment to the contrary, I do not believe that a program has yet been constructed which will play a complete game of chess. The nearest approach I know of is a program for the Manchester Machine by Prinz which will solve two-move chess problems, subject to certain restrictions. This program might be adapted to play a complete game, but it would be quite intolerably slow.

Chess presents two quite different sorts of difficulty which do not appear in the simple games. The first is that there are many types of men and moves so that at any stage there are a great many possible choices. The second is that as there is no complete theory of the game, it is necessary for the machine to look ahead for a number of moves and choose its move by some scheme of valuing the resulting position. The second of these difficulties is of much greater theoretical interest than the first, but it is the first, I think, which has made it impossible so far to produce a chess-playing routine.

For this reason, I have considered the much simpler game of draughts. In this game the moves are relatively simple, but it is still necessary to make the machine look ahead and choose its moves by a valuation scheme. I have succeeded in making a program for the Manchester machine which will in fact play a complete game of draughts at a reasonable speed. This program is a fairly typical example of a large logical program.

Representation of a Position

Draughts is played on the 32 white squares of a chessboard. For convenience we number these from 0 to 31 as shown in Figure 1.

There are only two kinds of pieces for each player—men, who can only move forwards, and Kings who can move forwards or backwards diagonally. We can represent a position completely by three 32-digit binary numbers which we shall call B, W, and K. Each digit in these numbers represents a square in the natural order—that is to say the least significant digit represents square 0 and the most significant digit square 31. The number B gives the positions of the Black men and Black Kings, W gives the positions of the White men and White Kings, while K gives the positions of the Kings alone

Black

0	1	2	3
4	5	6	7
8	9	10	11
12	13	14	15
16	17	18	19
20	21	22	23
24	25	26	27
28	29	30	31

White

Figure 1

of both colors. In each of the numbers a "1" indicates the presence and a 0 indicates the absence of the appropriate type of man. Thus, for example, the position in Figure 2 would be represented by

$$B = 1100\ 0000\ 0000\ 0000\ 0000\ 0000\ 0000\ 0000,$$

$$W = 0000\ 0000\ 0000\ 0000\ 0000\ 0000\ 0000\ 0011,$$

$$K = 0100\ 0000\ 0000\ 0000\ 0000\ 0000\ 0000\ 0010.$$

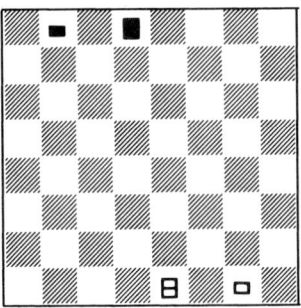

Figure 2

The positions of the Black Kings are given by the word B & K while the empty squares are given by $\sim$ B & $\sim$ W. This representation is not the most economical possible—it allows eight possible representations for each square of which only five are ever used—but it is simple and convenient.

Moves

If we indicate a move by the change in the square number, we see that there are six possible types of noncapture move ± 3, ± 4 or ± 5 (e.g., 14–17, 17–14,

14–18, 18–14, 9–14, 14–9) but at most four of these can be made from any square.

Let us first consider the $+4$ moves. These are possible (if the position allows it) from every square on the board except 28 to 31, so that the number $M_4 = 1111\ 1111\ 1111\ 1111\ 1111\ 1111\ 1111\ 0000$ represents the squares from which a $+4$ move is possible.

If we want to find the possible $+4$ moves for black, the number $B\ \&\ M_4$ will give the Black men which are on sailable squares, while $B\ \&\ M_4 \times 2^4$ will give the positions to which they will move. The move is only possible if the final square is empty, so that $Y = (B\ \&\ M_4) \times 2^4\ \&\ \sim B\ \&\ \sim W$ will give the squares to which Black men can actually make a $+4$ move.

The moves can then be considered individually by taking the nonzero digits of Y one at a time. If θ is one of these, so that it represents the square to which the Black man is moved, $\phi = \theta \times 2^{-4}$ represents the square from which it has been moved. Thus B', the resulting Black position, will be given by $B' = B \not\equiv \theta \not\equiv \phi$.

W will be unaltered, but to find K' we must determine if the moved was a King, and if not (i.e., if $\phi\ \&\ K = 0$) whether it has become a King during the move. This latter will be the case if $0 \geq 2^{28}$, i.e., if it has been moved to the last rank. Thus to find K' we perform the operations:

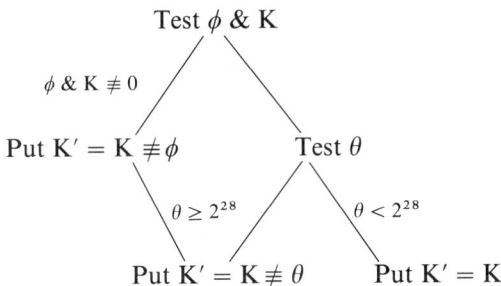

If we want to find the $+4$ moves for White, we must remember that as these are backwards moves, they can only be made by the White Kings so that the expression for the group of possible moves becomes

$$Y = (W\ \&\ K\ \&\ M_4) \times 2^4\ \&\ \sim B\ \&\ \sim W.$$

An exactly analogous procedure will apply for the other possible type of move. We can shorten the process somewhat by noticing that while a ± 4 move is possible from every square, only the combinations $(+5, -3)$ or $(+3, -5)$ are possible, it is therefore possible to combine the $+3$ and $+5$ moves together without ambiguity and take, for a Black move,

$$Y = \{(B\ \&\ M_3) \times 2^3 \not\equiv (B\ \&\ M_5) \times 2^5\}\ \&\ \sim B\ \&\ \sim W.$$

There are thus four types of noncapture moves to be considered for each position: $+4, -4, +3$ or $+5, -3, -5$. Single stage capture moves (i.e., moves capturing only one piece) consist of two noncapture moves in the same direction, but of different types (e.g., $+4$ followed by $+3$ or $+5$), with the final position empty and the intermediate one occupied by an opponent's piece. Thus one type of capture move for Black will be given by

$$Y = [\{(B \ \& \ M_3) \times 2^3 \not\equiv (B \ \& \ M_5) \times 2^5\} \ \& \ W \ \& \ M_4] \times 2^4 \ \& \sim B \ \& \sim W.$$

These are the moves which start with $+3$ or $+5$, followed by $+4$. There will be three other similar types of capture move.

There is a further difficulty about capture moves. This is that a capture move is not necessarily completed after one stage; indeed, in order to avoid being "huffed," it is essential not to terminate the move until no further captures are possible with the same piece. This feature, which is peculiar to draughts, introduces a very considerable complication into the program, and there is unfortunately no time to discuss it fully. In outline, however, the procedure is to enter the move-finding sequence repeatedly until no further captures can be found.

Valuation of Positions and Strategy

The chief interest in games-playing routines is probably in the development of a suitable type of strategy which will allow the machine to play a reasonably good game, and at the same time to play reasonably rapidly. It should be possible to graft almost any type of strategy into the move-finding scheme outlined above to produce a complete draughts-playing routine and then to evaluate the effectiveness of the strategy by direct experiments. I have done this with two rather simple types of strategy so far, and I hope to be able to try some rather more refined strategies in the future.

For demonstration purposes, and also to ensure that a record of the game is kept, and to take certain precautions against machine error, the move-finding sequence and its associated strategy have been combined with a general game-playing routine which accepts the opponent's moves, displays the positions, prints the move, and generally organizes the sequence of operations in the game. It is rather typical of a logical program that this organizing routine is, in fact, longer than the game-playing routine proper. As its operations, though rather spectacular, are of only trivial theoretical interest, I shall not describe them here.

The first, and simplest strategy to try is the direct one of allowing the machine to consider all the possible moves ahead on both sides for a specified number of stages. It then makes its choice, valueing the final resulting positions only in terms of the material left on the board and ignoring any positional advantage. There is an upper limit to the number of stages-ahead that can be considered, owing to limitations of storage space, actually six moves, three on each side, are all that can be allowed. In practice, however, time considerations provide a more severe limitation. There are on an average about ten possible legal moves at each stage of the game, so that consideration of one further

Black

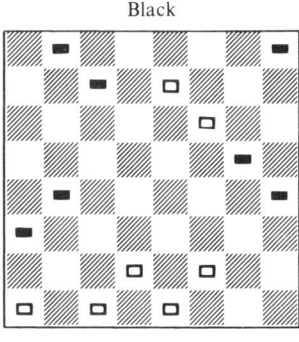

White

Figure 3

stage multiplies the time for making the move by a factor of about 10. The machine considers moves at the rate of about 10 per second, so that looking three moves ahead (those of its own and one of its opponent's), which takes between 1 and 2 minutes, represents about the limit which can be allowed from the point of view of time.

This is not sufficient to allow the machine to play well, though it can play fairly sensibly for most of the game. One wholly unexpected difficulty appears. Consider the position in Figure 3. In this position, the machine is aware that its opponent is going to King at the next move. Now a King is more valuable than a man—the actual values were 3 for a King and 1 for a man—so that if the opponent Kings the machine effectively looses 2 points. The only way it can stop this is by offering a man for sacrifice because then, by the rules of the game, the sacrifice must be taken at once. If it does this, it will loose only 1 point, and as it is not looking far enough ahead, it cannot see that it has not prevented its opponent from Kinging but only postponed the evil day. At its next move it is still faced with the same difficulty which it tries to solve in the same way, so that it will make every possible sacrifice of a single man before it accepts as inevitable the creation of an opponent's King. This, of course, is a fatal flaw in the strategy—and not one it would have been easy to detect without actually trying it out. An opponent who detected this behavior—and it is extremely conspicuous in play—would only have to leave his man on the point of Kinging indefinitely, the machine would then sacrifice all its remaining men as soon as the opportunity offered.

In order to avoid this difficulty, the second strategy was devised. In this the machine continues to investigate the moves ahead until it has found two consecutive moves without captures. This means that it will be able to recognize the futility of its sacrifice to prevent Kinging. It is still necessary to impose an overriding limit on the number of stages it can consider, and once more, considerations of time limit this. However, as no more is continued for more than two stages unless it leads to a capture, it is possible to allow the machine to consider up to four stages ahead without it becoming intolerably slow. This would mean that it would consider the sacrifice of two men to be of equal value to the creation of an opponent's King, and as there is a random choice between moves of equal value, it might still make this useless sacrifice. This has been prevented by reducing the value of a King from 3 to $2\frac{7}{8}$ points.

With this modified strategy the machine can play quite a tolerable game until it reaches the endgame, it has always seemed probable that a wholly different strategy will be necessary for endgames. The game given below, which is the first-ever played using the strategy, brings this point out very clearly.

Machine	Strachey	Machine	Strachey
11–15	23–18	18–23	26–22
7–11	21–17	23–27	22–17
8–12	20–16[a]	5– 8[i]	17–14
12–21 (16)	25–16 (21)	8–13	14– 9
9–14![b]	18– 9 (14)	19–23	9– 6
6–20 (16, 9)[c]	27–23	23–26[j]	31–22 (26)
2– 7[d]	23–18	27–31 (K)	6– 2 (K)
5– 8	18–14	7–10	2–7
8–13[e]	17– 8 (13)	10–15	21–16?[k]
4–13 (8)	14– 9	3–10 (7)	16– 9 (13)
1– 5[f]	9– 6	10–14	9– 6
15–19	6– 1 (K)	15– 9	6– 2 (K)
5– 9	1– 6?[g]	31–27[m]	2– 6
0– 5![h]	6–15 (10)	27–31[m]	6–10
11–25 (22, 15)	30–21 (25)	31–26[n]	10–17 (14)
13–17	21–14 (17)	19–23	29–25
9–18 (14)	24–21	26–31[p]	

[a] An experiment on my part—the only deliberate offer I made. I thought, wrongly, that it was quite safe.
[b] Not foreseen by me.
[c] Better than 5–21 (9, 17)
[d] A random move (zero value). Shows the lack of a constructive plan.
[e] Another random move of zero value. Actually rather good.
[f] Bad. Ultimately allows me to make a King. 10–14 would have been better.
[g] A bad slip on my part.
[h] Taking full advantage of my slip.
[i] Bad, unblocks the way to a King.
[j] Sacrifice in order to get a King (not to stop me Kinging). A good move, but not possible before 19–23 had been made by chance.
[k] Another bad slip on my part.
[m] Purposeless. The strategy is failing badly in the endgame.
[n] Too late.
[p] Futile. The game was stopped at this point as the outcome was obvious.

3.2. Some Studies in Machine Learning Using the Game of Checkers. I

Arthur L. Samuel

Originally published in: *IBM Journal of Research and Development*, vol. 3, 1959, pp. 210–229. Copyright © 1959 IBM Corporation. Reprinted by permission.

Abstract. Two machine-learning procedures have been investigated in some detail using the game of checkers. Enough work has been done by verify the fact that a computer can be programmed so that it will learn to play a better game of checkers than can be played by the person who wrote the program. Furthermore, it can learn to do this in a remarkably short period of time (8 or 10 hours of machine-playing time) when given only the rules of the game, a sense of direction, and a redundant and incomplete list of parameters which are thought to have something to do with the game, but whose correct signs and relative weights are unknown and unspecified. The principles of machine learning verified by these experiments are, of course, applicable to many other situations.

Introduction

The studies reported here have been concerned with the programming of a digital computer to behave in a way which, if done by human beings or animals, would be described as involving the process of learning. While this is not the place to dwell on the importance of machine-learning procedures, or to discourse on the philosophical aspects,[1] there is obviously a very large amount of work, now done by people, which is quite trivial in its demands on the intellect but does, nevertheless, involve some learning. We have at our command computers with adequate data-handling ability and with sufficient computational speed to make use of machine-learning techniques, but our

---

[1] Some of these are quite profound and have a bearing on the questions raised by Nelson Goodman (1954).

knowledge of the basic principles of these techniques is still rudimentary. Lacking such knowledge, it is necessary to specify methods of problem solution in minute and exact detail, a time-consuming and costly procedure. Programming computers to learn from experience should eventually eliminate the need for much of this detailed programming effort.

General Methods of Approach

At the outset it might be well to distinguish sharply between two general approaches to the problem of machine learning. One method, which might be called the *Neural-Net Approach*, deals with the possibility of inducing learned behavior into a randomly connected switching net (or its simulation on a digital computer) as a result of a reward-and-punishment routine. A second, and much more efficient approach, is to produce the equivalent of a highly organized network which has been designed to learn only certain specific things. The first method should lead to the development of general-purpose learning machines. A comparison between the size of the switching nets that can be reasonably constructed or simulated at the present time and the size of the neural nets used by animals, suggests that we have a long way to go before we obtain practical devices.[2] The second procedure requires reprogramming for each new application, but it is capable of realization at the present time. The experiments to be described here were based on this second approach.

Choice of Problem

For some years the writer has devoted his spare time to the subject of machine learning and has concentrated on the development of learning procedures as applied to games.[3] A game provides a convenient vehicle for such study as contrasted with a problem taken from life, since many of the complications of detail are removed. Checkers, rather than chess (Shannon, 1950a; Bernstein and Roberts, 1958a; Kister *et al.*, 1957; Newell *et al.*, 1958b), was chosen because the simplicity of its rules permits greater emphasis to be placed on learning techniques. Regardless of the relative merits of the two games as intellectual pastimes, it is fair to state that checkers contains all of the basic characteristics of an intellectual activity in which heuristic procedures and learning processes can play a major role and in which the processes can be evaluated.

---

[2] Warren S. McCulloch (1949) has compared the digital computer to the nervous system of a flatworm. To extend this comparison to the situation under discussion would be unfair to the worm, since its nervous system is actually quite highly organized as compared with the random-net studies by B. G. Farley and W. A. Clarke (1954). N. Rochester *et al.* (1956), and by F. Rosenblatt (1958).

[3] The first operating checker program for the IBM 701 was written in 1952. This was recoded for the IBM 704 in 1954. The first program with learning was completed in 1955 and demonstrated on television on February 24, 1956.

Some of these characteristics might well be enumerated. They are:

(1) The activity must not be deterministic in the practical sense. There exists no known algorithm which will guarantee a win or a draw in checkers, and the complete explorations of every possible path through a checker game would involve perhaps 10^{40} choices of moves which, at three choice per millimicrosecond, would still take 10^{21} centuries to consider.

(2) A definite goal must exist—the winning of the game—and at least one criterion or intermediate goal must exist which has a bearing on the achievement of the final goal and for which the sign should be known. In checkers the goal is to deprive the opponent of the possibility of moving, and the dominant criterion is the number of pieces of each color on the board. The importance of having a known criterion will be discussed later.

(3) The rules of the activity must be definite and they should be known. Games satisfy this requirement. Unfortunately, many problems of economic importance do not. While in principle the determination of the rules can be a part of the learning process, this is a complication which might well be left until later.

(4) There should be a background of knowledge concerning the activity against which the learning progress can be tested.

(5) The activity should be one that is familiar to a substantial body of people so that the behavior of the program can be made understandable to them. The ability to have the program play against human opponents (or antagonists) adds spice to the study and, incidentally, provides a convincing demonstration for those who do not believe that machines can learn.

Having settled on the game of checkers for our learning studies, we must, of course, first program the computer to play legal checkers; that is, we must express the rules of the game in machine language and we must arrange for the mechanics of accepting an opponent's moves and of reporting the computer's moves, together with all pertinent data desired by the experimenter. The general methods for doing this were described by Shannon in 1950 as applied to chess rather than checkers. The basic program used in these experiments is quite similar to the program described by Strachey in 1952. The availability of a larger and faster machine (the IBM 704), coupled with many detailed changes in the programming procedure, leads to a fairly interesting game being played, even without any learning. The basic forms of the program will now be described.

The Basic Checker-Playing Program

The computer plays by looking ahead a few moves and by evaluating the resulting board positions much as a human player might do. Board positions are stored by sets of machine words, four words normally being used to represent any particular board position. Thirty-two-bit positions (of the 36 available in an IBM 704 word) are, by convention, assigned to the 32 playing squares on the checkerboard, and pieces appearing on these squares are represented by 1's appearing in the assigned bit positions of the corresponding word. "Looking-ahead" is prepared for by computing all possible next moves, starting with a given board position. The indicated moves are explored in turn by producing new board-position records corresponding to the conditions after the move in question (the old board positions being saved to facilitate a return to the starting point) and the process can be repeated. This look-ahead procedure is carried several moves in advance, as illustrated in Figure 1. The resulting board positions are then scored in terms of their relative value to the machine.

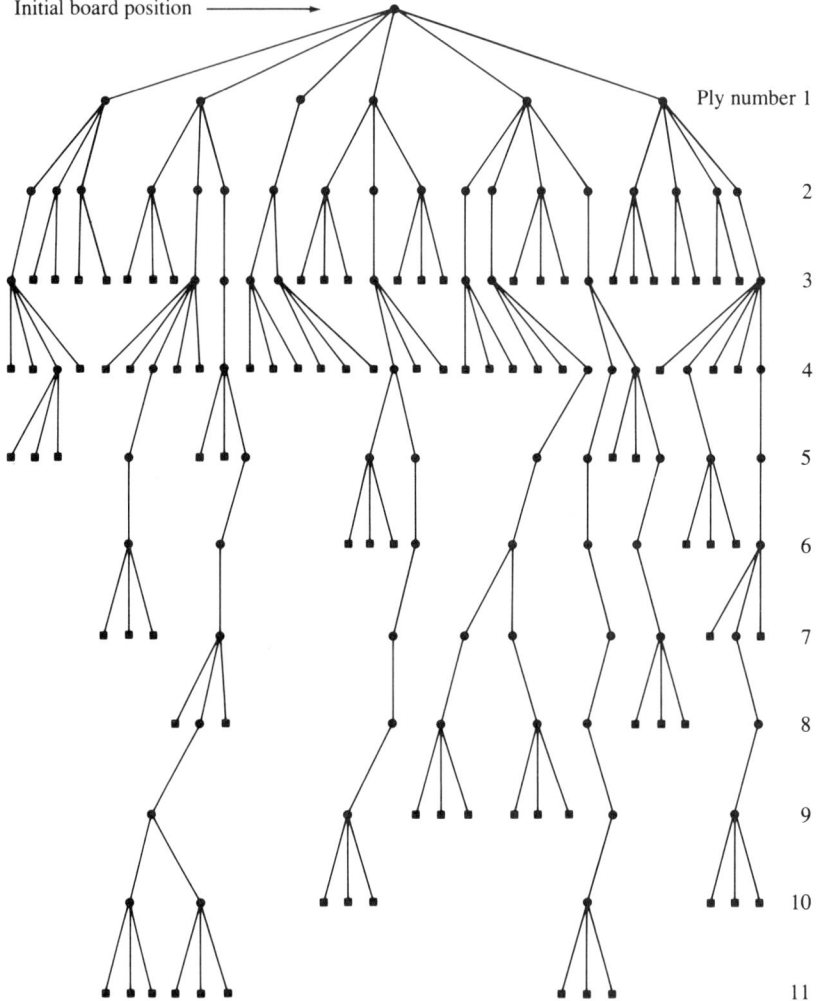

Figure 1. A "tree" of moves which might be investigated during the look-ahead procedure. The actual branchings are much more numerous than those shown, and the "tree" is apt to extend to as many as 20 levels.

The standard method of scoring the resulting board positions has been in terms of a linear polynomial. A number of schemes of an abstract sort were tried for evaluating board positions without regard to the usual checker concepts, but none of these was succesful.[4] One way of looking at the various terms in the scoring polynomial is that those terms with numerically small coefficients should measure criteria related as intermediate goals to the criteria measured by the larger terms. The achievement of these intermediate goals indicates that the machine is going in the right direction, such that the larger terms will eventually increase. If the program could look far enough ahead we need only ask, "Is the machine still in the game?"[5] Since it cannot look this far ahead in the usual situation, we must substitute something else, say the piece ratio, and let the machine continue the look-ahead until one side has gained a piece advantage. But even this is not always possible, so we have the program test to see if the machine has gained a positional advantage, etc. Numerical measures of these various properties of the board positions are then added together (each with an appropriate coefficient which defines its relative importance) to form the evaluation polynomial.

More specifically, as defined by the rules for checkers, the dominant scoring parameter is the inability for one side or the other to move.[6] Since this can occur but once in any game, it is tested for separately and is not included in the scoring polynomial as tabulated by the computer during play. The next parameter to be considered is the relative piece advantage. It is always assumed that it is to the machine's advantage to reduce the number of the opponent's pieces as compared to its own. A reversal of the sign of this term will, in fact, cause the program to play "give-away" checkers, and with learning it can only learn to play a better and better give-away game. Were the sign of this term not known by the programmer it could, of course, be determined by tests, but it must be fixed by the experimenter and, in effect, it is one of the instructions to the machine defining its task. The numerical computation of the piece advantage has been arranged in such a way as to account for the well-known property that it is usually to one's advantage to trade pieces when one is ahead and to avoid trades when behind. Furthermore, it is assumed that kings are more valuable than pieces, the relative weights assigned to them being three to two.[7] This ratio means that the program will trade three men for two Kings, or two Kings for three men, if by so doing it can obtain some positional advantage.

---

[4] One of the more interesting of these was to express a board position in terms of the first and higher moments of the White and Black pieces separately about two orthogonal axes on the board. Two such sets of axes were tried, one set being parallel to the sides of the board and the second set being those through the diagonals.

[5] This apt phraseology was suggested by John McCarthy.

[6] Not the capture of all of the opponent's pieces, as popularly assumed, although nearly all games end in this fashion.

[7] The use of a weight ratio rather than this, conforming more closely to the values assumed by many players, can lead into certain logical complications, as found by Strachey, *loc. cit.*

The choice for the parameters to follow this first term of the scoring polynomial and their coefficients then becomes a matter of concern. Two courses are open—either the experimenter can decide what these subsequent terms are to be, or he can arrange for the program to make the selection. We will discuss the first case in some detail in connection with the rote-learning studies and leave for a later section the discussion of various program methods of selecting parameters and adjusting their coefficients.

It is not satisfactory to select the initial move which leads to the board position with the highest score, since to reach this position would require the cooperation of the opponent. Instead, an analysis must be made proceeding *backward* from the evaluated board positions through the "tree" of possible moves, each time with consideration of the intent of the side whose move is being examined, assuming that the opponent would always attempt to minimize the machine's score while the machine acts to maximize its score. At each branch point, then, the corresponding board position is given the score of the board position which would result from the most favorable move. Carrying this "minimax" procedure back to the starting point results in the selection of a "best move." The score of the board position at the end of the most likely chain is also brought back, and for learning purposes this score is now assigned to the present board position. This process is shown in Figure 2. The best move is executed, reported on the console lights, and tabulated by the printer.

The opponent is then permitted to make his move, which can be communicated to the machine either by means of console switches or by means of punched cards. The computer verifies the legality of the opponent's move,

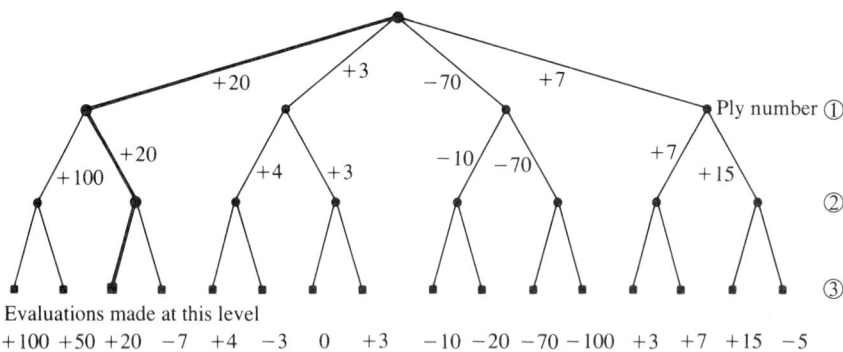

Figure 2. Simplified diagram showing how the evaluations are backed-up through the "tree" of possible moves to arrive at the best next move. The evaluation process starts at ③.

rejecting[8] or accepting it, and the process is repeated. When the program can look ahead and predict a win, this fact is reported on the printer. Similarly, the program concedes when it sees that it is going to lose.

Ply Limitations

Playing-time considerations make it necessary to limit the look-ahead distance to some fairly small value. This distance is defined as the *ply* (a ply of 2 consisting of one proposed move by the machine and the anticipated reply by the opponent). The ply is not fixed but depends upon the dynamics of the situation, and it varies from move to move and from branch to branch during the move analysis. A great many schemes of adjusting the look-ahead distance have been tried at various times, some of them quite complicated. The most effective one, although quite detailed, is simple in concept and is as follows. The program always looks ahead a minimum distance, which for the opening game and without learning is usually set at three moves. At this minimum ply the program will evaluate the board position if none of the following conditions occurs: (1) the next move is a jump; (2) the last move was a jump; or (3) an exchange offer is possible. If any one of these conditions exists, the program continues looking ahead. At a ply of 4 the program will stop and evaluate the resulting board position if conditions (1) and (3) above are not met. At a ply of 5 or greater, the program stops the look-ahead whenever the next ply level does not offer a jump. At a ply of 11 or greater, the program will terminate the look-ahead, even if the next move is to be a jump, should one side at this time be ahead by more than two Kings (to prevent the needless exploration of obviously losing or winning sequences). The program stops at a ply of 20 regardless of all conditions (since the memory space for the look-ahead moves is then exhausted) and an adjustment in score is made to allow for the pending jump. Finally, an adjustment is made in the levels of the break points between the different conditions when time is saved through rote learning (see below) and when the total number of pieces on the board falls below an arbitrary number. All break points are determined by single data words which can be changed at any time by manual intervention.

This tying of the ply with board conditions achieves three desired results. In the first place, it permits board evaluations to be made under conditions of relative stability for so-called dead positions, as defined by Turing (1953). Second, it causes greater surveillance of those paths which offer better opportunities for gaining or losing an advantage. Finally, since branching is usually seriously restricted by a jump situation, the total number of board positions and moves to be considered is still held down to a reasonable number and is more equitably distributed between the various possible initial moves.

---

[8] The only departure from complete generality of the game as programmed is that the program requires the opponent to make a permissible move, including the taking of a capture if one is offered. "Huffing" is not permitted.

As a practical matter, machine-playing time usually has been limited to approximately 30 seconds per move. Elaborate table-lookup procedures, fast sorting and searching procedures, and a variety of new programming tricks were developed, and full use was made of all of the resources of the IBM 704 to increase the operating speed as much as possible. One can, of course, set the playing time at any desired value by adjustments of the permitted ply; too small a ply results in a bad game and too large a ply makes the game unduly costly in terms of machine time.

Other Modes of Play

For study purposes the program was written to accommodate several variations of this basic plan. One of these permits the program to play against itself, that is, to play both sides of the game. This mode of play has been found to be especially good during the early stages of learning.

The program can also follow book games presented to it either on cards or on magnetic tape. When operating in this mode, the program decides at each point in the game on its next move in the usual way and reports this proposed move. Instead of actually making this move, the program refers to the stored record of a book game and makes the book move. The program records its evaluation of the two moves, and it also counts and reports the number of possible moves which the program rates as being better than the book move and the number it rates as being poorer. The sides are then reversed and the process is repeated. At the end of a book game a correlation coefficient is computed, relating the machine's indicated moves to those moves adjudged best by the checker masters.[9]

It should be noted that the emphasis throughout all of these studies has been on learning techniques. The temptation to improve the machine's game by giving it standard openings or other man-generated knowledge of playing techniques has been consistently resisted. Even when book games are played, no weight is given to the fact that the moves as listed are presumably the best possible moves under the circumstances.

For demonstration purposes, and also as a means of avoiding lost machine time while an opponent is thinking, it is sometimes convenient to play several simultaneous games against different opponents. With the program in its present form the most convenient number for this purpose has been found to be six, although eight have been played on a number of occasions.

Games may be started with any initial configuration for the board position so that the program may be tested on endgames, checker puzzles, etc. For nonstandard conditions, the program lists the initial piece arrangement. From time to time, and at the end of each game, the program also tabulates vari-

---

[9] This coefficient is defined as $C = (L - H)/(L + H)$, where L is the total number of different legal moves which the machine judged to be poorer than the indicated book moves, and H is the total number which it judged to be better than the book moves.

ous bits of statistical information which assist in the evaluation of playing performance.

Numerous other features have also been added to make the program convenient to operate (for details, see Appendix A), but these have no direct bearing on the problem of learning, to which we will now turn our attention.

Rote Learning and Its Variants

Perhaps the most elementary type of learning worth discussing would be a form of rote learning in which the program simply saved all of the board positions encountered during play, together with their computed scores. Reference could then be made to this memory record and a certain amount of computing time might be saved. This can hardly be called a very advanced form of learning; nevertheless, if the program then utilizes the saved time to compute further in depth it will improve with time.

Fortunately, the ability to store board information at a ply of 0 and to look up boards at a larger ply provides the possibility of looking much farther in advance than might otherwise be possible. To understand this, consider a very simple case where the look-ahead is always terminated at a fixed ply, say 3. Assume further that the program saves only the board positions encountered during the actual play with their associated backed-up scores. Now it is this list of previous board positions that is used to look up board positions while at a ply level of 3 in the subsequent games. If a board position is found, its score has, in effect, already been backed up by three levels, and if it becomes effective in determining the move to be made, it is a 6-ply score rather than a simple 3-ply score. This new initial board position with its 6-ply score is, in turn, saved and it may be encountered in a future game and the score backed up by an additional set of three levels, etc. This procedure is illustrated in Figure 3. The incorporation of this variation, together with the simpler rote-learning feature, results in a fairly powerful learning technique which has been studied in some detail.

Several additional features had to be incorporated into the program before it was practical to embark on learning studies using this storage scheme. In the first place, it was necessary to impart a sense of direction to the program in order to force it to press on toward a win. To illustrate this, consider the situation of two Kings against one King, which is a winning combination for practically all variations in board positions. In time, the program can be assumed to have stored all of these variations, each associated with a winning score. Now, if such a situation is encountered, the program will look ahead along all possible paths and each path will lead to a winning combination, in spite of the fact that only one of the possible initial moves may be along the direct path toward the win while all of the rest may be wasting time. How is the program to differentiate between these?

A good solution is to keep a record of the ply value of the different board

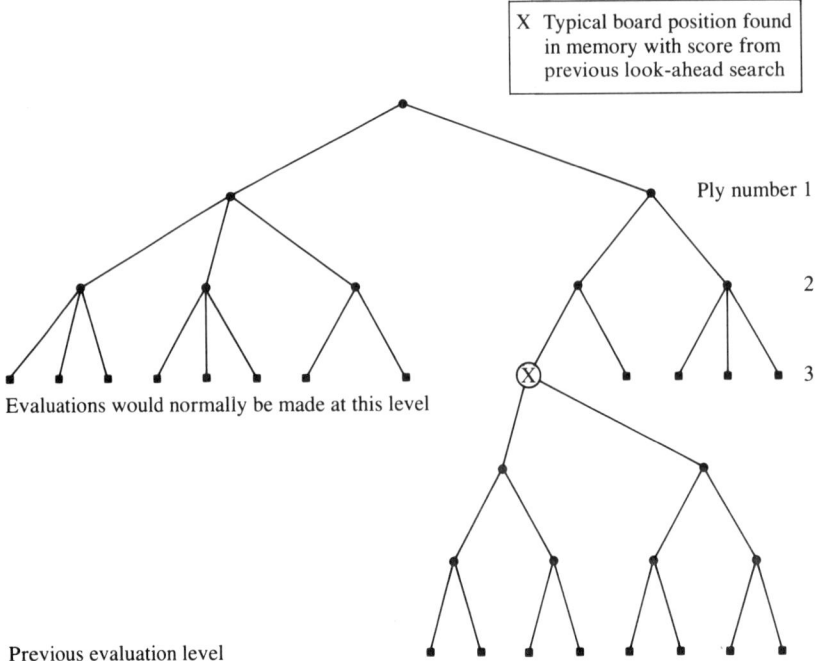

X Typical board position found
in memory with score from
previous look-ahead search

Ply number 1

2

3

Evaluations would normally be made at this level

Previous evaluation level

Figure 3. Simplified representation of the rote-learning process, in which information saved from a previous game is used to increase the effective ply of the backed-up score.

positions at all times and to make a further choice between board positions on this basis. If ahead, the program can be arranged to push directly toward the win while, if behind, it can be arranged to adopt delaying tactics. The most recent method used is to carry the effective ply along with the score by simply decreasing the magnitude of the score a small amount each time it is backed-up a ply level during the analyses. If the program is now faced with a choice of board positions whose scores differ only by the ply number, it will automatically make the most advantageous choice, choosing a low-ply alternative if winning and a high-ply alternative if losing. The significance of this concept of a direction sense should not be overlooked. Even without "learning," it is very important. Several of the early attempts at learning failed because the direction sense was not properly taken into account.

Cataloging and Culling Stored Information

Since practical considerations limit the number of board positions which can be saved, and since the time to search through those that are saved can easily become unduly long, one must devise systems: (1) to catalog boards that are saved; (2) to delete redundancies; and (3) to discard board positions which are not believed to be of much value. The most effective cataloging system found to date starts by standardizing all board positions, first by reversing the pieces and piece positions if it is a board position in which White is to move, so that all boards are reported as if it were Black's turn to move. This reduces by nearly a factor of two the number of boards which must be saved. Board positions, in which all of the pieces are Kings, can be reflected about the diagonals with a possible fourfold reduction in the number which must be saved. A more compact board representation than the one employed during play is also used so as to minimize the storage requirements.

After the board positions are standardized, they are grouped into records on the basis of:

(1) the number of pieces on the board;
(2) the presence or absence of a piece advantage;
(3) the side possessing this advantage;
(4) the presence or absence of Kings on the board;
(5) the side having the so-called "move," or opposition advantage; and finally
(6) the first moments of the pieces about normal and diagonal axes through the board.

During play, newly acquired board positions are saved in the memory until a reasonable number have been accumulated, and they are then merged with those on the "memory tape" and a new memory tape is produced. Board positions within a record are listed in a serial fashion, being sorted with respect to the words which define them. The records are arranged on the tape in the order that they are most likely to be needed during the course of a game; board positions with 12 pieces to a side coming first, etc. This method of cataloging is very important because it cuts tape-searching time to a minimum.

Reference must be made, of course, to the board positions already saved, and this is done by reading the correct record into the memory and searching through it by a dichotomous search procedure. Usually five or more records are held in memory at one time, the exact number at any time depending upon the lengths of the particular records in question. Normally, the program calls three or four new records into memory during each new move, making room for them as needed, by discarding the records which have been held the longest.

Two different procedures have been found to be of value in limiting the number of board positions that are saved; one based on the frequency of use, and the second on the ply. To keep track of the frequency of use, an age term is carried along with the score. Each new board position to be saved is arbitrarily assigned an age. When reference is made to a stored board position, either to update its score or to utilize it in the look-ahead procedure, the age recorded for this board position is divided by two. This is called *refreshing*. Offsetting this, each board position is automatically aged by one unit at the memory merge times (normally occurring about once every 20 moves). When the age of any one board position reaches an arbitrary maximum value this board position is expunged from the record. This is a form of *forgetting*. New board positions which remain unused are soon forgotten, while board positions which are used several times in succession will be refreshed to such an extent that they will be remembered even if not used thereafter for a fairly long period of time. This form of refreshing and forgetting was adopted on the basis of reflections as to the frailty of human memories. It has proven to be very effective.

In addition to the limitations imposed by forgetting, it seemed desirable to place a restriction on the maximum size of any one record. Whenever an arbitrary limit is reached, enough of the lowest-ply board positions are automatically culled from the record to bring the size well below the maximum.

Before embarking on a study of the learning capabilities of the system as just described, it was, of course, first necessary to fix the terms and coefficients in the evaluation polynomial. To do this, a number of different sets of values were tested by playing through a series of book games and computing the move correlation coefficients. These values varied from 0.2 for the poorest polynomial tested, to approximately 0.6 for the one finally adopted. The selected polynomial contained four terms (as contrasted with the use of 16 terms in later experiments). In decreasing order of importance these were:

(1) piece advantage;
(2) denial of occupancy;
(3) mobility; and
(4) a hybrid term which combined control of the center and piece advancement.

Rote-Learning Tests

After a scoring polynomial was arbitrarily picked, a series of games was played, both self-play and play against many different individuals (several of these being checker masters). Many book games were also followed, some of these being endgames. The program learned to play a very good opening game and to recognize most winning and losing end positions many moves in advance, although its midgame play was not greatly improved. This program now qualifies as a rather better-than-average novice, but definitely not as an expert.

At the present time the memory tape contains something over 53,000 board positions (averaging 3.8 words each) which have been selected from a much larger number of positions by means of the culling technqiues described. While this is still far from the number which would tax the listing and searching procedures used in the program, rough estimates, based on the frequency with which the saved boards are utilized during normal play (these figures being tabulated automatically), indicate that a library tape containing at least 20 times the present number of board positions would be needed to improve the midgame play significantly. At the present rate of acquisition of new positions this would require an inordinate amount of play and, consequently, of machine time.[10]

The general conclusions which can be drawn from these tests are that:

(1) An effective rote-learning technique must include a procedure to give the program a sense of direction, and it must contain a refined system for cataloging and storing information.
(2) Rote-learning procedures can be used effectively on machines with the data-handling capacity of the IBM 704 if the information which must be saved and searched does not occupy more than, roughly, one million words, and if not more than one hundred or so references need to be made to this information per minute. These figures are, of course, highly dependent upon the exact efficiency of cataloging which can be achieved.
(3) The game of checkers, when played with a simple scoring scheme and with rote learning only, requires more than this number of words for master caliber of play and, as a consequence, is not completely amenable to this treatment on the IBM 704.
(4) A game, such as checkers, is a suitable vehicle for use during the development of learning technqiues, and it is a very satisfactory device for demonstrating machine-learning procedures to the unbelieving.

Learning Procedure Involving Generalizations

An obvious way to decrease the amount of storage needed to utilize past experience is to generalize on the basis of experience and to save only the generalizations. This should, of course, be a continuous process if it is to be truly effective, and it should involve several levels of abstraction. A start has been made in this direction by having the program select a subset of possible terms for use in the evaluation polynomial and by having the program determine the sign and magnitude of the coefficients which multiply these parameters. At the present time this subset consists of 16 terms chosen from a list of 38 parameters. The piece-advantage term needed to define the task is computed separately and, of course, is not altered by the program.

After a number of relatively unsuccessful attempts to have the program generalize while playing both sides of the game, the program was arranged to act as two different players, for convenience called *Alpha* and *Beta*. Alpha generalizes on its experience after each move by adjusting the coefficients in its evaluation polynomial and by replacing terms which appear to be unimportant by new parameters drawn from a reserve list. Beta, on the contrary, uses the same evaluation polynomial for the duration of any one game. Program Alpha is used to play against human opponents, and during self-play Alpha and Beta play each other.

---

[10] This playing-time requirement, while large in terms of cost, would be less than the time which the checker master probably spends to acquire has proficiency.

At the end of each self-play game a determination is made of the relative playing ability of Alpha, as compared with Beta, by a neutral portion of the program. If Alpha wins—or is adjudged to be ahead when a game is otherwise terminated—the then current scoring system used by Alpha is given to Beta. If, on the other hand, Beta wins or is ahead, this fact is recorded as a black mark for Alpha. Whenever Alpha receives an arbitrary number of black marks (usually set at three) it is assumed to be on the wrong track, and a fairly drastic and arbitrary change is made in its scoring polynomial (by reducing the coefficient of the leading term to zero). This action is necessary on occasion, since the entire learning process is an attempt to find the highest point in multidimensional scoring space in the presence of many secondary maxima on which the program can become trapped. By manual intervention it is possible to return to some previous condition or make some other change if it becomes apparent that the learning process is not functioning properly. In general, however, the program seeks to extricate itself from traps and to improve more or less continuously.

The capability of the program can be tested at any time by having Alpha play one or more book games (with the learning procedure temporarily immobilized) and by correlating its play with the recommendations of the masters or, more interestingly, by pitting it against a human player.

Polynomial Modification Procedure

If Alpha is to make changes in its scoring polynomial, it must be given some trustworthy criteria for measuring performance. A logical difficulty presents itself, since the only measuring parameter available is this same scoring polynomial that the process is designed to improve. Recourse is had to the peculiar property of the look-ahead procedure, which makes it less important for the scoring polynomial to be particularly good the further ahead the process is continued. This means that one can evaluate the relative change in the positions of two players, when this evaluation is made over a fairly large number of moves, by using a scoring system which is much too gross to be significant on a move-by-move basis.

Perhaps an even better way of looking at the matter is that we are attempting to make the score, calculated for the current board position, look like that calculated for the terminal board position of the chain of moves which most probably will occur during actual play. Of course, if one could develop a perfect system of this sort it would be the equivalent of always looking ahead to the end of the game. The nearer this ideal is approached, the better would be the play.[11]

---

[11] There is a logical fallacy in this argument. The program might save only invariant terms which have nothing to do with goodness of play; for example, it might count the squares on the checkerboard. The forced inclusion of the piece-advantage term prevents this.

In order to obtain a sufficiently large span to make use of this characteristic, Alpha keeps a record of the apparent goodness of its board positions as the game progresses. This record is kept by computing the scoring polynomial for each board position encountered in actual play and by saving this polynomial in its entirety. At the same time, Alpha also computes the backed-up score for all board positions, using the look-ahead procedure described earlier. At each play by Alpha the initial board score, as saved from the previous Alpha move, is compared with the backed-up score for the current position. The difference between these scores, defined as *Delta*, is used to check the scoring polynomial. If Delta is positive it is reasonable to assume that the initial board evaluation was in error and terms which contributed positively should have been given more weight, while those that contributed negatively should have been given less weight. A converse statement can be made for the case where Delta is negative. Presumably, in this case, either the initial board evaluation was incorrect, or a wrong choice of moves was made, and greater weight should have been given to terms making negative contributions, with less weight to positive terms. These changes are not made directly but are brought about in an involved way which will now be described.

A record is kept of the correlation existing between the signs of the individual term contributions in the initial scoring polynomial and the sign of Delta. After each play an adjustment is made in the values of the correlation coefficients, due account being taken of the number of times that each particular term has been used and has had a nonzero value. The coefficient for the polynomial term (other than the piece-advantage term) with the then largest correlation coefficient is set at a prescribed maximum value with proportionate values determined for all of the remaining coefficients. Actually, the term coefficients are fixed at integral powers of 2, this power being defined by the ratio of the correlation coefficients. More precisely, if the ratio of two correlation coefficients is equal to or larger than n but less than $n + 1$, where n is an integer, then the ratio of the two term coefficients is set equal to 2^n. This procedure was adopted in order to increase the range in values of the term coefficients. Whenever a correlation-coefficient calculation leads to a negative sign, a corresponding reversal is made in the sign associated with the term itself.

Instabilities

It should be noted that the span of moves over which Delta is computed consists of a remembered part and an anticipated portion. During the remembered play, use had been made of Alpha's current scoring polynomial to determine Alpha's moves but not to determine the opponent's moves, while during the anticipation play the moves for both sides are made using Alpha's scoring polynomial. One is tempted to increase the sensitivity of Delta as an indicator of change by increasing the span of the remembered portion. This has been found to be dangerous since the coefficients in the evaluation polynomial and, indeed, the terms themselves, may change between the time of the remembered evaluation and the time at which the anticipation evaluation is made. As a matter of fact, this difficulty is present even for a span of one move-pair. It is necessary to recompute the scoring polynomial for a given initial board position after a move has been determined and after the indicated corrections in the scoring polynomial have been made, and to save this score for future comparisons, rather than to save the score used to determine the move. This may seem a trivial point, but its neglect in the initial stages of these experiments led to oscillations quite analogous to the instability induced in electrical circuits by long delays in a feedback loop.

As a means of stabilizing against minor variations in the Delta values, an arbitrary minimum value was set, and when Delta fell below this minimum for any particular move no change was made in the polynomial. This same minimum value is used to set limits for the initial board evaluation score to decide whether or not it will be assumed to be zero. This minimum is recomputed each time and, normally, has been fixed at the average value of the coefficients for the terms in the currently existing evaluation polynomial.

Still another type of instability can occur whenever a new term is introduced into the scoring polynomial. Obviously, after only a single move the correlation coefficient of this new term will have a magnitude of 1, even though it might go to 0 after the very next move. To prevent violent fluctuations due to this cause, the correlation coefficients for newly introduced terms are computed as if these terms had already been used several times and had been found to have a zero correlation coefficient. This is done by replacing the times-used number in the calculation by an arbitrary number (usually set at 16) until the usage does, in fact, equal this number.

After a term has been in use for some time, quite the opposite action is desired so that the more recent experience can outweigh earlier results. This is achieved, together with a substantial reduction in calculation time, by using powers of 2 in place of the actual times-used and by limiting the maximum power that is used. To be specific, at any stage of play defined as the Nth move, corrections to the values of the correlation coefficients C_N are made using 16 or N until $N = 32$, whereupon 32 is used until $N = 64$, etc., using the formula:

$$C_N = C_{N-1} - \frac{C_{N-1} \pm 1}{N},$$

and a value for $N > 256$ is never used.

After a minimum was set for Delta it seemed reasonable to attach greater weight to situations leading to large values of Delta. Accordingly, two additional categories are defined. If a contribution to Delta is made by the first term, meaning that a change has occurred in the piece ratio, indicated changes in the correlation coefficients are doubled, while if the value of Delta is so large as to indicate that an almost sure win or lose will result, the effect on the correlation coefficients is quadrupled.

Term Replacement

Mention has been made several times of the procedure for replacing terms in the scoring polynomial. The program, as it is currently running, contains 38 different terms (in addition to the piece-advantage term), 16 of these being included in the scoring polynomial at any one time and the remaining 22 being kept in reserve. After each move a low-term tally is recorded against that active term which has the lowest correlation coefficient and, at the same time, a test is made to see if this brings its tally count up to some arbitrary limit, usually set at 8. When this limit is reached for any specific term, this term is transferred to the bottom of the reserve list, and it is replaced by a term from the head of the reserve list. This new term enters the polynomial with zero values for its correlation coefficient, times used, and low-tally count. On the average, then, an active term is replaced once each eight moves and the replaced terms are given another chance after 176 moves. As a check on the effectiveness of this procedure, the program reports on the usage which has accrued against each discarded term. Terms which are repeatedly rejected after a minimum amount of usage can be removed and replaced with completely new terms.

It might be argued that this procedure of having the program select terms for the evaluation polynomial from a supplied list is much too simple and that the program should generate the terms for itself. Unfortunately, no satisfactory scheme for doing this has yet been devised. With a man-generated list one might at least ask that the terms be members of an orthogonal set, assuming that this has some meaning as applied to the evaluation of a checker position. Apparently, no one knows enough about checkers to define such a set. The only practical solution seems to be that of including a relatively large number of possible terms in the hope that all of the contributing parameters get covered somehow, even though in an involved and redundant way. This is not an undesirable state of affairs, however, since it simulates the situation which is likely to exist when an attempt is made to apply similar learning techniques to real-life situations.

Many of the terms in the existing list are related in some vague way to the parameters used by checker experts. Some of the concepts which checker experts appear to use have eluded the writer's attempts at definition, and he has been unable to program them. Some of the terms are quite unrelated to the usual checker lore and have been discovered more or less by accident. The second moment about the diagonal axis through the double corners is an example. Twenty-seven different simple terms are now in use, the rest being combinational terms, as will be described later.

A word might be said about these terms with respect to the exact way in which they are defined and the general procedures used for their evaluation. Each term relates to the relative standings of the two sides, with respect to the parameter in question, and it is numerically equal to the difference between the ratings for the individual sides. A reversal of the sign obviously corresponds to a change of sides. As a further means of insuring symmetry the individual ratings of the respective sides are determined at corresponding times in the play as viewed by the side in question. For example, consider a parameter which relates to the board conditions as left after one side has moved. The rating of Black for such a parameter would be made after Black had moved, and the rating of White would not be made until after White had moved. During anticipation play, these individual ratings are made after each move and saved for future reference. When an evaluation is desired the program takes the differences between the most recent ratings and those made a move earlier. In general, an attempt has been made to define all parameters so that the individual-side ratings are expressible as small positive integers.

Binary Connective Terms

In addition to the simple terms of the type just described, a number of combinational terms have been introduced. Without these terms the scoring polynomial would, of course, be linear. A number of different ways of introducing nonlinear terms have been devised but only one of these has been tested in any detail. This scheme provides terms which have some of the properties of binary logical connectives. Four such terms are formed for each pair of simple terms which are to be related. This is done by making an arbitrary division of the range in values for each of the simple terms and assigning the binary values of 0 and 1 to these ranges. Since most of the simple terms are symmetrical about 0, this is easily done on a sign basis. The new terms are then of the form $A \cdot B$, $A \cdot \bar{B}$, $\bar{A} \cdot B$, and $\bar{A} \cdot \bar{B}$, yielding values either of 0 or 1. These terms are introduced into the scoring polynomial with adjustable coefficients and signs, and are thereafter indistinguishable from the other terms.

As it would require some 1,404 such combinational terms to interrelate the 27 simple terms originally used, it was found desirable to limit the actual number of combinational terms used at any one time to a small fraction of these and to introduce new terms only as it became possible to retire older ineffectual terms. The terms actually used are given in Appendix C.

Preliminary Learning-by-Generalization Tests

An idea of the learning ability of this procedure can be gained by analyzing an initial test series of 28 games[12] played with the program just described. At the start an arbitrary selection of 16 terms was chosen and all terms were assigned equal weights. During the first 14 games Alpha was assigned the White side, with Beta constrained as to its first move (two cycles of the seven different initial moves). Thereafter, Alpha was assigned Black and White alternately. During this time a total of 29 different terms was discarded and replaced, the majority of these on two different occasions.

---

[12] Each game averaged 68 moves (34 to a side), of which approximately 20 caused changes to be made in the scoring polynomial.

Certain other figures obtained during these 28 games are of interest. At frequent intervals the program lists the 12 leading terms in Alpha's scoring polynomial with their correlation coefficients and a running count of the number of times these coefficients have been altered. Based on these samplings, one observes that at least 20 different terms were assigned the largest coefficient at some time or other, some of these alternating with other terms a number of times, and two even reappearing at the top of the list with their signs reversed. While these variations were more violent at the start of the series of games and decreased as time went on, their presence indicated that the learning procedure was still not completely stable. During the first seven games there were at least 14 changes in occupancy at the top of the list involving 10 different terms. Alpha won three of these games and lost four. The quality of the play was extremely poor. During the next seven games there were at least eight changes made in the top listing involving five different terms. Alpha lost the first of these games and won the next six. Quality of play improved steadily but the machine still played rather badly. During Games 15–21 there were eight changes in the top listing involving five terms; Alpha winning five games and losing two. Some fairly good amateur players who played the machine during this period agreed that it was "tricky but beatable". During Games 22–28 there were at least four changes involving three terms. Alpha won two games and lost five. The program appeared to be approaching a quality of play which caused it to be described as "a better-than-average player". A detailed analysis of these results indicated that the learning procedure did work and that the rate of learning was surprisingly high, but that the learning was quite erratic and none too stable.

Second Series of Tests

Some of the more obvious reasons for this erratic behavior in the first series of tests have been identified. The program was modified in several respects to improve the situation, and additional tests were made. Four of these modifications are important enough to justify a detailed explanation.

In the first place, the program was frequently fooled by bad play on the part of its opponent. A simple solution was to change the correlation coefficients less drastically when Delta was positive than when Delta was negative. The procedure finally adopted for the positive Delta case was to make corrections to selected terms in the polynomial only. When the scoring polynomial was positive, changes were made to coefficients associated with the negatively contributing terms, and when the polynomial was negative, changes were made to the coefficients associated with positively contributing terms. No changes were made to coefficients associated with terms which happened to be zero. For the negative Delta case, changes were made to the coefficients of all contributing terms, just as before.

A second defect seemed to be connected with the too frequent introduction of new terms into the scoring polynomial and the tendency for these new terms to assume dominant positions on the basis of insufficient evidence. This was remedied by the simple expedient of decreasing the rate of introduction of new terms from one every eight moves to one every 32 moves.

The third defect had to do with the complete exclusion from consideration of many of the board positions encountered during play by reason of the minimum limit on Delta. This resulted in the misassignment of credit to those board positions which permitted spectacular moves when the credit rightfully belonged to earlier board positions which had permitted the necessary ground-laying moves. Although no precise way has yet been devised to insure the correct assignment of credit, a very simple expedient was found to be most effective in minimizing the adverse effects of earlier assignments. This expedient was to allow the span of remembered moves, over which Delta is computed, to increase until Delta exceeded the arbitrary minimum value, and then to apply the corrections to the coefficients as dictated by the terms in the retained polynomial for this earlier board position. In this case, the difficulty which was mentioned in the section on instabilities in connection with an arbitrary increase in span, does not occur after each correction, since no changes are made in the coefficients of the scoring polynomial as long as Delta is below the minimum value. Of course, whenever Delta does exceed the minimum value the program must then recompute the initial scoring poly-nomial for then-current board position and so restart the procedure with a span of a single remembered move-pair. This overall procedure rectifies the defect of assigning credit to a board position that lies too far along the move chain, but it introduces the possibility of assigning credit to a board position that is not far enough along.

As a partial expedient to compensate for this newly introduced danger, a change was made in the initial board evaluation. Instead of evaluating the initial board positions directly, as was done before, a standard but rudimen-tary tree-search (terminated after the first nonjump move) was used. Errors due to impending jump situations were eliminated by this procedure, and because of the greater accuracy of the evaluation it was possible to reduce the minimum Delta limit by a small amount.

Finally, to avoid the danger of having Beta adopt Alpha's polynomial as a result of a chance win on Alpha's part (or perhaps a situation in which Alpha had allowed its polynomial to degenerate after an early or midgame advantage had been gained), it was decided to require a majority of wins on Alpha's part before Beta would adopt Alpha's scoring polynomial.

With these modifications, a new series of tests was made. It order to reduce the learning time, the initial selection of terms was made on the basis of the results obtained during the earlier test, but no attention was paid to their previously assigned weights. In contrast with the earlier erratic behavior, the revised program appeared to be extremely stable, perhaps at the expense of a somewhat lower initial learning rate. The way in which the character of the evaluation polynomial altered as learning progressed is shown in Figure 4.

The most obvious change in behavior was in regard to the relative number of games won by Alpha and the prevalence of draws. During the first 28 games

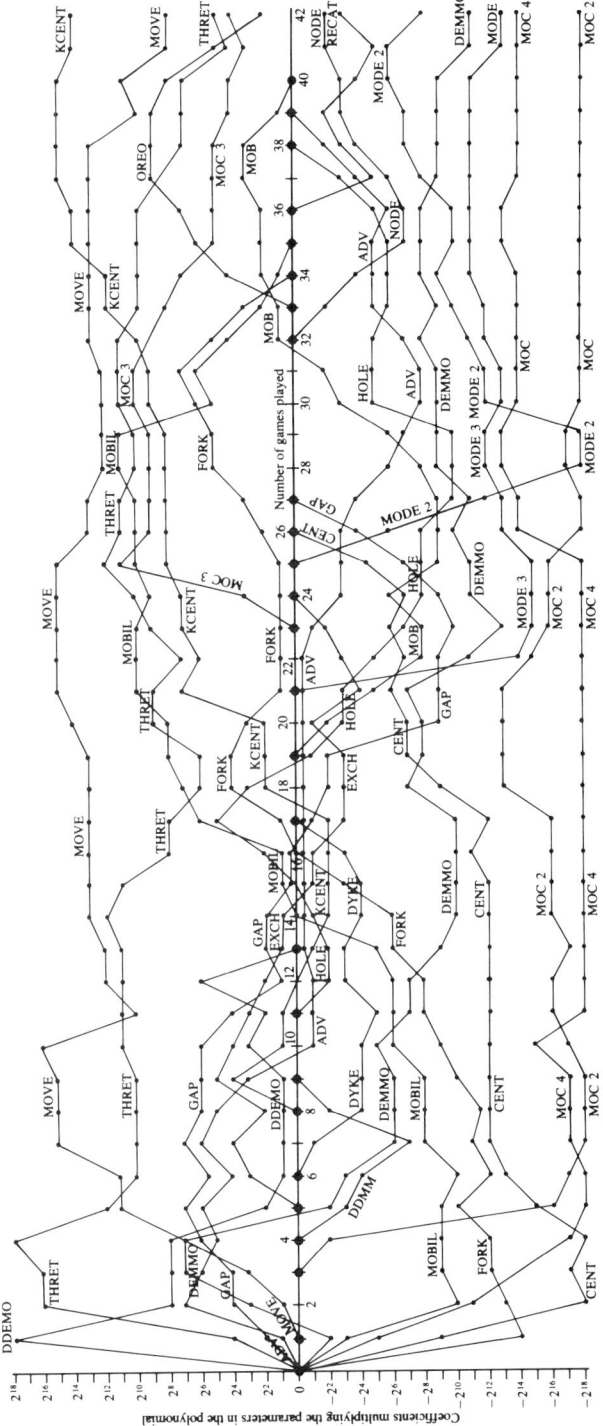

Figure 4. Second series of learning-by-generalization tests. Coefficients assigned by the program to the more significant parameters of the evaluation polynomial plotted as a function of the number of games played. Two regions of special interest might be noted: (1) the situation after 13 or 14 games, when the program found that the initial signs of many of the terms had been set incorrectly; and (2) the conditions of relative stability which are beginning to show up after 31 or 32 games.

of the earlier searies Alpha won 16 and lost 12. The corresponding figures for the first 28 games of the new series were 18 won by Alpha, and four lost, with six draws. In all cases the games were terminated, if not finished, in 70 moves and a judgment made in terms of the final positions. Unfortunately, these figures are not strictly comparable because of the decreased frequency with which Beta adopted Alpha's polynomial during the second series, both by design and because a programming error immobilized the adoption procedure during part of the tests. Nevertheless, the great increase in the number of losses and the prevalence of draws seemed to indicate that the learning process was much more stable. Some typical games from this second series are given in Appendix B.

As learning proceeds, it should become harder and harder for Alpha to improve its game, and one would expect the number of wins by Alpha to decrease with time. If secondary maxima in scoring space are encountered, one might even find situations in which Alpha wins less than half of the games. With Beta at such a maximum any minor change in Alpha's polynomial would result in a degradation of its play, and several oscillations about the maximum might occur before Alpha landed at a point which would enable it to beat Beta. Some evidence of this trend is discernible in the play, although many more games will have to be played before it can be observed with certainty.

The tentative conclusions which can be drawn from these tests are:

(1) A simple generalization scheme of the type here used can be an effective learning device for problems amenable to tree-searching procedures.
(2) The memory requirements of such schemes are quite modest and remain fixed with time.
(3) The operating times are also reasonable and remain fixed, independent of the amount of accumulated learning.
(4) Incipient forms of instability in the solution can be expected but, at least for the checker program, these can be dealt with by quite straightforward procedures.
(5) Even with the incomplete and redundant set of parameters which have been used to date, it is possible for the computer to learn to play a better-than-average game of checkers in a relatively short period of time.

As a final precautionary note, it should be stated that these experiments have not encompassed a sufficiently large series of games to demonstrate unambiguously that the learning procedure is completely stable or that it will necessarily lead to the best possible choice of parameters and coefficients.

Rote Learning versus Generalization

Some interesting comparisons can be made between the playing style developed by the learning-by-generalization program and that developed by the earlier rote-learning procedure. The program with rote learning soon learned to imitate master play during the opening moves. It was always quite poor during the middle game, but it easily learned how to avoid most of the obvious traps during endgame play and could usually drive on toward a win when left with a piece advantage. The program with the generalization procedure has never learned to play in a conventional manner and its openings are apt to be weak. On the other hand, it soon learned to play a good middle game, and with a piece advantage it usually polishes off its opponent in short order. Interestingly enough, after 28 games it had still not learned how to win an endgame with two Kings against one in a double corner.

Apparently, rote learning is of the greatest help, either under conditions when the results of any specific action are long delayed, or in those situations where highly specialized techniques are required. Contrasting with this, the generalization procedure is most helpful in situations in which the available permutations of conditions are large in number and when the consequences of any specific action are not long delayed.

Procedures Involving Both Forms of Learning

The next obvious step is to combine the better features of the rote-learning procedure with a generalization scheme. This must be done with some care, since it is not practical to update the previously saved information after every change in the evaluation polynomial. A compromise solution might be to save only a very limited amount of information during the early stages of learning and to increase the amount as warranted by the increasing stability of the evaluation coefficient with learning. For example, the program could be arranged to save only the piece-advantage term at the start. At some stage in the learning process the next term could be added, perhaps when no change had been made in the parameter used for this term during some fairly long period, say for three complete games. If and when the program is able to play an additional period without changes in the next parameter, this could also be added, etc. Whenever a change does occur in a parameter previously assumed to the stable the entire memory tape could be reviewed, all terms involving the changed parameter and those lower on the list could be expunged, and the program could drop back to the earlier condition with respect to its term-saving schedule.

Another solution would be to utilize the generalization scheme alone until it had become fairly stable and to introduce rote learning at this time. It is, of course, perfectly feasible to salvage much of the learning which has been accumulated by both of the programs studied to date. This could be done by appending an abridged form of the present memory tape to the generalization scheme in its present stage of learning and by proceeding from there in accordance with the first solution proposed above.

Future Development

While it is believed that these tests have reached the stage of diminishing returns, some effort might well be expended in an attempt to get the program to generate its own parameters for the evaluation polynomial. Lacking a perfectly general procedure, it might still be possible to generate terms based on theories as proposed by students of the game. This procedure would be at variance with the writer's previous philosophy, but it is highly likely that similar compromises will have to be made when one attempts to apply learning procedures to problems of economic importance.

Conclusions

As a result of these experiments one can say with some certainty that it is now possible to devise learning schemes which will greatly outperform an average person and that such learning schemes may eventually be economically feasible as applied to real-life problems.

Acknowledgments. Many different people have contributed to these studies through stimulating discussions of the basic problems. From time to time the writer was assisted by several different programmers, although most of the detailed work was his own. The forbearance of the machine room operators and their willingness to play the machine at all hours of the day and night are also greatly appreciated.

Appendix A. Programming Details

Approximate Size of Program

Basic checker-playing routine. . . . .   1,100 instructions
Input, move verification, and output . . . . . .   1,400 instructions
Game starting and terminating routines . . . . .   600 instructions
Loaders, table generators, dumping, etc. . . . . .   850 instructions
Statistical and analytical routines . . . .   700 instructions
Rote-learning routines . . . .   1,500 instructions
Generalization-learning routines. . . . .   650 instructions
Tables and constants for basic play. . . . . . .   700 words
Working space for basic play . . . .   2,000 words
Working space for generalization learning . . . .   500 words
Working space for rote learning . . . .   balance of memory

Approximate Computation Times

To find all available moves from given board position .   2.6 milliseconds
To make a single move and find resulting board position   1.5 milliseconds
To evaluate a board position (4 terms). . . . . . .   2.4 milliseconds

To find score for a saved board position (rote learning) .   2.3 milliseconds
To evaluate position (with 16 terms for generalization
learning) .   .   .   .   7.5 milliseconds

Board Representations

The standard checkerboard numbering system (see Appendix B) is used in communicating with the machine. A modified numbering system is used for internal computations, the numbers shown on the squares in Figure A-1 corresponding to the bit positions in an IBM 704 word. Any given board position is represented by four such words; one word (FA) containing 1's in those bit positions corresponding to squares containing pieces of the color whose turn it is to move and which normally move in a forward direction. To be specific, if it is Black's turn to move (i.e., if Black is "active") FA designates the location of all of Black's pieces, both men and Kings. Conversely, if White is active, FA designates the location of White's Kings only, since White's men can only move in the direction arbitrarily called *backward*. The other words designate, respectively: BA, backward active pieces; FP, forward passive pieces; and BP, backward passive pieces.

To conserve space when writing on tape, three words are used to record board positions with Kings, and only two words are used for board positions without Kings. These are saved in a standardized form, as explained in the text.

Possible moves are designated by five words; one word to indicate by its sign (with the word itself containing other information) whether the moves are jumps or not. (If a jump is available, only jump moves are saved.) The other four words designate the location of those pieces which can move in the four different diagonal directions: RF, for right forward; LF, for left forward; LB, for left backward; and RB, for right backward, respectively.

By reference to Figure A-1, it will be observed that a right-forward move results in an increase of four in the square designation, while a left-forward

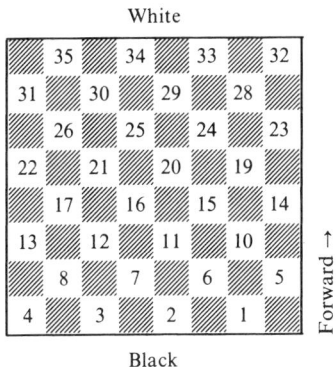

Figure A-1. Checkerboard notation for internal computations.

move results in an increase of five. Bit positions 9, 18, and 27 do not appear on the board. This notation makes it possible to compute available moves for all pieces simultaneously. Having previously computed a word called EMPTY, which contains 1's in locations corresponding to all unoccupied squares, one can compute RF, for the normal move case, in four instructions, as listed below (in IBM 704 symbolic language):

CLA	EMPTY	(puts word EMPTY into the accumulator);
ALS	four	(shifts word to left by four positions);
ANA	FA	(forms logical AND between EMPTY and FA);
STO	RF	(stores word as newly computed RF).

Jump moves are computed by a simple extension of this procedure. Multiple jumps are handled as a sequence of single jumps separated by null-reply moves.

Additional Time-Saving Expedients

Bit counting is done by a table-lookup procedure in a closed subroutine of 16 executed instructions (408 microseconds). This requires a 256-word table which is generated at the start by a 13-word program. Similar table-lookup procedures are used, to turn a word end-for-end, and to locate the 1's in a word for move reporting.

Multiplications are usually avoided. In several places where multiplication by small integers must be done, it is programmed in terms of shifts and logical operations.

During the look-ahead procedure a complete record is kept of the sequence of board positions currently under investigation. As a result, no computing is needed to retract moves.

Appendix B. Sample Games from the Second Series with Generalization Learning

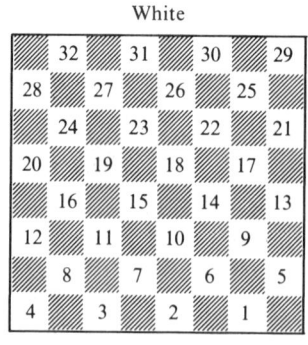

White

Black

Figure B-1. Square designations used in reporting games.

Typical Openings

The first eight moves of selected games in which Alpha played Black against Beta, showing the way in which different types of play were tried.

G-4	G-6	G-12	G-17	G-19	G-21	G-31	G-37	G-39	G-41	G-43
10–14	11–16	11–16	11–16	11–16	11–16	11–16	12–16	11–16	10–14	11–16
24–19	22–18	22–17	24–20	24–20	24–20	23–18	24–20	24–20	24–20	23–19
14–18	16–20	16–20	10–14	7–11	8–11	7–11	8–12	10–15	11–15	16–23
23–14	18–14	17–13	20–11	22–17	28–24	27–23	28–24	20–11	27–24	26–19
9–18	9–18	9–14	8–15	10–14	10–14	16–20	10–14	7–16	7–10	8–11
22–15	23–14	23–18	22–17	17–10	23–18	23–19	23–18	21–17	23–18	22–17
11–18	10–17	14–23	7–11	6–15	14–23	20–27	14–23	6–10	14–23	10–14
21–17	21–14	27–18	17–10	28–24	27–18	31–24	27–18	23–19	26–19	17–10

Typical Games

Sample games in which Alpha played White against forced Beta openings.

G-1	G-18	G-30	G-40	G-1	G-18	G-30	G-40
12–16	12–16	12–16	10–14	9–13	12–16	9–14	4– 8
24–19	24–20	24–20	24–20	1– 6	24–20	18– 9	1– 6
8–12	8–12	8–12	11–15	13–17	16–19	8–11	10–14
22–18	28–24	28–24	27–24	32–27	29–25	15– 8	6–10
10–14	10–15	10–14	7–10	16–20	13–17	4–11	14–17
26–22	22–18	22–18	23–18	18–14	10– 7	19–15	10–15
16–20	15–22	6–10	14–23	11–15	2–11	11–18	17–21
30–26	25–18	24–19	26–19	6–10	14–10	23–14	32–28
11–16	7–10	1– 6	10–14	15–18	19–23	13–17	5– 9
28–24	18–14	32–28	19–10	14– 9	21–14	9– 5	27–24
7–11	10–17	3– 8	6–15	Terminated	23–26	12–16	20–27
22–17	21–14	26–22	22–17	manually	10– 7	28–24	19–16
3– 8	9–18	9–13	2– 7		26–30	17–22	12–19
17–10	23–14	18– 9	17–10		25–21	6–10	15–22–31
6–15–22	6– 9	5–14	7–14		30–26	30–25	9–14
26–17	30–25	22–18	24–19		7– 3	1– 6	31–26
9–13	9–18	6– 9	15–24		11–15	25–21	14–18
17–14	26–23	25–22	28–19		14–10	5– 1	28–24
2– 7	3– 8	2– 6	14–17		5– 9	21–17	8–11
23–18	23–14	30–25	21–14		10– 6	24–20	24–19
16–23	1– 6	14–17	9–18		15–19	16–19	21–25
14–10	27–23	21–14–5	25–22		6– 1	20–16	30–21
7–14	6– 9	6– 9	18–25		26–22	17–13	Beta
18– 9	14–10	18–15	29–22		1– 6	6– 2	concedes
5–14	9–13	11–18	5– 9		9–13	13–17	
27–18–9	25–21	20–11–2	31–27		20–16	10– 6	
20–27	11–15	10–14	1– 5		19–23	Beta	
31–24	20–11	22–15	20–16		6– 9	concedes	
12–16	15–18	14–17	3– 7		23–27		
21–17	23–14	5– 1	22–17		16–11		
13–22	8–15	17–21	8–11		22–25		
25–18	24–19	25–22	17–13		11– 7		
1– 5	15–24	21–25	11–20		25–30		
9– 6	32–28	22–18	13– 6		7– 2		
5– 9	24–27	25–30	7–10		27–32		
6– 1	31–24	2– 6	6– 1		70 Move		
					termination		

Appendix C. Evaluation Polynomial Details for Second Series

Method of Computing Terms

The 16 terms called for in the evaluation polynomial are computed, individually, by taking the value of the appropriate parameter, as defined below, for the board position under consideration and subtracting the value of this same parameter computed for the board position just prior to the last move (with the necessary reversal in the definitions of active and passive sides). This difference is then multiplied by the corresponding program-computed coefficient, which can vary between -2^{18} and $+2^{18}$, and credited to the side which was passive on the board position under consideration.

Definitions of Parameters

ADV (Advancement)
The parameter is credited with 1 for each passive man in the fifth and sixth rows (counting in passive's direction) and debited with 1 for each passive man in the third and fourth rows.

APEX (Apex)
The parameter is debited with 1 if there are no Kings on the board, if either square 7 or 26 is occupied by an active man, and if neither of these squares is occupied by a passive man.

BACK (Back Row Bridge)
The parameter is credited with 1 if there are no active Kings on the board and if the two bridge squares (1 and 3, or 30 and 32) in the back row are occupied by passive pieces.

CENT (Center Control I)
The parameter is credited with 1 for each of the following squares: 11, 12, 15, 16, 20, 21, 24, and 25 which is occupied by a passive man.

CNTR (Center Control II)
The parameter is credited with 1 for each of the following squares: 11, 12, 15, 16, 20, 21, 24, and 25 that is either currently occupied by an active piece or to which an active piece can move.

CORN (Double-Corner Credit)
The parameter is credited with 1 if the material credit value for the the active side is 6 or less, if the passive side is ahead in material credit, and if the active side can move into one of the double-corner squares.

CRAMP (Cramp)
The parameter is credited with 2 if the passive side occupies the cramping square (13 for Black, and 20 for White) and at least one other nearby square (9 or 14 for Black, and 19 or 20 for White), while certain squares (17, 21, 22, and 25 for Black, and 8, 11, 12, and 16 for White) are all occupied by the active side.

DENY (Denial of Occupancy)
The parameter is credited with 1 for each square defined in MOB if on the next move a piece occupying this square could be captured without an exchange.

DIA (Double Diagonal File)
The parameter is credited with 1 for each passive piece located in the diagonal files terminating in the double-corner squares.

DIAV (Diagonal Moment Value)
The parameter is credited with 1/2 for each passive piece located on squares two removed from the double-corner diagonal files, with 1 for each passive piece located on squares one removed from the double-corner files and with 3/2 for each passive piece in the double-corner files.

DYKE (Dyke)
The parameter is credited with 1 for each string of passive pieces that occupy three adjacent diagonal squares.

EXCH (Exchange)
The parameter is credited with 1 for each square to which the active side may advance a piece and, in so doing, force an exchange.

EXPOS (Exposure)
The parameter is credited with 1 for each passive piece that is flanked along one or the other diagonal by two empty squares.

FORK (Threat of Fork)
The parameter is credited with 1 for each situation in which passive pieces occupy two adjacent squares in one row and in which there are three empty squares so disposed that the active side could, by occupying one of them, threaten a sure capture of one or the other of the two pieces.

GAP (Gap)
The parameter is credited with 1 for each single empty square that separates two passive pieces along a diagonal, or that separates a passive piece from the edge of the board.

GUARD (Back Row Control)
The parameter is credited with 1 if there are no active Kings and if either the Bridge or the Triangle of Oreo is occupied by passive pieces.

HOLE (Hole)
The parameter is credited with 1 for each empty square that is surrounded by three or more passive pieces.

KCENT (King Center Control)
The parameter is credited with 1 for each of the following squares: 11, 12, 15, 16, 20, 21, 24, and 25 which is occupied by a passive King.

MOB (Total Mobility)
The parameter is credited with 1 for each square to which the active side could move one or more pieces in the normal fashion, disregarding the fact that jump moves may or may not be available.

MOBIL (Undenied Mobility)

The parameter is credited with the difference between MOB and DENY.

MOVE (Move)

The parameter is credited with 1 if pieces are even with a total piece count (2 for men, and 3 for Kings) of less than 24, and if an odd number of pieces are in the move system, defined as those vertical files starting with squares, 1, 2, 3, and 4.

NODE (Node)

The parameter is credited with 1 for each passive piece that is surrounded by at least three empty squares.

OREO (Triangle of Oreo)

The parameter is credited with 1 if there are no passive Kings and if the Triangle of Oreo (squares 2, 3, and 7 for Black, and squares 26, 30, and 31 for White) is occupied by passive pieces.

POLE (Pole)

The parameter is credited with 1 for each passive man that is completely surrounded by empty squares.

RECAP (Recapture)

This parameter is identical with Exchange, as defined above. (It was introduced to test the effects produced by the random times at which parameters are introduced and deleted from the evaluation polynomial.)

THRET (Threat)

The parameter is credited with 1 for each square to which an active piece may be moved and in so doing threaten the capture of a passive piece on a subsequent move.

Binary Connective Terms

The abbreviations used for the terms of this type which have been employed are listed below, in the order of $A \cdot B$, $A \cdot \overline{B}$ $\overline{A} \cdot B$, and $\overline{A} \cdot \overline{B}$, where A and B are the two respective parameters heading the sublists of abbreviations.

Denial of occupancy— Total mobility	Undenied mobility— Denial of occupancy	Undenied mobility— Center control I
DEMO	MODE 1	MOC 1
DEMMO	MODE 2	MOC 3
DDEMO	MODE 3	MOC 2
DDMM	MODE 4	MOC 4

Evaluation Polynomial (First 12 Terms Only) After 42 Games, During Which a Total of 1039 Different Sets of Adjustments Were Made to the Terms and Their Coefficients

Term	Correlation coefficient	Sign of coefficient	Power of 2 used as coefficient	Times adjusted
MOC 2	0.45	−	18	84
KCENT	0.40	+	16	127
MOC 4	0.35	−	14	95
MODE 3	0.33	−	13	210
DEMMO	0.27	−	11	132
MOVE	0.19	+	8	91
ADV	0.19	−	8	739
MODE 2	0.19	−	8	55
BACK	0.14	−	6	6
CNTR	0.13	+	5	12
THRET	0.13	+	5	442
MOC 3	0.10	+	4	89

Discarded Terms During 42 Games

Term	Times adjusted before discard	Term	Times adjusted before discard
CORN	0	MODE 1	1
CRAMP	0	CENT	386
GUARD	0	MODE 4	0
EXPOS	162	FORK	400
DDMM	19	MOBIL	707
DYKE	115	POLE	11
MOC 1	1	HOLE	598
EXCH	445	GAP	792
DDEMO	53	MOB	608

Note added in proof: An additional 20 games have recently been played. Although some significant changes were noted, the general stabilization of the learning process suggested by Figure 4 has been confirmed. During this play, 412 more adjustments were made to the terms and their coefficients and 12 additions were made to the list of discarded terms.

3.3. Some Studies in Machine Learning Using the Game of Checkers. II—Recent Progress

ARTHUR L. SAMUEL

Originally published in: *IBM Journal of Research and Development*, vol. 11, 1967, pp. 601–617. Copyright © 1967 IBM Corporation. Reprinted by permission.

Abstract. A new signature table technique is described together with an improved book-learning procedure which is thought to be much superior to the linear polynomial method described earlier. Full use is made of the so-called "alpha–beta" pruning and several forms of forward pruning to restrict the spread of the move tree and to permit the program to look-ahead to a much greater depth than it otherwise could do. While still unable to outplay checker masters, the program's playing ability has been greatly improved.

Introduction

Limited progress has been made in the development of an improved book-learning technique and in the optimization of playing strategies as applied to the checker-playing program described in an earlier paper with this same title (Samuel, 1959). Because of the sharpening in our understanding and the substantial improvements in playing ability that have resulted from these recent studies, a reporting at this time seems desirable. Unfortunately, the most basic limitation of the known machine-learning techniques, as previously outlined, has not yet been overcome nor has the program been able to outplay the best human checker players.[1]

We will briefly review the earlier work. The reader who does not find this

---

[1] In a 1965 match with the program, the World Champion, Mr. W. F. Hellman, won all four games played by mail but was played to a draw in one hurriedly played cross-board game. Recently Mr. K. D. Hanson, the Pacific Coast Champion, has beaten current versions of the program on two separate occasions.

review adequate might do well to refresh his memory by referring to the earlier paper.

Two machine-learning procedures were described in some detail:

(1) A rote-learning procedure in which a record was kept of the board situation encountered in actual play together with information as to the results of the machine analyses of the situation; this record could be referenced at terminating board situations of each newly initiated tree-search and thus, in effect, allow the machine to look ahead further than time would otherwise permit.
(2) A generalization-learning procedure in which the program continuously re-evaluated the coefficients for the linear polynomial used to evaluate the board positions at the terminating board situations of a look-ahead tree-search. In both cases, the program applied a minimax procedure to back up scores assigned to the terminating situations and so select the best move, on the assumption that the opponent would also apply the same selection rules when it was his turn to play.

The rote-learning procedure was characterized by a very slow but continuous learning rate. It was most effective in the opening and endgame phases of the play. The generalization-learning procedure, by way of contrast, learned at a more rapid rate but soon approached a plateau set by limitations as to the adequacy of the man-generated list of parameters used in the evaluation polynomial. It was surprisingly good at midgame play but fared badly in the opening and endgame phases. Both learning procedures were used in cross-board play against human players and in self-play, and in spite of the absence of absolute standards were able to improve the play, thus demonstrating the usefulness of the techniques discussed.

Certain expressions were introduced which we will find useful. These are: *Ply*, defined as the number of moves ahead, where a ply of two consists of one proposed move by the machine and one anticipated reply by the opponent; *board parameter value*,[2] defined as the numerical value associated with some measured property or parameter of a board situation. Parameter values, when multiplied by learned coefficients, become *terms* in the learning polynomial. The value of the entire polynomial is a *score*.

The most glaring defects of the program, as earlier discussed, were:

(1) the absence of an effective machine procedure for generating new parameters for the evaluation procedure;
(2) the incorrectness of the assumption of linearity which underlies the use of a linear polynomial;
(3) the general slowness of the learning procedure;

---

[2] Example of a *board parameter* is **MOB** (total mobility): the number of squares to which the player can potentially move, disregarding forced jumps that might be available; the earlier paper describes many other parameters.

(4) the inadequacies of the heuristic procedures used to prune and to terminate the tree-search; and

(5) the absence of any strategy considerations for altering the machine mode of play in the light of the tactical situations as they develop during play.

While no progress has been made with respect to the first of these defects, some progress has been made in overcoming the other four limitations, as will now be described.

We will restrict the discussion in this paper to generalization-learning schemes in which a preassigned list of board parameters is used. Many attempts have been made to improve this list, to make it both more precise and more inclusive. It still remains a man-generated list and it is subject to all the human failings, both of the programmer, who is not a very good checker player, and of the checker experts consulted, who are good players (the best in the world, in fact) but who, in general, are quite unable to express their immense knowledge of the game in words, and certainly not in words understandable to this programmer. At the present time, some 27 parameters are in use, selected from the list given in Samuel (1959) with a few additions and modifications, although a somewhat longer list was used for some of the experiments which will be described.

Two methods of combining evaluations of these parameters have been studied in considerable detail. The first, as earlier described, is the linear polynomial method in which the values for the individual parameters are multiplied by coefficients determined through the learning process and added together to obtain a score. A second, more recent procedure is to use tabulations called "signature tables" to express the observed relationship between parameters in subsets. Values read from the tables for a number of subsets are then combined for the final evaluation. We will have more to say on evaluation procedures after a digression on other matters.

The Heuristic Search for Heuristics

At the risk of some repetition, and of sounding pedantic, it might be well to say a bit about the problem of immensity as related to the game of checkers. As pointed out in the earlier paper, checkers is not deterministic in the practical sense since there exists no known algorithm which will predict the best move short of the complete exploration of every acceptable[3] path to the end of the game. Lacking time for such a search, we must depend upon heuristic procedures.

Attempts to see how people deal with games such as checkers or chess[4] reveal that the better players engage in behavior that seems extremely com-

---

[3] The word "acceptable" rather than "possible" is used advisedly for reasons which relate to the so-called alpha–beta heuristic, as will be described later.
[4] See, for example, Newell et al. (1958b). For references to other games, see Samuel (1960).

plex, even a bit irrational in that they jump from one aspect to another, without seeming to complete any one line of reasoning. In fact, from the writer's limited observation of checker players he is convinced that the better the player, the more apparent confusion there exists in his approach to the problem, and the more intuitive his reactions seem to be, at least as viewed by the average person not blessed with a similar proficiency. We conclude[5] that at our present stage of knowledge, the only practical approach, even with the help of the digital computer, will be through the development of heuristics which tend to ape human behavior. Using a computer, these heuristics will, of course, be weighted in direction of placing greater reliance on speed than might be the case for a human player, but we assume that the the complexity of the human response is dictated by the complexity of the task to be performed and is, in some way, an indication of how such problems can best be handled.

We will go a step further and maintain that the task of making decisions as to the heuristics to be used is also a problem which can only be attacked by heuristic procedures, since it is essentially an even more complicated task than is the playing itself. Furthermore, we will seldom, if ever, be able to perform a simple test to determine the effectiveness of any particular heuristic, keeping everything else the same, as any scientist generally tends to do. There are simply too many heuristics that should be tested and there is simply not enough time to embark on such a program even if the cost of computer time were no object. But, more importantly, the heuristics to be tested are not independent of each other and they affect the other parameters which we would like to hold constant. A definitive set of experiments is virtually impossible of attainment. We are forced to make compromises, to make complicated changes in the program, varying many parameters at the same time and then, on the basis of incomplete tests, somehow conclude that our changes are or are not in the right direction.

Playing Techniques

While the investigation of the learning procedures forms the essential core of the experimental work, certain improvements have been made in playing techniques which must first be described. These improvements are largely concerned with tree-searching. They involve schemes to increase the effectiveness of the alpha–beta pruning, the so-called "alpha–beta heuristic"[6] and

---

[5] More precisely we adopt the heuristic procedure of assuming that we must so conclude.

[6] So named by Professor John McCarthy. This procedure was extensively investigated by Professor McCarthy and his students at MIT but it has been inadequately described in the literature. It is, of course, not a heuristic at all, being a simple algorithmic procedure and actually only a special case of the more general "branch and bound" technique which has been rediscovered many times and which is currently being exploited in integer programming research. See Land and Doight (1957) reported in Dantzig (1963); Rossman and Twery (1958); Little *et al.* (1963).

a variety of other techniques going under the generic name of tree pruning.[7] These improvements enable the program to analyze further in depth than it otherwise could do, albeit with the introduction of certain hazards which will be discussed. Lacking an ideal board evaluation scheme, tree-searching still occupies a central role in the checker program.

Alpha–Beta Pruning

Alpha–beta pruning can be explained simply as a technique for not exploring those branches of a search tree that the analysis up to any given point indicates not to be of further interest either to the player making the analysis (this is obvious) or to his opponent (and it is this that is frequently overlooked). In effect, there are always two scores, an *alpha value* which must be exceeded for a board to be considered desirable by the side about to play, and a *beta value* which must not be exceeded for the move leading to the board to have been made by the opponent. We note that if the board should not be acceptable to the side about to play, this player will usually be able to deny his opponent the opportunity of making the move leading to this board, by himself making a different earlier move. While people use this technique more or less instinctively during their look-ahead analyses, they sometimes do not understand the full implications of the principle. The saving in the required amount of tree-searching which can be achieved through its use is extremely large, and as a consequence alpha–beta pruning is an almost essential ingredient in any game playing program. There are no hazards associated with this form of pruning.

A move tree of the type that results when alpha–beta pruning is effective is shown in Figure 1, it being assumed that the moves are investigated from left to right. Those paths that are shown in dashed lines need never be considered, as can be verified by assigning any arbitrary scores to the terminals of the dashed paths and by minimaxing in the usual way. Admittedly the example chosen is quite special but it does illustrate the possible savings that can result. To realize the maximum saving in computational effort as shown in this example one must investigate the moves in an ideal order, this being the order which would result were each side to always consider its best possible move first. A great deal of thought and effort has gone into devising techniques which increase the probability that the moves will be investigated in something approaching this order.

The way in which two limiting values (McCarthy's alpha and beta) are used in pruning can be seen by referring to Figure 2, where the tree of Figure 1 has been redrawn with the uninvestigated branches deleted. For reasons of symmetry all boards during the look-ahead are scored as viewed by the side

---

[7] It is interesting to speculate on the fact that human learning is involved in making improvements in the tree pruning techniques. It would be nice if we could assign this learning task to the computer but no practical way of doing this has yet been devised.

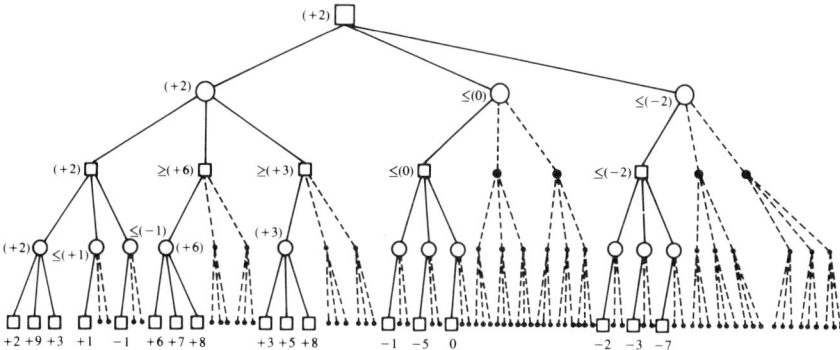

Figure 1. A (look-ahead) move tree in which alpha–beta pruning is fully effective if the tree is explored from left to right. Board positions for a look-ahead move by the first player are shown by squares, while board positions for the second player are shown by circles. The branches shown by dashed lines can be left unexplored without in any way influencing the final move choice.

whose turn it then is to move. This means that minimaxing is actually done by changing the sign of a score, once for each ply on backing up the tree, and then always maximizing. Furthermore, only one set of values (alpha values) need be considered. Alpha values are assigned to all boards in the tree (except for the terminating boards) as these boards are generated. These values reflect the score which must be exceeded before the branch leading to this board will be entered by the player whose turn it is to play. When the look-ahead is terminated and the terminal board evaluated (say at *board e* in Figure 2) then the value which currently is assigned the board two levels up the tree (in this case at *board c*) is used as the alpha value, and unless the terminal board score exceeds this alpha value, the player at *board c* would be ill-advised to consider

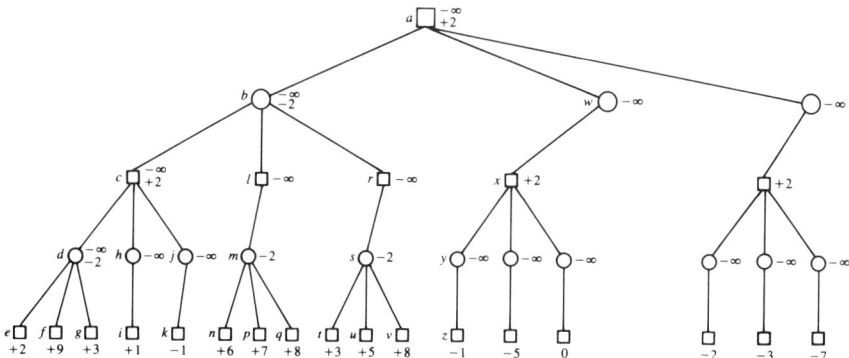

Figure 2. The move tree of Figure 1 redrawn to illustrate the detailed method used to keep track of the comparison values. Board positions are lettered in the order that they are investigated and the numbers are the successive alpha values that are assigned to the boards as the investigation proceeds.

entering the branch leading to this terminal board. Similarly, if the negative of the terminal board score does not exceed the alpha value associated with the board immediately above in the tree (in this case at *board d*) then the player at *board d* will not consider this to be desirable move. An alternate way of stating this second condition, in keeping with McCarthy's usage, is to say that the negative of the alpha value associated with the board one level up the tree (in this case *board d*) is the beta value which must not be exceeded by the score associated with the board in question (in this case *board e*). A single set of alpha values assigned to the boards in the tree thus performs a dual role, that of McCarthy's alpha as referenced by boards two levels down in the tree and, when negated, that of McCarthy's beta as referenced by boards one level down in the tree.

Returning to the analysis of Figure 2, we note that during the initial look-ahead (leading to *board e*) nothing is known as to the value of the boards, consequently the assigned alpha values are all set at $-\infty$ (actually within the computer only at a very large negative number). When *board e* is evaluated, its score ($+2$) is compared with the alpha at c ($-\infty$), and found to be larger. The negative of the score (-2) is then compared with the alpha at d ($-\infty$) and, being larger, it is used to replace it. The alpha at d is now -2 and it is unaffected by the subsequent consideration of terminal *boards f* and *g*. When all paths from *board d* have been considered, the final alpha value at d is compared with the current alpha value at *board b* ($-\infty$); it is larger, so the negative of alpha at d (now $+2$) is compared with the current alpha value at c ($-\infty$) and, being larger, it is used to replace the c value, and a new move from *board c* investigated leading to *board h* and then *board i*. As we go down the tree we must assign an alpha value to *board h*. We cannot use the alpha value at *board c* since we are now interested in the minimum that the other side will accept. We can however advance the alpha value from *board b*, which in this case is still at its initial value of $-\infty$. Now when *board i* is evaluated at $+1$ this value is compared with the alpha at *board c* ($+2$). The comparison being unfavorable, it is quite unnecessary to consider any other moves originating at *board h* and we go immediately to a consideration of *boards j* and *k*, where a similar situation exists. This process is simply repeated throughout the tree. On going forward the alpha values are advanced each time from two levels above and, on backing up, two comparisons are always made. When the tree is completely explored, the final alpha value on the initial board is the score, and the correct move is along the path from which this alpha was derived.

The saving that results from alpha–beta pruning can be expressed either as a reduction in the apparent amount of branching at each node or as an increase in the maximum ply to which the search may be extended in a fixed time interval. With optimum ordering, the apparent branching factor is reduced very nearly to the square root of its original value or, to put it another way, for a given investment in computer time, the maximum ply is very nearly doubled. With moderately complex trees the savings can be astronomical. For example, consider a situation with a branching factor of 8. With ideal alpha–beta pruning this factor is reduced to approximately 2.83. If time permits the evaluation of 66,000 boards (about 5 minutes for checkers), one can look ahead approximately 10-ply with alpha–beta pruning. Without alpha–beta this depth would require the evaluation of 8^{10} or approximately 10^9 board positions and would require over 1,000 hours of computation! Such savings are of course dependent upon perfect ordering of the moves. Actual savings are not as great but alpha–beta pruning can easily reduce the work by factors of 1,000 or more in real game situations.

Some improvement results from the use of alpha–beta pruning even without any attempt to optimize the search order. However, the number of branches which are pruned is then highly variable depending upon the accidental ordering of the moves. The problem is further complicated in the case of checkers because of the variable nature of the branching. Using alpha–beta alone the apparent branching factor is reduced from something in the vicinity of 6 (reduced from the value of 8 used above because of forced jump moves) to about 4, and with the best selection of ordering practiced to date, the apparent branching is reduced to 2.6. This leads to a very substantial increase in the depth to which the search can be carried.

Although the principal use of the alpha and beta values is to prune useless branches from the move tree, one can also avoid a certain amount of inconsequential work whenever the difference between the current alpha value and the current beta value becomes small. This means that the two sides have nearly agreed as to the optimum score and that little advantage to either one side or the other can be found by further exploration along the paths under investigation. It is therefore possible to back-up along the tree until a part of the tree is found at which this alpha–beta margin is no longer small. Not finding such a situation one may terminate the search. The added savings achieved in this way, while not as spectacular as the savings from the initial use of alpha–beta, are quite significant, frequently reducing the work by an additional factor of two or more.

Plausibility Analysis

In order for the alpha–beta pruning to be truly effective, it is necessary, as already mentioned, to introduce some technique for increasing the probability that the better paths are explored first. Several ways of doing this have been tried. By far the most useful seems to be to conduct a preliminary plausibility survey for any given board situation by looking ahead a fixed amount, and then to list the available moves in their apparent order of goodness on the basis of this information and to specify this as the order to be followed in the subsequent analysis. A compromise is required as to the depth to which this plausibility survey is to be conducted; too short a look-ahead renders it of doubtful value, while too long a look-ahead takes so much time that the depth of the final analysis must be curtailed. There is also a question as to whether or not this plausibility analysis should be applied at all ply levels during the main look-ahead or only for the first few levels. At one time the program used a plausibility survey for only the first two ply levels of the man look-ahead with the plausibility analysis itself being carried to a minimum ply of 2. More recently, the plausibility analysis has been applied at all stages during the main look-ahead and it has been carried to a minimum ply of 3 during certain portions of the look-ahead and under certain conditions, as will be explained later.

We pause to note that the alpha–beta pruning as described might be called a backward pruning technique in that it enables branches to be pruned at that time when the program is ready to back up and is making minimax comparisons. It assumes that the analyses of all branches are otherwise carried to a fixed ply and that all board evaluations are made at this fixed ply level. As mentioned earlier, the rigorous application of alpha–beta technique introduces no opportunities for erroneous pruning. The results in terms of the final moves chosen are always exactly as they would have been without the pruning. To this extent the procedure is not a heuristic although the plausibility analysis technique which makes it effective is certainly a heuristic.

While the simple use of the plausibility analysis has been found to be quite effective in increasing the amount of alpha–beta pruning, it suffers from two defects. In the first place, the actual amount of pruning varies greatly from move to move, depending upon random variations in the average correctness of the plausibility predictions. Second, within even the best move trees a wrong prediction at any one point in the search tree causes the program to follow a less than optimum path, even when it should have been possible to detect the fact that a poor prediction had been made before doing an excessive amount of useless work.

A Multiple-Path Enhanced-Plausibility Procedure

In studying procedures used by the better checker players one is struck with the fact that evaluations are being made continuously at all levels of look-ahead. Sometimes unpromising lines of play are discarded completely after only a cursory examination. More often, less promising lines are put aside briefly and several competing lines of play may be under study simultaneously with attention switching from one to another as the relative goodness of the lines of play appears to change with increasing depth of the tree-search. This action is undoubtedly prompted by a desire to improve the alpha–beta pruning effectiveness, although I have yet to find a checker master who explains it in these terms. We are well advised to copy this behavior.

Fortunately, the plausibility analysis provides the necessary information for making the desired comparisons at a fairly modest increase in data storage requirements and with a relatively small amount of reprogramming of the tree-search. The procedure used is as follows. At the beginning of each move, all possible moves are considered and a plausibility search is made for the opponent's replies to each of these plays. These moves are sorted in their apparent order of goodness. Each branch is then carried to a ply of 3; that is, making the machine's first move, the opponent's first reply and the machine's countermove. In each case the moves made are based on a plausibility analysis which is also carried to a minimum depth of 3-ply. The path yielding the highest score to the machine at this level is then chosen for investigation and followed forward for two moves only (that is, making the opponent's indicated best reply and the machine's best counterreply, always based on a plausibility analysis). At this point the score found for this path is compared with the score for the second best path as saved earlier. If the path under investigation is now found to be less good than an alternate path, it is stored and the alternative path is picked up and is extended in depth by two moves. A new comparison is made and the process is repeated. Alternately, if the original path under investigation is still found to be the best it is continued for two more moves. The analysis continues in this way until a limiting depth as set by other considerations has been reached. At this point the flitting from path to path is discontinued and the normal minimaxing procedure is instituted. Hopefully, however, the probability of having found the optimum path has been increased by this procedure and the alpha–beta pruning should work with greater effectiveness. The net effect of all of this is to increase the amount of alpha–beta pruning, to decrease the playing time, and to decrease the spread in playing time from move to move.

This enhanced plausibility analysis does not in any way affect the harzard-free nature of the alpha–beta pruning. The plausibility scores used during the look-ahead procedure are used only to determine the order of the analyses and they are all replaced by properly minimaxed scores as the analysis proceeds.

One minor point may require explanation. In order for all of the saved scores to be directly comparable, they are all related to the same side (actually to the machine's side) and as described they are compared only when it is the opponent's turn to move; that is, comparisons are made only on every alternate play. It would, in principle, be possible to make comparisons after every move but little is gained by so doing and serious complications arise which are thought to offset any possible advantage.

A move tree as recorded by the computer during actual play is shown in Figure 3. This is simply a listing of the moves, in the order in which they were considered, but arranged on the page to reveal the tree structure. Asterisks are used to indicate alternate moves at branch points and the principal branches are identified by serial numbers. In the interest of clarity, the moves made during each individual plausibility search are not shown, but one such search was associated with each recorded move. While the tree of Figure 3 exhibits the combined effect of several forms of pruning, some yet to be explained, the flitting from path to path is clearly visible at the start. In this case there were nine possible initial moves which were surveyed at the start and listed in the initially expected best order as identified by the serial

Figure 3. An actual look-ahead move tree as printed by the computer during play.

MOVE TREE		ALPHA	BETA	SCORE
15–19,23–16,12–19	1			00014
7–11,25–22, 5– 9	2			–00030
8–11,25–22, 4– 8	3			–00016
15–18,25–22,18–25	4			–00032
14–17,21–14,10–17	5			–00036
12–16,24–19,15–24	6			–06404
6– 9,13– 6, 2– 9	7			–00037
14–18,23–14,10–17	8			–00044
5– 9,24–19,15–24	9			00021
9 28–19, 8–11,25–22,11–15				00013
1 24–15,10–19,26–23,19–26				00010
9 22–18,15–24				00010
1 30–23, 8–12,25–22,14–18	**			00034
*12–16		00034		00021
*27–24		–00034		–00045
* 5– 9		00034		00024
*31–22, 7–10,30–26		–00034		–00105
*27–23		–00034		–00105
*26–22, 7–10,27–23,19–26			00034	00045
*30–26, 3– 7			00034	00036
*31–26, 3– 7			00034	00036

```
*24-15,10-19,23-16,12-19,26-23,19-26,30-23, 8-12,25-22     00034  00033
                                           *27-24          -00034 -00034
                                 *31-22, 7-10,30-26         -00034 -00045
                                           *27-23          -00034 -00105
                                                           -00034 -00105
              *26-22, 7-10                                  00034  00045
              *27-24, 7-10,24-15,10-19                      00034  00033

                                     27-20                -00034 -00010
                                    *15-22                        -00000
               * 4- 8                                      00034 -00036
               *11-16                                      00034 -00016

         * 7-11,19-15,11-18,21-17                          -00034 -00007
                        *10-19,23- 7                       -00034  00001
              *10-15,19-10, 6-15,13- 6                     -00034  00004
              * 1- 5                                        00034 -00032

    22-18,15-22,26-17,11-16,30-26, 8-11                     00034  00024
                                  *10-15                    00034 -17341
               * 5- 9,24-20                                -00034  00005
                        *14-18                              00034 -00041
    * 3- 8,22-17,15-19,24-15,11-18,28-24                   -00034  00031
                        *10-19,17- 3                       -00034  16023
               * 5- 9                                       00034 -00037
               * 6- 9                                       00034 -00105
               *14-18                                       00034 -00105
    *14-17,21-14,10-17,24-19,15-24,28-19                   -00034  00031
    * 6- 9,13- 6, 2- 9,29-25                               -00034  00032

9
3
```

Figure 3 (*continued*)

	MOVE TREE	ALPHA	BETA	SCORE
2	22-17,15-18,26-22,18-25,29-22,11-15	00034		-00030
	*12-16	00034		-00034
	* 2- 7,29-25		-00034	00023
	* 3- 7	00034		-00037
	*11-16	00034		-00030
	* 3- 7,22-17,15-19,24-15,11-18,28-24		-00034	00031
	*10-19,17- 3		-00034	16023
	* 5- 9	00034		-00037
	* 6- 9	00034		-00105
	*14-18	00034		-00105
	* 2- 7,24-19,15-24,28-19,14-17	00034		-00045
	* 5- 9	00034		-00045
	*11-16	00034		-00045
	*11-16,24-19	00034	-00034	00012
4	29-22,14-17,21-14,10-17,22-18, 6- 9,13- 6		-00034	00100
	*17-21	00034		-00030
	* 5- 9,24-19, 8-11	00034		-00007
	* 1- 5	00034		-00032
	* 7-11	00034		-00036
	* 8-11,23-18	00034	-00034	-00007
	* 7-11	00034		-00030
5	24-19,15-24,28-19, 5- 9,25-21, 9-14	00034		-00017
	*17-22	00034		-07432
	* 8-11,25-22	00034	-00034	00031
	* 7-10	00034		-00055

Move sequence	21	22	TOTAL
7			
23–18,15–22,25–18,14–23,26–19, 8–11,29–25	–00034		00030
* 9–14	00034		–00045
*14–23,27– 2,10–14,24–20, 8–11	00034		–15617
* 9–13	00034		–15620
*10–15,24–19	–00034		11614
* 3– 7	00034		–22205
8			
21–14, 6– 9,13– 6, 1–17,25–21,17–22,26–17	–00034		10416
* 2– 6	00034		–00105
* 2–18,26–23, 8–11,23–14	–00034		10436
*12–16	00034		–10370
* 8–11,24–15,15–24,28–19, 6– 9	00034		–00056
* 4– 8	00034		–00063
*15–18,26–22	–00034		06541
* 7–10	00034		–07410
6			
28–12, 8–11,23–18,14–23,27–18, 5– 9,21–17	–00034		06404
*11–15	00034		–07355
* 7–11,23–18,14–23,27–18, 5– 9	00034		–06446
*11–15	00034		–07353
* 5– 9,23–18	–00034		06422
* 6– 9	00034		–07364

PLY	3	4	5	6	7	8	9	10	11	12	13	14	15	16	17	18	19	20	21	22	TOTAL
USAGE	11	16	16	37	29	40	32	34	14	2	0	0	0	0	0	0	0	0	0	0	231
ENDS	0	8	1	12	5	12	11	24	13	2	0	0	0	0	0	0	0	0	0	0	88
2.	15–19	000342	1	1	1	9 29A21	16	15–19	7–11	8–11	15–18	2									

numbers. Each of these branches was carried to a depth of 3-ply and the apparent best branch was then found to be the one identified by serial number 9, as may be verified by reference to the scores at the far right (which are expressed in terms of the side which made the last recorded move on the line in question). Branch 9 was then investigated for four more moves, only to be put aside for an investigation of the branch identified by the serial number 1 which in turn was displaced by 9, then finally back to 1. At this point the normal minimaxing was initiated. The amount of flitting from move to move is, of course, critically dependent upon the exact board configuration being studied. A fairly simple situation is portrayed by this illustration. It will be noted that on the completion of the investigation of branch 1, the program went back to branch 9, then to branch 3, followed by branch 2, and so on until all branches were investigated. As a matter of general interest this tree is for the fifth move of a game following a 9–14, 22–17, 11–15 opening, after an opponent's move of 17–13, and move 15–19 (branch 1) was finally chosen. The 7094 computer took 1 minute and 3 seconds to make the move and to record the tree. This game was one of a set of four games being played simultaneously by the machine and the length of the tree-search had been arbitrarily reduced to speed up the play. The alpha and beta values listed in the columns to the right are both expressed in terms of the side making the last move, and hence a score to be considered must be larger than alpha and smaller than beta. For clarity of presentation deletions have been made of most large negative values when they should appear in the alpha column and of most large positive values when such values should appear in the beta column.

Forward Pruning

In addition to the hazardless alpha–beta pruning, as just described, there exist several forms of forward pruning which can be used to reduce the size of the search tree. There is always a risk associated with forward pruning since there can be no absolute assurance that the scores that would be obtained by a deeper analysis might not be quite different from those computed at the earlier ply. Indeed, if this were not so, there would never be any reasons for looking ahead. Still it seems reasonable to assume that some net improvement should result from the judicious use of these procedures. Two simple forms of forward pruning were found to be useful after a variety of more complicated procedures, based on an initial imperfect understanding of the problem, had been tried with great effort and little success.

To apply the first form it is only necessary to limit the number of moves saved for future analysis at each point in the tree, with provisions for saving all moves when the ply is small and gradually restricting the number saved, as the ply becomes greater until finally when the maximum feasible ply is being approached only two or three moves are saved. (The decision as to which are saved is, of course, based on the plausibility analysis.)

In the second form of forward pruning one compares the apparent scores as measured by the plausibility analysis with the current values of alpha and beta that are being carried forward, and terminates the look-ahead if this comparison is unfavorable. Rather than to apply this comparison in an unvarying way it seems reasonable to set margins which vary with the ply so that the amount of pruning increases with increasing ply. At low plies only the most unlikely paths can then be pruned, while fairly severe pruning can be caused to occur as the effective ply limit is approached. If the margins are set too high, then only negligible pruning will result, while if they are low or nonexistent, the pruning will be extreme and the risks of unwise pruning correspondingly large.

There are, then, several factors which may be experimentally studied, these being the magnitudes of the several forms of pruning and the way in which these magnitudes are caused to vary with the ply. The problem is even more complicated than it might at first appear since the various kinds of forward pruning are not independent. It seems reasonable to assume that the rate at which the margins are reduced in the last described form of forward pruning and the rate at which the number pruning is increased in the earlier described form should both depend upon the position in the plausibility listings of earlier boards along the branch under investigation. It is quite impractical to make a detailed study of these interdependencies because the range of possible combinations is extremely large and a whole series of games would have to be played for each combination before valid conclusions could be drawn. Only a very few arrangements have, in fact, been tried and the final scheme adopted is based more on the apparent reasonableness of the arrangement than upon any real data.

The Problem of "Pitch" Moves

In both of the above forms of forward pruning serious difficulties arise with respect to the proper consideration of so-called "pitch moves," that is, of moves in which a piece is sacrificed in return for a positional advantage which eventually leads at least to an equalizing capture if not to an actual winning position. In principle, one should be able to assign the proper relative weights to positional and material advantages so as to assess such moves correctly, but these situations generally appear to be so detail-specific that it is impossible to evaluate them directly in any way other than by look-ahead. Troubles are encountered because of the limited look-ahead distance to which the plausibility analysis can be extended; the equalizing moves may not be found and as a consequence a good pitch move may be pruned. A 2-ply plausibility search in which the analysis is terminated only on a nonjump situation will correctly evaluate move sequences of the type P, J, J, where P stands for pitch and J for jump (with N used later for nonjump moves which are not forcing) but it is powerless to evaluate sequences of the P, J, P, J, J type or of the P, J, N, P, J type. Both of these occur quite frequently in normal play. A 3-ply search will handle the first of these situations but will still not handle the second case. Unsatisfactory as it is, the best practical compromise which has been achieved to date seems to be to employ a 2-ply plausibility search for the normal nonpitch situation and to extend the search to 3-ply whenever the first or the second move of the plausibility search is a jump. As noted earlier a 3-ply search is customarily employed during the preliminary multipath phase of the analysis.

Several more complicated methods of handling this problem have been considered, but all of the methods tried to date have proved to be very expensive in terms of computing time and all have been discarded. One of these methods which seemed to be marginally effective consisted of a procedure for keeping a separate account of all pitch moves encountered during the plausibility search, defined in this case as sequences in which the first move in the search *is not a* jump and the second move *is* a jump. These pitch moves were sorted on the basis of their relative scores and a record was kept of the four best pitch moves. Of course some of these moves might have been also rated as good moves quite independently of their pitch status, either because most or all of the available moves were of this type or because the return capture was not delayed beyond the ply depth of the search. After the normal number of unpruned moves at any branch point had been explored, the best remaining pitch move (eliminating any already considered) was then followed up. Since most of the apparent pitch moves may in fact be sheer giveaway moves, it was quite impractical to consider more than a single pitch move but hopefully that apparent pitch which led to the highest positional score should have been the most likely move to investigate. This procedure causes a 2-ply plausibility search to salvage one likely candidate per move which could be of the P, J, N, J, J, type and it increases the power of the 3-ply plausibility search correspondingly. Unfortunately a rather high percentage of the additional moves so considered were found to be of no value and the bookkeeping costs of this procedure also seemed to be excessive.

As a further extension of this general method of handling pitch moves, it is possible to cause pitch sequences of the P, J, N, P, J type to be investigated using a 2-ply plausibility search. One need only specify that the main tree not be terminated when there is a jump move pending. While the cost of this addition might seem to be small, in practice it leads to the exploration in depth of extended giveaway sequences, and as a consequence it is of very questionable value.

Look-Ahead Termination

Regardless of the form or amount of forward pruning the time arrives along each path when it is necessary to terminate the look-ahead and evaluate the last board position. It is rather instructive to consider the termination as simply the end of the pruning process in which the pruning is complete. The use of a fixed depth for this final act of pruning, as previously assumed, is of course not at all reasonable and in fact it has never been used. In the earlier work (Samuel, 1959) much attention was given to the wisdom of terminating the look-ahead at so-called "dead" positions. With the current use made of the plausibility analysis this becomes a restriction mainly applicable to the plausibility analysis and it is of but little value in terminating the main tree itself. A limit is, of course, set by the amount of storage assigned for the tree but since the tree storage requirements are not excessive this should normally not be allowed to operate. If the plausibility analysis is at all effective one should be able to ration the computing time to various branches on the basis of their relative probability of being the best. For example, the initial path which survives the swapping routine during the initial look-ahead procedure should certainly be carried quite far along as compared with a path resulting from investigating, say, the fourth choice as found by the plausibility, when this is again followed by a fourth choice, etc., all the way through the tree.

The procedure found most effective has been that of defining a parameter called the *branching count* which is assigned a value for each board encountered during the tree search. To insure that all of the possible initial moves are given adequate consideration, identical values are given to the counts for the resulting boards after these initial moves. As each move originating with one of these boards is made, the branching count for the originating board is reduced by one unit and the resulting board after the move is assigned this new value as well. This process is repeated at each branch point down the tree until the branching count reaches zero, whereupon the search down this path is terminated (more correctly steps are taken to initiate termination unless other factors call for a further extension of the search, as will be explained later). Along the preferred branch, the branching count will thus be reduced by one unit for each ply level. For the second choice at any branch point a two-unit reduction occurs, for the third choice a three-unit, etc. The net result is that the less likely paths are terminated sooner than the most likely paths and in direct proportion to their decreasing likelihood.

Actually, a slightly more complicated procedure is used in that the branching count is set at a higher initial value and it is reduced by one unit when the move under consideration is a jump move and by four units when it is a normal move. This procedure causes the search to be extended further along those paths involving piece exchanges than along those that do not. Also the search is not permitted to terminate automatically when the branching count reaches zero if the indicated score for the move under consideration implies that this is in fact a preferred path. In this case the search is extended until the same depth has been reached along this path as had been reached along the previously indicated preferred path.

Tree Pruning Results

It has been found singularly difficult to assess the relative value of the various tree pruning techniques in terms of their effect on the goodness of play. Special situations can always be found for which the various forward pruning procedures are either very effective or quite inadequate. Short of very extensive tests indeed, there seems to be no very good way to determine the relative frequency with which these different situations occur during normal play. About all that has been done has been to observe the resulting game trees and to depend upon the opinions of checker masters as to the goodness of the resulting moves and as to the reasonableness in appearance of the trees.

As mentioned earlier, for each move that is tabulated in Figure 3 there was actually an auxiliary plausibility move analysis to a ply of 2 or more which is not shown at all for reasons of clarity. One can think of this as a fine brush of moves emanating from each recorded move. Examples of all types of pruning can be noted in this tree, although additional information is needed for their unambiguous identification. Checker experts all agree that such trees as these are much denser than they probably should be. Attempts to make them less dense by stronger pruning always seem to result in occasional examples of conspicuously poor play. It may well be that denser trees should be used for machine play than for human play, to compensate for deficiencies in the board evaluation methods.

Evaluation Procedures and Learning

Having covered the major improvements in playing techniques as they relate to tree-searching, we can now consider improvements in evaluation procedures, with particular reference to learning. We will first discuss the older linear polynomial scheme and then go on to consider the signature-table procedure.

Linear Polynomial Evaluations

While it is possible to allow for parameter interaction, for example, by using binary connective terms as described in Samuel (1959) the number of such interactions is large, and it seems necessary to consider more than pairwise interactions. This makes it quite difficult to depart very much from the linear case. Some improvement in performance resulted when the overall game was split, initially, into three phases (opening, midgame, and endgame) and more recently into six phases with a different set of coefficients determined for each phase. Various procedures for defining the phase of the game were tested, the simple one of making the determination solely in terms of the total number of pieces on the board seemed as good as any tried, and there were indications that little was to be gained by going to more than six phases.

The total number of parameters used at any one time has been varied from a very few to as many as 40. It has been customary to use all of the currently assessed successful parameters during the learning phase. A number of attempts have been made to speed up actual play by limiting the number of parameters to 5, 10, 15, or 20, selecting those with the larger magnitude coefficients. Five terms in the learning polynomial proved definitely inadequate, an improvement in going from 10 to 15 terms appeared to be barely discernible, and no evidence could be found for improvements in using more than 20 terms. In fact, there seemed to be some indication that a fortuitous combination of many ineffectual parameters with correspondingly low coefficients could, on occasion, override a more effective term and cause the program to play less well than it would with the ineffectual parameters omitted. In a series of six games played aginat R. W. Nealey (the U. S. blind checker champion) using 15 terms, the machine achieved five draws with one loss. The six poorest moves in these games as selected by L. W. Taylor, a checker analyst, were replayed, using 20 terms with no improvements and then using only 10 terms with a distinct improvement in two cases. There is, of course, no reason to believe that the program with the fewer number of terms might not have made other and more grievous errors for other untested board situations. Twenty terms were used during the games with W. F. Hellman referenced in footnote 1. No further work has been done on the linear polynomial schema in view of the demonstrated superiority of the "signature-table" procedure which will now be described.

Signature-Table Evaluations

The impracticality of considering all interparameter effects and the obvious importance of such interactions has led to the consideration of a number of different compromise proposals. The first successful compromise solution was proposed and tested on the Project Mac computer by Arnold Griffith, a graduate student at MIT. In one early modification of this schema, eight subsets of five parameters each were used, initially selected from 31 different parameters with some redundancy between subsets. Each subset was designated as a signature type and was characterized by an argument computed in terms of the values measured for the parameters within the subset for any particular board situation. The arguments for each signature type thus specify particular combinations of the parameters within the subset and serve as addresses for entering signature tables where the tabulated values are meant to reflect the relative worth to the computer's side of these particular combinations. In the initial Griffith scheme the values read from the eight different signature tables were simply added together to obtain the final board evaluation. Parameters which are thought to be somewhat related are grouped together in the individual subsets. While it would have been desirable to consider all possible values for each parameter and all possible interrelations between them, this quickly becomes unmanageable. Accordingly, the range of parameter values was restricted to but three values $+1$, 0, and -1; that is, the two sides could be equal or one or the other could be ahead in terms of the board property in question. Many of the board properties were already of this type. With each parameter limited to three values and with five parameters in a subset, a total of 3^5 or 243 entries in a signature table completely characterizes all possible interactions between the parameters. Actually since checkers is a "zero sum" game and since all parameters are defined symmetrically, it should be possible to reduce the table size roughly by two (122 entries instead of 243) by listing values for positive arguments only and taking values with a reversal of sign when negative arguments are evaluated. Allowing for 48 signature tables, eight signature types for each of the six different phases, we arrive at a memory space requirement for 5,856 table entries. Actually two words per table entry are used during the learning phase, as explained later, so the total memory requirement for the learning data is 11,712 words.

An example will make this procedure clear. Consider one signature type which might comprise the following five parameters: ANGLE, CENTER, OREO, GUARD, and KCENT, which will not be explained now but which all have to do with the control of the king row and the center of the board. Now consider the GUARD parameter. This can be assigned a value of 0 if both or neither of the sides have complete control of their back rows, a value of $+1$ if the side in question controls his back row while the opponent does not, and a value of -1 if the conditions are reversed. The other four parameters can be similarly valued, giving a ternary number consisting of a five-digit string selected from the set $-$, 0, and $+$ (where $-$ is used for -1, etc.), e.g., "$+-0--$" characterizes one particular combination of these five different parameters. This argument can be associated with some function value, a large positive value if it is a desirable combination, a near zero function value if the advantages to the two sides are about even, and a large negative value if it is a disadvantageous combination. Both the arguments and functions are symmetric; that is, the argument and function for the other side would be that gotten by reversing all signs. (In the $-$, 0, $+$ ternary system the first symbol in the list gives the sign and the processes of complementing and sign reversal are synonymous.) The argument for the other side would thus be $-+0++$, a negative number which would not be tabulated but the function value would be the negative of the value listed under $+-0--$, as it of course must be for the sum of the functions for the two sides to be zero.

The results obtained with this relatively simple method of handling parameter interactions were quite encouraging and as a result a series of more elaborate studies has been made using signature procedures of vary degrees of complexity. In particular, efforts were made:

(1) to decrease the total number of parameters by eliminating those found to be of marginal utility;
(2) to increase the range of values permitted for each parameter, initially increasing the range for certain parameters to permit seven values (-3, -2, -1, 0, $+1$, $+2$, $+3$) and more recently dividing the parameters into two equal groups—one group being restricted in range to five values; and

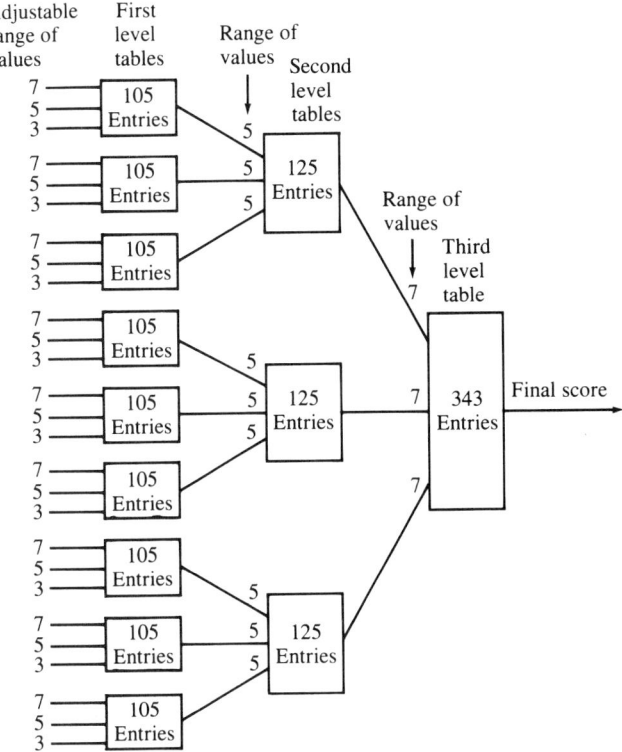

Figure 4. A three-level signature-table arrangement with 27 terms.

(3) to introduce a hierarchical structure of signature tables where the outputs from the first-level signature tables are combined in groups and used as inputs to a set of second level tables, etc.

Most of the experimental work has been restricted to a consideration of the two arrangements shown in Figures 4 and 5. These are both three-level arrangements. They differ in the degree of the correlation between parameters which is recognized and in the range of values permitted the individual parameters. Both are compromises.

Obviously, the optimum arrangement depends upon the actual number of parameters that must be used, the degree to which these parameters are interrelated and the extent to which these individual parameters can be safely represented by a limited range of integers. In the case of checkers, the desired number of parameters seems to lie in the range of 20–30. Constraints on the range of values required to define the parameters can be easily determined but substantially nothing is known concerning the interdependencies between the parameters. A series of quite inconclusive experiments was performed in an effort to measure these interdependencies. About all that can be said is that

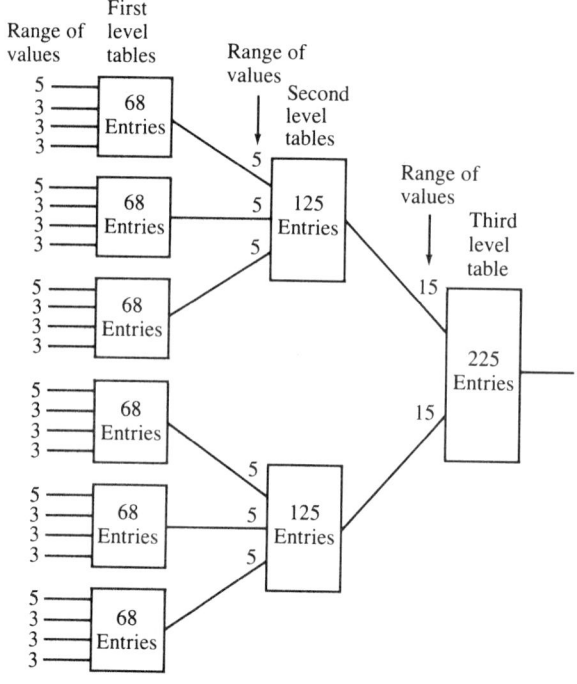

Figure 5. Revised three-level signature-table scheme with 24 terms.

the constraints imposed upon the permissible distribution of pieces on the board in any actual game, as set by the rules of the game and as dictated by good playing procedures, seem to produce an apparent average correlation between all parameters which is quite independent of the specific character of these parameters. The problem is further complicated by the fact that two quite opposing lines of argument can be advanced—the one to suggest that closely related terms be placed in the same subsets to allow for their inter-dependencies and the second to suggest that such terms be scattered among groups. The second suggestion can be made to look reasonable by considering the situation in which two parameters are unknowingly so closely related as to actually measure the same property. Placing these two terms in the same subset would accomplish nothing, while placing them in different sub-groups permits a direct tradeoff evaluation to be made between this property in question and the properties measured by the other parameters in both subgroups.

A few comments are in order at this time as to the supposedly symmetrical nature of the parameter data. While it is true that checkers is a zero-sum game and while it is true that the parameters are all defined in a symmetrical way, that is, as far as Black vs. White is concerned, the value of a board situation as defined by these parameters is actually dependent upon whose turn it is to play. A small but real bias normally exists for most parameters in favor of the side whose turn it is to move, although for certain parameters the reverse is true. The linear polynomial method of scoring is unfortunately not sensitive to these peculiarities of the different parameters since the partial scores for all types are simply added together. The signature table procedure should be able to take the added complication into account. Of course, the distinctions will be lost if the data are incorrectly stored or if they are incorrectly acquired. By storing the data in the uncompressed form one can evaluate this effect. More will be said about this matter later.

In the arrangement shown in Figure 4 there were 27 parameters divided into nine groups of three each, with each group being made up of one three-valued parameter, one five-valued parameter and one seven-valued parameter. Each first level signature table thus had 105 entries. The output values from each of these tables were quantized into five values and second-level signature tables were employed to combine these in sets of three. These second-level tables thus had 125 entries each. These outputs are further quantized into seven levels and a third-level signature table with 343 entries was used to combine the outputs from the three second-level tables into a final output which was used as the final board evaluation. Obviously, the parameters used to enter the first-level tables were grouped together on the basis of their assumed (and in some cases measured) interdependencies while the resulting signature types were again grouped together as well as possible, consistent with their assumed interdependencies. As always, there was a complete set of these tables for each of the six game phases. The tables were stored in full, without making use of the zero-sum characteristic to halve their size, and occupied 20,956 cells in memory. Outputs from the first-level tables were quantized into five levels and the outputs from the second level tables into seven levels.

The Latest Signature Table Procedure

The arrangement shown in Figure 5 used 24 parameters which were divided into six subgroups of four parameters each, with each subgroup containing one five-valued parameter and three three-valued parameters. In this case the first-level tables were compacted by taking advantage of the assumed symmetrical character of the data, although this is a dubious procedure as already noted. It was justified in this case because of the added parameter interactions which this made possible and because of a very large inverse effect of table size on speed of learning. This reduced the size of the first-level tables to 68 words each. The outputs from the first-level tables were quantized into five levels as before and the outputs from the second-level tables were quantized into 15 levels. The second- and third-level tables were not compacted, in an attempt to preserve some nonsymmetrical features. The total memory requirement for the tables as thus constituted was 10,136 words.

Before we can discuss the results obtained with the signature-table scheme it will be necessary to turn our attention to the various book-learning procedures.

Book Learning

While book learning was mentioned briefly in Samuel (1959), we will describe it in some detail as it was used throughout the studies now to be reported. Just as books speed up human learning, one might expect that a substantial increase in machine-learning speed might result if some use could be made of book information, in this case, the existing library of master play. To this end a reasonable sample (approximately 250,000 board situations) of this master play has been key punched and transcribed to magnetic tape. These are mostly draw games; in those cases where a win was achieved, data are used only from the moves made by the winning side. The program has been arranged to play through these recorded games considering one side, then the other, much as a person might do, analyzing the situation in terms of the existing evaluation procedures and listing the preferred move. This move is then compared with the book-recommended move and a suitable adjustment made in the evaluation procedure. This, of course, assumes that the book-recommended move is the only correct move, which it may not be, either because of a plurality of good moves or in some cases because of an actual error. However, if enough book moves are used, if the books are usually correct, and if the adjustments per move are of the proper size, the process should converge toward an optimum evaluation procedure, subject always to a basic limitation as to the appropriateness and completeness of the parameter list used.

While it still takes a substantial amount of machine time to play through the necessary book games, the learning process is very much faster than for learning from actual play. In the first place, the game paths followed are from the start representative of the very best play since the program is forced always to make the recommended book move before proceeding to considering the next move. Second, it is possible to assign values to be associated with the moves in a very direct fashion without depending upon the unreliable techniques which were earlier described. Finally, the analysis of each move can be extremely limited, with little or no minimaxing, since the only use made of the overall scores is that of measuring the learning, whereas in the earlier procedures these scores were needed to determine credit assignments to the parameters. The net effect of these factors is to make it possible to consider many more moves, at the rate of 300 to 600 moves per minute rather than the roughly one move per minute rate which is typical for actual games.

We will first explain how learning is achieved in terms of coefficients in a linear polynomial and then go on to the signature table case.

During the learning process, use must be made of the previously determined coefficients to perform the evaluation of all board situations either right after the initial moves or, if jump situations are encountered, at some terminating ply depth with the scores backed up by the minimaxing procedure. During this minimaxing, it is also necessary to back up the values of the parameter values themselves (i.e., the terms without coefficients), associated with the selected terminating board situations corresponding to the optimized path leading from each of the possible first moves. If there are nine possible moves, a 9×27 table will be produced in which the rows correspond to the nine different moves and the columns correspond to the 27 different parameters. On the basis of the book information, one row is indicated as being the best move.

The program must analyze the data within the table and accumulate totals which on the average indicate the relative worth of the different parameters in predicting the book move, and it must alter the coefficients to reflect the cumulative learning indicated by these totals. A variety of different procedures has been tested for accumulating totals; one of the simplest, surprisingly, the most effective, seems to be to simply count the number of moves, for each parameter separately, for which the parameter value is larger than the value associated with the book move and the number of moves for which the parameter value is smaller than the value associated with the book move. If these cumulated counts over all board situations examined to date are designated H and L, then one measure of the goodness of the parameter in predicting the book move is given by

$$C = (L - H)/(L + H).$$

This has the dimensions of a correlation coefficient. It would have a value of $+1$ if the parameter in question always predicted the book move, a value of -1 if it never made a correct prediction, and a value of 0 if there was no correlation between the machine indications and the book. The best procedure found to date is simply to use the values of the C's so obtained as the coefficients in the evaluation polynomial, although arguments can be advanced for the use of the values of the C's raised to some power greater than 1 to overcome the effect of several inconsequential terms overriding a valuable indication from some other term as mentioned earlier.

Typical coefficients as tabulated by the computer are shown in Table 1 based on roughly 150,000 board situations and using 31 functions during the learning process. The 19 terms per phase having the largest magnitude coefficients are listed. The play against Hellman mentioned earlier used this particular set of terms.

Book Learning Using Signature Tables

Extending the book-learning technique to the signature-table case is relatively easy. All that need be done is to back up the signatures corresponding to the signature types being used in a way quite analogous to the handling of parameters in the linear polynomial case. Taking the example used earlier, one

Table 1. Linear polynomial terms (parameter names and learned coefficients) as used in the games with W. F. Hellman. These coefficients resulted from an analysis of approximately 150,000 book moves.

Phase 1 — Terms and coefficients

GUARD	QUART	DIAGL	EDGES	FRONT	ANGLE	CENTR	NODES	DCHOL	ADVAN
0.33	0.29	−0.21	−0.20	−0.19	−0.18	0.14	0.13	0.11	−0.08
PINS	DYKSQ	FREE	EXCHS	THRET	STARS	PRESS	UNCEN	LINES	
0.07	0.07	0.06	−0.05	0.04	0.04	−0.04	0.03	0.02	

Phase 2 — Terms and coefficients

SPIKE	GUARD	EDGES	QUART	CENTR	ANGLE	FRONT	ADVAN	SHOVE	THRET
0.85	0.36	−0.24	0.23	0.21	−0.21	−0.19	−0.18	0.16	0.14
NODES	PINS	DCHOL	STARS	OFSET	HOLES	DIAGL	UNCEN	MOBIL	
0.13	0.11	−0.10	−0.09	0.09	0.09	−0.09	0.08	0.05	

Phase 3 — Terms and coefficients

SPIKE	KCENT	PANTS	GUARD	FRONT	CRAMP	ADVAN	EDGES	CENTR	STARS
0.88	0.48	0.42	0.37	−0.23	0.23	−0.23	−0.22	0.20	−0.19
QUART	ANGLE	THRET	DCHOL	PINS	SHOVE	NODES	UNCEN	OFSET	
0.19	−0.19	0.15	0.14	0.13	0.10	0.10	0.09	0.08	

Phase 4 — Terms and coefficients

SPIKE	GUARD	PANTS	KCENT	STARS	ADVAN	FRONT	THRET	ANGLE	EDGES
0.86	0.62	0.61	0.56	−0.30	−0.30	−0.27	0.26	−0.23	−0.22
DIAGL	CENTR	SHOVE	QUART	PINS	UNCEN	OFSET	DENYS	UNDEN	
0.22	0.20	0.18	0.16	0.12	0.11	0.09	0.09	−0.07	

Phase 5 — Terms and coefficients

GUARD	SPIKE	PANTS	KCENT	THRET	DIAGL	ADVAN	UNCEN	ANGLE	SHOVE
0.81	0.68	0.62	0.55	0.36	0.33	−0.32	0.27	−0.26	0.25
UNDEN	FRONT	DENYS	PINS	CENTR	EDGES	DYKSQ	QUART	DEUCE	
−0.22	−0.22	0.20	0.19	0.18	−0.16	−0.16	0.15	0.06	

Phase 6 — Terms and coefficients

PRESS	KCENT	UNCEN	UNDEN	DYKSQ	DENYS	SHOVE	DIAGL	SPIKE	THRET
−0.54	0.54	0.45	−0.41	−0.40	0.40	0.39	0.39	0.37	0.36
EXCHS	OFSET	ADVAN	PINS	ANGLE	FRONT	DEUCE	FREE	QUART	
−0.34	−0.26	−0.24	0.23	−0.23	−0.32	−0.16	−0.11	0.08	

signature corresponding to one possible move might be $+ -0- -$ (actually stored in the machine in binary form). Each signature type for each possible move is similarly characterized. Two totals (called D and A) are accumulated for each of the possible signature types. Additions of 1 each are made to the D totals for each signature for the moves that were not identified as the preferred book move and an addition of n, where n is the number of nonbook moves, is made to the A totals for the signatures identified with the recommended book move. The reason for adding n to the book move A totals is, of course, to give greater positive weight to the book-recommended move than is the negative weight given to moves that do not happen to correspond to the currently found book recommendation (there may be more than one good move and some other authority might recommend one of the other moves). This procedure has the incidental effect of maintaining equality between the grand totals of the A's and D's accumulated separately for all signatures in each table, and so of preserving a zero-sum character for the data.

When enough data have been accumulated for many different board situations, additions will have been made in the A and D columns against most of the signature arguments. The program then computes correlation coefficients for each signature defined in an analogous fashion to the earlier usage as

$$C = (A - D)/(A + D).$$

In the case of the third-level table these values are used directly as board evaluations. For the other two levels in the signature-table hierarchy, the actual values to be entered must be quantized so as to restrict the range of the tabulated values. This quantization has normally been done by first separating out all zero values and entering them into the tables as such. The nonzero values are then quantized by ranking the positive values and negative values separately into the desired number of equisized groups. The table entries are then made in terms of the small positive and negative integer numbers used to specify the relative ranking order of these groups.

This process of updating the signature tables themselves is done at intervals as determined by the rate at which significant data accumulate. During the intervals between updating, additions are, of course, continually being made to the tables of A's and D's.

There are several problems associated with this newer learning scheme. Reference has already been made to the space and time limitations which restrict the number of parameters to be combined in each signature type and restrict the range allowed for each parameter. The program has been written so that these numbers may be easily varied but this facility is of little use because of the very rapid rate at which the performance and the storage requirements vary with the values chosen. Values less than those indicated lead to performance but little different from that exhibited by the older linear polynomial experiments, while larger values greatly increase the memory requirements and slow down learning rate. A great deal of juggling is required in order to make even the simplest change if the operating times are to be kept within a reasonable range, and this still further complicates the problem of considering meaningful experiments.

This inverse effect of the table size on the learning rate comes about because of the need to accumulate data in the A and D columns for each signature table entry. The effect is, of course, compounded by the hierarchical nature of the table complex. At the start of a new learning run there will be no entries in any of the tables, the computed C's must all be set to zero and the program will have no basis for the minimaxing procedure. Depending upon the particular selection of the book games used there may, in fact, be a relatively long period of time before a significant fraction of signatures will have been encountered, and as a consequence, statistically unreliable data will persist in the C table. Not only will the individual function values be suspect but the quantizing levels will perforce be based on insufficient data as well. The magnitude of this effect will, of course, depend upon the size of the tables that the program is generating.

Palliative measures can be adopted to smooth the C tables in order to compensate for the blank entries and for entries based on insufficient data. Four of the more effective smoothing techniques have been found to be: (1) smoothing by inversion, (2) smoothing from adjacent phases, (3) smoothing by interpolation, and (4) smoothing by extrapolation. Smoothing is, of course, most needed during the early stages of the learning process but it also must be used during play even after a rather extensive learning run.

As a matter of fact, certain signatures are so improbable during book play (some may in fact be impossible) that voids are still found to exist in the signature tables, even after playing 100,000 book-game board situations. There is the reassuring thought that signatures not found during the learning process are also unlikely to be found during play. However, because of the very many board situations explored during the look-ahead process and presumably because of the consequences of making decisions on the basis of statistically unreliable entries, the quality of the play using unsmoothed data was found to be somewhat erratic until a fairly large amount of learning had been achieved.

It should be pointed out, that the smoothing techniques are employed as temporary expedients. All previous smoothed results are discarded and completely new calculations of values of C are made periodically during learning from the accumulated and uncorrupted A and D data. The effects of smoothing do persist, however, since the entries in the second- and the third-level tables, and hence the locations at which the A and D data are stored are influenced by it.

Smoothing by inversion is done by averaging positive and negative entries (with compensating sign inversions), and it is partially justified by the zero-sum symmetrical characteristic of the data.

Smoothing from adjacent phases is done by transferring data between phases. This is possible because of the random way in which data accumulate for the different phases, and it is reasonably valid because the values associated with a given signature vary but little between adjacent phases. This form of smoothing has been found to be of but limited utility since the same reasons which account for the absence of specific data for one phase often operate to prevent corresponding data from being generated for adjacent phases.

Smoothing by interpolation is based on the assumption that a missing correlation for a signature which contains one or more zeros in its argument can be approximated by averaging the values appearing for the related signatures where the zeros are individually replaced by a + and then by a −. In order for this to be effective there must be data available for both the + and cases for at least one of the zero-valued parameters. This form of smoothing assumes a linear relationship for the effect of the parameter to which the interpolation is applied. It is therefore, no better as far as this one parameter is concerned than the older linear polynomial procedure. This form of smoothing is quite ineffectual since all too often balanced pairs of entries cannot be found.

Smoothing by extrapolation may take two forms, the simplest being when entries are found for the zero value of some particular function and for either the + or the −case and a void for the remaining case is to be filled. All too often however, the more recalcitrant cases are those in which the zero entry only for some one parameter is found and substitute data are sought for both the + and the − case. Here we have recourse to the fact that it is possible to compute the apparent effect of the missing parameter from all of the pertinent data in the signature table, on the assumption of linearity. The program therefore computes a correlation coefficient for this parameter alone and uses this with the found signature data. Admittedly, this is a very dangerous form of extrapolation since it completely ignores all nonlinear effects, but is often the only recourse.

Signature-Table Learning Results

The results of the best signature-table learning run made to date are shown in Table 2. This particular run was arranged to yield comparable figures for both the newer signature-table procedure and the older linear polynomial procedure. Because of the great amount of machine time required (approximately 10 hours per run) it has not yet been possible to optimize:

(1) the choice of parameters to be used;
(2) the range of values to be assigned to these parameters;
(3) the specific assignments of parameters to signature types;
(4) the detailed hierarchical structure of the signature tables;
(5) the table sizes; and
(6) the various smoothing techniques which must be used during the early learning phases.

Table 2 reports the apparent goodness of play based upon a correlation factor defined as

$$C = (L - H)/(L + H),$$

Table 2. Correlation coefficients measuring the effects of learning for the signature-table procedure and for the linear polynomial procedure as a function of the total number of book moves analyzed. These tests used 27 parameters which for the signature-table score were grouped in the configuration shown in Figure 4.

Total number of book moves analyzed	Correlation coefficient, C	
	Signature-table case	Polynomial case
336	−0.08	−0.18
826	+0.06	−0.13
1,272	0.13	+0.06
1,769	0.18	0.10
2,705	0.27	0.15
3,487	0.31	0.16
4,680	0.34	0.15
5,446	0.36	0.16
8,933	0.38	0.19
10,762	0.39	0.20
14,240	0.40	0.21
17,527	0.41	0.22
21,302	0.41	0.23
23,666	0.42	0.23
30,173	0.43	0.24
40,082	0.43	0.25
50,294	0.43	0.26
55,165	0.44	0.26
66,663	0.45	0.26
70,083	0.45	0.26
90,093	0.46	0.26
106,477	0.46	0.26
120,247	0.47	0.26
145,021	0.47	0.26
173,091	0.48	0.26
183,877	0.48	0.26

where L is the accumulated count of all available moves which the program rates lower than its rating for the book-recommended move and H is the accumulated count of all available moves which the program rates higher than or equal to its rating for the book-recommended move. During this learning run the program looked ahead only a single ply except in those cases where jumps were pending. The observed correlation coefficients are fairly good measures of the goodness of the evaluation procedures without minimaxing. Coefficients were computed during the run both by using the signature table procedure and by the older linear polynomial procedure. These figures are tabulated in the second and third columns against the total number of moves in column 1. It will be observed that the coefficient for the polynomial procedure appears to stabilize at a figure of 0.26 after about 50,000 moves, while the coefficient for the signature-table procedure continues to rise and finally after perhaps 175,000 moves reaches a limit of 0.48. Interestingly enough, the signature-table coefficient was always larger than the polynomial coefficient even during the very early stage although a detailed analysis on a move-by-move basis, which cannot be easily reproduced here, did show that the signature-table method was the more erratic of the two during this stage.

It should be noted that these linear polynomial results are not directly comparable with the coefficients for individual terms as reported in Table 1, since for Table 1 the H values used in computing the C's did not include those moves rated equal to the book move while in Table 2 equals are included, and the computed coefficients are correspondingly lower. The discrepancy is particularly marked with respect to those parameters which are usually zero for most moves but which may be extremely valuable for their differentiating ability when they do depart from zero. Most of the terms with high coefficients in Table 1 have this characteristic. Furthermore, when minimaxing was required during the two tests it was based on different criteria, for Table 1 on the linear polynomial and for Table 2 on signature tables.

The results of Table 2 seem to indicate that the signature-table procedure is superior to the linear polynomial procedure even in its presently unoptimized form. It would be nice if one could measure this improvement in some more precise way, making a correct allowance for the difference in the computation times.

Perhaps a better way to assess the goodness of the play using signature tables is to list the fraction of the time that the program rates 0, then 1, 2, 3, etc. moves as equal to or higher than its rating of the book-recommended move. Typical figures are tabulated below, measured for a test lot of 895 representative moves after the program had learned by analyzing 173,989 book moves:

Moves higher or equal	0	1	2	3	4	5	6
Fractional times found	0.38	0.26	0.16	0.10	0.06	0.03	0.01

In view of the high probability of occurrence of two equally acceptable moves, the sum of the figures in the first two columns, namely 0.64, is a reasonable estimate of the fraction of time that the program would make an acceptable move without look-ahead and minimaxing. Look-ahead greatly improves the play and accounts for the difference between this prediction and the observed fact that the playing program tends to follow book-recommended moves a much higher fraction of the time.

Introduction of Strategies

The chief defect of the program in the recent past, according to several checker masters, seems to have been its failure to maintain any fixed strategy during play. The good player during his own play will note that a given board situation is favorable to him in some one respect and perhaps unfavorable in some second respect, and he will follow some fairly consistent policy for several moves in a row. In general, he will try to maintain his advantage and at the same time to overcome the unfavorable aspect. In doing this he may more or less ignore other secondary properties which, under different circumstances, might themselves be dominant. The program, as described, treats each board situation as a new problem. It is true that this procedure does not allow the program to exploit those human failings of the opponent that might have been revealed by the earlier play or to conduct a war of nerves intended to trick the opponent. Such actions have little place in games of complete information and can well be ignored.[8]

What may certainly be questioned is the failure to take account of the initial board situation in setting the goals to be considered during the look-ahead process. Were the program able to do this, then it could adopt a strategy for any particular move. If the program finally made a move that was consistent with this strategy, and if the opponent were unable to vitiate this strategy, then the program would, on the next move, again tend to adopt the same strategy. Of course, if the program had been unable to maintain an advantage by following its initial strategy, it might now find that a different strategy was indicated and it would therefore change its strategy. Nevertheless, on average, the program might follow a given strategy for several moves in a row and so exhibit playing characteristics that would give the impression of long-range planning.

---

[8] This statement can be questioned and, in fact, has been questioned by an anonymous reviewer who quite rightly pointed out that it would be desirable for the program to be able to define what is called "deep objectives," and, more importantly, to be able to detect such "deep objectives" on the part of a human opponent. The reviewer went on to say in part "—the good player will sometimes define a 'deep objective' and maneuver toward that point. He is always on the lookout for possibilities which will help him to get the better of the opponent. The opponent, unaware of his true objective until too late, does not defend adequately and loses.—It is most helpful to him to know that his opponent is not also playing a similar 'deep game.' I believe that the 'practical indeterminacy' of checkers makes the technique of 'deep' objectives by good players quite feasible. Indeed, I don't doublt the technique is part of the basic equipment of any champion player, however inarticulately he may describe it. This is perhaps the reason Hellman did better in the games by mail. He had time to study out appropriately 'deep' objectives and then to realize them. This is also what checker masters have in mind when they criticize the program's failure to maintain any fixed strategy during play."

This point of view finds support in the observation that those master players who have defeated the computer have all asked searching questions regarding the program, while good players who fail to win usually seem to hold the program in awe and generally fail to make any attempt to understand it.

This opens up what may be a fruitful line for additional research.

A possible mechanism for introducing this kind of strategic planning is provided by the signature table procedure and by the plausibility analysis. It is only necessary to view the different signature types as different strategic elements and to alter the relative weights assigned to the different signature types as a result of the plausibility analysis of the initial board situation. For this to be effective, some care must be given to the groupings of the parameters into the signature types so that these signature types tend to correspond to recognizable strategic concepts. Fortunately, the same initial-level grouping of parameters that is indicated by interdependency considerations seems to be reasonable in terms of strategies. We conclude that it is quite feasible to introduce the concept of strategy in this restricted way.

For reasons of symmetry, it seems desirable to pick two signature types for emphasis, that one yielding the highest positive value and that one yielding the most negative value for the most plausible move found during the initial plausibility analysis. This procedure recognizes the fact that to the opponent, the signs are reversed and his strongest signature type will be the first player's weakest one and vice versa. The simplest way to emphasize a particular strategy is to multiply the resulting values found for the two selected signature types by some arbitrary constant before entering a subsequent stage of the analysis. A factor of 2 (with a limit on the maximum resulting value so as not to exceed the table range) seemed reasonable, and this has been used for most of the experiments to date.

The results to date have been disappointing, presumably because of the ineffectual arrangement of terms into usable strategic groups, and as a consequence, this method of introducing strategies has been temporarily abandoned.

Conclusions

While the goal outlined in Samuel (1959), that of getting the program to generate its own parameters, remains as far in the future as it seemed to be in 1959, we can conclude that techniques are now in hand for dealing with many of the tree-pruning and parameter-interaction problems which were certainly much less well understood at the time of the earlier paper. Perhaps with these newer tools we may be able to apply machine-learning techniques to many problems of economic importance without waiting for the long-sought ultimate solution.

Acknowledgments. These studies were largely carried out while the writer was at the Thomas J. Watson Research Laboratories of the IBM Corporation, and while he was a Visiting Professor at MIT. More recently, the work has been supported in part by Stanford University and by the Advance Research Projects Agency of the Office of the Secretary of Defense (SD-183). The IBM Corporation has continued to aid the work by supplying time on an IBM

7094 computer at their San Jose Development Laboratories. Many individuals have contributed to these studies, and in particular, Arnold Griffith of MIT deserves commendation for suggesting the initial form of the signature-table procedure. The continuing interest and cooperation of the officers and player-members of the American Checker Federation has been most helpful.

CHAPTER 4

Scrabble

4.1. A Scrabble Crossword Game-Playing Program

STUART C. SHAPIRO and HOWARD R. SMITH

Originally published in 1977 as: Technical Report 119, Department of Computer Science, State University of New York at Buffalo. Reprinted by permission of Professor Stuart Shapiro.

Abstract. A program has been designed and implemented in SIMULA 67 on a DECSystem-10 to play the SCRABBLE Crossword Game interactively against a human opponent. The heart of the design is the data structure for the lexicon and the algorithm for searching it. The lexicon is represented as a letter table, or trie using a canonical ordering of the letters in the words rather than the original spelling. The algorithm takes the trie and a collection of letters, including blanks, and in a single backtrack search of the trie finds all words that can be formed from any combination and permutation of the letters. Words using the higher-valued letters are found before words not using those letters, and words using a collection of letters are found before words using a subcollection of them. The search procedure detaches after each group of words is found and may be resumed if more words are desired.

1. Introduction

The SCRABBLE Crossword Game is a well-known game considered to require a fair amount of intelligence, strategic and tactical skill, facility with words, and luck. Unlike most games in the artificial intelligence literature, it can be played by two or more players and is neither a zero-sum game nor a game of perfect information. For these reasons, game tree-searching procedures do not seem applicable. When humans play the game, a large easily accessible vocabulary seems to be the most important determiner of victory. One might, therefore, think that it would be easy to write a program that plays the SCRABBLE Crossword Game at championship level. However, several issues are not so clear: How should the lexicon be organized for maximum usefulness?; How should a program decide where to play?; How can a program take advantage of the small literature on the strategy and tactics of the game, e.g., (Conklin, 1976)?; What is the relative importance of a good memory for words vs. skillful decisions about what letters to use or not to use and where to play?

Our interest has focused on the organization of the lexicon. This lexicon differs from those usually used in natural language processing programs because of the use to which it is to be put. Usually, one is confronted with a possible word. One must determine if it is a word, and, if so, segment it into affixes and stem, and retrieve lexical information associated with the stem. One must allow for the possibility that the word is lexically ambiguous and that the segmentation can be done in several different ways. The problem for the SCRABBLE Crossword Game lexicon is, given a set of letters, to find all the words that can be made from any combination and permutation of them. This is a very different problem, but similar to the information retrieval problem of, given a set of keys find all records that contain any subset of them, or the pattern recognition problem of, given a set of features, some of which may be spurious, find all objects that might have given rise to them.

We have designed a lexicon and an algorithm for searching it. Around them, we have designed and implemented a program that plays the SCRABBLE Crossword Game interactively at a competitive, human level. We chose SIMULA 67 (Dahl *et al.*, 1966; 1968) for the programming language for reasons to be discussed below. In the sections below, we first briefly describe the program organization and the board-evaluation technique, then we discuss the lexicon and the lexicon-search algorithm in more detail.

2. Program Organization

Because our major concern was with the lexicon and associated algorithms, the rest of the program is the minimal required to play a reasonable game.

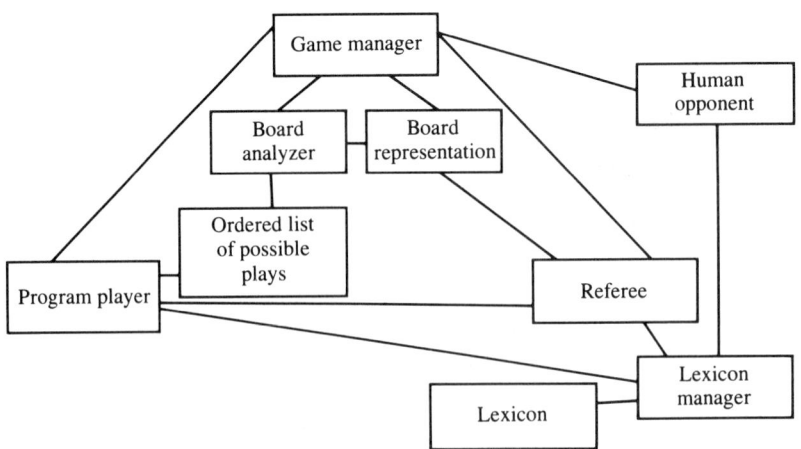

Figure 1. Organization of major program modules.

We will describe the program as it is, and in the final section of this paper indicate desirable enhancements.

The program is written to play a two-person game—the program player against one human opponent. Figure 1 shows the overall organization of the major program modules, which we shall describe below.

2.1. The Game Manager

The game manager handles interaction with the human opponent and keeps track of all game information. It deals out tiles to the human opponent and the program player at the beginning of the game and after each play. Dealing is done randomly (without replacement) from a list initialized correctly at the beginning of the game. The seed of the pseudorandom number generator is chosen by the human at the start of the game so that a game can be repeated to see the effect of learning new words. Whether the program or the human plays first is decided by randomly drawing a tile for each, according to the rules. The game manager's basic cycle is as follows:

(1) Print out the current board.
(2) Print out the human's rack and request an instruction. (The human's options at this point are described in Section 2.3.)
(3) If the human specifies a word to play, pass it to the referee for checking and scoring.
(4) If the referee says that the play is illegal (see Section 2.5), print an appropriate message and go to step (2).
(5) If the move was legal, update the board representation and the human's score, deal the human new tiles to replace the ones just used, print the score for the move just made and the new rack so the human can start thinking about the next move.
(6) Pass the human's move to the board analyzer for updating the list of possible plays.
(7) If the inspect mode is on, print the program player's rack.
(8) Get the program's move, update the board and the program's score, print the move and the score of the move.
(9) Pass the program's move to the board analyzer.
(10) Go to step (1).

The game ends when the human so specifies in step (2). Each player's total score is decreased by the value of the tiles in his/her rack, and the final scores are printed.

2.2. The Board Representation

The board is represented as a 15×15 array of SQUAREs. In interaction with the human, the rows are numbered 1–15 and the columns A–0, in the official manner (Conklin, 1976, pp. 33–34). Each SQUARE has a value as shown below:

Kind of SQUARE	Value
normal	0
double letter	1
triple letter	2
double word	3
triple word	4

If a SQUARE is occupied by a tile, it also contains the tile, an indication of whether the word using that tile is horizontal or vertical, and the value of a play using that tile as assigned by the board analyzer. Figure 2 shows how the board is printed before any play has been made.

	A	B	C	D	E	F	G	H	I	J	K	L	M	N	O	
1	4			1				4				1			4	1
2		3				2				2				3		2
3			3				1		1				3			3
4	1			3				1				3			1	4
5					3						3					5
6		2				2				2				2		6
7			1				1		1				1			7
8	4			1				3				1			4	8
9			1				1		1				1			9
10		2				2				2				2		10
11					3						3					11
12	1			3				1				3			1	12
13			3				1		1				3			13
14		3				2				2				3		14
15	4			1				4				1			4	15
	A	B	C	D	E	F	G	H	I	J	K	L	M	N	O	

Figure 2. How the board looks to the human before any words are played.

2.3. The Human Opponent

When it is the human's turn to move, the following options are available:

(0) terminate the game;
(1) play a word;
(2) pass without exchanging tiles;
(3) pass and exchange some tiles;
(4) have the total scores of both players printed;
(5) have the board and human's rack printed;
(6) access the lexicon manager (see Section 2.7);

(7) get general instructions for interacting with the program;
(8) get this list of options.

When the human plays a word, a notation close to the official notation of the SCRABBLE Crossword Game PLAYERS (Conklin, 1976, pp. 33–34) is used. The word is typed in with each letter already on the board preceded by a "$". When a blank tile is played, a "#" is typed followed by the letter it is being used as. For example, the play, $F#IRM, means that the player is using a blank, an R and an M from the rack and an F from the board, is using the blank as an I, and is spelling the word "firm." The location of the word is indicated by the official notation. For example, to place a word horizontally on row 12 from column K to column N, the notation is 12K–N. To place a word vertically on column C from row 13 to row 15, the notation is C13–15.

2.4. The Program Player

There are two basic ways to choose a play: (1) pick a place to play, then find a word that will fit; (2) pick a word to make, then find a place to put it. In either case, one might assign high priority to using or to not using certain tiles in the rack in order to keep the rack balanced or to build toward being able to make a bonus word (using all seven tiles on the rack). The second method is easier to use if the word chosen is made entirely from tiles in the rack, than if tiles from the board are also to be used (see Appendix, moves 3, 17, and 29). This is most appropriate when a bonus word can be made entirely from the rack. We decided to use the first method.

We adopted the following simplified approach. Possible places to play are tiles already on the board. If a tile is already being used in a horizontal word, only a vertical play will be considered and vice versa. This means that often valuable moves like 3, 17, 19, 21, 33, 35, and 39 in the Appendix will not be considered by this version of the program.

In certain situations, choice of a tile to play on puts obvious (to humans) limitations on possible words. For example, if we decide to play on a K in column N only words with a K as the last letter or second to last letter are possible. One might decide to build such limitations into the lexicon-search algorithm. However, this complicates situations where we decide to play on a centrally located tile. We decided to ignore such limitations in the lexicon lookup and use the referee to check each word found to see if it really fits where the players wants to put it.

The program player uses three parameters, MAXLOC, MAXWDS, and MINPT. It considers the best MAXLOC positions from the ordered list maintained by the board analyzer. For each position, it passes the tiles in its rack plus the tile at the position to the lexicon-search algorithm, and considers the first MAXWDS words found. Each word is passed to the referee along with its proposed location. The referee determines if the word really fits there, and if so, returns a score for the play. As soon as a play worth at least MINPT points is found, it is played. If no such play is found, the highest scoring play is made. If none of the MAXLOC × MAXWDS words are playable, the player exchanges all the tiles on its rack for new ones. Of course, if fewer than seven tiles are left to draw from, this exchange is illegal and the program just passes. In the game recorded in the Appendix, MAXLOC was 6, MAXWDS was 5 and MINPT was 14. Of the program's 25 moves, 6 were worth MINPT or more, 10 were worth fewer than MINPT, the program exchanged its rack 7 times, and passed twice. The average score for the 16 words actually played was 13.125. The average score for the human's 25 words was 13.88.

When the inspect mode is on, all positions and words that the program player considers are printed on the terminal.

2.5. The Referee

The referee is called by the program player with a proposed move and by the game manager with the human's move. In either case, a word and a location are passed to the referee, which checks the following (not necessarily in the order shown):

(1) The location and the length of the word are consistent.
(2) The word will not extend off the board.
(3) All letters except those preceded by "$" are on the player's rack.
(4) The word contains at least one tile from the board or is adjacent to a tile on the board in at least one place.
(5) The location places each letter preceded by a "$" where such a tile is already on the board and every other tile on an empty square.
(6) The two ends of the word are not adjacent (in the direction of the word) to nonempty squares.

If the referee is judging the human's move, it passes the word and all cross-words formed by the play to the lexicon-search routine. If one of these words is not in the lexicon, the human is asked if it really is a word. If the human responds "yes," the word is given to the lexicon manager for immediate insertion into the lexicon. If the response is "no," the current version of the program allows the play anyway.

If the play is legal, the referee computes its score, including the main word and all newly formed cross-words, and returns this to the caller.

2.6. The Board Analyzer

The board analyzer is called by the game manager after each move to update the values of the playable tiles and the ordered list of these positions. The analyzer begins by setting to 0 the value of each tile already on the board that has now been used in both directions. It then computes a value for each tile newly placed on the board by the play. If the play was vertical (horizontal), the value is the sum of the value of the square and the value of each unoccupied

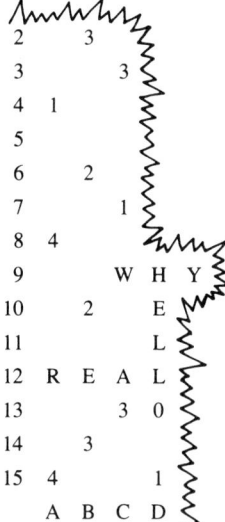

Figure 3. A section of the board after playing REA$L at 12A–D.

square in the same row (column), except that no square is included that is more than seven squares away from the tile being evaluated or that is beyond the closest occupied square. Those occupied squares are then reevaluated and the ordered list of playable positions is updated for the program player's next move. The values calculated by the board analyzer are stored in each evaluated SQUARE as mentioned in Section 2.2. For example, Figure 3 shows a section of the board after placing REA$L at 12A–D. The value of the L at 12D is changed to 0, the values of the R, E, and A is row 12 are set to 9, 8, and 4, respectively, and the W at 9C is reevaluated from 11 to 8.

We realize that the board evaluation scheme needs improvement, but it does provide a rough approximation to an adequate ordering of the playable positions and we were more concerned with the lexicon, to which we now turn.

2.7. The Lexicon Manager

The lexicon manager can perform the following operations:

(1) Insert a word into the lexicon.
(2) Delete a word from the lexicon.
(3) Check if a particular word is in the lexicon.
(4) Find words that can be formed from any permutation and combination of a set of tiles.

The referee uses operation (3) to check the human's plays and operation (1) when the human insists that a word that is not in the lexicon should be. The referee also uses operation (3) to check cross-words formed by plays proposed by the program player. The program player uses operation (4) to find possible words to play. The human can interact with the lexicon manager by choosing option (6) (see Section 2.3). He/She can then repeatedly use options (1), (2), or (4) before returning to the game. This option has been used by the authors for early editing of the lexicon. For example, we entered all legal two-letter words (Conklin, 1976, p. 156) this way.

Option (4) takes advantage of the SIMULA 67 *detach* facility by taking a set of tiles and a number, *n*. It returns approximately *n* words (see below), and then can either search the lexicon using a different set of tiles or can resume the search for more words using the original set of tiles. The availability of *detach* was the main reason for choosing SIMULA 67 as the programming language.

3. The Lexicon Data Structure

The lexicon was designed for the particular problem, "Given a collection of letters, find all words that can be formed from any combination and permutation of the letters, and find these words in approximately the order of their value in the SCRABBLE Crossword Game." Two key ideas were combined in the design of the data structure—letter tables (De La Briandais, 1959; Hayes, 1967; Lamb and Jacobsen, 1961), or tries (Knuth, 1973, pp. 481–487), and canonical ordering.

A letter table is a binary tree in which each node has the following four fields:

(1) a letter;
(2) information depending on the application;
(3) a success link to a subtree;
(4) a fail link to a subtree.

To look up a word in a letter table one starts at the root and follows fail links until a node is found whose letter is the first letter in the word. Then one looks up the remainder of the word in the success subtree of that node. When a node is found for the last letter in the word, the information field contains information about that word, e.g., lexical features. Note that as a word is looked up, all words formed from initial sub-sequences of the word are also found.

Consider the problem of designing a human readable anagram lexicon to find all words that can be formed from permutations of a given collection of letters. Take any word to be listed and reorder its letters according to any canonical ordering, e.g., alphabetical. List these re-spellings lexicographically based on the same ordering, and under each re-spelling list the original word. For example, to find anagrams of "live," look up "eilv," and find "evil," "live," and "vile."

Combining these two ideas, the data structure of our lexicon is a letter table

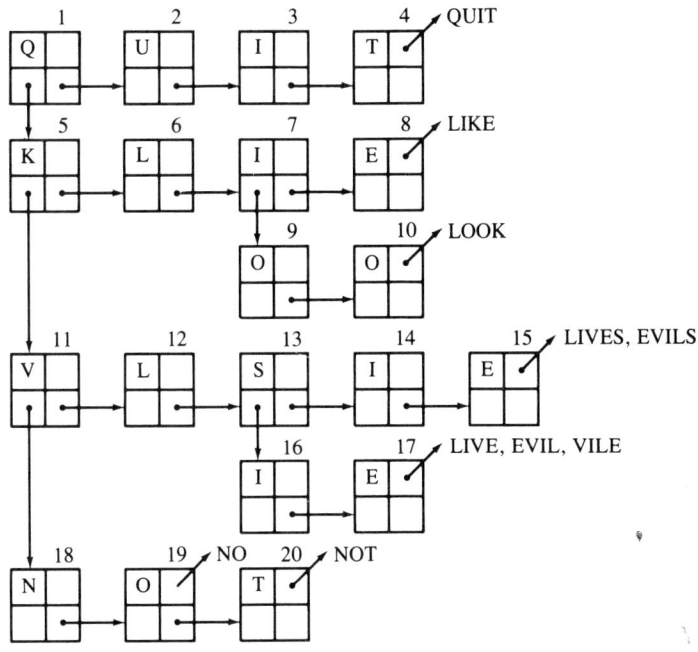

Figure 4. An example of the lexicon data structure.

using a canonical ordering of letters instead of the original spelling order. The information field of each node contains a list of the words formed from permutations of the letters which access the node. So that words can be found in approximately the order of their values in the SCRABBLE Crossword Game, the canonical ordering used is the value of the letters in that game. Among letters with the same value, the one with the least frequency in English is sorted first to increase the bushiness of the tree. The ordering used is:

ZQJXKVWYFHBPMCGDULSIRNOATE

Figure 4 shows a small lexicon using this data structure. The fields are shown as indicated below.

letter	words
fail	succ

Each node is numbered for reference in Section 4.

The lexicon is maintained in a sequential file on disk, ordered in the same way it is searched: letter field, words fields, success subtree, fail subtree. This file is scanned as the tree is searched and subtrees that are not needed are not stored in main memory.

4. The Lexicon-Search Algorithm

The search algorithm takes the lexicon tree and a list of letters in the canonical order. The list of letters may contain one or more occurrences of the blank, "#," which may match any letter and are initially placed at the front of the list. The search algorithm finds all words in the tree that are formed from any permutation and combination of the letters in the list. It finds words using the higher-valued letters before words not using them. It also finds words using a collection of letters before words using a proper subcollection of those letters. For example, if a word can be formed using all the letters in the list, this will be the first word found.

In the algorithm presented below, the procedure *detach* is to be understood as causing control to be returned to the original caller of the procedure in such a way that the current value of the local variables are available to the original caller, and so that the procedure may be resumed at the point right after the *detach*. Other variables and functions used are:

tree: a node of the lexicon tree
letters: a list of letters ordered as discussed above
nil: the empty list and the empty tree
letter(tree) ⎫
words(tree) ⎪
succ(tree) ⎬ the four fields of tree
fail(tree) ⎭
hd(letters): the first letter on the list
tl(letters): the list without the first letter
next-let(letters): the first non-# letter on the list, or nil if there is none
move-to-front(letter, letters): equal to letters, but with the first occurrence
        of letter moved to the front of the list
before(letter1, letter2): true if letter1 is before letter2 in the canonical
        ordering or if letter2 is nil, false otherwise
remove-next-let(letters): equal to letters with the first non-# letter removed.

The search algorithm is:

procedure findwords(tree, letters);
    while tree ≠ nil *and* letters ≠ nil *do*
        if letter(tree) = next-let(letters) *then*
            begin {lexicon node matches first non-# letter}
                letters ← move-to-front (next-let (letters), letters);
                findwords (succ(tree), tl(letters));
                if words (tree) ≠ nil *then detach*;
                letter ← tl(letters); {now ignore this letter and}
                tree ← fail (tree)   {continue searching}
            end

else if hd(letters) = ' # ' *then*
    {lexicon node does not match first non- # letter,
        but it can match the # }
    if before (letter(tree), next-let(letters)) *then*
        begin {allow the # to match the node}
            findwords (succ(tree), tl(letters));
            if words (tree) ≠ nil *then detach*;
            tree ← fail (tree) {the # can match something else}
        end
    else letters ← remove-next-let (letters)
                {we are past this letter, so ignore it}
else if before (hd(letters), letter(tree)) *then*
        letters ← tl(letters) {we're past this letter, so ignore it}
else tree ← fail(tree) {keep looking}

Table 1 shows a trace of this procedure on the lexicon of Figure 4 and the list of letters, # VSIE. Note that success links are followed recursively since we will later back up along these links, but fail links are followed iteratively since once following a fail link from a node we are no longer interested in that node or its success subtree. This is the method by which only those pieces of the tree in which we are interested are retained in main memory. Also note that since words are found in groups, if *n* words were wanted, at least *n* words, but possibly a few more, will be found.

One deficiency of this search algorithm is that when the program player picks a board position to play on and passes the tile at that position along with the tiles on its rack to the search algorithm, words that do not use the tile on the board may be returned. We want to be able to mark certain letters in the list as required to be used in the retrieved words. We will define the procedure findwords2 that takes a node of the tree and an ordered list of nodes, *n* with the following fields:

    letter(*n*):   a letter corresponding to an element of the
                   second argument of findwords;
    req(*n*):   true if letter(*n*) is required to be in the
                   retrieved words, false otherwise;
    done(*n*):   true if no node further on in the list is
                   required, false otherwise.

Given such a list with the letter and req fields set, it is easy to define the procedure setdone which returns the list with the done fields set properly. In the procedure below, letters is such a list after setdone has been applied, next-let(letters) returns the letter field of the first node in letters whose letter field is not #, next-req(letters) returns the req field of the first node in letters whose letter field is not #, remove-next-let(letters) removes from letters the

Table 1

Recursion level	Node of tree	Letter of tree	Letters	Test results	Action
1	1	Q	#VSIE	Q≠V, hd(LETTERS)=#, before(Q, V)	# matches Q, follow succ(1)
2	2	U	VSIE	U≠V, hd(LETTERS)≠#, before(V, U)	ignore V
2	2	U	SIE	U≠S, hd(LETTERS)≠#, ¬before(S, U)	follow fail(2)
2	nil		SIE		Return
1	1	Q	#VSIE	words(1) = nil	follow fail(1)
1	5	K	#VSIE	K≠V, hd(LETTERS)≠#, before(K, V)	# matches K, follow succ(5)
2	6	L	VSIE	L≠V, hd(LETTERS)≠#, before(V, L)	ignore V
2	6	L	SIE	L≠S, hd(LETTERS)≠#, ¬before(S, L)	follow fail(6)
2	nil		SIE		Return
1	5	K	#VSIE	words(5) = nil	follow fail(5)
1	11	V	#VSIE	V = V	move V to front, follow succ(11)
2	12	L	#SIE	L≠S, hd(LETTERS)=#, before(L, S)	# matches L, follow succ(12)
3	13	S	SIE	S = S	follow succ(13)
4	14	I	IE	I = I	follow succ(14)
5	15	E	E	E = E	follow succ(15)
6	nil		nil		Return
5	15	E	E	words(15) = LIVES, EVILS	Detach
5	15	E	E		ignore E and follow fail(15)

5	nil		nil	words(14) = nil	Return
4	14	I	IE		ignore I and follow fail(14)
4	nil		E	words(13) = nil	Return
3	13	S	SIE		ignore S and follow fail(13)
3	16	I	IE	I = I	follow succ(16)
4	17	E	E	E = E	follow succ(17)
5	nil		nil	words(17) = LIVE, EVIL, VILE	Return
4	17	E	E		Detach
4	17	E	E		ignore E and follow fail(17)
4	nil		nil	words(16) = nil	Return
3	16	I	IE		ignore I, follow fail(16)
3	nil		E	words(12) = nil	Return
2	12	L	#SIE		follow fail(12)
2	nil		#SIE	words(11) = nil	Return
1	11	V	V#SIE		ignore V, follow fail(11)
1	18	N	#SIE	$N \neq S$, hd(LETTERS) = #, $\neg$before(N, S)	ignore S
1	18	N	#IE	$N \neq I$, hd(LETTERS) = #, $\neg$before(N, I)	ignore I
1	18	N	#E	$N \neq E$, hd(LETTERS) = #, before(N, E)	# matches N, follow succ(18)
2	19	O	E	$O \neq E$, hd(LETTERS) $\neq$ #, $\neg$before(E, O)	follow fail(19)
2	nil		E	words(18) = nil	Return
1	18	N	#E		follow fail(18)
1	nil		#E		Return

first node whose letter field is not #, and move-to-front(letter, letters) moves to the front of letters the first node whose letter field is letter and if that node has a true req field returns setdone of the changed list. Lines in findwords2 that are different from corresponding lines in findword are marked by a "→" in the left margin.

procedure findwords2(tree, letters);
      while tree ≠ nil *and* letters ≠ nil *do*
          if letter(tree) = next-let(letters) *then*
              begin {lexicon node matches first non-# letter}
                  letters ← move-to-front(next-let(letters), letters);
                  findwords(succ(tree), tl(letters));
→   *if* words(tree) ≠ nil *and* done (hd(letters)) *then detach*;
→   *if* req(hd(letters)) *then* tree ← nil
→   *else begin* letters ← tl(letters);
→   tree   fail(tree)
→   *end*
              end
          else if hd(letter) = " # " *then*
              {lexicon node doesn't match first non-# letter, but
                    but it can match the #}
              if before(letter(tree), next-let(letters)) *then*
                  begin {allow the # to match the node}
                      findwords(succ(tree), tl(letters));
→   *if* words (tree) ≠ nil *and* done (hd(letters))
                          then detach
                      tree ← fail(tree) {the # can match something else}
                  end
→   *else if* next-req(letters) *then* letters ← nil
→   *else* letters ← remove-next-let(letters)
          else if before (hd(letters), letter(tree)) *then* {we've passed this letter}
→   *if* req(hd(letters)) *then* letters ← nil
→   *else* letters ← tl(letters)
          else tree ← fail(tree) {keep looking}

Notice that the req field keeps us from ignoring required letters, and the done field prevents words from being returned unless all required letters are included.

5. Conclusions

The lexicon data structure and search algorithm seem successful. The program player quickly makes use of high-valued tiles on the board or on its rack. There is still much room for improvement besides increasing the program's vocabulary. Implementing findwords2 would make the program player's search for words to play more efficient and more likely to yield playable words without changing the MAXLOC and MAXWDS parameters. The board evaluation scheme is still rather primitive. For example, the value of double letter squares should be twice the average value of the (still unplayed) tiles instead of 1. The program player should be modified to allow for playing words parallel to adjacent words and for extending existing words. Strategies such as maintaining a balanced rack and retaining high-frequency polygraphs to increase the future probability of a bonus word might be added. Even without these improvements, the program plays a competitive game against a human opponent.

Acknowledgments. The authors appreciate the work of Ben Shneiderman, Margaret Ambrose, and Barbara Rasche who along with the senior author, worked on a preliminary version of this program. Computer services were provided by IUPUI Computing Facilities as part of the Indiana University Computing Network.

Appendix

Table 2 provides a record of a complete game played between the program player and a human, DPF. DPF had previously played several rushed rounds against the program and consistently scored lower than the program. However, in the game presented here, he took advantage of his knowledge of the program's weaknesses. The game was played with the inspect mode on and took 17 minutes, 28.56 seconds of CPU time on a DECSystem-10 and 2 hours, 50 minutes, 39.05 seconds of real time. At the end of the game, there were 1,488 words in the lexicon.

Table 2

				Score			
				DPF		Program	
	Rack	Word	Location	Play	Total	Play	Total
1.	IFOHIOT	HOOF	8G–J	20	20		
2.	GSMHR☐B	F$\overline{\text{I}}$RM	J8–11			10	10
3.	LATIFIT	FAIL	K9–12	28	48		
4.	EZIGSHB	HO	I7–8			9	19
5.	ITYTTIT	THY	G7–9	14	62		
6.	AEZIGSB	LAZE	12K–N			26	45
7.	YCITTIT	YET	N11–13	6	68		
8.	UNOIGSB	BUSY	9D–G			9	54

Table 2 (*continued*)

	Rack	Word	Location	DPF Play	DPF Total	Program Play	Program Total
9.	DLCITIT	CULT	E8–11	12	80		
10.	PEDNOIG	ZIP	M12–14			32	86
11.	ONADIIT	SAID	F9–12	13	93		
12.	RPEDNOG	exchange rack					86
13.	AREONIT	PI	14M–N	22	115		
14.	GMRDNEI	DIME	12F–I			10	96
15.	AAREONT	MOAT	H12–15	18	133		
16.	ANRGRDN	RADAR	14G–K			8	104
17.	TEEAREN	ENTREE	O6–11	23	156		
18.	UAJTNGN	exchange rack					104
19.	ACISEAE	LAZES	12K–O	23	179		
20.	PUB□SGD	BUDG[E]T	15C–H			11	115
21.	RACIEAE	REBUGET	15A–H	33	212		
22.	INQIVPS	ON	13H–I			8	123
23.	UACIEAE	CAB	C13–15	14	226		
24.	EIQIVPS	exchange rack					123
25.	VNUIEAE	VAN	7M–O	10	236		
26.	ROGNLGI	exchange rack					123
27.	ANUIEAE	VANE	M7–10	8	244		
28.	EQVLUNI	exchange rack					123
29.	ITOUIAE	TO	O14–15	11	255		
30.	DEEOOKW	exchange rack					123
31.	JNIUIAE	JAR	A13–15	10	265		
32.	PGGRLVQ	RAP	N6–8			16	139
33.	ISNIUIE	ENDS	I12–15	17	282		
34.	EOGGLVQ	exchange rack					139
35.	WINIUIE	WRAP	N5–8	9	291		
36.	EDOWNSE	SNOW	5J–N			14	153
37.	OINIUIE	INN	L3–5	6	297		
38.	ONKEDWE	WINK	3K–N			22	175
39.	QGOIUIE	RAGE	10J–M	5	302		
40.	LUIOEDE	ELK	N1–3			14	189
41.	LQOIUIE	QUE	1L–N	22	324		
42.	EGUIODE	pass					189
43.	XOLOIIE	WISE	K3–6	9	333		
44.	EGUIODE	DE	6J–K			7	196
45.	EVXOLOI	LOIN	4I–L	4	337		
46.	EGUIOE	COG	13C–E			6	202
47.	EVXOI	EVIL	I1–4	8	345		
48.	EUIE	EVE	2H–J			8	210
49.	XO	LO	2N–O	2	347		
50.	UI	pass					210
51.	X	pass			347		
					339		208

	A	B	C	D	E	F	G	H	I	J	K	L	M	N	O	
1	4			1				4	E			Q	U	E	4	1
2		3				2		E	V	E			L	O		2
3			3				1		I		W	I	N	K		3
4	1			3				1	L	O	I	N			1	4
5					3						S	N	O	W		5
6		2				2				D	E			R	E	6
7			1				T		H				V	A	N	7
8	4			1	C		H	O	O	F		1	A	P	T	8
9			1	B	U	S	Y		1	I	F		N		R	9
10		2			L	A			R	A	G	E		2	E	10
11					T	I		M	I					Y	E	11
12	1			3		D	I	M	E		L	A	Z	E	S	12
13	J		C	O	G		1	O	N				I	T		13
14	A	3	A			2	R	A	D	A	R		P	I	T	14
15	R	E	B	U	D	G	E	T	S			1			O	15
	A	B	C	D	E	F	G	H	I	J	K	L	M	N	O	

Figure 5. The board at the end of the game of Table 2.

In Table 2, a letter already on the board is underlined and blanks are represented as a square. Figure 5 shows the board at the end of the game.

Bibliography

17.1. A Bibliography of Computer Games

David N. L. Levy

This bibliography contains every reference given in every one of the original papers reproduced in these volumes. I have also included a number of other references which I feel might be of interest to the reader. Since some of the papers in the present collection cross-refer to others, I have indicated below those references for which the original can be found herein. Such references are indicated thus: ***.

Although I have not attempted the impossible task of making this an absolutely complete bibliography of material on and relating to the computerization of strategy games, I believe that it does represent the most complete bibliography on the subject compiled to date. I have been compelled, for reasons of space, to omit many references to papers on computer chess, though the reader with a particular interest in that subject can refer to the Bibliography found in Levy (1988).

If any reader would like to suggest additional references which might be included in the Bibliography of any future edition, I will be pleased to hear of it via the publisher.

Abbreviations and Symbols

ACM   = Association for Computing Machinery
AISB   = British Computer Society Study Group for Artificial Intelligence and Simulation of Behaviour
IEEE   = Institute of Electrical and Electronic Engineers
IFIP   = International Federation for Information Processing
IJACI   = International Joint Conference on Artificial Intelligence
IRE   = Institute of Radio Engineers (later became IEEE)
SIGART = Publication of the ACM Special Interest Group on Artificial Intelligence
***   = This paper is reproduced in the present volumes.

Abrahams, G. (1951): *The Chess Mind*. Penguin, Harmondsworth.

Adelson-Velsky, G. M., Arlazarov, V. L., and Uskov, A. V. (1966): Programme playing chess. *Symposium on Theory and Computing Methods in the Upper Mantle Problem*.

Adelson-Velsky, G. M., Arlazarov, V. L., and Donskoy, M. V. (1975): Some methods of controlling the tree search in chess programs. *Artificial Intelligence*, **6**, 361–371.

Ajtai, M., Csirmaz, L., and Nagy, Zs. (1979): On a generalization of the game Go-Moku—I. *Studia Scientiarum Mathematica Hungarica*, **14**, 209–226.

Akl, S. G. and Newborn, M. M. (1977): The principal continuation and the killer heuristic. *Proceedings of ACM National Conference, Seattle, 1977*, pp. 466–478.

Akl, S. G. and Doran, R. J. (1983): A comparison of parallel implementations of the alpha–beta and scout tree search algorithms using the game of checkers. In Bramer, M. A. (1983), pp. 290–303.

Albion, H. (1980): Japanese openings. *Othello Quarterly*, **2**, no. 2, 3–5.

Alexis, M. and Wilson, C. Z. (1967): *Organizational Decision Making*. Prentice-Hall, Englewood Cliffs, New Jersey.

Anastasi, A. (1961): *Psychological Testing*. Macmillan, London.

Anderson, N. H. (1974): Cognitive algebra: Integration theory applied to social attribution. In Berkovitz, L. (Editor), *Advances in Experimental Social Psychology*, Vol. 7. Academic Press, New York.

Anderssen, I.: *Sure Tricks*. George Coffin, Waltham, Massachusetts.

Anstey, E. (1966): *Psychological Tests*. Macmillan, London.

Arden, B. W., Galler, B. A., and Graham, R. M. (1969): The MAD definition facility. *Communications of the ACM*, **12**, 432–439.

Arlazarov, V. L. and Futer, A. V. (1979): Computer analysis of a rook endgame. In Hayes, J. E., Michie, D., and Mikulich, L. I. (Editors), *Machine Intelligence* 9. Ellis Horwood, Chichester. Reprinted in Levy, D. N. L. (1988).

Armanino, D. (1959): *Dominoes*. David McKay, New York.

Atkinson, J. W. (1957): Motivational determinants of risk-taking behavior. *Psychological Review*, **64**, 359–372.

Atkinson, J. W. and Feather, N. T. (Editors) (1966): *A Theory of Achievement Motivation*. Wiley, New York.

Backus, J. W. *et al.* (1957): The FORTRAN automatic coding system. *Proceedings of the Western Joint Computer Conference*, pp. 188–198.

Bailey, D. (1977): The Eighth North American Computer Chess Championship, October 15–17, in Seattle. *Northwest Chess*, pp. 8–10.

Bakker, I. (1976): *European Computer Chess Championship Booklet*. Tournament Committee, Royal Dutch Chess Federation Office, Amsterdam.

Balzer, R. M. (1966): A mathematical model for performing a complex task in a card game. *Behavioral Science*, **11**, 219–226.

Banerji, R. B. (1969a): *Theory of Problem Solving—An Approach to Artificial Intelligence*. American Elsevier, New York.

Banerji, R. B. (1969b): An overview of game playing programs. Technical Report. Case Western Reserve University, Cleveland, Ohio.

Banerji, R. B. (1971): Similarities in games and their use in strategy construction. *Computers and Automata Proceedings of 21st Brooklyn Polytechnic Symposium*.

Banerji, R. B. and Ernst, G. W. (1971): Changes in representation which preserve strategies in games. *Proceedings of 2nd IJCAI*, pp. 651–658. A longer version appeared as a technical report of the same name published at Case Western Reserve University, Cleveland, Ohio.

Banerji, R. B. and Ernst, G. W. (1972): Strategy construction using homomorphisms between games. *Artificial Intelligence*, **3**, 223–250.

Bastian, A. L., Foley, J. P., and Petrick, S. R. (1962): On the implications and uses of a language for contract bridge bidding. *Proceedings of a Symposium on Symbolic Languages in Data Processing*, pp. 741–758. Gordon and Breach, New York. Also published as Air Force Cambridge Research Laboratories Research Report AFCRL-63-50.

Baudet, G. M. (1978): On the branching factor of the alpha–beta pruning algorithm. *Artificial Intelligence*, **9**, 177–199.

Baylor, G. W. and Simon, H. A. (1966): A chess mating combinations program. *Proceedings of the Spring Joint Computer Conference*, pp. 431–447. Reprinted in Levy, D. N. L. (1988).

Bell, A. G. (1967): Kalah on Atlas. In Michie, D. (Editor), *Machine Intelligence 3*, pp. 181–194. Edinburgh University Press, Edinburgh.

Bell, A. G. (1972): *Game Playing by Computer*. Allen and Unwin, London.

Bell, R. C. (1960): *Board and Table Games*. Oxford University Press, London.

Belladonna and Averelli, G. (1959): *Roman Club System of Distributional Bidding*. Simon and Schuster, New York.

Bellman, R. (1952): On games involving bluffing. *Rendiconti del Circolo Matematico di Palermo, Series 2*, **1**, 139–156.

Bellman, R. (1957): *Dynamic Programming*. Princeton University Press, Princeton, New Jersey.

Bellman, R. (1965): On the application of dynamic programming to the determination of optimal play in chess and checkers. *Proceedings of the National Academy of Sciences USA*, **53**.

Bellmann, R. and Blackwell, D. (1949): Some two-person games involving bluffing. *Proceedings of the National Academy of Sciences USA*, **45**, 600–605.

Benko, P. (1978): The "amateur" world champion: An interview with Max Euwe. *Chess Life and Review*, **33**, 410–413.

Benson, D. B. (1976): Life in the game of Go. *Information Sciences*, **10**, 17–9.***

Benson, D. B. (1979): A mathematical analysis of Go. In Heine, K. (1979a), pp. 55–64.

Benson, D. B., Evers, P., Miller, J., Tackett, M., and Starkey, D. (1976): Computerizing the game of Go. *Proceedings of Northwest '76: ACM Pacific Regional Symposium*.

Benson, D. B., Hilditch, B. R., and Starkey, J. D. (1979): Tree analysis techniques in TsumeGo. *Proceedings of 6th IJCAI, Tokyo*, pp. 50–52.***

Benson, D. B. and Soule, S. P. (1978): Legal Go: A formal program specification, Parts 1, 2, 3. Washington State University, Computer Science Department, Reports CS-78-45, 46, and 47.

Berg, C. C. (1972): Adaptive decisions under uncertainty. Ph.D. Thesis (in German), University of Mannheim, Mannheim.

Berlekamp, E. R. (1963): Program for playing double-dummy bridge problems—A new strategy for mechanical game playing. *Journal of the ACM*, **10**, no. 4, 357–364.***

Berlekamp, E. R., Conway, J. H., and Guy, R. K. (1982): *Winning Ways* (2 volumes). Academic Press, London.

Berliner, H. J. (1970): Experiences gained in constructing and testing a chess program. *Proceedings of IEEE Symposium on Systems Science and Cybernetics*, pp. 216–223.***

Berliner, H. J. (1973): Some necessary conditions for a master chess program. *Proceedings of the 3rd IJCAI*, pp. 77–85.

Berliner, H. J. (1974): Chess as problem solving: The development of a tactics analyzer. Unpublished Doctoral Thesis, Carnegie–Mellon University, Pittsburgh. Chapter 1 reprinted in Levy, D. N. L. (1988).

Berliner, H. J. (1976): Outstanding performances by CHESS 4.5 against human competition. *SIGART Newsletter*, no. 60, 12–13.

Berliner, H. J. (1977a): Two games from the Minnesota Open. *SIGART Newsletter*, no. 62, 9–10.

Berliner, H. J. (1977b): CHESS 4.5 vs. Levy. *SIGART Newsletter*, no. 62, 11.

Berliner, H. J. (1977c): *BKG—A program that plays Backgammon*. Computer Science Department, Carnegie–Mellon University, Pittsburgh.***

Berliner, H. J. (1977d): Experiences in evaluation with BKG, a program that plays backgammon. *Proceedings of the 5th IJCAI, Pittsburgh*, pp. 428–433.

Berliner, H. J. (1978): A chronology of computer chess and its literature. *Artificial Intelligence*, **10**, 201–214.

Berliner, H. J. (1979): On the construction of evaluation functions for large domains. *Proceedings 6th IJCAI, Tokyo*, pp. 53–55.

Berliner, H. J. (1980a): Backgammon computer program beats world champion. *Artificial Intelligence*, **14**, 205–220.***

Berliner, H. J. (1980b): Computer backgammon. *Scientific American*, (June 1980), 54–62.

Bernstein, A. and Roberts M. de V. (1958a): Computer vs. chessplayer. *Scientific American*, **198**, no. 6, 96–105.

Bernstein, A., Roberts, M. de V., Arbuckle, T., and Belsky, M. S. (1958b): A chess playing program for the IBM 704. *Proceedings of the 1958 Western Joint Computer Conference*, pp. 157–159. Reprinted in Levy, D. N. L. (1988).

Berry, M. J. A. (1983): A set of functions to play New Eleusis. In Bramer, M. A. (1983), pp. 256–262.

Billing, H. (Editor) (1961): *Lernende Automaten*. Oldenbourg, Munich.

Binet, A. (1894): *Psychologie des Grands Calculateurs et des Joueurs d'Echecs*. Hachette, Pairs.

Birkhoff, G. (1969): Mathematics and psychology. *SIAM Review*, **11**, no. 4, 429–449.

Birkhoff, G. and MacLane, S. (1965): *A Survey of Modern Algebra*. 3rd ed., revised. Macmillan, New York.

Bobrow, D. G. (1968): Natural language input for a computer problem-solving system. In Minsky, M. (1968), pp. 135–215.

Borel, E. *et al.* (1947): *Traite du Calcul des Probabilites et de ses Applications*, Vol. 4, part 2. Gauthier-Villars, Paris.

Botvinnik, M. M. (1970): *Computers, Chess and Long-Range Planning*. Springer-Verlag, Berlin and New York.

Botvinnik, M. M. (1975): Will computers get self-respect? *Sovietsky Sport*, June 15.

Bowden, B. V. (Editor) (1953): *Faster Than Thought*. Pitman, London.

Bradley, M. (1979): The game of Go—The ultimate challenge? *Creative Computing*, **5**, no. 3, 89–99.

Bramer, M. A. (Editor) (1983): *Computer Game-Playing: Theory and Practice*. Ellis Horwood, Chichester.

Bridge World (1967–1969): volume 38, no. 4 (January, 1967) through volume 40, no. 9 (June, 1969). Bridge World Magazine, New York.

Brieman, L. (1961): Optimal gambling systems for favorable games. *Fourth Berkeley Symposium on Probability and Statistics*, vol. 1, pp. 65–78.

Brown, D. J. H. (1979a): Is Go harder than chess? *Personal Computing*, **3**, no. 12.

Brown, D. J. H. (1979b): Hierarchical reasoning in the game of Go. *Proceedings of the 6th International Joint Conference on Artificial Intelligence, Tokyo*, pp. 114–116.

Brown, D. J. H. (1979c): Reasoning about games. *AISB Newsletter*, no. 32, 14–17.

Brown, D. J. H. (1983): Seeing is believing (or how to make Sabaki). In Bramer, M. A. (1983), pp. 177–184.

Brown, D. J. H. and Dowsey, S. (1979): The challenge of Go. *New Scientist*, **81**, 303–305.

Brudno, A. L. (1963): Bounds and valuations for shortening the scanning of variations. *Probl. Kibern.* **10**, 141–150.

Buckingham, R. A., Elithorn, A., Lee, D. N., and Nixon, W. L. B. (1963): A mathematical model of a perceptual maze test. *Nature*, **199**, 676–678.

Burroughs, (1968): B5500 information processing systems extended ALGOL (Language Manual). Equipment and Systems Marketing Division, Burroughs Corporation, Detroit.

Burstall, R., Collins, N. L., and Popplestone, R. (1971): *Programming in POP2*. Edinburgh University Press, Edinburgh.

Byrne, R. (1978): Fischer vs. the computer. *The New York Times*, July 30, p. 30.

Cahlander, D. (1977a): The Computer is a fish, or is it? *SIGART Newsletter*, no. 62, 8–9.

Cahlander, D. (1977b): Simultaneous play of CHESS 4.5 (unpublished).

Carley, G. L. (1962): A program to play contract bridge. M.S. Thesis, Electrical Engineering Department, Massachusetts Institute of Technology, Cambridge, Massachusetts.

Carson, N. D. (1966): *A Beginner's Guide to Go*. 4435 Mayfield Road, South Euclid, Ohio.

Cerf, J. (1980): Cerf vs. Mimura. *Othello Quarterly*, **2**, no. 4, 16–21.

Cerf, J. (1981): Machine vs. machine. *Othello Quarterly*, **3**, no. 1, 12–16.

Chamberlain, D. (1974): Towards the development of a decision-making model based on the game of poker. Term Project in Management Science, Portland State University, Portland, Oregon.

Charness, N. (1977): Human chess skill. In Frey, P. W. (1977a), pp. 34–53.

Cheatham, T. E., Jr. (1969): Motivation for extensible languages. *SIGPLAN Notices*, **4**, 45–49.

Christensen, C. and Shaw, C. J. (Editors) (1969): Proceedings of the Extensible Languages Symposium. *SIGPLAN Notices*, **4**.

Church, K. W. (1978): Co-ordinate squares: A solution to many chess pawn endgames. Undergraduate Thesis, Massachusetts Institute of Technology, Cambridge, Massachusetts. Reprinted in Levy, D. N. L. (1988).

Church, R. M. and Church, K. W. (1977): Plans, goals and search strategies for the selection of a move in chess. In Frey, P. W. (1977a), pp. 131–156.

Cichelli, R. J. (1973): Research progress report in computer chess. *SIGART Newsletter*, no. 41, 32–36.

Citrenbaum, R. L. (1970): Efficient representations of optimal solutions for a class of games. Technical Report SRC-69-5, Case Western Reserve University, Cleveland, Ohio.

Clark, M. R. B. (1977): A quantitative study of King and Pawn against King. In Clark, M. R. B. (Editor), *Advances in Computer Chess*, pp. 108–118.

Clarkson, G. P. E. (1963): A model of the trust investment process. In Feigenbaum, E. A. and Feldman, J. (1963), pp. 347–371.

COBOL (1961): Revised specification for a common business oriented language. Department of Defense, U.S. Government Printing Office, Washington, D.C.

Cohen, B. and Barrow, R. (1967): *The Bridge Players Encyclopaedia*. Paul Hamlyn, London.

Cohen, B. and Reese, T. (1938): *Acol System of Contract Bridge*. Toyner and Steele, London.

Colombera, D. (1979): Evolutionary strategies and the theory of games. In Heine, K. (1979a).

Condon, E. U., Tawney, G. L., and Derr, W. A. (1940): Machine to play game of Nim. U.S. Patent No. 2,215,544, Sept. 24th, 1940, U.S. Patent Office, Washington, D.C.

Conklin, D. K. (Editor) (1976): *The Official SCRABBLE Players' Handbook*. Crown Publishers, New York.

Continentwide Olympiad Fund Game (1967): American Contract Bridge League, Greenwich, Connecticut.

Conway, H. M. (Editor) (1963): *The Weather Handbook*. Conway Publications, Atlanta, Georgia.

Crawford, J. R. (1961): *How to be a Consistent Winner in the Most Popular Card Games*. Dolphin Books, Garden City, New York.

Csirmaz, L. (1980): On a combinatorial game with application to Go-Moku. *Discrete Mathematics*, **29**, 19–23.

Csirmaz, L. and Nagy, Zs. (1979): On a generalization of the game Go-Moku—II. *Studia Scientiarum Mathematica Hungarica*, **14**, 461–469.

Dahl, O. J., Myhrhang, B., and Nygaard, K. (1968): *The Simula 67 common base language*. Norwegian Computing Centre, Oslo.

Dahl, O. J. and Nygaard, K. (1966): Simula—an Algol-based simulation language. *Communications of the ACM*, **9**, 671–678.

Daly, W. G. (1961): Computer strategies for the game of Qubic. M.S. Thesis, Massachusetts Institute of Technology, Cambridge, Massachusetts.***

Dantzig, G. (1963): *Linear Programming and Extensions*. Princeton University Press, Princeton, New Jersey.

Davies, D. W. (1950): A theory of chess and noughts-and-crosses. *Science News*, pp. 40–64.

Davies, J. (1975a): *Life and Death*. Ishi Press, Tokyo.

Davies, J. (1975b): *Tesuji*. Ishi Press, Tokyo.

Davis, R. and King, J. (1976): An overview of production systems. In Elcock, E. W. and Michie, D. (Editors), *Machine Intelligence* 8. Wiley, New York.

De Groot, A. D. (1946): Het Denken van den Schaker. Reprinted as *Thought and Choice in Chess*. Mouton, The Hague, 1965. [Chapter VII A—"The Sequence of Phases"—is reprinted in Levy, D. N. L. (1988)].

De La Briandais, R. (1959): File searching using variable length keys. *Proceedings of the Western Joint Computer Conference*, pp. 295–298.

De Swaan Arons, H. (1983): The three-cushioned billiard game. In Bramer, M. A. (1983), pp. 263–273.

Dennis, J. B. (1959): MACRO-A conversion program for the TX-O computer. Memorandum M5001-5, Research Laboratory of Electronics, Massachusetts Institute of Technology, March 11, 1959.

Dijkstra, E. W. (1972): Notes on structured programming. In *Structured Programming*. Academic Press, New York.

Douglas, J. R. (1978): GM Walter Browne vs. CHESS 4.6. *Chess Life and Review*, **33**, 363–364.

Dowsey, S. (1973): Go and the computer. *Go Review*, **13**, no. 3, 72–74.

Dueball, F. (1960): *Das Gospiel*. Minden, Westfalia.

Edwards, D. J. and Hart, T. P. (1963): The alpha–beta heuristic. Massachusetts Institute of Technology AI Memo 30, Cambridge, Massachusetts.

Edwards, W. (1962): Subjective probabilities inferred from decisions. *Pschological Review*, **69**, 109–135.

Elcock, E. W. and Murray, A. M. (1967): Experiments with a learning component in a Go-Moku program. In Collins, N. L. and Michie, D. (Editors), *Machine Intelligence* 1, pp. 87–103. Oliver and Boyd, London.***

Elithorn, A. and Jagoe, J. R. (1969): The computer analysis of human problem-solving behaviour. *Proceedings of the NATO Symposium on the Simulation of Human Behaviour, Paris*, pp. 205–217.

Elithorn, A., Jagoe, J. R., and Lee, D. N. (1966): Simulation of perceptual problem-solving skill. *Nature*, **211**, 1029–1031.

Elithorn, A. and Jones, D. (Editors) (1973): *Artificial and Human Thinking*. Elsevier, Amsterdam.

Elithorn, A. and Telford, A. (1969a): Computer analysis of intellectual skills. *International Journal of Man-Machine Studies,* **1**, no. 2, 189–209.

Elithorn, A. and Telford, A. (1969b): Design considerations in relation to computer-based games. In Elithorn, A. and Jones, D. (1973), pp. 162–176.***

Elithorn, A. and Telford, A. (1970): Game and problem structure in relation to the study of human and artificial intelligence. *Nature*, **227**, 1205–1210.

Englebart, D. C. (1968): A research center for augmenting human intellect. *Communications of the ACM*, **11**, no. 11, 733.

Epstein, R. A. (1967): *The Theory of Gambling and Statistical Logic*, Chapter 8, pp. 270–301. Academic Press, New York.

Ernst, G. W. and Newell, A. (1967): *Generality and GPS*. Carnegie Institute of Technology, Pittsburgh.

Euwe, M. (1970): Computers and chess. In Sunnucks, A. (1970), *The Encyclopaedia of Chess*. St. Martins Press, New York.

Everett, Mellor, and Stanier, A. (1973): The Essex Tournament Bidding System. Privately circulated.

Falkener, E. (1961): *Games Ancient and Oriental and How to Play Them*. Dover, New York.

Farber, D. J., Griswold, R. E., and Polonsky, I. P. (1966): The SNOBOL3 programming language. *Bell Systems Technical Journal*, **45**, 895–944.

Farley, B. G. and Clarke, W. A. (1954): Simulation of self-organizing systems by digital computers. *IRE PGIT*, **4**, 76.

Feigenbaum, E. A. (1963): The simulation of verbal learning behavior. In Feigenbaum, E. A. and Feldman, J. (Editors) (1963).

Feigenbaum, E. A. (1968): Artificial intelligence: Themes in the second decade. *Proceedings IFIP Congress, Edinburgh*, vol. 2, pp. 1008–1022.

Feigenbaum, E. A. and Feldman, J. (1963): *Computers and Thought*. McGraw-Hill, New York.

Fikes, R. E. (1968): A heuristic program for solving problems stated as nondeterministic procedures. Ph.D. Thesis, Carnegie–Mellon University, Pittsburgh.

Findler, N. V. (1960a): Some remarks on the game "Dama" which can be played on a digital computer. *Computer Journal*, **3**, 40–44.***

Findler, N. V. (1960b): Programming games. Part (a) of Paper BI 3.3. *Summarized Proceedings of the First Conference on Automatic Computing and Data Processing, Australia.*

Findler, N. V. (1961): Computer model of gambling and bluffing. *IRE Transactions on Electronic Computers*, **EC-10**, no. 1, 97–98.***

Findler, N. V. (1969): Some new approaches to machine learning. *IEEE Transactions on Systems Sciences and Cybernetics*, **SSC-5**, 173–182.***

Findler, N. V. (1973): Computer experiments on forming and optimizing heuristic rules. In Elithorn, A. and Jones, D. (Editors) (1973), pp. 177–188.

Findler, N. V. (1977): Studies in machine cognition using the game of poker. *Communications of the ACM*, **20**, no. 4, 230–245.

Findler, N. V. (1978): Computer poker. *Scientific American* (July 1978), 112–119.

Findler, N. V., Klein, H., Gould, W., Kowal, A., and Menig, J. (1972): Studies on decision making using the game of poker. *Proceedings of IFIP Congress, LJUBLJANA*, pp. 1448–1459. North-Holland, Amsterdam.***

Findler, N. V., Klein, H., and Levine, Z. (1973): Experiments with inductive discovery processes leading to heuristics in a poker program. In Beckmann, Goos, and Kuenzi (Editors), *Proceedings of Conference on Cognitive and Systems*, pp. 257–266. Springer-Verlag, Berlin.

Findler, N. V., Klein, H., Johnson, R. C., Kowal, A., Levine, Z., and Menig, J. (1974): Heuristic programmers and their gambling machines. *Proceedings ACM National Conference, San Diego, California*, pp. 28–37.

Findler, N. V. and McKinzie, W. R. (1969): On a new tool in artificial intelligence research. *Proceedings International Conference on Artificial Intelligence*, pp. 259–270.

Findler, N. V., Pfaltz, J. L., and Bernstein, H. J. (1972): *Four High Level Extensions of FORTRAN IV: SLIP, AMPPL-II, TREETRAN and SYMBOLANG*. Spartan Books, New York.

Findler, N. V., Sicherman, G. L., and McCall, B. (1983): A multistrategy gaming environment. In Bramer, M. A. (1983), pp. 229–255.

Fine, R. (1941): *Basic Chess Endings*. David McKay, New York.

Fine, R. (1969): *Chess the Easy Way*. Cornerstone, New York.

First Microcomputer chess tournament (1978). *Chess Life and Review*, **33**, 363–364.

Foster, F. G. (1964): A computer technique for game-theoretic problems I: Chemin-de-fer analyzed. *Computer Journal*, **7**, 124–130.***

Frey, P. W. (Editor) (1977a): *Chess Skill in Man and Machine*. Springer-Verlag, New York. The second edition (1983) contained two additional papers not found in the original edition.

Frey, P. W. (1977b): An introduction to computer chess. In Frey, P. W. (1977a).

Frey, P. W. (1980a): Simulating human decision-making on a personal computer. *BYTE*, **5**, no. 7, 56–72.

Frey, P. W. (1980b): Machine Othello. *Personal Computing*, 89–90.

Frey, P. W. (1981a): The Santa Cruz Open Othello Tournament for computers. *BYTE*, **6**, no. 7, 26–37.

Frey, P. W. (1981b): Personal communication to P. S. Rosenbloom.

Frey, P. W. (1983): The alpha–beta algorithm: Incremental updating, well-behaved evaluation functions, and non-speculative forward pruning. In Bramer, M. A. (1983), pp. 285–289.

Frey, P. W. and Atkin, L. (1978–9): Creating a chess player. *Byte*, **3**, no. 10, 182–191; no. 11, 162–181; no. 12, 140–157; **4**, no. 1, 126–145.***

Fuller, S. H., Gasching, J. G., and Gillogly, J. J. (1973): An analysis of the alpha-beta pruning algorithm. Department of Computer Science Report, Carnegie–Mellon University, Pittsburgh.

Gardner, M. (1961): Mathematical recreations. *Scientific American*.

Gardner, M. (1962): Mathematical recreations. *Scientific American*.

Gardner, M. (1969): *The Unexpected Hanging and Other Mathematical Diversions from Scientific American*. Simon and Schuster, New York.

Gelernter, H. (1959): Realization of a geometry-theorem proving machine. *Proceedings of an International Conference on Information Processing, UNESCO, Paris*, pp. 273–282. Reprinted in Feigenbaum *et al.* (1963), pp. 134–152.

Gelernter, H., Hansen, J. R., and Loveland, D. W. (1960): Empirical explorations of the geometry-theorem proving machine. *Proceedings of the Western Joint Computer Conference*, pp. 143–147. Reprinted in Feignebaum, E. A. and Feldman, J. (1963), pp. 153–163.

Gillies, D. B., Mayberry J. P., and von Neumann, J. (1953): Two variants of poker. In Kuhn, H. W. and Tucker, A. W. (Editors), *Contributions to the Theory of Games*, Vol. II, Study 28. Princeton University Press, Princeton, New Jersey.

Gillogly, J. J. (1972): The technology chess program. *Artificial Intelligence*, 3, 145–164. Reprinted in Levy, D. N. L. (1988).

Gillogly, J. J. (1978): Performance analysis of the technology chess program. Ph.D. Thesis, Carnegie–Mellon University, Pittsburgh.

Gillogly, J. J. and Keeler, E. B. (1975): Playing the running game in backgammon. *Popular Bridge*, 9, no. 3, 34–38.

Goldman, A. J. and Stone, J. J. (1960): A symmetric continuous poker model. *Journal of Research National Bureau of Standards*, 64B, 35–40.

Goldwater, W. (1977): My game and animadversions. *Chess Life and Review*, 32, 313–314.

Good, I. J. (1965): The mystery of Go. *New Scientist*, no. 427 (January 21), 172–174.***

Good, I. J. (1968): A five-year plan for automatic chess. In Dale, E. and Michie, D. (Editors), *Machine Intelligence* 2, pp. 89–118. Edinburgh University Press, Edinburgh. Appendix F and Appendix H are reprinted in Levy, D. N. L. (1988).

Good, I. J. (1969): Analysis of the machine chess game, J. Scott (White), ICL-1900 versus R. D. Greenblatt, PDP-10. In Meltzer, B. and Michie, D. (Editors), *Machine Intelligence* 4, pp. 267–269. Edinburgh University Press, Edinburgh.

Goodell, J. D. (1957): *The Game of Ki*. Riverside Research Press, St. Paul, Minnesota.

Goodman, N. (1954): *Fact, Fiction and Forecast*. Harvard University Press, Cambridge, Massachusetts.

Goren, C. (1951): *Point Count Bidding*. Simon and Schuster, New York.

Goren, C. (1962): *Contract Bridge Complete*. Doubleday, New York.

Goren, C. (1974): *Goren's Modern Backgammon Complete*. Doubleday, New York.

Gorry, G. A. (1967): A system for computer-aided diagnosis. Ph.D. Thesis, Alfred P. Sloan School of Management, Massachusetts Institute of Technology. Reprinted as Massachusetts Institute of Technology Project MAC Report MAC-TR-44.

Graham, N. (1981): *Artificial Intelligence*. Tab Books, Blue Ridge Summit, Pennsylvania.

Green, H. S. (1983): Go and artificial intelligence. In Bramer, M. A. (1983), pp. 141–151.

Greenblatt, R. D., Eastlake, D. E. IIIrd, and Crocker, S. D. (1967): The Greenblatt chess program. *Proceedings of the Fall Joint Computer Conference*, pp. 801–810. Reprinted in Levy, D. N. L. (1988).

Griffith, A. K. (1966): A new machine learning technique applied to the game of checkers. Massachusetts Institute of Technology AI Memo 94. Cambridge, Massachusetts.

Griffith, A. K. (1974): A comparison and evaluation of three machine learning procedures as applied to the game of checkers. *Artificial Intelligence*, 5, 137–148.

Griffith, A. K. (1976): Empirical exploration of the performance of the alpha–beta tree search heuristic. *IEEE Transactions on Computers*, C-25, no. 1, 6–10.

Hafner, C. and Wilcox, B. (1974): LISP/MTS Programmers' Manual. Communication no. 302, Mental Health Research Institute, University of Michigan, Ann Arbor, Michigan.

Hardy (1973): The Popcorn Reference Manual, CSM-1. Essex University, Colchester.

Harris, L. R. (1977): The heuristic search: An alternative to the alpha–beta minimax procedure. In Frey, P. W. (1977a), pp. 157–167.

Hart, T. P. and Edwards, D. J. (1961): The tree prune (TP) algorithm. Massachusetts Institute of Technology AI Project Memo no. 30. R.L.E. and Computation Center, Massachusetts Institute of Technology, Cambridge, Massachusetts. Revised as Edwards, D. J. and Hart, T. P. (1963).

Haruyama and Nagahara (1969): *Basic Techniques of Go*. Ishi Press, Tokyo.

Hasegawa, G. and Brady, M. (1977): *How to Win at Othello*. Jove Publications, New York.

Hayes, D. G. (1967): *Introduction to Computational Linguistics*, pp. 92–94. American Elsevier, New York.

Hayes, J. and Levy, D. N. L. (1976): *The World Computer Chess Championship*. Edinburgh University Press, Edinburgh.

Heine, K. (Editor) (1979a): *Proceedings of IInd Seminar of Scientific Go-Theory*, Held at the 23rd European Go-Congress, Konigswinter, West Germany.

Heine, K. (1979b): Statistical research with the game of Go. In Heine, K. (1979a), pp. 33–45.

Heine, K. (1979c): Information content and value-counting. In Heine, K. (1979a), pp. 65–80.

Hilgard, E. R. (1956): *Theories of Learning*, 2nd ed. Appleton–Century–Croft, New York.

Holland, T. (1974): *Better Backgammon*. Reiss Games, New York.

Hubermann, B. J. (1968): A program to play chess endgames. Ph.D. Thesis (Technical Memo CS 106), Computer Science Department, Standford University, Standford, California.

IBM (1966): System 360 operating system: PL/1 language specifications. C28-6571-4. Data Processing Division, IBM Corporation, White Plains, New York.

Ishigure, I. (1973): *In the Beginning: The Opening in the Game of Go*. Ishi Press, Tokyo.

Iwamoto, K. (1972): *Go for Beginners*. Ishi Press, Tokyo.

Iwamoto, K. (1973): *The 1971 Honibo Tournament*. Ishi Press, Tokyo.

Jacobs, C. and Jacobs, E. (1979): Unbalancing your opponent. *Othello Quarterly*, **1**, no. 1, 3–5.

Jacoby, O. (1947a): *How to Figure the Odds*. Doubleday, Garden City, New York.

Jacoby, O. (1947b): *Oswald Jacoby on Poker*. Doubleday, Garden City, New York.

Jacoby, O. and Crawford, J. R. (1973): *The Backgammon Book*. Viking, New York.

Jastrow, R. (1978): Toward an intelligence beyond man's. *Time*, February 20th, p. 59.

Jensen, K. and Wirth, N. (1976): *PASCAL User Manual and Report*. Lecture Notes in Computer Science, Vol. 18. Springer-Verlag, New York.

Kaplan, E. (1965): *Competitive Bidding in Modern Bridge*. Fleet Publishing, New York.

Kaplan, E. and Shenwold, A. (1962): *How to Play Winning Bridge*. Collier, New York.

Kaplan, J. (1977): Let's go, big beige machine! *Sports Illustrated*, August 22, p. 42.

Karlin, S. and Restrepo, R. (1957): Multistage poker models. In Dresher, M., Tucker,

A. W., and Wolfe, (Editors): *Contributions to the Theory of Games*, Vol. III, Study 39, pp. 337–363. Princeton University Press, Princeton, New Jersey.

Kawabata, Y. (1972): *The Master of Go*. Knopf, New York.

Kay, N., Silodor, S., and Karpin, F. (1965): *The Complete Book of Duplicate Bridge*. Putnam, New York.

Keeler, E. B. and Spencer, J. (1969): *Proper Raising Points in a Generalization of Backgammon*. The Rand Corporation, P-4078, May 1969.

Keeler, E. B. and Spencer, J. (1975): Optimal doubling in backgammon. *Operations Research*, **23**, no. 6, 1063–1071.***

Kelly, J. L., Jr. (1956): A new interpretation of information rate. *Bell System Technical Journal*, **35**, 917–926.

Kelly, J. L., Jr. and Selfridge, O. G. (1962): Sophistication in computers: A disagreement. *IRE Transactions on Information Theory*, **IT-8**, 78–80.

Kendall, M. G. and Murchland, J. D.: Statistical aspects of the legality of gambling. *Journal of the Royal Statistical Society*, Series A.

Kent, E. W. (1978): The brains of men and machines. *BYTE* (January 1978), 11; (February 1978), 84; (March 1978), 74; (April 1978), 66.

Kerwin, J. and Reitman, W. (1973): Video game no. 3: A Go protocol with comments. Mental Health Research Institute, Communication No. 300, University of Michigan, Ann Arbor, Michigan.

Kierulf, A. (1983): Brand—An Othello program. In Bramer, M. A. (1983), pp. 197–208.

Kimble, D. P. (Editor) (1965): *The Anatomy of Memory*, Vol. 1. Science and Behavior Books, Palo Alto, California.

King, P. F. (1971): A computer program for positional games. Report 1107, Jennings Computer Center, Case Western Reserve University, Cleveland, Ohio.

Kishikawa, S. *Steppingstones to Go*. Tuttle, Rutland, Vermont.

Kister, J., Stein, P., Ulam, S., Walden, W., and Wells, M. (1957): Experiments in chess. *Journal of the ACM*, **4**, no. 2, 174–177.

Klein, H. (1970): *Heuristische Entscheidungsmodelle*. Galber, Wiesbaden.

Kleinmuntz, B. (1968): The processing of clinical information by man and machine. In Kleinmuntz, B. (Editor), *Formal Representation of Human Judgement*, pp. 149–186. Wiley, New York.

Knuth, D. E. (1968): *Fundamental Algorithms: The Art of Computer Programming*, Vol. 1. Addison-Wesley, Reading, Massachusetts.

Knuth, D. E. (1969): *Semi-Numerical Algorithms: The Art of Computer Programming*, Vol. 2. Addison-Wesley, Reading, Massachusetts.

Knuth, D. E. (1973): *Sorting and Searching: The Art of Computer Programming*, Vol. 3. Addison-Wesley, Reading, Massachusetts.

Knuth, D. E. and Moore, R. N. (1975): An analysis of alpha–beta pruning. *Artificial Intelligence*, **6**, 293–326.

Koffman, E. B. (1967): Learning through pattern recognition applied to a class of games. Ph.D. Thesis, Case Institute of Technology. Reprinted as Case Western Reserve University System Research Center Report SRC-107-A-67-45.

Kogan, N. and Wallach, M. A. (1964): *Risk Taking: a Study in Cognition and Personality*. Holt, Reinhart and Winston, New York.

Kogan, N. and Wallach, M. A. (1967): Risk taking as a function of the situation, the person and the group. *New Directions in Psychology*, Vol. 3, pp. 111–278. Holt, Reinhart and Winston, New York.

Koniver, D. (1963): Computer heuristics for Five-in-a-row. M.S. Thesis, Mathematics Department, Massachusetts Institute of Technology, Cambridge, Massachusetts.

Koppel, H. (1952): Digital computer plays Nim. *Electronics*, (November 1952), 155–157.

Korschelt, O. (1880): *The Theory and Practice of Go*. Translated and edited by King, S. P. and Leckie, G. G. (1966). Tuttle, Rutland, Vermont.

Kosugi, K. and Davies, J. (1970): 38 *Basic Joseki*. Ishi Press, Tokyo.

Kotok, A. (1962): A chess playing program for the IBM 7090. B.S. Thesis. Artificial Intelligence Memo No 41, Massachusetts Institute of Technology, Cambridge, Massachusetts. Reprinted in Levy, D. N. L. (1988).

Kramarczyk, W. (1979): Mistakes, strength and probability of winning. In Heine, K. (1979a), pp. 46–54.

Kuhn, H. W. (1950): A simplified two-person poker. In Kuhn, H. W. and Tucker, A. W. (Editors), *Contributions to the Theory of Games*, Annals of Mathematics Studies, no. 24, pp. 97–103. Princeton University Press, Princeton, New Jersey.

Lamb, S. M. and Jacobsen, W. H., Jr. (1961): A high-speed large-capacity dictionary system. *Mechanical Translation*, **6** (November 1961), 76–107.

Land, A. H. and Doight, A. G. (1957): An automatic method of solving discrete programming problems. In Dantzig, G., *LinearProgramming and Extensions*. Princeton University Press, Princeton, New Jersey.

Lasker, E. (1960): *GO and GO-MOKU, the Oriental Board Games*, 2nd ed. Dover, New York.

Lasker, E. (1977): But will it fly? *Chess Life and Review*, **32**, 314.

Lawrence, M. (1973): *How to Read Your Opponent's Cards: The Bridge Experts' Way to Locate Missing High Cards*. Prentice-Hall, Englewood Cliffs, New Jersey.

Lee, D. N. (1967): Graph-theoretical properties of Elithorn's maze. *Journal of Mathematical Psychology*, **4**, 341–347.

Lefkovitz, D. (1960): A strategic pattern recognition program for the game Go. M.S. Thesis, Moore School of Electrical Engineering, Philadelphia.

Lehner, P. E. (1979): Strategic planning in Go. *Proceedings of the IJCAI*, Tokyo, pp. 86–90. Reprinted in Bramer, M. A. (1983), pp. 167–176.

Lehner, P. E. (1981): Planning in adversity: A computational model of strategic planning in the game of Go. Ph.D. Dissertation, University of Michigan, Ann Arbor, Michigan.

Le-Ngoc, T. and Vroomen, L. C. (1982): Programming strategies in the game of Push-Over. *IEEE Micro* (August 1982), 58–68.***

Levner, D. (1976): Is brute force backgammon possible? *SIGART Newsletter*, no. 58 (June 1976), 20.

Levy, D. N. L. (1976a): *Chess and Computers*. Batsford, London. Reprinted in Levy, D. N. L. and Newborn, M. M. (1982).

Levy, D. N. L. (1976b): *1975 U.S. Computer Chess Championship*. Computer Science Press, Woodland Hills, California.

Levy, D. N. L. (1977a): Invasion from Cyberland. *Chess Life and Review*, **32**, 312–313.

Levy, D. N. L. (1977b): 1976 U.S. *Computer Chess Championship*. Computer Science Press, Woodland Hills, California.

Levy, D. N. L. (1988): *Compendium of Computer Chess*. Batsford, London.

Levy, D. N. L. and Newborn, M. M. (1980): *More Chess and Computers*. Computer Science Press, Rockville, Maryland.

Levy, D. N. L. and Newborn, M. M. (1982): *All About Chess and Computers*. Computer Science Press, Rockville, Maryland. [This work combines two earlier volumes: Levy, D. N. L. (1976a), together with Levy, D. N. L. and Newborn, M. M. (1980): *More Chess and Computers*. Computer Science Press, Rockville, Maryland.]

Lichtenstein, D. and Sipser, M. (1978): GO is *P*-space hard. *Proceedings of the 19th Annual Symposium on Foundation of Computer Science*, pp. 48–54.

Liskov, B. (1974): Programming with abstract data types. *SIGPLAN Notices*, **9**, no. 4, 50–59.

Little, J. D., Murty, K. P., Sweeney, D. W., and Karel, C. (1963): An algorithm for the travelling salesman problem. *Operations Research*, **11**, 972–989.

Liu, S. C. (1979): A mathematical theory of Wei-Chi (Go). In Heine, K. (1979), pp. 13–19.

London, R. L. (1968): Correctness of the ALGOL procedure ASKFORHAND. Technical Report no. 50, University of Wisconsin, Computer Sciences Department, Madison, Wisconsin.

London, R. L. and Wasserman, A. I. (1967): The anatomy of an ALGOL procedure. Technical Report no. 5, University of Wisconsin, Computer Sciences Department, Madison, Wisconsin.

Lopes, L. L. (1976): Model-based decision and inference in stud poker. *Journal of Experimental Psychology: General*, **105**, no. 3 (September, 1976), 217–239.

Luce, R. D. and Raiffa, H. (1957): *Games and Decisions*. Wiley, New York.

McCarthy, J. (1981): Personal communication to P. S. Rosenbloom.

McCarthy, J. *et al.* (1960): LISP I Programmers' Manual. Massachusetts Institute of Technology Computing Center and Research Laboratory for Electronics.

McCulloch, W. S. (1949): The brain as a computing machine. *Electrical Engineering*, **69**, 492.

McDonald, J. (1950): *Strategy in Poker, Business and War*. Norton, New York.

Maggs, P. B. (1979): Programming strategies in the game of REVERSI. *BYTE*, **4**, no. 11, 66–79.

Magriel, P. (1977): *Backgammon*. New York Times Book Co., New York.

Mano, Y. (1984): An approach to conquer difficulties in developing a Go playing program. *Journal of Information Processing*, **7**, no. 2, 81–88.***

Mano, Y. (1985): A technique for extending Pascal and an application to Pascal with module structures. *Transactions of the Information Processing Society of Japan*. (In Japanese.)

Mann, B. (1979): Untitled. *Personal Computing*, **3**, no. 6, 83–86.

Marion, L. R. (1966): Winning and non-losing strategies in games and control. Technical Report SRC 91-A-66-36. Case Western Reserve University, Cleveland, Ohio.

Markowitz, H. M. (1959): *Portfolio Selection*. Coules Commission Monograph, 16. Wiley, New York.

Marsland, T. A. (1976): 1976 Canadian computer chess workshop. *SIGART Newsletter*, no. 60, 22.

Marsland, T. A. (1977): A comprehensive list of computer chess literature. Technical Report TR77-4, Department of Computer Science, University of Alberta, Edmonton. Updated and reprinted as the Bibliography in Levy, D. N. L. (1988).

Mazlack, L. J. (1976): First North American Go-Moku tournament. *SIGART Newsletter*, no. 56 (February 1976), 2–3.

Mazlack, L. J. (1977): Analysis and results from the second Go-Moku tournament. *SIGART Newsletter*, no. 62 (April 1977), 11–12.

Michalski, R. and Negri, P. (1975): An experiment in inductive learning in chess endgames: the king–pawn case. In Elcock, G. W. and Michie, D. (Editors), *Machine Intelligence* 8. Ellis Horwood, Chichester.

Michie, D. (1966): Game playing and game learning automata. In Fox, L. (Editor), *Programming and Non-Numerical Computation*. Pergamon, Oxford.

Michie, D. (1976): An advice-taking system for computer chess. *Computer Bulletin* (December), 12–14.

Michie, D. (1977): David Levy challenge game, 1 April 1977. *SIGART Newsletter*, no. 62, 10–11.

Michie, D. and Bratko, I. (1978): Advice tables representations of chess endgame knowledge. *Proceedings of AISB Summer Conference, Hamburg*.

Michie, D. and Ross, R. (1970): Experiments with the adaptive graph traverser. Meltzer, B. and Michie, D. (Editors), *Machine Intelligence* 5, pp. 301–318. Edinburgh University Press.

Miles, M. (1968): *All Fifty-Two Cards: How to Read Bridge Hands the Way Bridge Experts Do*. Cornerstone Library, New York.

Millen, J. K. (1981): Programming the game of Go. *BYTE* (April 1981), 102–119.

Miller, G. A. (1956): The magical number seven, plus or minus two: Some limits on our capacity for processing information. *Psychological Review*, **63**, 81–97.

Miller (1973): Proposals for a better Chess Program. M.Sc. Thesis, Essex University, Colchester.

Minsky, M. (1961): Steps towards artificial intelligence. *Proceedings IRE*, **49** (January 1961), 8–30.

Minsky, M. (1968): *Semantic Information Processing*. MIT Press, Cambridge, Massachusetts.

Minsky, M. (1975): A framework for representing knowledge. In Winston, P. H. (Editor), *The Psychology of Computer Vision*. McGraw-Hill, New York.

Mittman, B. (1974): First world computer chess championship at IFIP Congress 74 Stockholm, August 5–8. *Communications of the ACM*, **17**, 604–605.

Moore, E. (1959): Annuals of the Computation Laboratory of Harvard.

Morehead, A. H. (Editor) (1964): *Official Rules of Card Games*. Crest Books, New York.

Morehead, A. H., Frey, R. L., and Mott-Smith, G. (1964): *The New Complete Hoyle*. Garden City Books, Garden City, New York.

Morris, L. and Morris E. (1951): *The Game of Go*. American Go Association, New York.

Morrison, M. E. (1976): Fourth Annual Paul Masson American Class Championship. *Chess Life and Review*, **31**, 553.

Morrison, M. E. (Editor) (1977): *Offical Rules of Chess*. David McKay, New York.

Moses, J. (1967): Symbolic integration. Ph.D. Thesis, Massachusetts Institute of Technology. Reprinted as Massachusetts Insitute of Technology Project MAC Report MAC-TR-47.

Murray, A. M. and Elcock, E. W. (1968): Automatic description and recognition of board patterns in Go-Moku. In Dale, E. and Michie, D. (Editors), *Machine Intelligence* 2, pp. 75–88. Oliver and Boyd, London.***

Murray, H. J. R. (1913): *A History of Chess*. Oxford University Press, London.

Murray, H. J. R. (1952): *A History of Board Games Other Than Chess*. Oxford University Press, London. Reprinted (1978), Hacker Art Books, New York.

Nado, R. A. and Reitman, W.: *Natural and Artificial Intelligence*. Lawrence Erlbaum Associates, Hillsdale, New Jersey.

Nagahara, Y. (1972): *Strategic Concepts of Go*. Ishi Press, Tokyo.

Nash, J. F. and Shapley, L. S. (1950): A simple three-person poker game. In Kuhn, H. W. and Tucker, A. W. (Editors), *Annuals of Mathematics Studies*, no. 24, pp. 105–116. Princeton University Press, Princeton, New Jersey.

Naur, P. (Editor) (1963): Revised report on the algorithmic language ALGOL 60. *Communications of the ACM*, **6** (January 1963), 1–17.

Neisser, U. (1967): *Cognitive Psychology*. Appleton-Century-Crofts, New York.

Neumann, J. von and Morgenstern, O. (1953): *Theory of Games and Economic Behavior*. Princeton University Press, Princeton, New Jersey.

Newborn, M. M. (1975): *Computer Chess*. Academic Press, New York.

Newborn, M. M. (1977a): The efficiency of the alpha–beta search on trees with branch-dependent terminal node scores. *Artificial Intelligence*, **8**, 137–153.

Newborn, M. M. (1977b): PEASANT: An endgame problem for kings and pawns. In Frey, P. W. (1977a), pp. 119–130.

Newborn, M. M. (1978a): Recent progress in computer Chess. In Alt, L. (Editor), *Advances in Computers*, Vol. 18, pp. 59–117. Academic Press, New York.***

Newborn, M. M. (1978b): Computer chess: Recent progess and future expectations. *Proceedings of 3rd Jerusalem Conference on Information Technology*, pp. 189–192. North-Holland, Amsterdam.

Newell, A. (1955): The chess machine. *Proceedings Western Joint Computer Conference*, pp. 101–110. Reprinted in Levy, D. N. L. (1988).

Newell, A. and Ernst, G. (1965): The search for generality. *Proceedings of IFIP Congress, New York, 1965*, pp. 17–24.

Newell, A. and Shaw, J. C. (1957): Programming the logic theory machine. *Proceedings of the 1957 Western Joint Computer Conference*, pp. 230–240.

Newell, A., Shaw, J. C., and Simon, H. A. (1958a): Elements of a theory of human problem solving. *Psychological Review*, **65** (March 1958), 151–166.

Newell, A, Shaw, J. C., and Simon, H. A. (1958b): Chess-playing programs and the problem of complexity. *IBM Journal of Research and Development*, **2**, 320–335.***

Newell, A., Shaw, J. C., and Simon, H. A. (1959): Report on a general problem-solving program. *Proceedings of International Conference on Information Processing.* UNESCO, Paris.

Newell, A., Shaw, J. C., and Simon, H. A. (1963): Chess-playing programs and the problem of complexity. In Fiegenbaum, E. A. and Feldman, J. (1963), pp. 39–70. [Also in *IBM Journal of Research and Development*, **4**, no. 2 (Oct. 1958), 320–335.]

Newell, A. and Simon, H. A. (1961): Computer simulation of human thinking. *Science*, **134**, 2011–2017.

Newell, A. and Simon, H. (1972): *Human Problem Solving.* Prentice-Hall, Englewood Cliffs, New Jersey.

Newman and Uhr, L. (1965): Bogart: A discovery and induction program for games. *Proceedings ACM National Conference*, pp. 176–186.

Nii, H. P. and Aiello, N. (1978): AGE ("Attempt to Generalize"): Profile of the AGE-0 system. Working Paper HPP-78-5, Computer Science Department, Stanford University, Stanford, California.

Nilsson, N. J. (1971): *Problem-Solving Methods in Artificial Intelligence.* McGraw-Hill, New York.

Olmstead, J. H. M. and Robinson, K. D. (1964): A treatise on the rules of Go. *Go Monthly Review* (Tokyo, Japan), **4**, no. 9, 87–103.

Olmstead, J. H. M. and Robinson, K. D.: Unpublished manuscript.

Parnas, D. L. (1972): A technique for software module specification with examples. *Communications of the ACM*, **15**, no. 5, 330–336.

Parson, D. (1959): *Fall of the Cards.* Little, Brown and Co., Boston.

Pearl, J. (1983): Game-searching theory: Survey of recent results. In Bramer, M. A. (1983), pp. 276–284.

Penrod, D. (1977a): *Computer Chess Newsletter*, no. 1. Santa Barbara, California.

Penrod, D. (1977b): *Computer Chess Newsletter*, no. 2. Santa Barbara, California.

Personal Computing (1980): Background and origins of Othello. 1980, pp. 87–88.

Pervin, Y. A. (1962): Algorithmization and programming of the game of dominoes. In *Problems of Cybernetics* III, pp. 957–972. New York, Pergamon Press. [Also in *Automation Express* (April 1959), 26–28.]***

Phillips, R. (1979): Writing an Othello program. *Othello Quarterly*, **1**, no. 3, 7–12.

Piasetski, L. (1976): An evaluation function for simple king and pawn endings. M.Sc. Thesis, McGill University, Montreal.

Pinkenburg, I. (1979): Trials in programming the game of Go. In Heine, K. (1979a), pp. 93–104.

Pitrat, J. (1968): Realization of a general game-playing program. *Proceedings IFIP Congress, Edinburgh*, pp. H120–H124.

Pitrat, J. (1971): A general game-playing program. In Findler, N. V. and Meltzer, B. (Editors), *Artificial Intelligence and Heuristic Programming.* Edinburgh University Press, Edinburgh.

Prentice, C. (1980): Report from London. *Othello Quarterly*, **2**, no. 4, 10–12.

Polya, G. (1954): *Mathematics and Plausible Reasoning*, Vol. I: *Induction and Analogy in Mathematics.* Princeton University Press, Princeton, New Jersey.

Pruitt, D. G. (1962): Pattern and level of rick in gambling decisions. *Psychological Review*, **69**, 187–201.

Quinlan, J. R. (1979): A knowledge-based system for locating missing high cards in bridge. *Proceedings of 6th IJCAI, Tokyo*, pp. 705–707.***

Raiffa, H. (1968): *Decision Analysis*. Addison-Wesley, Reading, Massachusetts.

Rayner, E. H. (1958): A study of evaluative problem solving. *Quarterly Journal of Experimental Psychology*, **10**, 155 and 193. Reprinted in Wason, P. C. *et al.* (Editors), *Thinking and Reasoning*. Penguin, London.

Reisman, S. (1972): Dominoes: A computer simulation of cognitive processes. *Simulation and Games*, **3**, no. 2, 155–163.

Reitman, W., Kerwin, J., Nado, R., Reitman, J., and Wilcox, B. (1974): Goals and plans in a program for playing Go. *Proceedings of the ACM National Conference, San Diego*, pp. 123–127.***

Reitman, W., Nado, R., and Wilcox, B. (1978): Machine perception: What makes it so hard for computers to see? In Savage, C. W. (Editor), *Perception and Cognition: Issues in the foundations of psychology*. Minnesota Studies in the Philosophy of Science, vol. 9, pp. 65–87. University of Minnesota Press, Minneapolis.

Reitman, W. and Wilcox, B. (1975): Perception and representation of spatial relations in a program for playing Go. *Proceedings of the ACM Annual Conference, Minneapolis*, pp. 37–41.***

Reitman, W. and Wilcox, B. (1978): Pattern recognition and pattern-directed inference in a program for playing Go. In Waterman, D. and Hayes-Roth, F. (1978), pp. 503–523. Academic Press, New York.***

Reitman, W. and Wilcox, B. (1979a): Modelling tactical analysis and problem solving in Go. *Proceedings of the Tenth Annual Pittsburgh Conference on Modelling and Simulation*, pp. 2133–2148.

Reitman, W. and Wilcox, B. (1979b): The structure and performance of the Interim.2 Go program. *Proceedings of 6th IJCAI, Tokyo*, pp. 711–719. Also in Heine, K. (1979), pp. 105–118.***

Reitman, W. and Wilcox, B. (1979): Artificial intelligence systems for policy analysis and planning? *First International Symposium on Policy Analysis and Information Systems* (1979).

Remus, H. (1961): *Lernversuche an der IBM 704*. Lernende Automaten, Munich, p. 144.

Remus, H. (1962): Simulation of a learning machine for playing Go. *Information Processing 1962* (*Proceedings of the IFIP Congress, Munich*), pp. 192–194. North-Holland, Amsterdam.***

Richards, R. (1981): The revised USOA rating system. *Othello Quarterly*, **3**, no. 1, 18–23.

Richter, H. (1976): The first German computer chess championship at Dortmund. *SIGART Newsletter*, no. 56, 2.

Riley, W. and Throop, T. (1969): An interactive bridge playing program. *Proceedings of the National Gaming Council, 8th Symposium, Kansas City, Missouri*.

Risticz, A. (1973): An investigation of the game of poker by computer-based analysis. Ph.D. Thesis, University of Adelaide, Adelaide.

Rochester, N., Holland, J. H., Habit, L. H., and Duda, W. L. (1956): Tests on a cell assembly theory of the action of the brain using a large digital computer. *IRE Transactions on Information Theory*, **IT-2**, no. 3, 80.

Rosenblatt, F. (1958): The Perceptron: A probabilistic model for information storage and organization in the brain. *Psychological Review*, **6** (November, 1958), 65.

Rosenbloom, P. S. (1982): A world-championship-level Othello program. *Artificial Intelligence*, **19**, 279–320.***

Rosenthal, G. (1954): *13 Line Go*. Published by author, 4009 Liberty Heights Avenue, Baltimore, Maryland.

Rossman, M. J. and Twery, R. J. (1958): Combinatorial programming. Abstract K7, *Operations Research*, **6**, 634.

Russell, R. (1964a): Kalah—The game and the program. Stanford Artificial Intelligence Memo no. 22, Stanford University, Stanford, California.

Russell, R. (1964b): Improvements to the Kalah program. Stanford Artificial Intelligence Memo no. 23, Stanford University, Stanford, California.

Ryder, J. L. (1971): Heuristic analysis of large tress as generated in the game of Go. Ph.D. Thesis, Stanford University, Stanford, California.

Sakata, E. (1971): *The Middle Game of Go*. Ishi Press, Tokyo.

Samuel, A. L. (1956): *IEE Proceedings*, 105, part B, pp. 452 et. seq.

Samuel, A. L. (1959): Some studies in machine learning using the game of checkers. *IBM Journal of Research and Development*, **3**, no. 3, 210–229. Reprinted in Feigenbaum, E. and Feldman, J. (1963).***

Samuel, A. L. (1960): Programming a computer to play games. In Alt, F. (Editor), *Advances in Computers*, Vol. 1, pp. 165–192. Academic Press, New York.

Samuel, A. L. (1967): Some studies in machine learning using the game of checkers, II—Recent progress. *IBM Journal of Research and Development*, **11**, no. 6, 601–618.***

Sander, P. T. and Davies, D. J. M. (1983): A strategic approach to the game of Go. In Bramer, M. A. (1983), pp. 152–166.

Sanechika, N. (1979): Recent developments in game playing programs. *Information Processing*, **20**, no. 7, 601–611 (in Japanese).

Sanechika, N. (1981): A model of evaluating moves in the game of Go. *Proceedings of the 22nd Convention of the Information Processing Society of Japan*.

Sanechika, N. (1982): Programming the decision process in Go. Technical Report of the Information Processing Society of Japan, June (in Japanese).

Sanechika, N., Ohigashi, H., Mano, Y., Sugawara, Y., and Torii, K. (1981): Notes on modelling and implementation of the human player's decision processes in the game of Go. *Bulletin of the Electrotechnical Laboratory*, **45**, no. 1–2, 1–11.

Scarne, J. (1961): *Scarne's Complete Guide to Gambling*. New York, Simon and Schuster.

Scheeling, T. (1966): *The Strategy of Conflict*. Harvard University Press, Cambridge, Massachusetts.

Schenken, H. (1963): *Better Bidding in Fifteen Minutes*. Simon and Schuster, New York.

Schenken, H. (1969): *Howard Schenken's "Big Club"*. Simon and Schuster, New York.

Schottenfeld, S. (1969): Five-card draw poker. Student Project at the Abraham Lincoln High School, Brooklyn, New York.

Science et Vie (1980): Push Over. In *Jeux et Strategies*, no. 2 (Avril–Mai), p. 7.

Scott, J. J. (1969): A chess-playing program. In Meltzer, B. and Michie, D. (Editors), *Machine Intelligence* 4, pp. 255–266. Edinburgh University Press, Edinburgh.

Segoe, K. (1960): *Go Proverbs Illustrated*. The Nihon Ki-in, Tokyo.

Selfridge, O. (1965): Reasoning in game playing by machine. In Sass, M. A. and Wilkinson, W. D. (Editors), *Symposium on Computer Augmentation of Human Reasoning*. Spartan Books, Washington, D.C.

Shannon, C. E. (1950a): Programming a computer for playing chess. *Philosophical Magazine*, **41**, no. 314, 256–275. Reprinted in Levy, D. N. L. (1988).

Shannon, C. E. (1950b): A chess-playing machine. *Scientific American*, **182**, 48–51.***

Shapiro, S. C. (1979): A Scrabble crossword game-playing program. *Proceedings 6th IJCAI*, pp. 797–799.

Shapiro, S. C. (1983): Scrabble crossword game-playing programs. In Bramer, M. A. (1983), pp. 221–228.

Shapiro, S. C. and Smith, H. R. (1977): A SCRABBLE crossword game-playing program. Technical Report no. 119, Department of Computer Science, State University of New York at Buffalo.***

Shaw, J. C., Newell, A., Simon, H. A., and Ellis, T. O. (1958): A command structure for complex information processing. *Proceedings of the 1958 Western Joint Computer Conference*.

Silver, R. (1967): The group of automorphisms of the game of 3-dimensional tic-tac-toe. *American Mathematical Monthly*, **74**, no. 3, 247–254.

Simon, H. A. (1955): A behavioral model of rational choice. *Quarterly Journal of Economics*, **29**, 99–118. Reprinted in Alexis, M. and Wilson, C. Z. (1967), *Organizational Decision Making*. Prentice-Hall, Englewood Cliffs, New Jersey.

Simon, H. A. and Chase, W. G. (1973): Skill in chess. *American Scientist*, **61**, 394–403. Reprinted in Levy, D. N. L. (1988).

Simon, H. A. and Feigenbaum, E. A. (1964): An information processing theory of some effects of similarity, familiarization, and meaningfulness in verbal learning. *Journal of Verbal Learning and Verbal Behavior*, **3**, 385–396.

Slagle, J. R. (1971): *Artificial Intelligence—The Heuristic Programming Approach*. McGraw-Hill, New York.

Slagle, J. R. and Bursky, P. (1968): Experiments with a multipurpose, theorem-proving heuristic program. *Journal of the ACM*, **15**, no. 1 (January, 1968), 85–99.

Slagle, J. R. and Dixon, J. K. (1969): Experiments with some programs that search game trees. *Journal of the ACM*, **16**, no. 2, 189–207.

Slagle, J. R. and Dixon, J. (1970): Experiments with the M & N tree-searching program. *Communications of the ACM*, **13** (March, 1970), 147–159.

Slate, D. J. and Atkin, L. R. (1977): CHESS 4.5—The Northwestern University Chess Program. In Frey, P. W. (1977a), pp. 92–118. Reprinted in Levy, D. N. L. (1988).

Slate, D. and Mittman, B. (1978): CHESS 4.6—Where do we go from here? *Proceedings of 3rd Jerusalem Conference on Information Technology*, pp. 184–188. North-Holland, Amsterdam.

Smith, A. (1956): *The Game of Go*. Tuttle, Rutland, Vermont.

Smith, C. A. B. (1968): *Journal of Recreational Mathematics*, **1**, 67.

Smith, M. H. (1973): A learning program which plays partnership dominoes. *Communications of the ACM*, **16**, 462–467.***

Soule, S. (1978): The implementation of a Go board. *Information Sciences*, **16**, 31–41.

Soule, S. and Marsland, T. A. (1975): Canadian computer chess tournament. *SIGART Newsletter*, no. 54, 12–13.

Stainer, A. (1974): BRIPP—A bridge playing program. Ph.D. Thesis, Essex University, Colchester.

Stanier, A. (1975): A bridge bidding program. *Proceedings of 4th IJCAI, Tbilisi*, pp. 374–378.***

Stanier, A. (1976): Planning to make tricks at bridge. *Proceedings of the AISB Summer Conference*, pp. 256–265.***

Starkey, J. D. (1979): The X–O–O heuristic in game tree analysis. *Proceedings of the 6th IJCAI, Tokyo*, pp. 842–844.

Stepoway, S. L. (1983): Reversi: An experiment in game-playing programs. In Bramer, M. A. (1983), pp. 188–196.

Strachey, C. S. (1952): Logical or non-mathematical programmes. *Proceedings of ACM Meeting at Toronto*, pp. 46–49, September 8–10.***

Stringham, G. (1980): Fundamental Othello misconceptions: Disc counting strategies. *Othello Quarterly*, **2**, no. 3, 3–7.

Sugawara, Y. and Sanechika, N. (1981): A method to recognize the strength situation in Go program. *Proceedings of 23rd National Conference of the Information Processing Society of Japan* (in Japanese).

Sullivan, G. (1981): Playing defensively. *Othello Quarterly*, **3**, no. 1, 24–31.

Sullivan, G. and Richards, R. (1981): Glossary of basic Othello terms. *Othello Quarterly*, **2**, no. 4, 8–9.

Tackett, M. J. (1976): A pattern recognition approach to Tesuji programming in Go. *Proceedings of ACM/CIPS Pacific Regional Symposium, Seattle*.

Takagawa, K. (1958a): *How to Play Go*. American Go Association, New York.

Takagawa, K. (1958b): *The Vital Point of Go*. American Go Association, New York.

Tan, S. T. (1972): Representation of knowledge for very simple pawn endings. Technical Memorandum MIP-R-98, Department of Machine Intelligence and Perception, University of Edinburgh, Edinburgh.

Teitelman, W. (1978): INTERLISP Reference Manual. California, XEROX Palo Alto Research Center, Palo Alto, California.

Thiele, T. N., Lemke, R. R., and Fu, K. S. (1962): A digital computer card playing program. Final Report, School of Electrical Engineering, Purdue University, Lafayette, Indiana. An edited version was reprinted in *Behavioral Science*, **8** (1963), 362–368.***

Thorp, E. O. (1962): *Beat the Dealer, A Winning Strategy for the Game of Twenty-One*. Random House, New York.

Thorp, E. O. (1969): Optimal gambling systems for favorable games. *Review of the International Statistical Institute*, **37**, no. 3, 273–293.

Thorp, E. O. (1975): Backgammon: Part 1, The optimal strategy for the pure running game. *Second Annual Conference on Gambling, South Lake Tahoe, Nevada.*

Thorp, E. O. (1978): End positions in backgammon. *Gambling Times,* October, November, December.***

Thorp, E. O. and Walden, W. (1964): A partial analysis of Go. *Computer Journal,* **7,** no. 3, 203–207.***

Thorp, E. O. and Walden, W. E. (1972): A computer assisted study of Go on $M \times N$ Boards, *Information Sciences,* **4,** no. 1, 1–33.***

Throop, T. A. (1962): The UNIVAC plays bridge. *Computers and Automation,* **11** (March, 1962), 3B–5B.

Tilley, J. (Editor) (1968): Go: *International Handbook and Dictionary.* Ishi Pres, Tokyo.

Toda, M. (1963): Report No. 1, Institute for Research, State College of Pennsylvania.

Travis, L. (1964): *Proceedings of the Spring Joint Computer Conference,* pp. 339 et. seq.

Turcan, P. J. (1983): A competitive Scrabble program. In Bramer, M. A. (1983), pp. 209–220.

Turing, A. M. (1953): Chess. Part of "Digital computers applied to games" in Bowden, B. V. (1953), pp. 286–295.

Tzannes, N. and Tzannes, V. (1974): *How Good Are You at Backgammon?* Simon and Schuster, New York.

Wallace, F. R. (1968): *Advanced Concepts of Poker.* I & O Publishing Company, Wilmington, Delaware.

Wasserman, A. I. (1970a): Achievement of skill and generality in an artificial intelligence program. Ph.D. Thesis, University of Wisconsin, Madison, Wisconsin.

Wasserman, A. I. (1970b): Realization of a skillful bridge bidding program. *Proceedings of the Fall Joint Computer Conference,* pp. 433–444.

Waterman, D. A. (1970): Gerneralization learning techniques for automating the learning of heuristics. *Artificial Intelligence,* **1,** 121–170.

Waterman, D. A. and Hayes-Roth, F. (Editors) (1978): *Pattern Directed Inference Systems.* Academic Press, New York.

Weizenbaum, J. (1961): How to make a computer appear intelligent—Five-in-a-row offers no guarantees. *Datamation,* **7,** 24–26.

Weizenbaum, J. (1963): Symmetric list processor. *Communications of the ACM,* **6,** 524–544.

Wiener, N. (1948): *Cybernetics.* Wiley, New York.

Wilcox, B. (1978–84): Computer Go. *American Go Journal,* **13,** no. 4, no. 5, no. 6; **14,** no. 1, nos. 5–6; **19.***

Wilcox, B., Reitman, D., and Reitman, W. (1978): Tutorial documentation for the INTERIM.2 Go program. IP-35, unpublished, University of Michigan, Ann Arbor, Michigan.

Wilkins, D. (1979): Using patterns and plans to solve problems and control search. Unpublished Doctoral Thesis, Stanford University, Stanford, California.

Williams, T. G. (1965): Some studies in game playing with a digital computer. Thesis, Carnegie Mellon University, Pittsburgh.

Winograd, T. (1972): *Understanding Natural Language.* Academic Press, New York.

Wirth, N. (1980): *Modula-2*. ETH, Institut fur Informatik.

Wulf, W. A., Russell, D. B., and Habermann, A. N. (1971): BLISS: A language for systems programming. *Communications of the ACM*, **14**, no. 12 (December, 1971), 780–790.

Yardley, H. O. (1961): *The Education of a Poker Player*. Pocket Books, New York.

Zadeh, N. (1974): *Winning Poker Systems*. Prentice-Hall, Englewood Cliffs, New Jersey.

Zadeh, N. and Koblinska, G. (1977): On optimal doubling in backgammon. *Management Science*, **23**, no. 8, 853–858.***

Zahle, T. U. (1979): A program of master-strength to play Five-in-a-row. *Proceedings EURO IFIP 79*, pp. 475–482. Elsevier, Amsterdam.***

Zemanek, H. (1961): Beschreibung von Lernvorgaengen. Lernende Automaten, p. 9. Munich.

Zobrist, A. L. (1969): A model of visual organization for the game of Go. *Proceedings of the Spring Joint Computer Conference*, pp. 103–112.

Zobrist, A. L. (1970): Feature extraction and representation for pattern recognition and the game of Go. Ph.D. Thesis, University of Wisconsin, Madison, Wisconsin.

Zobrist, A. L. and Carlson, F. R., Jr. (1973): An advice taking chess computer. *Scientific American*, **228**, no. 12, 92–105.

Index

Computer Games II, the companion volume to this book, is also edited by David Levy and covers the following games:

- Othello
- Go
- Go-Moku
- Bridge
- Dominoes
- Dama

- Poker
- Hearts
- Halma
- Qubic
- Push-Over
- Chemin-De-Fer

1988 ISBN 0-387-96609-9

Computer Chess Compendium
Edited by David Levy

The remarkable increase in strength of chess computers over the last ten years has resulted in a flood of books and articles on programming methods and new approaches to analyzing positions.

All important articles on the subject have now been collected together in one volume together with the best games by chess computers, including the first five World Microcomputer Championships. Every article has been transliterated into algebraic notation and an extensive bibliography provides scope for further research. This book will appeal to all chess players and computer enthusiasts, particularly those interested in artificial intelligence.

1988 ISBN 0-387-91331-9

 Springer-Verlag